D1244622

CAMPAIGN OF THE CENTURY

CAMPAIGN OF THE CENTURY

Kennedy, Nixon, and the Election of 1960

Irwin F. Gellman

Yale
UNIVERSITY
PRESS
New Haven & London

Published with assistance from the Louis Stern Memorial Fund.

Yale University Press books may be purchased in quantity for educational,
business, or promotional use. For information, please e-mail sales.press@yale.edu
(U.S. office) or sales@yaleup.co.uk (U.K. office).

Set in Postscript Electra type by Tseng Information Systems, Inc.
Printed in the United States of America.

Library of Congress Control Number: 2021937557
ISBN 978-0-300-21826-8 (hardcover : alk. paper)

A catalogue record for this book is available from the British Library.

This paper meets the requirements of ANSI/NISO Z39.48-1992 (Permanence of Paper).

10 9 8 7 6 5 4 3 2 1

To Honor the Memoirs of Three Extraordinary Individuals
Gloria and Robert Seeburger
and Their Daughter and My Wife
Gloria Gae Seeburger Gellman

CONTENTS

PREFACE: THE HISTORY WRITTEN
BY THE WINNERS

In January 1961, as Richard M. Nixon's staff began packing up his office and preparing to leave, the vice president still had official duties to perform. The Eighty-seventh Congress opened on Tuesday, January 3, and in his constitutional role as president of the Senate, Nixon had the task of convening that body at noon. He swore in the newly elected senators, announced the resignations of Senators John F. Kennedy of Massachusetts and Lyndon B. Johnson of Texas, and presided over a debate on reducing the number of votes needed to stop a filibuster.[1]

Nixon's term, as well as President Dwight Eisenhower's, would expire at noon on January 20, as set forth in the 20th Amendment to the Constitution. On Friday, January 6, Nixon had one other duty to carry out. The Constitution required the vice president to "open all Certificates" before a joint session of Congress, after which "the Votes shall then be counted" and the next president declared. The members of the Electoral College had already met in mid-December in each of the fifty states, cast their ballots, and declared Kennedy the winner.[2] The congressional vote counting was a constitutional formality.

The pageantry for the joint session began when two tellers carried the electors' ballots into the House chamber. Nixon, walking alone wearing a dark suit and a forced smile, followed them to the rostrum. There the session's cochair, Texas Democrat Samuel Rayburn, beginning his tenth term as speaker of the House, waited for him and then gaveled the senators and congressmen to order at 12:55 p.m. The vice president placed his arm around Rayburn's shoulder and wished him a happy seventy-ninth birthday.[3]

This was a carefully considered gesture. Since 1947, when Congressman Nixon first entered the House, Rayburn had grown to dislike him intensely.

Nixon's victorious senatorial campaign of 1950 had made him even more reprehensible in Rayburn's eyes, and then in the 1954 congressional elections, Nixon had allegedly called former president Harry Truman "a traitor" and Rayburn's Democrats "the party of treason." (The evidence shows that Nixon never made these remarks, but many Democrats believed he had.) The speaker not only disapproved of "Nixon's looks" but also considered him "a crook." At the height of the 1960 race, Rayburn wrote to Republican Congressman James Auchincloss from New Jersey: "I would dislike very much to see Nixon as President of the United States because I know him so well." Now the two men stood side by side on the rostrum.[4]

A century earlier, Vice President John Breckinridge, who at thirty-six had been the youngest man ever to become vice president (Nixon, elected at forty, was the second youngest) had lost the presidential race to Abraham Lincoln—Breckinridge's first political defeat. By the time he returned to Washington to serve out the rest of his term, seven southern states had seceded from the Union. Shortly after noon on February 13, 1861, Breckinridge led the senators from their side of the Capitol to the House of Representatives chamber on the other side for the ceremonial counting of electoral votes. Before a silent chamber, the vice president, "in an unfaltering voice," as historian James Klotter described it, announced that Lincoln had been duly elected president. He made no other statement but rose and marched his colleagues back to the Senate. It was the first time in American history that a vice president who had been defeated for the presidency formally ratified his rival's victory.[5]

Now this event occurred a second time. Nixon began the electoral count, which would last for more than an hour, by announcing the tally from Alabama: six votes for Senator Harry Byrd, Democrat from Virginia, and five for John Kennedy. The vice president remarked with a grin, "The gentleman from Virginia is now in the lead for the Presidency." When the tally was completed, Kennedy had received 303 electoral votes, Nixon 219, and Byrd 15.[6]

Before adjourning the joint session, Nixon, unlike Breckinridge, did not remain silent but asked the speaker for "permission" to make a brief statement in this "unprecedented situation." (Here, Nixon misspoke; he knew of Breckinridge's precedent.) He did not mention that a friendly reporter, Earl Mazo, had called his office just before he left for the House chamber, warning that some in the press gallery intended to write unfavorable stories about his conduct at the ceremony and suggesting that Nixon make some conciliatory statement.[7]

Speaking without notes, Nixon declared that his defeat and his opponent's victory provided an "eloquent example of the stability of our constitutional system and of the proud tradition of the American people of developing, respecting and honoring institutions of self-government." He had served fourteen years in elective office and had fought a hard campaign. He congratulated his onetime opponents and those elected to Congress and said it was "in that spirit" of congratulation that he declared Kennedy and Johnson the new president and vice president.[8]

After the long and tedious count, the chamber erupted with a prolonged ovation. Even Rayburn, who as speaker had never applauded a speech in the House chamber, clapped for Nixon's statement. (Nixon's gesture would lead to reconciliation between them — a fortunate one, because Rayburn would die of cancer less than a year later.) Senator Mike Mansfield, Democrat of Montana, commented: "What a way to go . . . with dignity and with head held high." Senator Hubert Humphrey, Democrat from Minnesota, said that the vice president's remarks would "go down as one of the truly historic messages. It was one filled with humility. It was a gracious and a very thoughtful pronouncement." *Time* magazine added that Congress and the galleries gave their ovation "to a good loser who makes a gracious gesture."[9]

From the Nixon who comes down to us from many historical descriptions, this is the last thing one would expect.

Given the vast number of books and articles that have been written about the election of 1960, it is remarkable how closely most authors' views follow Theodore White's *The Making of the President 1960*. White established a new approach to writing about elections. His book reads like a novel, presenting an insider's view of how the races evolved from the primaries through election night and beyond. Although many have questioned some of White's assertions, his overall narrative of the race, of a heroic senator defeating an unscrupulous partisan, has gone largely unchallenged.[10]

White was born in 1915. Raised in near-poverty, he received an exceptional secondary education, won a scholarship to Harvard University in 1934, and graduated summa cum laude in 1938 with a major in Chinese history. The following year, he left for China to serve as a lobbyist for Chiang Kai-shek's regime. Quickly disillusioned with the generalissimo's rule, he took a position with *Time* magazine as a war correspondent based in China. But he objected to the way his editor, Whittaker Chambers (later an enthusiastic Nixon defender), changed his stories to be more sympathetic to Chiang. Publisher Henry Luce consistently sided with Chambers, and White left *Time* in the summer of 1946. Right-wingers later unfairly charged him with favoritism toward the Chinese communists.[11]

White returned to the United States in 1953, worked for several magazines, and also wrote two novels. Sometime in the late 1950s he decided to write a book about the presidential election of 1960. The country was growing restless with the seeming complacency of the Eisenhower years, and many voters, he thought, were ready for a new political awakening. White wanted to work on his book full-time, without either the deadline pressure or editorial oversight that came with magazine or newspaper employment, so he persuaded the newly founded publisher Atheneum to give him a book contract with a sufficient cash advance to let him complete the project without distractions.[12]

As White wrote in his 1978 memoir, *In Search of History*, he planned to write about the campaign "as a story," featuring John Kennedy as the hero—"young, rich, heroic, witty, well read—and handsome." He had met Kennedy in 1956 and would follow him through the 1960 primaries, the general election, and into the Oval Office.

He could not have foreseen the impact of his work. After its publication in July 1961, *The Making of the President 1960* stood at No. 1 on the *New York Times* best-seller list for many weeks, won the 1962 Pulitzer Prize for general nonfiction, and sold more than four million copies; it is still in print. Reviewers' accolades matched the sales. James MacGregor Burns wrote in the *New York Times Book Review*, "No book that I know of has caught the heartbeat of a campaign as strikingly as Theodore White has done."[13] Sixty years after publication, it was still required reading in courses at some twenty American colleges and universities.

But the book had some unexpected consequences. By largely ignoring Kennedy's faults and highlighting Nixon's, it led subsequent writers to do the same. Those writers have also, following White's lead, minimized the roles of vice presidential candidates Lyndon Johnson and Henry Cabot Lodge, Jr. They have neglected President Dwight Eisenhower's passionate commitment to his vice president's victory and the extensive reporter bias against the Nixon campaign. They have perpetuated other errors as well.

White had the good fortune to write a book that crystallized, and even helped create, the Kennedy mystique. But despite the pride that journalists take in writing "the first draft of history," even he must have been surprised that there was no second draft.[14]

White's plan for his book never involved giving a balanced account. He became an advocate for JFK during the campaign and remained a supporter throughout his presidency.[15] He acknowledged some biases in his treatment of the race: eight months after *The Making of the President 1960* came out, he conceded in an interview with the *New York Post* that he had not been "too kind to Nixon. He comes out as something of a sad sack, an unsure man seeking approval."[16]

Few others seemed to have noticed. No sustained critique of White's method appeared in book form until 1995, when Joyce Hoffmann published *Theodore H.*

White and Journalism as Illusion, in which she analyzed his work as a mixture of reporting and fiction. He had become "enchanted," Hoffmann wrote, "with John F. Kennedy, the wealthy and sometimes ruthless politico whom White transformed into the clever and dashing hero of his book."[17]

In fairness to White, reporters in 1960 routinely avoided any discussion of a candidate's private behavior, so Kennedy's sexual addiction was not seen as a subject they should cover. They also usually ignored health issues. While President Eisenhower's heart attack and his other two serious illnesses had received extensive press coverage, the rumors that JFK had Addison's disease, a rare and sometimes life-threatening endocrine disorder, were avoided. Kennedy and his staff vehemently denied the rumors, and questions concerning his physical condition never surfaced during the general campaign.

As closely as he followed Kennedy, White never touched on anything that might damage his hero's image. Sometimes he was disingenuous. In defending JFK against allegations that his campaign had bought votes in the West Virginia primary race, White wrote that Attorney General William Rogers had conducted an "exhaustive study" of the primary and found "no evidence of wrongdoing."[18]

Many authors have convincingly demonstrated that the Kennedy campaign committed voter fraud in West Virginia. Whether this altered the outcome has not been analyzed, but the effect must have been significant. After the primary, Senator Barry Goldwater, Republican of Arizona, who chaired his party's senatorial finance committee, sent a former FBI agent to investigate the fraud rumors. He returned with sixteen affidavits from individuals who had participated in the contest and admitted that there had been fraud. Goldwater gave the affidavits to Rogers and never heard back from him, nor were the documents returned to the senator. White did not say where he got his information about an investigation by Rogers.[19]

He also did not mention the enormous sums of money with which the Kennedy campaign bribed primary voters to cast their ballots for JFK. He did not mention that Robert Kennedy instructed Franklin D. Roosevelt, Jr. (who was on the campaign payroll), to call JFK's primary opponent Hubert Humphrey "a draft dodger" and then denied that the Kennedys knew anything about the charge. He wrote nothing about President Eisenhower's important efforts that fall on behalf of his vice president. Nor has any serious historian subsequently examined these events. One can hardly blame White for what other writers failed to address—but it speaks to his book's powerful influence that it defined not only the tone but also the boundaries of many later histories of the campaign.

The adulation White heaped on Kennedy was matched by a tendency to patronize his general election opponent with amateur psychology. Nixon, White wrote, had emerged "from his impoverished middle-class youth" with "many strange qualities—the thrust of enormous internal drives, an overwhelming desire to be liked and, where he is rebuffed, a bitter, impulsive reflex of lash-backs." According to White, "Nixon was above all a friend seeker, almost pathetic in his eagerness to be liked." He "had great capacity for self-pity."[20]

This effort to pathologize Nixon was not new. While working at *Collier's* in 1956, White published an article describing him as "Tense, moody, introspective." He also repeated Democratic charges that Nixon had called his first congressional opponent, Jerry Voorhis, a communist in 1946, had done the same to Helen Gahagan Douglas during their 1950 Senate race, and in 1952 had tried to sabotage California Governor Earl Warren's effort to win the Republican presidential nomination. Despite these allegations, White gave a mixed assessment of Nixon, calling him "a magnificent campaigner" who "always shows best as an underdog battling against odds."[21]

White did his amateur psychoanalysis entirely at long distance. He had tried to interview Nixon for the piece without success. In January 1956, *Collier's* bureau chief Jim Derieux wrote James Bassett, a Nixon campaign aide, to say that the "infamous Teddy White" wanted to meet with the vice president. Ben Mandel, a former communist who had evolved into a virulent anticommunist crusader, chimed in later that month that White was "well known for his books and articles in support of Communist China." No interview took place.[22]

White tried again to approach the vice president for an interview on April 21, 1960, and received no answer. During the campaign, he talked to several Nixon staffers—Robert Finch, James Shepley, and Gabe Hauge—but could not get an audience. One time when he traveled with the Nixon campaign, he jumped aboard the reporters' car of the Dick Nixon Special with a "Kennedy for President" button pinned on his overcoat lapel. Nixon's personal physician, John Lungren, asked, "Why the decoration?" White replied, "I'm going with the winner."[23]

Shortly after the election, White wrote to the vice president that he was the "only major with whom I have not spoken." He had begun writing, he had a spring 1961 deadline, and this would be his last attempt at an interview. On November 29, Herbert Klein, Nixon's press secretary, replied that the vice president had "been away and we have a tremendous volume of work during these last few weeks which will preclude interviews of the type you would need." White, he added, should write the book without seeing Nixon.[24]

After the book came out and caused a sensation, journalist Victor Lasky, an avid Nixon defender, who most likely was relying on information from the former vice president himself, charged in a letter sent to multiple publications that White described events that never happened. White reported that Nixon had watched

Kennedy's acceptance speech at the Democratic National Convention from his home and commented that JFK had performed poorly. According to Lasky, the vice president had in fact watched the speech while attending a small dinner party at a friend's house and did not make any of the comments White attributed to him. In addition, contrary to White's account, Nixon thought "some time prior to the Democratic convention" that Kennedy would probably be his opponent and predicted that he must "select Lyndon Johnson as his running-mate." The general election, Nixon believed, would be hard fought, and he "foresaw . . . a close election."[25]

The Making of the President 1960 lavished praise on Kennedy for his treatment of reporters. Between forty and fifty of the best newsmen in the nation covered the election, according to White. Kennedy had been a journalist and was a Pulitzer Prize–winning author; the press "had become his friends and some of them, his most devoted admirers."[26] Nixon and his staff, on the other hand, were said to distrust journalists, and White wrote that the press grew hostile to them as a consequence. The negativity with which reporters portrayed Nixon, he suggested, was largely Nixon's own fault.[27]

Most authors agree that reporters abandoned their objectivity to advance Kennedy's candidacy. Ben Bradlee had been a reporter for fourteen years, mostly outside the United States, when he met Kennedy early in 1959 while working for *Newsweek*. They became Georgetown neighbors and close friends. Bradlee described JFK as "graceful, gay, funny, witty, teasing and teasable, forgiving, hungry, incapable of being corny, restless, interesting, interested, exuberant, blunt, profane, and loving." During the 1960 campaign, he wrote in his memoirs *Conversations with Kennedy* (1978), reporters usually protected Kennedy from his profanity and his uncomplimentary characterizations of people like Lyndon Johnson and Missouri Democratic Senator Stuart Symington.[28]

New York Times reporter Russell Baker could not believe how the press was seduced. "On the Kennedy campaign," he wrote, "a depressing number of really fine reporters lost their skepticism and went ga-ga over the candidate." Philip Potter of the *Baltimore Sun* surprised Baker by calling JFK "Jack" and pronouncing him "an absolute prince." Baker thought: *"Good Lord! They've brainwashed Potter!"* He had followed Nixon during his vice presidency and "would have gone gaily to the firing squad rather than call Nixon 'Dick' in the presence of another reporter." If Nixon and his staff thought the press was stacked against him, most likely it is because it was.[29]

Nixon read *The Making of the President 1960* shortly after it was released. Writing to Victor Lasky on August 24, 1961, he stated that he would use the last chapter of his forthcoming memoir, *Six Crises*, to correct "some of the more glaring inaccuracies." He wrote that chapter, largely from memory, over the last weeks of September and had the entire manuscript finished by the end of November.[30]

Six Crises was published remarkably quickly; it hit the stores in the spring of 1962. The sixth chapter of the book, "The Campaign of 1960," is the only one largely written by Nixon himself; the others were drafted by researchers. Its greatest shortcoming is that Nixon depended on his own recollections, which were inevitably selective, and relied on his staff only to answer specific questions. He did not use the massive number of documents he had assembled before, during, and after the contest to analyze the election.

Instead, he concentrated on several key issues, the most crucial of which was the presidential debates. Nixon had agreed to them because he did not want to seem afraid to defend the administration and his own record. In addition, he believed voters wanted them. In *Six Crises* he recounted all four debates, calling the first one "a setback—but not a disaster." He had concentrated too much on substance, not enough on appearance; he conceded that he did not look well due to his recent illness. In addition, Kennedy was as effective "as I have ever heard him." Nixon believed he had done far better in the three subsequent debates. Overall, they did not change voters' preferences but did solidify them.[31]

Nixon also focused on religion as a factor in the campaign. Many people, he knew, opposed any Catholic becoming president, but he rejected that stance. He agreed with Kennedy that a candidate's religion should not have any bearing in a presidential campaign. In spite of that commitment, Nixon's Catholic advisers were outraged at the Kennedy campaign's suggestion that people who did not vote for him were somehow religious bigots. Nixon wrote that his team wanted him to attack that premise, but he refused.[32]

He also addressed his refusal to comment on the arrest of Martin Luther King, Jr., in October 1960 or on the 1960–1961 recession that gave Democrats a rallying point. The latter, he thought, might have caused more blacks and workers to vote for Kennedy. Finally, he discussed the charges of irregularities in Texas and Illinois. Many supporters had wanted him to contest the outcomes in those states, but he refused. Any recount, he argued, would create chaos in the federal government, and in any case, Texas had no procedure by which a losing presidential candidate could demand a recount.[33]

Some minor aspects of White's account particularly irked him. White depicted Kennedy's performance at the annual Alfred E. Smith Dinner as masterful and ignored Nixon's. The former vice president offered a different recollection. The senator spoke first, he wrote, referred in bad taste to some partisan issues and sat down to "polite applause." Nixon then spoke extemporaneously and "received a prolonged ovation."[34]

Six Crises became a *New York Times* best-seller and a Book-of-the-Month Club main selection and sold several hundred thousand copies—but it had nowhere near the success of *The Making of the President 1960.* Kennedy read some of it. Although the two men had once had a cordial relationship, he had grown to despise Nixon during the campaign. When Bradlee asked the president if he had read Nixon's memoir, Kennedy replied: "I can't stand the way he puts everything in Tricia's mouth. It makes me sick. He's a cheap bastard." He was referring to a passage describing Kennedy's invitation to Nixon in May 1961 to come to the White House after the Bay of Pigs debacle. Nixon's fifteen-year-old daughter Tricia had taken the president's call and left a note by the phone for her father: "I knew it! It wouldn't be long before he would get into trouble and have to call on you for help."[35]

Of the many journalists and academics who have written on the election of 1960, only a few have tried to correct the imbalance in White's account. W. J. Rorabaugh's *The Real Making of the President*, Edmund Kallina, Jr.'s, *Kennedy v. Nixon*, and Laura Jane Gifford's *The Center Cannot Hold* represent real efforts to explain the election in a more meaningful context, with limited success.[36]

Others have been less rigorous. David Pietrusza, in researching *1960: LBJ vs. JFK vs. Nixon*, went to the Johnson and Kennedy libraries but never to Nixon's. Christopher Matthews may have spent several hours at the Nixon library while writing *Kennedy and Nixon*. Robert Dallek spent only a few sentences on the campaign in *Camelot's Court*, but he found enough space to assert, without a scintilla of proof, that "during the fall run against Republican Richard Nixon, break-ins of two Kennedy doctors' New York offices suggest that, like the 1968 Watergate burglary, the Nixon campaign was trying to steal medical records that could decide the election outcome." First, this incident occurred before the 1960 Democratic National Convention, and second, the Watergate break-in took place in 1972.[37]

While some of the neglect of Nixon's side of the campaign is perhaps personal, another part of the reason is institutional. The John F. Kennedy Presidential Library, in Boston, Massachusetts, is a relatively easy trip for writers, most of whom live on the East Coast; the Kennedy Foundation also provides funds for researchers. The materials on the 1960 election are well organized. Numerous memoirs favorable to Kennedy by aides such as Theodore Sorensen, Arthur Schlesinger, Jr., and John Kenneth Galbraith have received wide distribution.

Oral histories proliferated, were made available on microfilm, and are now often found online. And the glamour of the Kennedy presidency still shines.

The Nixon Presidential Library is in Yorba Linda, California, and until recently did not provide travel or research grants. Documents there are difficult to identify and find. The vast collection of primary sources for the pre-presidency includes more than two million pages of documents, and the major collection of these documents—865 manuscript boxes identified as the 320 Series—is organized alphabetically, not chronologically. Researchers cannot readily find information on the 1960 election, and there are no aides to assist them.[38]

The Kennedy scholar Bill Rorabaugh has pointed out that authors who have chosen to write about JFK can be placed in two categories: "Followers have expressed obsessive devotion, while bitter partisan opponents have found fault with all that he did or tried to do."[39]

In this book, for the first time, the Kennedy and Nixon campaigns are documented from extensive source material on both sides. Kennedy will not come out as a saint; his campaign was far more corrupt and ruthless than has been presented. Nixon will not come out as the villain or the foil; he ran a far cleaner operation than has been described. While the extremes of white and black occasionally surface, this narrative is mainly colored in shades of gray.

I will also correct many errors that are repeated so often they have become accepted as fact, even though the truth is readily verified. This unthinking repetition is not limited to popular writers who do no original research but rely on decades-old histories. One fable about the election that few historians have questioned concerns the significance of Kennedy's telephone call to Martin Luther King, Jr.'s, wife, Coretta, after her husband's arrest in late October. Harry Belafonte, in memoirs written a half-century after the election, claimed that the Kennedy campaign secretly sent out a pamphlet nationwide to African-American churches saying that Kennedy had saved King from incarceration. The Sunday before election day, black "ministers came right out and told their congregations how to vote. And those that could, did."[40] There is no evidence that this happened. While the pamphlet, known as the "blue bomb," exists, its distribution was far less than nationwide.

At the beginning of 2021, Paul Kendrick and Stephen Kendrick published *Nine Days*, a dramatic account of the arrest and release of Martin Luther King, Jr., in late October 1960. The authors then claimed that as the result of this event African Americans went to the polls in greater numbers and increased the share of their vote for Kennedy. There is no data (no polls or analysis of black voting) that supports that conclusion. The authors depended primarily on interviews and oral histories from Kennedy supporters like Sargent Shriver, Harris Wofford, Jr., and Louis Martin who exaggerated their influence during the King episode.[41]

The election did not mark a historic shift in African-American voting patterns. Seventy percent of black voters went for Franklin D. Roosevelt in 1936, and for the Democratic candidate in nearly every subsequent presidential election before 1960. (The one exception was in 1956, when Stevenson won 61 percent.) Sixty-eight percent of black voters cast their ballots for Kennedy in 1960.

In regard to the question of possible voter fraud, Kennedy received 303 electoral votes to Nixon's 219, with 269 needed to win. If the ballot fraud in Texas and Illinois had not occurred, Nixon probably would have won those states. Kennedy would have received 252 votes and lost to Nixon, who would have gotten 270. (Harry Byrd won the remaining 15.)

Winners—including the winners of elections—have generally written history from their own vantage point. With the 1960 race, the extreme contrast between Kennedy as hero and Nixon as villain has never been revised by a more balanced account. Part of the reason is that Kennedy's assassination has caused his entire life to be suffused in a mythic light. That makes for good propaganda, but not for accurate history. Two generations after the voting ended, it is long past time to tell the story without a partisan thumb on the scale.

CAMPAIGN OF THE CENTURY

JACK AND DICK

The presidential race of 1960 was a contest between two experienced politicians who had never lost an election. John F. Kennedy had won three House and two Senate races; Richard M. Nixon had won two House elections and one for the Senate, plus two as Eisenhower's running mate. Both seemed destined for the presidency and were consumed with the desire to win it.

Jack's birthplace, Brookline, Massachusetts, is almost three thousand miles from Yorba Linda, California, where Dick was born. Jack's father, Joseph Kennedy, graduated from Harvard, became one of the wealthiest men in America, and had served as United States ambassador to Great Britain under President Franklin Roosevelt. Dick's father, Frank, probably did not finish elementary school; his circle of acquaintants was limited to his grocery store customers and his fellow Quaker congregants. Jack's maternal grandfather, John "Honey Fitz" Fitzgerald, had been mayor of Boston and a United States congressman. His mother was raised as a devout Catholic, lived in comfort, and was well educated. Hannah Milhous's father, Franklin, was a successful nurseryman; both her parents were Quakers, making her a birthright Quaker.

Jack was a thin, sickly child who turned to books for relaxation. He attended exclusive private schools and graduated without distinction. Despite his scholastic record, he, like his father, graduated from Harvard. His education was enhanced by the family's frequent travel to Europe and elsewhere. In World War II, he volunteered for the navy and returned a hero. Joseph had initially fixated on Jack's older brother, Joseph Jr., to become the first Irish-Catholic president of the United States, but his dreams were dashed when Joe Jr. was killed during a dangerous wartime mission. With his death, Jack, the second son, was elevated to the role, by chance, not by choice.

Dick grew up in modest surroundings. His mother's family, the Milhouses, helped Frank provide for Hannah and their children. Dick was a high achiever as well as an enthusiastic if hopelessly untalented athlete. He went to public schools, Whittier College, and Duke University Law School, each time graduating third in his class. After passing the bar exam, he returned to his hometown and became a partner in a well-established local law firm. He and Thelma "Pat" Ryan married in 1940. A year later, Dick took a job with the Office of Price Administration in Washington, D.C., working there until he volunteered for the navy, which sent him to the South Pacific. Upon his return, he remained in the service until the end of 1945, negotiating the termination of military contracts. Shortly before the end of his enlistment, he unexpectedly received a telegram inviting him to be interviewed to run for Congress. He jumped at the chance.

The man Nixon defeated was a five-term incumbent, Jerry Voorhis. Several years after that election, stories began to circulate that Nixon had employed unscrupulous tactics to win. Voorhis and his allies charged that Nixon was beholden to wealthy backers, that he had lied about Voorhis's record, and that he had accused the congressman of being "soft on communism." Some alleged that Nixon had his supporters call voters on election day to tell them Voorhis was a communist. But the election did not center on communism, and no credible evidence was produced for the supposed phone calls. The claim that Nixon began his political career using unsavory practices belies the more likely explanation: Voorhis simply ran a lethargic campaign.[1]

Kennedy's political rise occurred in far different circumstances. He entered the 1946 Democratic congressional primary in Massachusetts's 11th District, a working-class area of Boston with a large Irish-Catholic constituency. His father chose the district after learning that Congressman James Curley, who represented it, was facing deep financial and legal difficulties. Joe Kennedy bribed Curley with a sizable amount of money to vacate his seat so that Jack could try to win it.[2]

Although the Kennedys were well aware of the systemic corruption that Boston-Irish politicians practiced, the family was wealthy and did not need to enrich themselves through influence peddling or other illegal activities. Jack Kennedy, according to Gerard O'Neill, an investigative reporter for the *Boston Globe*, relied on "ruthless pragmatism, which took no prisoners. Elections were no game, they were to get power to change things."[3]

During the campaign, Joe also helped manage the race from behind the scenes by supplying most of the staff and the money. Jack's mother, Rose, spoke in support of his candidacy; his sister Eunice held tea parties. JFK ran on his family name, his 1940 best-seller *Why England Slept*, his World War II heroics, and his Harvard ties. Witty, charming, and charismatic, he campaigned tirelessly, giving more than 450 speeches and greeting countless voters. When the 1946 primary results were tallied, he won with 40.5 percent of the vote. The primary victory in this heavily Democratic district assured a general election triumph, and when the votes were counted, he received 69,093 to his challenger's 26,007.[4]

Jack and Dick both entered Congress as young, thin, dark-haired navy veterans. According to Billy Sutton, Kennedy's first key congressional aide, they first met at the Washington Press Club in the capital. Sutton described spotting a "fellow over in the corner, a young fellow, very dapper dressed, from California. . . . He seemed to be the star of the show." JFK "was sort of taking things easy" when his aides pointed out Nixon. Ted Reardon, a Kennedy staff member, "brought Mr. Nixon over and introduced him to [JFK]. . . . Jack was all aglow. . . . He [Nixon] was the man who had defeated Jerry Voorhis. . . . It was a big thing to do and he did it, and [JFK] was quite elated over it, the surprise victory."[5]

Both freshmen congressmen were appointed to the House Committee on Education and Labor. When the committee convened at the beginning of January 1947, the freshman members drew straws for seniority. Jack drew the shortest straw for the Democrats and Dick did likewise for the Republicans. They sat at either end of a table facing each other. As Nixon recalled, they "were bookends on that committee."[6]

JFK was assigned offices in the Old House Office Building, room 322, and Nixon was placed in room 528. William Arnold, Nixon's first administrative assistant, described Jack and Dick as "fast friends." Nixon's secretaries remembered that they had a cordial relationship, as did Florida Democratic Congressman George Smathers, who was close to both men. Nixon recalled that they were "not buddy-buddy" but that Jack was "very personable" and, like him, "very shy." Jack agreed; both were introverts.[7]

As a congressman, Jack did not speak often on the House floor, but he did address specific issues that directly concerned him. He backed the Truman Doctrine and the Marshall Plan, but criticized the president for the loss of Mainland China and opposed the extension of the Reciprocal Trade Agreements Act. Domestically, he fought against the Taft-Hartley Act, which he considered damaging to his working-class constituency, vigorously supported the anticommunist provisions of the McCarran Act, voted to continue funding for the House Un-American Activities Committee (HUAC), and supported aid for veteran housing. He also tried to advance the interests of New England by demanding economic assistance to the entire region.[8]

Overall, his record in the House was undistinguished. House Speaker Rayburn described him as "a good boy" but not presidential material. Louisiana

Democrat Felix Hébert remembered that JFK "was nothing as a congressman." Reporter Walter Trohan said that he spoke only to promote himself: "For the most part he was lazy." Even the Harvard economist John Kenneth Galbraith, a Kennedy admirer, conceded that JFK "was not greatly effective as a legislator."[9]

Nixon nonetheless "came to have a high regard for [JFK's] ability as a legislator" and thought that Kennedy had a similar opinion of him. During committee hearings over the Taft-Hartley bill, which would reduce the power of unions, they questioned communist-leaning labor leaders who had infiltrated the unions and usually came to similar conclusions. But when the votes were tallied, Nixon, a conservative, voted to pass the bill and then to override President Truman's veto, while the liberal Kennedy voted against the bill and to sustain the veto.[10]

On April 21, 1947, during the fight over Taft-Hartley, Congressman Frank Buchanan, a Democrat from Pennsylvania, invited the two first-term congressmen to come to McKeesport, a heavily unionized steel town, to debate the legislation. This was the first Kennedy-Nixon debate. The affair was not well attended: Nixon argued against big labor, and union members booed. Kennedy favored the unions and got a better reception. After the debate, the two congressmen had dinner at the Star Diner, where they talked baseball.[11]

They left McKeesport together on the midnight train for a vote the next day at the Capitol. They drew straws for the lower berth and Dick won, but it did not matter because they stayed up all night talking. They discovered that during the war, both had been stationed at Vella Lavella in the South Pacific at the same time and might even have met there. They also discussed their experiences and their plans. Both strongly opposed communism and favored foreign aid (under the right circumstances) and the reciprocal trade agreements program.[12]

After Nixon won the primary for the California Senate seat in 1950, he faced Democratic Congresswoman Helen Gahagan Douglas in the general election. Jack came to Dick's office and asked to see him. The receptionist Dorothy Cox buzzed him in, and he handed Dick an envelope with $1,000 in cash. Dick was in for a tough fight against Douglas, Jack told him, and his father wanted to make a contribution. Dick recalled what Jack said: "I obviously can't endorse you, but it isn't going to break my heart if you can turn the Senate's loss into Hollywood's gain." After Jack left, Dick told his secretary he was "completely flabbergasted."[13]

Helen Gahagan Douglas contributed to Nixon's dark image. After her defeat, she proclaimed that her opponent had "impugned her loyalty and smeared her character." She and her supporters never conceded that she had failed to unify the Democratic factions or to assemble an effective, well-funded campaign organization.[14]

Many Democrats sided with her, charging that Nixon had won with smear tactics and asserting that he had publicly referred to Douglas as "the pink lady." William Arnold, who handled publicity for Nixon's campaign, remarked that he "bent over backwards to prevent criticism of him using unfair tactics." If Nixon did use that phrase, the quotation never made a single major California newspaper during the campaign. Manchester Boddy, Douglas's Democratic primary opponent, did run advertisements in his Los Angeles newspaper about "The Pink Lady," as well as ads attacking "Tricky Dick."[15]

Harvard historian Fredrik Logevall, in a sympathetic JFK biography published in 2020, described Nixon as a red baiter and a sexist. As evidence, he said that Nixon called Douglas "pink right down to her underwear" and added that this "sexism" was "as much a part of his tactics as red-baiting." Logevall failed to mention that Nixon never made this comment in public. He said it privately to Arnold, who later quoted it in a memoir. Logevall also did not mention that Douglas called Nixon a liar in newspaper advertisements, in which she also compared him to Stalin, Mussolini, and Hitler. Logevall's Harvard colleague Jill Lepore, in a book published the same year, not only repeated the same charge but, to underline Nixon's red-baiting tactics, erroneously gave Joe McCarthy a seat in the U.S. House of Representatives: "Nixon, like McCarthy, served on the House Un-American Activities Committee, where, like McCarthy, if with more polish and more subtlety, he gleefully accused a lot of other people of wearing pink underwear, too." McCarthy served only in the Senate, so he never could have been on any House committee.[16]

Neither historian wrote about Kennedy's reaction to the senatorial contest. Three days after Nixon defeated Douglas, Kennedy told a group of professors and students at Harvard that he was pleased with the results. Nixon recognized that while the $1,000 had come from Joe Kennedy, the son approved. Jack "was on my side in that campaign."[17]

Having watched his colleagues Smathers and Nixon win their Senate contests in 1950, Kennedy decided to go for it himself in 1952. Robert Kennedy, for the first time, managed his older brother's race. Kenneth O'Donnell, who had been on the Harvard football team with Bobby, and David Powers, who had served on earlier campaigns, joined Bobby on the staff. Larry O'Brien, an Irish-Catholic lawyer from Springfield, Massachusetts, directed the organization.[18]

The campaign was again a family effort. Kennedy's mother and several of his sisters held well-attended tea parties to advance his candidacy. Jack's father supplied funding, both conventional and otherwise. He made a $500,000 loan to John Fox, publisher of the *Boston Post*, that saved the newspaper from bankruptcy. A day later, the *Post* endorsed JFK, who well outperformed the head of the Democratic ticket. Even though General Dwight David Eisenhower defeated Illinois Governor Adlai Stevenson by 208,000 votes in Massachusetts, Jack's energetic campaigning and an uninspiring performance by the incumbent, Henry Cabot Lodge, Jr., resulted in a narrow triumph: Kennedy had 1,211,984 votes to Lodge's 1,141,247. He had upset Lodge with 51.5 percent of the vote.[19]

Nixon, meanwhile, had emerged as a popular Republican spokesman against communism. He had made his reputation by helping to expose Alger Hiss, the president of the Carnegie Foundation for International Peace and a former adviser to Franklin Roosevelt, as a likely communist. (Hiss, aided by many supporters on the left, denied the charge for the rest of his life; Nixon was finally vindicated only in 2009, years after his death, by the publication of *Spies*, in which John Earl Haynes and his coauthors provided indisputable evidence that Hiss had worked for Soviet military intelligence.)[20]

Nixon was rewarded in 1952 for his efforts by being chosen as Eisenhower's running mate. By any measure, his rise was meteoric, and he began to come under greater scrutiny. Ernest Brashear, a labor reporter who two years earlier had run unsuccessfully as a Democrat for the California state assembly, published a piece in the *New Republic* that September entitled "Who Is Richard Nixon?" The article recycled the old charges about Nixon's campaigns against Voorhis and Douglas, then turned to his legislative record, focusing mainly on the Mundt-Nixon bill, which Nixon cowrote and which was later merged into the Subversive Activities Control Act (also called the McCarran Act of 1950). The law required communist organizations to register with the United States attorney general and permitted government surveillance of persons suspected of being "subversives"; Congress had passed it over President Truman's veto. Brashear quoted the *New York Times* that the law "could be used to impose restrictions on freedom." Was Nixon "the man we want to place over our lives and within one heart beat of the most important temporal job in the world?" Brashear asked.[21]

While the *New Republic* appealed to a limited readership, the *New York Post*, a liberal newspaper at the time, enjoyed a much larger circulation. On September 18, it carried a story with the banner headline: "Secret Rich Men's Trust Fund Keeps Nixon in Style Far Beyond His Salary." The headline did not match the article. First, the fund was not secret; second, rich men were not the only contributors; and third, Nixon did not use the funds to enrich himself. They went to cover additional office expenses because he did not have the money to pay them himself. Even so, the allegations of corruption created a controversy around the candidate. Democratic newspapers and politicians demanded his resignation, and surprisingly, several influential Republican politicians and newspapers agreed. In an effort to absolve himself, Nixon gave the first nationally televised political speech in the nation's history—what is now known as the Checkers Speech. The response received by Nixon's staff was huge and overwhelmingly positive, but his opponents called it "maudlin."[22]

Kennedy congratulated his friend on his vice presidential nomination. After the Republican national convention, Jack sent Dick a handwritten note: "I was always convinced that you would move ahead to the top—but I never thought it would come this quickly. You were an ideal selection and will bring to the ticket a great deal of strength."[23]

Toward the end of the race, Dick and Jack were campaigning separately in Boston and their cars briefly happened to pass alongside each other. Dick and Pat saw Jack waving to them from his open convertible, and Dick waved back. Pat reminded her husband that Jack was running against Lodge and Dick should not give him a boost by greeting him.[24]

That January, Kennedy moved into room 362 of the Old Senate Office Building, directly across from room 361, Nixon's office as vice president. Sometimes the vice president would cross the hall to the senator's suite to talk to him, and Nixon and JFK often visited each other in their respective offices. Occasionally, Kennedy gave books to Nixon, including an inscribed copy of *To Light a Candle*, the autobiography of Father James Keller, founder of the Catholic inspirational group the Christophers. Kennedy also held a cocktail party for both staffs during his first year in the Senate.[25]

Jack did not belong to the Senate's inner circle. He did not play handball in the Senate gym; Dick did. Dick and Pat did not regularly socialize with Jack, though on several occasions, the Nixons went to small dinner parties at Kennedy's Georgetown home. On April 29, 1953, for example, they went to Kennedy's house for a reception to meet his sister Eunice, who shared the residence. They were, Nixon recalled, "gracious hosts." That September, the Nixons were invited to Jack and Jackie's wedding, but Dick declined because he had already committed to playing golf with the president in Denver.[26]

Once Kennedy was a senator, Jackie became a member of the Ladies of the Senate, which Pat Nixon chaired; they saw each other every Tuesday, when they dressed in white nurse's uniforms and rolled bandages. At the end of 1954, Jack asked Dick to write a letter of recommendation for membership in the Burning Tree Club. Dick wrote: "I have known Senator Kennedy for a number of years as a personal friend and he would make an excellent addition to the membership." Jack was accepted.[27]

When Jackie's father, John Bouvier III, died in the summer of 1957, the Nixons expressed their sympathies for her loss: "Parents are always very special people to all of us. It is hard to have them go no matter when." Jackie appreciated the note.

When Caroline was born in late November 1957, Dick and Pat sent a telegram to Jack welcoming him to the father-daughter club. Jackie responded: "If she grows up to be half as enchanting as your little girls I will ask no more of her." Jackie was saving the telegram for her daughter to read when she was able.[28]

Besides maintaining this personal relationship, the two men also discussed Senate business. On April 6, 1954, Kennedy said on the Senate floor that "to pour money, materiel, and men into the jungles of Indochina without at least a remote prospect of victory would be dangerously futile and self-destructive."[29]

Later, he and Nixon discussed the deteriorating conditions in Indochina, and Kennedy later recorded his recollection of the conversation on a Dictabelt. Nixon, he said, was angry with the British government because it had refused to provide air assistance to the French forces then surrounded at Dien Bien Phu by the Vietminh. Kennedy asked what the United States should do, and Nixon replied that it should support the French and the Vietnamese and hope they would successfully defend the fortress. He did not see any viable solution because the French were "really in bad shape over there." Later that month, speaking in Chicago about the worsening conditions in Indochina, Kennedy commented that if the vice president's statements were accurate, "we are about to enter the jungle and do battle with the tiger." Southeast Asia could not stay out of the communist orbit unless Indochina, India, Burma, and Indonesia united. Kennedy ended by calling for the French to grant Indochina independence.[30]

Many senators disapproved of Kennedy's work ethic. Maine Republican Margaret Chase Smith was among them. "His breezy style annoyed her," wrote her biographer Patricia Schmidt. "His indifference to the legislative process insulted her." Even Jack's close friend Senator Smathers rated him "not big as a senator." But the senior senator from Massachusetts, Republican Leverett Saltonstall, defended him. He had developed a "warm friendship" with Kennedy and believed that Jack was effective where he was deeply interested.[31] John Shaw, in his study *JFK in the Senate*, concluded: "There are no claims to landmark legislation, large accomplishments, or bold leadership." Kennedy "was not a great U.S. senator."[32]

Jack's chronically bad back grew worse. In late October 1954, he had spinal surgery that went terribly wrong due to a postoperative infection. A Catholic priest gave him last rites, but he survived and went through a protracted recovery. Nixon passed a message to Kennedy via Sorensen, assuring him that even though Kennedy was hospitalized, the narrow Democratic majority in the Senate would not be jeopardized. Jackie Kennedy replied for her husband on December 5, writing that this assurance took a load "off his mind" and that Nixon had been "kind and generous and thoughtful." Jack was frustrated being "cooped up in the hospital and wondering if it would affect everything in Washington." She added that there was not "anyone in the world he thinks more highly of than he does you—and this is just another proof of how incredible you are."[33]

Nixon answered on February 5, 1955, that he looked forward to seeing Jack return in the "very near future" and that Jack's staff was "working hard over there because I have stuck my head in a couple of times when I have gone home at a rather late hour and somebody is usually still there!" When Jack came back, Dick offered him the use of his formal office right off the Senate floor so that he would not have to walk the long distance from his office. Upon his return, the vice president sent a basket of fruit with a card: "Welcome home. Dick Nixon."[34]

While Kennedy was confined to bed rest, he started to draft *Profiles in Courage:* portraits of several senators who had exercised special examples of courage. It was finished with Sorensen's collaboration and went on to win a 1956 Pulitzer Prize. A copy of the book reached Nixon's desk on January 10, 1956, inscribed to Nixon "With the highest regards of his friend—Jack Kennedy." Nixon thanked the publisher: "I have a great deal of admiration and respect for my fellow colleague."[35]

Dick's friendship with Jack also brought him into contact with the senator's younger brothers. One day at the beginning of his vice presidency, Dick, as usual, came to his office early and found Edward "Ted" Kennedy, then a Harvard undergraduate, sitting on a suitcase outside his brother's closed office. Nixon invited him in for a cup of coffee, and they talked about his schooling.[36]

The vice president had more contact with Robert Kennedy, who worked for Senator Joseph McCarthy of Wisconsin. In 1953 he was appointed to the staff of the Senate Permanent Subcommittee on Investigations, but he soon quit because of friction between himself and the senator's two chief assistants, Roy Cohn and David Schine. The Democratic minority on the committee soon rehired him. Early in 1954, RFK telephoned Nixon's office to discuss one of its investigations and later met with the vice president, who signed a photograph: "To Bob Kennedy—with appreciation for his dedicated service to the nation from another investigator of an earlier vintage—Dick Nixon."[37]

Nixon recalled that Alice Longworth, former president Theodore Roosevelt's daughter, once described Bobby as "an eighteenth-century Jesuit priest" who lacked humor. According to Nixon, Bobby "was very intense, very hard-working, very dedicated." He fully supported McCarthy and McClellan, and they appreciated his loyalty.[38]

Nixon had a more complicated relationship with Eisenhower. When they took office in 1953, they were not well acquainted. They would later become, according to Nixon's unpublished memoirs, "friends, but not cronies." Ike did not consult with his vice president on his cabinet appointments, who generally did not have political experience. Nixon filled that void. During meetings at the

White House, he usually was the source of political advice. Throughout Ike's presidency, Nixon believed that anyone who could possibly damage the president was disposable. Senate majority whip Saltonstall recalled the vice president as "a very strong party man." Usually, he wrote, Nixon was "very quiet . . . seldom took the lead in the discussions, but when he did, his advice was very good."[39]

Ike carefully maintained his image as a man above partisan politics by doing little campaigning in the 1954 midterm elections. This stance left Nixon as the most prominent partisan Republican on the national scene. He campaigned tirelessly for Republican candidates and against Democrats over forty-eight days that fall. The tension between McCarthy, who even in steep decline commanded fervent supporters, and the avowedly apolitical president had left Republicans divided and, Nixon felt, often apathetic. Many political contests that year degenerated into mudslinging over communist associations.

Ike was not really so apolitical: behind the scenes, he routinely instructed Nixon how to counter the Democratic assaults against the administration. But neither was he devoted to the Republican Party, and it cost him. When the votes were tallied in November 1954, Republicans had lost sixteen House seats and two in the Senate. Eisenhower had lost his congressional majorities and would not regain them.[40]

Harsh words had been exchanged on both sides, and the bitterness over the election lingered. In the end, the Democrats, combining partisan rancor with a remarkable lack of self-awareness, decided it was largely Nixon's fault. Democratic National Committee chairman Paul Butler opened a "Chamber of Smears" to catalogue how Nixon had maligned Democrats during the races.[41]

Nixon, in his memoirs, recalled that he had to make some difficult decisions after the campaign. He knew the president would maintain a nonpolitical posture and that Democrats would not attack him because of his great popularity. As vice president, Nixon would lead the party's assaults on Democrats, and in turn would become a lightning rod for their counterattacks. The more effective he was in helping Republican candidates win elections, the bigger a target he would become. Reflecting on this, he "sometimes wondered where party loyalty left off and masochism began." Julie, his six-year-old, and Tricia, eight, "were reaching an impressionable age, and neither Pat nor I wanted their father to become the perennial bad guy of American politics." By the last week of the campaign, he was exhausted and decided that he would retire at forty-four and "pretty much be able to write my own ticket." He had one more speech to give, on election eve, and that would end his political career "unless exceptional circumstances intervened to change my mind."[42]

Dick also reflected on Pat's growing unhappiness. She was, he wrote, "a superb campaigner even though she is a very private person and much prefers home life to public life." The fund crisis in 1952, when adversaries questioned her husband's honesty, had made politics distasteful for her. Just after the 1954 elections, Pat and Dick had a tête-à-tête. She told him she was disillusioned with the party, the press, and others, and upset that Dick had received no credit for his tireless campaigning on behalf of Republican candidates; furthermore, the couple's social duties took time away from raising their daughters. By the time they went to sleep, she had persuaded him to leave the vice presidency and politics after 1956 and return to California. In his memoir, Nixon commented that this sourness about political life was a "passing phase" for him, but for her it was not. By the following year, however, "life became more bearable."[43]

By then, exceptional circumstances also had intervened. In the fall of 1955 the president was vacationing at his wife's family home in Denver, Colorado. Early on the morning of September 24, he awoke with chest pains and was transported to a nearby military hospital, where he was diagnosed with a severe heart attack. The announcement shocked the nation: the president might die.

Nixon was quickly apprised of Ike's condition, and as vice president, he spoke for the administration, reassuring the country that the government would function smoothly and that the president would fully recover. He received plaudits for handling this tense and delicate situation with assertiveness but without overstepping his authority. At cabinet meetings, he left the president's chair vacant, he remained in close contact with Ike during his convalescence, and he made it clear he was speaking for the president.

At the beginning of 1956, when the president returned to the White House, speculation arose over whether he would seek reelection. Those doubts were answered in mid-February when his physicians declared that their patient was sufficiently healthy to run again, and at the end of the month, Ike announced that he would seek a second term.[44]

But he made no mention of Nixon as his running mate. Late in 1955 and again in early 1956, Ike had told Nixon that if he won a second term, Nixon should take a cabinet position. Eisenhower was thinking in military terms. To move up to the next rank, he thought, Nixon should gain experience in a variety of settings, and the experience he most needed was running a large department. When he announced for reelection, Ike wanted to keep this option open. He later told the press that Nixon should "chart his own course." Nixon, thinking politically, knew this would be seen as a snub, and he was hurt and angry. When voters went to the polls in the New Hampshire primary in March, Nixon supporters cast a large number of write-in ballots for his renomination. Finally, after fretting for weeks, Nixon met with Ike on April 26 and asked to be his running mate. The president gladly agreed.[45]

But the delay and Ike's apparent uncertainty created an opening in some people's minds. On July 20, a month before the national convention, Harold Stassen, the administration's mutual security adviser, asked Nixon to step aside and proposed Governor Christian Herter of Massachusetts in his place. The press magnified Stassen's initiative into a "Dump Nixon" campaign, but it had no chance of success. Stassen had little influence in the GOP, Herter had no interest in the vice presidency, and by the time the convention opened, Nixon already had enough committed delegates to win the nomination. Stassen's motives were transparently opportunistic. He knew that Herter had no interest in being president and Nixon did; getting Nixon out of the way would clear a path for Stassen's own run for the Republican nomination in 1960.[46]

Republicans generally dismissed the assaults on Nixon's character. By the end of 1956, many in the party saw him as Ike's successor.

During the last year of Eisenhower's first term and the first year of his second, Kennedy, with little press attention, reviewed the duties of the president and vice president. As chairman of the Subcommittee on Reorganization of the Committee on Government Operations, he worked on the Hoover Commission's recommendations for amendments to the Constitution to make the executive branch more efficient and better organized. He rejected the introduction of an "Administrative Vice President." Presidents managed their administrative responsibilities, and Kennedy did not see any necessity for change. One proposal he did favor was abolishing the Electoral College, which he described as a "potentially dangerous anachronism." But the danger he saw was not the difference in voting power the system created between large and small states, only the potential that some electors might not follow the voters' wishes. He suggested that each state retain the same number of electoral votes and that these votes be automatically given to the winner of each state's popular vote. If no one candidate received a majority, he thought the House and Senate should hold an open roll call vote, one vote per legislator, to decide the winner.[47]

Kennedy began thinking about trying to become the 1956 Democratic vice presidential nominee in late 1955. He saw himself following Nixon's path: first the House, then the Senate, and then the vice presidency.

He had taken advice exclusively from Democrats, who inflated Adlai Stevenson's chances of winning a rematch with Eisenhower. On the morning of March 8, weeks before the New Hampshire primary, Kennedy announced that although

Massachusetts did not hold a primary, the time had come to announce his choice for the Democratic presidential nomination. He had supported Stevenson in 1952 and would stick with him. He would work for Stevenson's nomination at the convention and vigorously campaign for him during the general election.[48]

In the spring of 1956, rumors started circulating that he wanted to run with Stevenson. Kennedy had Sorensen prepare a sixteen-page analysis on how a Catholic vice presidential nominee would benefit the Democratic ticket. Large minorities of Democratic Catholics lived in fourteen states with 261 electoral votes, 5 short of an Electoral College majority. To shield Kennedy from accusations of self-promotion, John Bailey, a Catholic and the chair of Connecticut's Democratic Party, claimed authorship. It became known as the Bailey Memorandum.[49]

On July 1, as the convention drew close, JFK was interviewed on *Face the Nation*. The moderator, Stuart Novins, asked him to assess the Democrats' chances of defeating the Ike-Nixon ticket. Kennedy responded that even given the president's popularity, his party had a good chance of winning. Novins asked whether the Republicans should replace Nixon in view of Ike's health issues. Any effort to do so, Kennedy replied, would start "a hard political battle, those who wanted to keep him [Nixon] and those who did not, and it might split the Republican Party open, and it might lose them more than they would gain."[50]

While JFK was moving toward a decision to run for the vice presidency, his father wrote R. Sargent Shriver, Jr., one of his sons-in-law, that Ike was "the most popular man that we have seen in our time and to make attacks on him in the coming campaign is to me a sure way to commit suicide." Joe had shared this opinion with Stevenson two years earlier. In addition, he wrote to Shriver, the current peace and prosperity made the public uninterested in complicated issues that it did not comprehend. If he were Jack, he would base his "entire campaign on the possibility that Mr. Nixon would become President if anything happened to Eisenhower." Independents thought "badly enough of him [Nixon] as it is." Many did not even know why they disapproved of him: "You just hold up the spectre of Nixon as President and don't try to dot the i's or cross the t's."[51]

On July 23, the patriarch wrote his son questioning his decision to seek the vice presidential nomination. Stevenson would select his own running mate, and when Jack learned what kind of person Stevenson was considering, he could decide then whether that was attractive to him. If it was not, he needed to state publicly his preference to remain in the Senate and continue to serve the people of Massachusetts. Joe was willing to give a press interview backing whatever action his son took but noting that at present, Jack was dedicated to his state responsibilities. If Democratic Party officials thought he would help the national ticket, he would surely consider it; and "if he is nominated by his party, I am dead sure he will give a fine account of himself."[52]

To further strengthen his relationship with Stevenson, JFK worked within the Massachusetts Democratic Party to endorse him. He gained an unexpected advantage when asked to narrate *The Pursuit of Happiness,* a film shown at the national convention extolling the Democratic Party's virtues.[53]

The convention opened in Chicago on August 13. The film that JFK narrated was well received. Three days later he gave the nominating speech for Stevenson, telling his audience that Ike had been a lackluster president and only the Democrats could solve America's pressing domestic and foreign policy problems. As for Eisenhower and Nixon as candidates for reelection, he cautioned, "Our party will be up against two of the toughest, most skillful campaigners in its history—one who takes the high road, and one who takes the low." The delegates cheered wildly as he placed Stevenson's name in nomination.[54]

Once nominated, Stevenson surprised the delegates by allowing them to select his running mate. Senator Smathers nominated JFK, and on the first ballot, he and Senator Estes Kefauver from Tennessee ran first and second. When voting began on the second ballot, Kennedy came close to winning a majority, but the prospect of victory soon vanished. Delegations shifted to Kefauver, and by the end of the second ballot he had the nomination. On August 17, Kennedy again went to the podium and graciously conceded, calling on the delegates to make Kefauver's nomination unanimous.[55]

After his defeat, Kennedy told close friends: "I feel like the Indian who had a lot of arrows stuck in him and, when he was asked how he felt, said, 'It only hurts when I laugh.'"[56]

Jackie recalled that her bitterly disappointed husband had slept just two hours a night during five nights of the convention. Afterward, she said, he "was damned tired" and upset "for about a day or so." He also conceded that Kefauver, who had run in several primaries, deserved the victory. Jack telephoned his father, who was vacationing on the French Riviera. Rather than console his son, Joe congratulated him: "This is the best thing that's ever happened to you!" Jack also heard from Dick Nixon, who complimented him on his effort to win the vice presidential nomination and said he would have made a stronger candidate than Kefauver.[57]

Arthur Schlesinger, Jr., agreed, writing JFK that he "clearly emerged as the man who gained the most during the Convention. You hit the bull's eye on every one of your appearances; and your general demeanor and effectiveness made you in a single week a national political figure." Schlesinger suggested that

Jack add to his national presence by campaigning vigorously for the ticket and meeting people across the nation.[58]

At the close of the convention, a pregnant Jackie Kennedy told her husband and Smathers to take a "boat trip" to relax. According to Smathers, he and Jack chartered a forty-five-foot sailboat in the Mediterranean and went on a two-week cruise. On August 23, Jackie was rushed to the hospital with internal hemorrhaging and had a stillborn daughter, Arabella. Jack did not learn of his wife's loss until three days later, when he telephoned from Genoa, Italy. At first he saw no reason to return, but Smathers told him that this neglect might ruin his marriage and thus damage his political future. Smathers recalled: "I was going to get him back there even if I had to carry him." Jack arrived at Boston's Logan Airport on August 28 and immediately went to comfort his wife.[59]

The FBI learned more about Kennedy's Mediterranean cruise in July 1959. James Dowd, an FBI attorney, spoke with Lee Holley, "a very ardent Democrat" and a former marine who had worked his way through Georgetown Law School with a part-time job as a Senate office guard. Some years earlier, checking Kennedy's office one evening, Holley was angered to find evidence of the senator's "damn poor judgment." On his desk for anyone to see was a photograph of a group of men and women partying on a yacht. Kennedy's "extracurricular activities," Holley said, "were a standard joke around the Senate Office Building."[60]

During the fall campaign, Jack followed Schlesinger's advice and spoke out for the Democratic ticket across the nation. Ike had failed in domestic legislation, he said, by not passing enough new social programs, and in foreign affairs by failing to move against European colonialism or to confront the Soviet menace.[61]

Stevenson, meanwhile, asked Bobby Kennedy after the convention to join his campaign staff as an observer. After spending six weeks on the campaign, Bobby concluded that it was "the most disastrous operation" he had ever seen. The Stevenson staffers wasted far too much time arguing over inconsequential issues. Bobby lost confidence in Stevenson and voted for Ike.[62]

The president campaigned at his convenience, while Nixon went at it full-bore. By the close of the contest, Stevenson was following Joe Kennedy's advice: he regularly warned audiences that Eisenhower was likely to die before the end of his term, making Nixon president; to prevent this calamity, the nation must vote for Stevenson.

During the closing days of the campaign, two international events drew national attention. A revolt in Poland against Soviet occupation that summer sparked a larger, more violent rebellion in Hungary in late October. After the Hungarian government fell, the Soviet army invaded on November 4, just two days before the election. Also in late October, British, French, and Israeli troops attacked the Suez Canal, then controlled by Egypt. Eisenhower, the committed internationalist and proven military hero, showed his mettle by exercising restraint in both cases, pointedly refusing to support Britain and France in the Suez. But the crises took the wind out of Stevenson's sails: his campaign's call for reduced military spending looked decidedly unconvincing. Ike won by a landslide, with a margin of more than nine million votes, or 57 percent to 43, and carried forty-one of the forty-eight states. But he was the first president since 1848 whose election came without his party winning a majority in at least one house of Congress.[63]

The Kennedys assessed the many mistakes they had made at the Democratic convention. Bobby, who managed his brother's failed attempt at the vice presidential nomination, had never been to a Democratic convention and had not grasped how it operated. RFK knew he would have to have a better grasp of the rules in order to prevent a similar defeat if his brother ran for the presidency in the future. Next time, he would master the rules, make deals with the delegates, determine the delegate count, and maintain effective communications.[64]

2

Team Kennedy

Just days after Eisenhower's landslide victory in 1956, Jack Kennedy decided to seek the presidency. Right before Thanksgiving dinner at the family's large white house overlooking the Atlantic Ocean in Hyannis Port, Massachusetts, Jack and his father talked privately. When they sat down at the dinner table, Jack told the family he intended to run for the White House.[1]

He saw three potential Democratic rivals for the 1960 nomination: Senators Hubert Humphrey from Minnesota, Stuart Symington from Missouri, and Lyndon Johnson from Texas.

Humphrey, identified with the northern liberal faction of the party, had become mayor of Minneapolis in 1945 at the age of thirty-four. At the 1948 Democratic national convention, he gave a keynote address passionately proclaiming that his party must champion the cause of civil rights. He ran for the Senate that year and won, and remained in the vanguard of liberal causes. He publicly announced his candidacy in July 1959. The same factor that made him popular among liberals, his support of civil rights, made southern Democrats staunchly oppose his candidacy. He was seen as a regional candidate who lacked the funds to mount a serious race, and his declaration never sparked any national enthusiasm.[2]

At 6-foot-2 and 183 pounds, the gray-haired William Stuart Symington, Jr., looked like a president. He was born in 1901 and graduated from Yale in 1923. He served as the first secretary of the air force from 1947 to 1950, won election to the Senate two years later, and was convincingly reelected in 1958. He joined the attack on McCarthy's excesses and vigorously supported his censure. By the beginning of 1957, former president Truman was pushing Symington's candidacy, and the Democratic power broker Clark Clifford, who had known Symington for twenty-five years, emerged as his principal campaign adviser. During Eisenhower's second term, Symington voiced dire warnings about a "missile gap" and believed the president was lying to the country when he said that there was not one. But his strength was undercut by distinct weaknesses. He decided not to participate in any primaries; nor did he have the finances to match Kennedy's. More important, he did not seem to have the compulsive drive that a candidate must have.[3]

Kennedy's third and most significant threat was Lyndon Johnson. Born in 1908, he had been consumed with politics for almost his entire adult life. He had won election to the House of Representatives in 1936 and lost his first Senate contest in 1941 to W. Lee "Pappy" O'Daniel by 1,311 votes through massive fraud. Following that defeat, he started to amass a personal fortune, buying radio and television stations in the Lone Star State. When he again tried for the Senate seat in 1948, he won by 87 votes using the same corrupt practices—such as buying votes and ballot stuffing—that had been employed against him seven years earlier, earning the nickname "Landslide Lyndon." Robert Caro, Johnson's principal biographer, wrote that he "displayed a willingness to do whatever was necessary to win: a willingness so complete that even in the generous terms of political morality, it amounted to amorality."[4]

In 1952, as a forty-four-year-old freshman senator, Johnson rose to minority leader with support from the party's southern wing and especially from Richard Russell of Georgia. LBJ matured into a master of insider manipulation and was famous for applying "The Treatment": towering over most of his colleagues at 6-foot-3, he would put his arm around a senator's shoulder, lean in close, and apply thick layers of Texas charm until the other senator gave in.[5]

Johnson usually cooperated with Ike on foreign policy and differed over domestic legislation. When he criticized the administration's Vietnam policies in May 1954, this was an exception. He also led the unanimous Democratic effort to censure McCarthy. Johnson easily won reelection in 1954; the Democratic Party regained a Senate majority, and he became, at forty-six years old, the youngest majority leader in Senate history.[6]

LBJ survived a serious heart attack on July 2, 1955, and that autumn, Joe and Bobby Kennedy had a meeting in New York with the powerful Washington attorney Thomas Corcoran, in which they asked him to approach Johnson to run for the presidency in 1956. Joe would fund the campaign on the condition that LBJ select JFK as his running mate. Johnson declined the offer.[7]

Johnson voted for Kennedy to be Stevenson's running mate at the 1956 Democratic convention. This was not a sign of Johnson's high opinion of his colleague.

He once described JFK's performance in the Senate as "pathetic." LBJ's administrative assistant, George Reedy, labeled Jack a "lightweight." Bobby Baker, who served as secretary to the majority leader and worked closely with LBJ, said that JFK "didn't give a damn about the Senate."[8]

At the start of Eisenhower's second term, LBJ started to speak like a candidate, but like most other contenders, he denied interest in the presidency. He helped guide the Civil Rights Act of 1957 through the Senate and won plaudits for that accomplishment. Columnist Joseph Alsop, on March 18, 1958, told Johnson he was "probably the most admired man at present in Washington."[9]

The next year, Alsop reiterated his support for LBJ, and Speaker Rayburn also pushed him to run. Johnson clubs appeared around the country, while he continued to deny any presidential aspirations. But he also booked a six-day political tour of Kentucky, Missouri, Iowa, Kansas, and Arizona. Even though none of these states had a primary, LBJ believed that he had potential support in each of them.[10]

Johnson's strength and weakness were his southern roots. The South gave him an unshakable base but limited his appeal outside the region. He tried calling himself a westerner, but that distinction never gained traction. As master of the Senate, he won praise for passing legislation from the groups that benefited, and resentment from those who opposed the bills.

Additionally, Adlai Stevenson remained a potential phantom candidate. From 1957 to 1960 he repeatedly declared that he was not a candidate. The attention flattered him, he insisted, but his name should not be placed on any primary ballot. He would not eliminate himself from consideration but would not make any overt effort for the nomination. When a movement to draft him started to build momentum toward the end of 1959, he wrote: "I will not lift a finger for the nomination; indeed, don't want it."[11] Yet he did not endorse anyone else.

Stevenson's political contacts with Kennedy began during the 1956 Democratic convention. On July 6, before the convention, Stevenson met with his staff, telling them he admired JFK as a potential running mate, "but he's too young"; Stevenson also cited "his father, his religion." Twenty days later, he specifically dismissed Kennedy because of his Catholic faith.[12]

After losing the presidential race in 1956, Stevenson remained in contact with Kennedy, congratulating him on his overwhelming reelection to the Senate in 1958. Press gossip disrupted such pleasantries. Columnist Rowland Evans, Jr., wrote on May 30, 1959, that Stevenson told friends that LBJ was the most "capable" Democratic candidate, followed in order by Humphrey, Kennedy, and Symington. If none of these reached a majority, Stevenson might accept nomination as a compromise candidate. He wrote all four on the first of June, declaring that he had "never discussed the relative merits of Presidential candidates with anybody at any time."[13]

With Stevenson's status muddying the primary waters, Eleanor Roosevelt, the former first lady and a powerful Democratic leader, attacked Kennedy in print and in her speaking engagements. Since her husband's presidency she had viewed Joseph Kennedy as a Hitler appeaser and anti-Semite who had broken with her husband. She had enthusiastically backed Stevenson for the presidency twice and was encouraging him to run again in 1960.[14]

In her memoir *On My Own*, she noted that during a meeting in her hotel room at the 1956 Democratic convention, JFK had refused to condemn McCarthy and McCarthyism. Disappointed, she responded by refusing to support his vice presidential nomination. At the end of March 1958, Kennedy appeared on CBS's *Face the Nation* and claimed to have approved of McCarthy's censure. The former first lady found him unconvincing.[15]

The exchange grew more adversarial on December 7, when Eleanor went on ABC's *College News Conference*. She said that Kennedy's father had "been spending oodles of money all over the country and probably has a paid representative in every state by now." JFK quickly wrote her that these statements were false. She answered that Joe Kennedy had publicly stated that he "would spend any money to make his son the first Catholic President of this country." And she had another concern: "Building an organization is permissible, but giving too lavishly may seem to indicate a desire to influence through money." JFK replied that his father had "not spent any money around the country" and he himself had no paid representatives in any state.[16]

JFK wrote her again on January 22, 1959, saying he hoped they would meet in the near future. Eleanor replied by telegram on January 29: "My dear boy I only say these things for your own good I have found in lifetime of adversity that when blows are rained on one, it is advisable to turn the other profile." The reference was to Kennedy's *Profiles in Courage*, a quality she not so subtly implied that he lacked. She told audiences across the nation that she thought Kennedy understood "what courage is and admires it but had not quite the independence to practice it."[17]

Why had JFK not repudiated McCarthy? He and McCarthy had met when they both entered Congress in 1947. They had double-dated and McCarthy was a guest at the Hyannis Port compound that summer; Joe Kennedy liked him, and he dated several Kennedy daughters. To help Jack against Henry Cabot Lodge in 1952, McCarthy did not campaign in Massachusetts, and in return, Joe Kennedy contributed to McCarthy's reelection race. When McCarthy was married the following year, Jack attended the ceremony.[18]

Jack also publicly defended McCarthy. In February 1952, at the one hundredth anniversary of the Harvard Spee Club (of which Jack had been a member as an undergraduate), Fred Eaton, a distinguished alumnus, stressed in a speech that he was proud that Harvard had not produced a spy like Alger Hiss or anyone like McCarthy. JFK interrupted: "How dare you couple the name of a great American patriot with that of a traitor!"[19]

When the Senate voted to censure McCarthy in December 1954, Kennedy was hospitalized from the infection that followed his spinal surgery. He and Republican Senator Alexander Wiley of Wisconsin were the only two members of the Senate not to make public statements, nor did JFK ever refer to the censure or speak out.[20]

Kennedy built a powerful organization to defeat the other contenders for the nomination. His family remained his principal anchor. Grace Burke, who worked as a secretary in Kennedy's Boston office from 1946 to 1963, recognized that the Kennedys were "very close to each other." If any member were attacked, "the whole family would take offense at it. . . . They were very loyal. And very loyal to people they knew."[21]

Joseph Kennedy, obsessed with making his son the first Irish-Catholic president, was then one of the richest men in the United States. Jack was the candidate, but his seventy-two-year-old father propelled Jack's political career, making recommendations and providing funding. He had impressed upon his children that the Boston Brahmins resented him and his Irish ancestors, who "quickly found that the promise of America was tarnished by anger, distrust, and fear." From these beliefs and his business success, he instilled in his children the idea that winning was everything. He often said to them, "we don't want any losers around here."[22]

During World War I, he had formed a cordial relationship with Assistant Secretary of the Navy Franklin D. Roosevelt, and when Roosevelt ran for the presidency in 1932, Kennedy pitched in as a major fundraiser. As a reward, he was named the first chairman of the Securities and Exchange Commission and then the chairman of the Maritime Commission. Added prestige came when the president appointed him the United States Ambassador to the Court of St. James's in 1938. As Hitler drove Europe closer to war, the ambassador aligned himself with British appeasers. He did not keep these opinions to himself or hide his anti-Semitism. These factors and the ambassador's opposition to FDR's run for a third term made him expendable. The president removed him from his post in the winter of 1940, and he never regained his influence inside the White House.[23]

Powerful Democrats despised him. Former New York governor W. Averell Harriman condemned the "shyster tactics" Joe employed in his business dealings. Harry Truman recalled a meeting at the Ritz Carlton Hotel during the 1944 presidential campaign in which Kennedy attacked FDR for taking the United States into war. He asked Truman: "What the hell are you doing campaigning for that crippled son of a bitch that killed my son Joe?" Truman says he replied, "If you say another word about Roosevelt, I'm going to throw you out that window."[24]

Because of his controversial career, Joe stayed out of the limelight. He offered advice and supplied the money. The amount Joe lavished on his son's campaign was never disclosed, but it was the subject of jokes. When Jack spoke at the Gridiron Club in Washington on March 15, 1958, he pretended to pull a telegram from his father out of his breast pocket: "Dear Jack: Don't buy a single vote more than is necessary—I'll be damned if I'm going to pay for a landslide!" The audience laughed and applauded.[25]

But it was no joke: Jack's father spent a staggering amount. The family did not release its expenditures on polling, the opening of the campaign's capital headquarters, or hiring additional staff. In the summer of 1959, the family also purchased a $385,000 twin-engine Convair CV-240, named *Caroline* after Jack's two-year-old daughter. It was the first private aircraft used in a presidential campaign and had a desk, galley, and bedroom.[26]

Robert Kennedy played a critical role in the campaign. Born November 20, 1925, Bobby was eight years younger than Jack and had a small part in the first congressional race, knocking on doors for his brother. His sister Jean called him "fiercely competitive"; journalist John Bartlow Martin liked him "from the start"; he and Arthur Schlesinger formed a long-lasting friendship. Others found him vindictive and ruthless. After the 1952 Senate race, Sorensen described Bobby as "militant, aggressive, intolerant, opinionated, somewhat shallow in his convictions." The congressman who replaced JFK in the 11th district, Charles "Tip" O'Neill, Jr., thought Bobby considered everyone outside the family "disposable" and "had the personality of a casket handle. He was just a miserable kid." Harvard economist John Kenneth Galbraith, an early Jack Kennedy supporter, kept his distance from Bobby but noted that his "commitment was complete. You were either for the cause or against it, either with the Kennedys or a leper. There was no room for ambiguity, indecision or a middle ground."[27]

Bobby spent most of his energy from 1955 through the summer of 1959 working as chief counsel on the Rackets Committee and writing *The Enemy*

Within, about corruption inside labor unions. He resigned his job on September 10, 1959, and by New Year was ready to manage his brother's campaign.[28]

Ted Kennedy, the last of the nine children, was born on February 22, 1932. Like his older brothers, he went to private schools, and entered Harvard. But as a freshman in 1951, he was expelled for having another student take an exam for him. He enlisted in the army, reentered Harvard in 1953, and graduated in 1956. He followed Bobby to the University of Virginia Law School the following year and got his degree in time to assist in his brother's primary campaigns.[29]

Ted was nominally in charge of representing his brother in the western states. Columnist Robert Novak described him as "robust, trim, and good-looking." He "was brand-new on the job and didn't know anything about them [the western states]. . . . He had the reputation of a playboy but also seemed a lightweight." That opinion was partly accurate, but Ted worked energetically for his brother throughout the primaries and general election.[30]

Jean, the eighth child, married Stephen Smith in 1956. Then twenty-nine, he was admitted to the inner circle, and Ted looked on him as another brother. His family, "one of the foremost of New York waterfront families," owned Cleary Brothers, which operated tugs and barges in upstate New York and New York Harbor. Steve graduated from Georgetown University with a history major and had fought in the Korean War before entering the family business. After his marriage, he managed Park Agency, Inc., a Manhattan financial company with $300 million in Kennedy family assets. On January 1, 1959, Smith opened a nine-room suite with his name on the door in the 517 Esso Building on 261 Constitution Avenue, at the foot of Capitol Hill. After the senator announced for the presidency, the suite became the national headquarters of Senator John F. Kennedy for President.[31]

Eunice, the Kennedys' oldest daughter, had married Sargent Shriver in May 1953, when he was thirty-seven and she was thirty-one. According to sister Jean, they were "the perfect match." They were devout Catholics. Sarge, according to Harris Wofford, who worked with him on civil rights during the 1960 campaign, "belonged to the old Maryland Catholic aristocracy, unlike the Kennedys." He was a Yale graduate who had managed the Chicago Merchandise Mart, the world's largest commercial building and the largest wholesale design center, after the patriarch bought it in 1945. Besides this business, Sarge worked through the Catholic Church to end racial segregation in the Chicago schools and was active in local Democratic politics. Jack, Bobby, and other family members never fully admitted Shriver to the family's inner circle because, Wofford said, he was "too liberal."[32]

Patricia Kennedy and the movie star Peter Lawford married in the spring of

1954. Lawford and Jack had a cordial relationship by 1956, but the brothers never confided in him; he was too indiscreet. He did serve a purpose; movie stars fascinated Jack, and Lawford introduced him to Frank Sinatra, Sammy Davis, Jr., Judy Garland, and others. By the summer of 1958, Lawford had become friends as well as business partners with Sinatra. Peter introduced Jack to Frank at his Malibu home that summer, and Kennedy had Sinatra as his guest at the Mayflower Hotel in the capital. During the following winter, Sinatra attended a Kennedy fundraiser in Los Angeles, and the senator was a guest at Sinatra's Palm Springs estate.[33]

In 1960, there were not yet ethics laws mandating strict separation between congressional employees and paid campaign workers, and the senator's staff did an exceptional job of promoting his candidacy. Ted Sorensen drove himself almost to exhaustion when traveling with the senator seeking support for his nomination. Born on May 8, 1928, Ted had gone to public schools in Lincoln, Nebraska, and then attended the University of Nebraska for his law degree, tying for first in the class. Rather than remain in the Midwest, he moved to the capital and found a job in the Federal Security Agency; in 1952 he moved to a Senate committee on railroad retirement chaired by Paul Douglas, Democrat from Illinois. When the committee finished its task at the end of the year, Douglas recommended him to JFK. Within a year, he had become the senator's chief speechwriter and confidant; JFK, in turn, had become Sorensen's "hero" and would remain so for the rest of Ted's life. A quarter century after Kennedy's death, Sorensen wrote: "John F. Kennedy was so blessed with the gifts of reason, intellect, and vitality that eloquence came naturally to him." One observer commented in the summer of 1960: "when Jack's injured, Ted bleeds."[34]

Kennedy hired Pierre Salinger as his press secretary. One of his principal assignments was to cozy up to reporters. After the candidate announced, Salinger took the media on a tour of the Senator John F. Kennedy for President headquarters, which had grown in size to ten employees, with a half dozen phones, soon to be linked by a switchboard. Copies of the Kennedy campaign movie were stacked in a far corner, and newspaper clippings covered the office walls. A red, white, and blue plastic hat had "Kennedy for President" around the band and on the flat top a smiling photo of the candidate.[35]

The senator also brought in Larry O'Brien and David Powers, who had assisted in his earlier campaigns. Bobby Kennedy brought his administrative assistant, friend, and Harvard football teammate Kenneth O'Donnell into the campaign. Bob Wallace also worked on the staff and served as an advance man to induce Democratic politicians to endorse the senator. Mike Feldman was ostensibly employed as a legislative assistant, but he spent most of his time doing opposition research on Nixon and writing speeches.[36]

Four months after Steve Smith opened the campaign's Washington headquarters, the family met for a strategy session at the patriarch's Palm Beach estate. Jack convened "the Summit" with his father, Bobby, Smith, Harris, Sorensen, O'Donnell, O'Brien, Powers, and Salinger. Sitting on beach chairs facing the ocean, they went through a state-by-state analysis and discussed possible opponents like Nixon and Nelson Rockefeller. Joe promised to provide whatever money was necessary; Bobby was appointed campaign manager. A second large gathering was held toward the end of October for campaign planning, and finally, in December, Joe, Jack, Jackie, Bobby, his wife, Ethel, and Paul Fay, Jr., and his wife met at the Palm Beach home, where Bobby, who had not yet resigned as chief counsel to the Senate Permanent Subcommittee on Investigations, demanded an update from his brother on the status of the campaign planning.[37]

In fact, Bobby was already working on campaign strategy. One of his advisers was Henry "Scoop" Jackson, recently reelected to his Senate seat from Washington. A committed anticommunist liberal and a national defense hawk, he believed in the missile gap; he had also worked with Jack and Bobby Kennedy while serving on the Subcommittee on Investigations.[38] Jackson would become a staunch Kennedy loyalist.

Jack also had an advantage that few recognized; he had started his career as a reporter and was friends with many of the Georgetown set who worked as columnists. He was especially close with Joseph Alsop, whom he had met right after he entered Congress. Jack and Jackie moved into a house in Alsop's Georgetown neighborhood in 1957. Ted Kennedy had met Alsop at the University of Virginia Law School Student Legal Forum, and on August 4, 1958, wrote the columnist that his brother's campaign was "gathering momentum with each week" and that Jack wanted "to extend to you his best wishes."[39]

In a *Washington Post* column, Alsop informed his readers that he was a Republican and would probably support Lyndon Johnson for the Democratic nomination, but that Kennedy should be considered a serious contender for several reasons. He did not act like a politician; his efforts at labor reform were extremely popular; and he had overwhelming support among Catholics.[40]

Alsop was being disingenuous. He had already written to a colleague that Kennedy would be the Democratic nominee: "It will be entertaining at any rate, to have a President of the United States who strongly resembles a marine enlisted man, only slightly withered by time, with a wife who is very beautiful, very young, and unconventionally intelligent."[41]

Also in 1957, Ben Bradlee and his wife, Toni, returned to the capital after six years in Europe and bought a home in Georgetown a few months before Jack and Jackie purchased one "only a few yards from ours." The couples met while wheeling baby carriages and became friends. Ben happened to be a Harvard graduate and a *Newsweek* reporter. He sporadically reported on the senator in 1959, and after he announced for the presidency, Bradlee covered the candidate full-time.[42]

Kennedy even seduced the skeptical Robert Novak, who thought the senator "was the most attractive political personality that I have met . . . handsome, witty, charismatic, and very nice to me."[43]

Not everyone agreed. *New York Times* reporter Russell Baker thought Kennedy "looked like a kid." His desk was in the Senate's last row, a part of the floor "reserved for greenhorns," and he was seldom at it. But Baker conceded that Kennedy "was blessed with a personality beguiling to reporters."[44]

Future Pulitzer Prize winner Patrick Sloyan had enrolled at the University of Maryland, College Park, on the G.I. Bill and had been a professional journalist since leaving the army in 1957, working part-time for the *Washington Evening Star* and the *Baltimore News-Post*. He heard JFK speak at the University of Maryland in April 1959 about Thomas Jefferson and James Madison's political activities before the 1800 presidential election. Sloyan wrote that he "was spellbound by his speaking style and sparkling humor." After the presentation, he walked up to Kennedy and asked whether his Catholicism would damage his presidential chances. The reaction surprised him: "The humor washed from his face. His eyes and mouth hardened. His elation from the crowd's applause vanished." He replied: "No, my religion will be an asset. America is a religious nation and Americans will respect my religion." He moved on to the next questioner and gave Sloyan "another dirty look."[45]

Baker and Sloyan were in the minority. The media gave Jack and Jackie widespread positive coverage. They were regularly photographed as the ideal couple, and journalists gave them extensive interviews.

Despite focusing most of his energies on his run for the White House, Kennedy also attended to his senatorial duties. One task in the first session of the 85th Congress was to head a committee to select the five senators who exemplified "The Senate's Distinguished Traditions." On May 1, 1957, he announced the results: Henry Clay of Kentucky, Daniel Webster of Massachusetts, John Calhoun of South Carolina, Robert La Follette of Wisconsin, and Robert Taft of Ohio.[46]

This assignment was not nearly as consequential as the pending civil rights legislation in the summer of 1957. This issue was not a high priority for him, and he participated only sporadically in the debate. When the bill came up for Senate consideration, Kennedy voted with the southern senators three times. First, he voted against curbing the filibuster. Next, the normal procedure was that bills went to the appropriate committee for hearings — in this case, the judiciary committee, chaired by James Eastland of Mississippi, who would bury it. Forty-five senators voted to send the bill directly to the Senate floor, while thirty-nine opposed. Kennedy voted with the minority. Finally, JFK joined the 51–45 majority who voted that those accused of violating the act would have the right to a jury trial, an innocuous-sounding measure that in fact meant that defendants facing all-white southern juries would be acquitted.[47]

For his stances on the bill, Kennedy received praise from his southern colleagues and condemnation from liberals. The British historian Nick Bryant, in *The Bystander: John F. Kennedy and the Struggle for Black Equality*, calls JFK's actions "opportunistic and unprincipled."[48]

Kennedy's positions were firmer on foreign affairs, and he used his position on the Senate Foreign Relations Committee to boost his foreign policy credentials. Although his attendance at committee meetings was sporadic, he had often traveled abroad and was deeply interested in the subject. Shortly after joining the committee, he called for a permanent Middle East peace based on military assistance, a solution to the Palestinian refugee problem, and economic assistance to India and other developing countries.[49]

On July 2, 1957, he gave a speech on the Senate floor in which he said the United States had to confront both Soviet and Western imperialism in Asia and Africa. Algeria was offered as his primary example. France, he said, would have to face the fact that its colony deserved independence. Even though the United States did not wish to antagonize a European ally, the administration, the senator declared, had to stand for anticolonialism and independence.[50]

The speech drew strong criticism: those who supported the French government called it premature to grant Algerian independence. After six days of heated reaction, JFK added that if the United States did not join the forces of anticolonialism, the communists could take hold throughout the developing world, asserting that in the "world-wide struggle against imperialism, the sweep of nationalism is the most potent factor in foreign affairs today."[51] The next month, he continued his assault by attacking the administration's policies toward Poland. In a Senate speech, he called Eisenhower's rollback policy in Eastern Europe a failure. Poland, he said, should receive economic assistance and developmental loans for the Poles to create better conditions.[52]

The launching of *Sputnik* that October made headlines everywhere. The Soviets had won a spectacular public relations victory. The media exaggerated the satellite's significance, as did some Democrats. Eisenhower did not panic; he knew the United States had a commanding lead over the Soviet Union in strategic capability. But, unable to convince the public that the nation was secure, he was forced to increase military spending.[53]

Two weeks after the launch, Kennedy spoke at the University of Florida in Gainesville. "Many Americans," he said, "shocked at our failures, dismayed at our setbacks, fearful of our course, are asking themselves" whether the United States could compete with the Russians. He answered that it certainly could and called on Americans to spend more money teaching physical sciences and mathematics in secondary schools.[54]

Reiterating the theme that Eisenhower had failed and that the nation had fallen behind the Russians, Kennedy called for a bolder global strategy supported by greater expenditures. To promote his presidential aspirations and demonstrate his acumen on defense policy, he addressed his Senate colleagues on August 14, 1958, attacking the administration on the "missile gap" and accusing it of placing budgetary restraint ahead of defending the homeland.[55]

What JFK did not realize was that there was no missile gap: it was a myth based on unverifiable speculation over Soviet missile construction. Kennedy believed the worst, but he also, as Fred Kaplan writes in *The Wizards of Armageddon*, "milked the missile-gap phenomenon for political capital." Shortly after he became president, his administration admitted that the gap never existed.[56]

Besides attacking Eisenhower from his Senate seat, throughout 1957 and 1958 Kennedy spoke to Democratic groups promoting himself and his party. On May 23, 1957, he addressed the Democratic Party of Cook County, Illinois, optimistically predicting future Democratic victories. Republican prosperity, he said, did not extend to all sectors of the economy: farmers were in trouble and schools were overcrowded. A month later, speaking before the Jefferson-Jackson Day Dinner in Rockland, Maine, he held that the GOP was complacent and that "only the Democratic Party has the enthusiasm and the determination and the new ideas necessary to meet these problems and crises."[57]

Kennedy also addressed independent groups. On November 27, 1956, just after he decided to seek the presidency, he told a Zionist organization that Soviet penetration of the Middle East posed a threat to Israel. On January 20, 1958, he addressed the Woman's Club of Richmond, Virginia, about the Soviet threat in the political and economic arenas, and a month later he compared Soviet and American scientific and educational advances at the Loyola College Alumni Banquet in Baltimore as well as at the Social Science Foundation in Denver. In June he told the graduating class at the University of Wisconsin, Madison, that he hoped scholars would also become politicians.[58]

In the fall of 1958, Kennedy interrupted his speaking schedule to run for reelection. He had already run against his opponent, Vincent Celeste, in the heavily Democratic 11th congressional district in 1950, receiving 87,699 votes, or 82 percent, against Celeste's 18,302, or 17 percent. Eight years later, the outcome was predictable: Kennedy won reelection with 73 percent of the vote against Celeste's 26 percent. The margin was 874,608, the largest for any Senate candidate that year. He was the first candidate ever to carry every city and county in Massachusetts. Even FDR never took more than 60 percent of the state's vote.[59]

Kennedy continued to serve on the Rackets Committee, where his brother Bobby was chief counsel. After the Democrats regained control of the Senate in January 1955, John McClellan of Arkansas had become chairman, and the committee had become known as the McClellan Committee. Its investigations focused on corruption in government procurement programs, influence peddling, and conflict of interest. During hearings with David Beck, the president of the Teamsters Union, Bobby's interrogation was so devastating that Beck resigned. After Jimmy Hoffa succeeded him as the union's president, the chief counsel linked him to gangsters.[60]

JFK was also appointed chairman of the Subcommittee on Labor and Public Welfare, where he teamed up with New York Republican Irving Ives to draft the Labor-Management Reporting and Disclosure Act of 1958. The bill was designed to regulate union pensions, health and welfare funds, union funds, union democracy, and the resolution of labor-management disputes, but it died in the House.

The following year, Kennedy reintroduced the bill, but the public wanted a corrective to the alliance between some unions and organized crime. McClellan, in his capacity as chairman of the committee on labor and public welfare, added a workers' bill of rights to protect the rank and file from corrupt union bosses. As the bill, originally somewhat lenient, became harsher toward unions, Kennedy stopped trying to moderate it, and it was eventually passed as the Landrum-Griffin Act. Signed on September 14, 1959, the law made the Department of Labor a referee on unions' internal operations; prohibited secondary boycotts and organizational picketing; and required unions to hold elections of national officers every five years and elections of local officials every three years.[61]

Unions generally supported Democrats, and with the understandable exception of the Teamsters Union, they favored Kennedy. Labor gave him a perfect score on his votes in Congress. R. Alton Lee, in his book *Eisenhower and Landrum-Griffin*, writes that the senator had "established a good rapport with union leaders in trying to protect their interests and emerged from the battle with his reputation as a leader greatly enhanced." Even in failure, his efforts on behalf of labor "undoubtedly promoted his candidacy for the presidency in 1960."[62]

To promote his liberal credentials, at the end of June, Kennedy proposed an amendment to repeal provisions of the National Defense Education Act of 1958 that required an affidavit of loyalty from anyone applying for a loan or grant from federal funds. When this bill was being debated, no one had questioned its loyalty section. After its passage, higher education advocates overwhelmingly wanted it repealed. Such requirements, Kennedy declared, were "repugnant to our history, our traditions, our laws, and our basic philosophy."[63]

Kennedy also resumed his speaking schedule. Before a Democratic crowd in Philadelphia, he compared FDR's leadership with Ike's failure to lead. In Oregon, Idaho, and Colorado, he talked about the administration's inability to solve water resource issues. In Milwaukee he warned about the Soviet threat.[64]

As his visibility rose, Kennedy became one of the first politicians to take polling seriously. Gallup and other companies reported their findings on general trends in the press, but he wanted more detailed information. His first large campaign expense was a personal check for $5,000 paid to Louis Harris at the beginning of 1958, to conduct polls in the primary states measuring Kennedy against Democratic contenders as well as against Nixon and other Republicans. At a price of $2,500 to $4,000 per poll, depending on the size of the sample, Harris surveyed voters in California, Oregon, Florida, Maryland, Ohio, and Massachusetts. In addition to testing his strength against various opponents, the surveys showed how well Kennedy was doing with various constituencies—Catholic and Protestant voters, for example—and how much his personal image of youth and energy affected voters.[65]

Kennedy's success showed up in the polling throughout 1959. He and Stevenson were virtually tied among Democrats, but independents favored the senator. Gallup results had Kennedy consistently coming in either first or second for the Democratic presidential nomination. When Gallup narrowed the choice to Stevenson or Kennedy in February, April, and June, it found them virtually tied. When Democratic county chairmen were asked their preference in October, Kennedy came in first and Symington second. When Gallup asked voters about Kennedy's personal qualities, they responded to his youth, energy, attractiveness, wealth, truthfulness, and intelligence, and thought he was a good family man. *Newsweek* called him "the frontrunner" in the second week of November, while noting that he still faced stiff opposition.[66]

The California poll conducted by Mervin Field on March 8, 1959, released in that state's major newspapers, further confirmed Kennedy's growing popularity. Three months earlier, Field had called Stevenson the "relatively unchallenged" Democratic front-runner. That had changed. When voters were asked which man they wanted as president, Stevenson led Kennedy 29 percent to 23;

but when asked which would make the stronger candidate, they chose Kennedy, 27 percent to 23.[67]

While Kennedy ran as a devoted husband to an attractive wife and a young daughter, he faced a potentially explosive encounter that could have ended his candidacy. Mrs. Florence Mary Kater owned a Georgetown home near an apartment that the senator sublet to his receptionist, Pamela Turnure, then in her twenties. Evelyn Lincoln, the senator's private secretary, described Turnure as "a pretty girl who many visitors said looked like Jackie." As the senator was leaving her apartment on July 11, 1958, at 1:00 a.m., Kater took a photograph of Kennedy trying to hide his face. A devout Catholic, she was outraged by this apparent adultery. She sent the photo to major media outlets, believing voters had the right to know about Kennedy's personal conduct. He claimed, she protested, to be "an ideal family man" who was "above all reproach," but that image was an illusion.[68]

Most journalists at the time would not touch such personal subjects. Reporters from a minor newspaper in Washington wrote a short article on Kater's charges, but no large papers or other outlets picked up the story.

The press also failed to uncover Kennedy's most closely guarded secret. He ran as an athletic and energetic candidate and asked his private physician, Dr. Janet Travell, for a written statement about his physical condition. She replied on July 21, 1959, to his "request for a medical statement concerning your health," saying she was doing so on the condition that her name would "not be used in connection with this statement in any publication." Her letter made three assertions: (1) he had had two back surgeries and currently his back was "entirely well"; (2) he had "never had any abnormal pigmentation of the skin or mucous membranes," meaning that he had never had Addison's disease; and (3) he had "tremendous physical stamina" and a "fine physique and remarkable vitality."[69]

Each of these statements was untrue.

Kennedy had back problems for most of his adult life, causing the left side of his body to be shorter than the right side. He had first injured his back in 1937, when he spent two hours on an Italian beach pushing his car off the sand and onto the asphalt. Three years later, he aggravated the injury while playing tennis. When his PT boat was destroyed in 1943, his time swimming in the ocean and caring for his men added to the injury. His first spinal surgery to lessen his pain, performed in 1944, was unsuccessful.[70]

Both the Lahey and Mayo clinics advised against another surgery, but he found surgeons in New York City willing to operate. On October 21, 1954, he underwent surgery that fused his lower spine with a metal plate. A postoperative infection almost killed him. After his recovery, he had additional surgery in February 1955 to remove the plate.[71]

JFK's family and friends were acutely aware of his back troubles. Kenny O'Donnell observed that Jack "always had crutches in the car, which he would use when his back really bothered the hell out of him and when nobody was looking." Salinger added that JFK used a "canvas back support about eight inches wide, strapped around his waist." He wore a jacket to hide the brace from the public.[72]

Jackie Kennedy's recollection was more poignant: Jack, she said, "was always campaigning on crutches. It was so pathetic to see him go up the steps of a plane, or the steps to a stage or something on his crutches . . . because he looked so vulnerable." Once at the podium, she added, he was in complete control.[73]

During a trip to London in September 1947, Kennedy was diagnosed with Addison's disease, a rare and fatal illness in which the adrenal glands stop producing hormones. When he was autopsied in 1963, his adrenal glands were gone. When the Mayo Clinic announced in April 1949 that DOCA, desoxycorticosterone acetate, helped control Addison's disease, JFK gained a normal life expectancy. By the following year, he was taking commercially available cortisone and his condition improved. He had a crisis in the fall of 1951 on a trip to Okinawa after he failed to take his medicine, but he never let it happen again.[74]

Kennedy repeatedly lied about his illness. On July 19, 1959, Arthur Schlesinger recorded in his journal a conversation with the senator, who said he had had fevers associated with malaria that "produced a malfunctioning of the adrenal glands" but was now "perfectly OK." He never had Addison's symptoms, "yellowed skin, black spots in mouth, unusual vulnerability to infection," and added that "no one who has Addison's disease ought to run for President; but I do not have it and have never had it." He denied having ever taken cortisone for "adrenal deficiency."[75]

After Kennedy's medical records were released, almost four decades after his death, several historians and physicians visited the John F. Kennedy Library and Museum to examine the files. His first serious illness came when he contracted scarlet fever at five years old. Throughout his childhood at various boarding schools, he complained of different illnesses. In the summer of 1930, he had his tonsils and adenoids removed. While at Choate preparatory school, he was often sick with colds, flu, and ear infections, and occasionally hospitalized with high fevers.[76]

Between 1953 and 1957, he was admitted to hospitals on nine separate occasions with back pain, urinary tract infections, and gastrointestinal problems. Historian James Giglio, who examined his medical records in consultation with several physicians, concluded that JFK had a preoccupation with death: "The pain continued for much of Kennedy's life—the product of surgical trauma, arthritis, weakened muscles and recurrent infections."[77] One physician, Lee Mandel, wrote that JFK "had the most complex medical history of anyone to occupy the White House." In addition to painkillers, he routinely took hot baths that, according to Mandel, may have served to "relax some muscle spasms, but other than the benefit of heat there would be no intrinsic medical value."[78]

Kennedy hid both his sexual adventures and his compromised health throughout his exhausting three-year campaign to create a positive public image for himself, from which he emerged as the front-runner for the Democratic presidential nomination. Many reporters heard the rumors about his adultery but did not pursue them. Few knew the true state of his health. Neither the extent of his illnesses nor his sexual behavior became known to the American public until long after his death.

In December 1959, the Democratic governor of Connecticut, Abraham Ribicoff, became one of the first politicians to endorse JFK for president. He then wrote the senator to say he believed this was not "a strategic mistake." Kennedy, he wrote, had singular ability "to make a split second decision from the heart and the viscera as well as the mind." Ribicoff hoped the New Year would "bring good health and success at the end of the rugged and often lonely road."[79]

Kennedy's secrets remained hidden while he prepared to announce for the presidency.

3

THE UNIFIER

At the end of 1956, the Republican National Committee summarized the results of Eisenhower's landslide electoral victory. Although the percentage of eligible voters who had gone to the polls was down 2.6 points from four years earlier, turnout was still 60.4 percent, the second-highest in recent history. Ike had defeated Stevenson by 9,559,788 votes. Republicans had gained 1,700,000 voters over 1952, and Ike had won majorities in all eight of the nation's geographical regions. For Democrats, it was the worst defeat in eighty-four years. The party lost 1,300,000 voters from the previous presidential election. The bright spot for the Democrats was that they still controlled both houses of Congress, marking the first time since 1848 that the winning presidential candidate's party failed to carry either house.[1]

Democrats had another reason for optimism. Even before the second inaugural, some were already referring to Ike as a lame duck. The 22nd Amendment had made him the first president who was barred from running for a third term. This prospect was especially disconcerting to Republicans because Gallup polls showed that Ike was the most admired man in the world and would likely have won another term if he were willing and able to run.[2]

The president voiced his displeasure at Republican congressional losses. To enlarge the party's appeal, he started talking about something called Modern Republicanism. That nebulous term was not meant as a rejection of basic Republican principles — it did not appear to mean much at all — but some party members believed, mistakenly, that he was trying to alter fundamental tenets.[3]

Nixon loyally supported the president's domestic and foreign policy priorities and depended on him for assignments. He held to a consistent schedule. He got up at 7:00 a.m., had breakfast with his family, and arrived at his Senate Office

Building suite by 8:30 or 9:00. He scheduled four to six meetings each morning in his formal office off the Senate chamber and left for the Senate floor around noon. When the Senate was engaged in routine business, he let someone else preside and returned to his office. Lunch usually consisted of a sandwich and a glass of milk, after which he tried to keep his schedule open to finish his work. He left his suite between 6:30 and 7:00 p.m. and tried to get to sleep before midnight.[4]

His wife, Pat, was his greatest asset. Nixon's mother, Hannah, usually watched the children when the Nixons left the capital to campaign. Tricia graduated from the Horace Mann Public Elementary School in June 1958, and that September, the Nixons enrolled her and Julie in the private Sidwell Friends School to expose them to Quaker teaching in line with their faith. The school had been segregated until 1956, when it "initiated a plan of progressive integration," starting with kindergarten and integrating grade by grade each year. When the girls entered, the school had "a few" black students but no black teachers or instructors.[5]

Nixon's vice presidential staff contained four male employees. His executive assistant was William Key and his legislative aide was Charles McWhorter, who had been the chairman of the 500,000-member Young Republican National Federation. When Admiral Arthur Radford, the chairman of the Joint Chiefs of Staff, learned how small Nixon's staff was, he selected two military men to work for him for the entire second term, paid out of the military budget. Colonel Robert Cushman, Jr., came from the Marine Corps and was tasked with handling national security matters; Major James "Don" Hughes came from the air force and served as the vice president's appointment secretary. Both wore civilian clothes while they worked in the office.[6]

The twelve people on the secretarial staff were all women. Heading the list were Rose Mary Woods, who would remain with Nixon until the end of his presidency, and Loie Gaunt, his office manager. Both women were devoted to him professionally and were considered part of the family. He did not have any discretionary funds for a separate campaign staff.[7]

Within the administration, William Rogers was Nixon's closest friend and ally. He and Nixon were born in the same year and both came from humble beginnings. Rogers went through New York City public schools, graduated first in his high school class, and attended Colgate University on a scholarship. He graduated fifth in his class from Cornell Law School in 1937. During World War II, he joined the navy and fought in the Pacific. Nixon met him in 1948, when Rogers was an attorney on the Senate Executive Expenditures Committee during the Hiss investigation.[8]

After a stint in private practice, Rogers joined the Eisenhower administration as deputy attorney general, with Nixon lobbying on his behalf. When Attorney General Herbert Brownell retired in 1957, the president promoted Rogers. He and Nixon talked frequently about politics and sports, and they vacationed together. John Lungren, Nixon's personal physician, described Rogers as "handsome and vain, highly intelligent and ingratiating," and a "yes-man."[9]

At the beginning of the 1957 congressional session, the vice president prepared for debate on the civil rights bill the administration had proposed the previous year. Despite opposition from segregationists, the Civil Rights Act of 1957 became law in September. Those who opposed it were pleased that it had been watered down; those who promoted it intended to press for more. What many overlooked was that the act gave the nation a federal Civil Rights Commission that would expose segregationist practices and a civil rights division within the justice department with power to prosecute those who violated black people's civil rights.[10]

The same month the bill was signed, the confrontation at Little Rock, Arkansas, over school integration matched Eisenhower against Governor Orval Faubus. The struggle ended when Ike sent the 101st Airborne to escort nine black students to their classes at Central High School.[11]

The launching of *Sputnik*, the first manmade satellite to orbit in outer space, pushed civil rights from the headlines and replaced it with the threat of Soviet military superiority. Ike tried to prevent public hysteria over the accomplishment but could not, and he was forced to yield to demands for increases in defense spending.[12]

Capping off a tumultuous year, in late November the president had a mild stroke that temporarily incapacitated him. This announcement initially caused Wall Street losses and brief speculation about whether the president would finish out his second term or if Nixon would become president.[13]

At the same time, the recession of 1957–1958 damaged support for the administration. Nixon pushed for increased spending, but the president rejected that option; the vice president also called for a tax cut to improve the economy, but the president rejected that as well. He feared inflation and believed that balancing the budget and limiting spending increases would ultimately restore economic growth. The downturn lingered for fourteen months, through the 1958 elections.[14]

Furthering damaging Republican chances, the White House chief of staff, Sherman Adams, was found to have accepted gifts from a millionaire named Bernard Goldfine, raising cries of corruption. Although Adams claimed that he never provided favors in return for the gifts, Democrats charged that he was using his office to peddle influence and called for his resignation. Ike defended Adams at first, but finally had to ask him to resign. Adams did so in late September 1958, but the taint of scandal lasted.[15]

Nixon campaigned furiously from September to election day, and even the president entered the contest toward the closing days. Their efforts were ineffective. The GOP suffered its worst loss since FDR's 1936 landslide. In 1956, Democrats had 49 senators and Republicans 47; two years later, Democrats had 64 and Republicans 34. In 1956, Democrats had 234 House members and the Republicans had 201; after 1958, there were 283 Democrats and 153 Republicans. Democrats controlled 29 governorships and Republicans had 19 in 1956; two years later, Democrats had 34 and Republicans 14. Republicans also suffered a net loss of 686 seats in state legislatures.[16]

Intraparty strife in California exemplified and amplified GOP troubles. Senator William Knowland, the Republican most often mentioned as an alternative to Nixon for the 1960 presidential nomination, ran for governor in the state. He made this decision because he detested the incumbent Republican governor, Goodwin Knight, and wanted to get him out of office. Rather than endure a bloody primary and risk defeat, Knight decided against challenging Knowland and instead, in what became known as the "Big Switch," ran for the Senate seat Knowland had vacated in order to run for governor. This accommodation did not create harmony. Instead, both men and their partisans savagely attacked one another during their campaigns, fracturing the party. Knowland and Knight each lost by more than a million votes, and neither was ever elected to public office again.[17]

At his press conference on November 5, the day after the devastating losses, the president said he saw no need to change any of his policies. He would continue as before and fight against any unnecessary spending proposed by Democrats.[18]

Writing to British Prime Minister Harold Macmillan six days later, Ike said he viewed the disappointing election results with "some detachment." He was not "an expert politician" and could not comprehend why voters did not understand that more federal assistance meant more government control. One of the Republican Party's faults, he suggested, was that it divided over the nebulous labels of liberals and conservatives. It was also plagued by "internal strife." The Democrats were equally divided, but they united at election time. Ike represented the better of the two parties and wanted to reorganize and revitalize the GOP, but as president he had a "somewhat broader [duty] than that of a mere politician."[19]

Nixon also issued a statement on November 5. Democrats deserved the victory because they had worked for two years whereas Republicans had campaigned for two months. Politics had turned into a "year-round business," and until his party recognized that, results like those of 1958 were "inevitable." He added that the GOP would start planning the next day "for the victory which will be ours in November 1960."[20]

In an interview right after the election, Nixon said that his goal over the next two years was "to help the administration make a good record." He would work to rebuild the party by finding candidates, organizing the operation, and getting finances. Republicans had to convince voters that they were doing what was best for them; they could not take "the far right position." He himself sometimes "took unpopular stands," such as on civil rights, which he considered "a moral issue." Voters' largest concern in 1960 was "probably going to be the economic issue." He opposed the big government that Democrats advocated: "The role of the government will get bigger, and the role of individuals will get smaller." It was necessary to save American capitalism. As for the 1960 nomination, the winner would be the candidate "who happens to best fit the qualifications that the public want in a President at that time." The primaries and the convention would dictate the nomination. If it went to someone else, he was "completely resigned to it."[21]

The GOP had "to move out the deadwood and get our best people in the spots where we need drive and imagination to take the action which must be taken to rebuild the Party." He favored "a general housecleaning" but added that the party needed "to find people in each state who are both able and willing." Labor unions were growing in popularity, and businesses in many areas were viewed "as a necessary evil." Business spent too much time promoting antilabor propaganda, and the many Americans who were union members reacted badly to attacks on labor. The business community should focus on positive issues instead.[22]

Amid the general disaster, some Republicans had won important contests. In races for governor, Mark Hatfield won in Oregon, Christopher Del Sesto won in Rhode Island, and Nelson Rockefeller defeated New York's incumbent Governor Averell Harriman. In senatorial races, Hugh Scott was elected in Pennsylvania and Kenneth Keating in New York, and Barry Goldwater was reelected in Arizona.[23]

With his reelection victory, Goldwater emerged as the leader of Republican conservatives. Born in 1909 of Jewish ancestry, he had fought in World War II as a pilot and then returned to Phoenix, where he was elected to the city council in 1949 and reelected two years later. He upset the two-term Democratic incumbent senator, Ernest McFarland, in 1952, running an energetic campaign and winning by 6,725 out of approximately 260,000 votes cast.[24]

Goldwater became involved with Nixon just before Christmas 1953, when Nixon's father became critically ill on an American Airline flight, forcing an emergency landing in Phoenix. He was hospitalized with a gastric hemorrhage. Goldwater learned about the crisis and kept the vice president informed about his father's condition. They began working closely together after Goldwater became chair of the Republican senatorial campaign committee, in 1955.

Goldwater backed Ike in his first term despite his worry that the party was relying on him too heavily. The party was more important than the man, he wrote Nixon in the middle of December 1958: "The principles of the Party are more important than both." The presidency was significant, but "there's too much of the idea prevalent in the Party and out of it that Ike is all we have."[25]

Still, Goldwater worked energetically for Ike's reelection. Not until afterward, when he decided that the president favored big government and approved excessive funding, particularly in foreign aid, did Goldwater break with Eisenhower, calling the president's New Republicanism a "dime-store New Deal."[26]

The breach did not extend to Ike's vice president. One day before Eisenhower announced his intention to seek reelection in 1956, Goldwater made a statement supporting Nixon for reelection. In July, he called Nixon "the best vice president that has been around since I can remember and I think that that is the general opinion of the American public."[27]

Shortly after the 1956 presidential election, Nixon described Goldwater as "one of the most able and well-liked men in the United States Senate." Goldwater, that winter, invited the vice president to speak in Phoenix because he was "immensely popular." Nixon and Pat made another appearance in February 1958, thanking Goldwater and his "enthusiastic workers" for their "fine work" for his state and his party.[28]

Goldwater ran for reelection that fall, once more against McFarland. The campaign became heated when unions spent large amounts of money attacking Goldwater for his opposition to labor before the McClellan Committee and for his antiunion activities in the Senate. He fought back with equal ferocity and ended up winning 56 percent of the vote.[29]

In December, Goldwater wrote Nixon suggesting that the GOP move to the "right of center" but not to the "extreme right." Democrats, he believed, controlled the "left of center," and the vice president needed to champion conservatism. "If you will proclaim the party and its principles as being someplace to the right, a place of your selection, then I can assure you that your team will begin to build, its strength will grow, and in 1960, not only you, but the party will be successful." Nixon was the party leader, wrote Goldwater, because the president had not shown "any evidence of interest in politics or frankly, any evidence of interest in the future of our party."[30]

The vice president replied on the last day of December. He would devote the first two weeks of January to thinking about how to rebuild the party. If it did not change, the presidential nomination in 1960 would be worthless: "We owe it to the Party and to the country to make an all out fight for the principals [*sic*] in which we believe."[31]

While Goldwater lobbied Nixon to embrace conservative principles, the vice president confronted a challenge from the newly elected governor of New York, Nelson Rockefeller, who was emerging as the party's liberal spokesman. An heir to one of the largest family fortunes in the United States, Rockefeller had served in the Roosevelt administration as assistant secretary of state for Latin American Affairs and then worked under Truman. He held a variety of jobs during Eisenhower's first term, including undersecretary of Health, Education, and Welfare and, starting in 1954, special assistant to the president for cold war planning. When he asked for expanded authority in foreign affairs and defense planning, Ike refused. Given no new duties, at the end of 1955 he resigned from the administration and returned to New York.[32]

Nixon and Rockefeller met in the summer of 1953 and saw each other occasionally thereafter at social events. Rockefeller filled in for the vice president at an event, and Nixon appreciated his substitution, referring to Rockefeller as "a good guy." When Rockefeller's wife, Mary, learned that the Nixons were going to spend part of their 1954 summer vacation in Maine, she wrote Pat Nixon, inviting them to visit their house at Seal Harbor. Rockefeller remained on cordial terms with Nixon after leaving Washington. The two men were especially in tune on foreign policy and viewed each other as political allies.[33]

Beginning in January 1956, Rockefeller helped organize Salute to Eisenhower dinners and encouraged both Ike and Nixon to run for reelection. After the March primary in New Hampshire, Rockefeller expressed his delight with the outcome, "especially the write-in for Mr. Nixon" to be renominated for the vice presidency. That summer, as the general election approached, he watched the vice president's television appearance on ABC and wrote him afterward to say he was "terrific. You have lots of friends that are all for you." Rockefeller himself was "with you."[34]

In the middle of January 1957, Nixon highlighted a "close association and friendship" since meeting Rockefeller. Both had argued for an economic program in the Middle East, and the administration was spearheading that effort. By spring, Rockefeller was writing the vice president about the need to increase expenditures for foreign and domestic programs and hoped to discuss his special studies project.[35]

Early in 1958, Rockefeller decided to run against Governor Harriman. That January, speaking at the annual luncheon of the Women's National Republican Club in New York City, Nixon singled out Rockefeller as the man to beat Harriman. Nelson was sitting two seats away and smiled broadly when the remark drew loud applause.[36]

Rockefeller received the Republican nomination for governor on August 25. The president congratulated him and wished him luck. To help himself win, Rockefeller pressured New York Congressman Kenneth Keating to run for the Senate. Keating's district was in upstate New York, and his entrance into the race would help Rockefeller attract those regional voters. After Keating rejected the idea, Rockefeller asked for Nixon's help. The vice president spoke to Keating, saying that both he and the president hoped the congressman would run, and that they would support him. Keating relented and joined Rockefeller's team.[37]

Believing that New York Democrats and independents disapproved of both Ike and Nixon, Rockefeller ran on local issues. On October 23, at the height of the contest, Nixon fulfilled his pledge to support Keating's senatorial campaign by appearing with him on television. Rockefeller was campaigning outside the city, and he neither greeted the vice president nor wanted to. They had breakfast together the next day, however, and posed for photographs. Rockefeller soundly defeated Harriman, 55 percent to 40 percent.[38]

Ike, after congratulating Rockefeller on his victory, spoke with his friend Slats Slater, who thought that the anti-Nixon faction of the party would gravitate toward Rockefeller. If Rockefeller did not get the nomination, however, Slater thought a Nixon-Rockefeller ticket "had a real chance to win."[39]

On November 22 Rockefeller met with the vice president in Washington. Denying any interest in a 1960 presidential bid, he told Nixon he expected to serve his full four-year term and that they would work together to build the GOP and encourage the best possible candidates to run for office. Nixon was skeptical: he anticipated that Rockefeller would become a candidate. A few days after the meeting he called the governor-elect "one of the best candidates I have ever seen."[40]

Feeling that the party's liberal and conservative factions were coalescing, Ike held an all-day meeting with Republican leaders at the White House on January 5, 1959, to unite the party in advance of the RNC gathering in Des Moines, Iowa, that would begin preparations for the 1960 elections. The president urged the party to publicize Republican principles year-round. Nixon reiterated Ike's recommendations, emphasizing that if it hoped to win in 1960, the party needed better organization and better candidates. RNC Chairman Meade Alcorn then addressed the conference with a nine-point program that included recruiting two million additional precinct workers and a committee to promote the party's principles, hold regional training sessions, concentrate on recruiting young people, especially on college campuses, and work daily on fundraising activities.[41]

In March, the president confided to his diary that he was "somewhat frustrated in his efforts to rejuvenate the Republican Party." His 1956 landslide, he felt, "should be a lesson to the Republicans who failed to carry the Congress . . . in 1956 or 1958." He thought people like Goldwater were not uniting: "There were just 'too many leaders' running in too many directions at once."[42]

Alcorn resigned his chairmanship in April and was replaced by Kentucky Senator Thruston Morton. To keep him informed of the administration's activities, the president invited Morton to attend the legislative leadership meetings at the White House. But the change did not bring any improvement. After breakfast with Ike at the White House, the vice president recorded his impression: "President was concerned about the defeatism in the Party. . . . Defeatism in our Party is the worst thing that confronts us."[43]

Speaking before the Young Republicans in June, he argued that the party had to advertise its successes: "The Republican Administration produced the things that the Democrats promised." The GOP wanted more money in the people's pockets, the Democrats more money for the federal government to spend. "Our programs work and theirs don't." Republicans, he concluded, needed to be aggressive in pushing their conservative politics.[44]

Goldwater, again selected as head of the Republican Senate Campaign Committee, promoted his own brand of conservatism. That spring he addressed an audience of 150 Mississippi Republicans and called Chief Justice Earl Warren a "socialist." The South had to accept the Supreme Court's decision in *Brown v. Board of Education*, he added, but sending federal troops to Little Rock, as Eisenhower had done, was a "mistake." Nixon was a "conservative" and thus more acceptable to the South than any Democrat. Appearing a few days later on *Face the Nation*, Goldwater said that the vice president's approach to civil rights was "more like most of us who feel that this problem cannot be solved by forceful means but it will be solved by understanding people in the South who are already moving in that direction."[45]

Rockefeller was inaugurated as New York governor early in 1959 and quickly became the most visible spokesman for the party's liberal wing. At that point, according to his brother David's memoirs, Nelson was already planning to run for the presidency. He expected to increase his visibility, and his brothers, especially Laurance, would contribute generously to this effort.[46]

Almost immediately after taking office, Nelson showed his appetite for large outlays on a variety of programs, and new taxes to pay for them. The *Times's* Russell Baker thought the governor was a new force in the GOP, while Nixon represented the status quo. Rockefeller had won convincingly in 1958, while the party's huge losses elsewhere had hurt Nixon. Rockefeller also had instant access to the New York media, which, Baker wrote, had started to promote the idea that "Nixon can't win." Columnist Marquis Childs predicted in early April that Rockefeller would be the GOP nominee.[47]

Baker and Childs, however, did not reflect the rank and file of the Republican Party. Many conservative regulars fervently backed Nixon because they saw him as mirroring their values, and they had watched him campaigning for their candidates for more than a decade. Partisans resented the Rockefeller buildup and the Nixon teardown.[48]

At a White House press conference in July, Robert Donovan asked the president about possible Republican presidential candidates. Ike replied that his list of ten or more "middle-of-the-roaders" included both Nixon and Rockefeller, whom he would gladly support. He would remain neutral unless some extremist gained strength, and once the candidate was chosen, he expected the challengers to unite behind him and not indulge in lingering vendettas.[49]

Speaking to reporters at the annual governors' conference in San Juan, Puerto Rico, the next month, Rockefeller denied any intention of seeking the presidency. The next afternoon, his family staged an extravagant lunchtime "coming-out party" for five hundred guests at the Dorado Beach and Golf Club, which had been developed by Nelson's brother Laurance. The governor told the press he would not "under any circumstances" run for vice president, and that he had fixed early November as the date for deciding whether he would challenge Nixon for the presidential nomination. That decision would depend on how each man stacked up in public opinion polls against likely Democratic opponents. If the polls gave him a better chance of winning than the vice president, he would run; otherwise he would not. Rockefeller refused to promote the "Nixon can't win" theme, but he suggested that the vice president could not appeal to enough dissident Democrats and Independents to win.[50]

At his White House press conference a week later, the president repeated that he had identified eight or ten Republicans whom he would energetically support for president. He would not give out the list, but he hoped the party would select a "vigorous . . . straightforward, hard-hitting" candidate "who honesty be-

lieves in the philosophy that would hopefully be expounded in the national platform." Once the general election campaign began, he would accept the speaking
requests from the candidate that fit into his schedule. He would campaign to
strengthen "moderate government, sound, middle-of-the-road government in
this country."[51]

On August 18, while Nixon was vacationing in Virginia Beach, Ike memori-
alized his position in a "most secret possible basis" letter. He had spoken with
Rockefeller that morning and said he was worried that both their staffs saw issues
that did not exist. He emphasized to Rockefeller how much he appreciated
Nixon's service as vice president, and he told Nixon that "people can be politically ambitious if they so desire without necessarily becoming personal antago-
nists."[52]

Nixon and his staff monitored Rockefeller's activities with the expectation that
the governor would enter the race. Robert Finch had a southern Californian political ally, Fred Haffner, acting as a spy on the governor's exploratory committee.
Herb Klein learned that Rockefeller intended to run as "a strong, vigorous executive, in direct contrast to Eisenhower." Given that some liberal Republicans had
come out for Rockefeller, Charlie McWhorter proposed to balance them with
governors who would endorse Nixon.[53]

When Walter Trohan of the *Chicago Tribune* expressed concern over a Rockefeller buildup in early June, the vice president asked Finch to "keep in close
touch" with Trohan, "get intelligence from him—feed him our stories." Toward
the end of October, Nixon asked for the texts of Rockefeller's statements, and
at the start of November he asked for "some good research done on NAR's private business failures." By the middle of the month, Nixon's supporters were
reminding reporters of Rockefeller's admiration for the vice president and demanding that the governor answer questions about where he stood on domestic
and foreign issues.[54]

Rockefeller asked for and was granted the opportunity to speak at the thirteen-
state Republican Western States Conference in Los Angeles on November 12.
The day before his departure, addressing the annual meeting of the National
Conference of Christians and Jews, he praised Kennedy as "an attractive, popular
and useful public servant." The possibility that a Catholic might be nominated
president was a "landmark of a growing maturity" among Americans. He also
told the audience that he endorsed the *Brown* decision and thought it had "accelerated a social evolution" across the nation.[55]

On the West Coast, Rockefeller made thirty-five public appearances in four
days. About seventy-five supporters greeted him on his arrival at the Los Angeles
airport. Edward Shattuck, the RNC committeeman from California, led the

official welcoming delegation wearing a silver-and-blue Nixon button on his lapel. The car that drove the governor to his hotel bore a Nixon sticker. During his initial press conference, the governor referred to Nixon as "our great Vice President" and predicted a warm welcome the next time he visited New York. Answering a question about the White House, he called the Eisenhower administration "superb" and refused to say whether he expected to enter the presidential contest. He reiterated that under no circumstances would he run for the vice presidency. At a dinner that evening, he found himself giving his address while standing in front of a huge photograph of Nixon, flanked by pictures of Eisenhower and Lincoln. Hundreds in the audience had sticking out of their breast pockets a red, white, and blue emblem reading "Nixon, 60, Now." Rockefeller sat down to polite applause.[56]

Goldwater followed the governor. Earl Mazo, covering the event for the *New York Herald Tribune*, was surprised that when he was introduced, the senator received "a demonstration of enthusiasm that dwarfed the Rockefeller applause." Goldwater told the audience he had traveled to forty-three states and found the vice president the overwhelming choice of party workers for the presidential nomination. Afterward, at a press conference, he commented that Rockefeller had not gained enough experience to seek the nomination. The party wanted Nixon, he said, and the governor's trip west had not changed that consensus: "Rockefeller just didn't catch fire politically."[57]

In San Francisco on November 13, Rockefeller again received a polite reception. The professional politicians supported the vice president, and the governor refused to say whether he had made any decision on running against him. He continued on to Eugene, Oregon, where he spoke at the University of Oregon and called Governor Hatfield a "wonderful" vice presidential prospect. This was followed by short stops in Seattle, Washington, and Boise, Idaho, where the welcome was more enthusiastic. Then he flew back to New York.[58]

Rockefeller's first national political experience persuaded him to abandon the "Nixon can't win" strategy. He would never again question the vice president's vote-getting ability. By December, he had changed his stance to "Nixon shouldn't win." In the middle of the month, he traveled to seven states in seven days: Indiana, Missouri, Minnesota, Wisconsin, Oklahoma, Texas, and Florida. Many observers, including Nixon's staff, saw this trip as a prelude to the governor's announcement of his candidacy. During his speeches, the sharpest break he made with the administration came when he called for a resumption of nuclear weapons testing, which Ike had banned in October 1958.[59]

Texas presented hurdles Rockefeller could not clear. By the time he landed there, the Republican leadership was already committed. The Nixons had gone in October to Fort Worth, where they received a tumultuous welcome, and to Dallas to open the state fair, also to a frenzied reception. Maurice Carlson, president of Reliance Life and Accident Insurance Company of America, wrote the vice president: "Both you and Mrs. Nixon took Texas by storm, and we are proud and honored that you came to see us in this great State, which is a Nixon stronghold."[60]

Rockefeller completed his second tour on December 18. Some predicted he would formally enter the race for the presidency before Christmas or in the first week of January. Instead, on December 26, he shocked most political observers by issuing a statement that he was not running for the presidential nomination because it would take too much time away from his job as governor.[61]

Ike, who had left for a vacation in Georgia the day after the governor's announcement, had no comment until his press conference on January 13, 1960, when Robert Pierpoint of CBS News asked for his reaction to Rockefeller's withdrawal. He replied that he "was just as astonished as anybody else, but I just take his statement at face value."[62]

The president had already anticipated that his vice president would be the party's nominee. At a cabinet meeting on November 27, Ike commented that if Nixon succeeded him he would have to hold down taxes and expenditures. Two days before the New Year, the president wrote Nixon to say he owed him "a debt . . . that I can never repay but which I shall always remember."[63]

The vice president released a statement on the same day as Rockefeller's, acknowledging the governor as a national leader: "He is a man destined for continuing leadership in the Republican Party and the nation in the years ahead." But he stayed silent on his own plans.[64] He had his own reservations about Rockefeller, but like Eisenhower he took "the disclaimer at face value." The governor, he noted, had not said he would not be a candidate, and commentators did not know what course he would follow. Nixon would be better able to "accurately appraise the effect of his announcement" in a few weeks. Meanwhile, he would "keep a close eye on the situation."[65]

A quarter century later, Nixon reminisced that Rockefeller was "a very attractive individual. . . . He not only was rich, but he [was] very gregarious. He'd usually come up—'Hiya, fella!' That's the Rockefeller trademark." Some people disliked his personality, but Nixon thought "you could have a good talk with him. He could be very candid, and . . . he could be perhaps a bit on the devious side. He was a good politician." Rockefeller also could be very "blunt." He unconsciously was a snob, "but when you're that rich and have had everything on a silver platter all your life, it's very difficult not to show just a little bit of that arrogance."[66]

At this point in his career, poised for a run for the presidency, Nixon's position in the GOP may be understood in relation to three men. Eisenhower, who had never been a traditional politician, was briefly invigorated to revitalize the party after the 1958 elections but soon became absorbed in domestic and foreign policy concerns. Unwilling to risk his image as the nonpartisan chief executive, he avoided involvement in the race to succeed him, except to say that he opposed extremism. By the start of 1960, some Republicans saw him as perpetuating the New Deal and were counting the days until the end of his term.

Rockefeller, having won the office of governor of New York in his first election at any level, confronted the needs of his state by increasing spending and taxes. While he perceived these acts as practical moves, he unwittingly made himself a major symbol of East Coast Republican liberalism.

Goldwater, coming from a far different environment, saw himself as representing the views of the constituency that sent him to the Senate—views that resonated with large numbers of voters across the nation, especially in the South and the West. He was no more an ideologue than Rockefeller, but he found himself cast as the spokesman for the party's right wing.

Nixon was a skilled and energetic campaigner who had spent the past three election cycles earning Republican leaders' loyalty in the way that counted most: by traveling to their states and districts to help them raise funds and get elected. He appealed to both conservatives and liberals in the party, and many of them enthusiastically endorsed him for the presidency. With Eisenhower, Rockefeller, and Goldwater each having shown his limits, the task of unifying the party fell to Nixon.

4

THE LEAST ATTRACTIVE CANDIDATE

On November 28, 1958, when asked who might be his Democratic challengers, Nixon replied: John Kennedy, Lyndon Johnson, Stuart Symington, Adlai
Stevenson, and others.[1]

The vice president failed to mention Senator Hubert Humphrey. Yet the two
had known each other since their time in the Senate, where they had continually clashed. In September 1954, for example, after Nixon linked Democrats with
socialism, Humphrey responded that the vice president should be careful calling
the "American economy socialistic because . . . he's apt to convince people in
other parts of the world that socialism really works for the American people."[2]

Their political differences never became personal. Humphrey wrote to Nixon
in August 1955 that he was "most grateful to you for the friendly manner in which
you have treated me. We have had our difficulties in politics but you have never
permitted those differences to affect or influence your actions insofar as I am
concerned." Nixon answered: "The test of democracy in action is our ability not
to allow those differences to destroy friendly relations between members of the
two parties."[3]

In the fall of 1959, as both men prepared for the primaries, the vice president
wrote Humphrey again. They had differed in the past and would probably do
so in the future, but Nixon respected "a person who will speak out and work for
what he believes, and this you have surely done." That winter, on a speaking tour
in his native South Dakota, the senator attacked the administration's agricultural
program as a "fraud." If elected, he would replace it with a family farm program
development act that would fit the farmers' needs. Meanwhile, as a senator he
had no plan to compromise with the administration.[4]

The vice president did not ignore Senator Symington as a dark horse contender. He had easily won reelection in 1958 and constantly attacked the administration for failed agricultural policies, inadequate defense spending, and the alleged missile gap. His greatest strength as a presidential aspirant was that former president Truman was fully behind him.[5]

Nixon viewed Lyndon Johnson as a worthy challenger. Most of those who offered impressions of their relationship have misunderstood it. George Reedy, Johnson's administrative assistant, recalled that his boss called the vice president "that fascist so-and-so," which, coming from Johnson, meant "any unpleasant person." James Rowe, Jr., capital lawyer, FDR staffer, and close Johnson counselor, believed that he disliked Nixon. From the Republican side, White House press secretary Jim Hagerty portrayed their interactions as "cool and correct" and said they were "bitter political enemies." Senator Clifford Case, Republican from New Jersey, thought Johnson "had absolutely no use for him at all."[6]

Johnson himself offered a radically different view. In his memoirs, he wrote that he disagreed strongly with Nixon's political philosophy, but "I never shared the intense dislike of Richard Nixon felt by many of my fellow Democrats." Having served with Nixon in both the House and Senate, Johnson wrote, he "considered him a much-maligned and misunderstood man. I looked upon Nixon as a tough, unyielding partisan and a shrewd politician, but always a man trying to do the best for his country as he saw it."[7]

Nixon discussed his feelings toward Johnson in several oral histories. As a senator, Johnson was "the most effective legislative leader of the century." He wielded power well and was "persuasive" as well as "ruthless." He "did everything big. He drank big, and he was a big man." Nixon recalled a midnight Senate session in which LBJ finished off two bottles of liquor and still maintained total control. He disapproved of the senator's excesses but thought he and Johnson "got along very well" and "respected each other."[8]

The two met for the first time in February 1948 at Bethesda Naval Medical Center. While carrying his daughter Tricia, Nixon slipped on ice and broke both his elbows. He went to the hospital and found himself sharing a room with a Texas congressman who had also fallen on the ice. A "very handsome, vigorous young man bringing a big bowl of chili," according to Nixon's recollection, came to visit. That was LBJ. Nixon described him as "a fashion plate" who wore cufflinks when most congressmen did not, and a "very impressive-looking fellow." The three men shared the chili.[9]

In July 1953, over dinner with Emmet John Hughes, a speechwriter for Eisenhower, the vice president described his admiration for LBJ: "We have nobody to compare with him—he's something of a cold fish personally but smart as hell."

During Ike's second term, Nixon added that he admired Johnson because he was "always able to keep in mind the major objectives." Sometimes he compromised, "but in the end he gets the major part of his program through."[10]

Not that Nixon and Johnson always agreed. In May 1954, Johnson ridiculed Nixon by suggesting that maybe Checkers, the family dog, had come up with the administration's Indochina policy. FDR's dog, Fala, said Johnson, would never propose such a policy. Later that month, the vice president warned Ike that LBJ would use delaying tactics to block the president's proposals. Toward the end of May, the Nixons gave a black-tie dinner for the Senate's majority and minority leaders, but the partisanship did not abate. Nixon proceeded to make such a vitriolic attack on former secretary of state Dean Acheson's Asia policy that both Johnson and the current secretary, John Foster Dulles, agreed it was over the top.[11]

A few years later, during the debate over the jury trial amendment to the 1957 civil rights bill, the majority leader charged the vice president with staging "a concerted propaganda campaign" against the amendment. After LBJ engineered enough votes for its passage, Nixon called it "one of the saddest days in the history of the senate, because this was a vote against the right to vote."[12]

But these battles did not define their relationship. Johnson seldom hesitated to ask the vice president for the occasional favor. In October 1954 he was "*most anxious*, if not insistent," to have Nixon speak at the annual convention of the National Association of Retail Druggists in Houston. The senator asked him personally because this was "a very influential group" and approximately seven thousand to nine thousand representatives would be in attendance. Nixon accepted the invitation, placing one condition on his appearance. He would give a nonpartisan address without mentioning the upcoming off-year elections. He would not have to endorse any Republican running for the House or the Senate in Texas so as not to support anyone running against Johnson, who was running for reelection. He promised to say nothing "uncomplimentary as far as the Minority Leader is concerned!"[13]

Johnson asked Nixon to make a side trip to his ranch, an hour by plane from Houston. The senator had improved the property to use it as a showpiece to entertain famous guests. The vice president could not accommodate him because he had already agreed to speak at a fundraiser for what Nixon described as "the poverty-stricken Republicans!" LBJ expressed his displeasure on October 5: "A Democrat would never have turned down a good friend for a few lousy shillings." He thought the Texas Republicans were "sufficiently well-heeled to permit you to relax with an old friend for a few hours."[14]

Johnson, who had already assured his 1954 reelection by discouraging any opposition, did little campaigning. According to the political commentator William White, he concentrated on speaking for Democrats in the West and "appointed himself, without defining his mission in public, to be Nixon's principal adversary." He did not attack the vice president directly, however, but instead focused on Democratic achievements.[15]

Johnson easily won reelection and returned to the Senate in January 1955 as majority leader. That July he suffered a serious heart attack. While he was recuperating at Bethesda, one of the "biggest lifts in his morale," according to reporter Earl Mazo, was the president's visit; the vice president came later. Nixon told LBJ he looked "fit" and complimented him on his leadership skills, especially his bipartisan cooperation on foreign policy. They discussed some legislative business. Nixon never told LBJ he had arranged Eisenhower's appearance. When Johnson returned to his Texas ranch for rehabilitation toward the end of August, Nixon wished him a speedy recovery, and LBJ again invited the Nixons to visit.[16]

Nixon welcomed Johnson back to the Senate in January 1956 as the chamber stood and applauded. The vice president then waited outside to pose for photographs with the majority leader and put his arm around Johnson, who wrote that he was "deeply moved" by the gesture and cherished Nixon's "warm friendship." Nixon replied: "It's always a pleasure to travel the 'two-way street' that runs between us."[17]

The cordial relationship continued throughout 1956. That spring, LBJ's secretary, Juanita Richards, said that her boss had "never known a man any fairer than Dick Nixon." Johnson wrote the vice president in early August that he counted Nixon among his "closest friends." Nixon reciprocated, praising LBJ for his leadership and friendship, which he would "value . . . in all the years to come." In December, Nixon wrote Johnson: "One of the compensations for the knocks that a fellow gets in this business of ours is the opportunity for the friendship which we have enjoyed."[18]

In February 1957, LBJ wrote that he had "a little retreat" where he rested for a few minutes and did some of his "best thinking." He wanted an autographed photograph of Nixon and had chosen a place for it. The vice president signed it "with deep appreciation for the wise counsel and friendship of a fine Senator and a great American."[19]

Evaluating LBJ as a presidential contender in the winter of 1958, Nixon said he was "the ablest Democrat" and "would make a good President," but he had two strikes against him: "his heart attack and Texas." Earl Mazo wrote in June 1959 that the vice president doubted a southerner could be nominated for the presidency, but he thought Johnson was "the best qualified Democrat to be president."[20]

✔ ✔ ✔

While Nixon recognized Johnson as a formidable political figure, Nixon did not see him as his main opponent for the presidency. Jack Kennedy was. Nixon considered JFK "a good personal friend" and had "a very high regard for him as an able senator and campaigner; he's very attractive and formidable."[21]

To the vice president, the senator's greatest asset was his weak competition. Humphrey was an underfunded candidate who would have a hard time expanding his appeal beyond the Midwest; Symington had Truman's backing but little else; Johnson was a southerner; Stevenson had lost twice. Nixon's pollster, Claude Robinson, pointed out JFK's liabilities: "youth, inexperience, wealth, and religion." Nixon thought Kennedy would overcome them.[22]

He had been receiving information on Kennedy's campaign activities since early 1957, when Timothy Murphy, a Boston lawyer, predicted that JFK would "be a strong contender for the Democratic Presidential nomination in 1960." Kennedy, Murphy reported, was developing positions on both foreign and domestic affairs and building close ties to organized labor.[23]

That July, Kennedy's speech in favor of Algerian independence received harsh reviews inside the administration. Eisenhower learned its contents on the day of its delivery, and at a White House legislative leadership meeting, the president opined that the Algerians "lacked sufficient education and training to run their own government in the most efficient way." Still, Ike went on, the United States had fought a revolution to gain its freedom and could not object if Algerians did the same. Republicans should not publicly attack Kennedy, but they might chide him "a bit for pretending to have all the answers." The vice president added that Algerian independence could result in "a terrible revolution," with one million Europeans fighting against eight million Algerians. The United States, he advised, should work on the French to prepare the Algerians for independence. To press hard for immediate action, however, would anger the French government.[24]

A month later, on August 13, Nixon had his assistant Charles McWhorter draft a memorandum comparing him with Kennedy. Nixon had visited forty countries and "had unprecedented experience in international affairs." Kennedy did not. Nixon was a firm defender of civil rights, while the senator had "been characterized by opportunism and an obvious desire to obtain the Democratic nomination for President in 1960." When the civil rights bill was before the Senate in 1957, "Kennedy," wrote McWhorter, "did not take part in the debate . . . but sat on the sidelines hoping to be spared any brickbats which would come from exerting leadership in this area." Finally, Nixon worked for prosperity and was not controlled by any interest group. Kennedy accepted orders from labor bosses.

He had "demonstrated his weakness of character in bowing . . . to the dictates of Southern politicians on civil rights and to the dictates of big labor on economic matters."[25]

When Kennedy ran for reelection in 1958, Nixon watched his campaign closely. RNC chairman Meade Alcorn spoke in Newton, Massachusetts, on April 7, claiming that the senator had been infected with the presidential bug and had flip-flopped on agricultural issues. For five years he had voted for flexible price supports, but he now favored fixed, rigid controls. He flip-flopped on the civil rights bill and had viciously attacked French policy in Algeria. Even worse, he had become a puppet of big labor.[26]

McWhorter also noted Kennedy's strategy of eliminating opponents through primaries. As the best-known Democratic candidate, he wanted to prevent any of his adversaries from gaining unexpected momentum before the convention. McWhorter thought "the primaries may be somewhat bitter," but "they will contribute to making for a more harmonious convention by shaking down the number of candidates. Here is where Kennedy's investment in a public relations program will pay off handsomely."[27]

Nixon did not campaign in Massachusetts in 1958 because he hoped to avoid questions about facing Kennedy as a presidential candidate. Asked about Kennedy that fall, he said he knew Jack well and "happen[ed] to have a fairly high regard for him." He saw no reason to campaign for some unknown against him. At the end of October, asked whether Kennedy's religion would be a liability, Nixon replied that the United States was ready for a Roman Catholic president.[28]

Early in 1959, Kennedy visited Nixon in his office off the Senate floor to ask him not to bring up his thousand-dollar gift for Nixon's Senate race against Helen Gahagan Douglas. Nixon agreed and did not ask for any concessions in return, nor did Kennedy offer any.[29]

Nixon continued to speak positively about Kennedy throughout that year. On June 11, he told members of the Commonwealth Club in San Francisco not to write off Kennedy because of his religion. In July, Father John Cronin sent a letter to the editor of the *New York Times* denying innuendos that Nixon welcomed Kennedy as an opponent because Nixon could defeat him on religious grounds. Cronin wrote that he had "been a close personal friend of the Nixons for twelve years. I know his faults better than most persons here in Washington. Bigotry is not one of them."[30]

On June 19, Nixon and Kennedy boarded the same airplane from Washington to Chicago and posed for photographers upon their arrival at Midway Airport, shaking hands with Jackie standing between them. The *New York Times* called them the leading presidential candidates in their respective parties.[31]

Later that summer, the *New York World-Telegram and Sun* reported that the two men had offices across from each other. They said hello, according to the story, but never stopped to chat. That was false, but an accompanying cartoon had Nixon and Kennedy looking out of their offices. The cartoonist Bill Pause sent the original to Kennedy, who asked Nixon to autograph it. He obliged: "To my friend & neighbor Jack Kennedy with best wishes for almost anything!"[32]

On November 12, Nixon spoke at a dinner honoring Congressman Melvin Laird in his hometown of Wisconsin Rapids; Kennedy happened to be barnstorming in nearby Marshfield the same day. Three days earlier, Secretary of Health, Education, and Welfare (HEW) Arthur Flemming had warned about contaminated cranberries due to possible carcinogenic herbicides. The caution severely damaged sales. Kennedy's home state of Massachusetts also grew cranberries, and on his arrival, he drank two glasses of cranberry juice. Not to be outdone, Nixon had several helpings of cranberry sauce at dinner. Kennedy later told an audience that he felt fine. If he and Nixon died from eating cranberries, he said, "I shall have performed a great public service by taking the Vice President with me." Nixon's press secretary called this incident "the first debate."[33]

A month later, Nixon told *Washington Post* reporter Chalmers Roberts that Kennedy "was going somewhere" and might do well in the primaries. But the Democrats still might nominate Stevenson.[34]

Nixon had viciously attacked the former Democratic presidential candidate during his two campaigns against Eisenhower, earning the former Illinois governor's lifelong enmity. As Earl Mazo was completing a Nixon biography, in late October 1958, Stevenson permitted Mazo to quote his comment on Nixon's use of Stevenson's deposition in the Hiss case: he had called it "vile and contemptible and obviously intended to mislead." During Stevenson's presidential campaigns, Nixon had never stopped "distorting issues or demeaning his office." As for the 1960 presidential nomination, "The idea of Nixon being a candidate for President of the United States, the most exalted office on earth, is something I find hard to believe possible." In his biography of Stevenson, John Bartlow Martin wrote that he "never stopped despising Nixon."[35]

Stevenson actively worked to damage Nixon's presidential aspirations. In January 1958, Margaret Halsey sent the former governor an article from the *New Republic* entitled "Beware the Tender Trap," comparing Nixon to Hitler and concluding that the vice president's drive to run for the presidency was "an attempt to debase the moral currency."[36]

The magazine promoted the article. Selig Harrison, an assistant editor, had gone to Harvard with Nixon aide Charlie McWhorter, and the two had lunch at the National Press Club in early May. Harrison said that in advance of the 1958 elections, the magazine was looking for a gimmick to increase its circulation, then at thirty-three thousand. It had sent out a mailing to one hundred thousand people offering the Halsey article, which Harrison thought was in "questionable taste," and ten more issues for a dollar. Harrison described the response, eight or nine thousand acceptances, as "fantastic" and "unprecedented." The Halsey offer was "an experiment in increasing circulation and was not intended to set off any irrational and hysterical attack" on the vice president.[37]

A month after the article appeared, Stevenson met with his former speech-writer Stanley Frankel and William Blair, Jr., one of his law partners. Blair and Stevenson had already talked with several others, including Democratic activist Marietta Tree and Governor Averell Harriman, about the need to stop the "Nixon danger" and "to arrest [his] growing popularity." Stevenson considered Nixon the "greatest menace the country faces." He and Blair wanted Frankel to come up with a plan of action. He could include others, but "better NOT discuss with any *talkers*."

Frankel wrote a memorandum that included planting items with the popular gossip columnist Walter Winchell and anti-Nixon newspapers. Someone might write a novel about an immoral politician like Tricky Dick, exposing his dark side. Frankel shared the memo with Leonard Robinson, an executive editor with the book publisher Henry Holt, who replied on March 12 that he liked the idea, but he never did commission such a novel.[38]

Frankel also was the brother-in-law of another of Stevenson's law partners, Newton Minow. A week later he learned the memo was circulating and worried that others who were not sympathetic would find out. He asked Frankel to discuss the memo with him and Bill Blair around April 1. First, he would see Stevenson to discuss how to proceed. Minow cautioned: "Don't let it [the memo] out of *your* hands. please." *Your* was underlined three times.[39]

In early June, Blair wrote Frankel that he and Marietta Tree had talked about the idea with John Steinbeck, who had a cordial relationship with Stevenson. He "was entirely sympathetic" but refused to write the novel, urging instead "a frontal attack" as a "more effective and straight-forward approach."[40]

Tree answered Frankel in the middle of July that she had received several letters from Blair "regarding our project." She also mentioned an idea proposed by Arthur Schlesinger, Jr.: since Nixon was the likely Republican candidate in 1960, someone needed to write a serious Nixon biography and get it out before the election. Schlesinger thought John Bartlow Martin was the best choice, as he had worked for the Stevenson campaigns but this attachment was not well known.

Schlesinger had already spoken with Charles Bolte, executive vice president at the Viking Press, who liked the idea and would provide a big enough advance for research and writing.[41]

Toward the end of November, William Costello, who had never written a book, signed a contract with the Viking Press to write a Nixon biography. Costello had been a reporter since 1929 and had most recently been in Asia and South America before returning to Washington as a political reporter in 1955. At the start of 1959 he was the Mutual Broadcasting Company's White House correspondent and was heard daily on over 458 stations. Nixon's press secretary, Herbert Klein, told his boss that Costello was "a liberal and strongly internationalist in his stand." He was "thought of as a very sharp reporter who has been out of the country for quite a while."[42]

As late as the second week of August 1959, Costello was still conducting research, asking Nixon's office for information on his recent Russian and Polish trips. He was still broadcasting daily, and two-thirds of his manuscript had been submitted to the publisher. The completed manuscript, written in less than a year, was submitted in the middle of September and was released at the end of the year. When asked what he thought, Stevenson said he had not read the book but had been "told it is excellent."[43]

No direct evidence proves that *The Facts about Nixon: An Unauthorized Biography* resulted from Stevenson's Nixon phobia. But the same Charles Bolte who favorably responded to Schlesinger's proposal is thanked in Costello's preface for having "conceived and nurtured the project."[44]

The volume made the best-seller list of the *New York Times Book Review* on February 7, 1960. That June, the *New Republic* endorsed Kennedy for president and started to publish excerpts from the book, and by the end of the year it had excerpted two-thirds of it.

Costello defended his book as "pretty scholarly, factual and objective." He had "made an extravagant effort to be accurate about facts," and readers who wrote to him had found only about a half-dozen errors. In fall 1960, the chief researcher for the book wore a Kennedy button at a deposition for a lawsuit regarding the book. She now worked for the DNC and "freely admitted research for the book came exclusively from the DNC—that they have three cabinets devoted to RN." Nora de Toledano, wife of syndicated columnist Ralph de Toledano and a Nixon advocate, thought the book was "worse than the articles; worst hatchet job yet—appalling and incredible."[45]

Criticism of Nixon from other Democratic Party leaders continued nonstop. Eleanor Roosevelt regularly belittled the vice president. At the end of 1955, she had called him "the least attractive" Republican presidential candidate. During a *Meet the Press* interview on September 16, 1956, she disagreed with many Republicans who thought Nixon had "matured." The vice president had accused her friend, Helen Gahagan Douglas, of being a communist during the 1950 California senatorial race when he knew the charge was false. (Roosevelt later admitted that Nixon never called Douglas a communist, but maintained that he had clearly implied it.) Later she added: "I doubt if Eisenhower can stand a second term and I doubt if the country can stand Nixon as President." The next year, in an interview with Mike Wallace, she again called Nixon "the least attractive" candidate for 1960. His presidency "would worry" her, she said, because his "convictions are not very strong."[46]

Truman regularly lambasted Republicans. He and Nixon had had several heated exchanges during the 1952 race. Truman attacked Ike in San Francisco for betraying his liberal backers by turning away from Governor Warren as his running mate in favor of "another Californian who is not worthy to lace his shoes." Two days later, Nixon answered: "No one has stooped so low as Truman in his attack on Eisenhower." In Truman's home state of Missouri, Nixon called him "one of the poorest Presidents we ever had."[47]

The acrimony reached another level when Nixon, speaking in Texarkana, Texas, claimed that Truman, Acheson, and Stevenson were "traitors to the high principles in which many of the nation's Democrats believe." Truman took the comment as a deep personal insult. Nixon later explained that he meant Truman had abandoned the principles of the Democratic Party and "left millions of Democrats with no home," but given the national furor over such actual traitors as Julius and Ethel Rosenberg, Nixon's role in bringing down Alger Hiss, and McCarthy's damaging attacks on Truman's state department, it was, at the very least, an extremely poor choice of words. Truman never accepted Nixon's explanation, and according to his aide Ken Hechler, always viewed him with contempt.[48]

On October 1, 1958, Truman declared that the Democratic Party had "about a dozen good candidates" for president, and he preferred Nixon as the Republican candidate because "We can lick him." Seventeen days later, the former president held a press conference in which he accused Nixon of "character assassination" and "slander" of Jerry Voorhis and Helen Gahagan Douglas in his campaigns against them and repeated his contention that Nixon would be the easiest Republican to beat in 1960. In November, Nixon told Earl Mazo that Truman had said "rather libelous [things] about the President and the administration and myself."[49]

Many in the media agreed with the Democrats. Nixon's relationship with the press was always complicated. He possessed a moody intensity on which it was easy to project one's political fears, and reporters, whether sympathetic or not, were not immune to this temptation. *New York Times* reporter Russell Baker, who first met him in late 1958, recalled in his memoir that Nixon "was cursed with a personality reporters loved to loathe. . . . There were darknesses in his soul that seemed to leave his life bereft of joy."[50]

Nixon had by this time developed long-standing distrust of the press. In December 1958 he wrote to his successor in the House, Pat Hillings, "I am getting rather bored with the constant effort that is required to 'win over' the skeptical American news reporters who cover me on my trips abroad and on campaigns. Most of them seem to be favorably impressed while the trip is going on, but apparently they get so much heat from some of their friends that they soon get out their carving knives again." The only way to keep the press honest was through question-and-answer interviews on television.[51]

Nine days later, he was still thinking about his press relations. Derogatory articles, he wrote to *New York Times* reporter Max Frankel, presented a serious problem that was difficult to counteract. The only effective method was a letter to the editor. Although he could file libel suits, they were costly and time-consuming, and the courts looked skeptically on such suits from politicians: "We are considered fair game for almost anything anybody wants to say about us!"[52]

Richard Rovere routinely attacked the vice president in the *New Yorker,* as did Doris Fleeson in her nationally syndicated column. Another columnist, Marquis Childs, was disappointed with the policies of the Eisenhower administration and believed Nixon would continue the status quo. Drew Pearson used his columns as well as radio and television to smear Nixon personally and professionally. James Reston of the *New York Times* disliked Nixon and his politics. Reston's biographer considered the two men poles apart: "Reston tended to be sunny and optimistic, forgiving and broadminded, easy and confident in his dealings with others. Nixon was dark, full of self-doubt—even self-loathing—and afflicted with a self-fulfilling paranoia about the Eastern establishment press." Herbert Block, who published his cartoons under the name Herblock, routinely depicted both Nixon and McCarthy as unshaven louts, reinforcing the public's identification of them as two of a kind.[53]

Other reporters tried to be impartial. *Washington Post* reporter Chalmers Roberts saw Nixon as "a man of intelligence, drive, decision-making ability, yet he is close to being a demagogue in the way he capsulized ideas, as with Democrats and war. He is infected with the Madison Avenue selling ideas; he is . . . a pitchman in many respects." Robert Donovan, when he became the Washington bureau chief for the *New York Herald Tribune* in late 1957, expected to maintain the cordial relations with the vice president that his predecessors had. He thought reporters believed that "Nixon was suspicious of them." Yet many "respected him for his drive and intelligence." The *New York Times's* Arthur Krock, despite his close connection to the Kennedy family, wrote complimentary articles about the vice president.[54]

Nixon's rivals for the presidency, Democratic leaders, and liberal columnists and reporters routinely portrayed the vice president in the worst possible light. Even when their claims were patently false, many partisan Democrats took them as fact.

5

Not a Political Type

On January 2, 1960, forty-two-year-old Senator John Kennedy entered the Senate Office Building caucus room, which was packed with reporters and supporters, and reading from a prepared text, announced his candidacy for the presidency. It was, he said, "the most powerful office in the Free World," where "the most crucial decisions of this century must be made in the next four years." The major issues of the campaign were ending the arms race, maintaining the freedom of developing nations, rebuilding American science and education, preventing the collapse of the farm economy, and stopping urban decay. Prosperity must be extended to all Americans without increasing either inflation or unemployment. Kennedy also wanted "to give direction to our traditional moral purpose."

In the previous forty months, he had talked to Democrats in every state and was convinced he could "win both the nomination and the election." Any Democrat who aspired to the nomination needed to run in the primaries; he was entering the New Hampshire primary and would announce "other primaries as their filing dates approach."[1]

During the following press conference, Kennedy said he would not accept the vice presidential nomination "under any circumstances." He did not see any fundamental differences between himself and Senator Humphrey, who had already declared they were both "liberal Democrats." He acknowledged that the first Catholic Democratic presidential nominee, Alfred Smith in 1928, had lost because of his religious affiliation, but he did not think religion would play a major role in this election. McCarthyism had damaged the United States both domestically and abroad, he said, but he avoided any discussion of his personal relationship with McCarthy. He supported the bill then coming before the Senate because the military budget was insufficient; he would consider a tax increase, if necessary, to pay for it. He would not recognize the People's Republic of China but was willing to change his opinion if the PRC stopped its aggressive policies. He was considering entering the primaries in Wisconsin, Ohio, Florida, California, Maryland, the District of Columbia, Indiana, Nebraska, and Oregon. Finally, because Democrats would have decided on their candidate by May, he did not foresee any deadlock at July's national convention.[2]

After the questions were finished, Jack's thirty-year-old wife, Jackie, seated at the back of the room, came forward for pictures with her husband. *Time* and *Newsweek* were already calling her "one of America's most photographed women."[3]

Three days after this announcement, Jack and Jackie had their neighbors Ben Bradlee and his wife, Toni, over for dinner. Ben, then the Washington bureau chief for *Newsweek*, invited one of his reporters, James Cannon, to record an interview with Kennedy, who, unknown to Cannon, was already recording various thoughts in his Senate office. The senator claimed he was "not a political type" and that at the start of his career, his highest goal might have been Massachusetts governor. He smoothly related for Cannon his family background, how he entered the "political profession," and how he came to his present position.

He began by saying that "politics has become one of our most abused and neglected professions," yet politicians made "the great decisions of war and peace, prosperity and recession, the decision whether we look to the future or the past." If citizens were interested in what government decided, "government service is the way to translate this interest into action. . . . The natural place for the concerned citizen is to contribute part of his life to the national interest."

Kennedy then described how he came into politics. His family had always been interested in public affairs, and many had held elected office. Through college and World War II, he himself had never considered running. The patriarch had chosen that path for Joseph Jr. Even after his brother died in the war, Jack had no interest in politics as a profession. He tried reporting but felt he was only observing, not participating in events. He thought about law school but soon abandoned the idea.

Once he began running for Congress in 1946, he "realized how satisfactory a profession a political career could be." His family's prominence was an advantage, but he had not lived in Boston for a decade. He started to campaign early and continued that practice throughout his career, noting that "most aspirants for public office start much too late." To become well known to voters, a candidate had to meet as many of them as possible: "For the politician to make a dent in the consciousness of the great majority of the people is a long and laborious job, particularly in a primary where you don't have the party label to help you." To be a contender you had to be willing "to submit yourself to long, long, long labor."

In the House he had found it frustrating to be just one of 435 members. After six years in Congress, he challenged and upset an incumbent senator, Henry Cabot Lodge, Jr. In the Senate he became one of 96. Shortly after entering the Senate he concluded that while Congress helped make decisions, it was "the President who controls and who can affect results." That was when he decided to seek the presidency.[4]

The first polls after the announcement were dispiriting because of Kennedy's lack of name recognition. The Gallup poll on February 7, 1960, had Nixon defeating him by several points, and beating Stevenson by a greater margin. A California poll eleven months earlier had had Kennedy with 48 percent and Nixon with 39 percent.[5]

Through the first quarter of 1960, Kennedy's in-house pollster, Louis Harris, surveyed the primary states that he was entering as well as a few he was not. Harris conducted interviews in Florida, Michigan, and Indiana during January and found that Kennedy polled well against Nixon in those states. He also learned that the senator's image had "become well known across this country." In Indiana, Harris reported, "the two outstanding candidates from both parties are Nixon and Kennedy," a pairing that promised "a lively dogfight."[6]

By mid-February, according to *Time* magazine, the Kennedy campaign had "the smoothest-running, widest-ranging, most efficient personal organization in the Democratic Party today. It has men, money and brains" and was "the most savvy and hard-nosed group put together in U.S. politics since . . . '48."[7]

Kennedy supplemented his professional staff with an academic brain trust, including many members from Harvard. Arthur Schlesinger, Jr., supplied historical context; John Kenneth Galbraith provided economic data; and Archibald Cox, from the law school, consulted on labor matters. Walt Rostow from MIT advised on foreign policy as well as economics.[8]

James MacGregor Burns, a well-respected historian and political scientist, was excluded. He was a liberal Democrat who had been a delegate to the 1952 and 1956 Democratic national conventions, the latter time voting for Kennedy as the vice presidential nominee. In 1958, Burns ran for Congress in the heavily Republican western part of Massachusetts. He and Kennedy appeared together at one campaign stop, where Burns lamented that he was having trouble raising money for his campaign. Burns told me four decades later that Kennedy, in response, "handed me a wad of cash."[9]

After Burns lost his election, Sorensen approached him to write a Kennedy biography, and Burns enthusiastically agreed. By September 1959 he had a finished draft and sent it to Kennedy, who was displeased. He and Sorensen met with Burns, after which the author made at least two dozen changes. He deleted negative references to Helen Gahagan Douglas and Joe McCarthy; Kathleen Kennedy's death while flying to a liaison with a married man; unflattering references to Joseph Jr.'s character; and the actual authorship of *Profiles in Courage*.[10]

Burns claimed in his preface that the senator had given him "full access to past and current files." But while he saw a great deal of material, he did not examine any of Kennedy's medical records. He also never mentioned Kennedy's contribution to his congressional campaign. Historian Michael O'Brien, in his exhaustive biography of Kennedy, wrote that "behind the scenes the book's highly respected author, under severe pressure, had agreed to many concessions favorable to Kennedy—some of them major. In fact, the book was significantly less objective than it appeared."[11]

None of this background was public when Burns's book, *John Kennedy: A Political Profile*, came out in January 1960 to excellent reviews. It was the first biography of the senator to depict him as a serious presidential aspirant.[12]

Kennedy still lacked major liberal support outside the academic community. To win the nomination, he needed the backing of prominent liberals within the Democratic Party, many of whom disapproved of his relationship with McCarthy and his tepid support for the Civil Rights Act of 1957. In addition, Eleanor Roosevelt and Harry Truman detested Joe Kennedy for his break with FDR.

Kennedy sought a breakthrough by courting Chester Bowles, who had become an activist in the civil rights struggle, had been governor of Connecticut from 1949 to 1951, and had won a House seat in 1958. Since the current governor, Abraham Ribicoff, and state Democratic chairman John Bailey were vocal Kennedy backers, Bowles had to reach some accommodation with the senator or weaken his standing in the state.[13]

The senator began meeting with Bowles in the summer of 1959, and by September, Bowles had decided to support JFK with a major condition. He was friendly with Stevenson and Humphrey and told Kennedy that he would not campaign against them. Even with that caveat, at the end of January 1960 the senator asked Bowles to be his "chief foreign policy adviser," and at the start of February, Bowles accepted the position. He claimed to be "the first liberal to come out for Kennedy," and in fact he was the first notable liberal to do so.[14]

Humphrey had announced three days before Kennedy. The most liberal of the Democratic contenders, he focused on civil rights and farm issues. He was one of the founders of Americans for Democratic Action (ADA) and advertised that attachment. When speaking before the Capital Press Club, an organization of black reporters, he mentioned twice that he might appoint an African American to his cabinet. He was committed to the primaries in Wisconsin, South Dakota, and the District of Columbia and optimistically predicted that he would reach the convention with between 150 to 225 delegates, far short of the 761 he would need to win on the first ballot but enough to make him a potential compromise candidate in the event of a deadlock. Even then, he knew he faced "an uphill fight."[15]

Stuart Symington had similar hopes. Before announcing his candidacy in early March, he continually attacked the administration for its failure to spend enough on defense and for its dismal agricultural record. His longtime friend and Washington power broker Clark Clifford managed his campaign, but his greatest asset was the backing of his fellow Missourian Harry Truman. With that powerful support, the senator felt he could skip the primaries and concentrate on the twenty states that chose their delegates by party caucus. James Olson, Symington's biographer, believed the senator "had little stomach for the struggle."[16]

Humphrey and Symington were long shots. Kennedy's greatest threat came from Senate majority leader Lyndon Johnson, who could control a large bloc of southern delegates. Speaker Rayburn was his passionate advocate. He and LBJ were more than friends; the senator thought of "Mr. Sam" as a father figure, and Rayburn looked on Johnson as a son.[17]

Writing to Truman at the end of August 1959, former secretary of state Dean Acheson called LBJ "the ablest man in national public life today. He has thousands of faults," but even with those weaknesses, he was "a giant among pygmies." A ticket of LBJ for president with Kennedy for vice president, Acheson thought, could "turn the tide for the great struggle of our time."[18]

Johnson's strategy was to gain recognition for his work as majority leader during weekdays and travel the nation on weekends to win delegates. He flew to Chicago for a luncheon address on January 21, 1960, for instance, and then went to New York City to speak at a dinner honoring Congressman John Rooney. Johnson declared that the nation "must quit running away from the problems of bigotry—whether race, creed or section." During World War II, no soldier asked a fellow soldier's religion or what part of the country he came from. Johnson then specifically referred to the fact that he was a southerner and Kennedy was a Catholic. Voters must ignore such things, he said, and select the next president based on who was "best qualified to lead this country in the face of the Communist threat."[19]

Kennedy was deeply concerned that the others might make some deal to stop him, and he especially worried about Stevenson, who repeatedly declared that he was not a candidate but would accept a draft. Millions of Democrats were still "madly for Adlai" even though he had twice lost to Eisenhower. By the start of 1960, draft clubs had opened in five states. There were efforts to collect a million petition signatures urging him to run.[20]

That January, Stevenson received an offer of help from an unexpected source. On the sixteenth he visited Soviet Ambassador Mikhail Menshikov at his embassy in the capital. Khrushchev, the ambassador told Stevenson, had "voted for you in his heart in 1956." The premier knew his views on "disarmament, nuclear testing, peaceful coexistence, and the conditions of a peaceful world," and he and the Presidium saw the former governor as the best candidate to improve bilateral relations. Menshikov wanted to know how his government could help Stevenson's campaign. A week later, Stevenson wrote to say that he would not accept any Soviet assistance and advised Khrushchev not to interfere in the presidential race.[21]

Eleanor Roosevelt thought Stevenson was the only "mature person" running for the nomination. He would not enter any primaries, but she considered primaries unimportant. In May 1960 she reported in her "My Day" column that in her travels throughout the nation she had "found an underlying ground swell for Adlai Stevenson on the part of the ordinary Democrat who hasn't much official power but who does make up the majority of the Democratic vote."[22]

On May 3, after a lecture at the University of Virginia in Charlottesville, a "smart-aleck" kid asked Truman: "What's going to happen when the Pope moves into the White House?" He responded: "It's not the Pope I'm afraid of, it's the Pop.... Old Joe Kennedy is as big a crook as we've got anywhere in this country."[23]

Kennedy's decision to enter a number of primaries was meant to give him both delegates and positive publicity. The nation had seventeen primaries, which chose about 40 percent of each party's convention delegates. For Democrats, that amounted to 624 out of 1,521 delegates. Kennedy, as a New Englander, was fortunate that the first primary was in New Hampshire, where none of his major opponents even entered. JFK started his New Hampshire campaign in its largest city, Manchester, at a press conference with Jackie beside him and a heavy January snowfall outside. He predicted that "no candidate will be elected as the Democratic nominee who has not run in at least one or more state primaries."[24]

On the eve of the balloting, Republican Governor Wesley Powell released a prepared statement to the press accusing Kennedy of a "softness toward communism." Kennedy labeled it a smear, and Nixon repudiated it. While the two men had differences, said Herbert Klein on the vice president's behalf, "they have always been in complete agreement in their unalterable opposition to communism at home and abroad."[25]

On Tuesday, March 8, Kennedy received 43,372 votes, more than any previous Democratic candidate in a New Hampshire primary. The traditional Republican advantage over Democrats in ballots cast was more than two-to-one; this time Kennedy cut the difference to three-to-two. The victory improved his poll numbers nationwide: the Gallup poll, which had 32 percent of Democrats favoring him as their nominee in January, now put him at 35 percent.[26]

In New Hampshire, Kennedy had run unopposed close to his home turf. Wisconsin would be his first major test. Humphrey was his only adversary, and coming from the neighboring state of Minnesota, he thought he had the advantage. He hoped that Wisconsin Governor Gaylord Nelson would act as a favorite-son candidate on his behalf, but freshman Senator William Proxmire prevented it. Kennedy had campaigned for Proxmire in 1958, and now he was repaying the debt. If the governor ran as a favorite son on behalf of Humphrey, Proxmire would challenge him in the primary. Kennedy and Humphrey, he argued, should face off directly.[27]

Wisconsin had 30 delegates: 2½ from each of the ten congressional districts and 5 for the winner of the statewide vote. The state had a population of four million, of whom 1.2 million were Catholics and 1.5 million were Protestants. Primary voters could cast their ballots across party lines.[28]

Once his spectacular New Hampshire results came in, Kennedy grew optimistic, even cocky about his chances in Wisconsin. Late winter and early spring was Wisconsin's "mud season," full of what Pat Lucey, Wisconsin Democratic chairman and Kennedy supporter, described as "dull, dark, cold days." Beginning on February 16, Kennedy, sometimes with Jackie, spent twenty-nine days campaigning there, waking at 5:00 in the morning and ending late at night, making seven to nine appearances per day and giving more than 250 speeches. He insisted that he rest for an hour to ninety minutes before dinner, and that he have free time at noon and an hour in the hotel in the morning. He used these periods to rest his back and maintain contact with his Senate office.[29]

As in New Hampshire, the campaign was well organized and efficient. From the summer of 1959, the Kennedys paid Jerry Bruno of Proxmire's staff to handle the preliminaries until they established their operation. Bobby managed the campaign and also spoke throughout the state. Ted addressed various groups and took his first ski jump to promote his brother's candidacy. Rose, the seventy-year-old mother, and her daughters Eunice, Pat, and Jean held "Coffee with the Kennedys," where they visited homes, met the ladies present, promoted Jack, and then went to the next house. Sargent Shriver managed the campaign in the first and second districts, while volunteers manned the other eight. Someone from the Kennedy campaign visited every town with a population greater than three hundred—at least once and usually several times.[30]

Humphrey campaigned as an underdog, a traditional politician focusing on agriculture issues, which were critical to voters in the three districts that bordered Minnesota. He maintained the same hectic schedule as his opponent, but without nearly the same financial support. His wife, Muriel, handed out her famous beef soup recipe while their twenty-one-year-old daughter, Nancy, and sons Hubert Jr., Robert, and Dougie helped out. Political allies from Humphrey's home state, including Governor Orville Freeman and Senator Eugene McCarthy, joined his campaign, as did former baseball star and civil rights leader Jackie Robinson and Helen Gahagan Douglas.[31]

Shortly before both candidates made their last campaign pushes, five thousand anti-Catholic pamphlets, postmarked from Minnesota, flooded into Wisconsin's rural Catholic areas. Both the Kennedy and Humphrey camps denied responsibility. Nixon, recalling this incident almost three decades later, described the pamphlets as "vicious anti-Catholic" literature. Even with his denials, Humphrey was presumed guilty. Nixon noted that "the Kennedy people did nothing to dissuade them."[32]

Bobby Kennedy had reasons to stay silent. No one mentioned Paul Corbin, whom Bobby had met when both worked for Joe McCarthy. They became such close friends that Corbin converted to Catholicism with Ethel and Bobby as his godparents. After Bobby hired Corbin to organize Wisconsin's seventh district, Corbin orchestrated the anti-Catholic mailing and also distributed similar material in Catholic neighborhoods to stimulate votes for Kennedy.[33]

JFK found the final tally a disappointment: six districts went for him and four for Humphrey. Given the optimism coming from his supporters after New Hampshire, anything less than a landslide was a defeat. He won the popular vote, 56.5 percent to Humphrey's 43.5, but the breakdown by district was disturbing. He had won all fourteen counties with populations that were more than 35 percent Catholic, but only twenty of the thirty-seven with lower Catholic populations. Humphrey easily won the two farming districts (third and ninth) and narrowly won in the second and tenth. He won where the Protestant vote was the highest, showing that religion was a major issue.[34]

Both the Kennedy and Humphrey forces were bitter about the other side's tactics, and at the end the campaign grew rough. Humphrey, knowing he was behind in the polls and resentful of Kennedy's seemingly endless supply of money, stormed the state reminding listeners that he could "not win by competing in glamour or in public relations. . . . The Kennedy forces are waging a psychological blitz that I cannot match. I'm not the candidate of the fat cats."[35]

Shortly after the primary, the Kennedys met at Joe's mansion in Palm Beach, Florida. Jack had decided to enter the primary in West Virginia, where the population was about 95 percent Protestant. During the meeting, Joe opposed the idea: "It's a nothing state and they'll kill him over the Catholic thing." The son answered: "Well, we've heard from the Ambassador, but we're going to go into West Virginia and we're going to win."[36]

Jack saw that he had to confront the religious issue directly. Addressing the American Society of Newspaper Editors in the capital on April 21, he asked reporters to concentrate on facts. He supported the First Amendment's guarantee of religious freedom and assured his audience that ecclesiastical pressure would not influence his decisions. As a senator, he had voted against federal aid to parochial schools and opposed appointing an ambassador to the Vatican. He opposed using United States foreign aid funds for birth control unless in the public interest.

Reporters continually asked the same questions, he said, and he gave the same replies. What troubled him was that the media analyzed voters and candidates solely on religion, while voters cast their ballots for many reasons. He rejected any suggestion of a special religious test only for presidential candidates. He was "not the Catholic candidate for president" and hoped "to avert a religious spectacle." If he lost the election due to his religion, it would mean bigotry had triumphed.[37]

While Kennedy's forces fanned across West Virginia for the May 10 balloting, his name was on the ballot in several earlier primaries. On April 12, with no Democrats on the Illinois ballot, he received 64.6 percent of the write-in vote. Massachusetts voters cast their ballots fourteen days later and gave him almost 93 percent of the write-in vote without any opposition; there was no primary contest with candidates on the ballot. At the start of May, Indiana gave him 81 percent of the Democratic vote with token opposition.[38]

West Virginia remained Kennedy's principal focus. The challenges were far different from those of his earlier primaries. Some commentators held that West Virginia had never recovered from the Great Depression. From 1950 to 1960, it was the only state in the Union to lose population every year. Its unemployment rate of 15 percent was three times the national average. Many in the state were dependent on surplus government food.[39]

For a Catholic candidate, an additional problem was that only ninety-five thousand of West Virginia's 1.9 million residents were Catholic. Fifty-nine percent claimed no religious affiliation at all, and church membership was among the lowest in the nation. Voters had, however, recently elected two Catholics to the state supreme court. The state also had a long history of bought elections. "Slating" was a common practice: candidates paid local officials such as sheriffs or county clerks to print lists distributed by poll workers so that voters would cast their ballots for an entire slate.[40]

Humphrey entered the West Virginia primary early in February with what looked like a commanding lead. He had gone there several times in the past year and hoped to rely on Protestant, union, and black voters, as well as a large "Stop Kennedy" contingent. He and his family campaigned tirelessly, but he did not have the money to hire a large organization or buy slates. Rein J. Vander Zee directed the Humphrey campaign starting in January. He recalled that the Kennedys spent "a massive, massive influx of money." He added that the winner was decided by "who could bring the most money to their game." The obvious answer was the Kennedys. As the balloting approached, Humphrey and his supporters once again grew intense and bitter. He declared at one campaign appearance: "I can't afford to run through this state with a little black bag and a checkbook." At another, he added: "I don't think elections should be bought." On May 4, six days before the vote, he and Kennedy held a one-hour joint television appearance in which they limited themselves to attacks on Republican policies. They addressed each other politely and there were no angry exchanges. In the final days of the race, Humphrey emphasized his standing as the underdog.[41]

Kennedy's staff made this campaign personal. They viewed Humphrey as a spoiler with no chance of winning the nomination, whose only purpose was to lead a stop-Kennedy movement. Larry O'Brien recalled: "Perhaps the toughest political fight I've ever been in was the 1960 Kennedy-Humphrey primary race in West Virginia. It was no holds barred." Kenny O'Donnell described a campaign staff determined that "in winning they would make sure Humphrey paid a price."[42]

The Kennedys had an endless supply of money to pay staff, make massive numbers of telephone calls, and attract volunteers. They promoted JFK's personality, especially his wartime heroism and call for religious toleration. He spoke across the state until he was hoarse. His family accompanied him and championed his cause.[43]

Kennedy had another enormous advantage: the endorsement of Franklin D. Roosevelt, Jr. He already had campaigned for Kennedy in Wisconsin, but the Roosevelt name had special sway in West Virginia. Charles Peters, Jr., who lived in the state and worked on the Kennedy campaign, was among many who urged Kennedy to take advantage of "the power of the Roosevelt name." Peters believed Junior's intervention could mean the difference between victory and defeat. For many West Virginians, FDR Jr. "was almost God's son coming down and saying it was all right to vote for this Catholic, that it was permissible, and it wasn't something terrible to do."[44]

FDR Jr. did more than speak in favor of Kennedy; he spoke against Humphrey, labeling him a draft dodger for not joining the armed forces during World War II while failing to point out that Humphrey was deferred twice on medical grounds. When Humphrey heard this accusation, he called it "gutter politics." Jack and Bobby Kennedy disavowed it, leaving FDR Jr. alone saddled with this false allegation.[45]

The election took place on a drizzly, dreary day; just 57 percent of registered Democrats went to the polls. By midnight, Humphrey had suffered such a devastating loss that he ended his candidacy. After he graciously conceded, Bobby Kennedy went to Humphrey's headquarters and walked over to kiss Muriel Humphrey. She refused, but her husband went to the airport to meet Jack Kennedy, who was flying from the capital. They shook hands, and Humphrey left while Kennedy spoke to the press.[46]

Humphrey saved his bitterness for his memoirs, where he wrote that while the Kennedy campaign had a "beautiful exterior," underneath it "there was an element of ruthlessness and toughness that I had trouble either accepting or forgetting." Ted Kennedy, in his memoirs, wrote of Humphrey, "It took years for his private bitterness to heal."[47]

Humphrey lost for a variety of reasons, but the difference in financial resources between the two campaigns stands out. Because of the way campaign expenditures were reported in 1960, there are no hard figures. Kennedy may have spent as much as $4 million (about $35 million in 2020 dollars) on staff, material, television and radio time, and other needs.[48]

One person quipped that if the Kennedys came to West Virginia again, the state would be out of its depression. Raymond Chafin, Democratic chairman for Logan County, initially decided to back Humphrey, who gave him $2,000 for his support. Chafin returned the money and shifted to Kennedy at the end of April, telling JFK he needed "about 35," meaning $3,500, for the election. A few days before the balloting, someone from Kennedy's staff told Chafin to meet a plane that afternoon because Kennedy was sending him "something to work with." Robert McDonough, who was running the Kennedy campaign in the state, handed Chafin two briefcases with "heavy seals." They contained more than $35,000. Logan County gave Kennedy 55 percent of its vote.[49]

On the day of the primary, "dirt farmers, hillbillies and unemployed coal miners," according to *Time* magazine, sold their votes "for a half-pint of whiskey" in the depressed southern part of the state. One poll watcher said that along with the whiskey, voters received two to five dollars in cash. Others also claimed to see whiskey and money passed for votes. After the results were posted, Paul Corbin bragged about handing out ten-dollar bills to get votes.[50]

Charges of vote buying surfaced after the election. Senator Goldwater, as chair of the Republican senatorial campaign committee, hired a former FBI agent, who also was an attorney, to investigate. The man sent back sixteen affidavits from individuals who confessed "to criminal conduct." One admitted to distributing a half-pint of Kentucky moonshine whiskey plus two dollars to each person voting for Kennedy; in all, he gave out some twelve gallons of whiskey. Goldwater gave the affidavits to Attorney General William Rogers, who did nothing with them.[51]

The FBI received allegations of vote buying, moving polling places, and Logan County officials pulling "machine levers for local citizens." Even though some reporters claimed that the FBI was conducting an investigation, no one was charged with any illegal activities.[52]

The religious issue never materialized. Dan Fleming, in his exhaustive study of the contest, expressed disappointment at the media for failing to realize that Kennedy would easily win and for believing that the Catholic issue would make the election close. *New York Times* and *Washington Post* reporters, he wrote, "badly misread the election" and overdramatized religion.[53]

The Nebraska primary was held the same day as West Virginia. Kennedy received 88.7 percent of the vote, again drawing the highest total of any Democrat since FDR. A week later, Maryland gave him 70.3 percent and more votes than any previous Democrat.[54]

The May 20 primary in Oregon, with seventeen delegates at stake, was Kennedy's seventh and last. Senator Wayne Morse, running as a favorite son, bitterly opposed him because he thought Kennedy was lazy, and also that he was responsible for the passage of the Landrum-Griffin Act, which Morse believed sold out labor. His charges did not resonate with voters. Kennedy received 51 percent of the vote—once again, the highest Democratic vote total in the state's history—to Morse's 31.9 percent.[55]

The day after the Oregon primary, at the urging of his advisers, Kennedy flew to Stevenson's farm in Libertyville, Illinois, to ask for his support. Afterward, the senator called the meeting "rather unsatisfactory" and could not understand why Stevenson refused to endorse him. Larry O'Brien, in his memoir, wrote that Kennedy found Stevenson "cool and aloof" and confused as to the purpose of the visit. The senator "was furious" that his political advisers had put him in the position of making a pilgrimage to Stevenson only to be rejected.[56]

Yet in a letter to Schlesinger, Stevenson described his initial impression of Kennedy as "entirely satisfactory." He was impressed with Kennedy's foreign policy views, and if he was not yet ready to endorse him, neither would he participate in any stop-Kennedy effort. He did not think Kennedy understood the difficulties Stevenson faced with his own supporters. He even offered to help with the Catholic issue. The former governor saw JFK as "very self-confident and assured & much tougher and blunter than I remember him in the past."[57]

Kennedy had other worries: certain uncomfortable facts were threatening to come to light. In June 1959, while completing his Kennedy biography, James MacGregor Burns had read a *Boston Post* item about a rumor that the senator had Addison's disease. Later that month, Burns asked Kennedy for "the full record of your health background." Instead of being referred to the physicians who had treated him for Addison's, Burns was told to contact Dr. Janet Travell. She insisted that he had only "a mild case of adrenal insufficiency" that he had contracted as a result of the PT-109 episode and was now fully rehabilitated. Nor did he have the most striking physical sign of Addison's, "deep pigmentation or tanning of the skin." Furthermore, she reported, he had "tremendous physical stamina" and "above-average resistance to infections, such as influenza."

Burns consulted Dr. Alexander Preston, a physician and family friend, who in turn contacted two experts. On August 21, Preston informed Burns that he doubted Travell's honesty; Burns should discuss the disease directly with the senator. In late September, Preston further cautioned Burns that he should find out what treatment Kennedy had received for "adrenal insufficiency." But Burns seems to have ignored this advice: his book reinforced the fiction that Kennedy did not have the illness.

Burns wrote: "While Kennedy's adrenal insufficiency might well be diagnosed by some doctors as a mild case of Addison's Disease, it was not diagnosed as the classic type of Addison's Disease, which is due to tuberculosis." Other medical problems could create problems with the adrenal glands, but Kennedy was getting routine checkups and taking medication when necessary. But the phrase "classic type of Addison's Disease" was deceptive. It is insignificant that Kennedy's condition did not arise from tuberculosis. He required daily medication to stay alive.[58]

When *Newsweek* reporter James Cannon asked him about his medical history at that dinner with the Bradlees on January 5, 1960, three days after he announced for the presidency, Kennedy recalled that his father thought any possibility of a political career "was hopeless" because of his poor health. Ben Bradlee recalled seeing him in the late 1940s as a congressman looking "like the wrath of God. . . . You weighed 120, and you were bright green." Kennedy agreed: he "looked like a cadaver" and continued: "It was atabrine [a drug for malaria], malaria, and probably some adrenal deficiency." At one point, he said, "Drew Pearson's man" had asked him if he had Addison's disease, and "I said no, God, a guy with Addison's Disease looks sort of brown and everything."[59]

These rumors about Kennedy's health were still circulating quietly among journalists in the summer of 1960, but the public heard nothing. They also heard nothing about his sexual behavior. In addition to following Kennedy since the early 1940s, the FBI had followed Frank Sinatra's activities for some years because of his association with left-wing causes and his connections to gangsters. The parties he went to came under the bureau's scrutiny, including those attended by Kennedy and his brother-in-law Peter Lawford. On March 22, 1960, a criminal informant told special agents that *Confidential* magazine had recently assigned one of its local reporters in southern California to check rumors of a sex party at Sinatra's Palm Springs home while Kennedy and Lawford were guests there. The following week, "a notorious private investigator" who was also an FBI informant said that the magazine had already obtained signed affidavits from "allegedly two mulatto prostitutes in New York" about an "indiscreet party" with the three men in a New York hotel room.[60] When the three stayed at the Sands Hotel in Las Vegas, Nevada, "show girls from all over town were running in and out of the senator's suite."

The same FBI report, dated March 29, says that during a stop in Miami, Florida, airline hostess Susan Stalling was sent to visit Kennedy. At the start of April, a confidential informer corroborated the sex rumors about Sinatra, Kennedy, and Lawford. Drew Pearson recorded in his diary: "When Kennedy wants a girl in Miami, [Senator George] Smathers produces her." Pearson wrote that Associate Supreme Court Justice William Douglas "described Smathers as a good-time boy who had a bad influence on Kennedy and was only worth something when you wanted to get a girl in Miami."[61]

Sinatra introduced Judith Campbell (later Judith Exner) to Kennedy on February 7, 1960. They had dinner at the Sands and lunch the next day. On the twelfth he called from Fresno, California, and sent her a dozen red roses, followed by lunch at Warner Brothers on the twenty-fourth. They met at the Plaza Hotel in New York City on March 7, the day before the New Hampshire primary, and according to Exner had intercourse for the first time. According to her memoir, on April 6, the day after the Wisconsin primary, they slept together at Kennedy's Georgetown home. They saw each other again at a Miami hotel on the twelfth, after which he left her two thousand dollars.[62]

While waiting for the results of the West Virginia primary, the Bradlees and Kennedys again had dinner at their home. Jack decided that the couples should go to the movies to pass the time while waiting for the results. They went to one theater where the picture was half finished and decided to go elsewhere. Jack took them to the Plaza Theater, which specialized in pornographic films, where they saw *Private Property*, about a horny housewife who takes up with hoodlums. (The movie was on the Catholic Legion of Decency's list of condemned films.) Jackie later recalled that the couples saw "some strange movie. . . . It was some awful, sordid thing about some murder in California . . . just morbid." The movie was "terribly" depressing, and they went home to wait for the results.[63]

Reporters at the time generally did not write about such things. Bradlee vividly illustrated how his reporting changed toward sexual issues over three decades. In 1960, he mentioned only that Jack and Jackie spent a quiet evening with friends at home. In his memoir, *A Good Life*, released in 1995, he provided a detailed account of going to see the pornographic movie.

Six days before the Oregon primary, Florence Kater, who had tried to expose Kennedy's affair with Pamela Turnure in the summer of 1958, confronted him at a University of Maryland political rally. She carried an enlarged photograph of him leaving the apartment and asked him why he was trying to hide his face and why he was trying to have her husband fired from his job. As she was being escorted out of the gymnasium, Kennedy's supporters called out: "It looks like Tricky Dick! It looks like Tricky Dick!"

The *Washington Star* ran a brief article the next day about "a heckler." Kennedy's staffers told reporters that the picture was a fake created by Wisconsin "religious fanatics." Three *Washington Star* photographers came to Kater's door the following morning to tell her the article had gotten them into trouble. Kater described exactly where the photo was taken, and the reporters left convinced that the picture was authentic.[64]

After that meeting, James McInerney, a former assistant attorney general and troubleshooter for Joe Kennedy, visited the Katers and suggested that they stop distributing the photograph. McInerney, according to Drew Pearson, had been hired by Joe Kennedy "to handle Jack's girls when they want to be paid off." Some time later, Congressman William Bates, accompanied by Senator Kennedy, told Mr. Kater that he would lose his job if he bothered the senator any more.[65]

During the campaign, the public never learned about this side of Jack Kennedy. Louis Harris's polls showed that his image as a family man was central to his success as a presidential nominee. Interviewees appreciated his political talents—he was smart, engaging, witty, and energetic—and considered it a major strength that he was a practicing Catholic and a faithful husband, with an attractive wife and a young daughter.

The candidate learned from these polls, and during the primaries he matured into an exceptional campaigner. Always trying to perform better, he recognized that he needed to improve his speaking. He often asked Jackie as well as Robert Healy, the political editor of the *Boston Globe* and the only reporter to follow him throughout his primary contests, for their opinions. They said that sometimes he spoke too quickly; he had loudness issues and a Harvard-Boston accent. After the Democratic convention, he hired David McClosky, a professor of voice at Boston University, to coach him on his speaking skills. They worked out a set of hand signals that allowed McClosky to sit in the Senate gallery or in the audience at speaking events, giving Kennedy instant feedback on his delivery.[66]

By the time the primaries were finished, Kennedy had become superbly adept at two things: how to show the voters what he wanted them to see, and how to conceal what he did not want them to see. He approached the Democratic convention with his image intact.

6

The Whippersnapper
and the Riverboat Gambler Team Up

John Kennedy had swept all seven primaries he had entered. In five he ran unchallenged, and he decisively defeated Humphrey in the other two. Going into the summer, Louis Harris's surveys showed his client doing far better than the other Democratic contenders in every state except South Carolina, where Lyndon Johnson narrowly beat him. Gallup provided added encouragement: by the end of June, 51 percent preferred Kennedy over other Democrats in national polls.[1]

One impediment to Kennedy's march to the Democratic nomination was his need to convince African Americans to vote for him despite his poor voting record on civil rights. This issue had come to the fore in February 1960, when four black college students went to a Woolworth's department store in Greensboro, North Carolina. One bought a tube of toothpaste, and then the group went to the lunch counter and asked to be served coffee. Even after the waitress refused to wait on them, they remained seated. Some white people violently removed them. Sporadic sit-ins with scant newspaper coverage had been staged in the past, but the Greensboro incident ignited the spark that started a national firestorm.[2]

Kennedy was pulled in opposite directions. Southern political leaders, whom he needed for the nomination, opposed integration, while black leaders, whom he also needed, demanded it. He met with entertainer Harry Belafonte and retired athlete Jackie Robinson as well as Martin Luther King, Jr., to win their support. NAACP executive secretary Roy Wilkins sometimes harshly criticized the senator and sometimes supported him.[3]

Kennedy also confronted charges that he was too inexperienced for the presidency. On May 1, a U-2 spy plane had been shot down over Soviet airspace, and rather than destroy the plane and commit suicide, the pilot, Francis Gary Powers, allowed himself to be captured. Four days later, Soviet Premier Nikita Khrushchev produced plane fragments and the pilot for the world to see. Eisenhower, on May 11, admitted that he had ordered the flight and earlier ones to prevent a surprise Soviet attack on the United States. A summit in Paris with the leaders of France, Great Britain, the United States, and the Soviet Union had already been scheduled for mid-May. Both Ike and Khrushchev flew to the French capital, but Khrushchev refused to proceed without an apology from the president. The summit collapsed before it began.[4]

Kennedy suggested that Eisenhower should have apologized. He received severe criticism for attacking the president and suggesting any apology to the Soviet leader. Many found his remarks opportunistic; they raised questions about his judgment. Later, when asked about his statement, Kennedy muttered that Ike should have expressed "diplomatic regrets" and not an "apology."[5]

To draw attention to Kennedy's gaffe, Lyndon Johnson sent a cable to the president signed by himself, Speaker Rayburn, Senate Foreign Relations Committee Chairman William Fulbright, and Adlai Stevenson. They claimed to be "shocked" that Khrushchev "would meddle in an American election for the apparent purpose of coping with his own domestic problems." The Soviet leader should keep out of American politics.[6]

On June 14, Kennedy spoke in the Senate chamber to explain his position. He favored an arms control agreement but called for a stronger military that would end the "missile gap" and enable America to fight limited wars anywhere in the world. He wanted to strengthen NATO (North Atlantic Treaty Organization) and the Organization of American States (OAS) and provide economic assistance to developing nations. Since the administration's "liberation" policy in Eastern Europe had failed, there had to be a new approach to the impasse in Berlin and to the Soviet satellites in general. Finally, he would not recognize the People's Republic of China or allow it to join the United Nations.[7]

Johnson had emerged as Kennedy's most serious opponent for the nomination. Eisenhower had told *New York Times* columnist Arthur Krock that Johnson was the "best qualified Democrat to succeed him," and others on the White House staff agreed. Press secretary Jim Hagerty recalled that in the last years of his presidency, Ike told several people that Johnson "would be a fine president." Presidential assistant Bryce Harlow remembered that Ike believed "that in many ways Lyndon would make a great president." Ike respected his leadership abilities.[8]

Kennedy did not share this opinion. On May 22, he told Arthur Schlesinger that LBJ was "a chronic liar" and that "he has been making all sorts of assurances to me for years and has lived up to none of them." Three weeks later, he described Johnson as a "riverboat gambler."[9]

George Smathers, who had been best man at Kennedy's wedding and was now one of LBJ's legislative lieutenants, admired Johnson as "a great majority leader." At first, he did not take JFK's candidacy seriously and did not believe that, as a Catholic, Kennedy could be elected president. LBJ, he later recalled, called JFK "an abomination." He thought the two "abided each other, but they didn't like each other really." They came from "totally different backgrounds." Nixon remembered Johnson describing Kennedy as "a young whippersnapper who was much too ambitious considering his experience and who wasn't qualified to be President."[10]

At the beginning of June, even though LBJ headquarters had opened, the candidate still had made no formal announcement. He pointed out that as majority leader he had critical responsibilities that prevented him from campaigning. In the middle of the month, nineteen editors of the Scripps-Howard newspaper chain declared LBJ "the ablest and strongest" Democratic candidate. At the same time, nineteen major American newspapers ran ads urging Johnson to become "an active candidate." *Newsweek* on June 20 named him the ablest man in the Senate.[11]

Congress recessed in mid-July so that both national parties could prepare for their conventions. Johnson understood that he had to persuade enough Democratic delegates to vote against Kennedy to deny him a first-ballot majority. With that objective in mind, he spoke to Stevenson on May 19 about stopping Kennedy. If Stevenson could gather four hundred delegates, then those, combined with Johnson's delegates, would deny JFK the majority. Johnson hoped to emerge as the candidate on subsequent ballots, but if he failed, he would support Stevenson. The former governor replied that he was not a candidate, did not expect to get that number of delegates, and would not join a stop-Kennedy effort. Nor would he endorse Kennedy, or interfere with a draft movement.[12]

Fog hung over Stevenson's candidacy. The *New York Times* ran a full-page ad on May 22: "America Needs Adlai Stevenson." At least thirty-two states had established Stevenson headquarters. Many Democrats wished for a Stevenson-Kennedy ticket, even though JFK had said that he would refuse second place under any circumstances.[13]

Adding to the confusion, on June 8 the *New York Times* published an open letter to "Fellow Liberals" signed by Columbia historian Henry Steele Commager, Galbraith and Schlesinger of Harvard, and ADA founder Joseph Rauh, Jr. All had enthusiastically backed Stevenson in his two previous presidential bids but now endorsed JFK because he "was an active candidate" who supported liberalism.[14]

Eleanor Roosevelt thought differently. On June 10, in her column "My Day," she wrote that she and others wanted the convention to nominate Stevenson for president and Kennedy for vice president, calling this the "best and strongest ticket." She then telephoned Stevenson to urge him to accept a draft, and on June 20, a full-page ad in the *New York Times* announced that she had been named the honorary chairwoman of the Stevenson for President Committee.[15]

Stevenson appreciated his supporters' efforts and disapproved of the pressure Kennedy had placed on him. The former governor thought he had launched Kennedy into the national spotlight at the 1956 Democratic convention and had done nothing to impede the senator's rise since then. He was especially provoked that Kennedy's advocates were warning him that unless he endorsed the senator, he would not be considered for secretary of state.[16]

In the third week of June, Stevenson wrote: "Kennedy's tactics are coercive, but effective, and if he is nominated—all will be well, but if he slips the victims will turn on him like wolves." He "was bright and able but too young and unseasoned for the presidency." He also would lose the general election because of his faith. Johnson was too regional to be a strong contender, and Symington was unqualified. If the convention deadlocked, Stevenson thought, it might turn to him.[17]

In the second week of June, Kennedy told Schlesinger, "I understand for the first time that Adlai is helping me by doing nothing—that he could do me considerable harm by raising his finger." William Attwood, who wrote speeches first for Stevenson and then for Kennedy, had dinner with Jack on June 14 at his Georgetown home and told him that Stevenson was not a candidate and would not lead a stop-Kennedy effort. Jack and Jackie agreed that Stevenson's posture helped Symington and Johnson. Stevenson later asked Attwood for a summary of the meeting. Attwood wrote that he saw in JFK "a mixture of cockiness and uncertainty, a consuming drive to win and a total absorption in political strategy," and he mentioned the point about naming the former governor to a cabinet post. Stevenson replied: "How could I ever go to work for such an arrogant young man?"[18]

Symington's strategy was to stay out of the primaries and avoid friction with the other contenders. He would speak on the Senate floor about the various issues that he specialized in, like defense and farming, and he would address audiences across the nation. After announcing for the presidency, he called for peace through defense, better health care, education, and slum clearance. If the

convention deadlocked, he hoped that this broad agenda would make him attractive as the compromise candidate.[19]

Harry Truman, Symington's most powerful advocate, said even before the primaries were finished that they did not "mean a hoot." As for Kennedy, the former
president described him as "a fine young man" and said "I know and like him."
But at the end of June, Truman announced that he would not attend the convention because it was "fixed" in favor of Kennedy. He preferred Symington,
Johnson, and eight others for the nomination. On the last day of June, CBS televised Truman's news conference in which he denounced Kennedy. The Democratic Party, he said, needed "a man with the greatest possible maturity and experience to be its presidential nominee." Nixon thought the former president's
action might force a reevaluation of JFK's nomination but then changed his
mind: "The Democratic pros, when they go up against the gun, cannot take the
risk of denying him the nomination."[20]

On Independence Day, Kennedy answered Truman's allegations. He would
not, he said, "step aside at anyone's request." He was running for the presidential nomination. Second, the Democratic convention was not rigged. Third, his
campaign had not applied "improper pressure on the delegates." He had made
no promises to anyone. Last, in response to Truman's suggestion that he was not
ready for the presidency, he answered that he had spent eighteen years in his
country's service: four in the military and fourteen in Congress. He had won
every primary he had entered, while neither Symington nor Johnson had even
contested any. At forty-three years old, he proclaimed that the nation's leadership
was passing to a new generation "to cope with new problems and new opportunities." The White House required someone with his "strength and health and
vigor." He was ready.[21]

India Edwards, cochairwoman of Citizens for Johnson, held a press conference within twenty-four hours to refute Kennedy's claim that he was in excellent
health. With John Connally, who also worked for LBJ, standing at her side, she
objected to Kennedy's "muscle flexing in boasting about his youth," with its im-
plication that LBJ, due to his heart attack, was too sick to run. Kennedy, she said,
had Addison's disease, and several physicians had told her that he could not survive without cortisone. She called him a "spavined little hunchback," a phrase no
newspaper would print.[22]

The Kennedy campaign responded instantly, deploring LBJ's desperate reliance on "despicable tactics." Kennedy's press secretary, Pierre Salinger, stated
that Kennedy's energetic campaign clearly demonstrated his robust health.
Robert Kennedy added that his brother never had the "ailment described classi-

cally as Addison's Disease, which is a tuberculose [*sic*] destruction of the adrenal gland."[23]

The campaign released a letter written on June 11 signed by physicians Eugene Cohen, "a world-renowned endocrinologist," and Janet Travell, Kennedy's personal doctor, both of whom had been treating him for more than five years. In a cover letter not released, the two doctors stated: "[That] your adrenal glands do function has been confirmed by a leading endocrinologist outside of New York City." But the physician's name was not disclosed, nor was any evidence included.[24]

Travell and Cohen addressed five points contained in the senator's medical records: (1) since 1957, except for a brief laryngitis attack in April 1960, "no health problem has handicapped your efforts"; (2) "Your health is excellent"; (3) Kennedy was capable of serving in the presidency "without need for special medical treatment, unusual rest periods or other limitations"; (4) his strenuous campaign activities during the primaries illustrated his "superb physical condition"; and (5) his "adrenal glands do function."[25]

The next day, July 5, Johnson announced his candidacy, emphasizing that the next president "should be a working president" with the essential experience, an indirect slap at Kennedy. During the question-and-answer session that followed, George Cheely of CBS News asked about the health issue. The Kennedy team, Johnson replied, had urged him to "repudiate the irresponsible statements" of his supporters. Both he and Kennedy were in good health. When asked if he would run for the vice presidency, he surprised many listeners by not rejecting the idea.[26]

With attention suddenly focused on the candidates' health, the press asked about Nixon's physical condition. Dr. Walter Tkach, the assistant White House physician, had conducted an examination of the vice president at Walter Reed Hospital on April 25, concluding "that the Vice President's health is excellent in all respects." Vice presidential press secretary Herb Klein said on July 7 that he was not trying to make health an issue, but he referred reporters to the results of Tkach's exam.[27]

By July 7, LBJ was on his way to Los Angeles for the convention, predicting that he would be the Democratic nominee. At a stop in Chicago, he hinted that the convention was rigged. Stevenson, interviewed at his farm in Illinois, said he was "not informed of any rigging," and Symington concurred.[28]

Several days before the convention opened, the Manhattan office of Dr. Eugene Cohen, the endocrinologist who had cosigned the letter attesting to Kennedy's good health, was burglarized. No valuables or drugs were taken. Nothing was missing except patients' records filed under K, which were ransacked and left on the floor. Cohen believed that the burglars were searching for his files on Kennedy, but they were undisturbed.[29]

Kennedy's private physician, Dr. Janet Travell, later claimed there was an attempted burglary of her office at the same time. She did not mention this in her 1968 memoir *Office Hours,* but in her oral history at the Kennedy Library, she said someone had "just sliced the door and they tried to break the lock."[30]

Travell's recollection cannot be relied upon. She lied about Kennedy's health, and Cohen's subsequent letters to President Kennedy and his personal physician, Rear Admiral George Burkley, further call her veracity into question. On November 12, 1961, Cohen wrote the president that Travell sought personal advancement and had placed "her own interests . . . above yours." He described her as a "venomous creature" with limited skills: "We were stuck with a deceiving incompetent, publicity-mad physician."[31]

Historian Robert Dallek, relying on Travell's oral history in his 2003 JFK biography *An Unfinished Life,* speculated that Richard Nixon's operatives might have been responsible for the break-ins as a prelude to Watergate. Dallek did not consult Cohen, who was still alive at the time. The historian incorrectly stated that the burglary of the physician's office occurred during the general election campaign; it occurred before the Democratic convention. Nixon had no reason to order it. Don Hughes, his appointment secretary, who was constantly at the vice president's side, did not believe that his boss had ordered any break-in. Nixon asked his personal physician, John Lungren, about Addison's disease and concluded that since this illness did not affect JFK's mind, it was not "a legitimate issue." He never raised it in the general election.[32]

Dallek was granted access to Kennedy's medical records while writing *An Unfinished Life.* He concluded that the senator had deceived the public. "By hiding the extent of his ailments he denied voters the chance to decide whether they wanted to share this gamble" on his ability to serve as president. Dallek doubts that Kennedy "could have been nominated, much less elected, if the public had known what we now know about his health."[33]

Theodore Sorensen, JFK's most fervent defender, disagreed. After the medical records were made public, he admitted, forty-eight years after the election, that he, Bobby Kennedy, and the press office "may have obscured the stark truth." But unlike Dallek, Sorensen insisted that "even if more medical information had been disclosed," JFK "would have won."[34]

Kennedy, of course, never explained why he lied about his Addison's disease and his other serious health problems; except in the days before the convention and toward the end of the campaign, they were never an issue while he was alive.

Lee Mandel, M.D., and historian James Giglio, who have written extensively on Kennedy's health, believe that above all else, he was concerned with his image. He must be seen as energetic and vigorous or he would lose one of his most charismatic qualities as a politician. His attractiveness and credibility would suffer.[35]

Another potential embarrassment as the convention approached came from a Drew Pearson column claiming that Republicans planned "to bring out the Jack Kennedy contribution of $1,000 to help Nixon defeat Mrs. Helen Gahagan Douglas." When reporters asked Herb Klein about this, he replied that Nixon had "no knowledge of a contribution from Kennedy in that or any other campaign." Nixon, of course, knew this was false: Kennedy had personally handed him the money. The accusation never arose during the campaign.[36]

Kennedy's civil rights stand was a far more controversial subject, and as the convention approached, his team worried about wavering support and potentially low turnout among black voters. Jackie Robinson, who had left baseball in 1956 to become a spokesman for the Chock Full O'Nuts coffee shop chain, a *New York Post* columnist, and an NAACP executive board member, distrusted and spoke out against Kennedy because the senator had entertained the segregationist governor of Alabama, John Patterson, and the leader of the state's White Citizens' Council, Sam Engelhardt, for breakfast at his Georgetown home. Patterson, in turn, had been the first influential southern politician to endorse JFK.[37]

In March and April, Robinson campaigned energetically for Humphrey in Wisconsin. When Bobby Kennedy accused the Minnesota senator of paying Robinson to attend his rallies, Robinson angrily called Bobby a liar—he had not received any money—and labeled JFK the "fair-haired boy of the Southern segregationists."[38]

Over the next two months, JFK tried to change Robinson's opinion and to clarify his civil rights record. He made a statement in late May saying he had supported the 1960 Civil Rights Act and tried to strengthen it. He had made no commitment to Patterson and Engelhardt regarding civil rights. Further, he supported the sit-in movement and disagreed with Truman's position on it. Robinson would have none of it: in his column on June 3 he again called Kennedy the segregationists' "fair-haired boy" and added that he was "not fit to be President."[39]

In his column a week later, on June 10, Robinson endorsed Nixon. Responding by letter at the end of the month, Nixon agreed with Robinson that "no political party or special interest group can take the American Negro vote for granted."[40]

Chester Bowles arranged an evening meeting between Kennedy and Robinson at Bowles's Washington home on June 29. Robinson later told Nixon that in the meeting, JFK admitted that he did not know many African Americans or understand "the Negro problem." Robinson came away angry, thinking Kennedy had little interest in civil rights. Two days later, the senator sent Robinson a letter saying that he appreciated Robinson's position on "first-class citizenship for all Americans" and hoped he understood that they both sought the same goals. He met with many individuals, he wrote, including segregationists, but that did not mean he accepted their views.[41]

Robinson reprinted the letter in his *Post* column of July 6, adding that JFK had "limited experience" with African Americans. The senator impressed him, he wrote, but he would not endorse his candidacy. Instead, he would watch Kennedy's actions closely. JFK was "a little late in seeking to make himself clear, after 14 years in Congress. But if he is sincere, there is still time to catch up." In his autobiography, Robinson was more pessimistic, commenting that the senator knew nothing about black people and that when they met, Kennedy would not look him "in the eyes."[42]

Marietta Tree, an avid Stevenson advocate, arrived in Los Angeles on Saturday, July 9, two days before the start of the convention. She wrote to her husband that JFK's victory was a foregone conclusion. The delegates were saying, "He's going to win anyway, so we might as well vote for him."[43]

Stevenson arrived the same day, to the largest demonstration of any candidate. Remaining cool and detached, he said he would run for the White House if the party drafted him, but he was not optimistic "in view of the aggressive ambitions of others." The chances for a draft were crushed on Sunday, when Chicago Mayor Richard Daley announced that the delegation from Stevenson's home state of Illinois would cast 59½ of its 69 votes for JFK on the first ballot.[44]

Almost simultaneously with Daley's statement, Eleanor Roosevelt landed in Los Angeles. Stevenson supporters greeted her with banners championing his nomination. At two party dinners that evening, she still held out hope that her "undeclared candidate, Mr. Stevenson" would receive the nomination.[45]

Roosevelt's dream of a Stevenson draft and Johnson's entrance into the contest did not alter Symington's strategy. He remained hopeful that the convention would deadlock and turn to him as the compromise candidate. Despite the Kennedy bandwagon he tried to keep his delegates firmly committed and even searched for more.[46]

Johnson looked to Stevenson to help propel a stop-Kennedy effort, but the former governor vacillated. *Time* magazine put the Senate majority leader on its cover as its pick to win the nomination. Johnson was pleased with *Time* and denounced Bill Lawrence of the *New York Times* for predicting a first-ballot victory for JFK.[47]

Newsweek, predicting a JFK victory, had put him on its cover that Sunday. He had arrived in Los Angeles on the ninth; Jackie, who was four months pregnant and had a history of difficult pregnancies, stayed in Hyannis Port.[48]

The FBI had not stopped monitoring Jack's sex life. As the convention was starting, the local office in Los Angeles interviewed a "high-priced Hollywood call girl" about a telephone call the night of July 10 from Fred Otash, a Los Angeles private detective "convicted of horse race fixing," in which he asked her about "sex parties" involving Kennedy, Sinatra, Lawford, and Sammy Davis, Jr. Although she denied any knowledge of them, he asked her for the names of any other girls who might have been present. Local agents then talked to Otash. He implied that *Confidential* magazine was trying to find someone to "spy" on JFK's hotel room and that the magazine was "looking for dirt on Kennedy or Lawford" to use for a series of articles before the November election. That evening Otash called a woman to ask her to arrange an introduction to JFK and offered to equip her with a recording device for any JFK "indiscreet statements." She refused.[49]

In her memoir, Judith Campbell Exner writes that on the first night of the convention, Kennedy invited her for an evening rendezvous. He had booked a suite at the Beverly Hilton, and upon her arrival, she saw that there was another woman in the bedroom. She refused to participate in a threesome and left.[50]

By the time Jack arrived in Los Angeles, Bobby was directing daily operations with his team already in place. He had learned well from the failed effort to win the 1956 vice presidential nomination. *Newsweek* reported that RFK ran "one of the most smoothly organized machines ever seen at a national convention." Twenty-five to forty individuals sat before him at morning briefings, and he had several telephone lines coming into the suite. The staff, according to Larry O'Brien, had "set up an elaborate intelligence system" to monitor each delegate and alternate, with a separate file for each. Trusted staff members served as liaisons to each delegation and relayed daily reports. On the convention floor, staffers carried walkie-talkies for instant communication.[51]

Much of the Kennedy clan was there. The patriarch remained out of sight at a nearby mansion, providing money and advice. Ted assisted with various delegations, and Eunice, Patricia, and Jean lobbied for their brother. Brothers-in-law Steve Smith and Sargent Shriver worked with various delegations. JFK's alter ego Ted Sorensen prepared the speeches JFK gave before the various groups. Kenny O'Donnell and Larry O'Brien gave directions to the staff; Schlesinger and Galbraith concentrated on liberal backers.[52]

Kennedy, who was fascinated by movie stars, had support from Hollywood. Sinatra held a party for Kennedy's sister Eunice the day Jack arrived, and the following evening, the Democratic Party held a fundraiser at the Beverly Hilton with a guest list that included Sinatra, Lawford, Judy Garland, Tony Curtis, and Janet Leigh. When Sammy Davis, Jr., was introduced, the Mississippi and Alabama delegates booed.[53]

The campaign had booked every space throughout the hotel so that television cables could run only to Kennedy's suite. The other candidates, to get on television, had to arrange to be interviewed outside the hotel. Jack Lindquist was a Disney employee assigned to recruit Democratic VIPs to visit Disneyland, and to accomplish this, he tried to set up a ten-by-ten-foot trade show booth on the hotel's mezzanine level. He saw Bobby, who approved it on one condition. Lindquist had to return the next day with five thousand dollars in cash. He brought the money, which he considered a bribe; Bobby took the funds without giving Lindquist a receipt. But he got his booth.[54]

On June 19, Republican Senator Hugh Scott from Pennsylvania had published an open letter to JFK, mocking him for his Senate absenteeism: "We don't want to bore you, Jack. If you have time, drop in and if not, just send one of the other Kennedys down." On July 12, Scott gave Jackie Robinson his colleague's "nonvoting record" in the Senate. He had missed twenty-seven of the thirty-six votes on amendments and passage of the 1957 civil rights bill. Of the fifty-six quorum calls or votes in night sessions, Kennedy was present for very few. The one time Kennedy did weigh in on the bill, he voted with the majority to remove Title III, which would have given the attorney general injunctive power to protect voting rights and other civil rights. Blacks and liberals were disappointed, Scott concluded, while southerners were gleeful: "The whole problem with Senator Kennedy has been that he does not take his responsibilities seriously, especially when his own ambition intervenes."[55]

Despite this criticism, Governor David Lawrence of Pennsylvania, known as "the leader of the big-city bosses," announced that sixty-eight of his eighty-one delegates would vote for JFK. Governor Pat Brown of California proclaimed his preference for JFK, as did Herschel Loveless of Iowa and George Docking of Kansas, all favorite sons. Even though Kennedy did not get the total vote from these delegations, the bandwagon seemed to be rolling.[56]

Tuesday was devoted to the presentation of the party platform, the least-watched day of the convention. Chester Bowles, the chairman of the Committee on Platform and Resolutions, was irate that the "Kennedy people showed almost no interest." When Bowles presented the platform, the civil rights plank, promising an end to discrimination in voting, education, housing, lunch counters, and employment, drew the most attention. The 1957 and 1960 Civil Rights Acts would be vigorously enforced. Ten southern delegations filed a minority report objecting to the plank, but they were overruled.[57]

Wednesday, the most watched day, featured the nomination of the presidential candidates. Before the balloting started, Robert Kennedy held his morning briefing and concluded that his brother had 740 delegates, 21 short of the 761 needed for nomination. He instructed his staff to keep the committed firm and find the needed delegates.[58]

The roll call began at 10:07 p.m. After West Virginia and Wisconsin cast their votes, Kennedy had 750 votes. The Wyoming delegation was the last, with 15 votes. The Kennedy team thought they had 8½ of those 15 and were 2½ shy of a first-ballot victory. Ted stood in the midst of the delegation. When the entire delegation went for his brother, he grabbed the Wyoming standard and waved it wildly. When the first ballot was completed, after some vote-switching, Kennedy had received 806 votes. He left his room and briefly appeared on the convention floor.[59]

Nixon watched Kennedy's speech. He had foreseen JFK's victory six months earlier: "It will be a tough scrap all the way, because he has unlimited money, a superb organization and a rare ability to project himself effectively on television." Some reporters thought Kennedy would be the easiest Democrat to beat, but Nixon thought otherwise. The only question that remained was whether Lyndon Johnson could be persuaded to accept the vice presidential slot: "That would be about as formidable a ticket as they could nominate."[60]

With the presidential nomination complete, attention turned immediately to this question. Rumors flourished about likely running mates: Humphrey, Symington, and others. Johnson was occasionally mentioned, but few thought he would leave the powerful Senate majority leader's post for what was then seen as a far less important position. On the flight to the West Coast, JFK told Ben Bradlee that he doubted Johnson would ever take the second spot.[61]

That Wednesday evening, Kennedy offered the position to Symington, who asked for the night to consider it. By the following afternoon, the nominee had reneged on the offer. Without consulting Bobby, Jack went to Johnson's suite and offered him the vice presidency. Johnson accepted.[62]

Until that moment, the Kennedy and Johnson staffs had bitterly fought and belittled each other. Kennedy portrayed LBJ and his supporters as hicks. Johnson perceived the wealthy Kennedy clan as political interlopers undeserving of the nomination. Bobby and Lyndon despised each other. These personal feelings were immaterial to JFK. If he wanted to win, he had to carry the South, and Johnson was the logical choice.[63]

Speaker Rayburn had already tried to convince Johnson that becoming JFK's running mate was the only way to beat Nixon. Supreme Court Justice William Douglas recalled in his memoirs sitting with the speaker sipping bourbon and branch water before the convention. Mr. Sam said of Nixon: "Look at his profile from each side, look him in the eyes. You can see what kind of a person he is. I hate to say it, Bill, but that man is a crook."[64]

Liberals were dismayed. Chester Bowles called the selection a "shock to everyone [that] greatly unnerved the liberals in general." UAW president Walter Reuther was angry. Schlesinger was sickened and remained cool toward Kennedy afterward. The historian saw the candidate "to be a devious and, if necessary, ruthless man."[65]

Eleanor Roosevelt, who learned of Kennedy's decision while flying back to New York, thought LBJ was the logical choice. He had come to the convention with the second-most delegate votes; he was from Texas and that would please the South; and he was an experienced politician.[66]

The day after Johnson's selection, Jackie Robinson wrote in his column that the Democratic Party had produced the strongest civil rights plank in its history and then jeopardized its value by making Johnson its vice presidential nominee. In choosing him, the party was making "a bid for the appeasement of Southern bigots. . . . This sell-out reveals about Kennedy . . . a naked, damaging truth: Kennedy is willing to ruthlessly gamble with the rights—and the very lives—of millions of Southern Negro Americans in order to satisfy his own personal ambition." Kennedy and Johnson, recognizing this fear, met with black delegates to assure them that the Democratic ticket would advance the civil rights cause.[67]

Dean Acheson wrote Truman two days after the convention that Johnson would be less valuable as vice president than he was as majority leader. As Acheson saw it, "Jack and his team were the only 'pros' in Los Angeles," and Johnson or Symington as the nominee would not have been "any better." The present ticket was the best the Democratic Party had. "It will not raise great enthusiasm, but neither could any other ticket."[68]

On Friday afternoon, July 15, JFK accepted his party's nomination at the 105,000-seat Los Angeles Coliseum. The 80,000 spectators made it look half-filled. Arthur Schlesinger wrote in *A Thousand Days* that JFK looked "very tired" after the week's events. *Time* magazine noted that he fidgeted in his chair, fingered his lips and ears, spoke to his neighbor, and scraped gum off his right shoe. Before starting his address, entitled "The New Frontier," he saluted Johnson, Stevenson, Symington, and Truman and then spoke about the issue of his Catholic faith. He expected to meet foreign and domestic problems with leadership that the current administration did not provide. The New Frontier offered a choice "between the public interest and private comfort—between national greatness and national decline—between the fresh air of progress and the stale, dank atmosphere of 'normalcy'—between determined dedication and creeping mediocrity."[69]

Nixon watched on television as Kennedy attacked him for supporting the status quo and carrying out the unpopular policies of conservatives like Senators Goldwater and Everett Dirksen of Illinois; just as damning, the vice president supported the controversial farm programs of Secretary of Agriculture Ezra Taft Benson's. Kennedy added that throughout his political career, Nixon had "often seemed to show charity toward none and malice for all." He had "spoken or voted on every known side of every known issue." Millions of voters would reject him because he "did not measure to the footsteps of Dwight D. Eisenhower" (a remark that, according to Nixon, "was below the belt" but which the media largely ignored). James Reston wrote in his column that JFK had given a masterful address. Nixon asked for someone whom Reston respected to write a letter to the editor, thinking that this would force the columnist and other reporters "to follow a single standard and not a double standard as far as campaign tactics are concerned."[70]

Galbraith, a day after the address, wrote the candidate that he liked the New Frontier language and the references to defense and Khrushchev. But he thought the references to religion were a bad idea, and he hoped Kennedy would drop them from future speeches. He then moved on to more serious flaws. The speech "was essentially unfinished. It was badly in need of editing and polish." Kennedy had to focus on his strength, "straightforward exposition." When he ventured on "oratorical flights," he gave "a reasonable imitation of a bird with a broken wing." Schlesinger later called JFK's delivery "uncertain and at times almost strident."[71]

With all his imperfections, Jack Kennedy had overcome tremendous obstacles to win the presidential nomination. The party's only living ex-president, the politically active widow of its greatest president, its nominee in the previous two presidential campaigns, and its highest-ranking elected official had all opposed him. Yet they could not mount an effective stop-Kennedy movement. Kennedy's strategy of entering primaries, negotiating with influential Democratic bosses, and working energetically to attract delegates had kept him moving toward victory.

Nor had the Kennedy clan repeated the confusion and chaos that surrounded Jack's bid for the 1956 vice presidential nomination. The family was prepared. Bobby met regularly with his staff and received constant updates on the delegate count, and the others all had specific assignments that they handled well. By the time the balloting began, Jack and Bobby knew that victory was close.

At the same time, Kennedy's hubris is perplexing. He lied about his health and recklessly had an adulterous encounter on the very night the convention opened. He may be excused for not knowing the FBI was following him, but he also seemed oblivious to the more mundane possibility that some tawdry magazine might expose his behavior. Bobby, an attorney who had gained fame revealing union corruption, had to understand his liability if the bribe he demanded from Disneyland were to become known. The brothers, in their arrogance, did not seem to consider these possibilities.

Shortly before the Democratic convention opened, Nixon sized up his opponent's three biggest strengths: money from his family and from labor unions; a superb organization; and his positive image with voters. Kennedy's Catholicism, Nixon thought, probably would not hurt him. Some Protestants might reject him, but the increased turnout from Catholics would compensate. As for weaknesses, Kennedy gave "the appearance of immaturity," while Nixon struck voters as more experienced and mature. Defeating Kennedy would thus depend on Nixon's success in getting voters to cast their ballots based on the man, not the party.[72]

Part of this calculation, Nixon wrote in July to Milton Eisenhower, the president's brother, was "the almost frightening weakening of the Republican Party throughout the country. Present indications are that I will have to run 7 to 8 percentage points ahead of the Party in most States in order to win." Ike had done this, "but it will take an extraordinary effort if I can pull it off this time." Nationwide, Democratic registrants outnumbered Republicans by fifteen million to twenty million. A Gallup poll in mid-July asked: "If the congressional elections were held today, which party would you like to win?" The response was Republicans 40 percent, Democrats 60.[73]

The economy was another potential trouble spot. In March, Nixon had talked with Arthur Burns, former chairman of the Council of Economic Advisers under Eisenhower, who predicted a recession. By mid-April, with the economic news worsening, Nixon thought the administration might have to take some preventive action, like lowering taxes or increasing federal spending to stimulate the economy. Two months later, the business climate looked like it might significantly affect the election. When Gallup asked respondents who would keep the country prosperous, Democrats led Republicans by 46 percent to 26. Voters who concentrated on domestic issues, Nixon predicted, would gravitate toward Democrats, "who inevitably can and will promise more than we will."[74]

Nixon's advantage lay with voters who looked primarily to foreign affairs. In a Senate speech in mid-June, Kennedy claimed the Soviet Union had expanded its military and economic capabilities while the United States had lost ground. The vice president knew he could not let this negative portrayal go unchallenged or allow Democrats to have "a monopoly on new ideas in the international field." He needed to "take a strong, firm line on Communism and not let them get away with the idea that all that is needed is a fresh, new approach." He planned "to wrap Stevenson around Kennedy's neck," along with Chester Bowles—JFK's two principal foreign policy advisers.[75]

Nixon also hoped to win African-American votes by attacking Kennedy and Johnson on civil rights. LBJ had spent his entire career voting against civil rights bills. When the 1957 civil rights legislation went to the Senate, both Johnson and Kennedy voted to refer the legislation to the judiciary committee, chaired by John Eastland of Mississippi, which would have killed the bill. They also voted with the majority to pass an amendment requiring jury trials for defendants accused of civil rights violations. Given the behavior of all-white juries in the South, this amendment severely weakened enforcement of the bill.[76]

Eisenhower hardly knew Kennedy. Henry Cabot Lodge recorded in a memo on January 13, 1960, the president's opinion that "all the Democratic candidates were a rather sorry lot," but that of these contenders, "Kennedy was the strongest vote getter." JFK wrote the president on March 30 that he hoped that Ike would work on a nuclear test ban treaty and assuring him that, if elected, he would support that effort. Ike replied that he was trying to negotiate "a fair and just agreement for the cessation of nuclear testing."[77]

The president discussed JFK in two interviews with the *Times*'s Arthur Krock. On April 7, Ike called him "immature" and said he was appalled that Kennedy might be nominated. Three months later, he labeled Kennedy an "inexperienced boy." Raymond Saulnier, chairman of the Council of Economic Advisers, recalled forty years later that Republicans saw Kennedy as "a pleasant fellow, but without any very distinguished legislative history."[78]

Jackie Kennedy recalled that her husband had no high regard for Ike, either. George Smathers said that JFK did not "think very highly of him" at "any time." Smathers himself saw Ike as "a great conciliator" with no "great ability."[79]

Ike was more ambivalent toward Johnson. They had worked together closely, and Rayburn, Eisenhower, and Johnson would often share a late-afternoon drink in the White House while discussing legislative and diplomatic issues. Speaking with Krock on July 6, Eisenhower speculated that LBJ would be the best Democratic nominee. The JFK-LBJ ticket, he thought, was "just a marriage of convenience." In spite of the differences within the party, "Democrats . . . manage to get together when the chips are down, like brothers."[80]

But according to William Ewald's *Eisenhower the President*, Ike distrusted

LBJ, saying at one point, "That fellow's such a phony." As for Speaker Rayburn, President Eisenhower complained, "That fellow . . . would doublecross you." But he knew he needed them to pass his legislative agenda.[81]

Once JFK and LBJ were nominated, the president set aside his personal opinions and sent them telegrams asking if they wanted "to have periodic briefings on the international scene" from the CIA. They accepted the offer.[82]

Ike's assessment of the Democratic ticket was the least of Kennedy's problems. Truman, Eleanor Roosevelt, Stevenson, and other powerful Democrats had vigorously attacked him. Now, having won the nomination, he had to unite his party behind him.

7

THE WAITING GAME

At the beginning of January 1960, Nixon instructed his staff to avoid committing him to any "cocktail/reception dinner type of thing any more than absolutely necessary." While Congress was in session, because of his crowded schedule, he would stay in the capital and handle the majority of his appointments in the Senate Office Building. When the president returned to the White House in early January from Georgia, Nixon barely had time to shake his hand and welcome him home.[1]

With the election approaching, Pat Nixon received more press attention. She stressed that her first duty was to her family. When meeting with female reporters, she refused to discuss the possibility of becoming First Lady. She had not chosen a public life and expected to remain "the silent partner" in the political team of Pat and Dick.[2]

Barring some catastrophe, Nixon was virtually assured of the GOP nomination. Republican Governor Mark Hatfield of Oregon telephoned on Friday, January 8, to tell him that his name had been placed on the state's primary ballot. Nixon consented but added that he would not "actively campaign in any primary states" because he had to be in Washington to promote the administration's agenda.[3]

Nixon turned forty-seven years old on Saturday, January 9. Without fanfare, Herbert Klein called a twenty-minute press conference for about a dozen reporters. Sitting in the vice president's chair at the Senate Office Building, Klein declared that Nixon had "willingly" authorized that his name be placed on the presidential primary ballots in New Hampshire, Ohio, and Oregon. There would be no formal statement because the media already assumed he was running.[4]

At the start of the New Year, Nixon did not have a national campaign headquarters or a paid speechwriter. Rose Mary Woods contracted pneumonia in early January and did not return to the office until the end of February, at which time she began handling campaign trips. Vice presidential assistant Robert Finch did some organizational work by establishing Nixon Clubs, which were economically self-sustaining and needed to attract independents to embrace GOP principles. H. R. Haldeman did the advance planning.[5]

Nixon's first public appearance after announcing for the presidency was at the University of Florida, Gainesville, where ten thousand spectators heard him answer questions from a five-man panel on the administration's foreign and domestic policies. The next day he stopped in Miami for a press conference at a jammed Miami Beach Municipal Auditorium.[6]

From that first encounter with the public and the press, he emphasized that "if I should be elected, . . . I will try to carry out, implement and build upon" the constructive programs Ike had initiated. He pledged that he would conduct "a hard-hitting campaign on the great issues before the American people," while making no "personal attacks"; he declined to speculate whether the Democratic nominee would do any "mudslinging." He complimented the Democratic contenders. Jack Kennedy was "a very serious student of public affairs." Nixon and Stuart Symington were "good friends" and played golf together. Lyndon Johnson was "a very able man."[7]

Nixon tried to focus on the issues. Speaking before the California Newspaper Publishers Association during the first week of February, he predicted that international affairs "would override all domestic issues in the . . . campaign." Khrushchev, he argued, would not attack the United States because he knew the United States would retaliate and destroy the Soviet Union. There was no deterrent gap: the United States had adequate forces to prevent any adversary from attacking its territory. In the middle of February, Nixon declared that the United States was "stronger than any other country in the world."[8]

Discussing United States–Cuba relations, Nixon acknowledged that Fidel Castro had risen because of the previous regime's corrupt practices. Castro had lately taken an anti-American posture and seemed to be overtly friendly to communist regimes. The Cubans could choose the government they preferred, but the United States would try to protect American businesses against confiscation. The vice president urged patience and hoped that the Cubans would adopt a democratic system.[9]

In the second week of April, the vice president answered questions before another packed auditorium, at Stanford University. One questioner asked about European colonialism in Africa. Nixon had visited the continent three years earlier and asserted that the communists were trying to gain influence there.

In the coming decade the free world would need to keep Africa out of the communist orbit. The situation in South Africa was tragic, Nixon said: the minority white government denied blacks equality of opportunity. Extremists on both sides had to be avoided.[10]

The vice president spent considerable time discussing economic issues as a champion of private enterprise. In the second week of January, he started to study how to increase United States economic growth to 3 percent a year; a month later, he saw an urgent need to reform the American tax structure. Toward the end of April, speaking before the American Society of Newspaper Editors, he laid out a broad program of what he labeled "progressive conservatism."[11]

One especially controversial issue was the administration's agricultural policy. During World War II, encouraged by price supports, farmers expanded planting to produce the maximum crops. After the war, they did not lower production, causing prices to drop and increasing their dependence on price supports. Ike tried to move toward a free market by making these price supports flexible instead of rigid. Some farmers objected when surpluses increased and prices stayed low. The president employed programs to keep some products off the market and take farmland out of production, but these efforts did not end the surpluses. By the time he left office, production had soared and prices had plummeted.[12]

Ike's secretary of agriculture, Ezra Taft Benson, a staunch conservative, followed the president's stands on holding down inflation and balancing the budget, as well as on moving farmers off of federal assistance and toward a free-market economy. But when he tried to wean farmers off subsidies, some farming sectors, especially in the Midwest, vehemently objected. Calls to replace him accelerated in Ike's second term. But the president never wavered; Benson stayed.[13]

On the last day of 1959, Benson announced that Nixon "would make a good President." The secretary continued to promote the administration's farm policies and link them to Nixon. In January, he said on *Meet the Press* that he and the vice president agreed on the administration's agricultural programs. In mid-February, he told *Face the Nation* that Nixon had helped draft the president's upcoming farm message to Congress. Anyone who sought the Republican presidential nomination, he emphasized, must back the administration's farm policies. Privately, Benson had begun to worry that Nixon planned to jettison those policies for political expediency. He wrote in his diary: "I wish I had more confidence in the Vice-President's ability to provide wise leadership for the nation."[14]

Nixon knew Benson was a political liability. Early in 1960, *Newsweek* reported that the vice president did not plan to speak before farm groups until after the GOP convention. In March, when asked at a press conference whether Nixon was going to alter the administration's farm program, Ike replied that Nixon's "desire for an agricultural program of his own" was "all right." The next month, because Benson had been so rigid, the vice president began to work with anti-Benson Republicans and Democrats to find some solution to the price-support problem.[15]

Civil rights was another complex issue. Eisenhower and Nixon both thought they had made good progress on civil rights initiatives. Ike had made Nixon chairman of the President's Committee on Government Contracts in his first year in office, with a mandate to provide black citizens greater job opportunities. The Eisenhower administration, with Nixon's energetic support, had gotten the Civil Rights Act of 1957 through Congress; the law established a civil rights division in the justice department and a Civil Rights Commission that would expose segregationist practices. The president had also sent the 101st Airborne into Little Rock, Arkansas, in September 1957 to protect African-American students who had entered Central High School. He and Nixon had met with many black leaders. In 1960, they helped pass a second Civil Rights Act, but southern opposition made it largely ineffective.[16]

Ike wrote his sister-in-law Lucy that most southerners agreed "that we must make some progress toward achieving political and economic equality among all individuals regardless of race." He thought his southern friends were knowledgeable on racial matters, sometimes amused and other times resentful, and were not worried by the sit-ins that had begun that year. The implications of these protests had been distorted, making southerners anxious about "the possibility of an undesirable social mingling."[17]

The vice president viewed the sit-ins as an "essentially moral" issue, not a legal one, and sought input from African Americans. He kept in regular contact with the highest black appointee on the White House staff, E. Frederic Morrow, and with Val Washington, the African-American director of minority affairs for the GOP. Nixon had met Martin Luther King, Jr., on his trip to Africa in 1957, and they had formed a cordial relationship. William Rentschler, president of Stevens Candy Kitchens, had lunch with John Johnson, the publisher of *Ebony*, in May 1959 and reported "he had nothing but kind words for the Vice President. He thinks very highly of him . . . and almost surely can be counted on to join the Nixon 'team' for '60."[18]

On June 22, meeting with fifty African-American ministers from the Eastern Shore of Maryland, Nixon said that civil rights should be regarded as "a part of the national security structure." The United States had to set an example to the international community or it would "lose the struggle for the hearts and minds of the world's peoples."[19]

Nixon's most vocal advocate in the black community was Jackie Robinson, whom he had met at the Republican national convention in 1952. Six years later, the vice president wrote him that he had played football at Whittier College "and held down the Varsity Bench for four years! However, that did not diminish [my] genuine interest in sports, and there is nothing I would rather do now than to see a good football or baseball game."[20]

In his *New York Post* column, Robinson wrote on December 30, 1959, that he favored Humphrey for president based on his strong civil rights record. But he thought Nixon would not be easy to beat and that his own civil rights record might attract African-American voters. Many Democrats vehemently opposed him, and when Robinson asked why, they replied that they deplored the methods Nixon had used against Helen Gahagan Douglas in 1950. Robinson dismissed those objections; the vice president had matured since taking office: "If it should come to a choice between a weak and indecisive Democratic nominee and Vice President Nixon, I, for one, would enthusiastically support Nixon."[21]

Robinson's opinion of Nixon did not extend to the president. In a column on January 20, he deplored Eisenhower's statement expressing doubts about securing black voting rights in the South. Ike had not, he wrote, provided convincing leadership for black civil rights: "Negroes have been patient for nigh onto a hundred years, and now our patience is rapidly wearing thin." The president had the "moral obligation" to take the lead.[22]

Robinson did not reveal that for several weeks he had been moving toward backing Nixon. Fred Lowey, an influential New York Republican, had had lunch with Robinson on March 29 and concluded that he "would come on the Nixon band wagon." The vice president was Robinson's second choice after Humphrey. Lowey urged Nixon to meet with him: "Robinson is more or less considered sort of a God up here."[23]

The two men had lunch on May 10, along with Attorney General Rogers and Secretary of Labor James Mitchell. After the meeting, Mitchell drove Robinson to the airport and commented that their guest was "more convinced then [*sic*] ever of the rightness of his support of Nixon." Robinson wrote the vice president the next day that he enjoyed the conversation but wondered whether Nixon could "erase the image left by Eisenhower as far as Civil Rights is concerned."[24]

The bond between them strengthened in June. On the third, the vice president supplied copies of his civil rights votes, rulings, and positions to Robinson. He agreed with Robinson that the nation needed to take advantage of the 17 million black citizens to win the ideological struggle against communism. To deny the nation their talents and energy "would be stupidity of the greatest magnitude." In the middle of the month, Robinson wrote another laudatory column about the vice president, and a day before month's end, Robinson had dinner with Nixon at his home.[25]

Answering a question at the University of Florida in mid-January, the vice president said that the United States had "made progress without going to extremes." The audience applauded when he asserted that everyone had the right to vote. In California, he said that integration was a national issue; he opposed racial prejudice and called for the country to stand up against it. He conceded that integration would take time. Accepting an award for patriotism at the University of Notre Dame, he called on his listeners to be proactive in civil rights "to help in leading the fight in your communities and in this country against prejudice and for the realization of equality of opportunity for all our people."[26]

Early in May, in a meeting with Arthur Krock of the *New York Times*, Nixon said he disagreed with Ike's civil rights approach: "The President alone can exercise the essential moral leadership against racial discrimination, and should do so." A few days later he broadened that viewpoint before the Catholic Press Association: "We must not only recognize our obligation to avoid action based on prejudice and discrimination—because the law says so—we must recognize that we avoid such action because it is right to do so."[27]

Nixon could not afford to alienate the president; his most crucial task in the first half of 1960 was getting Ike's approval for his nomination. In the middle of January, he described the president as a strong leader who exercised "cool judgment." Later that month, speaking at "Dinner with Ike" at the Chicago International Amphitheatre, he vowed to build on the president's policies. Nixon praised his leadership, rejecting Democratic attacks. Republicans were proud of the administration's record, and the party was moving away from bigger government and toward free enterprise. In foreign affairs, Ike was leading the free world to victory against Khrushchev's threat to peaceful competition.[28]

That same day, Eisenhower wrote a confidential memo, assuming Nixon would be the presidential nominee, enumerating potential candidates for the vice presidency and cabinet posts. He shared these thoughts with Nixon a month later. Toward the end of January, he held another press conference where Thomas Schroth from the *Congressional Quarterly* said that at a recent Democratic campaign dinner the speakers denounced the administration, and someone [Senator Humphrey] referred to the vice president as a "juvenile delinquent." Ike responded: "I couldn't comment except to laugh."[29]

At a White House press conference later in the month, Marvin Arrowsmith of the AP said that some California Republicans were surprised that Ike had not referred to Nixon in his Los Angeles address. Ike replied that he did not like to mention individuals until after the nomination. He and Nixon, he continued, had had a close association and he had "admiration and respect for the Vice President." A number of Republicans could run for the presidency, but "I am not dissatisfied with the individual that looks like he will get it, not by any manner of means."[30]

The president was clearly moving toward an endorsement. On March 12, the Washington Gridiron Club held its annual off-the-record dinner with 546 guests, including the president, who sat to the right of the club president, John O'Brien, Washington bureau chief of the *Philadelphia Inquirer*. Nixon was on O'Brien's left. The president said that it would save a lot of trouble if, for the future, everyone at his table moved over two places.[31]

Merriman Smith of UPI asked the president at his press conference on March 16 whether he would comment on his Gridiron remarks. Ike answered that he had a "personal preference or even bias with respect to this upcoming presidential race": he definitely favored Nixon. The two men never had "a specific difference in our points of view on any important problem for 7 years." Immediately afterward, Ike telephoned Nixon in New York and told him what he had said: he was "biased in favor of Nixon for President."[32]

Ike had a private conversation with Arthur Krock in April in which he said that at least six Republicans could fill the presidency, but "none had qualifications superior to Nixon's." He had had no intention of damaging the vice president's career when he suggested, in 1956, that Nixon take a cabinet position. Nixon considered the offer, Ike said, but thought an appointive position would be viewed as a demotion.[33]

In May, Ike answered two letters from his brother Edgar's wife, Lucy, who accused Nixon of a "liberal me-too attitude." The president responded that he believed in a middle-of-the-road approach to governing and opposed any type of extremism. He defended his principles of cutting federal expenditures and balancing the budget. Republicans wanted to provide Americans with self-respect and thereby strengthen the country; Democrats refused to accept this obligation. Vice President Nixon, Ike maintained, would extend his legacy: "The country must be made to see the difference between Nixon and any one of his prospective opponents and . . . it should rally to the cause of the policies and philosophies that he espouses."[34]

Rather than acknowledge Ike's support for Nixon, some journalists repeated rumors of the friction between Ike and Dick. In the April 1960 issue of *Esquire*, for instance, Joseph Kraft's story "IKE vs. NIXON" purported to shed "new light on the political and personal relationship of the President and his Vice President." Kraft held that their different upbringings, educations, and professional careers meant that they could not have a close bond, and that as president, Ike routinely kept Nixon "in the dark about his most important plans." Kraft concluded that this distant relationship was the reason Ike did not choose Nixon to succeed him but instead "allowed circumstances to thrust upon him his heir apparent."[35]

Nixon's normally unruffled press secretary, Herb Klein, wrote his first-ever letter of complaint to a magazine, asking "to set the record straight." He "was shocked" that *Esquire* would publish a "hatchet article" that was "peppered with factual inaccuracies" and contained "fallacious conclusions." Among the article's errors were the claims that Ike never gave Nixon "any major assignments"; that Ike had played football whereas Nixon was a spectator; and the president had acted cautiously toward Khrushchev while Nixon had a "verbal brawl with" him.[36]

Contrary to the picture presented by Kraft, who later served as a speechwriter for the Kennedy campaign, and others, the president often looked for ways to enhance his vice president's standing. On April 21, Ike telephoned Nixon from Augusta, Georgia, to talk about the United States–Soviet summit that was to open in Paris on May 16. If the president left the gathering after a week to keep an engagement in Lisbon, Portugal, on May 23, Ike wondered, "could (and should politically)" the vice president "take over?"[37]

On May 1, fifteen days before the summit opened, Francis Gary Powers's U-2 spy plane was shot down in Soviet airspace, effectively scuttling the Paris summit. The day before it had been scheduled to convene, Nixon appeared on WNTA-TV's *Open End*, with David Susskind as the moderator. The vice president admitted that he was "privy" to the missions and approved of them. Ike's first duty, he emphasized, was national security, and therefore the president was justified in authorizing the U-2 flights to protect the United States from a surprise attack.[38]

At a breakfast on May 18 in Syracuse, New York, the vice president said that Ike had told him Khrushchev was planning to break up the summit before the U-2 incident, and after the airplane was shot down, the premier used it as the reason to cancel the meeting. The collapse rested "squarely on the shoulders of Mr. Khrushchev." In Buffalo later that day, Nixon suggested that if Khrushchev wanted an apology from the president, perhaps he should apologize in turn for sending spies into the United States, which the Soviet Union had been doing since the 1930s. He said that while Khrushchev was giving a disarmament speech to the United Nations on September 18, 1959, two Soviet spies attached to the United Nations Secretariat diplomatic personnel had been arrested in Springfield, Massachusetts, as they tried to obtain information from an American citizen.[39]

Nixon did not miss this opportunity to attack his potential Democratic rivals. On May 27 he called out Stevenson, Symington, and Kennedy, in that order. The previous week, Stevenson had told a Chicago audience that the president had handed the Soviet dictator "the crowbar and sledgehammer to wreck this [summit] meeting"; Symington charged Ike with causing a "humiliating disaster" in France that damaged American prestige; and Kennedy had called on the president to apologize to Khrushchev. A reporter asked Nixon whether he thought Stevenson and Kennedy had taken a "soft" approach to communism and been guilty of "appeasement." The vice president replied that those two and Symington were "out of step" with Democratic politicians and voters in "attempting to make a partisan issue" out of the incident.[40]

Nixon continued to send the White House polls confirming that the summit's collapse had not damaged Ike's prestige or Nixon's standing. He took the stand "that the American people will not allow Khrushchev to interfere with the selection of a President either way."[41]

Nixon's refusal to campaign in the primaries did not prevent his political allies from placing his name on every primary ballot. In New Hampshire, during the 1956 primary, he had received a huge write-in vote of more than 22,000. With the support of the state's leading Republican politicians and 8,000 volunteers, on March 8 he received 65,204 votes; Rockefeller, in second place, drew 2,745—just 3.8 percent of the total.[42]

Nixon was entered in five primaries in April: Wisconsin, Illinois, New Jersey, Massachusetts, and Pennsylvania, where he ran unopposed. On April 26, with Senator Hugh Scott managing his campaign, he got 968,538 votes in Pennsylvania, beating Ike's total of four years earlier.[43]

William Scranton, who was starting his political rise, was delighted with the vice president's triumph. A 1946 Yale Law School graduate who came from a prominent Pennsylvania family, Scranton was appointed a special assistant to the secretary of state in the summer of 1959. Nixon congratulated him on his appointment. Bill wrote back in December that he held Nixon in "high esteem" and wanted his assistance for the economically distressed areas especially in northeastern Pennsylvania because this issue would heavily figure in the 1960 elections. Scranton announced for the tenth congressional district in January. In early February, vice presidential assistant Charlie McWhorter wrote that Scranton had a "blueblood background but a helluva nice guy and RN stalwart." Scranton won his primary, congratulated Nixon on his victory, and promised to back him in the general election.[44]

One of Pennsylvania's seventy delegates to the national convention was Harold Stassen, who had tried to orchestrate a "Dump Nixon" movement at the

1956 convention—an effort that succeeded only in alienating him from many Republicans. After the primary, Stassen sent out a questionnaire that attempted to make it appear that Nixon would carry only five states in the general election. He suggested Rockefeller, Henry Cabot Lodge, Robert Anderson, and Fred Seaton as better possibilities. If Nixon won the California primary "in impressive numbers," Stassen would end his opposition; otherwise he would advocate drafting another nominee. In May, Nixon won the delegates from Ohio, Indiana, Nebraska, and Oregon.[45] By the end of the month, the Associated Press reported that he had passed the number of delegates needed to win a first-ballot nomination.[46]

Nixon paid scant attention to most primaries, but California was an exception. Nearly 60 percent of the state's voters were registered as Democrats. The only way the GOP could overcome that three-to-two disadvantage was if large numbers of Democrats crossed party lines to vote Republican.[47]

The vice presidential assistant specializing in California politics, Robert Finch, wrote on January 22 that he was firmly convinced "that is absolutely necessary to carry the state," especially southern California. To do so, Nixon would have to counteract the "viciously anti-Nixon" stories in the *Fresno Bee*, the *Sacramento Bee*, and other opposition newspapers. In the second week of April, he began hearing about "stepped-up word of mouth attacks"—that he did not "go to church—he is anti-Semetic [*sic*], anti-Catholic, etc." Such charges, when they appeared, "should . . . be answered where appropriate." The vice president also understood that Democrats were "embarking upon a huge whispering campaign with regard to 'something being wrong' with our campaign against [Helen Gahagan] Douglas." Nixon thought he should ignore it, or else "a very reasonable article . . . probably would serve a useful purpose."[48]

Nixon loyalists mounted a massive effort. Republicans sent a get-out-the-vote mailer with a request for donations just before the primary. It drew the most money ever received in a primary campaign, about twenty-five thousand dollars in small contributions. Gemma O'Brien, who had worked on the vice president's secretarial staff in the capital and had moved to California, managed "operation Telephone." She explained: "We got to make a big showing in the primary for the psychological effect." The Republican effort succeeded, and the party used this operation in the general election to win the state.[49]

The voting in the presidential primary, on June 7, surprised Republicans. Nixon received 1,517,652 votes (58.6 percent of Republican voters), while Governor Brown, without Kennedy on the ballot, won 1,354,031, 67.7 percent of Democratic voters. Republicans were overjoyed that the vice president had outpolled the governor. The California victory was an important milestone. Finch declared: "People now believe with justification that Nixon and the Republicans can carry California."[50]

Nixon had swept all of his primaries. Of the 5.5 million Republicans who voted, 4.9 million, nearly 90 percent, had chosen him.[51]

Some loyalists were disappointed that he had not actively campaigned. He explained why to Raymond Moley, a conservative columnist for *Newsweek*. Republicans had to accept that Democratic contenders were going to receive the spotlight, "so that once we start our campaign we can keep it at a high tempo until Election Day." Nixon had asked British Prime Minister Harold Macmillan at Camp David what he thought of the strategy, and Macmillan had endorsed it. Many of Macmillan's supporters had wanted him to start campaigning several months before his own election, but "he waited until his opponents overreached themselves with their pie in the sky promises and then took them on with a very effective counter-attack three weeks before the election."[52]

The vice president did not want to "start campaigning too early and to have nothing left for the stretch." He had already planned his long-range strategy: the "time to be fresh and strong, both mentally and physically, is the month before election. Then the speeches that are made will have lasting impact which could affect votes—now they may affect standings in the polls but by the time the election comes around they will be pretty well forgotten."[53]

Nixon followed his potential opponents' activities, especially Kennedy's. Gallup and other polling organizations had been conducting presidential surveys starting in 1959. Until mid-July that year, Nixon had trailed Stevenson and Kennedy. But late that month, sent to Moscow to attend the opening of the American National Exhibition in Moscow, the vice president engaged with Khrushchev in what became known as the Kitchen Debate, widely perceived as a rhetorical victory for Nixon's approval ratings and consumer capitalism. After that confrontation, the vice president never again polled behind Stevenson and ran better than Kennedy for the rest of the year.[54]

Nixon and Kennedy had much in common. One of the senator's aides told Father Theodore Hesburgh, president of the University of Notre Dame, that "the real problem is that the Senator and the Vice President are very much alike in many ways. Jack thinks a great deal of Dick, and has always respected him highly for his performance in the Senate, as Vice President. This doesn't get talked about very much, but it's very real fact."[55]

The polling illustrated how closely matched the two contenders were: they continually switched narrow leads just over 50 percent. Following the U-2 crisis and the summit collapse, the voters rallied behind the president and were drawn to Nixon's theme of experience and tough-mindedness. He could deal with

Khrushchev. Pollster Samuel Lubell discovered that the American public did not blame the Republicans for the summit failure: nearly 85 percent of respondents praised Ike for his "dignity," and three out of four stuck with their initial choice for president. Nixon had received a "small boost" due to the anxiety over war. In mid-June, Nixon wrote his pollster Claude Robinson that according to the latest polls, "if foreign policy is uppermost in the people's mind we will do well."[56]

Nixon started to follow Massachusetts's politics in 1957 and began commenting on JFK's candidacy in 1957 and 1958. In 1958 he explained to a dinner audience that professional Democratic politicians might reject Kennedy due to uncertainty over his Catholic faith, but rank-and-file voters would not. If they thought their chances of winning the presidency were slim, the party's leaders might nominate Kennedy. But Nixon believed "that Kennedy would be a much harder candidate to defeat than Stevenson" and that "a Catholic candidate on the Democratic ticket would have much more political pulling power than most of the professional politicians realize."[57]

On January 19, 1960, Nixon was leaving a private luncheon in Manhattan at the Colony Restaurant when he ran into the patriarch, Joseph Kennedy, along with Ted and his wife, Joan. They all shook hands. Nixon told the father that his son was "doing very well" in his race for the presidential nomination and was a "fine guy" despite their political differences. Joe replied, "John thinks the same of you."[58]

Twenty-three years after this exchange, Nixon provided additional dialogue. Joe said: "I just want you to know how much I admire you for what you've done in the Hiss case and in these—this Communist activity of yours." He added: "If Jack doesn't get it, I'll be for you."[59]

The patriarch shared a far bleaker impression of the vice president with Sorensen on February 24, 1960: "I continually hear about Nixon's experience and I . . . think for the most part that *experience* is a term usually used to describe a lifetime of mistakes." Three months later, Joe wrote the British press baron Lord Beaverbrook: "If I were betting, I would bet that Jack will get the nomination and will have no great difficulty with Nixon."[60]

Throughout the first five months of 1960, Nixon continually found himself answering questions about the patriarch's son. In the middle of January, campaigning in Miami Beach, Florida, he responded to a speech at the National Press Club in Washington in which Kennedy labeled Theodore Roosevelt and Abraham Lincoln strong Republican presidents and Eisenhower a weak one. Nixon said that while the senator was "a very serious student" of politics, he missed the point of presidential leadership by highlighting personalities instead of accomplishments. By that more important measure, Ike was a strong leader.[61]

Nixon also evaluated the primaries Kennedy had entered. Ahead of the race in West Virginia between Humphrey and Kennedy, Nixon speculated that it might "become the most important primary in recent American history" because it would test whether the candidates were judged on the issues.[62]

On April 10, he predicted that if JFK won in West Virginia, he would win the nomination, but if he lost, that did not mean he had lost the nomination. Eight days later, Nixon received a confidential memo saying that if JFK lost, Stevenson or Symington would offer him the vice presidential place, and he would accept it. Kennedy's reason, Nixon surmised, was that if he refused to take the second spot, the Democratic Party would never nominate him for president. If he became the running mate and the presidential candidate lost, the party would nominate him in 1964 because of his cooperation in 1960.[63]

After JFK won the West Virginia primary, Arthur Krock reminded Nixon that he had predicted it weeks earlier.[64]

8

No Capacity for Sensible Advice

Nelson Rockefeller's surprise announcement at the end of 1959 that he would not challenge Nixon for the nomination had shocked his followers. By the New Year, rumors were circulating that he would accept a draft; that he would boycott the Republican convention; that he was reconsidering and would challenge the vice president after all. One fact was indisputable. He would not endorse Nixon.[1]

In January his withdrawal was already suspect. The seventy or eighty researchers he had hired for his primary campaign remained on the payroll. California businessmen were organizing a draft movement. Addressing a "Salute to Eisenhower" dinner toward the end of January, Rockefeller lavished praise on the president and failed to mention the vice president. He called on the GOP to recruit more "crusaders" and move from the status quo to offering innovations. At the start of February, the *Denver Post*, which had supported Ike in his two presidential campaigns, called for a concerted draft-Rockefeller effort.[2]

The governor's supporters no doubt agreed that they were a distinct minority. At the end of January, RNC chair Thruston Morton appeared on *Meet the Press* and highlighted Nixon's support. The vice president had 67 percent approval within the party, and Rockefeller probably would not run unless the vice president "stubbed his toe." Morton added that he had received assurances that Rockefeller would work for Nixon in the general election.[3]

Morton did not know that Rockefeller's chief political counselor, Frank Jamieson, had died of cancer on the same day as the *Meet the Press* interview. When Rockefeller's advisers changed, so did the advice he received. He now relied on Emmet Hughes, whom he had hired as a speechwriter and foreign policy expert a few weeks earlier. Hughes had been an Eisenhower speechwriter, but when he asked for a high diplomatic post, Secretary of State Dulles refused, and the president supported that decision. He left the administration angry and disappointed. Working for Rockefeller gave him an opportunity to embarrass both the president and the vice president by having an important party figure subject them to criticism.[4]

Henry Kissinger, a Harvard government professor, also became a major resource for the governor. He had met Rockefeller in 1955, and the following year Rockefeller had hired him to work on the Special Studies Project. Kissinger gained national prominence in 1957 with his best-selling book *Nuclear Weapons and Foreign Policy*, which advocated limited nuclear war.[5]

Henry Cabot Lodge read the book and recommended it to Ike. The president did not know Kissinger but found the book "very provocative." While he did not agree with all of it, he sent acting Secretary of State Christian Herter some excerpts that General Andrew Goodpaster, a presidential foreign policy adviser, had prepared. Herter, Ike believed, would find the book "interesting and worth reading." The president wanted his opinion kept confidential to avoid any publicity "because I have frequently been embarrassed by press reports as to my 'reading habits.'"[6]

By the following summer, Kissinger was writing speeches for Rockefeller, having him oppose nuclear test bans without sufficient verification and advocate aggressively resisting Soviet threats in Berlin. By submitting these arguments, Kissinger was breaking with Eisenhower's policies. By the time of the U-2 debacle and the collapse of the Paris summit in May 1960, Kissinger had become Rockefeller's chief foreign policy adviser.[7]

Kissinger had been the protégé of Harvard professor William Elliott, dean of the Harvard Summer School and founder of the Harvard International Seminar. Elliott served as a foreign policy adviser to the vice president and sent him a copy of Kissinger's book in July 1957, shortly after it was published. Nixon had already read it and had written Kissinger that it was "most stimulating and constructive." When Nixon asked Elliott the following summer to recommend some young men whom he could hire to write for him, Elliott named Kissinger.[8]

Between the summers of 1958 and 1959, Kissinger invited the vice president several times to come to Cambridge and speak at the Harvard Seminar. Nixon declined for a variety of reasons. But after Kissinger published an article in the *New York Times Magazine* on September 6, 1959, entitled "The Khrushchev Visit—Dangers and Hopes," concerning the Berlin crisis and the administration's options, the vice president sent him a letter saying that his article "was a superb analysis of the factors involved in the Khrushchev visit. . . . In major respects my views coincide exactly with those you expressed." Nixon thought so highly of the piece that he mentioned it in a speech given in New York.[9]

Kissinger's opinions of Nixon depended on who was asking. When Mike Wallace interviewed Kissinger in the summer of 1958, he asked whom Kissinger looked to for leadership in the United States. Kissinger answered that he disliked discussing personalities, but that Nixon "in his public utterances recently has shown an awareness of the situation." But once Rockefeller started to campaign, Kissinger considered the vice president an unworthy opponent.[10]

Not all spokesmen within his state pleased the governor. In the middle of November 1959, Peter Flanigan, an investment banker with Dillon Read and Co., opened a New Yorkers for Nixon Committee in Manhattan. Thirty-seven individuals served on the board with prominent members like William Robinson, chairman of Coca-Cola Company and one of Ike's social friends, and Frank Gifford, star halfback for the New York Giants.[11]

Ike had eliminated the governor from presidential contention in early January. But he didn't speak to Rockefeller about it until late March, after he publicly endorsed Nixon, at which point he called the governor to explain that he had done so "quite deliberately" because the governor "was no longer in the race." During his press conference on the thirtieth, the president suggested that Rockefeller would be an acceptable vice presidential candidate, along with "a score of Republicans of real stature." A week later, Ike told Arthur Krock of his concern that the governor's withdrawal made it look like the GOP was "boss-controlled" and Nixon was a product of this monopoly. He had asked Rockefeller to come out for Nixon publicly and thought he would do it shortly.[12]

But despite his formal withdrawal, Rockefeller was not acting like someone who was entirely out of the race. In late April he gave addresses in Chicago and Philadelphia attacking the administration for the communist global successes because of "our failure to create larger political structures in which freedom can flourish." The United States, he argued, lacked "a clear sense of purpose and dedication" and tried to substitute military and economic actions "for the vital and lacking political acts of creation." He suggested that the United States develop a Western Hemispheric economic union through the UN and that the United States place its nuclear weaponry under NATO supervision. He insisted that he was not criticizing the administration or running for president. Reporters were skeptical.[13]

The Philadelphia visit caught the attention of the Nixon campaign. William Scranton, who had been one of Rockefeller's hosts and was running for a Pennsylvania congressional seat, called vice presidential assistant Charles McWhorter to tell him that Rockefeller had "displayed an appalling ignorance of the nature of the chronic unemployment problem in the state." Scranton did not want anyone in the vice president's office to think that he was "selling out to Rockefeller," but intended to educate him when they next saw each other.[14]

The president wrote the governor on May 5 after reading both speeches. As generalities, they were eloquent and "admirable." The difficulties arose when Rockefeller did not keep to the "middle-of-the-road," where most people stood. Progress took time. The Soviets would block Rockefeller's calls for a UN-run Western Hemispheric economic union and would be outraged at any effort to place nuclear weapons under NATO control. Besides, the administration had worked very hard to strengthen the nation's existing economic and political alliances. Ike encouraged Rockefeller to continue making speeches, but to eliminate such extremes.[15]

After the U-2 incident and the collapse of the Paris conference, the governor suggested that those debacles called for a national debate. The Republican Party did not attack him for this position but tried to accommodate him. RNC chairman Morton offered Rockefeller his choice of a keynote speech or either the temporary or permanent chairmanship of the convention. Rockefeller instead announced that he would not attend the convention. A week later he reversed himself: he would go to the convention and accept a draft, if offered.[16]

His allies were eager to make this happen. L. Judson Morhouse, the New York Republican chairman and a Rockefeller loyalist, refused to endorse the vice president. At the start of May, Morhouse had urged the ninety-six-member New York delegation to go to the party's convention uncommitted, arguing that the governor had widespread national appeal beyond the GOP and needed to head the ticket. Rockefeller, he stressed, "should not be ruled out of consideration for the presidency—and . . . he should not rule himself out." The governor disassociated himself from Morhouse's statement.[17]

Another ally, Republican New York Senator Jacob Javits, had encouraged Nixon in January to prove "that his thinking is modern and forward looking and is not rooted in a stand-pat attitude." By late May, Javits assumed that Nixon had the nomination and that the New York delegation would work for a liberal platform. But in June, liberal Senator John Sherman Cooper of Kentucky called for Rockefeller to declare his candidacy so that he and Nixon could debate critical issues on the national stage afforded by the convention.[18]

The vice president closely followed the governor's actions. He asked his staff for the latest information on Rockefeller's schedule so that he could consider it when making up his own. While the vice president was gathering delegates, Gallup polls gave Nixon sizable leads over Rockefeller: in December 1959, 66 percent to 19; January 1960, 84 percent, with no mention of the governor; May 1960, 75 percent to 13.[19]

Reporters regularly asked Nixon to comment on his relations with Rockefeller, and the vice president publicly took the governor at his word that he was not a rival candidate. In February, Nixon expressed appreciation that the governor had complimented him for looking forward, not backward. He and Rockefeller had been "good friends" while both worked for the administration, and he hoped Rockefeller would play "a very prominent part in developing our program in the future."[20]

But as the convention approached, the governor's coyness began to try Nixon's patience. In a background interview on May 3 with Arthur Krock, Nixon criticized Rockefeller for not endorsing him. The columnist wrote that the vice president felt the governor's "continued avoidance of endorsing him is out of character." Ike had recently telephoned Rockefeller, asking him to endorse Nixon, and Rockefeller had replied that an endorsement would be "'more effective' just before the convention." Nixon disagreed.[21]

In his television interview with David Susskind twelve days later, Nixon said that Rockefeller had "a perfect right to withhold his endorsement of the Republican candidate until the Republican convention meets." After the candidate was selected, he was certain Rockefeller would support him.[22]

The governor continued to deny that he was running for the presidency, but his actions suggested otherwise. He had committed to traveling to North Dakota in June to campaign for two-term Republican Governor John Davis against Congressman Quentin Burdick, who in 1958 had become the first Democrat the state ever elected to the House. A special election was being held on June 28 to replace Senator William Langer, who had died in office. Both Davis and Burdick were popular in the state, and the election shaped up as extremely close.[23]

On June 1, Nixon advance man H. R. Haldeman talked with Mark Andrews, the national committeeman from North Dakota, about Rockefeller's appearances. The governor's advance men and public relations people had taken his itinerary away from the local Republicans, Haldeman reported, and he seemed more interested in bolstering his own cause than in backing Davis. Andrews complained that the state GOP was "so excited over the possibility of shaking hands with $200,000,000 [that] they have completely lost interest in working on the Senatorial campaign and instead are working on arrangements for the Rockefeller visit."[24]

The governor arrived by chartered plane on the afternoon of June 2. Before landing, he and a group of aides told *Newsweek* senior editor Harold Lavine that

Nixon was almost certain to get the nomination, but in politics, miracles did happen. By saying he would accept a draft, the governor had made himself newsworthy, and the press followed him. He hoped to force the convention to adopt a liberal platform because he thought the GOP could not win on Ike's record. His aides added that if Kennedy won the Democratic nomination, he would destroy Nixon in the general election.[25]

Rockefeller held a press conference after landing and stated that his single reason for coming was to support Davis. When a reporter asked about a draft, he answered: "It's a little windy but I haven't translated it into a draft yet." A sign outside the entrance to Fargo's new Civil Memorial Auditorium read: "An Evening with Rockefeller: Free N.D. milk and N.Y. apple pie." Governor Davis's name did not appear. At that evening's rally, Rockefeller argued that a Davis victory would inspire Republicans elsewhere to increase their efforts. Hundreds of listeners filed by after the speech to shake Rockefeller's hand, urging him to declare for the presidency.[26]

The next day the governor spoke at a rally in a Valley City park, went to a picnic near Jamestown for fourteen hundred guests, took a walking tour of Bismarck, held a press conference, and attended a box supper in Mandan. He repeatedly called for converting much of the United States' farm surplus into a food reserve to feed Americans for up to a year after a nuclear attack. This was necessary, he said, because the failure of the Paris summit had revived cold war tensions and made "greater preparedness" essential.[27]

Rockefeller pronounced himself pleased with the reception he received. He had met the rank-and-file and had charmed them. He still was not an active candidate, but if a draft came, he would accept it. Near the end of his trip, a reporter asked: "Do you feel a draft now?" He answered, "I don't feel a draft—but it's not stuffy either."[28]

Back in New York, perhaps feeling himself a legitimate contender, Rockefeller had Emmet Hughes prepare a statement critical of the administration's foreign and domestic policies, based on research that the Rockefeller Brothers Fund would later publish under the title *Prospects for America: The Rockefeller Panel Reports*. Without revealing the statement's contents or outlining an agenda, Rockefeller telephoned the White House on Monday, June 7, and made an appointment to have breakfast with the president the next morning. Ike then called Nixon to ask whether he thought the meeting should be on the record. Nixon said yes.[29]

Rockefeller met with the president on Tuesday for two hours. He spoke largely in generalities, saying he wanted to add a billion dollars to the defense budget without stating how it would be spent. He also took the occasion to attack Nixon's failure to be clear on "certain issues." While Ike mostly listened, he specifically asked the governor to address the convention.[30]

Reporters waiting for Rockefeller outside the White House wanted to know if he was being drafted for the nomination. Avoiding an answer, he said he had told the president that the vice president needed to make his positions clear, before the convention, on urgent national issues. In his memoirs, Ike wrote: "I had unwittingly been made a party to the quarrel."[31]

The president was furious. Drew Pearson wrote in his diary on June 8 that Ike was "boiling at" Rockefeller. Three weeks later, Slats Slater recorded in his diary that the president was "irked" by Rockefeller's remarks, and they were uppermost in his current thinking.[32]

Rather than hurting his rival, Rockefeller's actions galvanized GOP leaders to unite behind Nixon. Ray Bliss, the Ohio state chairman, compared his statement to Harold Stassen's "Dump Nixon" flop in 1956. Many party leaders were angry that Rockefeller would castigate the first Republican president in two decades. Others believed he was breaking with the administration in the belief that if Nixon lost, he could say "I told you so" and try to win a leadership position after November.[33]

Ike was unaware that Rockefeller had directed Emmet Hughes to draft a statement the day before their breakfast. Rockefeller and Hughes finished it on the flight back to New York and had it mimeographed as soon as they landed. The governor went directly from the airport to a meeting with the state's Republican leadership, after which he distributed the twenty-seven-hundred–word statement to reporters. It was highly critical of the administration. The governor called for an added $3 billion for the military budget and a half billion more for civil defense, for a total of $3.5 billion more to the defense budget. The U-2 fiasco and the summit failure, the statement asserted, showed the need for a reorganization of the government to better address such situations. The governor advocated compulsory arbitration in labor disputes that endangered national welfare. As for civil rights, he demanded a far broader program than the administration had enacted. He also called for federal aid to education, medical assistance to the elderly under Social Security, and economic help to low-income farmers. He criticized Nixon for his role in settling the 1959 steelworkers' strike, calling the deal inflationary.[34]

Eisenhower talked with Nixon after that day's National Security Council meeting ended, shortly before 4:00. The governor, he said, had not given him any inkling of what was coming, and Ike did not want Nixon to think Rockefeller had his approval.[35]

At a Republican leadership meeting on Wednesday morning, he chided Rockefeller for meddling in foreign affairs. In their meeting, Ike said, the governor had made a vague mention of adding a billion dollars to the defense budget, without specifying how it should be used. He had never mentioned $3.5 billion, or civil defense. Ike had explained to the governor how carefully the budget was prepared. Now he suggested that Nixon acknowledge that Rockefeller, "as a prominent Republican," had the right to express his opinions. He might be urged to give a major address at the convention as a sign of "fair play." Senate minority leader Everett Dirksen said that the governor's "unfortunate" remarks damaged America's relations with its allies and with other nations that depended on the United States. Secretary of Defense Thomas Gates added that he was surprised by the statement because he and Rockefeller were friendly, and the governor knew that Gates had "the defense matter under constant review."[36]

After the meeting, Nixon headed to Camden for a testimonial dinner for freshman Congressman William Cahill. Before that event, he held a press conference in a small, stuffy room filled with about a hundred reporters. When asked about Rockefeller's statement, Nixon replied that the claim that the United States' global standing was at its worst since World War II damaged American prestige. He was proud of the administration's record in defending the homeland. Acknowledging that the governor was a prominent GOP leader, Nixon noted that this was his forty-sixth press conference in the previous five months, and he had answered many questions concerning the major issues of the day. There was no mystery about where he stood. He thought adding $3.5 billion to the defense budget was unnecessary. He opposed compulsory arbitration and health care for the elderly; he approved of federal aid to education for construction in needy school districts.

Nixon challenged Rockefeller to question him on television about the issues. He would not, he said, ask the governor to be his running mate, but Rockefeller should appear before the platform committee to present his proposals. Within three hours after Nixon finished, Rockefeller replied that there would be no debate until Nixon stated his views.[37]

Ike wrote Nixon that his handling of the press conference was "excellent"; he hoped it would blunt Rockefeller's challenge and "keep a potentially explosive situation from getting out of hand." Virgil Pinkley, editor and publisher of Associated Desert Newspapers, wrote Nixon that Ike had answered some of the governor's charges, and he expected him "to continue to use the 'soft answer' in the hope that no more wrath will develop than seems presently to be in evidence." He also thought Nixon had to "leave the door open for Nelson to support the ticket with at least some degree of enthusiasm" after the convention.[38]

That evening, Rockefeller called the White House twice wanting to speak with Ike. The first time he called, he told Ann Whitman, the president's private secretary, that he was not criticizing the administration but the "lack of leadership on the Vice President's part, in promulgating a program for the future, changing needs of our country." Insisting that he did not want to damage the party, he asked Whitman to ask the president whether "he should become an avowed candidate." The first time he called, Whitman replied that he should make his own decision and that it was inappropriate to ask the president. When he called again, he simply asked to "chat."[39]

The president returned the call that evening but failed to reach the governor. On Friday, June 10, Rockefeller did not call because he was opening the British Exhibition at the Manhattan Coliseum, with Prince Philip, husband of Queen Elizabeth II, in attendance. The vice president was there too: he arrived first, around 10:00 a.m. When the governor came in, Nixon said: "Glad to see you again, Nelson." He responded with an equally insincere "Hiya, fella. Nice to see you again!"

On Saturday morning, June 11, the president telephoned Oveta Hobby, who had been HEW secretary when Rockefeller was the undersecretary. She believed that "Nelson has great possibilities," but his statement was "so sad." Ike asked her to call Rockefeller, explaining that he was incorrect calling the party unimaginative "and not looking forward." She remarked that Nixon was "not easy." Ike replied that he "was growing in stature daily, that people respected him."[40]

Then Ike called Rockefeller, who asked whether he should run for president. At first the president hesitated; then he said that Rockefeller should not have unnecessarily alarmed Americans over the size of the military budget. As for Nelson's "becoming an active candidate," the president noted that he had already quit the race once and did not want to become "off again, on again, gone again, Finnegan." Even though the governor could have someone nominate him at the convention, Ike thought his "chances were very remote." He "trusted Nelson's common sense" and hoped that the governor would not hurt his standing within the party by attacking the administration. In addition, Nelson should not become "a lone wolf." He could not get by with only independent support; he also had to have backing within the GOP. Ike used one of his favorite sayings: "Do not make mistakes in a hurry." He advised the governor to write his own speeches and pledge to support whomever the convention nominated. If Nixon lost in November, Nelson would be one of the favorites for 1964. The governor seemed to agree to Ike's suggestions. He did make "some minor criticism of the Vice President." Although he had spoken out on some issues, he had not included all of them.[41]

Rockefeller might not have recognized Eisenhower's reference to the popular song "Off Again, On Again, Gone Again, Finnegan," released in 1910, or understood the president's uncomplimentary reference to it. Andy Finnegan was a railroad section boss who caused a crash with ten deaths, a husband who had marriage problems, and a construction worker who fell twenty-two stories, landing on a policeman.[42]

The president also saw "the fine hand of Emmet" Hughes in selling Rockefeller on the idea of the critical statement. Ike wrote Henry Luce, the publisher of *Time* and *Life* and a previous employer of Hughes: "Nelson is being too much influenced by a man who has no capacity for giving sensible advice."[43]

On Sunday, June 12, the president left the capital for a two-week goodwill tour of four major Asian cities: Manila, Seoul, Taipei, and Tokyo. Nixon approved of this initiative and was gratified to see how well the president was received in the Philippines. He hoped that Japanese protocol regarding guests would "prevail over the rabble-rousing lefts who, while they are large in numbers, still are a tiny minority of the whole population." But the Japanese canceled Ike's visit because of threats of widespread rioting.[44]

That morning, Rockefeller appeared on *Meet the Press* and that evening on *Open End* with David Susskind. He reiterated that he was a loyal Republican and was not trying to block Nixon's nomination. He would not declare himself a candidate, but if it were offered, he would accept a draft. He would not take the second spot. He hoped that Nixon would address the major issues confronting the nation before the convention, as this would make winning the election much easier. He promised to campaign energetically for the ticket in the general election. Finally, he called Ike a great leader.[45]

Later that week, Nixon wrote Robert McClure, a political supporter, that he could not yet "appraise the effect of the Rockefeller blast, but . . . I am doing everything that I can to avoid replying in kind." The governor, Nixon told loyalist Tim Murphy on June 16, had stirred up excitement, and the coming months would "not be dull and uneventful." Later he told another supporter that he had "tried to keep a potentially explosive situation from getting out of hand."[46]

The Rockefeller-Nixon exchanges subsided. On June 17, Herb Klein told the press that early the following morning the vice president and his wife would take a four-day trip of three midwestern farm states, to campaign for two Republican senatorial candidates and "touch" on the farm issue.[47]

His most important stop came on Monday, June 20, in North Dakota. He had two objectives: to address farmers' complaints about the administration's policy on agricultural price supports, and to prop up the Republican candidate, Governor John Davis, against Democratic Congressman Quentin Burdick in that month's special election for a United States Senate seat. Burdick was running on the slogan "Beat Benson with Burdick," meaning Ezra Taft Benson, and Davis was trying to disassociate himself from the unpopular secretary of agriculture. If Nixon did not go to North Dakota, he might be blamed for Davis's defeat. But if he went and Davis lost anyway, it might look like the state was renouncing the entire administration, Nixon included.[48]

The vice president, his wife, and their party landed at the Williston airport, where they were warmly welcomed by Governor Davis. Nixon spoke at the American Legion convention before five thousand; gave a press conference in Fargo; and spoke at a dinner in Minot, where he argued that the Democratic Congress had hurt farmers by not passing the president's agricultural legislation. He declared that Rockefeller's recommendation for a year's supply of grain reserves in the case of a nuclear attack had merit and offered two other proposals: increased commercial uses of farm products, and distribution of U.S. food surpluses to the world's hungry. The *Minot Daily News* editorialized on Nixon's visit: "It was tumultuous while it lasted, a donnybrook that drew . . . more persons jamming into the auditorium for a free GOP barbecue and a chance to see Nixon and his wife in person."[49]

While he had directly confronted some of the difficulties with the administration's agricultural policy, Nixon did not look upon his Minot address as putting forward a "Farm Program." He meant to make some constructive suggestions toward alleviating certain problems. As for his assist to Davis, he earned the governor's gratitude and burnished one of his greatest political assets: his reputation for helping fellow Republicans in their election campaigns.[50]

Davis lost the June 28 election. In the early returns, he held a tiny lead in the cities and towns, but it vanished when the rural areas reported. When the votes were counted, Burdick received 104,593 and Davis had 103,475. The governor had gone down to defeat by 1,118 votes.[51]

Shortly after the results were posted, Secretary Benson met with the president to discuss agricultural issues. Ike stated that he was considering presenting to the UN the "Food-For-Peace proposal" that Nixon had advanced. They agreed that there would be no changes to the administration's farm policies, and the administration should introduce a wheat bill to Congress to support that crop.[52]

The last stop of Nixon's forty-five-hundred–mile swing came on June 20 in St. Louis. Before attending to his packed schedule, he and Pat celebrated their twentieth wedding anniversary with a cake. He addressed the national convention of the Junior Chamber of Commerce (JCC) where he attacked both Rockefeller and liberal Democrats for claiming that the Soviet economy was ahead of the United States'. Analyzing economic growth, he noted, was "becoming the . . .

political parlor game of our time." But "growthmanship," as he called it, translated into a government-managed economy. Asserting that the "primitive" Soviet economy was racing ahead of America's was not correct: American economic growth, he said, was far superior to the Soviets'. America "has been and will continue to be the dynamic, creative productivity of private rather than government enterprise."[53]

This was his last tour before the Republican convention. He had given eighteen addresses in six cities; he had spoken to party "fat cats" and GOP stalwarts. *Time* magazine described "mercilessly crowded schedules, jostling crowds, exploding flashbulbs, endless lines of hands to be shaken. . . . The crowds were bigger and more enthusiastic than he expected." *New York Daily News* reporter Frank Holeman concluded after covering the trip: "If you are making any bets on the national elections this fall, here's a friendly little tip: don't be a sucker. Don't give long odds against Nixon."[54]

Rockefeller responded to Nixon's "growthmanship" comment in a television interview. He advocated a faster rate of national economic expansion and said he was "a little concerned . . . by this trying to sort of turn this very basic question off as a light parlor game." On another occasion, he commented that Japan's cancellation of the president's visit demonstrated the shortcomings of American foreign policy and a failure "to assess realistically the facts before us and to define realistic purposes and actions to meet them." He also proposed sweeping civil rights initiatives, implicitly criticizing Eisenhower for his failure to use his executive powers and challenging Nixon to take a more aggressive stand. In a speech to thirty-five hundred African-American Baptist Sunday school teachers, he outlined a program under which blacks would be guaranteed voting rights, equal job opportunities, and an end to segregation in schools and public and private housing. Though he did not directly blame the president, he implied that many of these measures could have been accomplished by executive orders, without Congress's approval. As the governor left, the ministers rose, singing: "Mine eyes have seen the glory of the coming of the Lord."[55]

If Rockefeller believed he was improving his image, the Gallup Poll of June 24 said otherwise. The survey asked Republican county chairmen who they preferred as their presidential nominee: Nixon 79 percent, Rockefeller 8. When asked who they thought would receive the nomination, it was Nixon 95 percent and Rockefeller 2.[56]

When Eisenhower returned from his Asian tour on the morning of June 26, Nixon greeted him at Andrews Air Force Base. In addition to having the Tokyo visit canceled, Ike had been greeted with large protests in Manila. The president called the mission "pretty good" and resumed his White House schedule.[57]

Nixon wrote Milton Eisenhower about Ike's Manila greeting and his potential dangers of left-wing rioting in Japan. Milton answered in confidence that he had an idea for a new agency for a "total strategy for peace." He offered this proposal because Nixon's "election is essential to the future of the nation and . . . the winning of peace is going to call for imaginative additional efforts, some of which will surely be calculated risks."[58]

Asked about his relations with Rockefeller at an end-of-the-month press conference, Nixon pointed out that they agreed on many things. "I do not see any difference that cannot be reconciled once we go through the convention, have these issues thrashed out in the platform, and of course in meetings that take place between us." He noted with approval the governor's decision to attend the convention and tried to discourage any movement to draft him for vice president. After the convention, he knew, the governor would actively support him.[59]

The president did not show Rockefeller the same regard. During his press conference on July 6, Ike told reporters that the governor was a "dedicated, honest, hard-working man" with whom he disagreed over the state of the American military. That evening, he called the governor "a well-meaning fellow" but overambitious.[60]

Despite both men's denials, the press continued to speculate about a Nixon-Rockefeller ticket. The governor was not interested "in the slightest," and the vice president confirmed that Rockefeller had rejected any thought of being his running mate. Reporters were not convinced. On one key point, though, Rockefeller had not budged. With the convention now very close, the governor had not endorsed Nixon's nomination.[61]

9

"ONE OF US"

Rockefeller's efforts to derail Nixon's nomination put him distinctly in the minority. An overwhelming number of Republican partisans enthusiastically supported Nixon. Others who had opposed him throughout his political career reversed their opinions. Ronald Reagan was one. He had voted for FDR and then for Truman, and had become president of the Screen Actors Guild in 1947 as what historian Kiron Skinner described as "a very active and militant Democrat." That year, Congressman Nixon, then serving on the House Un-American Activities Committee, wrote his mentor Herman Perry that Reagan was "classified as a liberal" and that he wanted him called before HUAC to testify at a public hearing.[1]

Reagan did radio spots for Helen Gahagan Douglas in the 1950 Senate contest in California but voted for Ike in 1952. Still, he did not approve of Nixon, writing: "Pray as I am praying for the health and long life of Eisenhower because the thought of Nixon in the White House is almost as bad as that of 'Uncle Joe [Stalin].' . . . Nixon is a hand picked errand boy with a pleasing façade and naught but emptiness behind. He has been subsidized by a small clique of oil and real estate pirates, he is *less than honest* and he is an ambitious opportunist completely undeserving of the high honor paid him."[2]

But Reagan's political views were changing. By June 1959, the speeches he gave as General Electric's spokesman bore titles like "Business, Ballots, and Bureaus"; they promoted free enterprise and opposed government interference. The income tax was unfair and violated "the old-fashioned philosophy that the least government is the best government." The exception was defense spending against communist aggression. Freedom, according to Reagan, "occurred in a Capitalistic system—indeed there could be no individual liberty without Capitalism." He questioned the "Tax and tax, spend and spend, . . . elect and elect" mentality.[3]

Still a registered Democrat, Reagan watched the Democratic convention on television and sent his reactions to Nixon. The speeches were insignificant, he wrote, but he "heard a frightening call to arms" from the delegates. Kennedy was "a powerful speaker with an appeal to the emotions." Republican liberals might want to echo his call for bigger government and more spending, Reagan warned, but doing so would not gain votes. After speaking in thirty-eight states that year, he was convinced the nation was "economically conservative." JFK, on the other hand, was a dangerous left-winger: "Under the tousled boyish hair cut it is still old Karl Marx—first launched a century ago. There is nothing new in the idea of a government being Big Brother to us all. Hitler called his 'State Socialism' and way before him it was 'benevolent monarchy.'" Nixon should demand that Democrats give specifics on how much their programs would cost. Nixon filed Reagan's letter with a note attached: "Use him as speaker whenever possible. He *used* to be a liberal!"[4]

With just over two weeks to go before the Republican convention, Rockefeller still refused to endorse Nixon. During the United States Governors' Conference, Indiana's Republican governor, Harold Handley, an ardent Nixon supporter, surprised Rockefeller by trying to embarrass him into signing a petition pledging "full and loyal support" to the vice president for the presidential nomination. The petition had already been given to reporters with a press release saying every Republican governor had signed it. Rockefeller handed the paper back unsigned, saying, "You guys are some artists, aren't you?"[5]

At the time, Charles Percy, the chairman of the platform committee, and Gabriel Hauge, executive secretary for the RNC to the platform committee, were negotiating with the governor, hoping to gain his endorsement in exchange for some planks in the platform. Percy telephoned the president on July 8 and said that he and Hauge had spent three hours with Rockefeller that morning and were going to ask him to come before the platform committee to present his views, "hopefully on a *positive* note." The governor had drawn up "a bill of particulars" for Nixon, which Percy was to deliver to him that day.[6]

Rockefeller then made his case to the platform committee. On foreign policy, he wanted the United States to lead regional confederations of free countries; on national defense, he called for $3.5 billion of additional spending; on arms control, he opposed "total disarmament" and advocated resumption of underground nuclear testing; on labor, he argued that the president be empowered to end long strikes; on agriculture, he wanted to help marginal farmers find other jobs and also expand "Food for Peace" exports; he was for economic growth; and he called for federal health insurance for Americans over sixty-five, to be paid for through Social Security payroll taxes.[7]

Ike called Hauge and recounted his efforts to persuade Rockefeller to run for the vice presidency. Rockefeller, Ike said, did not see it as "his duty" to accept the second spot: "He has a personal ambition that is overwhelming. Next to the Presidency, he considers the governorship of the State of New York the next most important job in the country." The president was willing to talk to Nelson again but believed "it would be futile." Still, he continued, there was an option. If Nixon promised to serve no more than one term, Nelson might become his running mate. But Eisenhower doubted that Nixon would agree; if he did, "it would have to be completely confidential, a gentleman's agreement." If Hauge arranged an interview between the president and the governor at the convention, Ike would do his best to make his case.[8]

Nixon also realized he had to minimize Rockefeller's objections to the platform, or else the disagreements could result in a damaging floor fight at the convention. The "Rockefeller thing has to be worked out," he wrote in a staff memo. He had "made every possible overture" to the governor and "would be glad to talk to him." He was willing to have someone act as an intermediary to get them together.[9]

Early on July 22, Nixon talked to former attorney general Herbert Brownell, who was friendly with Rockefeller. Brownell advised a meeting, and Nixon called the governor that afternoon. That evening, he flew to New York City and went directly to the governor's apartment for a private dinner. From 10:00 p.m. into the wee hours of the morning, Nixon, Rockefeller, and his adviser Emmet Hughes worked through the platform. The governor telephoned Charles Percy at 4:30 a.m. to give him the changes. Nixon also released a short statement saying that everyone agreed with the "basic philosophy" of the platform and that he and the governor concurred on the "important issues." Rockefeller unilaterally issued a "joint" statement, which the press labeled the "Compact of Fifth Avenue."[10]

The vice president flew back to Washington for a hastily called press conference. He said that the media had exaggerated the differences between himself and the governor; they agreed on principles. Both favored a strong civil rights plank, increased defense spending, and maximum economic growth. They disagreed on compulsory labor arbitration, the amount of additional defense spending, and health insurance for the elderly. Nixon did not mention the $3.5 billion in added defense spending that Ike had opposed. As for a Nixon-Rockefeller ticket, the governor would not consider second place, and the subject was "a closed book."[11]

Conservatives were distraught at the news of a secret agreement sprung on them by the liberal Eastern Establishment. They already distrusted Ike for embracing parts of the New Deal instead of dismantling it; some now talked of forming a third party, with Goldwater at the top of the ticket. He had emerged as the party's principal conservative leader and had his name on a best-selling new book, *The Conscience of a Conservative*, which advocated leaving enforcement of civil rights to individual states, overturning the *Brown* decision, ending farm subsidy programs, passing "right-to-work" legislation for those who did not want to join unions, eliminating welfare programs, and battling communist regimes everywhere in the world.[12]

In April, Goldwater had privately warned the vice president that "a liberal Nixon would alienate the conservative core of the GOP," and he needed those voters to win the general election. The same month, he told *U.S. News and World Report* that his "good friend" must not veer to the left in an effort to win votes. Nixon could win the presidency by standing on "conservative" principles and attracting Republican Party volunteers who would enthusiastically persuade Democrats and independents to follow their lead. "People are desperately looking for a man who will give them 'conservative' leadership," Goldwater emphasized—someone who would "tell the farmers to get back under the law of supply and demand, get the chiselers off the welfare rolls, tell people that their welfare depends on themselves, not on the Federal Government."[13]

Goldwater was furious about the Nixon-Rockefeller announcement. He had talked with Nixon on the morning of July 22 and received no hint about any meeting with Rockefeller. Now he feared that Nixon was "moving farther to the left than I ever hoped he would." The agreement, drawn up a thousand miles from the convention, seemed like a "surrender to Rockefeller," an "American Munich," and he promised to lead the fight against this "unprecedented last-minute attempt" to appease "a spokesman for the ultra-liberals."[14]

At a press conference on the twenty-third, Goldwater said he expected southerners and conservatives to help him defeat the plank calling for federal aid to education and assistance to the elderly, as well as the civil rights plank. Nixon had assured him, he claimed, that the platform would not call for federal action to fight racial discrimination in private employment. While he opposed segregation, enforcement of civil rights was a matter for the states, not the federal government. Speaking before the Illinois Federation of Republican Women at the convention two days later, he could easily have started a delegate uprising, but he refrained.[15]

Adding to the week's complications, Secretary Benson surprised many by announcing on July 23 that he endorsed Rockefeller as the GOP candidate with the "best chance" of defeating Kennedy, because he would appeal to Republicans, Democrats, and independents. Benson found Rockefeller "somewhat too liberal" on some issues but felt he would make a "great President."[16]

Nixon called the president, who was in Newport, Rhode Island, at 12:30 p.m. that day. He had not told Eisenhower about his meeting with Rockefeller, and the president told him it "was being interpreted by the Convention as Nixon undercutting the President." Late that afternoon, Ike told press secretary Hagerty that he would not be involved in the selection of the vice president unless asked, nor would he try to influence the platform. When reporters asked about the Nixon-Rockefeller agreement, Hagerty replied, "No comment."[17]

The following day, platform committee chairman Percy telephoned Ike, saying "he would give the President $100 for every word in the platform he would be unhappy with." Percy added that Rockefeller had caused some "confusion and bitterness" within the committee by releasing the agreement unilaterally. He and the president discussed civil rights, Social Security coverage for the elderly, a Western Hemispheric alliance, and nuclear testing. Talking later to Congressman Melvin Laird, the vice chairman of the platform committee, who had helped negotiate the changes, Eisenhower was clearly upset, "angry about defense plank," and he implied that Nixon might have to choose between his support and the governor's.[18]

Nor was he mollified by the platform's easy passage. He telephoned Nixon to tell him about Percy and Hauge's "unhappiness" that the agreement was "at variance" with the platform committee's decisions. Its members, the president said, believed he was "being publicly repudiated." Nixon replied that no such repudiation was intended. He thought the committee members were upset with Rockefeller's unilateral statement, and he was trying to find common ground without surrendering to Rockefeller so that the governor could "be with us and not against us." Ike answered that he wanted a platform "that would be good for the Republicans"; Nixon answered that it was "a ringing endorsement of everything the Administration has done."[19]

Arriving in Chicago on Sunday, July 24, Nixon instructed his small Secret Service detail and the Chicago police to let the crowd touch him. His directive caused chaos. One agent said: "The crowd moved in like a juggernaut. The girls [Julie and Tricia] turned white with fear."[20]

Rockefeller appeared on Meet the Press the same day. Asked about the likelihood of his being nominated president, he conceded that Nixon would be the party's nominee. As for his relationship with Goldwater, he was comfortable with the Arizonan in the Republican Party.[21]

The convention opened the next day at the Union Stockyards Amphitheatre, with Congressman Walter Judd from Minnesota giving the keynote address. A charismatic speaker and a favorite of the conservative wing for his crusade in support of the Nationalist Chinese leader Chiang Kai-shek, Judd gave the address he had been waiting a decade to deliver. Republicans, he proclaimed, offered the nation its best chance for peace and continued prosperity. Accepting Kennedy's challenge of making foreign policy the key issue in the campaign, he accused the Democrats, particularly FDR and Truman, of selling out to the Russians.[22]

Tuesday was devoted to the president. His prime-time address was seen in 16.7 million homes, the convention's second-largest television audience. Ike called on Republicans to unite and elect the next president, and then devoted the remainder of the speech to his administration's accomplishments. He had kept the peace and expanded economic growth. As for the future, "I glory in the moral, economic and military strength of this nation, in the ideals that she upholds before the world, and in her readiness to assist the less fortunate of the earth to obtain and enjoy the blessings of freedom." He failed to mention his vice president.[23]

The convention's third day belonged to Nixon. That evening, the platform was accepted and was followed by the nominating speeches. Governor Hatfield gave one of the shortest presidential nominating addresses in American history, only 288 words, but he left little to the imagination. He never mentioned Kennedy but pointedly noted that "the White House is not for sale," a clear reference to the Kennedy fortune. Nixon had the experience the country needed, and the courage displayed in his confrontations from Caracas to the Kremlin. He was "one of us" and had "known hard times" and "hard work." Hatfield did not need to say "unlike Kennedy."[24]

Governor Paul Fannin of Arizona followed by nominating Goldwater. This was a residue of the Rockefeller-Nixon agreement: angry conservatives had demanded that Goldwater's name be placed in nomination. Immediately after being nominated, Goldwater addressed the delegates. He appreciated the honor, he said, but he asked that his name be withdrawn and that Republicans, particularly conservatives, back Nixon. Even though he and others disagreed with some platform planks, the GOP platform was far superior to Democratic "socialism." Conservatives represented a minority and lacked the votes to win the battle against socialism by themselves. In the future, however, they would take control of the party: "Now let's put our shoulders to the wheel of Dick Nixon and push him across the line. . . . Let's grow up, conservatives."[25]

The delegates finished voting just before midnight. Ike sent Nixon a telegram: "I am delighted that you are at last free to speak freely and frankly in expressing your views on the present and future of our great country." He prayed that he would pass the presidency on to Nixon.[26]

Nixon's next priority was choosing a running mate from among many contenders. On June 27, *Newsweek* had stated that Michigan Congressman Gerald Ford, Jr., was "rapidly becoming first choice of important Nixon strategists." He came from the Midwest and had served in the House for six terms; he was the same age as the vice president and was "Nixon's type." Talking to Thomas De-Frank almost a half-century later, Ford said, "Dick Nixon and I were longtime close friends. I mean, for years."[27]

Dick and Jerry had met in 1949. Nixon was starting his second term in the House when Jerry was elected. Both lived in the Virginia suburbs, and they carpooled together to the Capitol. Both were charter members of the Chowder and Marching Club, a small group of Republican congressmen who lobbied for legislation that they favored. After Nixon won the vice presidency, Ford became one of his strongest advocates and often invited him to speak in Michigan. He praised Nixon's performance during Ike's heart attack and wrote the president supporting his friend for renomination in 1956 because he was "the most able, constructive and conscientious public official I have ever known."[28]

Nixon returned the friendship. At one point after Ford contacted the vice president's office, Nixon assured him that "a recommendation from you always gets flagged for special attention." When Ford ran for a fifth term in 1958, Nixon had the Republican national congressional committee contribute five hundred dollars to his campaign. In December 1959, as Ford's supporters were beginning to campaign to put him on the Republican ticket as vice presidential nominee, Nixon wrote journalist Raymond Moley that Ford was "one of my closest friends in the House" and, as an influential member of the House appropriations committee, "one of the leaders in the fight for the economy."[29]

Nixon mentioned Ford in his memoirs as one of the six men on his short list for vice presidential nominee in 1960. The *Washington Daily News* placed him third behind Morton and Lodge. On July 11, Moley wrote in *Newsweek* that Nixon was looking for a running mate "who would be entirely in sympathy with his policies, who would be sufficiently articulate to represent him at home and abroad, who would assist him in carrying the immense burdens of the Presidency, and who is vigorous enough to carry such a load as he, himself, has carried for President Eisenhower." The column was titled "Ford for Vice President?"[30]

Lodge was ten years older than both Nixon and Ford. Born in Massachusetts to a prominent political family, he graduated from Harvard cum laude in 1924 and began reporting for the *Boston Transcript* and then the *New York Herald Tribune*. After deciding that journalism was not his calling, he ran for the state legislature in 1932 and won. He declared for the United States Senate three years later, at the age of thirty-four, and was the only Republican to unseat a Democratic opponent in the Democratic landslide of 1936. After winning reelection, he resigned his seat in 1944 to serve in World War II, becoming the first senator since the Civil War to see combat. He left the army as a lieutenant colonel, again ran for the Senate, and was elected in 1946. He ran for reelection in 1952 while helping to manage Eisenhower's presidential bid. Ike won. Lodge lost to John Kennedy, and Ike appointed him ambassador to the United Nations.[31]

As Ike's second term drew to a close, Lodge was rumored to be a dark horse for the presidential nomination. After he raised his visibility by escorting Khrushchev on the latter's 1959 visit to America, pundits wrote of him as a vice presidential prospect. Hints surfaced at the start of 1960 that he might become Nixon's running mate. Influential Republicans like former House speaker Joseph Martin, Jr., came out for him, and columnist Roscoe Drummond in the *New York Herald Tribune* called him a "forceful speaker" who mirrored Nixon's foreign policy positions. During the United Nations debates over the U-2 incident, Lodge had done well, outmaneuvering the Russians and making himself a principal contender for the vice presidential nomination.[32]

Lodge's prestige grew throughout June. He had "stood up" to Khrushchev. In July, a *Life* editorial called for his nomination as vice presidential candidate. As the convention approached and world events made national headlines, more advocates championed his cause. The day before the convention, Rockefeller suggested that he might nominate Lodge. On the second day of the convention, *Boston Globe* Washington correspondent Robert Healy declared that the ambassador was already writing his acceptance speech.[33]

Lodge had met Eisenhower during the war, was one of the first to see him as a potential president, and had even entered Ike in the 1952 New Hampshire primary without the latter's knowledge. At the end of 1957, Ike wrote Lodge and alluded to "the intimacy of our long friendship." In a press conference a few days later, the president stated that he would keep a "'hands off' policy" toward the presidential election, but added in the same breath that he "admired" Lodge, thought he was "wonderful," and especially approved of his "enthusiasm." He was not focusing on any one contender but had his "eye on three or four." He mentioned Nixon and then suggested that Lodge "would make a wonderful President." A year later he had settled on a Nixon-Lodge ticket as the best one for the Republican Party.[34]

As the convention approached, the president lobbied actively for Lodge. Six days before it opened, he told Gabe Hauge: "Two men of stature would be Nixon and Lodge, they would appeal to thinking people." The headline on Roscoe Drummond's Sunday column on July 24 read: "Ike Would Like Lodge to Run with Nixon." On the day of Nixon's nomination, Ike held a private luncheon before leaving Chicago for Denver. Nixon was one of the guests, and he asked each of the others, including Percy, Len Hall, and Milton Eisenhower, to write down his vice presidential choice. They favored Lodge almost unanimously.[35]

Nixon, who was well aware of Ike's preference, had known Lodge since both men were senators, and they had become close friends when Lodge helped manage the Eisenhower campaign in 1952. After the 1956 presidential contest, Lodge, then at the United Nations, told Nixon, "You have confounded your enemies, impressed the circle of your friends and stand as a public figure of real stature before the nation."[36]

The interaction between Nixon and Lodge increased during Eisenhower's second term, especially concerning foreign policy, on which each developed great respect for the other's acumen. At the end of 1959, Nixon asked Lodge to provide "new ideas for speeches" on foreign policy that would advocate "some constructive new programs." As a political adviser to Nixon's primary campaigns, Lodge pushed the vice president toward cautious engagement with communist states and a stronger stand on civil rights for minorities.[37]

They also discussed the upcoming convention. At the start of the year, Lodge said he did not want to be considered as Nixon's running mate, but three months later, the vice president wrote Lodge about a talk he had with Republican Senator John Williams of Delaware. Williams, an "ultra-conservative," told Nixon that Lodge "was the best candidate for Vice President" even though he "was more identified with the liberal camp." That June, Lodge was the only vice presidential contender whom Nixon invited to join his "very small group of advisors" to discuss "long range policy problems" that might come up in the campaign.

The movement toward Lodge accelerated in July. On the ninth, Len Hall, working at the Nixon for President national headquarters in Washington, wrote Lodge that a poll of the delegates and alternates at the 1960 convention showed that 389 favored Lodge as the vice presidential nominee; 290 were for Goldwater, followed by 280 for Thruston Morton. The same day, Nixon sent Lodge a poll showing that when asked which of both parties' presidential candidates were likely to do the best job with the Russian leaders, 22 percent of respondents chose Nixon, followed by Lodge (21 percent), Stevenson (18 percent), and Kennedy (10 percent).[38]

As the convention opened, Lodge was attending a United Nations Security Council meeting where the Soviet Union introduced a resolution to investigate the espionage activities of an American RB-47 reconnaissance plane that Soviet fighters had shot down on July 1. Two of the six-man crew had survived the crash. The council voted down the resolution by nine to two (the Soviet Union and Poland). Lodge offered his own resolution for an investigation of Soviet behavior during the incident, asserting that the American plane had not committed any type of "aggression" and charging the Soviet Union with acting hypocritically, since its planes and ships had been spying off the Alaska coast and East Coast for years.[39]

Nixon saw Lodge as urbane, handsome, suave, and articulate. He had received massive newspaper coverage. The nation had watched him forcefully defend the United States in televised Security Council sessions. He had spoken out against communist activity in Congo and Laos and against the rise of Castro in Cuba. Lodge was a national celebrity. He also added balance and seasoning to the ticket: he came from Massachusetts and was fifty-eight, while Nixon was from California and was forty-seven. The vice president hoped for another edge over Kennedy as well. Lodge had a wealth of experience in foreign affairs, and if the election centered on global issues, as Nixon preferred, his résumé would be advantageous.

As the delegates were casting their votes to nominate him for president, Nixon invited Walter Judd to his suite at the Blackstone Hotel. He had to choose, he said, between Lodge and Judd. The congressman replied that he would have accepted the position, but he assumed that Nixon had already decided on Lodge because the ambassador was said to be writing his acceptance speech. Nixon then asked Judd to nominate Lodge, and Judd graciously accepted.[40]

Just after midnight, Nixon called a meeting of some three dozen Republican politicians. Richard Kleindienst was invited to the gathering as the chairman of the Arizona Republican Party. In his book *Justice*, Kleindienst remembered that the vice president told the group that his decision on a running mate came down to three individuals: Morton, Lodge, and Judd, but that Judd had asked that his name be withdrawn because of his poor health.

That left Morton and Lodge. Illinois Governor William Stratton led off the discussion by advocating Morton, with support from several others. After they finished, former New York governor and two-time GOP presidential nominee Thomas Dewey spoke for Lodge, arguing that he had greater public exposure than Morton. Archconservative John Bricker, a former senator from Ohio who had been Dewey's running mate in 1944, said that even though he seldom agreed with the governor, this time he did. Bricker did not mention that he and Lodge had been warm friends for years. The group agreed that Morton was the favorite of the party politicians, while Lodge had national popularity. When the vice president asked for a vote, the assemblage answered that the decision was his. He chose Lodge.[41]

Nixon announced his choice to reporters at 2:30 a.m. Central time. Only then did he telephone Lodge with the offer, which he accepted. By 5:00 p.m. Eastern time, Lodge and his wife had reached New York International Airport, better known as Idlewild, in Queens, held a press conference, and boarded a jet for Chicago. The plane landed at O'Hare around 6:15. The entire Massachusetts delegation greeted him, as did a sudden downpour, and both accompanied him to his suite at the Palmer House in downtown Chicago.[42]

Lodge arrived at the Union Stockyards Amphitheatre just in time for his name to be placed in nomination. Congressman Judd spent the first part of his nomination speech praising Nixon, who had "met every situation with extraordinary competence, skill and success." As for Lodge, Judd started with his accomplishments, noting that as a tank commander in Africa during World War II, he had won a Bronze Star for bravery. He continued fighting through France and Germany, returned to the United States, was returned to the Senate, and then became American ambassador to the United Nations. Eight Republicans, including Congressman Ford, gave seconding speeches.[43]

In his acceptance speech, Lodge thanked the assemblage for the honor it had conferred upon him. He promised to "give the campaign everything I've got," warned of the communist menace and predicted that the United States would triumph, saluted Eisenhower for keeping the nation safe and free from Americans fighting abroad, and paid tribute to Nixon as "a man you like, you feel warmly about him." Americans needed to be well educated, the elderly had to be cared for, farmers should have a decent standard of living, and civil rights advances were an imperative. He never mentioned the opposition.[44]

Rockefeller then came to the podium for a seven-minute speech to introduce the vice president. First he praised Ike, and then he stated that while both national parties fought for freedom and against totalitarianism, the GOP principle of free enterprise was far superior to the big government advanced by the opposition. He ended his address by describing Nixon as "a man of experience, . . . a man of courage, . . . a man of vision and of judgment" who would unite the nation. He ended his speech dramatically with the candidate's name: "Richard E. Nixon!"[45]

Some delegates gasped and others shouted "No!" The band started playing, anticipating Nixon's entrance; the demonstration began; the flop was dismissed. The governor did not make this slip on purpose. He had dyslexia, a reading impairment that he kept secret.[46]

Nixon had been writing his speech for two weeks, and thinking about it for considerably longer. He wrote Charles Percy in May: "There is nothing more deadly than a formal speech on television in my opinion and I intend to avoid them whenever possible." He had studied the speeches of other presidents as a guideline and had composed several drafts at Camp David without help from

speechwriters. He planned to deliver the address "with very little if any reference to the text." He also had some elements planned as early as April 19, such as
"visiting all 50 states." Several days before the convention opened, Nixon had a
telephone conversation with Herter, who had succeeded the terminally ill John
Foster Dulles as secretary of state. Herter recorded: "Kennedy had been pretty
rough personally" on Nixon, and he would try "not to be personally tough on
Kennedy."[47]

The speech, which took forty-eight minutes to deliver, was the most watched
event of the convention. It began with praise for Americans in general and the
Republican Party in particular. While Rockefeller and Goldwater had displayed
unity, the Democrats had shown they were fragmented. Nixon pledged to work
to benefit all segments of society. He would emphasize what was right with the
United States and not concentrate on its shortcomings. He would provide leadership.[48]

Kennedy's call for bold, young leaders was appealing, but Nixon countered
that the maturity of Charles de Gaulle, Harold Macmillan, and Konrad Adenauer deserved praise. Kennedy, by contrast, had "made the rash and impulsive
suggestion that President Eisenhower could have apologized or sent regrets to
Mr. Khrushchev for the U-2 flights, which the President had ordered to save our
country from surprise attack."[49]

The assemblage interrupted the address sixty-five times with applause, which
on two occasions lasted more than a minute. The first came when Nixon said the
United States had to challenge the Soviet propaganda claims: "When Mr. Khrushchev says our grandchildren will live under Communism, let us say his grandchildren will live in freedom." The second came just before the end, when the
vice president referred to a comment by Abraham Lincoln during the Civil War.
Someone asked Lincoln whether he believed "God was on his side. His answer
was: 'My concern is not whether God is on our side, but whether we are on God's
side.'" With that, he accepted his party's presidential nomination.[50]

Nixon considered this address the best he ever made. Others called it "great,"
"a classic," "magnificent." Ike congratulated the Nixon-Lodge ticket: "Your combined wisdom and knowledge of the affairs of government, both at home and
abroad, will be a telling factor in the campaign that lies ahead." The president
was confident that Republicans, "a large majority of the independent voters,"
and "a great many discerning Democrats," would "insure victory at the polls."[51]

The race was on.

10

MENDING FENCES

With the nomination secured, John Kennedy expected to use the second half of July and all of August preparing for the race, which would begin in earnest around Labor Day. Even though he had promised Jackie he would take a week's vacation at the family's summer home in Hyannis Port, he rested for only two days before getting back to what he did best: winning an election. He had won three consecutive House races beginning in 1946, defeated the popular incumbent Henry Cabot Lodge, Jr., for the Senate in 1952, and been reelected six years later with the highest vote total of any senator in Massachusetts history. In every case he had successfully united Massachusetts Democrats for the general election. Now he had to unite a far more fractious party across the whole country.

On July 21, he announced that he would begin traveling the country around September 1, visiting "as many States as time will allow" in every section of the country. He would start in Hawaii and Alaska because they were "symbols of the New Frontier." Alaska, newly admitted as the forty-ninth state, personified "a pioneer spirit which we all need to recapture in these difficult times." Hawaii, the fiftieth state, represented "peoples of many races and national origins living and working together in peace and harmony." It was also "a bridge to Asia."[1]

A week later he held a press conference at Hyannis Port, predicting "a hard-fought campaign" in which the main issue was "which candidate, which party understands the sixties and the problems we are going to face, which is ready to move forward, and which wants to stand still?" Just as Eisenhower, eight years earlier, had run as the candidate of change, Kennedy now advertised that it was time to get the nation moving again.

Like all Democratic campaigns of that era, Kennedy's appealed to Roosevelt's New Deal coalition. Early in August, United Auto Workers president Walter

Reuther enthusiastically backed JFK, and toward the end of the month, the AFL-CIO gave its "full and unstinting" endorsement. The candidate reached out to Jewish voters during the High Holy Days of Rosh Hashanah and Yom Kippur. The campaign also established a civil rights division, announcing through a press release that African Americans would "be integrated on a functional basis in all parts of the campaign."[2]

Throughout August, the candidate vigorously attacked Secretary Benson's failed agricultural programs. He called "the decline in farm income the nation's prime domestic problem" and continually tied Nixon to "the Benson farm program which he helped to write."[3]

Kennedy discussed issues in broad terms. Both parties, he said, were for strengthening the armed forces, providing greater economic security for Americans, and improving the slumping farming sector; but the Democrats would do a much better job. He was dissatisfied with American military power in comparison with that of the USSR or the People's Republic of China. While the United States was currently equal to its adversaries, he warned, it risked falling behind in the future. If America did not take "immediate action," the communist nations would soon be stronger than the United States.[4]

The nominee focused his attention far more on foreign policy than on domestic problems. He was an avid cold warrior who viewed the Soviet Union as America's principal threat, and his positions rested on this premise. After his nomination, he received unexpected help from President Eisenhower, who ordered CIA director Allen Dulles to give the Democratic ticket an intelligence briefing. Dulles met with Kennedy on July 23 at Hyannis Port and five days later with Johnson at his Texas ranch. The two briefings covered the same material: Chinese and Soviet military actions; the capabilities of Soviet missiles and long-range bombers; nuclear testing; and the RB-47 episode, in which Soviet planes had shot down an American plane. Kennedy and Johnson were especially concerned with Berlin, Cuba, and the Congo, because these subjects might arise during the campaign.

Kennedy asked about Soviet missile development, and Dulles suggested he discuss the issue with the defense and state departments but added that he would talk to the president when the National Security Council met on July 25. The candidate also asked about the possibility that China might soon attack the offshore islands in the Taiwan Straits, and the status of negotiations on the nuclear test conference. He asked to have another briefing after he returned to Washington but left the time undetermined. On several other occasions Dulles confidentially gave the candidate synopses of foreign broadcasts and comments on both national tickets.[5]

Kennedy consulted many other foreign policy experts throughout the campaign, but in his speeches, he generally presented his own views. Speaking to the Veterans of Foreign Wars convention toward the end of August, he warned that American "security and leadership are both slipping away from us—that the balance of world power is slowly shifting to the Soviet–Red Chinese bloc." The Castro regime in Cuba was moving into the communist orbit, and there were many other threats in Latin America, Africa, and Asia. The United States needed "a defense second to none." The basis of that defense included the economy, a response to the *Sputnik* challenge, and better science education in the public schools. He wanted the American model to be "Always First."[6]

JFK had left the Democratic convention still needing to solidify his party behind him. He solicited Chester Bowles's support because he needed liberal backing. Ted Sorensen told Bowles that he would be appointed secretary of state if he came out for JFK before the convention. Two days after the convention, Bowles met with the candidate and found him noncommittal over the appointment. The two met again at the start of August. They agreed on the need to "freshen up" and change the Eisenhower administration's "warmed over" global initiatives, which had "failed." A week later, Kennedy announced that Bowles's assistance would be "invaluable" during the campaign. Bowles, however, worried that Kennedy was ambivalent toward the promised cabinet position and commented that the nominee's staff was "suspicious of outsiders and anxious to keep them at arm's length." However much the Kennedys needed liberal support, Bowles was never considered a loyalist and never included in the campaign's inner circle.[7]

Kennedy also worked to mend fences with his primary opponents. At the convention, Humphrey had applauded the party's planks on civil rights and medical insurance for the elderly, both of which he had championed, but he did not encourage Minnesota delegates to vote for Kennedy's nomination. He did, however, vigorously support Johnson as Kennedy's running mate. During the campaign, Humphrey worked diligently to see that the Democratic Party won Minnesota.[8]

Symington, who already had a cordial relationship with Kennedy and agreed on the need for a large increase in military spending, readily cooperated. He accepted without rancor Kennedy's decision to withdraw his offer of the vice presidency. During the first week of August, he visited Kennedy, who announced that his friend would study how to strengthen the defense department.[9]

The bigger fish required more work. Adlai Stevenson had recognized the inevitable at the convention and agreed to introduce the nominee. Forgotten were the Kennedy staff's pressure for an endorsement and Stevenson's refusal to succumb to lobbying. In his nominating speech, the former candidate praised JFK's strengths: "He is a man brave and strong in his own right. He is a man who embodies the hopes of the generation, which is rising to power in the world. He is a man whose passion for peace was bred in the agony of war." That address helped ease the friction, but JFK knew he had yet to secure Stevenson's "active" and "vigorous support." Stevenson was still the leader of the Democrats' liberal wing, and many of his followers refused to back Kennedy.[10]

On July 31, the two men met at Hyannis Port. Stevenson found the talks "agreeable, their mood optimistic & efficiency high." Kennedy asked the former governor to campaign far more than he had anticipated. JFK especially wanted Stevenson's help in the New York race and with black and Jewish voters. He wanted to know "how to get the reform group, the independents and Stevenson people to really work for him" and "how to meet the youth and inexperience charge." After the meeting, the two leaders held a press conference in which the former governor pledged to give his enthusiastic backing to the Democratic ticket.[11]

Even though Kennedy assured the former governor that he, not Bowles, was the front-runner for secretary of state, Stevenson was skeptical. Sometimes Kennedy mentioned the appointment to him; other times he remained coy about it. In spite of this tentative commitment, Stevenson did campaign for the ticket, concentrating largely on foreign policy.[12]

Stevenson was the key to an even more iconic figure: Kennedy needed to win the backing of Eleanor Roosevelt, who had shown only mild enthusiasm for him after the convention. She believed her party governed better than the Republicans, having passed "all forward looking legislation which we have today," and she was fatalistic about current affairs. "Young men," she wrote to a Mrs. W. E. Degeest, were "taking the leadership in nation after nation, so perhaps it is better to have youth to deal with youth." In her "My Day" column on July 26, she expressed appreciation for some of Kennedy's decisions, like his forming a foreign policy advisory group led by her friend the former New York governor Averell Harriman. Harriman would campaign to win that state and so would she. Democrats needed to take over the White House because America needed "new and imaginative thinking." The United States looked forward to change, and she hoped "youth and wisdom will be combined."[13]

Despite this praise, Mrs. Roosevelt remained uncertain about the candidate. On August 11, she wrote Stevenson that the presidential nominee would have difficulty winning California and New York, and added: "I wish people who meet him didn't feel he is such a cold & calculating person." She invited Kennedy to Hyde Park three days later; they met at her Val-Kill cottage on the twenty-fifth anniversary of the signing of the Social Security Act. In his speech that day,

Kennedy applauded the former first lady as "a true teacher . . . [whose] very life teaches a love of truth and duty and courage." He continued by praising her husband for passing the Social Security legislation and then turned to his own plans: providing better medical care for the elderly, broadening Social Security benefits, and expanding housing and employment opportunities for the aged.[14]

Then the nominee and Mrs. Roosevelt had a private lunch. She asked for his assurance that he and Stevenson had similar philosophies and that Adlai was at least under consideration for secretary of state. With Kennedy's answers, Eleanor's perception of him markedly improved. Once he pledged to work closely with Stevenson, he became for her "a man who could learn. I liked him better than I ever had before because he seemed so little cock-sure, and I think he has a mind that is open to new ideas." She thought many of his actions were driven by political ambition but hoped he was "interested in helping the people of his own country and mankind in general." She believed he would mature with time and felt "he would make a good President if elected."[15]

Having decided to back him, Mrs. Roosevelt agreed to serve as the cochair of the New York State Citizens Committee for Kennedy. In her "My Day" column on August 17, she described JFK as "a likeable man with charm" who would be a fine president. In the same column five days later, she wrote that he had "an outstanding record for voting right on questions that involve the well-being of the people of our country as a whole."[16]

There was one last hurdle. Former president Truman had promoted Symington for the presidency and stated that Kennedy was too young and inexperienced for the White House. When Truman realized his candidate had no chance at the nomination, he boycotted the convention, claiming that the Kennedys had rigged it. Coaxing Truman onto Kennedy's side required intercession by allies. First, Johnson had lunch with him and asked him to support the ticket. Connecticut Governor Abraham Ribicoff, an old friend of the president and a close Kennedy ally, phoned him and persuaded him to campaign for JFK because the country needed a Democratic president.[17]

Kennedy held a news conference on August 2 on the lawn of his Hyannis Port home to announce that he had talked with Truman and that he would make the pilgrimage to Independence, Missouri. On August 20, Truman greeted him on the steps leading up to his library. They talked privately before going to the auditorium, where three dozen reporters were waiting. The former president dominated the gathering, promising to campaign across the nation. He had not had a "give 'em hell style" during his 1948 presidential race. Republicans made up that nickname, he said, because he told the truth. He declared he would "continue to tell the truth, and they will still think it is hell." The presidential nominee asked Truman to support him by campaigning in Missouri, which he proclaimed Democrats would overwhelmingly win. Truman would also campaign in New York, concentrating on foreign affairs, agriculture, and economic policy.[18]

Kennedy also had to be assured of his running mate's commitment to a sign of unity. After the convention, Johnson was aware of many southerners' negative feelings about his appearance on the Democratic ticket, given the platform's strong civil rights plank. In a speech in Cheyenne, Wyoming, on July 26, Johnson charged that the Republican Party's liberal and conservative factions were hopelessly split, but he made no mention of the growing split in his own party.[19]

Johnson traveled with his wife, Lady Bird, to Hyannis Port to meet with Jack and Jackie on July 30, their first meeting since the convention. They opened their press conference by calling for party harmony, and then discussed the legislative items for the upcoming congressional session: at the top of the list were medical care for the elderly, housing, aid to education, and a federal minimum wage.[20]

James Rowe, who had directed Johnson's convention effort, visited Jack and Bobby Kennedy at Hyannis Port in mid-August. After that meeting, he wrote Johnson that the Kennedys wanted him to serve as a liaison between themselves and Johnson because they were not well acquainted with Texas politics. Rowe worried that the Kennedys might try to interfere with the Johnson campaign, and he warned that John Connally, who was working for LBJ, had to be as tough as Bobby Kennedy and know how to "handle" him. The Kennedys pressured Rowe to accept the strategy that JFK should confine his campaign "almost exclusively" to the industrial states, while Johnson should concentrate on the South, Midwest, and West. Rowe, worried that Connally would stack Johnson's whole organization with Texans, recommended to LBJ that he needed advisers from the North and West. When campaigning outside the South, Rowe suggested, "you might well have a Negro traveling with you." His concerns about Kennedy interference in Johnson's activities proved unfounded.[21]

The candidates would run largely separate campaigns, and each would hedge his bets. To protect himself against defeat, LBJ persuaded the Texas legislature to pass a bill allowing him to appear twice on the Texas ballot: as the Democratic vice presidential candidate and as a candidate for reelection to the Senate. Kennedy guarded against any damage Johnson might do in the South by bringing Florida Senator George Smathers into the campaign. He announced on August 19 that his friend would become the assistant DNC chairman, in charge of the eleven southern and border states, plus Texas and Oklahoma.[22]

Johnson was probably unaware that FBI director J. Edgar Hoover had in his inner office an Official and Confidential file on him that dated back to October 1956. Its subjects included voting irregularities in Laredo, Texas, during LBJ's

1954 reelection campaign, as well as reports concerning Lady Bird Johnson's ownership of the KTBC radio station in Austin, as well as television stations in Waco and Weslaco. In the spring of 1958, the FBI received complaints that Johnson had violated Texas election laws in past elections. None of these questions received an extensive FBI examination. Hoover had to be circumspect with the Johnsons. LBJ had power as Senate majority leader and could cause difficulties for the FBI.[23]

At the center of the campaign, of course, were the Kennedys themselves. The media presented Jackie as young, attractive and fashionable, shy and quiet. The photographic images of the happy couple were for public consumption. Jackie knew that her husband, like her father and father-in-law, was a serial adulterer. After the 1960 election, Drew Pearson wrote in his diary that rumors had circulated that "she will get a divorce if Jack loses" and that she had been "unhappy ... for some years."[24]

Even though Joe Kennedy had to stay out of sight during the campaign, on September 12, 1960, *Newsweek* featured the patriarch on its cover, with a five-page article entitled "The Mystery of Joe Kennedy" that emphasized his positive traits as a husband and father, his net worth of some $400 million, and his many charitable contributions. It noted that he had been charged with being a Hitler appeaser and an anti-Semite while serving as ambassador to Great Britain and that he had broken with FDR during the 1940 presidential election. As was customary at the time, it did not mention his notorious adultery. At an earlier press conference, a reporter asked JFK whether his father had removed himself from the campaign because he was too "controversial." The candidate answered: his father was "not going to participate actively in the campaign. . . . But I will be talking to him, frequently." That was his last comment on the subject.[25]

After the convention, Arthur Schlesinger grew closer to the candidate, writing him that he deserved to win because he was "a man of first-rate intelligence, authority and decision." The historian also called the choice of LBJ as running mate "a wise and brave move." Early in August, Schlesinger drove to Hyannis Port to see Jack and Jackie. To the historian, Jack "was warm, funny, quick, intelligent and spontaneous." Later that month, Schlesinger went to a national board meeting of the Americans for Democratic Action, with almost sixty people attending, and tried to gin up enthusiasm for his candidate. Most were hostile to Kennedy but would still support him.[26]

In late August, thinking the campaign was off to a slow start, Schlesinger urged Kennedy to get "liberals, the reformers, the intellectuals" involved. The selection of Johnson as vice president had dampened the momentum. "The kinetic people were set back and put off a bit." Even though they favored the Democratic ticket, they were not crusading. Kennedy had to emphasize his credentials: "You should take a strong liberal line from now on." Republicans controlled the press, he argued, and "to develop enthusiasm we have no choice but to give the enthusiasts something to believe in."[27]

The journalist Eric Sevareid had published a column early in 1960 claiming there was no real difference between Kennedy and Nixon. Kennedy, angry about this thesis, had encouraged Schlesinger to write a book about the differences between the two candidates. He finished the manuscript in a few months, and *Kennedy or Nixon: Does It Make Any Difference?* reached bookstores at the start of September. It was an immediate best-seller. Kennedy was a positive force, the book argued, while Nixon was the opposite.[28]

The Harvard economist John Kenneth Galbraith also counseled JFK. A prolific author, Galbraith advocated greater federal control over the economy and objected to the Eisenhower administration's call for less of it. He encouraged others to join the Kennedy camp and made recommendations on how to conduct the campaign. Toward the end of July, Galbraith wrote Jack that "Nixon's claim to vast experience in a period of trouble and peril is going to be one of our most difficult and perhaps our most difficult issue." JFK should highlight Nixon's scant diplomatic experience, he suggested, by contrasting the vice president's few moments with Khrushchev at the Kitchen Debate in Moscow with his own years of service on the Senate Foreign Relations Committee.[29]

While both sides were preparing for the campaign, Democrats concentrated on a special session of Congress, where they had large majorities, in early August. The Senate would convene at noon on August 8 and the House a week later. When the Senate opened, Nixon appeared at the rostrum; Kennedy entered the chamber shortly before noon and conferred with Johnson, who, as majority leader, decided which bills to bring up for votes. Here, Johnson was in charge and Kennedy was subordinate to him; their positions would be reversed in six months.[30]

Eisenhower overshadowed the Democratic agenda by presenting a special message to Congress containing more than twenty proposals he wanted it to consider. Republicans offered a civil rights bill, which Democrats united to crush. *New York Times* reporter Tom Wicker wrote that LBJ demonstrated "that he was ready to use abrupt and ruthless parliamentary tactics to achieve the ends of the Democratic party." Kennedy, who had pledged to implement his party's civil rights plank, did not promote any of this legislation.[31]

Kennedy and Johnson had certain priorities. One was medical care for the elderly. JFK proposed to tie the program to Social Security so that it would be adequately financed. During the session he presented an amendment to the Social Security legislation that would extend medical insurance to nine million elderly citizens. He also sponsored a bill to raise the federal minimum wage from $1 an hour to $1.25. Even though the Senate overwhelmingly passed it by a vote of 62–34, it failed in the House. None of the major bills that Kennedy had energetically pushed were enacted into law.[32]

The GOP, seeking to damage the Democratic ticket, labeled it the "do-little" session. After Congress adjourned, *Time* magazine summarized the results. "Candidate Kennedy's defeat marked the collapse of the high political hopes he had brought to Washington two weeks earlier: hopes of getting through Congress a parcel of New Frontier welfare measures that would pay off in votes in November." As the session was drawing to an end, former secretary of state Acheson wrote to Truman that Johnson was "not nearly as smart as he and [a] lot [of] his admirers think."[33]

Kennedy's ambitious proposals were out of character. During his fourteen years in Congress he had energetically pushed only a single labor bill and had not had his name on any major piece of legislation. In an oral history in June 1963, Johnson described JFK as "pathetic as a Congressman and as a Senator. He didn't know how to address the chair." Many congressional colleagues agreed.[34]

Neither the failure of the special session nor his unproductive legislative record seriously hurt JFK's campaign. Democrats were united on one overriding principle: to see that Richard Nixon did not win the presidency. Stevenson, Eleanor Roosevelt, and Truman led the attack on him as unfit to hold office.

Stevenson passionately detested Nixon and regularly commented on how awful he was. In the middle of January 1960, he wrote: "People just don't like him or trust him—for good and obvious reasons." Stevenson could not understand "that a man with his background of slander, abuse, innuendo, expediency and resort to all the most devious political devices should ever occupy an office which we have tried for generations to exalt in the esteem of young people and the world."[35]

Truman had declared, even before he reconciled with Kennedy, that he would vote for the Democratic ticket and "not vote for Nixon." After meeting with Kennedy, he added: "Nixon is impossible."[36]

Eleanor Roosevelt was equally vehement. Before the Democratic convention, she predicted: "If Mr. Nixon is nominated on the Republican ticket you can look for a tough and unscrupulous campaign."[37]

While Democrats attacked Nixon for his shortcomings, Kennedy had serious problems hidden from view. Kennedy suffered from a multitude of undisclosed physical problems, including venereal disease and often excruciating episodes of back pain. One of his speechwriters during the campaign, John Bartlow Martin, wrote of seeing the senator in his hotel room in Baltimore "stretched out flat on his bed, his face grimacing in pain from his back, his eyes glazed."[38]

Kennedy also presented himself as a devoted husband, but throughout his marriage, he had repeated sexual encounters with other women. In 1955, he spent a week in Sweden having sex with an aristocrat named Gunilla von Post, and during his presidential campaign he slept with Judith Campbell.[39]

The Kennedys probably were unaware that FBI director Hoover had extensive Official and Confidential files on Joseph, Jack, and Bobby. One of the FBI's deputy directors, Cartha DeLoach, commented in his memoir that the JFK file shocked the director, who had a cordial friendship with the patriarch "and probably did not want to be responsible for a report that would damage the political career of old Joe's promising son." DeLoach also was aware of five other files on JFK "involving sexual misconduct."[40]

On July 13, the day of JFK's presidential nomination, Hoover received a nine-page memorandum detailing the bureau's association with Joseph, Jack, and Bobby Kennedy. The summary concluded that the FBI had "enjoyed friendly relations with Senator Kennedy and his family" since World War II.

In their occasional correspondence, Hoover addressed the father, who had been a special service contact for the FBI office in Boston, as "Dear Joe." The elder Kennedy was also on a first-name basis with Special Agent David Murphy, Jr., of the Washington, D.C., office, and with Special Agent William Carpenter, resident agent at Hyannis, Massachusetts, who had attended Jackie and Jack's wedding in 1953.

Hoover had sent Joe, Jack, and Bobby autographed copies of his book *Masters of Deceit*, as well as *The FBI Story*, for which he had written a foreword. He had talked to Bobby several times while Bobby served as chief counsel to the McClellan Committee. In his book *The Enemy Within*, Bobby praised Hoover for giving "absolutely invaluable" advice to the committee.

The FBI file on Jack, though mostly concerned with "allegations of immoral activities," meaning his sex life, also contained some positive material. The director had written him in November 1954 wishing him a speedy recovery from back surgery, congratulated him in 1956 for winning the Cardinal Gibbons Medal, and congratulated him again on his reelection to the Senate two years later. Some of the file came from material that may or may not be reliable, including allegations of "hoodlum connections" that were largely "unsubstantiated." So that mob bosses could gain access to JFK, Frank Sinatra had been cultivating Jack's brother-in-law Peter Lawford when he worked on Jack's 1958 reelection campaign.

The "allegations of immoral activities" in the file started in World War II, including his relationship with Danish journalist Inga Arvad, who was married at the time. Other reports alleged that Kennedy had been "compromised" with a woman in Las Vegas and that he and Sinatra had orgies in Palm Springs, Las Vegas, and New York City. *Confidential* magazine intended to hire someone to spy on JFK's hotel room at the Democratic convention to get "dirt" on JFK to use before the election.[41]

While some in the media knew about JFK's sexual promiscuity, they never exposed it. The press at this time generally refrained from this type of reporting, which was considered sensationalist. Instead, reporters and columnists concentrated on Kennedy's youth, his smile, his political acumen, how his family members all pitched in on the campaign, and how efficiently his organization had operated to win the nomination.[42]

After the Democratic convention, the theologian Reinhold Niebuhr, who taught at the Union Theological Seminary in New York City, wrote disapprovingly to Schlesinger about the "thinness" of Kennedy's religious beliefs and personal morality. Union President Henry Van Dusen also wrote Schlesinger about widespread rumors of JFK's extramarital affairs in Britain. If the rumors were accurate, his "dubious morals" made him unfit for the presidency. Niebuhr had told Van Dusen that Kennedy would sleep with anyone.

The historian sent Van Dusen's letter to Stevenson, along with a cover note asserting that the gossip was exaggerated and that he had heard similar tales about FDR, Truman, and Stevenson himself. He believed JFK's philandering episodes had all occurred before 1955, and he had "heard no reliable account of any such incident in recent years." The stories Van Dusen was circulating were "out of date" and "largely unsubstantiated." Anyway, even if JFK was a womanizer, Schlesinger did "not see how they bear essentially on Kennedy's capacity to be President," especially given that Nixon was the alternative.[43]

None of this reached the media. Americans read adoring newspaper articles about Jackie and Jack's lifestyle and saw photographs of an attractive couple with a small child. Kennedy was presented as an experienced politician who had successfully united the Democratic Party and would lead the country toward a New Frontier.

Kennedy highlighted his public life and concealed his private one. His family and loyalists promoted this image and hid the realities concerning his health and his promiscuity. Those who knew about these liabilities, including reporters, maintained the fiction as was the tradition at that time, and his physical infirmities and reckless adultery remained concealed long after his assassination.

The period from the end of the Democratic convention until the beginning of

September was, for Kennedy, a time of gathering his allies for battle. He needed both Bowles and Stevenson to help ensure liberal support. He never trusted them, but he solicited their cooperation. Schlesinger, Galbraith, and other intellectuals had twice supported Stevenson for the presidency and switched to Kennedy. They did not penetrate the inner circle either. Eleanor Roosevelt and Harry Truman had championed others for the nomination and belittled Kennedy, but as loyal Democratic partisans, after the convention they endorsed the standard bearer.

Lyndon Johnson had finished in second place for the presidential nomination. The Kennedy and Johnson staffs had each fought for their candidate, and each side harbored animosity toward the other. This conflict evaporated once the nominees were joined on a single ticket. It would reemerge later, but not in 1960. During the campaign, they minimized friction by letting each side run its own contest.

Kennedy entered September having assembled a team pulling in the same direction. Trust rested first with his family and next in his loyalists. Others were not expected to reach that status. He had their endorsements. That was enough.

11

UNITING REPUBLICANS

The Republicans were less fractious than their opponents. The vice president left Chicago having dominated the convention and with a platform that the delegates generally agreed upon. Rockefeller and Goldwater, who led the party's liberal and conservative factions, had both pledged their allegiance to the ticket.[1]

To maintain his momentum, Nixon held a news conference the day after the convention, July 29. The race had begun, and he would not take a vacation until after election day. He had entered the contest, he said, as the "underdog. . . . Anyone running on the Republican ticket would have a hole in his head unless he said that he was starting behind." Even if he won the presidency, he would almost certainly face a Democratic Congress.

The vice president answered questions about other issues, and the mood once again relaxed. He saw "national security" as the first priority, and he would not increase taxes unless for national defense. He was ambitious to stop the "great erosion" of Republican strength in the Midwest. The next day he met with midwestern Republican congressmen and farm delegates to hear their views on agricultural policy.[2]

He was ambivalent about his running mate. Sixteen years after the election, Nixon reflected that choosing Lodge had been a mistake. He had favored Thruston Morton, but Lodge's foreign policy views were closer to Nixon's own. Lodge was far more liberal on domestic issues, however, and in hindsight, Nixon believed he had not run an energetic campaign.

Eisenhower unequivocally preferred Lodge, and that, for Nixon, was the deciding factor. Lodge had been the United States ambassador to the United Nations since 1953. Because television routinely carried UN debates that showcased the ambassador defending America against Soviet criticism, he had gained widespread national exposure. Lodge was also strongly committed to civil rights and would help in winning black voters.[3]

At the news conference, the vice president announced that Lodge would remain at the UN until mid-August. Before Lodge received the vice presidential nomination, Ike had asked him to try to reopen the Geneva talks that the Soviets had walked out of in June. The ambassador agreed, even though a breakthrough was unlikely. In a letter to the *St. Louis Post-Dispatch*, he wrote that "it would be inappropriate for me to make political speeches" while he was UN ambassador. He had never done that during his tenure and would not start now. "It would be selfish and irresponsible for me to leave before this unfinished business has been finished."[4]

Lodge appeared before the disarmament commission on August 16 and the following day sent his resignation letter, effective September 3, to the president, who accepted it with "deep regret." Before Lodge left the UN, Rowland Evans, Jr., wrote about how he was perceived. On television, Evans wrote, he was always the one coolly provoking Russian anger: "Whenever he says 'hot' there is the Russian shouting 'cold'; whenever he wags a finger, there is a Russian shaking a fist." When the Gallup Poll asked voters for "enthusiasm quotients" for Nixon and Kennedy, the former received a score of 43 and the latter 42. When the same question was posed for Lodge and Johnson, their respective scores were 45 and 30. Gallup concluded that Lodge added more to the Republican ticket than Johnson to the Democratic.[5]

Cliff Roberts, a member of Eisenhower's "Augusta gang," a group of wealthy acquaintances who played golf with him in Augusta, Georgia, recalled: "Behind the scenes Ike was doing everything that he could to help Nixon." In a meeting with the president after his return to Newport, Nixon and Lodge asked him not to campaign in the early stages. They wanted to save him for the closing days.[6]

Ike was fully committed to the Nixon-Lodge ticket, a combination he had favored since the beginning of 1960. He had worked closely with both men and believed his legacy was central to a Republican triumph in 1960. Shortly after the convention, he wrote to HEW Secretary Arthur Flemming that he told the delegates "of the necessity for continuing the policies and programs for which the Republican Party stands"—by which he meant his own policies and programs.[7]

Eisenhower had a low opinion of the political opposition, especially Stevenson. After listening to his acceptance speech at the 1956 Democratic convention, Ike declared: "I think he's a bigger faker than all the rest of them." Cliff Roberts, in his oral history, commented that Ike saw Stevenson as "a pretty little fellow, not too much depth."[8]

The necessity of a Republican victory became even more urgent in Ike's eyes after the Kennedy-Johnson team was chosen. Milton Eisenhower, the president's youngest brother and his closest White House adviser, remembered that Kennedy's nomination surprised most of the White House staff. According to Cliff Roberts, the president had had limited contact with Kennedy but viewed him as "a weak-minded youngster . . . that had no particular ability, leadership ability, and we were probably in for tough times." If the Democratic ticket won, it would mean excessive federal spending. Ellis Slater, another Augusta gang member, quoted Ike as saying that "if Kennedy gets in we will never get them out—that there will be a machine bigger than Tammany Hall ever was—the size of the Kennedy family alone means this to a degree." At an October 11 meeting, the president's science adviser, George Kistiakowsky, noted Eisenhower's belief "that the Democratic candidates either talk nonsense or lie." He launched into an extended discourse "on how incompetent Kennedy is compared to Nixon, that even the more thoughtful Democrats are horrified by his selection."[9]

Ike felt no better about Lyndon Johnson, who had been Senate majority leader for almost six years, meaning that Ike had to work with him to get legislation passed. The president at a breakfast meeting in October repeated his negative opinion of LBJ: he was "the most tricky and unreliable politician in Congress."[10]

Eisenhower's primary focus that summer was on foreign affairs. Relations with Cuba had worsened as Castro drew closer to the Soviet Union. Belgium had granted independence to the Congo, leading to an immediate civil war, with the communists supporting the first prime minister, Patrice Lumumba, and the United States favoring his opposition. The United States was demanding the bodies of the dead airmen and the return of two survivors from the RB-47 shot down by the Soviets over the Barents Sea, but the Russians refused to comply. Ike faced the issues of resolving the partition of Berlin, emerging problems in Southeast Asia and China, and an ongoing conflict in the Middle East.

Influential Republicans took encouragement from Ike's enthusiasm for the Nixon-Lodge ticket. Goldwater, despite his dismay over the "American Munich" agreement between Nixon and Rockefeller just before the convention, had given a speech in support of Nixon's candidacy that was a high point of the convention and the starting point of his own quest for the presidency four years later. During the campaign he would give 125 speeches in twenty-six states for Nixon-Lodge; afterward, he wrote that Nixon "lost, but the conservatives won." Many Goldwater speeches consisted of an attack on Kennedy's "socialistic" plans. "To win the elections of 1960," he told audiences, "the Republicans must once again proclaim their devotion to a limited government which is the servant and not the master of the people." This was a struggle of free enterprise against government interference in private lives.[11]

Rockefeller also joined the bandwagon. In the first week of August he announced plans to elect Republicans nationwide. The vice president had made New York a priority, and the governor opened the campaign headquarters there to support the ticket. On the fourth of the month he flew upstate to campaign. The Nixon-Rockefeller relationship was complex, but, as *Newsweek* reported, one overriding reality was paramount: "Nixon must take New York to become President. Rockefeller must hold New York to survive." Toward the end of the month, Nixon told his staff they must "keep a constant line of communication open with Rockefeller and his people." He wanted his principal campaign advisers to call the governor "personally from time to time."[12]

Nixon wrote that the reelection campaign for his friend Jerry Ford's Michigan congressional seat had "the earmarks of being one of the most rigorous in modern political history." Ford had been a dark horse candidate for the vice presidential nomination, and even though he was not chosen, he gave a seconding speech for Lodge. After the convention, Ford and Nebraska Senator Roman Hruska became cochairs of the RNC Speakers' Bureau, which helped arrange appearances, make media contacts, and act as a clearinghouse for speakers.[13]

While leaving the campaign administration to the professional politicians, Nixon concentrated on Democrats trying to link Nixon to Agriculture Secretary Benson wherever possible, because of the administration's unpopular policies on price supports and federal assistance for the sale of farm surpluses. Many in the farm belt called for Benson's resignation.

After the convention, Benson wrote the vice president that voters had a clear choice "between the economic monstrosity which the Democrats call their agricultural plank, and the sound, broad, forward-looking plank which was adopted in Chicago." Those who loudly opposed Ike's agricultural programs had made Benson "a scapegoat which, to some extent, limits my help to you." He nonetheless offered his assistance to the campaign.[14]

Senator Morton had been unanimously reelected RNC chairman at the convention. On August 8, he announced that John "Cliff" Folger would serve as chairman of the national finance committee. Two months earlier, Leonard Hall had telephoned Folger, who was United States ambassador to Belgium from 1957 to 1959 and a wealthy investment broker, asking him to act as Nixon's chief fundraiser. He replied: "If it's money you need, . . . I'll shake the trees and see what comes down."[15]

Pat Nixon fully supported and fiercely defended her husband, but she was a very private person who did not enjoy campaigning. She stood by her husband's side through most of the contest, shook hands with voters, and cooperated in photographic opportunities. She generally did not make speeches.[16]

Arthur Burns, who had been chairman of the Council of Economic Advisers during Eisenhower's first term, was Nixon's closest economics adviser. He agreed with Nixon on encouraging economic growth through investment and capital improvements rather than consumer spending. During the 1958 recession, they argued that tax cuts would be the best way to bring about a recovery; Ike rejected that advice and also decided against increasing federal spending.[17]

The vice president selected Len Hall, who had been the RNC chairman from 1953 to 1957 and also directed Nixon's 1956 reelection campaign, as his general campaign manager. Hall believed Nixon was "the best-prepared candidate" he had ever known.[18]

Robert Finch was appointed campaign director, reporting directly to the vice president. Senator Nixon had met him in southern California in the early 1950s and was impressed with his political skills. He had run unsuccessfully for the House of Representatives in 1952 and 1954, and then was elected Republican chairman for Los Angeles County. Nixon had brought him to the capital as an administrative assistant at the beginning of 1959 to serve as liaison with Congress and the White House. Finch wrote on August 6 to an Illinois Republican, Robert Spinell, that he was "daily more aware of the rightness of our cause. Dick Nixon must be elected—and he will be." Six days later, Finch wrote another supporter that he had no illusions about the coming battle: the Kennedy machine was the best-organized and best-financed campaign team in American history. In this race, "you can throw away the rule book."[19]

Herbert Klein had first met the candidate in 1946, as a reporter for the *Alhambra Post-Advocate* during Nixon's first congressional race. They became friends, and Nixon had employed him as a press secretary in the 1956 and 1958 campaigns. Klein left his post as an editor for the *San Diego Union* and joined the vice president's staff in the spring of 1959 as press secretary during Nixon's trip to the Soviet Union that July. He would emerge as the chief campaign spokesperson.[20]

Six years after the election, Klein compared the Nixon and Kennedy organizations. They were "similar," but "the Nixon campaign was better organized than Kennedy's in terms of timing, logistics, etc. Among the advantages Kennedy had were a great majority of the registered voters." Later, in his 1980 memoirs, Klein seems to have changed his mind. He reflected that the Nixon organization's "major weakness" was that it had three managers: the vice president, Hall, and Finch. "The result was constant overlap and confusion compounded often by the candidate frequently sending out duplicate instructions." Nixon did not delegate effectively and "managed strategy poorly."[21]

Finally, Nixon employed H. R. Haldeman, an advertising executive, to lead the advance team, whom Klein nicknamed the "frog men" because they leaped in front to make arrangements. Haldeman had worked as an advance man in the 1956 presidential campaign and now directed a nineteen-man team. Planning for their activities began in the spring of 1960, at which point Haldeman brought in his college roommate and friend John Ehrlichman as his "key assistant." Don Hughes, the vice president's appointment secretary, described the frogmen as "the finest group that could have been put together, and . . . the campaign would have been a shambles without them."[22]

The vice president wrote a constant stream of memoranda on issues requiring action. Starting in August, he suggested all-day meetings on agriculture, education, science, foreign affairs, the economy, the elderly, civil rights, urban matters, and other subjects, as a counterattack on those who claimed his organization was "poor." He asked for an analysis of the key differences between the Democratic and Republican platforms that he could use against Kennedy during the race. He tried to secure videotapes of his acceptance and other speeches for his files as well as for television usage.[23]

Nixon was "extremely anxious to develop an effective program for using retired people as campaign workers." He specifically wanted individuals who had retired from the armed forces. They tended to be conservative, were generally overlooked by employers, had executive experience, and wished to be "useful."[24]

He managed his own schedule. His department heads were instructed to get him back to the capital on the weekends whenever feasible. This would give him time with his daughters, allow him to "get fresh clothes for the next swing," and let him work on his speeches. Finally, the first two weeks of his schedule would not be released without his approval. He wanted to control "the timing for announcing it" so as to prevent the Democrats from using his appearances to plan their own.[25]

The vice president was particularly upset at "the obvious unobjectivity and unfairness of most" newspapers. Kennedy, in his acceptance speech, had personally attacked him, while Nixon, in his own address, had taken the "high road" toward his opponent. The campaign had "to do a better job of hammering home the line that . . . [the Democrats] have already started on the low road." The *Washington Post*, he complained, had used anti-Nixon journalists to attack him, and the *New York Times* columnist James Reston had insinuated that someone had written Nixon's acceptance speech for him, and he had memorized it.[26]

Nixon also insisted that Kennedy be criticized for accepting support from Alabama Governor John Patterson and others "who are anathema to the liberals on the Civil Rights issue." He must be asked at every press gathering whether or not he welcomed their backing, in the same way journalists had hounded Eisenhower about where he stood on McCarthy. Eisenhower supporters like Secretary of the Treasury Robert Anderson and HEW secretary Oveta Culp Hobby must be approached to back Nixon rather than Kennedy. The *Washington Daily News* had reported that Kennedy received a 100 percent rating from organized labor's Committee on Political Education, which had campaigned against Republicans running for political office. That story should be widely circulated to "conservative business men and others" before Kennedy began asking for their financial contributions.[27]

Kennedy was getting support from top business and education leaders and was winning over Stevenson "eggheads," African Americans, and farmers. Nixon had to solicit similar individuals before Kennedy could get their commitment.[28]

Toward the end of August, Nixon prepared a list of speakers for the campaign, with notes on their strengths and weaknesses. Congressman Walter Judd, from Minnesota, could go anywhere: "He has unusually strong appeal for educational groups, university students, religious groups and youth generally." Senator Goldwater had "tremendous appeal" and "would be extremely effective" with conservatives, especially in the South, Southwest, and Rocky Mountain states. Lodge should not go to rural areas; he would be "most effective . . . in metropolitan areas and along the seaboards." Oregon Governor Hatfield should stay on the Pacific Coast and the Rocky Mountain states, addressing youthful audiences and women voters, because he was "handsome and good-looking." Women voted "more on emotions than through logic," and this had "to be appreciated and handled accordingly." Rockefeller had to be kept away from the South and from strongly "anti-civil rights" groups and should concentrate on "New York, California and liberal states."[29]

The campaign began as soon as Nixon returned to the capital after the convention. After meeting with Eisenhower in Newport, Rhode Island, the vice president flew out to the West Coast. Before leaving, however, he responded to the Kennedy camp's charge that he was a man without beliefs. "Mr. Kennedy," he told reporters, "has started on the low road and he intends to keep on it. . . . I don't think Mr. Kennedy wants to do this. I think it is his advisers. He is doing it to satisfy the extremists in his party. I will not get into personalities as he did. I will leave the low-road business to him." Throughout the campaign, Nixon would not attack Joseph Kennedy for his anti-Semitism or for his break with FDR.[30]

Pat and Dick opened the campaign in Reno, Nevada. Jim Bassett, the vice president's scheduler, declared: "As a standing rule, Pat Nixon stays with the Vice President during his visits, except for occasional individual appearances within the town they happen to be visiting." Reno had declared August 1 Pat Nixon Day, and the vice president used the occasion to draw a sharp distinction between his and her upbringing and that of the wealthy Kennedys. Pat, he noted, was born in Nevada. Her mother had died when she was twelve, and her father five years later. She had helped raise her three brothers and had worked her way through college. When she and Dick got engaged, she helped to pay for the engagement ring because she was making more as a high school teacher than he made as a struggling lawyer. He concluded by saying she would always be his "First Lady."[31]

On August 2, the Nixons flew into Los Angeles International Airport, where the vice president tested some themes he would use throughout the race. He attacked Kennedy as a pessimist and argued that the United States was not behind the Soviet Union militarily, economically, or educationally. Defending the administration's record, he asserted that the nation led the world in all of these areas.[32]

Later, at a press conference, he criticized Secretary Benson for refusing to explore alternative solutions to farm problems. Both candidates agreed on strengthening relations with America's allies, Nixon said, but they differed over labor. The Democrat intended to weaken the Taft-Hartley Act to get union bosses' support. Nixon would not: he expected to represent labor and business equally. He would draw some labor votes, he thought, because of the Republican prosperity.[33]

Nixon returned to his hometown of Whittier that evening and spoke at Whittier College, his alma mater. Thousands lined the streets to welcome the Nixons, and fifteen thousand spectators saw him speak at Hadley Field, where as a third-stringer on the football team he had watched most games from the sidelines. He reminisced about compulsory chapel at the Quaker college and segued into his major themes. Above all, the students learned dedication to peace. He promised to keep it by maintaining the nation's military strength. He would use diplomacy, but with firmness. Racial discrimination damaged American prestige internationally and was a moral problem at home; Americans had to solve it. He repeated his pledge to campaign in all fifty states.[34]

Nixon then flew to Hawaii, becoming the first major United States official to visit the newest state. For two days, he toured the four most populated islands to tumultuous receptions. He gave speeches and held press conferences reiterating his themes on military preparedness and racial toleration, adding a partisan note that this election presented a choice between government control and free enterprise. At press conferences, he answered questions about local concerns such as interaction with Japan and nonrecognition of the People's Republic of China.

He said he favored suspending nuclear testing during negotiations with the Russians. If they did not deal honestly, the testing could resume. As for Cuba, the United States was carefully watching Fidel Castro for signs of his political direction.[35]

He arrived in the capital in time for the start of the special session of Congress on August 9. The day after it opened, Nixon and Johnson clashed when LBJ led Democrats in killing the administration's civil rights bill. Nixon angrily criticized Johnson for refusing to take it up; he responded that the civil rights bill had been tabled because the Republicans were using it to "disrupt" the Senate agenda. These tactics, said Johnson, "may get a headline, but they get no statute."[36]

The vice president supported the numerous proposals Eisenhower had offered to Congress. Nixon opposed Kennedy's minimum wage increase to $1.25 an hour and favored the president's lesser increase, to $1.10. He also rejected Kennedy's proposal for care for the aged through Social Security, which he considered socialistic, in favor of the Republican plan of voluntary insurance with federal participation. In the end, the session was a bust.[37]

With Congress in session, Nixon kept his campaign trips brief. On August 13, he went to Portland, Maine, where he expected to carry the state for the Republican ticket, and on August 17, he flew to Greensboro, North Carolina, a state Eisenhower had barely lost in 1956 and where Nixon saw a possible victory. Addressing a jam-packed War Memorial Auditorium, he repeated his major topics and then turned to civil rights. The lunch-counter sit-in movement had begun in Greensboro. When he declared his support for its objectives, the crowd grew silent. When he proclaimed, "I recognize that law alone is not the answer to the civil rights problem," they cheered.[38]

Two weeks later, he appeared in Birmingham, Alabama, where a large crowd greeted him and Pat. Admirers ripped several buttons off his jacket, and Pat lost her white gloves. He offered a challenge: "It is time for the Democratic candidates to quit taking the South for granted. And it is time for the Republican candidates to quit conceding the South to the Democrats." His loudest cheers came when he said of relations with the Soviet Union, "America must be firm, but at the same time, not belligerent."[39]

The same day, the Nixons continued on to Atlanta, where some 200,000 people—nearly half of the city's population—came out to see them. The vice president's convertible drove through downtown in "an almost blinding confetti storm." He told an enthusiastic audience of 45,000 that no Democratic presidential candidate in a quarter century had "bothered to campaign in Georgia," but he would not concede the South. He asked Georgians to "vote for the best man regardless of his party label." As he later wrote in *Six Crises*, "The party of Schlesinger, Stevenson, and Bowles was a far cry from the party of Jefferson, Jackson, and Wilson."[40]

Between southern trips, Nixon spoke in Detroit to the Veterans of Foreign Wars, whom he assured that American military strength was "second to none any place in the world." While he saw no need to raise taxes at that moment, it might become necessary to maintain military superiority. He attacked Kennedy, without mentioning him by name, for advocating that Ike apologize to the Russians for the U-2 incident. The American president, he said, "must not and never should apologize or express regrets for trying to protect the security of this country against surprise attack." As for Castro, the United States had "the power . . . to throw him out of office any day that we would choose, but getting rid of Castro is not the answer alone." The United States had to offer some acceptable alternatives to the islanders and to the rest of Latin America.[41]

The next evening Nixon appeared on Jack Paar's *Tonight Show*. Kennedy had appeared in June. The line to be part of the live audience—the theater seated only about two hundred—had started forming at 5:30 a.m. Paar, as host, combined jokes with serious material, and the vice president did the same. He cautiously predicted that he would win and asked voters to cast their ballots based "on the issues" and "on the basis of leadership." He and Kennedy had a "friendly" personal relationship, but they disagreed "on some great issues." Nixon did not think "that this campaign will be a personal campaign from the standpoint of personal animosity. I would hope not." Toward the end of the broadcast, Pat joined her husband onstage, and Nixon asked Paar for and received an autograph for their daughters. The usual audience of approximately 7.5 million to 8 million jumped to around 11.3 million for the Nixons' guest appearance.[42]

Pat usually traveled with her husband. When he was chairing the Senate during the special session, she occasionally toured by herself. On August 20, she flew to Meriden, Connecticut, in a pouring rain to celebrate "Pat Nixon Day." Her grandfather Patrick Ryan had lived in Bethel for years, and her father, William, was born there. First cousin Alice Lynch, from Ridgefield, chatted with her. Pat told a crowd of twelve hundred that the Nixons had "always campaigned as a team. . . . I've always made the miles with him."[43]

A week later, she attended the Erie County Republican family picnic in Buffalo, New York. Reflecting on the enthusiastic welcome in North Carolina, Alabama, and Georgia, she predicted that her husband would win and would carry some of the Solid South. That was the extent of her political views. Asked about her domestic life, she said her main concern was to keep her daughters away from politics. "Campaigning is very hard on little girls. . . . We want them to grow up as normal children."[44]

✔ ✔ ✔

While the Nixons campaigned, the president was busy answering reporters' questions about the proposals he had submitted to the special session of Congress.[45] He also had to combat talk of recession. On August 8, he and Nixon telephoned Pete Jones, an industrialist, philanthropist, and Augusta gang member, from the Oval Office. The Democrats were "trying to build up a full blown depression," the president said, but the economy, with the exception of the steel industry, was "in good shape," and he wanted Jones "to talk a little optimistically, not pessimistically, these next three months." Jones answered that oil industry volume "was at an all time high," as was "the use of electrical energy." Both were "good indices" of the economy's strength.[46]

Two days later, the president at his weekly press conference declared that the economy was showing no signs of recession or depression. His labor department was reporting decreased unemployment and increased employment. David McDonald, president of the United Steel Workers, immediately challenged this assessment, seeing "the possibility of a real recession developing."[47]

With just five months to go in the White House, Ike started to reflect on his presidency, writing *Time* and *Life* publisher Henry Luce of the difficulty of having had a Republican majority in Congress only for his first two years. The rest of the time he had had to use "methods calculated to attract cooperation" from antagonistic Democrats. Even so, he had been able to govern. He worried that the American government had "become too complex, and too pervasive in its influence on all our lives for one individual to pretend to direct the details of its important and critical programming."[48]

At the Republican convention, he had tried to express his "basic philosophy" and convince his listeners "of the necessity for continuing the policies and programs for which the Republican Party stands." He wanted to impress on them the reasons for the foreign and domestic policies he had advocated.[49]

The president told a press conference on August 10 that "the Nixon-Lodge ticket is going to do well." He would do whatever he could to help it. Ike was pleased that Nixon was "starting a fight as rapidly as he can, and he is going to wage it right down to the last minute of the campaign." He did not think his vice president would "take anything for granted."[50]

The president also defended Nixon privately. Some had incorrectly claimed that he was a member of the NAACP; a local California chapter in 1946 had made him an honorary member. Ike, in his letter to Luce, wrote that he had noticed some southern Democratic "disaffection." The South, he suggested, thought Johnson had "betrayed them, while Mr. Kennedy they believe to be a complete 'radical.'" Nixon, on the other hand, had "been a moderate in his political philosophy." As for integration, the vice president had "consistently argued that education and understanding are much more important than rigidly conceived laws in bringing about improvement in the racial situation." Both Ike and Nixon believed that people attempting to vote needed to be protected, and federal court orders had to be enforced.[51]

On a telephone call on August 19 with Republican Party officials, Ike said that although he did not enjoy motorcades, he would ride in eight or ten "to try to arouse enthusiasm." One reason he had run for reelection in 1956 was "to generate new life into the Republican Party." He felt he had not succeeded and would "devote the rest of the time to trying to do so." He "would do almost anything to avoid turning his chair and the country over to Kennedy."[52]

The president also helped organize Volunteers for Nixon. Ike had established his own committees during his two election campaigns, and they had raised considerable money. He asked Cliff Roberts to raise funds for Nixon and then persuaded a hundred people to write checks averaging one thousand dollars—a feat Roberts found "remarkable." The president was pleased and allowed his name to be used as a donor. Roberts wrote Nixon toward the end of the month that Ike's friends had given money to his campaign and "enthusiastically" supported him. Nixon had two advantages, Roberts wrote: the president's record, and "the President's willingness to campaign for you."[53]

On August 24, Ike held the 190th news conference of his presidency. Sarah McClendon of the *El Paso Times*, noting the president's praise for Nixon during the campaign, asked what "big decisions" the vice president had helped make. Ike answered, "no one participates in the decisions." He had been a career army officer, and he used his subordinates for advice. As the commander, he made the decisions. Any questions that intimated a lack of authority on his part irritated him.

The questions continued—on domestic and foreign affairs, and on Kennedy's religion. The last questioner, Charles Mohr from *Time*, returned to McClendon's inquiry regarding Nixon's experience and the Republican claim that he "had a great deal of practice at being President." Ike repeated that Nixon had been a valued adviser, but the president made the decisions. The vice president had "taken a full part in every principal discussion." Mohr pressed the issue, asking "if you could give us an example of a major idea of his that you had adopted in that role as the decider." Ike cut him off, possibly irritated by the repetition, and as he was leaving the podium, he said: "If you give me a week, I might think of one. I don't remember." Some in the audience chuckled. Almost simultaneously, Jack Bell of the Associated Press thanked the president, ending the conference.[54]

Jules Witcover, who covered the conference for the *Syracuse Herald-Journal*, recalled his astonishment: "The answer brought unbelieving looks throughout the room." Radio and television immediately featured it, and newspapers carried "GIVE ME A WEEK" as a banner headline. The DNC printed the questions and answers to circulate during the campaign.[55]

At a press conference in Detroit on the same day, Nixon was asked to respond to the issue of his role in the administration. He agreed that Ike was correct. Eisenhower consulted many advisers, "but when it comes to the power of decision only the President can and should make decisions." Jack Paar that evening asked something similar. Nixon answered that the president had upgraded the vice president's office, "so that instead of just being a gavel pounder over the Senate, he actually is used in foreign policy, in domestic policy, and in a lot of other important matters."[56]

The day after the press conference, Nixon reacted to criticism by the *Washington Post*. On one hand, he played no role in the administration's decision making, but on the other hand, the paper featured Kennedy's assault on him as "responsible for the decisions of retreat and defeat." Nixon thought some letters to the editor "with a facetious and devastating line that they are being somewhat contradictory . . . would be quite effective and might get under their skins."[57]

Ike normally held weekly press conferences, but he did not hold his next one until September 7. At that one, no reporter asked a follow-up question about Nixon's role in the administration.[58]

The day after the August 24 press conference, as "Give Me a Week" stared out from every newsstand in the country, Ike apologized to Nixon "for a poor choice of words." The same day, Stephen Hess, who worked on the White House staff, asked Eisenhower's son, John, what his father was thinking. John replied that Ike meant he wanted to end the conference and would answer the question the following week.[59]

Nixon looked back on these events while in the White House. Speaking to Secretary of Treasury John Connally on July 21, 1971, the president thought that Ike had treated him "extremely well," but he was not included in decisions until the last two or three years, at which point he had to be. In an unpublished memoir written in 1976, Nixon wrote that he did not believe Ike made the unfortunate statement intentionally, and that Ike's private secretary, Ann Whitman, had told Rose Mary Woods that the president "was in one of his rather moody states that whole week." And during an interview with Frank Gannon in 1983, Nixon remembered that after the press conference, the president called him and said: "You've got to answer this. . . . Every time anybody raises that goddamned 'Give me a week' thing, it just raises my blood pressure."[60]

In hindsight, Nixon felt that the remark had hurt his campaign. Senator Pres-

cott Bush from Connecticut agreed. It "was a very damaging remark; . . . it de-
meaned Nixon and hurt him badly." Former senator William Knowland in his
oral history concurred.[61]

Three authors, out of many, described this event with a particular lack of objectivity. Garry Wills, in *Nixon Agonistes* (1969), argued that the president continually belittled Nixon, culminating in the August 24 "harsh affront." Ike's real
purpose in making this and other earlier remarks, Wills asserted, was to demonstrate that the two leaders never had an intimate relationship. Jeffrey Frank's *Ike
and Dick* (2013) used the incident to describe how little the president thought
of Nixon and to claim that the remark personally offended the vice president.
Robert Dallek, in *Camelot's Court* (2013), wrote that Ike's answer was more a reflection of "his reluctance to back Nixon's reach for the White House than [of]
Nixon's performance as vice president." None of these descriptions is supported
by anything Eisenhower said or did, during the campaign or at any other time.[62]

Notwithstanding Ike's gaffe, Nixon did well in August in asserting leadership
of his party. Even Harold Stassen, who had tried to get Nixon removed from the
Eisenhower ticket in 1952 and 1956 to advance his own presidential ambitions,
congratulated him on his "unanimous nomination for President" and wrote that
he expected to enthusiastically support the ticket. Nixon had achieved what he
needed: unity within the GOP.[63]

Nixon also had the opportunity to try out some major themes. He had to identify with the successes of the Eisenhower years. He promoted his experience in
foreign affairs and pledged to act firmly but with restraint. Lodge, who also had
vast diplomatic knowledge, would do the same. Both put out the message that
neither Kennedy nor Johnson was prepared to shape American diplomacy. A
Nixon-Lodge administration would be far superior in dealing with the Russians
and their allies, especially China and Cuba. In domestic matters, Republicans
staked out their position as the party of private enterprise while claiming that
Democrats promised more spending for federal programs without divulging how
they were going to pay for them. The Democrats, Nixon asserted, made promises
that could not be fulfilled; Republicans were prudent.[64]

Throughout his speeches and press conferences, Nixon repeated his fifty-
state campaign pledge and promised not to concede any state to the Democrats. Some had few electoral votes; he would visit those just once. Others, with
more electoral votes, would be visited more often, particularly if the race was
close there. He would not exclude New England, Kennedy's backyard, or the
Democratic South. His early forays in the South raised expectations that some
southern states might be ripe for the taking.

Nixon was especially concerned about California. The humiliating defeats of

William Knowland for governor and Goodwin Knight for senator in 1958 had left the state Republican Party in shambles. By 1960, California had 3,676,495 registered Democrats and 2,519,975 Republicans—a Democratic advantage of more than a million voters.[65]

Nixon realized that the California race would be a tough, close battle, but winning there was imperative. It was his home state; failure to carry it might doom not only his 1960 campaign but even his future as a politician. The vice president was so concerned that he hired Stanley McCaffrey, a boyhood friend who was serving as executive assistant under University of California President Clark Kerr, to work on the campaign. By the start of June, McCaffrey's duties were clear: help Nixon win California. He was the sole staff member who was responsible for a single state.[66]

Fortunately for the vice president, Californian Republicans were already uniting. At the statewide convention in early August, political fences were mended, and the party's leaders predicted Nixon would carry the state "by a substantial majority." Congressman Robert Wilson from San Diego echoed that sentiment; his county organization was "united and enthusiastic" and would carry his county that fall. The GOP had to get Republican voters to turn out at a rate 7 or 8 percent better than the Democrats and also lure some Democrats to vote for the Nixon-Lodge ticket.[67]

Nixon seemed ready to start campaigning nonstop by the beginning of September.

A simple car door dramatically changed his plans.

12

Starting the Contest

From the number of telephone calls to and from the vice president that his private secretary, Rose Mary Woods, noted in her boss's daily logs, it is clear that FBI director J. Edgar Hoover had taken a close interest in Nixon's campaign since at least the beginning of 1960. He wrote to Nixon in June that although Kennedy was "very popular" and had "sufficient capital to finance his campaign," Nixon was "more able than all of the Democrats put together."[1]

The director grew even more involved in July. His daily logs show two telephone calls from Woods and one from Nixon before the convention. On the sixth, he sent Nixon a *Wall Street Journal* editorial questioning Kennedy's argument that age should not be used to judge a presidential candidate's qualification for office. Youth was not a factor, the article said, but seasoning was: "The problems confronting a President demand maturity and experience, regardless of age." The next day, Hoover scribbled a short note to Dick: "May our country be blessed with having you guide our destiny for many years to come. Best wishes, Edgar."[2]

Fourteen days later, Hoover called Woods, asking her to relay some campaign advice. Some spokesman other than the candidate, he suggested, should point out—without referring to any other candidate—that Nixon was healthy and had "no restrictions or limitations on what [he] can do." Hoover had recently learned that while visiting New Jersey Governor Robert Meyner in June, Kennedy had "fainted—apparently quite a few people know about this." He thought someone should highlight Nixon's "perfect physical condition."[3]

Voters gave an energetic Nixon a warm welcome everywhere he went. During his visit to Greensboro, North Carolina, in the middle of August, he ignored the Secret Service recommendation for crowd control, and in the crush of spectators, his left knee banged against his car door. At that moment, he was more concerned about his torn pants than about the injury.[4]

The knee bothered him for nine days. His appointment secretary, Don Hughes, thought he "looked terrible" and "sallow." In his unpublished memoir, Nixon writes that he was physically exhausted and lost ten pounds. During the *Tonight Show* telecast on August 24, Jack Paar asked, "something wrong with your leg?" Nixon answered no. Two days later, he complained of "nagging pain in my right knee." (He meant his left.)[5]

On Saturday, the sore burst, with pus emerging from the knee, spreading the infection. He saw Dr. Walter Tkach, the assistant White House physician, who treated the infection with antibiotics and sent him to Walter Reed General Hospital to see whether he needed further treatment.[6]

Dr. Raymond Scalettar, a specialist in arthritis and rheumatic diseases, became the vice president's attending physician. After examining what he described as a "swollen hot joint," Scalettar drained fluids from the knee and took specimens for laboratory analysis. The culture indicated hemolytic *Staphylococcus aureus* infection.[7]

Nixon asked thirteen doctors for their opinions, and only Scalettar told him that he had to be admitted to the hospital as a "precautionary measure to avoid any possible permanent damage." Nixon fought the idea of being hospitalized, but the doctor's diagnosis did not allow for any option. So he wrote the Reverend Billy Graham that he had decided to stay "because of the doctor's warning that further infection might lay me up at the critical period during the campaign. I thought it would be better to be out of action now so that I would be in good shape in the critical three weeks before election."[8]

The vice president was admitted to Walter Reed Hospital on August 29 with the estimate of a two-week stay. Ike authorized that Nixon be placed in Ward #8 on the third floor, the presidential suite. His leg was immobilized, placed in traction with a weight device, and he was treated with arthrocentesis (draining fluids from the joint via a needle) and multiple antibiotics, including penicillin and erythromycin. When he had a bad reaction to one antibiotic, Scalettar stayed with him through the night.[9]

A stream of political figures came to visit. President Eisenhower sat with him. Before his arrival, the vice president told Scalettar that he did not want to shave until just before Ike's visit and joked that the president would say that Nixon should have recovered faster. During the visit, Ike talked about the knee injury that ended his football career at West Point. The two men also discussed the campaign, congressional legislation, and a recent Organization of American States meeting.[10]

One other visitor at Walter Reed was Nixon's main competitor for the Republican nomination; Nelson Rockefeller interrupted his vacation to fly to the capital, and the governor answered questions from reporters while wearing an "I'm for Nixon" button on his lapel.[11]

Jack Kennedy sent a sympathetic telegram, and Nixon replied with a note of appreciation, saying he hoped JFK had "no similar accident. Much against my will, I am trying to do what the doctor orders. I hope to be back on the campaign trail before too long."[12]

Lyndon Johnson visited Nixon on September 2, along with Republican Senate minority leader Everett Dirksen. LBJ recalled that after he suffered a severe heart attack in July 1955, his first official visitor was the president, and the second was Nixon. He commented that the vice president had had "a bad break . . . but before long he'll be back out there mixing it with us."[13]

Nixon made certain that his press bulletins, on which Scalettar collaborated with press secretary Klein, gave optimistic news. The bulletin on August 30 stated that Nixon's infection was "localized in his knee joint" and he was "progressing satisfactorily." He felt "very well," had "no fever," his appetite was "good and his general physical condition is excellent." On September 1, the doctors were "encouraged by his progress. . . . He had excellent rest during the night . . . has no fever and continues to be in very good spirits."[14]

Nixon conducted his campaign from his hospital room, concentrating on Democratic attacks, especially the charge that the United States was "second-rate militarily, scientifically, etc." and that under Eisenhower the nation's "prestige and power have been allowed to wane." The vice president also wanted to implement a strategy of "whacking" JFK's advisers, not just the nominee himself. "Everytime anyone whacks him they scream [bigot]." He hoped that a friendly reporter would ask JFK "to repudiate Truman's attack on RN's integrity with regard to this religious thing." After Walter Reuther, president of the United Automobile Workers, called the vice president "Tricky Dick," Nixon said that a reporter should ask the candidate: "Do you agree with this type of attack?"[15]

Nixon and Klein were grateful when Ralph de Toledano, a Nixon advocate, wrote columns defending their campaign. The journalist and Nixon partisan Victor Lasky helped with a story about Robert Kennedy's "harangue about the critics of his brother," a piece the vice president thought should receive wide circulation.[16]

To provide supporters with ammunition, Nixon asked for a mailing list of approximately ten thousand Republican politicians and volunteers, as well as opinion makers, newspaper editors, and radio and television journalists and producers, to receive campaign material. VIPs needed special attention; their letters had to be answered. "We really catch hell when any important person doesn't get a responsive answer when he takes the trouble to send in a suggestion for a speech or the campaign itself."[17]

Nixon also wanted to concentrate on "the seven major states (including Texas)." He asked for weekly reports on each of them until election day, with the latest polls and volunteer organizations. California was a priority. Nixon contemplated the "drastic move" of sending Stanley McCaffrey, a boyhood friend from Whittier High School who began working for the campaign in June, "out there on a fulltime basis to take over the California campaign" and to provide a "fresh approach [and] even with his lack of experience might be the answer to our problems." He eventually did it; it would be his most important personnel move.[18]

The vice president also focused on southern weeklies and large and small dailies, asking his press staff who was handling these newspapers. Several editors had attended receptions during his southern stops. To those who had endorsed him, he wanted to send letters expressing his gratitude. The southern states had to be handled delicately. Democratic Senator Harry Byrd of Virginia, in "a very confidential meeting" with White House chief of staff Jerry Persons, recommended that Nixon and possibly Lodge speak in his state. Goldwater had spoken there, calling for a "two-party system in Virginia" and saying that the election's objective "was to make Virginia Republican." This, Nixon felt, was a mistake. Republican speakers needed to emphasize that they were not "making the South Republican—but [were there] for the purpose of carrying the South for the Nixon-Lodge ticket."[19]

Secretary Benson expected to campaign in the South despite other prominent Republicans' objections. If he went there, Nixon thought, he should discuss the economy, not farm issues. Nixon had talked to Benson about his schedule. Although Republicans could not prevent him from campaigning, Nixon thought "the hopeless states in the South [were] the best ones" for him to visit. Benson would do the least harm in Georgia, Alabama, Mississippi, and Louisiana. The vice president also favored the current program of tobacco price supports, which Benson opposed. Republican Senator John Cooper, from Kentucky, supported it and did not want Benson campaigning in his state. The RNC, Nixon argued, "must keep him out of the Midwest—he must not go in there for anything."[20]

FBI director Hoover added his own counsel. While vacationing in southern California, the director had lunch with Virginia Murchison, the wife of oil millionaire Clint Murchison, on September 8; she wanted to give Nixon a fundraising luncheon in Dallas. Even though Texans were Democrats, she said, they supported Ike and Dick. Hoover later wrote that Robert Lehman, head of Lehman Brothers, favored Nixon and planned to give the campaign $100,000 because he objected to Joseph Kennedy's anti-Semitism.[21]

Nixon "sneaked out of the hospital Sept. 9—no release," having been there for twelve days. He told the press that the doctors had "completely checked the infection." Pat wrote that her husband seemed "to have the knee infection quite cleared up." Ten days after his release, Nixon said the knee was better.[22]

Jack Kennedy began his general election campaign in New Hampshire on September 2, embarking on a hectic schedule that would take him to seventeen states in eighteen days. From New Hampshire he went to Maine and then to San Francisco. He flew to Anchorage, Alaska, becoming the first presidential candidate to campaign in the forty-ninth state, continued to Detroit for a Labor Day address, and then stopped in Idaho, Washington, and Oregon. On September 8, he began a two-day whistle-stop tour by train from northern California to southern California, finishing in San Diego three days later.[23]

At each stop, Kennedy emphasized party: he was the Democratic presidential nominee running against the Republican. He did this because, out of the roughly 103,400,000 registered voters in the country, Gallup Polls estimated 55 percent to 59 percent were Democrats, while 38 percent to 41 percent identified as Republicans. In raw numbers, this came to roughly 56.8 million Democrats, 40.4 million Republicans, and 6.2 million undecided. Using different sources, the *Washington Post* had reported that Democratic registration exceeded Republican by at least 12.5 million.[24]

During his events, Kennedy answered questions about the failure of the special session of Congress, which had adjourned at the beginning of September. Rather than concede that Democrats had failed to pass any meaningful legislation, he insisted that major bills would have been passed under a Democratic president. As long as the nation had a divided government, with a Republican in the White House and Democrats controlling the House and Senate, legislation would be stalemated.[25]

With 66 Democrats in the Senate and 34 Republicans, it was mathematically impossible for Republicans to take control of that chamber. The House had 281 Democrats to 155 Republicans; it would take a tidal wave for the GOP to win a majority. Democrats held 34 governors' seats against 16 Republicans. Of the nation's 177 largest cities, 128 had Democratic mayors against 49 Republicans. On top of these advantages, Democrats had done a far better job of registering new voters.[26]

Everywhere he spoke, Kennedy addressed distinct parts of the party's constituency. He called for a new civil rights bill to appeal to liberals and African Americans, pledged to protect Israel to win Jewish voters, and advocated changes in the Taft-Hartley Act to capture union workers' votes. He also included local issues: in New England, returning manufacturing jobs and reducing unemployment; in Alaska, protecting natural resources; in Idaho, farming; in Washington and Oregon, managing water resources; and in California, conservation and farming.

Despite these efforts and the large Democratic advantage in registration, he and Nixon remained virtually tied throughout September. Gallup, in three polls, indicated that voters were almost equally split over which party would be able to solve the nation's major problems. But Gallup also found that a recession would benefit Democrats because they offered better economic security. When asked which party was more likely to keep the United States out of World War III, more than a third saw Republicans as the "party of peace," while the Democrats were favored by just over a fifth. Pollster Samuel Lubell reported early in the month: "Never in all my years of interviewing have I found the American people more troubled and more shaken over what the future holds."[27]

Kennedy was beginning to view Nixon as an enemy. When Brian Lamb interviewed Arthur Schlesinger, Jr., for C-SPAN in December 2000, Lamb said he had heard that Kennedy and Nixon were friends. The historian disagreed: they were not "pals"; Kennedy thought Nixon had "no class," and he had been no more than civil to the vice president while in the Senate. Ben Bradlee offered a more nuanced view. Before the election, Kennedy's cordial relationship with Nixon had caused chagrin to JFK's supporters. But he came to despise his opponent during the campaign, telling Bradlee: "Anyone who can't beat Nixon doesn't deserve to be president."[28]

Kennedy's staff, none of whom were ever friendly with Nixon, had assembled a long list of talking points against him. The journalist William Attwood, who began working for JFK in August, loathed the vice president. "Nixon is the most vulnerable candidate we could hope for," he wrote, "and may become the Democrats' greatest campaign asset." He helped draft a speech for Adlai Stevenson to give in late September that would attack Nixon "with all barrels."[29]

At a speech in Alexandria, Virginia, on August 24, Kennedy said that the vice president's leadership in foreign policy had produced a record of "retreat, defeat, and weakness." But once Nixon entered Walter Reed Hospital, Kennedy refused to mention him as long as he remained there.[30] Nixon had not taken advantage of Kennedy's absence from the Senate due to his back surgery in 1955, and Kennedy may have been responding in kind.

On his whistle-stop tour of Nixon's home state, aboard a thirteen-car Southern

Pacific special train that retraced Truman's 1948 campaign trip through the Sacramento and San Joaquin Valleys, Kennedy emphasized that the contest was not simply about himself versus Nixon: "This is a contest between two political parties, between the histories of those parties, and between their promises and the record for the future." Democrats had promoted progressive legislation, he declared, while the Republicans stood for the status quo.[31]

James Powell, a speech professor at California State College (now University), Long Beach, analyzed Kennedy's early addresses in a 1968 article in the journal *Western Speech* and found them uneven. He described JFK's voice as "taut and tense, his delivery rapid and rushed." His Boston accent sometimes made him hard to understand. Vigor became "viga" and Cuba turned into "Cubar." He had good eye contact but talked at 240 words a minute (the normal rate was 100), seldom smiled, and spoke from the throat instead of from the diaphragm. In spite of these flaws, Powell concluded, "Kennedy's vigorous advocacy of change, delivered in his earnest way, came through to audiences and served to complement his theme of urgency."[32]

Kennedy hired experts to help him improve his delivery. David McClosky, a voice and speech therapist, traveled with the candidate to coach him on speaking from the diaphragm like an actor. After two days on the California tour, he told the press that Kennedy had developed "voice fatigue" and would rest on Saturday, without any speaking engagements.[33]

On the morning of September 8 in his running mate's hometown of Boston — an interesting choice given that Kennedy was then in California — Johnson opened his campaign and was warmly received, with 100,000 people lining the streets in ninety-degree heat as his motorcade slowly moved through downtown. Every few minutes he jumped out of his car and shook hands with onlookers. At his press conference he told reporters that he expected to win every state "after a hard fight." The principal issue in the race was the need for new (Democratic) leadership to restore prestige and "give the country confidence and freedom. We're tired of being slapped around in all parts of the globe. . . . We're tired of dictators and would-be dictators who think they can thumb their noses at the United States with impunity." Castro had attacked the United States for its interference in the island's domestic affairs, and mobs in Japan had forced Eisenhower to cancel his trip there. The United States could not accept that kind of treatment.[34]

That evening LBJ spoke at Symphony Hall to a full house. He pointed out that JFK "defeated me fairly and squarely for the nomination, and when he came to my room and asked me to help him to win the election as president of all

America, and when I saw how big he could be I felt I could be big enough to help him." He also highlighted his central theme: "Under no single administration in American history has the position of our Nation in the world declined so far or so fast as it has under the administration of the Republican Party."[35]

After this northern visit he returned to Texas, where he joined Kennedy on September 11 for a two-day tour to build unity. Among other issues, conservative Democrats who had previously supported LBJ were hostile toward JFK and the Democratic platform. Many Texans, feeling that Johnson had deserted them by being on the ticket with Kennedy, had become "Democrats for Nixon." Others in the LBJ camp did not know whether he should be a national or regional candidate. He had to carry the South; but he also had to campaign across the country.[36]

Johnson recognized that the Democratic ticket faced serious problems in his state and across the former Confederate states. Even before the conventions, commentators noted the South's discontent with the national Democratic Party, particularly its stand promoting civil rights. By the time Johnson and Kennedy met in Texas, the Gallup Poll banner headline read: "Two Tickets Neck-and-Neck in South." The pollster reported that 47 percent of southerners supported Kennedy-Johnson and 45 percent were for Nixon-Lodge, with 8 percent undecided.[37]

Speaker Rayburn was angry with his fellow Texans. He was pleased with the Kennedy-Johnson ticket even if others were not. Writing on August 12, he noted that some Texas Democrats had not supported Truman and Stevenson for president and now planned to vote for Nixon: "I just wonder how long some of these people will have to vote Republican in order to acknowledge that they are Republicans." If the state's Democrats united, he observed, they would "overwhelmingly" carry the state. As for the vice president, "a lot of people, especially women, just do not like Nixon's looks."[38]

Even before Kennedy and Johnson arrived in Texas, Lady Bird Johnson and Kennedy's mother and sisters held a series of tea and coffee rallies to charm voters. They failed to convince conservative Democrats who opposed the party's national platform and were getting ready for the state convention to oppose it. Some speculated that the candidates had come to the state only to generate enthusiasm for the ticket at the convention. Texas Governor Price Daniel made certain that the disgruntled Democrats were silenced. The convention gave the Kennedy-Johnson team its full backing.[39]

During the two-day swing on September 12 and 13, Kennedy and Johnson worked together smoothly. Afterward, the Kennedy organization allowed Johnson carte blanche in Texas and across most of the South. But LBJ supporter

James Blundell recalled that Johnson felt ignored by both Kennedy and his organization. He was disappointed and hurt for the rest of the campaign; the Kennedy team never again asked him to make a joint appearance with Jack.[40]

At the start of September, Nixon received some welcome information. His pollster, Claude Robinson, told him that the race was "close, but I think you are going to win." On his first day out of the hospital, he and his opponent would start out tied. Meanwhile, his surrogates began attacking Kennedy. On September 5, Secretary Benson praised the vice president and charged JFK with a "complete flip-flop" on his agricultural voting record and a "complete reversal" of his voting in other areas after he was "bitten by the presidential bug." HEW Secretary Arthur Flemming held a news conference the next day to charge JFK with "completely distorting the facts" on the vice president's social-welfare positions. Flemming was incensed that Kennedy had described Nixon as "the man and the party who oppose decent wages for our teachers . . . and medical care for our aged."[41]

While hospitalized, Nixon also focused on the role of his running mate, Henry Cabot Lodge, Jr. *Newsweek* speculated that he was chosen for geographic balance, while *Time* declared that his selection had met with widespread national approval. Nixon wrote Henry Luce, *Time*'s publisher, to emphasize how firmly he believed that Lodge was the right choice. He had "tremendous appeal among women voters and is the only one of the four candidates who is completely 'non-controversial.' Americans had watched Lodge for eight years on television speaking for the United States against the likes of [Soviet Foreign Affairs Minister Andrei] Gromyko."[42]

The vice president had been promoting his running mate's experience since the convention. On July 29, he declared that if elected, Lodge would have a major diplomatic presence. On August 1, Nixon ordered his staff to give Lodge briefing summaries on major issues so that he would "not get caught off base by press conference questions." In the last week of August, the vice president recorded a speech for the Zionist Organization of America in which he promised that Lodge, "one of the most skilled diplomats of our times," would have "primary responsibility" for negotiating an Arab-Israeli settlement.[43]

Lodge knew how to cooperate with the liberal and conservative wings within the GOP. When Goldwater had won his 1958 senatorial reelection, Lodge had written him calling the victory "a bright spot in a cloudy sky." Goldwater, he said, should be proud of his accomplishment, and if Lodge could "be of service and trust," the senator should call on him.[44]

Yet he was far more comfortable with his party's liberal wing. His letters to Rockefeller began "Dear Nelson," and in the governor's replies, Lodge was "Dear

Cabot." When Nelson won the governorship of New York, Cabot was effusive: "Throughout the campaign you stood for all the best things and you did so with intelligence, honesty and warmth." Lodge had worked "for your kind of Republicanism through all my public life," and he found Rockefeller's triumph gratifying and inspiring. Lodge was "completely at your disposal if there is any way in which I can be of help to you."[45]

In New York City in the last week of August, Rockefeller told reporters that the Republicans would carry his state in November and also that he would be the principal speaker at Republican rallies in Pennsylvania. When asked to comment on Kennedy's contention that the Eisenhower administration had acted with "weakness and timidity" in the Middle East, the governor responded that the Arab-Israeli conflict had to be resolved. But the fighting was decades old, and any solution would be difficult.[46]

With Nixon hospitalized, Lodge filled in for him on September 3 alongside Governor Rockefeller in the Catskills. The many resorts that earned the region the nickname the Jewish Alps were then in their heyday, and Jewish New Yorkers swelled the region's summertime population from forty thousand to more than ten times that. A million Jewish vacationers might be there over the holiday weekend.[47]

The governor used his private Beechcraft airplane to fly himself, the ambassador, and New York Attorney General Louis Lefkowitz from New York City to Liberty airport. After landing, Lodge answered reporters' questions. One asked him whether he had come there to court Jewish voters. Lodge replied that the question was inappropriate: he was traveling across the nation to meet Americans of all persuasions. The group then drove to Grossinger's Hotel for a kosher lunch. Lodge and Rockefeller shook hands with a largely enthusiastic crowd.[48]

Lodge praised Nixon's "tough intellectual fibre" and described him as "rich in experience. . . . There is rough weather ahead . . . and we need an experienced captain on the bridge." Echoing his acceptance speech at the convention, he highlighted three points: strengthening "military power," improving "the kind of community we have," and progressing "in the field of human rights." He singled out "the great American Ralph Bunche," who had "given such brilliant leadership" as the UN representative in Lebanon in 1958, Laos in 1959, and most recently in the Congo.[49]

On Labor Day, Lodge and Rockefeller toured the New York beaches by helicopter, changing their sweated-through shirts for new ones at each stop. Lodge, imposing at almost 6-foot-3, "in shirtsleeves, drenched in perspiration," greeted bathers with good humor. The trip began at the Jones Beach Guard Station on Long Island, where one woman was thrilled to meet "that good-looking guy who talks back to the Russians on TV." They went on to Jacob Riis Park in Rockaway, Queens, and finally to Coney Island, where Lodge ate two frankfurters at Nathan's Famous restaurant. Mobs of enthusiastic beachgoers made crowd control almost impossible for the police, and the governor added to their difficulties by telling the guards: "That's all right, let them come through—we want to get to meet the people." Rockefeller acted like a candidate, shaking hands with everyone and saying: "So NICE to see YEW."[50]

On the evening of September 6, Lodge gave his first major campaign speech, before thirty-two hundred at a GOP rally in Abington, Pennsylvania, a town that generally voted 3.5-to-1 Republican. Before the speech, a reporter asked him whether he might be better situated as secretary of state; he snapped back that the Republican convention decided where he belonged. Another correspondent asked about Rockefeller's earlier criticism of Nixon; Lodge said he would not comment on "loaded questions."

In his address to the party faithful, he repeated his pledges to strengthen the military and the economy as well as improve living standards. He praised the Eisenhower administration's record and described Nixon as a man of "tough, penetrating, resilient intelligence" who had proven that he would "stand up to the Russians." The election was not a traditional partisan battle between Republicans and Democrats. "The basic contest is the life and death struggle between the Communists on the one hand, and those who insist on being free on the other."[51]

Lodge met with Eisenhower in the White House on the morning of September 7 to discuss the upcoming UN general assembly session, campaign plans, and a future foreign policy address. Afterward, he called Nixon to discuss how he could be most effective in the campaign. They settled on a division of responsibilities: Nixon would exhort Republican partisans to campaign vigorously for the ticket; Lodge would focus on Democrats and independents and go to urban areas that Republicans normally did not reach. Lodge, Nixon wrote, could "do things that nobody else can do and that means putting him in with Democrats and Independents where he can give his 'God, mother and country' pitch and waggle his finger at Gromyko—thereby reminding people of his television performances at the United Nations."[52]

Lodge next returned to Massachusetts for a two-day homecoming on September 7 and 8. He rode in motorcades through Worcester, Lowell, and Boston to promote the ticket, the reelection of Senator Leverett Saltonstall, and the election of John Volpe as governor and Augustus Means as lieutenant governor. He told reporters: "In the cold war, you've got to follow the maxim of Stonewall Jackson: 'mystify, mislead and surprise.'" Asked to elaborate, he said the campaign's specific plans could not be "put out in public." Two days later, he left for Washington for a public appearance with the president and vice president.[53]

On Monday morning, September 12, Ike rode out to Friendship International Airport, south of Baltimore, in a driving rainstorm with 35-mile-an-hour wind gusts caused by Hurricane Donna. He told those assembled that the weather was a good omen because he had begun his 1952 presidential campaign in Abilene under similar conditions. Nixon and Lodge would build upon his accomplishments, he predicted, but they would never be satisfied with the status quo and would fight for peace and disarmament without compromising national security. He was saying goodbye, he said, "to two of my very best friends in Government as they start on this pilgrimage, this campaign, for the benefit of the United States and the free world. I believe they are, I repeat, the finest team that all America could have chosen for this effort."[54]

Nixon answered by welcoming the opportunity to build on Eisenhower's record of bringing "peace, prosperity and progress" to Americans. He highlighted his principal campaign theme: "the great overriding issue . . . is keeping the peace without surrender and extending freedom throughout the world." Nixon, who had recently signed himself out of the hospital, walked Ike to his limousine in the pouring rain without a raincoat. The president implored photographers to allow his vice president to get back indoors; he did not "want him to get sick."[55]

Kennedy's press secretary Pierre Salinger responded that at the Democratic convention, "we made public a complete medical statement on Sen. Kennedy. . . . Anyone who has traveled with Sen. Kennedy throughout the campaign could have no doubt as to the state of his health."[56]

Nixon asked his private physician, Dr. John Lungren, to explain Addison's disease to him. Since it did not affect the senator's mind, the vice president dismissed it. In an interview twenty-three years later, he concluded: "A campaign is more difficult than being president and anybody that can go through a presidential campaign is healthy enough to be president."[57]

Many years later, in 1984, Dr. Scalettar published an article in the *Journal of the American Medical Association* entitled "Presidential Candidate Disability" in which he discussed presidential candidates' health as well as alcohol and drug abuse. These issues, he suggested, might "result in the victory of a candidate elected not necessarily by the will of the people but by default because of an opponent's medical illness." Reviewing Nixon's illness, he noted that the vice president left the hospital "still complaining of stiffness in his left knee and favoring his left lower extremity when he walked." He started campaigning without "adequate convalescence and rehabilitation." Five days later, "he experienced a raging fever and shaking chill. Antibiotics were again prescribed." Nixon was fatigued, had lost weight, and was generally in "poor physical condition." This was readily apparent in the first presidential debate.

The American voter, Scalettar wrote, had the right to know the candidates' physical condition. "Yet no mechanism exists today to replace an infirmed or deceased presidential candidate after the major political party conventions have named their candidates." Candidates needed to provide "as much as possible about the health and well-being." Since the article's publication, no legislation has addressed these issues.[58]

In the summer of 2001, Scalettar added another disturbing element. He had personally told Nixon that he should not leave the hospital when he did. Under current rules, the doctor would have insisted that the vice president sign a statement that he was being released against medical advice. Jack Golden, the Secret Service agent assigned to the vice president, agreed that Nixon should not have left. He still had shivers and was perspiring and pale.[59]

Both Nixon and Kennedy knew the importance of appearing to be in excellent health. The vice president distorted his wellness after leaving Walter Reed, but recovered enough during the campaign to run a vigorous contest. Kennedy had a variety of serious illnesses and suffered some excruciating episodes throughout the race. Each subordinated his health issues and succeeded in creating a false impression. Winning superseded all else.

John F. Kennedy (back row, second from right) and Richard Nixon (to the right of Kennedy) as freshmen Congressmen in 1947. The group is not identified. Reni Newsphoto Service. Courtesy of the Richard Nixon Presidential Library and Museum.

The Nixon vice-presidential office staff with Pat Nixon. (From left to right) Loie Gaunt, office manager; Dorothy Cox, receptionist; P. J. Everts, secretary; Pat Nixon; Rose Mary Woods, the vice president's private secretary; Margaret Brock, a personal friend of Pat's. Courtesy of the Richard Nixon Presidential Library and Museum.

Lyndon Johnson at a dinner with Jackie Kennedy at the Sheraton Park
Hotel, Washington, D.C., January 23, 1960. Frank Muto.
Courtesy of the LBJ Presidential Library.

Jack Kennedy at the same dinner (see previous photo) with Lady Bird Johnson.
Frank Muto. Courtesy of the LBJ Presidential Library.

Nixon and
Eisenhower at the
Jumbo Jamboree box
supper given by the
National Republican
Women's Conference
at the Uline Arena in
Washington, D.C.,
on April 4, 1960.
Courtesy of the
Dwight D. Eisenhower
Presidential Library
and Museum.

Nixon with Julie, Pat, and Tricia at the Republican National Convention in Chicago,
July 1960. Courtesy of the Richard Nixon Presidential Library and Museum.

Nixon and Lodge greet members of the press after accepting the
presidential and vice-presidential nominations, July 25, 1960.
Courtesy of the Richard Nixon Presidential Library and Museum.

Nelson Rockefeller
visiting Nixon at
Walter Reed Hospital,
September 1, 1960. Signal
Corps Photographic
Laboratory, Walter
Reed Army Medical
Center, Washington,
D.C. Courtesy of the
Rockefeller Archive
Center.

JFK and LBJ in Austin, Texas, September 1960. Speaking before a group of ministers there, Kennedy declared that he was the Democratic candidate for President, not the Catholic candidate. Frank Muto. Courtesy of the LBJ Presidential Library.

Eisenhower at the Nixon campaign kickoff event, Friendship Airport, Baltimore, September 12, 1960. Courtesy of the National Park Service. Dwight D. Eisenhower Presidential Library and Museum.

Robert F. Kennedy shaking hands with a supporter, Sugar Creek, Missouri, November 1960. J. W. Porter for the *Kansas City Star.* Courtesy of the Harry S. Truman Library and Museum.

Harry S. Truman arriving for a Kennedy campaign event in Nashville, Tennessee, October 20, 1960. Courtesy of the Harry S. Truman Library and Museum.

Election Day: Three young Kennedy supporters in front of the Iolani Palace, Honolulu, Hawaii, November 8, 1960. Courtesy of the Harry S. Truman Library and Museum.

JFK speaking to reporters in Hyannis Port, Massachusetts, the morning he was declared the winner. Courtesy of the John F. Kennedy Presidential Library and Museum.

Nixon and Kennedy meeting at Key Biscayne, Florida, November 14, 1960. Courtesy of the Richard Nixon Presidential Library and Museum.

Kennedy and Eisenhower in the Oval Office during the presidential transition.
Courtesy of the John F. Kennedy Presidential Library and Museum.

John F. Kennedy is sworn in as the 35th U.S. president, January 20, 1961.
Courtesy of John F. Kennedy Presidential Library and Museum.

13

The Catholic Candidate

John Kennedy had begun his political career representing a heavily Irish-American congressional district. There his religion was not an issue, either initially or when he twice ran for reelection. Nor did he confront a major assault on his religious beliefs in his 1952 race for the Senate against incumbent Henry Cabot Lodge.

This changed in 1956, when he decided to seek the vice presidency. Before the Democratic convention, Ted Sorensen wrote a memorandum arguing for JFK to be Stevenson's running mate. To give the Kennedy organization plausible deniability as to authorship, John Bailey, state chairman of the Connecticut Democratic Party and a Catholic, claimed responsibility for the report, which became known as the "Bailey Report." It argued the existence of a "Catholic vote" that would support "a well-known Catholic candidate or a ticket with special Catholic appeal." Two-thirds of Catholics usually voted Democratic, and they were heavily concentrated in the northeastern urban centers, which represented a large bloc of electoral votes. If they united behind a coreligionist, that "could refashion this [Catholic] base . . . and begin a new era of Democratic victories."

The report briefly mentioned New York Governor Alfred Smith's race against Secretary of Commerce Herbert Hoover in 1928. Smith was the first Catholic to win a major party's presidential nomination, and he had lost in a landslide to the first Quaker presidential nominee. The report dismissed that defeat: "1928 was a Republican year, regardless of who was on either ticket."[1]

Robert Slayton, in his biography of Smith, *Empire Statesman*, offered several reasons why the candidate lost. He was a "wet" and called for the repeal of Prohibition. He spoke with a heavy New York accent and represented an urban, immigrant base at a time when the nation was experiencing a major nativist revival.

Groups like the Ku Klux Klan were on the rise and conducting hate-filled, violent campaigns against Jews, African Americans, and Catholics. Anti-Catholic propaganda included the idea that the Vatican expected to rule the world and would impose a theocracy on the United States. According to Slayton, Smith anticipated that the election "would be a fair fight" in which voters would examine "the record." Instead, in what Slayton describes as "a spasm of intense cruelty," he was viciously attacked for his Catholicism.[2]

The Bailey Report nearly persuaded enough delegates at the 1956 Democratic convention to nominate Kennedy for the vice presidency, but instead, by the slimmest margin, he suffered his first political failure. The Stevenson-Kefauver ticket lost to Eisenhower-Nixon in a landslide, and JFK launched his quest for the 1960 presidential nomination just days later.

Eisenhower had won almost half of Catholic voters in 1952; four years later, he again won just less than half. During the 1958 off-year elections, Catholics returned to their party, with as high as 85 percent voting Democratic in some elections. According to Lyman Kellstedt and Mark Noll, two-thirds of Catholics regularly went to church in the 1950s and approximately 65 percent identified as Democrats. Since World War II, that percentage had decreased; but the 1960 presidential election "marked the high point of Roman Catholic support for the Democratic party."[3]

Nixon was a birthright Quaker and steeped in that faith's beliefs. He did not encounter any religious issues that affected his early political career. While many in his church were pacifists, he had joined the navy in World War II, and few doubted his willingness to use military force to defend American interests. A couple of decades after the 1960 election, he reflected on why he had not used his Christian background as a political asset. He was embarrassed and uncomfortable, he said, using the word "God" in public appearances.[4]

He had often addressed religion as vice president. Shortly after the 1952 inauguration, he gave a televised address called "Back to God—Go to Church." In 1955 he was the principal speaker of the Second National Conference on Spiritual Foundations. After moving to Washington, the Nixon family joined the Westmoreland Congregational Church; they later switched to the Metropolitan Methodist Church because it was more conveniently located.[5]

Nixon routinely made appearances at Catholic events and corresponded with influential members of the Catholic hierarchy. Father John Cronin, whom he met in 1947, remained a trusted adviser. In the summer of 1957 Cronin told Nixon that Kennedy would be his principal competitor for the presidency. Since the vice president rose from a humble upbringing and lacked Kennedy's vast family wealth, he would have to rely on volunteers, a superior organization, and the efficient use of campaign funds. In April 1959, Cronin added that the Catholic clergy did not think highly of Kennedy. He routinely sent copies of the vice president's speeches to the Catholic hierarchy. Even with this counsel, Cronin stayed out of the 1960 presidential contest.[6]

The vice president also met Father Theodore Hesburgh, president of the University of Notre Dame, whom he described as "one of the ablest men in the field of education today." In 1954, Nixon spoke at Notre Dame about its commitment "to teach young men to be loyal to God and country." He wrote Francis Cardinal Spellman, archbishop of New York, and visited the archbishop of Boston, Richard Cardinal Cushing, in the fall of 1955 to discuss communist activities in Latin America. Four years later, Archbishop Cushing wrote FBI director Hoover: "No one can ever accuse the Vice President of being apathetic or indifferent to Communism."[7]

America in the 1950s was a religious country. Almost half the population regularly attended church, according to Gallup Polls, and more than 90 percent said they believed in God. By 1960, 114 million of the nation's 180 million people had religious affiliations. Gallup reported that two-thirds of voters were Protestant, just over a quarter were Catholic, and 4 percent were Jewish.[8]

In 1960, *Time* magazine noted that Roman Catholics in the United States were experiencing a "population explosion." From 1950 to 1959, their numbers had increased 35.8 percent, to almost 44 million, while the nation as a whole grew by 16.6 percent. By 1960, according to the U.S. census, 22 percent of Americans were Catholics. Gallup found that 68 percent of Americans were willing to vote for a Catholic for president, compared with 62 percent in 1940. In 1958, seven Catholic candidates, all Democrats, had won governorships, and eight had won Senate seats, increasing the number of Catholic senators to twelve. Again, all were Democrats.[9]

In March 1959, the Gallup Poll reported that just over half of those interviewed knew that Kennedy was Catholic; 40 percent of Catholics were unaware of it. On March 3, columnist Fletcher Knebel published "Democratic Forecast: A Catholic in 1960" in *Look* magazine. He asserted that Catholicism was no longer a handicap for a presidential candidate and might even help. Kennedy, quoted in the piece, made several points. First, he said, the Constitution stated that "no religious test shall ever be required as a qualification to any office or public trust under the United States." Second, to ease any anxieties over his ties to the pope, he emphasized that "the separation of church and state is fundamental to our American concept and heritage and should remain so." He opposed the appointment of an American ambassador to the Vatican as well as federal aid to parochial schools.[10]

The Catholic press, according to historian T. David Lisle, commented that JFK's "remarks had most certainly been ill-advised not to say somewhat presumptuous." His pledge that the pope would not dictate policy to him, made to calm Protestant fears, troubled some Catholic commentators. Despite widespread criticism, the article brought attention both to Kennedy and to how he would address his religious beliefs as president. Throughout the campaign, according to Lisle, the Catholic press "remained consistently . . . frank, lucid, thoughtful, refusing to succumb to paranoia or reverse bigotry."[11]

On December 21, 1959, *Newsweek* reported on its own survey of how Catholics felt about a Catholic running for the presidency. The majority believed there was far less anti-Catholic sentiment than in 1928, and they saw no conflict for a president between "being a loyal American and a good Catholic." Still, they worried that if a Catholic president made mistakes, they would be blamed on his religion or "on the Pope." They wanted one of their own to run and win to end the thinking that a Catholic could not become president. When asked their preferred candidate, the name most often mentioned was Kennedy's.[12]

At the beginning of 1960, *U.S. News and World Report* reported on the Louisiana gubernatorial primary race of January 9, which pitted New Orleans mayor deLesseps Morrison, a Catholic, against former governor James Davis, a Protestant. After Davis won, Louisiana politicians generally agreed that religion had played a significant role. Morrison carried every parish (county) where Catholics held a majority and lost almost all of the Protestant-majority parishes.[13]

Kennedy's religion might have changed voter preferences. Before it became an issue, he was running ahead of Nixon, but as his Catholicism became better known, Nixon pulled ahead, 53 percent to 47. When Kennedy won the Wisconsin primary in April, he achieved his highest margins in the urban, industrial Catholic districts; Humphrey carried the rural Protestant ones, which were also closest to his home state of Minnesota. Kennedy decided to face off against Humphrey in West Virginia's May primary even though that state was about 95 percent Protestant.[14]

Interrupting that campaign to appear before the American Society of Newspaper Editors on April 21, Kennedy spoke heatedly about "the religious issue." No one had paid much attention to his religion, he said, until he decided to run for the White House. The media were preoccupied with how his religion had affected the Wisconsin primary outcome, but he downplayed its significance and criticized the press for not focusing on the major issues confronting the nation. He had repeatedly declared that as president he would not respond to "ecclesiastical pressures or obligations," and he objected to being "the only candidate required to answer those questions." Some of his decisions as a senator, he emphasized, displeased the Catholic Church. He had voted for aid to the communist nation of Yugoslavia, for example, and approved the nomination of James Conant as the first United States ambassador to West Germany, even though Conant vehemently opposed federal aid to parochial schools. If a bill came to his desk to provide foreign aid for birth control, he would base his decision on what was best for the public interest, not his personal religious beliefs.[15]

Dan Fleming, Jr., who has written the most authoritative book on the West Virginia primary, says that the outcome was never in doubt; Kennedy led comfortably throughout the race, and Humphrey lost in a landslide. Fleming concluded: "The media focus on and dramatization of the religious issue was overdone to the point that they fell prey to their own efforts to keep a good story going. The national press did not have its finest hour." In their preoccupation with religion, reporters failed to look into the seemingly endless money the Kennedy organization poured into the race.[16]

Seven days after that primary, the Vatican daily newspaper, *L'Osservatore Romano*, deflated the triumph by claiming that the Church's jurisdiction extended to all activities, including political views. This rekindled the debate within the Catholic press over Kennedy's policy positions.[17]

In his acceptance speech at the Democratic convention on July 15, Kennedy acknowledged that many thought the Democratic Party had taken "a new and hazardous risk" by nominating a Catholic for president. He agreed that he was a risky choice but congratulated his party for having "placed its confidence in the American people, and in their ability to render a free, fair judgment." The party could be assured that he would "uphold the Constitution and my oath of office—and . . . reject any kind of religious pressure or obligation that might directly or indirectly interfere with my conduct of the Presidency in the national interest." He pledged: "My decisions on any public policy will be my own—as an American, a Democrat, and a free man."[18]

During a campaign stop in Seattle on September 6, reporter Bill Buskirk asked Kennedy how he would answer the attacks on his Catholicism, especially in the South. Responding that some would never vote for him, he said he did not believe "that anyone would throw away their vote by voting for me or against me because of my religion, rather than the things for which I might stand."[19]

Campaign manager Bobby Kennedy gave his opinion of "the religious question" in a letter at the end of August to Congressman Morgan Moulder, Democrat from Missouri. Many people had "a genuine desire to make a judgment based on the facts." During the West Virginia primary, the issue of JFK's religion was "acute," and at first he "ran considerably behind." But after the senator confronted the issue "forthrightly and . . . spoke out and conveyed his convictions on this subject there was a tremendous switch in voter sentiment." Voters were persuaded to vote for him through "a vigorous but sympathetic effort." If the general election campaign adopted the West Virginia model, it would yield the same result: "The so-called religious issue will evaporate."[20]

To address the issue, the campaign established a community relations committee. On August 24 it announced that James Wine, Jr., "a lay Protestant leader" and former associate general secretary of the National Council of Churches, had been hired as a special assistant to Kennedy "to help combat" religious opposition. Writing to the Reverend Eugene Blake of the United Presbyterian Church on September 7, Wine asserted that all religious communities had to state "what . . . we really mean when we say religious freedom and the full exercise of religious liberty." Voting for JFK might not resolve this, but all faiths had to embrace "an enlightened attitude."[21]

The campaign committee received many letters concerning Kennedy's membership in the Knights of Columbus. He was also rumored to have sworn an oath—which the campaign described as "bogus"—to an ultraconservative Baptist minister named Mickey Johnson. Johnson had written Kennedy in early 1958 to complain about Catholic persecution of Baptist missionaries and to threaten that if Kennedy did not clarify his positions on many issues, especially the separation of church and state, Baptists would oppose his candidacy.[22]

At first, Joe Kennedy did not think religion would be a critical factor, but by the start of 1959 he had changed his mind. He was outraged that Pope John XXIII and members of the American Catholic hierarchy refused to champion his son's candidacy. The only exception was Richard Cardinal Cushing, archbishop of Boston and a Kennedy loyalist. After all the money Joe had given to Catholic charities, he was livid, and he vowed to end his donations to the Catholic Church—except those to Cushing.[23]

Lyndon Johnson commented on the religious issue in the first week of August. Speaking in Texas, he said that the last time the nation voted against a Catholic, it had suffered the Great Depression. The *El Paso Times* responded that if LBJ was claiming the nation had been punished because of Smith's defeat, "he'd better stop right now and do some soul searching." Toward the end of the month, Lady Bird Johnson declared that religion would not be decisive in the Lone Star State because Texans were too "broadminded." The Johnsons, she pointed out, were Baptists and not anti-Catholic.[24]

Truman began promoting the Democratic ticket by attacking Nixon as prejudiced. He said on August 5: "While he stands at the front door proclaiming charity and tolerance, his supporters are herding the forces of racial, religious and anti-union bigotry by way of the back door." The vice president understood "what is going on," said Truman, who asked his audience to reject religious prejudice and accept that every American had the right to hold office. Since religion did not prevent a man from joining the armed forces and defending the nation, "it surely ought not to bar him from holding public office."[25]

Harvard professors offered their advice. In late August economist John Kenneth Galbraith told Kennedy that his religion was a serious problem in the farm belt that had to be addressed forcefully. Kennedy's only option was a televised speech that would offer a solution to the agricultural crisis and also "deal directly with religion" by assuring his audience that any fear of his Catholic beliefs was "groundless." Arthur Schlesinger, Jr., added his thoughts in early September, telling Bobby that some people believed Jack's "victory would mean that your co-religionists would take over the Democratic party and convert it into a Demo-Christian party." That idea was "illogical and self-pitying, but it exists."[26]

Eisenhower had long believed that the nation needed more spiritual values and less secularism. He had offered a short prayer during his first inaugural speech, and soon after taking office, he had become the first (and so far only) president to be baptized while in the White House. Under his administration, the National Day of Prayer and the National Prayer Breakfast became annual events, the words "under God" were added to the Pledge of Allegiance, and "In God We Trust" first appeared on United States currency.[27]

Ike also appointed several Catholics to high positions. William Brennan, Jr., was selected for the Supreme Court; Clare Boothe Luce became ambassador to Italy; and James Mitchell served as secretary of labor. When the president traveled to the Vatican in 1959 to visit Pope John XXIII, he became only the second American president to have an audience with the pope (Woodrow Wilson was the first, forty years earlier). Historian Craig Keller writes that Eisenhower "accepted Roman Catholicism as constituting one of the nation's vital religions."[28]

By spring 1960, questions about religion were coming up at the president's press conferences. On April 27, Ray Scherer of NBC asked how Ike felt about religion's being injected into political campaigns. The president cited Article VI of the Constitution, which bars any religious test for public office, and quoted the First Amendment: "Congress shall make no law respecting an establishment of religion or prohibiting the free exercise thereof."[29]

In a press conference on August 24, Edward Morgan of ABC News said that several sources had commented on the rise of anti-Catholic sentiment during the campaign and asked whether Eisenhower personally objected to religious issues being raised. The president replied that while religion "should not be an issue . . .

I am not so naïve that I think that in some areas it will not be." Some people had "strong emotional convictions and reactions" about religion. He would never recognize a candidate's beliefs as "a legitimate question."[30]

At the president's next press conference, two weeks later, Kenneth Scheibel of Gannett Newspapers noted that the vice president refused to discuss religion during the campaign. The president answered that he and Nixon had agreed they would "never raise, and never mention" religion in the upcoming race. He did not believe in "voicing prejudice," and he assured his audience that he felt "none." The vice president held the same view. Religion should be "one of those subjects that could be laid on the shelf and forgotten until after the election is over."[31]

Nixon had been responding to questions about Kennedy's ambitions since October 1958, when, in reply to a reporter's question, he said that the United States had changed dramatically since the 1928 election. Kennedy was "an able man, an effective opponent and a good campaigner" whose religion would not affect his presidential aspirations and would not be "a liability."[32]

The following year, Nixon said that Catholics did not vote as a bloc but "as their conscience dictates," and they would be offended if anyone suggested otherwise. The decline of religious prejudice illustrated the country's growing political maturity.[33]

Before primary voting began, in February 1960, Nixon was again asked about Kennedy's religion, and he replied that several candidates thought it could be an issue. But "it should not be an issue." In the middle of May, as Kennedy was winning every primary he entered, the vice president suggested "that aggressive anti-Catholics will do more to drive Republican Catholics and independent Catholics into the Kennedy ranks than all his [Kennedy's] campaigning could possibly do." He could not, however, do anything "to stop their foolish statements."[34] In a letter to Ike's brother Milton written on the day Kennedy was nominated, Nixon wrote that his prediction about JFK had come true: "The so-called religious issue" would help Kennedy more than it hurt him.[35]

Behind the scenes, Nixon worked to get prominent Catholics to serve on his campaign committees. He wanted to do this quietly but also make sure people knew he had Catholic support. He told his public relations advisers to give out information, especially to the Catholic press, regarding key people on his staffs who were Catholics, even including stenographers like receptionist Betty McVey.[36]

In a press conference shortly after his nomination, a reporter said that since religion was being raised in the campaign, there was "talk abroad that probably you'll name Billy Graham as part of your Cabinet." Nixon replied: "Religion will be in this campaign to the extent that the candidates of either side talk about it. I shall never talk about it and we'll start right now."[37]

Reporters often asked Nixon about Graham. Ordained as a Baptist minister, he had helped to restore the revivalist tradition through his "crusades," which emphasized individual conversion and simple moral choices rather than complex issues. He presented modern politics as equally simple: a struggle between God and communism.[38]

Graham had met Ike in Paris when Eisenhower was NATO's commander in chief. After Eisenhower became president, Graham participated in his prayer breakfasts at the White House and the National Prayer Day. Both men agreed that the way to achieve civil rights was by changing people's hearts and proceeding with moderation. Graham compared Eisenhower to Lincoln and ultimately concluded that he was the greatest president in American history.[39]

In the spring of 1959, the evangelist started offering the president political advice. In March, he wrote that he was "delighted" to see the president "standing up to the Russians" because they had to be stopped. The president, he cautioned, must "not allow extreme Liberal churchmen to advise you that war is the ultimate evil." God sometimes sanctioned a just war.[40]

A year later, Graham wrote that when the president was scheduled to travel to Moscow, he should attend a Baptist service, or any Protestant service, the Sunday before. Since his invitation came from "professed atheists," his attendance "might be one of the most historic events of your administration." On May 20, Graham expressed his approval of the president's address regarding the Paris summit and his terrible disappointment with "the attitude of Stevenson, Kennedy and others. . . . They have hurt themselves." In early August, he saw the president battling against Kennedy-Johnson legislative proposals and urged him to "send so many dramatic messages to Congress that you could keep Kennedy and Johnson off-balance and capture the headlines during that period."[41]

Graham started to comment on the upcoming election in early August. Ike's convention address "was absolutely superb," and the president should campaign vigorously for Nixon, who had "a fighting chance only if you go all out." The president needed to concentrate on "key states from Kentucky to Texas." At the beginning of September, Graham predicted that religion was "shaping up as the most decisive of all the issues." The president's popularity had never been higher, and his "all-out support for Nixon and Lodge could be one of the strongest factors in the campaign."[42]

Graham also began forming a close bond with the vice president. Senator

Clyde Hoey, a Democrat from North Carolina, had introduced them during lunch in the Senate cafeteria early in Nixon's first term, and they played golf together that afternoon. Though they met only on rare occasions, Graham considered the vice president "the most able man in the Republican Party" but feared that "extreme right-wingers" might have too much influence over him. To win the presidency, Nixon would have to "take a middle-of-the-road position."[43]

The two men grew closer during Eisenhower's second term. At a religious service at Yankee Stadium on an oppressively hot summer day in 1957, with 100,000 people inside and an overflow crowd of 20,000 outside, Graham preached as Nixon sat with him on the platform. This was the first time a vice president had attended one of the evangelist's crusades.[44]

Graham often wrote Nixon with advice on his run for the presidency. Toward the end of 1957, he commented that the vice president's "political stock is extremely high, although I fear there are many factors working against any Republican being elected in 1960." Kennedy was receiving laudatory press coverage, and while he would be a "formidable foe, . . . the religious issue would be very strong and might conceivably work in your behalf."[45] In November 1959 he urged the vice president to attend church regularly to obtain the backing of American churchgoers.[46]

In the spring of 1960, Graham attended the Southern Baptist Convention, which drew about fifteen thousand delegates, and where the *New York Times* reported that he supported Nixon for the presidency without publicly mentioning him by name. Graham reported to the vice president: "Nearly all seemed to be strong Nixon supporters—if Kennedy is the Democratic nominee!" If JFK ran, Nixon might win several southern states. Just before the Republican convention, he advised Nixon to choose Rockefeller as his running mate.[47]

The evangelist sent Nixon a letter on August 23, saying he had spent three days with Martin Luther King, Jr., at the Baptist World Alliance convention in Rio de Janeiro. King told Graham that Kennedy had invited him to his Georgetown home and they had talked for three hours, leaving King "greatly impressed and just about sold." But Graham thought he had neutralized King, and if Nixon saw him briefly, "it might swing him. He would be a powerful influence."[48]

Graham would be preaching in Germany through September and would return to the United States in the first week of October. At a conference in Switzerland with twenty-five "outstanding American clergymen," he had talked with the Reverend Dr. Norman Vincent Peale, and the two had decided to open an office in the capital on September 8 to supply material on Kennedy and a Catholic presidency to religious leaders throughout the nation. Graham and Peale wanted the vice president to include more religious references in his speeches, and Peale was "coming out flat-footed for you in a sermon on or about October 9. He says this will be extremely costly to him but feels that he must speak out at all costs."[49]

Graham should have added that, while in Switzerland, he had said publicly that "a man's religion cannot be separated from his person. . . . The religious issue is deeper than in 1928. People are better informed today." Protestants might be hesitant to vote for Kennedy because his church was "not only a religious but also a secular institution, with its own ministers and ambassadors."[50]

As the general election campaign began and the media continued to comment on the "religious issue," *Newsweek* and *Time* ran articles on Graham's role in the upcoming election. In an interview with *Time*, Graham said that JFK's religion "was a legitimate issue in the campaign and would be decisive in the outcome."[51]

After these articles were published in late August, Graham sent letters to both magazines declaring that he was not involving himself in the religious issue. Clearly in anticipation of their release, he wrote to Nixon, "I am not so much opposed to Kennedy as I am *for you*." He would "do all in my power to help you get elected." The Protestant attack, he claimed, was in response to the Catholic bloc: "At all cost you must continue to stay a million miles away from the religious issue at this time." Kennedy had hired "a clever, brilliant, Protestant attorney by the name of Vine [James Wine]" to organize Protestants for JFK. Graham closed by saying he would "probably come out openly for you—but not on religious grounds—but on the grounds that you and Lodge are best equipped to steer the Nation in the next four years."[52]

Nixon wrote back on August 29, pointing out that after the press had covered the Nixons when they attended church services, a Kennedy supporter complained to one of Nixon's friends that he had deliberately injected "the religious issue into the campaign by allowing my picture to be taken going to church. This shows that you just can't win on that issue!" He hoped ministers would encourage people to vote: "This completely avoids any so-called religious prejudice and simply assures that the decision on November 8 will be made by a majority of all the people."[53]

The man Graham met with in Switzerland, Norman Vincent Peale, led the Marble Collegiate Church in Manhattan, where his two Sunday sermons always drew overflow crowds. His books, led by *The Power of Positive Thinking* from 1952, had sold more than four million copies; his syndicated column, "Confident Living," ran in 196 newspapers; his radio show, *The Art of Living*, was broadcast on sixty NBC stations; and his monthly magazine, *Guideposts*, was distributed nationwide. Politically, he was a Republican who had backed Thomas Dewey for the presidency in 1948. In 1952, he advised ministers to stay away from politics but added, "when there was a moral involved they should speak up in this case for Eisenhower and Nixon."[54]

Peale first wrote to Nixon in the winter of 1956, after hearing him speak before the National Republican Club in New York City. Calling the address "one of the truly great speeches by a political leader in recent years," the minister encouraged Nixon to seek the presidency if Ike did not run. Even though his calling was "quite apart from politics," Peale wished "to be registered as an original Nixon man."[55]

On April 12, 1960, just before the state's primary campaign began, Peale spoke in Charleston, West Virginia, expressing doubts about whether Kennedy, as a Catholic, should be president. He worried about an incident in 1950 in which JFK refused to speak at an interfaith meeting after consultation with Dennis Cardinal Dougherty. If he listened to the cardinal's advice then, "what would he do under other circumstances? Should any ecclesiastical authority be able to interfere with the freedom of a public official of the United States?"[56]

On April 19, the vice president wrote in a memorandum to his staff that someone should see Peale and ask him to mail Bela Kornitzer's *The Real Nixon* to every Protestant minister possible. Peale could add a short note saying that while he was not in politics, he knew Nixon, who always stopped in his church when in New York City. A month later, Peale provided such a letter: the vice president was "misunderstood by some of my friends," and Kornitzer's book would help them understand the man.[57]

On the first of August, Peale informed Nixon that he was deeply concerned about the presidential election and could not believe that voters would choose Kennedy over him. He had spoken with Graham, and they agreed they "must do all within our power to help you." The vice president was "a real statesman" and was being challenged by "an insatiable opportunist with vast sums of money at his disposal."[58]

Others agreed. Fundamentalists, according to historian Warren Vinz, passionately "hated and feared Roman Catholicism." Historian William Martin adds that fundamentalist and evangelical Christians despised the Roman Catholic Church "as the institution identified in the book of Revelation as the whore of Babylon, an integral part of the Antichrist's evil plan for world domination."[59]

Bruce Felknor, the executive director of the Fair Campaign Practices Committee, reported on August 24 that mailings of anti-Catholic literature were coming from "nearly every part of the country." He had never seen this amount of hateful material: "There is a substantial danger that the campaign in 1960 will be dirtier on the religious issue than it was in 1928."[60]

Toward the end of August, the Minnesota Baptist Convention passed a resolution opposing the election of a Catholic president. Other Southern Baptist conventions and Methodist organizations took similar positions. On September 4, the *New York Times* published a long front-page article in its Sunday edition reporting that anti-Catholicism was widespread in parts of the South. Fundamentalists and Masons opposed JFK on religious grounds. The Southern Baptist Convention, with 9.6 million followers and thirty-one thousand ministers, declared that many southern Baptists would vote Republican. The head of the convention, the Reverend Dr. Ramsey Pollard, announced that he would not vote for a Catholic as president: "I think the vast majority of Southern Baptist ministers and laymen will vote against Kennedy. . . . Most of us feel he is a devout Catholic, a splendid young man. But we do not feel he can dissociate himself from the Roman Catholic hierarchy." The 150-member General Presbytery of the Assemblies of God in Missouri, an evangelical church with a million members, unanimously voted to oppose a Catholic president.[61]

Speaking before the Senate on August 30, Estes Kefauver, Democrat from Tennessee, declared: "The country is being flooded once again with false and libelous anti-Catholic materials. There is every likelihood that this hate campaign will get worse." The next day, Virginia Governor J. Lindsay Almond, Jr., a Democrat, blamed Nixon for telling his staff not to talk about religion. While Republicans publicly said they would not make religion an issue, Almond declared, they were tolerating a hate campaign that could make Kennedy lose "substantial support" in his state. Alabama Governor John Patterson claimed that the GOP was exploiting the religious issue, but JFK would not be damaged because Alabama voters "are more tolerant than ever before."[62]

Peale returned from Switzerland on September 6. The next day he traveled from New York to Washington, D.C., to meet behind closed doors at the Mayflower Hotel with a group of 150 Protestant ministers and laymen from thirty-seven denominations. According to the *New York Times*, Peale identified the group as "more or less representative of the evangelical, conservative Protestants."

Peale chaired the gathering alongside Dr. Daniel Poling, another prominent Protestant minister, editor of the influential monthly *Christian Herald*, and an unsuccessful Republican candidate for mayor of Philadelphia. Poling was also a longtime Kennedy antagonist. As a congressman in 1950, Kennedy had accepted Poling's invitation to speak at an interfaith fundraiser in memory of four army chaplains who died on the troop ship Dorchester in 1943, including Poling's son, Clark. Kennedy canceled at the last moment on advice of the archdiocese of Philadelphia.[63]

Kennedy had written an apologetic letter to Poling a few weeks before the 1960 convention. He would have come, he said, representing Massachusetts or Congress, not as "a spokesman for the Catholic Church." His congressional record on the separation of church and state was "well known." Any "further pursuit of this ancient misunderstanding" would not serve "the cause of brotherhood." He hoped to work with Poling to take "whatever steps are necessary to set the record straight."[64] This attempt at damage control was unsatisfactory. Poling never forgave him.

The "Peale group," as it came to be known, released a two thousand–word manifesto on September 7, stating that "the religious issue remains a major factor in the current political campaign." In a preamble, the group claimed that it was not prejudiced and acknowledged that Kennedy had declared that the Catholic Church would not influence his decisions. But they were alarmed that the church "insists he is duty-bound to submit to its direction."[65]

The manifesto listed five points. First, the Roman Catholic Church was a political and religious institution, and a Catholic president would come "under extreme pressure" to follow its diplomatic line, including appointing a representative to the Vatican. Second, the church believed that Protestants were "heretical and counterfeit and that they have no theoretical right to exist." Third, where the Catholic Church dominated, it denied "equal rights for all of other faiths." In Spain and Colombia, for instance, Protestant missionaries had "been arrested, imprisoned and otherwise persecuted because of their religion." Fourth, the Catholic Church in the United States was attempting to "break down the wall of separation of church and state," including lobbying for federal aid to parochial schools. Kennedy had voted several times for Catholic Church initiatives. As president, he would shape legislation and would not "be able to withstand altogether the determined efforts of" his church to provide money "and favors for its schools and institutions." Finally, under canon law, a Catholic president could not go to interfaith gatherings or worship in a Protestant church without ecclesiastical permission. This violated the separation of church and state. Kennedy was not at fault for this situation. The Catholic Church created it by being both a religious and "a temporal state."[66]

Those present chose Peale to speak to the press. A conferee warned: "Say one wrong word, and the press will murder us—by next week we'll be out of business." Peale joked: "Pray for us while we are talking to those reporters."[67]

Their prayers were not answered. Peale faced a barrage of criticism as soon as the manifesto was published. Three days after the meeting, he severed ties with the organization and canceled his media and speaking engagements. The following week he wrote that reporters had distorted his role and the purpose of the

gathering, and that the best-qualified candidate should win the election. It was objectionable that the conference was labeled the "Peale group," and he offered to resign from his pulpit over his "unwise" actions. The offer was of course refused.[68]

Just one day after the Peale group released its manifesto, the Liberal Party of New York put out a statement by Dr. Reinhold Niebuhr, the party's vice president and the recently retired vice president of the Union Theological Seminary: "Dr. Peale and I disagree on everything, religiously and politically." Even as they claimed to reject bigotry, Niebuhr wrote, the Peale group showed a "blind prejudice" against the Catholic Church and did not recognize the independence of American Catholics who held high political offices. The Liberal Party, which had endorsed Kennedy, said it repudiated the false issue of the candidate's beliefs.[69]

But notwithstanding his personal and professional antipathy toward Peale, Niebuhr had his own doubts regarding Kennedy. That summer he had told Henry Van Dusen, president of the Union Theological Seminary, that if the rumors of Kennedy's reckless philandering were true, his "dubious morals" made him unfit for the presidency. As the campaign commenced, however, his disapproval of the "ruthless" Kennedy family, the "thinness" of JFK's religious convictions, and his personal conduct disappeared. As a liberal Democrat who never voted Republican, Niebuhr rationalized that compared with Nixon, Kennedy was the lesser of two evils.[70]

Joe Kennedy, returning from a trip abroad, wrote the newspaper publisher Lord Beaverbrook on September 9 that he had come back to the United States to find that the presidential election was not between a Republican and Democrat but between a Catholic and Protestant. His son had given anti-Catholicism "a bad licking in West Virginia" and would lick it again. "But with the Baptist ministers working in the pulpit every Sunday, it is going to be tough. . . . They have a hell of a nerve to be talking about freedom for the world when we have this kind of a condition right here in our country." The Kennedys needed "to fight this thing with everything we have. And that is what we are going to do."[71]

The same day, Kennedy spoke from the rear platform of his train in Modesto, California, about many campaign issues. A heckler interrupted him, asking whether "all Protestants are heretics." He replied: "No, and I hope you don't believe all Catholics are." Later that day, at a press conference in Burbank, he was asked about the Peale group's statement that he would be "under extreme pressure from" the Catholic hierarchy to bring "American foreign policy into line with Vatican objectives." He refused to respond.[72]

Lyndon Johnson gave a press conference on the ninth deploring the attacks on Kennedy's Catholicism. If the United States supported a religious test for office,

he said, we might as well "tear up the Bill of Rights and throw our Constitution into the wastebasket." At another press conference the next day, he objected to "hatemongers" and "hate literature." Few Americans considered religion an issue, he said; "most Americans think that all people should have the right to worship God as they please." Later he added that what church one belonged to did not matter, "as long as you believe in God and worship as your conscience dictates."[73]

Nixon, hospitalized when the articles on the Peale group appeared, recalled a quarter century later that he and Pat often went to Peale's church when they were in Manhattan, and he considered Vincent "one of my closest friends." Peale, he said, "was heartbroken when he realized that the statement he endorsed might have caused such a negative uproar against me." Nixon, in turn, was upset by how the media had "savaged" Peale.[74]

He wrote to Clare Boothe Luce, then the United States ambassador to Italy, that he wanted to keep religion out of the election. He detested anti-Catholic literature, he told Luce, and had heard rumors that it was being mailed out where there were high concentrations of Catholic voters. He did not think Kennedy would do this, "but I wouldn't put this past the likes of Reuther, et al." He worried that "the effect may well be to drive the small percentage of Catholic voters who are still on our side to vote for Kennedy out of protest." That the selection of the president "might be affected by a completely extraneous issue" was "disheartening to a degree I find hard to describe."[75]

The vice president appeared on *Meet the Press* on September 11. When NBC correspondent Herbert Kaplow asked him about Kennedy's Catholicism, the vice president said he never doubted Kennedy's loyalty and that America's image abroad would suffer substantially if the election were seen to turn on religion. He said he had ordered "all of the people in my campaign not to discuss religion, not to raise it, not to allow anybody to participate in the [anti-Catholic] campaign. . . . I will decline to discuss religion and will discuss other issues in order to keep the minds of the people on the issues that should decide this election and to keep them off of an issue that should not enter into it." He hoped that he and Kennedy would agree on "a cutoff date" to "refrain from raising the issue."[76]

Kennedy listened to Nixon's interview on the radio while driving from Santa Monica to the airport. Upon his arrival, he told reporters that he agreed with the vice president that any religious debate should end "right now." Nixon quickly endorsed his opponent's declaration. Kennedy did not mention that he and Sorensen had spent most of the weekend working on a speech that would directly address the religion issue.[77]

JFK knew that anti-Catholic extremists would always vote against him. The Peale group's manifesto, however, came from more mainstream and influential Protestants. He needed to answer them, and his speech before the Greater Houston Ministerial Association on September 12 was the opportunity to do it. Kenneth O'Donnell, Bobby Kennedy's Harvard roommate and a close Kennedy counselor, advised Jack against giving any religious speech in Texas. He agreed with Lyndon Johnson and Sam Rayburn: "They're mostly Republicans and they're out to get you." Kennedy rejected that counsel: "This is as good a time as any to get it over with. I've got to face it sooner or later."[78]

Johnson flew into El Paso on September 11; he and Rayburn were to meet with Kennedy when he arrived there the following morning. They held rallies in El Paso and Lubbock. At the Alamo in San Antonio, protesters greeted JFK with signs: "We don't want the Kremlin and the Vatican" and "We want the Bible and the Constitution." When introducing JFK, LBJ shouted above the hecklers and reminded them of Kennedy's heroism on PT-109. "When Jack Kennedy was saving those Americans, they didn't ask him what church he belonged to." The party then flew on to Houston.[79]

In a ministerial association of eight hundred members, normally fifty regularly attended, in a region with more than one thousand Protestant churches. No Jewish or Catholic clergy were members. Kennedy began his forty-minute address before a gathering of six hundred to one thousand clergymen and laymen at 9:00 p.m. Twenty-two Texas television stations carried the event.[80]

Kenny O'Donnell recalled that JFK was "as restless as a caged tiger." He started by first reminding his listeners that while his principal topic was the "so-called religious issue," the major subjects of the campaign, like the spread of communism to Cuba and poverty in West Virginia, were far more pressing. The election should focus on which candidate was better prepared to solve those problems. Yet he had to direct this address to his religious beliefs. He repeated his earlier statement that he was "the Democratic Party's candidate for President, who happens also to be a Catholic."[81]

He had fought in the Pacific during World War II, and his older brother, fighting in Europe, had died in a plane explosion; no one then had asked them if they had "divided loyalty" because of their beliefs. He had visited the Alamo earlier that day. James Bowie and Davy Crockett gave their lives alongside Fuentes, McCafferty, Bailey, Bedilio, and Carey. There was no religious test, and no one knew whether they were Catholics or Protestants, or held some other beliefs.

Kennedy made one startling promise he had never uttered before. If he were president and his office required him "to either violate my conscience or violate the national interest, then I would resign the office." Later, in the question-and-answer period, he provided a murky correction: he meant to say conflict "with my conscience." He did not think such a situation would occur, and he hoped others would act similarly.[82]

Texas Democrats praised the address. Religious leaders expressed differing opinions. Some ministers were upset because they felt Kennedy had been treated discourteously. The Catholic press and priests remained neutral. Through most of the campaign, Catholics were on the defensive, and some Catholic conservatives opposed Kennedy's candidacy. Rabbi Robert Kahn of Temple Emanu El in Houston said that JFK had resolved any doubts about his independence from his church. While many Christian ministers agreed, Dr. Tim Trammell, minister of the First Baptist Church of Kilgore, thought that since JFK was a loyal Catholic and his church opposed the separation of church and state, he should not be president. The editor of the *Baptist Standard* concurred, as did many other Baptists. One influential Texas minister, Dr. W. A. Criswell of Dallas, had not attended but said that a friend who did called the event "the biggest farce he ever saw in his life." He added that Kennedy had lied when he said the Catholic Church had no real means of punishment if he disobeyed them. All Catholics, Criswell said, feared excommunication. All Catholics therefore needed to be "barred from public office." Many Baptists formed political organizations to vote against Kennedy; some joined Democrats for Nixon or Texans for Nixon.[83]

Lyndon Johnson raised the Catholic issue for the rest of the campaign, repeating the line that Kennedy's older brother died in a plane explosion during World War II and that his copilot was Wilford Wiley of Forth Worth, Texas: "When those boys went out to die so that you could live, nobody asked them what church they went to."[84]

After the Houston appearance, the Kennedy campaign continually invoked his address. In the middle of October, *Time* magazine reported that, to the surprise of local California Democrats, the DNC had distributed Kennedy's speech to eight television stations in prime time. It also ran in Colorado, Wyoming, Minnesota, Michigan, New York, and Vermont, and also across the South. Republicans were upset; they had agreed to stop talking about religion. Democrats, however, knew that broadcasting the speech where there was a high concentration of Catholics such as New York, Seattle, and San Francisco kept "the issue bubbling." Kennedy forces admitted that Republicans were not exploiting the issue, but their reasoning for broadcasting the address was that "crackpot mail against a Catholic President [is] flooding mailboxes, particularly in the South and the border states."[85]

✔ ✔ ✔

In a speech on September 12, Truman declared that the religious issue in national politics was "finally dead" and that both Kennedy and Nixon had agreed "to lay aside this whole religious issue for good." Because he backed Kennedy, he told his listeners, many "ignorant, bigoted people" had written him letters calling him names for supporting a Catholic. RNC chairman Morton accused the former president and other Democrats of keeping "the religious issue inflamed." Democrats, he charged, were using it for "their own political advantage." New York Republican Congressman William Miller, a Catholic and chairman of the Republican congressional campaign committee, argued that the Democratic Party was using the film of the Houston gathering to depict JFK as a martyr against a fundamentalist inquisition and unite Catholics to vote for their coreligionist.[86]

Also speaking on September 12, Henry Cabot Lodge said that religion should not be a campaign issue. As an Episcopalian, he did not want anyone to vote for or against him because of his religion. The younger of his two sons, Henry, had married a Catholic woman, and their three children were being raised in that faith. He would not want them barred from seeking the presidency. His other son, George, had two sons being raised Episcopalian, and Lodge did not want them barred either.[87]

Billy Graham added another dimension in a September 24 letter to Nixon marked "Urgent & Confidential." The evangelist wrote Nixon that he had to be "very careful" in the existing political climate. Having seen how the press had savaged Peale, the evangelist wrote, he did not want to get involved in the religious issue. But as the campaign intensified, he thought he might "be forced to take a more open stand if I feel it will help your cause, but we shall wait further developments."

Friends had told him, Graham wrote, that the religious issue in the West Virginia primary "was hardly a whisper when the Kennedy people began to talk about it and they have continually fanned the flames." The minister was "convinced that the religious tide that may be running slightly against you at the moment *must* be turned." He had spoken in June to a Democratic leader who said Democrats were planning to use the religious issue "to put their crowd in the White House," "to solidify the Catholic vote," to "split the Protestant vote," to "present Mr. Kennedy as a persecuted martyr," "to create sympathy for him," and to "obscure the primary issues in the campaign." Graham wanted Eisenhower, Rockefeller, Dewey, and Javits to speak out against bigotry.[88]

Gallup's two polls in mid-September and the first week of October confirmed that religion both helped and hurt Kennedy. Catholics, who traditionally voted

Democratic, had cast 49 percent of their ballots for Eisenhower in 1956. Two years later, in the congressional elections, three-quarters voted for Democrats. Current polling showed approximately three-fourths of Catholic voters expecting to vote for Kennedy. Protestants usually voted Republican, and six out of ten intended to vote for Nixon.[89]

In the second week of October, Truman, a Baptist, visited San Antonio where he attacked Baptists and other Protestant groups for their anti-Catholic attitude. He told them: "If you vote for Nixon, you ought to go to hell." In Waco, he spent half of a thirty-minute address castigating religious intolerance and the dissemination of "hate literature," saying "I bow my head in shame and pray to God to forgive these people for what they do." The opposition to Kennedy did not come because he was a Catholic, he suggested, but because he was a Democrat. He accused Nixon of "paying lip service" to religious toleration while accepting "any vote that may come his way by reason of religious intolerance."[90]

One of the most extreme declarations came from a United Automobile Workers pamphlet entitled "Which Do You Choose? Liberty or Bigotry?," which was sent to autoworkers in Detroit. The cover showed the Statue of Liberty and a hooded Klansman. The Michigan Fair Election Practices Committee condemned this as inflammatory. Walter Reuther apologized, saying he had not seen the pamphlet before publication, and Eisenhower denounced it for implying that a vote for Nixon was a vote for bigotry.[91]

The annual Alfred E. Smith Memorial Foundation dinner was held on October 19, sponsored by the archbishop of New York, Francis Cardinal Spellman, the most powerful Catholic priest outside of Rome. He had vigorously supported McCarthy's anticommunist crusade, as had his friend and benefactor Joe Kennedy. They had met in the mid-1930s and formed a cordial relationship in which the archbishop counted on Joe for donations, and Joe used Spellman for introductions to influential businessmen.[92]

The 1960 campaign severed that bond. Even before the primaries began, the patriarch realized that Spellman and the Catholic hierarchy did not support his son. Jack Kennedy had publicly opposed the church on key issues like federal aid to parochial schools and an American ambassador to the Vatican.[93]

Shortly before the dinner, Joe Kennedy asked Clare Boothe Luce "to do Jack a big favor." Nuns were crowding the front seats at many JFK rallies to draw attention to the school funding issue, and he wanted her to persuade Spellman to make them stop. He said of Spellman, "The SOB hates me." But if he wanted "a Catholic in the White House, he'd better keep those goddam nuns from hogging all the front rows. This isn't an ordination—it's an election!"[94]

Both Kennedy and Nixon accepted Spellman's invitation to speak. The archbishop specifically asked the vice president to attend and even booked his hotel room. JFK spoke first, remarking that the cardinal had brought together "two political leaders who are increasingly apprehensive about the November election, who have long eyed each other suspiciously, and who have disagreed so strongly, both publicly and privately"—Nixon and Rockefeller. The audience laughed.[95]

These witty barbs continued until Kennedy turned to a comparison of the 1928 election with that of 1960. Some believed, he said, "that the religious convictions of the candidates will influence the outcome more than their convictions on the issues." But he thought the two elections were "very different. Regardless of the outcome, and regardless of these similarities, I do not believe the American voter in 1960 is the same as the American voter of 1928. For we live in a different world."[96]

Nixon told fewer jokes but received more applause. On religion, he said that it "should not be an issue in a campaign . . . and it will not be, certainly, if those of us who are of goodwill—as Senator Kennedy is, and I am, and we would trust our supporters will be—do everything we can to keep the real issues before the American people by not discussing religion."[97]

The next day, three Catholic bishops in Puerto Rico brought the Vatican's role in domestic politics back into the news by sending out a pastoral letter urging parishioners to vote against Governor Luis Muñoz Marín's bid for reelection because of Muñoz Marín's approval of birth control and his opposition to religious education. The Kennedy campaign immediately responded, declaring that Kennedy "considers it wholly improper and alien to our democratic system for church men of any faith to tell the members of their Church for whom to vote or for whom not to vote." On October 26, the Vatican said that under certain circumstances, the church had a duty to provide political direction, but it implied that this principle did not, at the moment, extend to the United States. Some Protestants saw this as proof that the Catholic Church was willing to interfere in a nation's domestic politics.[98]

During the closing days of the campaign, Nixon's Catholic staffers were outraged that Kennedy supporters had suggested that if voters did not vote for their candidate, they were bigots. The vice president later conceded that he "probably made a mistake in resisting the strong recommendations of virtually every one of my advisers two and a half weeks before the election that I should take the issue on frontally rather than to continue to ignore it."[99]

One Catholic on Nixon's campaign staff, Peter Flanigan, had taken leave from a New York investment firm and started working for Nixon against Rockefeller's challenge by establishing New Yorkers for Nixon in October 1959. By the summer of the following year, Flanigan had become the national director of the Volunteers for Nixon-Lodge, managing "non-party support" to influence Democratic and independent swing voters. Forty-three years after the election, Flanigan was still angry that the vice president refused to appeal to the Protestant vote while Kennedy freely appealed to the Catholic vote.[100]

While drafting his chapter on the election in *Six Crises*, Nixon sent his research assistants a memo on the religious issue. It was, he wrote, the first topic to be acted upon. He wanted to show how Kennedy and his associates used it, how Nixon handled it, and how it helped Kennedy more than it hurt him. The former vice president also wanted to refute the suggestion that if Kennedy had been Protestant, he would have won by a larger margin. Nixon wanted these points "covered in a terse, factual, objective way."[101]

Most authors ignored Nixon's call for objective analysis. Sorensen declares in *Kennedy* that Nixon handled "the religious issue very shrewdly." He deplored mentioning it and asked both candidates not to discuss it, Sorensen argues, but religious leaders who were opposed to Kennedy and his religion continued to use it against him. The unstated assumption is that Nixon could have somehow stopped the anti-Catholic forces.[102]

Several scholars have exploited Sorensen's theme, adding to Nixon's perfidy while ignoring the vast amount of evidence against this interpretation. Daniel Williams, without serious primary research, falsely claims in "Richard Nixon's Religious Right" that the vice president developed an evangelical anti-Catholic coalition. Shaun Casey, also with virtually no research to support his claim, asserts in *The Making of a Catholic President* that Nixon purposely tapped into the anti-Catholic feeling that foreshadowed the rise of the religious right, and that he pitted Protestants against Catholics by exploiting Protestant fears of what a Catholic president might do. "Nixon chose to fan the flames of intolerance in a manner that he could not publicly acknowledge." Finally, historian Robert Dallek concludes, again without any research in the relevant primary sources, that "Nixon and the Republicans shrewdly kept the issue alive by continually deploring efforts to discuss it."[103]

The truth is more complicated. The anti-Catholic sentiment in the country in 1960 was certainly real and a problem for the Kennedy campaign. JFK and his advocates used his religion when it worked to his advantage and ignored it when it did not, and they were not above letting a surrogate like Truman periodically reignite the controversy. Nixon, on the other hand, did not think religion was a winning issue for him. The conservative Protestants who were most likely to be swayed by anti-Catholic sentiment were also likely to oppose Kennedy on grounds having nothing to do with his faith. But the more loudly the anti-Catholic extremists shouted their support for Nixon, the more tainted he became in the eyes of the moderate and liberal voters he needed to win over. He had strategic reasons for wanting to keep religion out of the campaign.

Nixon is not blameless. While none of his correspondence with Graham, Peale, and others shows him egging on religious bigotry, he could have urged them to stop, or even to preach tolerance. That he did not, despite his evident discomfort with their actions, is evidence of his willingness—like Kennedy's—to accept what advantage he could get in a close race without dirtying his hands. Ultimately, however, Graham and Peale were only giving their followers what they wanted. Nixon could not have stopped the anti-Catholic voices from being heard. To make either candidate a hero or a villain is contrary to the facts.

14

The Great Debates

Without question, the iconic moments of the Kennedy-Nixon race were the four televised debates—the first ones between presidential candidates in United States history. Theodore White's *The Making of the President 1960* devotes a chapter to them that has set the tone of almost all subsequent writing on the subject. Most of the chapter deals with the first debate and the events leading up to it. White claims that opinion polls gave Kennedy the victory in that first one as well as the next three, but that the debates as a whole "did little to advance the reasonable discussion of issues."[1]

Nixon's *Six Crises*, published a year after White's book and meant in many ways as a response to it, also spends one chapter on the 1960 election. It is the only chapter Nixon wrote himself. He assigned his research assistants to examine the press reaction to the debates and argued that their effect on the vote was "apparently greatly over-estimated." Other issues, such as the recession and unemployment, were more critical.

After Kennedy was assassinated in November 1963, some staffers who had worked on the campaign also published accounts of the debates. Schlesinger wrote in his journal at the end of March 1962 that Nixon had lost the first debate "on substance while Kennedy concentrated on image," and in his 1965 history of the Kennedy presidency, *A Thousand Days*, he briefly made the same point. Sorensen's *Kennedy*, published the same year, described how his boss had "won the debates" by looking better, being better prepared, and gaining greater exposure. Writing in the *New York Times* op-ed section on the fiftieth anniversary of the first debate, Sorensen sought to correct several "myths," especially the idea that, contrary to his own claim, the debates had not swayed that many voters. According to Sorensen, they had increased Kennedy's support with the Democratic base, in the South, and with independents. Without them, he said, Kennedy "would never have been elected President."[2]

Ted Kennedy wrote in his memoirs that his brother had "psyched out" Nixon in the first debate and had won because he was more charismatic. Kennedy's press secretary, Pierre Salinger, declared that Kennedy had come across "on TV as a mature, knowledgeable, attractive man. Nixon came across with all the sincerity of an actor reading a toothpaste commercial." Other staff members, including Richard Goodwin, Kenny O'Donnell, and Lawrence O'Brien, reinforced these opinions. Kennedy, they all wrote, had given an outstanding performance and had won the election because of it. The longtime Democratic operative Clark Clifford believed Kennedy ran a brilliant race, and he could not think of any "significant error" made by the campaign. Explicit and implicit in their portrayals was that Nixon campaigned poorly.[3]

These accounts, all based on partisan recollections of events, laid the foundation for subsequent historical studies. In the sixty years that have passed since the campaign, almost all the research on the debates had until now been done at the Kennedy presidential library. No one had done significant archival research on the subject at the Nixon, Eisenhower, Johnson, or Lodge repositories.

Both Kennedy and Nixon were experienced debaters, and they had met in this arena before. As first-term congressmen in the spring of 1947, they had traveled to McKeesport, Pennsylvania, to debate the Taft-Hartley Act: Kennedy, who had been elected with union support, opposed it while Nixon favored it. In 1952, JFK appeared on television with Senator Lodge, and in May 1960 he faced off against Humphrey in the West Virginia primary. Nixon had been a varsity debater in high school and college, and during his first race for Congress, in 1946, he and the incumbent, Jerry Voorhis, debated five times.[4]

The idea of a face-to-face meeting between the candidates had circulated early in 1960. Well before the nominating conventions—before Nixon and Kennedy had even established themselves as the respective nominees—Congress had been working to suspend Section 315 of the Federal Communications Act of 1934, which required broadcasters to allow political candidates equal time to present their views. Since they could not give coverage to major candidates without offering the same opportunity to marginal candidates, broadcasters simply sold time to those who could afford it—paid time being exempted from the equal-time rule. In the spring of 1960, Congress began hearings on suspending the rule until election day so that the two principal candidates could debate without having to share the stage with third-party candidates, but also without having to buy time, which was costly. Congress passed Joint Resolution 207 in late July, and the president signed it on August 24.[5]

Nixon was the better-known candidate, and the debates would give Kennedy exposure that he badly needed. But the vice president could not find "a way to avoid debates without appearing to be afraid to face the challenger." On May 9, he wrote Senator John Pastore, Democrat from Rhode Island, opposing the suspension of equal time, which also required television stations and networks to provide facilities and time to qualified presidential candidates for free. Broadcasting was a private industry, he argued, which should not be compelled in this way, and candidates should manage their own campaigns without being forced to use television. A week later, without any explanation, he changed his position, announcing on the David Susskind show that he was willing to debate his Democratic opponent.[6]

In the fall of 1960, Americans owned 52 million television sets; eighty-five of every hundred families owned at least one; 60 percent of viewers turned to television for political information. The U.S. census reported that 88 percent of all homes had televisions. Ownership in urban areas stood at 91 percent, 82 percent in rural regions. The population also had just under 100 million radios. Counting both radio and television, it was estimated that 100 million Americans would tune in to the debates.[7]

To heighten interest even more, NBC board chairman Robert Sarnoff wrote both Kennedy and Nixon as soon as the Senate had passed the resolution suspending free time. Anticipating that the House and the president would approve, Sarnoff offered them slots in prime time. CBS and ABC made similar offers the same day. Kennedy accepted without reservation and assigned his television adviser, Leonard Reinsch, to negotiate the particulars. Without consulting his staff, Nixon accepted the invitation at the press conference following his nomination, saying he wanted "a full and free exchange of views without prepared texts or notes and without interruption."[8]

In early September, Herb Klein met with Reinsch, Sorensen, and Salinger. They decided that there would be no studio audiences, and a panel of four reporters would question the candidates. Besides production staff, the only others in the studio would be the moderator, three print reporters, two radio/television representatives, and two photographers. The rest of the press corps would watch the debate on a monitor in an adjacent studio. September 26 and October 7, 13, and 21 were chosen for the broadcasts.[9]

The campaigns agreed that the first debate would focus on domestic issues and the last on foreign policy, a plan urged by the Nixon campaign. The vice president, Klein recalled, reasoned that interest in the debates would grow. Republican Congressman Robert Wilson remembered that Nixon thought he would lose on social issues, a Democratic strength, but win on foreign policy, a Republican strength.[10]

By drawing of lots, CBS was chosen to host the first face-to-face debate, in Chicago on September 26. In preparation for the first debate, CBS director-producer Don Hewitt met on September 8 with Ted Rogers, Nixon's television consultant, along with Reinsch and William Wilson from Kennedy's staff. The candidates should arrive at the studio an hour before the broadcast so that the advisers could view each man on television. Each candidate would also take care of his own makeup. A week later, the two parties met with Hewitt in Chicago and approved an informal sketch of the set.[11]

Kennedy arrived in Chicago early Saturday morning, September 24, and remained in seclusion with his staff, preparing for the debate. On Sunday he made a quick flight to Cleveland, where he received a tumultuous reception from 370,000 spectators as his motorcade traveled through the city to a Democratic rally. He returned to Chicago that afternoon.[12]

According to Eisenhower's close friend and World War II colleague Homer Gruenther, Ike opposed the debates. No matter "how effective" Nixon was, the debates would enhance Kennedy's image because he was "less known to the voters." On September 15, he wrote Nixon to say he had received "excellent receptions" on his trips and that his friends "are with you and all the best to yourself." The president still was displeased that Nixon had agreed to debate Kennedy.[13]

Nixon completed his campaign swing on Saturday, September 24, in St. Paul, Minnesota, boarded a plane and arrived in the capital on Sunday at 4:30 a.m. Clearly aware of Ike's disapproval, he called the event "risky for both sides." Nixon told Ike that he had decided "to play it in a low key. He was going to be gentlemanly, let Kennedy be the aggressor." Nixon "could not be too tough" because of the religious issue. He had to be positive "and not try to be too slick" but instead "knowledgeable, good humored." The president added that Kennedy had "been very inconsistent," and Nixon should not be "concerned about Kennedy looking bad."[14]

The decision to refrain from attacking Kennedy was not popular with several of Nixon's supporters. New York Senator Jacob Javits's brother, Ben Javits, urged him to go on the offensive. James Stahlman, publisher of the *Nashville Banner* and a conservative Republican, thought the vice president was being too tolerant toward Kennedy: "It is all right to be kind to the other fellow on a reciprocal basis, but when he is whacking at you with razors and hatchets, . . . it's time for you to go at him with brass knucks."[15]

Nixon flew to Chicago the evening of the twenty-fifth. He had told his staff that his schedule had to "be left flexible . . . so that under no circumstances (and I repeat, no circumstances) we are caught in a situation where I do not have a full day for preparation the day the television debate takes place. These appearances will be infinitely more important than any stops we may make."[16] He violated his own rule, however, by speaking the day of the event, September 26 at 11:00 a.m. before the annual convention of the United Brotherhood of Carpenters. Then he returned to his hotel, where he studied the campaign issues until he left for the television studio.[17]

Ted Rogers had been Nixon's television adviser in the 1952 presidential campaign and had occasionally assisted the vice president during the 1960 primaries. After the convention he worked for the campaign full time. While briefing the vice president en route to the studio, Rogers observed that Nixon did not look well and did not seem to understand "the *magnitude, the tension, the pressure*" that was building up.[18]

Nixon's two-car procession arrived at the studio at 7:30 in the evening. Kennedy came ten minutes later with his brother Bobby. As the two men approached each other, the senator said: "Glad to see you," and they shook hands. Both candidates took stills with network executives. Five minutes later, they went into the studio, a cavernous room once used for horseback riding, ice-skating, and televised wrestling matches. More stills were taken of them on the set while Hewitt oversaw last-minute technical adjustments. Then they retired to separate rooms to prepare for the telecast.[19]

CBS president Frank Stanton wanted "to be sure that no stone was left unturned in having the arrangements as near perfect as possible on this historic occasion." He had sent his best technical personnel from the New York headquarters to be certain the broadcast went smoothly.[20] Both staffs, according to Hewitt, had the same opportunity before the broadcast to examine the set. Kennedy's staff was satisfied "with the way he looked, requested no changes of any kind and also declined the services of our makeup expert." The senator did not make any requests but sent back to his hotel for a blue shirt that he changed into shortly before the program. Just before airtime, Bobby told Jack: "Kick him in the balls."[21]

Nixon arrived in the studio seven minutes before broadcast time, and Kennedy came in four minutes later. He wore a dark blue suit; he was tan and used a little makeup. Nixon was dressed in a light gray suit and was still recovering from his hospital stay. He had lost five pounds and felt that his shirt collar was too large. Rogers said that his client needed professional makeup. Hewitt asked whether Nixon wanted any; he had flown Frances Arnold, one of the best television makeup artists, in from New York for that purpose. Campaign manager Len Hall and Attorney General Rogers replied, "We are satisfied with the way he looks." Nixon also told Klein and Rogers that he would not wear makeup because Humphrey had worn pancake makeup for a debate in the West Virginia primary, and Kennedy attacked him for his false face. Instead, Everett Hart, who served as a consultant to the vice president, applied a product called Lazy Shave to hide his five o'clock shadow. In his memoirs, Klein admitted that the staff did not concentrate enough on the candidate's appearance.[22]

Howard K. Smith from CBS News acted as the moderator, sitting behind a desk with the protagonists sitting at chairs on either side. When answering a question, each man would stand and go to a podium.[23]

Kennedy spoke first. His eight-minute opening statement emphasized his dissatisfaction with the status quo. Even though the debate was meant to concentrate on domestic issues, he mentioned Khrushchev's global communist offensive and the threat posed by the Chinese. He then shifted to the reasons for his dissatisfaction. The United States' economic growth needed to be increased. American farmers were producing surpluses, some of which were rotting for lack of buyers. Teachers were poorly paid, and the Soviet Union was producing more engineers and scientists than the United States. Blacks, Mexicans, and Puerto Ricans were being denied their constitutional rights. Many elderly citizens could not support themselves on their Social Security checks.

Kennedy tried to distance himself from the accusation that Democrats spent too much. He did not "believe in big government, but I believe in effective governmental action. . . . If the United States fails, then the whole cause of freedom fails." He asserted that the current generation, like Franklin Roosevelt's, had a "rendezvous with destiny," and he concluded: "It's time America started moving again." Throughout the entire program, he hardy smiled.[24]

Just before the debate, the reporter Earl Mazo thought Nixon "looked like the wrath of God," but he smiled repeatedly throughout the program. Whereas Kennedy pointed out the administration's failures, the vice president highlighted its successes. The American economy was not "standing still"; wages and family income were growing much faster than under Truman, and inflation was under control. The country had greatly expanded school construction and hydroelectric power. Republicans advocated programs that increased educational possibilities and had a proposal to provide medical care for the aged.

Kennedy, said Nixon, wanted the federal government to "spend more than I would have it spend." The Democratic platform would cost, each year, at least $13.2 billion and perhaps as much as $18 billion more than the government was currently spending. The additional cost of the Republican platform would be between $4 billion and $4.9 billion a year. The Republican programs would spur the American people's entrepreneurial spirit, but Kennedy's proposals would "have a tendency to stifle those creative energies." Last, Nixon countered Kennedy's claim that Republicans lacked "compassion for the poor, for the old, and for others that are unfortunate." Without mentioning his humble upbringing or Kennedy's wealth, the vice president said he understood what it meant "to be poor" and how it felt to be unemployed.[25]

With the opening statements completed, the four newspapermen had time for ten questions. Each candidate answered five, and each had a chance to rebut. Bob Fleming of ABC News asked Kennedy about the charge that he was not as experienced as Nixon; Kennedy responded that their "experience in government is comparable" and noted the sharp differences between the two political parties. He led the Democratic Party, which had produced presidents like Woodrow Wilson, FDR, and Truman, while the vice president's Republican Party had spent the previous twenty-five years fighting against federal aid to education, medical care for the elderly, the Tennessee Valley Authority, and national resources development. Kennedy had given the vice president many openings to challenge him, but when asked to respond, rather than challenge those claims Nixon replied, "No comment."[26]

For the remainder of the question-and-answer segment, the contenders stuck to their talking points. Nixon wanted voters to cast their votes for the man, not the party. He had greater experience; he opposed greater government expenditures and favored free enterprise. Kennedy held that he had similar experience. He favored more federal programs but claimed that he would balance the budget. He attacked Eisenhower's agricultural program for its inability to raise farm prices and connected the unpopular Secretary Benson to the vice president.[27]

When asked about the Democrats' failure during that summer's special session of Congress to pass legislation on increasing the minimum wage, medical care for the aged, school construction, or aid to education, Kennedy replied that the bills would have passed under a Democratic president. Nixon answered that even with their large majorities in both houses, the Democrats could not form a consensus even to send a bill to the president for his signature or veto.[28]

Sander Vanocur from NBC News raised Eisenhower's comment about Nixon's contributions to his administration: "If you give me a week, I might think of one." Nixon answered that this was probably "a facetious remark." He had advised Eisenhower on many issues, but the president made the decisions. Kennedy responded that the real issue was "which candidate and which party can meet the problems that the United States is going to face in the '60s."[29]

In *Six Crises*, Nixon charged that Vanocur had posed this question to hurt his election chances: "To millions of unsophisticated televiewers, this question had been most effective in raising a doubt in their minds with regard to one of my strongest campaign themes and assets—my experience as Vice President." Forty-five years later, Vanocur denied that the question was meant to damage Nixon.[30]

When the questioning was completed, each candidate had three minutes and twenty seconds for summation. Nixon came first and used the time to defend Eisenhower's record. He agreed with Kennedy on several points, but they had fundamental differences. Kennedy "would rely too much on the Federal Government on what it would do to solve our problems, to stimulate growth." Republicans emphasized volunteerism and private enterprise. Kennedy responded that the Republicans had not met the external challenge from the Soviet Union or domestic challenges such as providing medical care for the aged. If voters were satisfied with current conditions, they should vote for Nixon. If they believed "that we have to move again in the sixties," they should cast their ballots for him.[31]

After the broadcast, Kennedy and Nixon shook hands. The vice president said: "It was a good sharp exchange of views." As photographers entered the studio to take pictures of the two men for the morning newspapers, Nixon started to poke his finger into Kennedy's chest. According to Kennedy, he did it for the photographers "so he would look like he was laying down the law to me, like I am some young kid, he is laying down the law about foreign policy or communism. Nice fellow!"[32]

This debate drew the largest television audience ever for a political event. Nielsen Television Index reported that out of the total of 45 million United States homes with televisions, 66.4 percent viewed the debate for at least six minutes. Others estimated that 70 million to 75 million people watched some or all of it.[33]

After the debate, moderator Howard K. Smith said he believed that both candidates had sidestepped the questions, but "Nixon was marginally better." After reviewing the replay, however, Smith felt that Kennedy had won. Kennedy later told him, Smith said, that "he won the election that night."[34]

Three individuals were chosen by lot to represent the press services and the newspapers in the studio: Everett Irwin of United Press International, Arthur Edson of the Associated Press, and Thomas Ross of the *Chicago Sun-Times*. Interviewed that evening, Irwin said that each candidate had showed respect for the other. Ross thought Nixon had displayed "calm self-assurance," while Kennedy showed no emotion.[35]

Joseph Costa, the chief photographer for the Chicago *Sunday Mirror Magazine*, was also in the studio and was interviewed three days after the debate. He pointed out that "the paleness of the whole picture, coupled with the fact Mr. Nixon was wearing a much lighter suit than was the Senator, added up to a much less pleasing visual impression than was derived from the Kennedy picture."[36]

Stanton recalled forty years later that he visited both candidates in their preparation rooms after the debate. He spoke only briefly with Nixon: the vice president had left without his briefcase and coat and was returning to his hotel. Stanton next called on Kennedy, who was seated, talking on the telephone; "his sleeves were wet with perspiration down to his wrists." Stanton thought he was probably talking to Jackie, who had watched the debate in Hyannis Port. Jack, according to Stanton, asked what she had thought. Stanton heard her answer: "You were superb."[37] After hanging up the phone, Jack proclaimed: "We sure took this one." Chicago mayor Richard Daley had been at the studio, and as he and Kennedy walked down the hall, the mayor told him he had not been an enthusiastic supporter, but now "I'm going to change my mind, and tell my men to go all out for Kennedy."[38]

Russell Baker, the *New York Times* reporter, watched the contest from a television monitor in an unused studio across the hall from the debate studio. He did not look much at the monitor but instead listened while taking notes. He found the debate "dull" but gave Nixon "a slight edge."[39]

Most newspapers called the debate a tie or gave Kennedy a slim victory. James Reston of the *New York Times* argued that Kennedy had gained because he had answered the charge of his immaturity and inexperience, "but it was a fielder's choice, settling nothing." Carroll Kilpatrick wrote in the *Washington Post* that both men did well: "They calmly but firmly disagreed with each other on the means America should adopt to meet its goals." Roscoe Drummond wrote in the *Chicago Sun-Times* that the debate was "superb," with no knockouts. Two days later, Walter Lippmann, in his column "Today and Tomorrow," expressed surprise that Kennedy, not Nixon, was the aggressor.[40]

Before the debate, Gallup Polls had the candidates tied. Independents favored Nixon, while young voters went for Kennedy. Separate surveys in the Midwest, South, Mountain, and Pacific states showed similar results. Gallup gave Democrats a distinct edge that party strength did not shift. At the beginning of October, Gallup reported that potential Democratic voters outnumbered Republicans, 56.8 million to 40.5 million.[41]

After the debate, in his suite at the studio, Kennedy adviser Kenny O'Donnell recalled that his boss had painted Nixon as a threat: "Something is very wrong. He is very unsure of himself. We have to win this election. He would be very dangerous as president. He would not be good for the country." Over dinner in his hotel room after the debate, the senator added, "We owe it to this country to keep Richard Nixon out of the White House."[42]

After dinner, Kennedy went to the airport and boarded his private plane, the *Caroline*, for the flight to Ohio. According to Sorensen, his boss was "confident and happy." Democrats universally believed that the senator had won. What partisans savored, according to Clark Clifford, was that Kennedy had eliminated the issue of "experience versus youth."[43]

Arriving on Tuesday morning in Cleveland, Kennedy found even larger crowds than two days earlier. Press secretary Salinger reported that "the people were coming off the walls." At 7:00 a.m., conservative Democratic Senator Frank Lausche from Ohio, who had been lukewarm to Kennedy's candidacy, and Governor Michael DiSalle rode in a motorcade through downtown to enthusiastic receptions.[44]

Ten of the eleven southern governors who met in Hot Springs, Arkansas, for the Southern Governors Conference abandoned their lukewarm backing of Kennedy and sent a telegram endorsing him. Lyndon Johnson, who rested at his ranch during the debate, returned to campaigning in the Midwest on September 27. Without mentioning the debate, he attacked Nixon on "maturity and experience." For the first time, he highlighted the economic recession, placing the blame on the administration and "Shifty Dick." At a stop in Ohio on September 29, he predicted a win of "landslide proportions."[45]

Some Nixon supporters listened on the radio. Dudley Swim, from Pebble Beach, California, wrote: "Your voice and delivery easily took command over the voice and delivery of Kennedy. You were the best by a wide margin." Sindlinger & Co., a research firm, found that Kennedy won the debate on television by a wide margin, but Nixon routed the senator on the radio.[46]

The Sindlinger study was published on November 7, 1960, in *Broadcasting*, the weekly business magazine for television and radio. Its findings gave rise to the claim that radio listeners thought that Nixon won on substance, while the television audience believed Kennedy looked better and won on image. The difference in looks was probably accentuated by Kennedy's better wardrobe choice and Nixon's recent illness. The vice president did not do as well as his opponent, but not because of appearance or substance. His Republican partisans were disappointed that he agreed with his adversary too often and did not mount a fierce attack on his policies. However, the first debate did not cause a massive swing of millions of votes for Kennedy. The Gallup Poll following the debate had not changed.[47]

A few partisans congratulated Nixon on his performance, but at least fifty indi-

viduals expressed their unhappiness. Based on scores of letters, Stanley McCaffrey, a staff member, summarized his supporters' disappointment. Nixon looked
"gaunt and haggard, tired, even sick," he needed a different color suit and better
makeup, he was too defensive and gentle with Kennedy, and he had to take
the offensive, maximize his experience and be tougher. But the vice president,
McCaffrey wrote, had not suffered "an irreparable loss."[48]

The vice president's pollster, Claude Robinson, concurred. Professional politicians reacted badly to Nixon's performance; he needed to act more presidential,
he agreed too much with Kennedy, and he needed to "slug it out more." Neither
man won, but "Kennedy could stand up and slug with the best." He had shaken
off the image of being "immature."[49]

Vice presidential nominee Lodge had invited Pat Fergurson of the *Baltimore
Sun*, Allen Otten from the *Wall Street Journal*, Tom Wicker of the *New York
Times*, and Murray Fromson from NBC News to watch the debate in his hotel
room. The morning after the broadcast, Wicker wrote, Lodge and his staff were
"acting like they had been killed. They knew Nixon had lost." Fromson vividly
recalled what Lodge said decades later: "That son of a bitch has blown the election."[50]

But on the day he flew off to campaign in Kansas City, Missouri, Lodge wrote
in a memo that he did not think the debate "was particularly decisive" or that
Nixon was "particularly hurt." "The image Nixon portrayed of a mature, reasonable logical individual was far above the Kennedy image but Kennedy did better
than anyone expected in terms of showing vigor, confidence although some felt
this bordered on arrogance." But the vice president seemed to be on the defensive and looked "terribly tired and gave the appearance of allowing Kennedy to
take the initiative away from him." Nixon spent too much time defending the
Eisenhower administration. A better move would have been to "take pride in it
and move on to" his own proposals. The memo closed with an understatement:
"Kennedy appeared to exploit the opportunity better than you might have."[51]

Even though Lodge had changed his tone from the night before, this was the
Nixon campaign's lowest point. He supposedly should have easily defeated Kennedy, but the senator performed better than was expected, and Nixon did not
crush his challenger.

The Nixons flew to Memphis, Tennessee, and upon their arrival at the airport,
an elderly lady with an oversized Nixon button greeted him. Hugging him in
front of press cameras, she announced: "Don't worry, son. Kennedy beat you last
night, but you'll get him next time." This was not just an embarrassing accident.
The Kennedys had hired Dick Tuck to replace Paul Corbin as their dirty trickster.
Even before the first debate, Tuck had traveled on Nixon's campaign plane with a

fake press pass and used a recorder to tape Nixon so that Kennedy could use what the vice president was saying as he prepared for the debate.[52]

Nixon described Tuck's bond to the Kennedys as sinister. Twenty-three years after the election, Nixon recalled: the Kennedys were "smart," "rich," and "ruthless." They did "anything to win." The media classified Tuck's operation as "fun and games" because reporters liked him. Nixon belittled his impact, but it was "quite irritating to be heckled and to have your schedule screwed up." The Kennedys hired Tuck to spy on Nixon's operation, understanding his value; "they played hardball."[53]

Many reporters fondly referred to Tuck as someone who enjoyed "a career of political pranks and subterfuge, [who] specialized in tormenting Richard Nixon." Tuck described himself as "not surreptitious" and said he had not hidden what he had done and that he "never tried to be malicious." We can judge his lack of malice from what Tuck said after Nixon resigned from the presidency: "We drove the rat out."[54]

The president did not watch the debate because he was preparing to address the UN General Assembly. British Prime Minister Harold Macmillan, in New York for the speech, had taken time to watch the debate and told Ike, "Your chap's beat." When the president asked why, the prime minister answered, "One of them looked like a convicted criminal and the other looked like a rather engaging young undergraduate."[55]

The day after the debate, Eisenhower wrote in his diary that "the man representing the 'Ins' should never take on an 'Out' in a debate." The latter could "say anything he wants since there is no test of responsibility or ability to make good on proposals."[56] Ike's press secretary, James Hagerty, obtained a kinescope copy of the debate for the president, who watched it with movie star and the president's television consultant, Robert Montgomery, and several others. They thought Nixon looked sickly and agreed too much with Kennedy, who, in Hagerty's opinion, received a significant boost from the broadcast.[57]

Later, the president wrote the actor Freeman Gosden with his analysis. Both men, he thought, looked "ill at ease sitting in chairs." In the future, the candidates "should sit behind a table or closed-in bench." That way the audience would not notice any discomfort. Nixon, moreover, "was not well made up." He looked tired and "there was perspiration on his chin," which gave "an adverse impression." But despite the vice president's appearance, "the debate was somewhat even." Kennedy highlighted "his wishful thinking for America against the Republican's outlining facts and issues." The president complimented Nixon for displaying "sincerity and knowledgeability" but thought that on "a few occasions" he needed to project "more authority." Nixon should emphasize facts over impressions so that voters understood the fundamental difference between the candidates' positions.[58]

Also speaking before the UN General Assembly on the day of the debate was Fidel Castro, who limited his address to four and a half hours. He attacked United States imperialism, hinted at using force to get the Americans to leave the Guantánamo Bay naval base, and called on Latin Americans to overthrow their present regimes. As for the presidential candidates, Castro described them as "brainless" and "ignorant." A few days later, appearing on television in Havana, he called them "cowardly hypocrites" and "two ignorant, beardless kids . . . puppets who are toys of the great interests."[59]

For the first week of October, Kennedy campaigned throughout the Midwest. He continued to criticize the Benson farm policies, blamed the president and vice president for the recession, and advocated stronger civil rights measures. Stopping in St. Louis for a hundred dollar–a–plate fundraiser, he appeared with former president Truman, who praised the nominee as the future president and attacked Nixon as a "me too" candidate who had abandoned Republican programs for Democratic ones. In a letter to former secretary of state Dean Acheson on October 9, Truman called Nixon "a dangerous man. Never has there been one like him so close to the Presidency."[60]

While in Missouri, Kennedy also spoke about closing "the missile gap," modernizing America's conventional forces, and giving the nation "defensive strength." He continued to insist that a missile gap existed even though Director of Central Intelligence Allen Dulles and Secretary of Defense Thomas Gates had briefed him on Soviet military capabilities. A few weeks after Kennedy entered the Oval Office, Secretary of Defense Robert McNamara announced at a press background briefing that there was no missile gap.[61]

While Kennedy was in the Midwest, his running mate traveled to the East Coast. Everywhere he went, Johnson attacked the vice president as "the greatest misjudger of the decade" on foreign affairs and placed Lodge in the same category. Republicans as a party pitted "class against class, race against race and religion against religion." Nixon responded by quoting a line that LBJ had supposedly uttered during the 1956 Democratic convention: "I am not now and never have been an advocate of civil rights. I don't think I ever will be." Johnson denied saying it and accused the Republicans of "below the belt politics." Nixon, he charged, knew the statement was misleading, and by quoting it he was resurrecting McCarthyism.[62]

Nixon, meanwhile, toured the Midwest, as well as North Carolina, Virginia, New Jersey, New York (where Rockefeller campaigned with him all day), Tennessee, and Philadelphia. He began making more references to Kennedy's wealth. During one address, he declared that Democrats were spending voters' money on extravagant programs: "It isn't Jack's money, but it's your money and that's what the American people are aware of."[63]

He also hit back at Kennedy's criticisms of Eisenhower. During an evening address in Evansville, Indiana, he said, "If Mr. Kennedy would stop looking so hard for things that are wrong with America's position and America's prestige, he would not have made such a reckless and irresponsible attack on the President. . . . The Senator owes it to his party and to his country to cease these irresponsible attacks."[64]

At the beginning of October, Ike gave a five hundred–dollar contribution to the Nixon campaign. When the president talked later to Nixon, he said he needed more "zip" in the next debate.[65]

On October 2, Republicans launched a Truth Squad to follow Kennedy wherever he appeared and point out his misstatements. On the third, Republican Senator Hugh Scott from Pennsylvania held a press conference, declaring that Kennedy had missed 331 of 1,189 Senate votes, one quarter of the total, from 1953 to 1960. "This is no job for a playboy," Scott concluded. Nixon wrote Scott to say the speech "was absolutely superb and that your own inimitable brand of ammunition was highly effective."[66]

The second debate was in Washington, D.C., on Friday, October 7. The vice president arrived in the capital early that morning. He had gained five pounds by drinking a milkshake at every meal and another one in midafternoon. He listened to his television consultant, Ted Rogers, who handled his makeup and lighting. Before Nixon left for the studio, Stan Lawrence, a freelance makeup artist from New York, applied his makeup.[67]

Kennedy wore a dark suit and refused any makeup. He, Bobby, and a few aides arrived at NBC's Washington studio at 6:45 p.m. and immediately complained about the temperature. Nixon had asked for it to be set at sixty-four degrees to minimize his perspiration; the thermostat was raised to seventy degrees. Two minutes before the 7:30 airtime, Kennedy appeared, and Nixon came on the set a minute later.[68]

This broadcast took place on the 102nd anniversary of the Lincoln-Douglas debate for a United States Senate seat in Galesburg, Illinois. Approximately twenty thousand people had attended in Galesburg, while more than sixty million saw the Kennedy-Nixon exchange, more than the total number of voters in the 1956 presidential election. The Nielsen Television Index reported that 27,979,000 TV homes watched the debate, a decrease of 2,034,000 from the first round, and the audience percentage was 61.9 percent, down from 66.4 percent.[69]

The candidates did not make opening and closing statements this time. The moderator was Frank McGee from NBC; four correspondents took turns asking questions, and the nominees alternated answering and responding to each other's answers. Arthur Edson, the only reporter who watched both debates from the studios, saw a distinct difference. Both men were primed to get in "the strongest jabs and were barely cordial to each other."[70]

The reporters had time to ask thirteen questions, with no overarching theme: five questions had to do with domestic issues and eight were on foreign policy. Nixon changed his approach. Gone were the half dozen times in the first meeting that he agreed with the senator. He agreed once, on the need to make careful preparations for any summit with Khrushchev. Neither man smiled. The exchange was sometimes biting. Kennedy attacked the administration for its failure of moral leadership in promoting civil rights, and Nixon replied that Eisenhower had shown leadership while Kennedy's running mate, Lyndon Johnson, had opposed all civil rights legislation. Both men said they would try to avoid tax increases but would allow them if necessary. The vice president denied that the nation was in a recession and predicted that if Kennedy enacted the proposals in the Democratic platform, he would have to raise taxes. Kennedy rejected this assumption. The two men also differed on importance of party. Nixon urged voters to cast their ballots for the better candidate, and Kennedy promised that his party would pass landmark social legislation while Republicans would defend the status quo. Kennedy blamed the administration for Castro's rise; the vice president rejected that assertion. He criticized the senator for suggesting that the president apologize to Khrushchev for the U-2 incident. Kennedy replied that Republicans had grossly exaggerated what he had said.[71]

The most contentious exchange came on the next-to-last question, when Edward Morgan of ABC News asked Kennedy about his statement that the offshore islands of Quemoy and Matsu, five miles from the Chinese mainland and defended by Chiang Kai-shek's troops, were beyond the United States' defense perimeter. The senator, citing several authorities, replied that the two tiny islands were indefensible and nonessential, and should be abandoned. Nixon disagreed "completely." While conceding that the islands themselves were insignificant, he insisted that the principle was crucial. They were located "in the area of freedom," and if they were surrendered, "we start a chain reaction" that would end with the Communists trying to conquer Taiwan. "This is the same kind of woolly thinking," he continued, "that led to disaster for America in Korea." He hoped that if Kennedy were elected, he would "change his mind."[72]

James Michener, the author and Democratic chairman from Bucks County, Pennsylvania, watched this exchange. Of Kennedy's position, he said: "Oh, I wish he hadn't said that!" Michener had visited Quemoy and Matsu, and after the debate he wrote two articles supporting Nixon's position. In a report on the debate to his Democratic colleagues, he wrote, "We lost a lot of votes on this Quemoy-Matsu business."[73]

In interviews after the broadcast, Nixon said, "We had a good exchange." The two talked about their campaigns and what the vice president labeled "crowds-manship," a controversy between their respective press secretaries about which candidate drew the larger crowds. Nixon affirmed that he was getting "great crowds." When he told the senator, in parting, that he would see him next week, Kennedy coolly responded, "Next week, and I'll give you my best."[74]

Bobby Kennedy told his brother, "You were great," but the staff thought the vice president had scored over Quemoy-Matsu. The euphoria that followed the first encounter had disappeared. The vice president had had a better perfor-mance, Bobby told his brother, because Nixon "had no way to go but up. If he hadn't improved tonight, the campaign would have been over."[75]

Kennedy's private remarks had a far different tone. Nixon had been "playing dirty" by lowering the studio's temperature and changing the lighting. JFK told Arthur Schlesinger that his opponent refused to discuss the issues and instead made "little speeches." He tried to correct Nixon's "misrepresentations" but had little time to get his points across. After the broadcast, Kennedy went up to Nixon to shake hands, and as they chatted, the vice president saw a photographer ap-proach and started to wave his finger in Kennedy's face as he did with Khru-shchev in the Kitchen Debate. Nixon, the senator concluded, was "a shit—a total shit."[76]

The senator also spoke with *New York Times* publisher Arthur Sulzberger, re-marking that Nixon "was a damn fool to agree to debate with me on an equal-time TV basis." He again complained that the vice president tried to trick him by altering the temperature and the lighting. Despite these actions, Kennedy was pleased with the debates. During an interview with journalist C. L. Sulzberger, Kennedy said the press was "largely pro-Nixon and has been building Kennedy up as a naïve, inexperienced young man. Now he can come before the whole nation and show his true colors."[77]

Asked for his verdict on the second debate, Kennedy called it a tie. The vice president had gained "an emotional edge" in the Quemoy-Matsu exchange by using the "don't give-the-Commies an-inch" theme. But Kennedy would not budge from his stand: the islands were indefensible.[78]

Nixon left the studio elated. At a traffic light, a motorist shouted out to him: "You really clobbered him tonight." When he reached his house, one of his daughters welcomed him at the door: "Daddy . . . you did great!"[79]

Nixon's side was jubilant. Ike phoned him immediately after the broadcast to congratulate him. Maryland Republican Senator J. Glenn Beall wired the vice president that he was "terrific." South Carolina's Democratic governor, James Byrnes, told Robert Finch he was pleased with the vice president's performance. Nixon had not only rebounded but, as Kennedy did in the first debate, had energized his supporters.[80]

Polls suggested that Nixon had done better, but like the first debate, this one changed few people's minds. The Gallup Poll had Kennedy at 49 percent and Nixon at 46. Another poll had Nixon at 49.9 percent, Kennedy at 43.9, and 6.2 percent undecided or giving no answer. Two other polls troubled Republicans. Democrats still maintained a 55 percent to 36 lead in party affiliation, and they led Republicans in congressional races, 55 percent to 39.[81]

In the middle of October, Nixon wrote a supporter that he had always felt "that a good deal of politics is timing. Pace and tempo is something one has to feel and judge as he goes along." He was "optimistic without being over-confident. Right now the campaign is close."[82]

With six days to go before the third debate, Kennedy toured Kentucky, Ohio, Georgia, South Carolina, Pennsylvania, and New York. Enthusiastic crowds regularly welcomed him, and he concentrated on his major issues: moving forward versus standing pat, the loss of American prestige abroad, and economic recession at home. In Ohio he talked about the decline of steel production. He stopped in Warm Springs, Georgia, where FDR had sought relief from polio, to promote the similarities between himself and the former president. He charged that Nixon's position on Quemoy and Matsu "may involve American boys in an unnecessary or futile war."[83]

The vice president, visiting Wisconsin, Minnesota, Montana, Colorado, Utah, New Mexico, and California, criticized Kennedy for his lack of foreign affairs experience and "bad" judgment. United States prestige around the globe was high. The administration supported the independence of West Berliners, and the situation in the Congo was not as worrisome as Kennedy had painted it. As for Cuba, "the Cuban people will reassert their right to freedom and progress through freedom rather than without." And he would not turn Quemoy and Matsu over to Red China.

Nixon firmly opposed Kennedy's social legislation, saying it would increase the size of government and stifle free enterprise. He maintained that the senator also exaggerated the current economic downturn, and as for agricultural policy, Kennedy's proposals would not solve farmers' problems. Speaking at the Mormon Tabernacle in Salt Lake City, he praised Benson's integrity and received an endorsement from David McKay, the eighty-seven-year-old president of the church.[84]

Two days before the third debate, Nixon made a major staffing change. Secretary of the Interior Fred Seaton had been traveling with him from the start of the campaign. Now, with a month to go before the election, Seaton returned to Washington to direct the campaign as a "sort of chief of staff." At Nixon's request, Seaton told the campaign team that the candidate wanted a speech that would lay out a "program for economic progress," "a summary of what are the most radical elements of the Democratic program and platform," a plan for greater defense spending, and a program for overcoming the "space gap" to make the United States first in space. The day before the third debate, Nixon instructed Seaton to write questions on Quemoy-Matsu as soon as possible. By the morning of the debate, Nixon had his ammunition. Speaking at breakfast, he asserted that in 1955, Kennedy had voted with just ten other senators not to defend Quemoy and Matsu; seventy senators, including Lyndon Johnson and the majority of Democrats, rejected this proposal.[85]

The day before the debate, Nixon spent the morning filming campaign spots and being interviewed by NBC reporters Chet Huntley and David Brinkley. Telling an audience that abandoning Quemoy and Matsu "would lead to war or surrender," he called on his rival to explain why Republicans were wrong about his proposals and to tell Americans how much his programs would cost. The public, he declared, had "a right to see the price tag."[86]

While Nixon was attacking Kennedy in Los Angeles, the senator had a full schedule in New York City. He and Jackie went to Eleanor Roosevelt's apartment for breakfast. The former first lady and the candidate then held two rallies in Harlem, one for the Puerto Rican community and another for the black community. The latter event featured Congressman Adam Clayton Powell, Jr., who vehemently attacked Nixon for signing a covenant promising not to sell his home in the Washington suburbs to African Americans or Jews. Powell charged that a Florida Grand Dragon of the Ku Klux Klan had endorsed the vice president, and Nixon had not repudiated the endorsement. Nor had he rejected the support of southern white Protestant ministers who objected to Kennedy's Catholic faith. The KKK, the minister proclaimed, was "riding high again in this campaign. If it doesn't stop, all bigots will vote for Nixon and all right-thinking Christians and Jews will vote for Kennedy rather than be found in the ranks of the Klan-minded."[87]

The third debate, hosted by ABC on October 13, was a transcontinental program with Nixon, the moderator, and four panelists in Hollywood, and Kennedy in New York City. The network called this arrangement "the most technically complicated broadcast in television history"; it required five hundred people, including two hundred technicians, and twelve cameras. The nominees appeared on identical sets and wore similar attire for the proper lighting. Kennedy declined any makeup, while Nixon had light makeup applied. He had completely recovered from his knee injury. Because it was so technically complex, there is only one brief shot of Kennedy reacting to one of Nixon's statements.[88]

As in the second debate, there were no opening or closing statements, and the reporters again asked thirteen questions. Both candidates began the broadcast robust and combative, clashing on almost every issue and accusing each other of misrepresentation. The acrimony began with the first question, from NBC's Frank McGee, on the Quemoy-Matsu debate. Kennedy called the vice president "trigger-happy," and Nixon responded that three Democratic presidents had led the United States into war during the twentieth century, versus no Republicans. When the Eisenhower administration came into office, it ended the Korean War. The next five questions all dealt with foreign affairs, and the debate grew heated.

When the discussion turned to domestic matters, *New York Herald Tribune* columnist Roscoe Drummond quoted Congressman Powell's accusations against Nixon and added that Democratic Governor Michael DiSalle of Ohio had made similar charges. Kennedy repudiated them and agreed that religion should not be an issue in the campaign. The argument then moved to corruption in labor unions, the oil depletion allowance, government spending as reflected in the parties' platforms, economic growth, and tax loopholes.

The only light-hearted moment came when Charles Von Fremd of CBS News asked whether Kennedy should get Truman to apologize for a previous comment. During an earlier press conference, the former president accused Nixon of never telling "the truth in his life." At dinner afterward, he referred to "damn Republicans" and caused an uproar by saying if anyone voted for the vice president, "you ought to go to hell." The senator answered that he could not control the seventy-six-year-old former president or change his language: "Perhaps Mrs. Truman can, but I don't think I can."[89]

After the debate, Earl Mazo joined Nixon in his suite. When the reporter entered, he found the vice president sitting in a chair with his legs up, "nursing a Scotch and soda." He felt fine and believed he had done well. The president missed the broadcast but heard excellent reports. In a telephone call the next day, he told Nixon "not . . . to be so glib, to ponder and appear to think about something before answering the question." The press generally regarded it as Nixon's best performance to date.[90]

Watching his monitor before the program, Nixon had seen Kennedy shuffling notes, and he mentioned this to reporters. He did not use notes, which were against the rules; he depended on his memory. He insisted that he was not upset, but a reporter observed that his "face was rigid, his lips taut, and his voice rose" when he talked about the notes. John Daly, the ABC vice president for news and public affairs, said that he understood that both men would "ad lib without prepared text or notes." When confronted, press secretary Salinger first said there was no such agreement; he then amended his position and said his candidate had only read a quotation from the president. David Wise of the *New York Herald Tribune*, who was present in Kennedy's studio, said he saw the candidate with seven or eight pieces of paper arranged by subject.[91]

After a small flurry of interest, the notes issue faded. During the week between the third and fourth debates, Kennedy traveled to Michigan, Colorado, the Middle Atlantic States, Ohio, Florida, and New York. He joked that Nixon's makeup did not improve his looks and asserted that "the Republican Party has stood against progress and so has Mr. Nixon." Between them, they had failed to pass legislation to help the elderly or for housing, urban renewal, or aid to education.

Kennedy also announced assistance for freedom fighters to overthrow Castro. As for Latin America, he would initiate an Alliance for Progress with a twelve-point program including student exchange, technical assistance, long-term development loans, land reform, and private investment. He pledged to bring a new "tone" to the White House. He would provide "moral leadership" and establish a "ministry of the best available talent" for federal employees. Using a "code of ethics," he would prevent conflicts of interest and other corrupt practices.[92]

Like Kennedy, Nixon maintained a frantic pace and appeared optimistic. He toured California, moved on to Arizona, Oklahoma, Illinois, Connecticut, Florida, and Delaware, and ended in New York. Conservative leaders like Goldwater and liberals like Rockefeller enthusiastically came out for him. The vice president criticized his opponent as "immature" and continued to attack his "frightening foolishness" on Quemoy and Matsu. Nixon claimed that Kennedy would run an administration like Truman's by raising taxes and tolerating corruption. The vice president also wanted to "set the record straight" on the Kennedy campaign's misstatements of where Republicans stood on issues like defense, health, and civil rights. He also offered positive measures. He intended to initiate a global "peace offensive" against the communists. He would hold four regional summits with representatives of free nations and would introduce legislation to revise the tax code to stimulate growth. In Florida, he told listeners that he would "quarantine the Castro regime in the Americas."[93]

On Sunday, October 15, White House press secretary Hagerty said Kennedy had misstated the administration's position on Quemoy and Matsu to make it sound more aggressive than it actually was. The next day, Secretary of State Christian Herter said that Nixon should call on Americans to unite behind the president on the islands and ask Kennedy to "surrender" his position for the sake of national unity. That Friday, Admiral Arthur Radford, a former chairman of the Joint Chiefs of Staff, met with Nixon and said afterward that if Kennedy did not change his position, "we might have a war on our hands in the Pacific."[94]

Both candidates prepared for the fourth debate in their hotels, Kennedy at the Carlyle and Nixon ten blocks away at the Waldorf Astoria. The format used in the first debate was repeated: eight-minute opening and five-minute closing statements. The questions were limited to foreign policy. The moderator made the introductions, and four newsmen asked a total of seven questions, with the candidates given two and a half minutes for each answer and one and a half minutes for rebuttal.[95]

After Moderator Quincy Howe of ABC News started the broadcast, Nixon gave his opening statement: he defined the principal goal of American diplomacy as keeping the peace without either surrender or war. By refusing to support the defense of Quemoy and Matsu, he said, Kennedy would undermine that aim. The senator replied that the vice president had distorted his position, but more significant, Kennedy believed American foreign policy worldwide had been a dismal failure under the current administration. The United States had not adapted its policies to meet current exigencies, and a change was needed to restore American prestige abroad.

With the opening statements completed, Frank Singiser of Mutual News asked the first question to the vice president. Nixon wasted no time in attacking Kennedy or in making the next day's headlines: he lambasted Kennedy's suggestion that the United States aid the exiled Cuban forces in overthrowing Castro militarily, saying that "Kennedy's policies and recommendations for the handling of the Castro regime are probably the most dangers—dangerously irresponsible recommendations that he's made during the course of this campaign." The administration's policy of quarantining the island, Nixon said, would lead to the dictator's ouster.

Kennedy made the first closing statement by wrapping himself in FDR's mantle and comparing Roosevelt's success with Republican failure. The Republican Party, he pronounced, had "stood still really for twenty-five years—its leadership has. It opposed all of the programs of President Roosevelt and others." Meanwhile, "a new generation of Americans . . . have now taken over in the United States, and . . . they're going to put this country back to work again." He closed by repeating the campaign's major theme: "We must get America moving again."

The vice president ended the debate by challenging Kennedy's basic assertion: "America is not standing still. It has not been standing still." The administration had made far greater strides in housing, schools, civil rights, and slum clearance than the Truman government had, and "anybody that says America has been standing still for the last seven and a half years hasn't been traveling in America. He's been in some other country."[96]

This final debate contained the one moment in the campaign when Nixon admitted to being "personally . . . mad" at his opponent. Kennedy had been regularly attacking the administration over Cuba, and just before the debate began, the senator had released a statement calling for "direct aid to the rebel forces in and out of Cuba." Nixon believed that DCI Dulles had briefed Kennedy about the covert aid being given to Cuban rebels then training in Central America, and that the senator then used this secret information to his advantage. After the broadcast, Nixon telephoned Fred Seaton, who confirmed that the CIA had given Kennedy a briefing on Cuba. The vice president supported the aid, but had remained silent so as not to disclose a CIA operation. But Nixon flirted with the truth when he responded that quarantining was enough.

Nixon was angry with Dulles for revealing the operation to Kennedy, but he was not the culprit. Alabama Governor Patterson, a staunch Kennedy partisan, knew that his state's Air National Guard was flying missions to Central America to aid the rebels. The governor flew to New York to see Kennedy at his hotel before the debate and informed him of the clandestine activity.

Public interest remained strong: the Nielsen Television Index reported that the audience for the last debate was almost as large as for the first. Viewership throughout the evening never fell below 50 percent of television homes. Polling showed the nation divided on who had won, and the polls themselves seemed divided on voter engagement. A Gallup Poll on October 19 declared that many voters lacked enthusiasm; two days later, another Gallup survey found interest in this election higher than in either of the Eisenhower-Stevenson contests.[97]

The debates ended on a sour note. From October 10 onward, Kennedy lobbied for a fifth one, and negotiations continued throughout the month without resolution. The senator really was not interested, but he sensed that Nixon was unwilling, and he wanted to goad the vice president by suggesting he was afraid of another broadcast. Nixon replied that he actually was willing to debate again and the senator was acting immaturely. By the end of the month, negotiations had broken off, with each side accusing the other of "bad faith."[98]

No impartial judge analyzed the debates. Kennedy and many others felt he had triumphed. To researchers Percy Tannenbaum, Bradley Greenberg, and Fred Silverman, "Kennedy did not necessarily win the debates, but Nixon lost them." The senator's image improved, they argued, and Nixon's declined.[99]

After the last debate, Ted Rogers wrote that Kennedy, with nothing to lose, had established himself "as the man who can stand up to RN. RN and the Debate Platform provided the cast and stage to make Jack Kennedy a star." Rogers thought Hewitt and Stanton had conspired against Nixon in the first debate, writing after the election that he believed "with all my heart this was a put-up job against RN."[100]

Thinking back on the broadcasts a year later, Nixon reflected that he had concentrated too much on substance and not enough on appearance. While he did not look robust in the first round and his suit clashed with the set, these were symptoms of a larger miscalculation on his part. He purposely did not act like the no-holds-barred campaigner his partisans anticipated. He had decided to throw off his opponent by being more reserved than expected, a tactic he abandoned in later rounds.[101]

In retrospect, he saw that Kennedy gained ground, in that the broadcasts made him better known. Nixon decided he might have been better off accepting "what loss of face would have [been] involved in making that decision [to reject debates] in order to avoid the greater risk of giving my opponent the visibility which he needed."[102]

Schwerin Research Corporation, a pioneering advertising and marketing company that conducted extensive polling and tested more than fifty thousand commercials, concluded that the debates were "the cornerstone" of Kennedy's electoral victory. Despite this finding, Horace Schwerin, SRC's president, did a number of studies comparing two prominent individuals who appeared together on television. All things being equal, he found that the more they appeared, the more viewers found them similar. Many pundits did not find much to distinguish between Kennedy and Nixon. Viewers too may have noticed more commonalities than differences.[103]

Polls taken from July until November showed the election as too close to call, and the debates did not change the percentages. The Kennedy proposition that the debates were the deciding factor in the election seems an exaggeration. To the extent that Kennedy's problem was to get himself seen as Nixon's equal, he gained by fighting his opponent to a draw. But even given his superior performance in the first round—the one enshrined in the JFK legend—there is no plausible argument that the debates decided the election. Other factors were far more important.

15

THE DEMOCRATS' FRANTIC FINALE

Kennedy spent the days after the fourth debate campaigning in the Midwest, promoting his message of change. He began talking about "the Nixon Gap," a variation on the "missile gap," to highlight the differences between the vice president's voting record and his current promises. He routinely charged that Nixon was responsible for the worsening recession and foreign policy failures.[1]

The Kennedy campaign hired the African-American reporter Louis Martin, a two-term president of the National Newspaper Publishers Association, to be one of two chief assistants in its civil rights division. He ran an extensive operation that included advertisements in African-American newspapers, radio ads, and outreach to influential leaders such as black ministers. Martin knew that Kennedy's civil rights record was mediocre at best. In 1957, when the Little Rock crisis erupted, his statement supporting the president's actions had been carefully worded to avoid offending southern sensibilities. Black leaders did not see him as someone who fought aggressively for civil rights initiatives.[2]

Before winning the nomination, Kennedy tried to entice influential black leaders like the retired baseball star Jackie Robinson to support him. Robinson not only refused but became a vocal opponent of Kennedy's candidacy. Martin Luther King, Jr., also refused him. JFK was more successful in recruiting Harry Belafonte, even though Belafonte recognized that Kennedy lacked a strong commitment to civil rights.[3]

Adam Clayton Powell, Jr., also refused Kennedy at first. The pastor had led the 152-year-old Abyssinian Baptist Church congregation in Harlem since the 1930s and had been elected to the House of Representatives in 1945, emerging as a major political force in the black community. According to Harris Wofford, Jr., shortly before the 1960 convention the Kennedys secured Powell's backing "with the help of a sizable financial inducement" of fifty thousand dollars. For that, he appeared in thirty-two cities in fourteen states, praising the Democratic ticket while lambasting Nixon for the restrictive covenant he had signed for his suburban Washington home in 1951, even though a 1948 Supreme Court decision had declared such covenants unenforceable.[4]

Sargent Shriver headed the civil rights division for the Kennedy campaign and later recalled that his brother-in-law "was not a wild pro-black guy." Wofford, who had a warm relationship with the King family, was Shriver's principal assistant, along with Martin. Before hiring Wofford at the beginning of May, Sorensen took him to lunch and warned him not to get close to Shriver; the Kennedys viewed him as "the house Communist—too liberal, unduly idealistic, a Boy Scout." In an oral history, Wofford conceded that JFK did not "know much about Negroes and Negro issues." Chester Bowles, a major civil rights activist, accompanied Kennedy to many meetings before civil rights groups and recalled that "on almost every occasion he was uneasy and occasionally contentious."[5]

In his opening statement in the first debate, Kennedy alluded to Lincoln's proclamation that the United States could not be "half slave and half free," highlighting the disparities between whites and blacks in education and employment. Four days later, during a question-and-answer session, he said that if elected, he would sign an executive order ending discrimination in federal housing and force American companies doing business with the federal government to hire without regard to race, creed, or color. (As president, he failed to act energetically on these promises.)[6]

A few weeks later, Kennedy's civil rights commitment was tested. Dr. Martin Luther King, Jr., and thirty-five activists were arrested on October 19 for demanding service in the tearoom at the Rich's department store in downtown Atlanta. Standing before municipal judge James Webb, the group argued that they were protesting peacefully and had done nothing wrong. But a recently passed Georgia law made it a misdemeanor for a person to refuse to leave private property after being asked to do so by an owner or owner's representative.[7]

On Sunday, October 23, the city dismissed all charges against the demonstrators with a single exception. Only King remained in jail. He was on probation after having been convicted of a minor traffic offense, and his participation in the sit-in violated his probation. Judge J. Oscar Mitchell of the DeKalb County civil and criminal court issued a restraining order demanding that King show cause why he should not be sent to prison. At his hearing two days later, the courthouse was first cleared after a bomb threat. After reconvening in a packed and racially segregated courtroom, with African Americans on the left and whites on the right, Mitchell revoked King's suspended sentence on driving without the nec-essary permit and ordered the minister to serve four months at Georgia State Prison in Reidsville, the state's largest penitentiary. King left before dawn and arrived at Reidsville at 8:00 a.m. Until he was "classified," warden R. P. Balkcom said, he would be confined to a solitary cell.[8]

After the judge pronounced his sentence, Coretta King telephoned Wofford to say how worried she was that her husband would be harmed in prison. Wof-ford asked Shriver to telephone JFK, who was at O'Hare Airport, to ask him to call Coretta to express his sympathy. Kennedy did, and after they talked, Coretta told reporters that JFK understood her anxiety over her husband's arrest and "was very much concerned about both of us." That evening at the Mt. Zion Second Baptist Church in Atlanta, the Reverend Ralph Abernathy, who had worked closely with King, was the featured speaker. Before a mass meeting of five hun-dred supporters, he said he would rather be with King at the prison "down on the road gang" to show his stand against segregation.[9]

In a hearing the next morning, October 27, Mitchell granted bail while King appealed his original traffic conviction. Speaking to the press, the judge said that he had gotten pressure from advocates of both sides, including Bobby Ken-nedy, who had telephoned to ask whether King had a constitutional right to bail. But his decision, Mitchell maintained, was based strictly on the law. When re-porters asked Bobby about the judge's revelation, he said that he had made the call after receiving many inquiries about King, and that that was the extent of his involvement. He was not interfering in the court's actions. When a reporter asked John Kennedy to confirm that he had called Coretta King, he did, adding, "I had nothing to do with his release." He mentioned this incident one other time during the rest of the campaign.

King's attorney, D. L. Hollowell, rented an airplane, flew to the prison to meet his client, and returned with him to Atlanta. When reporters asked him which candidate he supported for president, King answered that he headed a non-partisan organization and would not publicly announce his choice. That night, Martin Luther King, Sr., "Daddy King," copastor with his son at the Ebenezer Baptist Church, told an enthusiastic audience of eight hundred that he was switching his vote from Republican to Democratic because of Kennedy's action. Daddy King said he had initially opposed the Democratic nominee because of his Catholic faith, but "he has the moral courage to stand up for what he knows is right. . . . I've got all my votes, and I've got a suitcase, and I'm going to take them up there and dump them in his lap." His son spoke next. Avoiding any mention of his choice for president, he declared that his eight-day jail confinement should show his followers how to "master the art of creative suffering." African Americans, he said, "must be prepared to suffer, sacrifice and even die. . . . Freedom is not free." Segregation must end, whatever the cost.[10]

At a press conference at the start of November, King praised Kennedy for his moral courage: "His act impressed a large number of Negro voters all over the country." If Kennedy became president, King predicted, he would act positively on civil rights. He reiterated that as the leader of a nonpartisan organization, he could not endorse anyone. "But for fear of being considered an ingrate, I want to make it palpably clear that I am deeply grateful to Senator Kennedy for the genuine concern he expressed in my arrest." According to Belafonte, the "Kennedys were furious" that King withheld his endorsement.[11]

That failure did not prevent Shriver from approving a pamphlet entitled "'No Comment' Nixon versus a Candidate With a Heart, Senator Kennedy," referred to as the "Blue Bomb" because it was printed on blue paper. The Kennedy campaign and various unions sent thousands of these flyers to voters, though probably not the two million that Wofford claimed or the three million that Martin alleged. Many African Americans read about King's arrest and jail time in mainstream newspapers like the *Atlanta Constitution* and the *New York Times*, as well as approximately 140 black weekly newspapers. Others learned about the incident by word of mouth.[12]

The impact of the telephone call from Kennedy to Coretta King has been cited as the primary reason black voters cast their ballots for Kennedy. When asked how one or two million copies of the Blue Bomb were circulated on the Sunday before the election at black churches across the nation, Wofford admitted that this might have been an exaggeration. He believed the pamphlet was only one part of the successful civil rights effort that his division mounted, and it succeeded because it was distributed in Chicago and Washington.[13]

While this was going on, Nixon was campaigning in the Midwest. His civil rights record was far better than Kennedy's: he had chaired the President's Committee on Government Contracts, which worked to integrate the workforces of firms that did business with the federal government; he had supported *Brown v. Board of Education* as a moral imperative; and he had lobbied vigorously for the Civil Rights Act of 1957. Harold Tyler, the director of the civil rights division of the justice department in 1959 and 1960, said Nixon was the only member of the executive branch who was interested in civil rights legislation and regularly called him for updates.[14]

Nixon's staff had been notified about the need to move aggressively on civil rights. Louis Lautier, Washington bureau chief of the National Newspaper Publishers Association, wrote Nixon's political adviser Charles McWhorter on

October 10, complaining that "little or nothing is being done to win the Negro vote beyond the efforts of the Vice President himself." Lautier was being flooded with DNC press releases praising Kennedy's record and downplaying Nixon's achievements, but he was getting nothing from Republicans. Neither the RNC nor Volunteers for Nixon were "doing an effective job," and the Nixon campaign was performing abysmally: "If the situation is not corrected immediately and some effective work done to get Negroes to vote for Nixon and Lodge, the election could be lost."[15]

After Kennedy telephoned Mrs. King on October 26, she told the press that neither Nixon nor his staff had contacted her: "He's been very quiet." When her husband was interviewed at the end of the month, he not only praised Kennedy for his "courage" but added that he objected to being labeled a "Nixon man." The minister had spoken with the vice president on several occasions but would not endorse him or anyone else.[16]

The Kings were unaware of the debate going on within the justice department. On October 18, Deputy Attorney General Lawrence Walsh read an Associated Press story concerning King's arrest and saw an opportunity to help the Nixon campaign with black voters by getting King out of jail. He, Harold Tyler, and other staffers worked all afternoon on possible legal steps to free him. One option discussed and rejected early that evening was a presidential statement that Ike was appalled King had been put in prison.[17]

On October 31, a few days after King was released, Walsh dictated to White House press secretary Jim Hagerty a draft of a letter for the president to send to the governor of Georgia: "It seems to me fundamentally unjust that a man who has peacefully attempted to establish his right to equal treatment free from racial discrimination be imprisoned on an old, unrelated and relatively insignificant charge, driving without a license." Walsh then went to the White House to personally lobby for Ike's approval, but according to Walsh, the president "did not want to be drawn into the controversy." Walsh next telephoned Attorney General Rogers, who was traveling with Nixon. Rogers said that Nixon would not release any statement without Ike's blessing. It never came. Tyler recalled that "the whole episode was probably the biggest disappointment I have had in my entire career of public service."[18]

Nixon wrote Jackie Robinson on November 4 to explain why he had not intervened. He had "frequently counseled with Dr. King," he wrote, "and [I] have a great respect for him." But he did not want to make a "grandstand play" because the progress over civil rights required "consistent application of the principles which we know are sound."[19]

Ike never directly mentioned the incident, but when he did allude to it, it was to express his disappointment with African Americans. During a meeting with industrial leaders at the White House five weeks after the election, he asserted that a "couple of phone calls" had helped the Democratic totals even though his administration had worked diligently on voting rights and public school integration and at desegregating the nation's capital. Even his efforts to pass civil rights legislation had moved black voting less than 2 percent from Democratic to Republican between 1952 and 1956.[20]

Kennedy advocates as well as many journalists and historians have grossly exaggerated this episode's impact. Taylor Branch argues in *Parting the Waters*, which won a Pulitzer Prize, that in the 1956 presidential election, blacks voted 60 percent Republican to 40 percent Democratic, but that in 1960 they went 70 percent Democratic. This, Branch claims, was a seismic shift: "Two little phone calls about the welfare of a Negro preacher were a necessary cause of Democratic victory." But he does not cite any polling data in making his claim. The source he cites—an article in the NAACP magazine *The Crisis*—does not mention vote shares at all.[21]

This spectacular shift in the black vote never happened. The proportion of African Americans voting for each party hardly changed between 1956 and 1960. In 1956, according to Gallup and other polls, Eisenhower received between 36 and 39 percent of the black vote and Stevenson between 61 and 64 percent. Kennedy, according to the Gallup Poll, received 68 percent of the black vote and Nixon 32 in 1960. The Democrats' 4- to 7-point improvement simply reflects Stevenson's landslide loss in 1956; Kennedy's share is close to the historical average from 1936 to 1952. As for Daddy King's promise of "a suitcase full of votes" for Kennedy, Nixon won all nine predominantly black districts in Atlanta. In the Kings' hometown, there was no seismic shift.[22]

While Sargent Shriver and his staff were working on civil rights issues, Lyndon Johnson tested some of his own themes on the weekend of October 7. He described the vice president as an ineffective leader and warned that if Nixon won the presidency, it would create a "stalemate government" because Nixon could not gain bipartisan cooperation. (He could speak to this issue with authority because, as Senate majority leader during a Nixon presidency, he would have a major say in providing that cooperation.) Johnson stumped through Maryland ridiculing Nixon's claim of experience and attacking him on civil rights, pointing out that when Republicans controlled both houses of Congress, in 1953 and 1954, they did not present any civil rights legislation. But once Johnson became majority leader, Congress began to pass civil rights bills: one in 1957 and another in 1960. The vice president, he added, had a "Dixie speech" and a "northern speech." On *Meet the Press*, he associated the struggle for civil rights with religious bigotry against Kennedy's Catholicism: "We have a real duty as public servants to protect the constitutional rights of every American citizen regardless of race or religion or region."[23]

Johnson's black chauffeur, Robert Parker, had a different recollection of the majority leader: "Whenever I was late, no matter what the reason, Johnson called me a lazy, good-for-nothing nigger. He especially liked to call me nigger in front of southerners and racists like [Georgia Senator] Richard Russell. It was . . . LBJ's way of being one of the boys."[24]

Starting from the capital on Monday, October 10, Johnson traveled through eight southern states in five days, ending in New Orleans on Friday, October 15. The trip was billed as a whistle-stop tour aboard his thirteen-car train, the LBJ Victory Special (which others named the Cornpone Special). He traveled 3,811 miles, stopped at sixty towns, gave fifty-seven speeches, and entertained 1,247 southern politicians in his private Pullman car. Democratic Senators Harry Byrd, from Virginia, and Strom Thurmond, from South Carolina, were notably absent from Johnson's visitor list.

Johnson emphasized he was the great-grandson of a Confederate soldier from Georgia, while Kennedy was the "Catholic grandson of a poor Irish immigrant." Lady Bird pointed out that her mother and father owned a three thousand–acre plantation in Alabama that she frequently visited. The farther south the Johnsons went, the more pronounced his drawl and folksy manner grew.

His first stop was in Culpeper, Virginia. As his train pulled in, "The Yellow Rose of Texas" blared out from the station loudspeakers. Johnson briefly spoke from the rear platform and was still talking as the train pulled out. "What has Nixon ever done for Culpeper? What have the Republicans ever done for you?" he shouted as he receded down the track. At almost every event, he lashed out at the vice president for his "smear campaign," his lack of experience, his duplicity on civil rights, and the loss of Cuba under the Eisenhower-Nixon administration. The vice president was an "apostle of discord."

Johnson welcomed the endorsement of a multitude of southern segregationists. Georgia's most powerful politician, Senator Herman Talmadge, reluctantly backed Kennedy-Johnson but frequently pointed out that the Senate majority leader had removed the most obnoxious provisions from the 1957 civil rights bill and "thwarted" moves by the Senate's "extreme liberals." In Atlanta, Senator Russell, according to Johnson's secretary Robert Baker, advised Johnson not to mention civil rights. In Mississippi, Senator John Stennis told audiences that the majority leader had "taken the lead in defeating vicious and radical legislation that would materially injure us." Johnson finished his journey convinced that the

Republican tide in the South had turned and that Democratic solidarity would bring a Kennedy-Johnson victory.[25]

Not everyone agreed. George Reedy, the candidate's press secretary, later wrote that his boss had two faces on the train trip: "one that of a magnificent inspiring leader; the other that of an insufferable bastard." Almost twenty-two years after the journey, Senator Smathers, who rode on Johnson's train, remembered that Lady Bird became furiously angry in Miami, shouting, "You're working him too hard" and "You're killing my husband." He had had a serious heart attack in the summer of 1955 and was not healthy. At the end of the tour, Johnson did not ride in the parade, leaving that to Lady Bird and Smathers, but joined them at New Orleans City Hall, where he spoke.[26]

Johnson campaigned in battleground states from the middle of October until the end of the month. Throughout his tour, he criticized the Republicans on their failure to prevent the communist takeover of Cuba, their belligerence on Quemoy and Matsu, their inaction on unemployment, and the decline in American prestige. He specifically thrashed Nixon for his unsavory political practices. Because the vice president was losing, Johnson asserted, he was "panicky," "throwing the punches of a desperate man" and using "smear tactics in a last desperate attempt to elect their ticket."[27]

No one attacked Nixon more viciously than former president Truman, whose audiences called on him to "give 'em hell." Speaking in San Antonio in mid-October, he declared that the vice president had "never told the truth in his life." In Virginia, he lashed out at Nixon as a "political hatchet man." A week later in Louisiana, he accused him of winning his elections to the House and Senate by questioning his opponents' loyalty; he also implied that Nixon was a pawn of wealthy contributors.[28]

Stevenson may have despised Nixon even more than Truman did. Shortly after the nominating conventions, the former governor wrote that the vice president was "one of the few people in my life I really deeply distrust and dislike." He expected "a brutal campaign" with Nixon taking "the high road" but his supporters attacking Democrats for "being soft on communism, appeasement, etc."[29]

Beginning in October, Stevenson traveled to New York and North Carolina, advising enthusiastic crowds to keep Nixon's "dangerous impetuosity" out of the White House. Most Democrats, he remarked, would stay with the party and actively support Kennedy; Nixon was losing "confidence and enthusiasm even among the Republicans." JFK would win easily, and the election would be "as much a defeat for Nixon as a victory for Kennedy."[30]

Eleanor Roosevelt, who vehemently opposed a Nixon victory, wrote to Kennedy on October 24 that she could not "feel safe till the last week is over because with Mr. Nixon I always have the feeling that he will pull some trick at the last minute." Six days before the vote, she wrote in her "My Day" column that "Nixon has tried to be outgoing and his pretty wife says she loves campaigning because she loves people." But the vice president's crowds, she observed, were not responding. Kennedy identified with the people and would draw strength from them.[31]

Before returning to Texas for the final four days of the race, Johnson predicted a Democratic landslide larger than the FDR sweep of 1936. Texas Republicans, he warned, were trying "to destroy Texas influence in Washington — to take from us our leadership in Congress and to keep us from acquiring leadership in the executive branch." If Texans did not vote for Democrats, his party "would not soon come here again to select a national nominee. . . . Texas would be cut off from the opportunity to share during our lifetimes."[32]

Johnson welcomed Kennedy to Texas on Thursday, November 3, at the Amarillo airport. A sign greeted them: "This Group of Baptists is for Kennedy." At an airport rally later that day in Wichita Falls, Johnson said: "A buzzard is a nasty bird; a skunk is a stinking cat. But what makes me really hold my nose is a Nixon Democrat." At the end of the rally, Kennedy flew off and Johnson remained to fulfill his pledge that Texas would vote Democratic.[33]

On the day that Johnson was greeting Kennedy, the *Dallas Times Herald* published a political advertisement sponsored by the Dallas County Citizens for Kennedy and Johnson, with thirty-five hundred names of people who supported the Democratic ticket. The next day, Republicans in the city reported that they had checked the names and discovered that about six hundred were dead. Nixon's supporters, according to the *Dallas Morning News*, viewed the ad as the city's "hottest political story." Banker and former school board president R. L. Thomas not only complained that he had never authorized the use of his name but added, "I have Nixon sign in my front yard." Arthur Baron, another supposed signer, said he would not vote for LBJ "for dog catcher."[34]

Johnson's packed schedule on November 4 included a well-publicized stop at the Baker Hotel in Dallas. Waiting for Johnson's motorcade was the conservative Congressman from Dallas, Bruce Alger, who carried a sign: "LBJ Sold Out to Yankee Socialists." John Tower, a political science professor who was challenging LBJ for his Senate seat, also was present. Before LBJ arrived, Republican women passed out pamphlets and Nixon-Lodge buttons. Some in the crowd of eleven hundred began to express their venom toward the candidate. LBJ recalled eight years later that Alger and Tower, both Republicans, "had whipped up a lot of mink-coat fascist-type women. I was regarded as left wing in Texas. There was a great revulsion that I had joined the ticket with the Pope of Rome."[35]

Sue Connally, a *Dallas Morning News* reporter, was at Johnson's elbow when the heckling and jostling started, as the candidate and his wife entered the Baker Hotel. They turned around and crossed the street, heading for the Hotel Adolphus lobby, taking almost a half hour to travel seventy-two feet. Republicans booed and chanted: "We want Nixon." Democrats answered, "We want Kennedy." The demonstrators were orderly and there was little physical violence, although Lady Bird, visibly upset but silent, was shoved by protesters while walking in front of her husband. LBJ could have avoided the confrontation by allowing the police to clear the way through a side entrance, but he refused their protection. After the incident, he said: "If the time ever came when I couldn't walk through the corridors of hotels in Dallas I want to know it."[36]

Saturday, the day after the hotel disturbance, Johnson flew to New York to join Kennedy for their first joint appearance since early in the campaign. Returning home on Sunday, he told partisans at rallies: "If elected, Jack Kennedy and Lyndon Johnson will work their fingers to the bone for you." Johnson's travels, forty thousand miles across forty states, finished that evening.[37]

He had cause for concern. There were many signs that Kennedy had not overcome his handicaps—his religion and a Democratic platform that some considered radical—in a state whose capture was the reason Johnson was on the ticket. In mid-October, the Belden Poll, the most reliable one in the state, reported 44 percent of voters favoring Nixon versus 39 percent for Kennedy, with 17 percent undecided. At the end of the month, Louis Harris, Kennedy's pollster, had Kennedy with 49 percent, Nixon with 41, and 10 percent undecided. Many in the Texas press considered the race too close to call.[38]

Kennedy, meanwhile, was frantically racing toward his own finish line, making charges and responding to countercharges. Reporter Eric Sevareid castigated both presidential candidates for their refusal to answer questions that troubled Americans. Except for a brief impromptu press conference on the day after he telephoned Coretta King, JFK concentrated on winning the states his campaign considered pivotal. On October 27, the *New York Times* endorsed the Democratic ticket for the first time since 1944. Three days later, *Time, Newsweek*, and *U.S. News and World Report* all reported Kennedy in the lead.[39]

From November 1 through the seventh, Kennedy kept up a frenzied pace, usually attracting large, enthusiastic crowds. On the first of the month, he flew to Los Angeles, where he made special appeals to Hispanics, blacks, and unions and pledged to raise teachers' salaries. In San Francisco he proposed a "peace corps" that would select young men for three-year terms to provide technical assistance to "underdeveloped" countries.

He went to four southwestern states his campaign considered doubtful, including Texas. In his speeches he blamed the Republicans for the slumping oil industry and the "Republican recession." His last two days were spent in the industrial Northeast. Eleanor Roosevelt stood alongside him in New York City, showing her support and anointing him as an heir to Franklin Roosevelt's legacy. He ended his campaign in Boston and then went home to Hyannis Port to await the results.[40]

Jack Kennedy had reason to be optimistic. He had been a reporter shortly after the close of World War II and knew how to cater to his former colleagues. In the 1950s, many reporters were heavy drinkers and smokers, and Salinger tried "to make the campaign as easy for the press to cover as possible" by supplying them with ample quantities of liquor and tobacco. When a new reporter was assigned to cover Kennedy, Salinger immediately introduced him to the candidate. Usually that reporter sat with the candidate on the *Caroline*'s next flight.[41]

Some reporters and columnists had been longtime friends. Charles Bartlett, a correspondent for the *Chattanooga Times* and columnist for the *Chicago Sun-Times*, had introduced Jack to Jackie in 1951 and later attended their wedding. Ben Bradlee, who reported for *Newsweek*, recalled that he wanted "his friend and neighbor to be president." According to Bradlee, Jack was comfortable with reporters, "liked the press and spoke the same language." A month before the Democratic convention, another Georgetown neighbor, syndicated columnist Joseph Alsop, wanted to bet Charles Devens, a classmate at Groton and Harvard, twenty-five dollars even money that Kennedy would defeat Nixon. After the convention, the columnist visited the Hyannis Port compound and "found the whole experience not only extremely gay, but also rather moving. For it is moving to see Jack going into this hard campaign with his special combination of a hard grasp of its problems and a high heart." The day of the election, Alsop wrote that Kennedy was "the first American politician I have ever known who seemed to me to have the promise of true greatness."[42]

William Lawrence, a *New York Times* correspondent, started playing golf with Kennedy at Hyannis Port after the convention, and became a partisan during the campaign. In his memoirs he admitted that Nixon had "some legitimate reasons for disliking me." At one point, Nixon's private secretary Rose Mary Woods overheard Lawrence make a comment that she felt "was unfair to Nixon" and poured a drink over his head. In the summer after the election, Nixon remarked that Lawrence "never missed an opportunity to knife us during his career."[43]

Female reporters also sided with Kennedy. Sarah McClendon, who had become a national press corps member in 1944, saw some flaws, but he gave her hope for the future. She found him "charming," and during the debates, his "good looks, his way with words and his charisma . . . came across most strikingly over the tube." Helen Thomas, according to her colleague at UPI Patrick Sloyan, elevated Jackie and her children "to a new category reserved for Britain's royal family."[44]

Television journalists also favored Kennedy. Edward R. Murrow, Eric Sevareid, and Robert Pierpont from CBS News backed him. Sander Vanocur from NBC News said that Kennedy joked and laughed with the press while Nixon was frigid. Herb Klein believed Vanocur's coverage was "looked upon by many close to Nixon as a prime example of biased reporting."[45]

Salinger wrote that the press treated his candidate well and saw Nixon as "aloof and inaccessible." Ben Bradlee described him to Kennedy as "different, joyless, strangely dull, almost hostile." Russell Baker saw Kennedy as "blessed with a personality beguiling to reporters," while Nixon "was cursed with a personality reporters loved to loathe." Most journalists were Democrats, and "if you were a Democrat in the 1950s, you were expected to despise Nixon, whether you despised him or not." Baker recalled: "A depressing number of really fine reporters lost their skepticism and went ga-ga over the candidate."[46]

Joan and Clay Blair condemned the press's behavior in their 1976 book *The Search for JFK*, charging that the Kennedys shrewdly manipulated the media to help Jack win. Journalists did not do their due diligence and instead accepted the Kennedy spin: "The American people seem all too glad to be given comic-strip heroes to believe in, and woefully unwilling to consider human complexity in the very human beings who want to lead them."[47]

While the Blairs did not refer to the "Canons of Journalism" adopted by the American Association of Newspaper Editors in 1923, they certainly could have: "News reports should be free from opinion or bias of any kind." Journalism ethicist Stephen Ward said in an interview that in the 1960 presidential election, these codes "called for objectivity in reporting, independence from government and business influence, and a strict distinction between news and opinion." At best, the press corps blurred this distinction.[48]

Pollsters had the race close, but most put Kennedy in the lead. The Gallup Poll on October 28 had him ahead of Nixon 46 percent to 43, with 11 percent undecided. On November 4, Gallup released another survey showing that Kennedy had surged to 53 percent, with Nixon at 45 percent. In its final poll, on November 6, Gallup found Kennedy at 49 percent, Nixon at 48, and 3 percent undecided.[49]

Kennedy was worried. At his stop in San Francisco on November 3 he told his friend Paul Fay, "If the election was tomorrow I'd win easily, but six days from now it's up for grabs."[50]

One problem for the Democrats in the last two weeks of the campaign was that they had about half the advertising funds the Republicans had. Democrats needed money in the closing days of the race in the battleground states to counteract Republican ads. With two days left until the balloting and several states still in doubt, they had spent almost three-quarters of their budget, and by November 7 they had less than 20 percent left to counter the massive outpouring of Republican advertisements.[51]

Two potentially explosive issues did not draw media attention. In the last three weeks before the voting, Florence Kater renewed her protests. On November 5, Drew Pearson wrote: "There is a woman parading in front of the White House with a picture of Kennedy taken as he left his girlfriend's house with his hands over his face to keep from being photographed." Pearson and his associate Jack Anderson had discussed Kater with Kennedy over breakfast the previous March. She was clearly trying to embarrass him, Pearson wrote in his diary, "but apparently it hasn't hurt. Judging from the women who are eager to touch his hand and kiss him, it may even help him."[52]

The other issue, which would remain hidden until long after Kennedy's death, was the state of his health. Early in the morning of November 6, he campaigned in Waterbury, Connecticut, alongside Governor Ribicoff and then flew to Boston. As soon as he landed, Kennedy called the governor: "Jesus, Abe . . . there's a medical bag floating around and it can't get in anybody's hands. I don't know where it is. . . . You have to find that bag. It would be murder. This is the day before the election." When the bag was recovered, Kennedy said, Ribicoff must call him no matter what time it was. Ribicoff telephoned the commissioner of the state police, Leo Mulcahey, and told him to find the bag and bring it to the governor's mansion. It was delivered around 3:00 a.m., and as instructed, Ribicoff telephoned, saying, "We got the bag." Kennedy answered, "O.K., keep it and don't let anybody see it until after the election's over."[53]

As he waited for the results, Kennedy could reflect on his nonstop campaign from beginning to end. He had focused on the industrial states, where his fellow Catholics made up a large portion of the voting population and where registered Democrats significantly outnumbered Republicans. If he could persuade his party to vote for him, he could win easily. He had spent much of the campaign trying to achieve that solidarity by appealing to his party's fear of Nixon.

Kennedy portrayed himself as a committed cold warrior in foreign affairs and as a liberal on domestic policies. As for his stand on civil rights, he mentioned it very little, but after his phone call with Coretta King his campaign's civil rights division framed him as a crusader on the issue—something he had never been.

Kennedy's two most damaging secrets were daily realities on the campaign. Many reporters and campaign associates knew about his spinal operations, his need to wear a back brace, and the frequent pain he suffered, but this was not reported. He successfully denied having Addison's disease. His sexual liaisons were also an open secret. Many reporters knew about them, but Florence Kater, marching in front of the White House with a photograph of Kennedy leaving a mistress's apartment, could not get her charges reported in the press. On November 21, *U.S. News and World Report* published an article entitled "The President-Elect Is Not a Playboy."[54]

Lyndon Johnson, too, presented himself as a cold warrior and a liberal on domestic issues. His primary objective was to win the South, especially his home state of Texas. He campaigned as an advocate for civil rights, even though while he served as Senate majority leader his closest allies had been racist senators. During the campaign, they reminded supporters that Johnson had weakened civil rights legislation, a claim he never denied. He called his black chauffeur racist epithets to raise his credibility with segregationists.

Johnson was permitted only a single joint appearance with Kennedy outside of Texas. The campaign let him manage his own state's operations but put Smathers in charge of the campaign in other southern states. This was a harbinger of how Kennedy, as president, would treat his vice president.

Johnson, too, called for Democrats to remain in the party and focused a great deal of energy on denigrating Nixon's record. He knew better, but he returned to the theme when it seemed appropriate. Sitting in the White House on March 6, 1965, President Johnson trivialized Nixon's role in the Eisenhower presidency: "Dick Nixon tried to make out like he had something, but . . . Eisenhower cut his guts out and didn't want Nixon to have *any* power. And although Nixon bragged about how he ran everything if you'll look at these confidential records down here, they treated Nixon just like he wasn't *here*."[55]

Truman, Stevenson, and Eleanor Roosevelt, who had initially wanted others to win the Democratic presidential nomination, increasingly rallied behind the nominee. At first, they grudgingly considered Kennedy the best of the worst, but they grew increasingly sincere in their support through the campaign.

Nixon recognized the Democratic strategy. The opposition could not personally attack Eisenhower because of his high approval ratings. The Democrats' best path to victory was to separate Nixon from Eisenhower, laying the administration's failures at Nixon's feet while simultaneously claiming he was too far out of the loop to deserve credit for its successes. Some of the accusations were erroneous, but many Americans accepted them. The vice president received high marks from his Republican base, but for his entire career, he had to live with false claims that he could never effectively refute.

16

Nixon's Plan for Winning

From his experience as Eisenhower's running mate, Richard Nixon believed that the last two or three weeks leading up to the presidential election were the most critical period of the race. This was when most undecided voters made up their minds about the candidates.

One of the vice president's major assets in his plan for victory was Billy Graham. After playing a prominent role in establishing the Peale group in Switzerland, Graham had remained in Europe, watching as the group imploded in the United States. The evangelist grasped the disastrous consequences of either seeming to be anti-Catholic or of visibly opposing the anti-Catholic assembly, and he assiduously avoided reporters. He wrote to Nixon on September 24: "I cannot possibly get involved in the religious issue. Not only would they crucify me, but they would eventually turn against you." He thought Nixon was "doing great" and said he "believe[d] with all my heart that you are going to win."[1]

When Graham returned to the United States in the second week in October, he seemed to change his position. Protestant theologians like Reinhold Niebuhr and John Bennett had openly endorsed Kennedy; did not he too have the right to express his opinion? He sought the advice of Henry Luce, who suggested he write an article for *Life* magazine about why he favored Nixon. Graham wrote it in less than an hour, heaping praise on Nixon, describing his greatest qualities as his "sincerity" and his deep religious beliefs. He would be as great a president as Lincoln in leading the United States through the crisis years ahead. Graham concluded with a disclaimer: "I am not against Mr. Kennedy. I am simply for Mr. Nixon." If the senator won, Graham expected to support him.[2]

After the election, Graham wrote to Nixon to tell him what had happened. Shortly before the article's publication date, Luce told Graham that he had received an angry telephone call from Kennedy, demanding that Luce balance Graham's piece by having Niebuhr or some other Protestant clergyman write a pro-Kennedy piece. The next morning, Senator Smathers, Governor Luther Hodges of North Carolina, and Governor Frank Clement of Tennessee called on Graham to withdraw the essay. In fairness to Kennedy, Luce had deferred the article until the following week. Feeling that "the Lord had intervened in some strange and mysterious way," Graham replaced his piece with one on the responsibility of voting, not mentioning Nixon. It came out in *Life*'s November 7 issue.[3]

Asked by Nixon in May 1961 for his recollections about the article for the campaign chapter of *Six Crises*, Graham wrote that he had "tried desperately to reach you personally," but instead had to discuss the issue with a staffer, who "seemed terribly indecisive" about whether or not to publish. He did not receive "a definite green light" until after Luce pulled the first article. Nixon defended his staff's indecision by pointing out that he himself did not know how to handle the matter. Kennedy and his campaign advocates, especially Governor Hodges, had "used the religious issue shamelessly," Nixon told Graham, and he felt "it would be irresponsible on my part to follow the same tactics." Nixon's memoir differed from Graham's recollection. According to *Six Crises*, Nixon vetoed Graham's *Life* endorsement.[4]

Despite this disagreement, Graham continued to offer Nixon advice on the campaign. Three issues, he wrote on October 17, would decide the election: Nixon must take a strong stand on Cuba, show how his administration would halt communist advances, and demonstrate how Democrats were exploiting the religious issue to "solidify the Catholic vote" and "split the Protestants." He urged the vice president to "speak out more strongly about the need of spiritual revitalization, dependence on God and prayer." Nixon should also emphasize that Kennedy, if he won, would repudiate Ike's agenda. The president himself should campaign in Texas, Pennsylvania, Ohio, and California. Graham promised Nixon that "thousands of prayer meetings have been organized across America to pray about this election."[5]

In addition to the evangelist's blessing, the vice president benefited from party solidarity. Rockefeller and other liberal Republicans intensified their campaign schedules in October. At the end of the month, the governor wrote his "Fellow Republicans" that the Nixon-Lodge ticket offered "the American people that leadership of courage and judgment, experience and responsibility that the times demand." The governor visited eight states that month, making some 195 addresses, and planned another 80 or 90 speaking engagements before election day. Referring to Kennedy's principal weakness, he stressed that this was "no time for on-the-job training" and urged Republicans to work as hard as they could during the last eight days before the voting.[6]

Conservatives also coalesced behind the ticket. From September 10 until the end of the race, Goldwater gave 126 speeches in twenty-six states in front of 185,000 people. Southerners greeted him especially warmly. He called Johnson "the forgotten candidate" and said sarcastically of Kennedy, "sometimes I wonder how Jack gets that sailboat back to harbor." In foreign affairs, Goldwater said the United States should forcefully overthrow Castro. As for domestic issues, he opposed federal aid to education because the government should not be involved: "The family has an obligation to educate children through local school boards and local taxes."[7]

Some Democrats who had moved toward conservatism spoke out for Nixon. Ronald Reagan, formerly a liberal Democrat, had once objected to a Nixon vice presidency. In the winter of 1952, the actor considered him an awful choice, but still cast his ballot for the Republican ticket. Over the following eight years, Reagan's political beliefs had changed dramatically. After Nixon returned from his trip to Moscow in the summer of 1959, Reagan thanked him "for the great step you took in starting us back to the uncompromising position which is our heritage and responsibility."[8]

During the 1960 race, Joe Kennedy asked Reagan to campaign for his son, but he refused, citing "big government" as "the real enemy." Journalist, novelist, and screenwriter Adela Rogers St. Johns, a Nixon adviser from California, wrote the vice president on September 2 to urge him to get actor James Cagney and screenwriter and producer Jerry Wald to persuade Reagan to come out publicly for Nixon. She also thought that Walt Disney might be "the right man . . . [to] get Ronnie Reagan to come along." Reagan did and asked Nixon if he should change his party registration from Democrat to Republican. The vice president thought Reagan would be more effective as a Democrat for Nixon.[9]

While the vice president appealed to Reagan, Nixon also paid close attention to civil rights because the administration had performed far better in this area than the Democrats. Eisenhower had desegregated schools, theaters, hotels, and restaurants in Washington, D.C., appointed J. Ernest Wilkins an assistant secretary of labor, the highest post held by an African American in almost thirty years, named other blacks to influential posts, and made E. Frederic Morrow the first African American to serve on the White House executive staff. He had spearheaded the passage of the 1957 civil rights law, which he called his "biggest success," as well as another civil rights bill in 1960. He had ordered troops to Little Rock, Arkansas, to enforce a court order to allow black children into public schools. He began to eliminate segregation in the armed forces—an action Truman had ordered but never enforced—and ended the practice of excluding black people from major White House events.[10] Nixon had emerged as the leading civil rights advocate within Ike's administration.[11]

Both parties adopted strong civil rights planks in their platforms, employed black advisers, and made efforts to end discrimination in campaign travel. On the Nixon campaign, the civil rights issue was "only fragmentarily handled by a small staff"—about five people—"under Val Washington and with little money." Nor did Nixon visit many black urban areas, because the Republican Party had no organization there.[12]

Morrow had been a member of the White House staff since 1955. In late 1958, he wrote Nixon and other Republican leaders that the GOP was losing close elections because the party, despite its good record on civil rights, did not reach out to black voters. The RNC did not spend money to recruit black registrants or ask black citizens for their vote. Morrow declared "emphatically and categorically there cannot be a Republican victory in 1960 until this situation is faced squarely and honestly." Starting in early 1959, he sent repeated messages to RNC chairman Morton and members of Nixon's staff, urging them to reach out to African Americans. But as he sadly noted in his memoir, "Often the notes were ignored or the replies innocuous. It was maddening."[13]

At the end of 1959, Morrow complained directly to the vice president. Since joining Ike's campaign staff in 1952, he had tried to bring more blacks into the Republican Party, but "simple opportunities are muffed by the Party as a whole." No prominent black citizens had been invited to speak at any presidential dinner. Morrow suggested that if "some prominent Negro could be given just five or ten minutes to appear on a program, it would make a great deal of difference in our public relations." In January 1960, Nixon decided that Morrow should be giving speeches and asked Ike to assign him to his campaign staff.[14]

Morrow confirmed the abysmal situation that Val Washington faced as RNC director of minority affairs. In the second week of September, Ike gave Morrow a leave of absence from the White House so that he could work on Nixon's staff. As he wrote later, Leonard Hall had promised him "a prominent and vital place in the campaign hierarchy, but it did not materialize." He did not receive any budget: "No literature, no workers, no assistants." When African-American leaders telephoned him to ask for material, he had nothing to give them.[15]

Jackie Robinson emerged as the most prominent African American supporting the vice president's campaign. During the campaign, his opposition to Kennedy grew vehement. Kennedy knew little about black Americans; he had chosen Lyndon Johnson, a southern segregationist, as his running mate; and he had had breakfast with Alabama Governor John Patterson and Alabama White Citizens Council chairman Sam Engelhardt. Patterson had campaigned for his position by holding a photograph showing whites in Little Rock kicking a black man in the stomach. He showed this alongside a sign saying: "This is how I will treat them if you make me your governor." Kennedy admitted that this meeting was his "greatest burden" while seeking the nomination, but he claimed that civil rights had not been mentioned during the breakfast. Robinson was not convinced: "I admit to being naïve, but I'm not that naïve."[16]

While Robinson hesitated over his endorsement, in May 1960 he used his column in the *New York Post* to record his favorable impressions of Nixon, Attorney General Rogers, and Secretary of Labor James Mitchell. In his column on June 10, he supported Nixon as a serious presidential candidate. After the Republican convention, the former baseball star expressed his approval of the Nixon-Lodge ticket.[17]

In early September, Robinson received a leave of absence from his job at Chock Full O' Nuts to campaign for the Republican ticket as an unpaid volunteer. He accepted the position, he said, because Nixon was "better qualified" and "more aggressive on civil rights" than Kennedy. The *Post* immediately suspended his column for the campaign's duration. On election day, *Post* editor James Wechsler fired Robinson, ostensibly because he had not informed Wechsler that he was campaigning for Nixon.[18]

Robinson toured one hundred cities for the Nixon campaign, covering sixty thousand miles. In early October, he introduced Nixon in Newark, New Jersey, as "a man who says the same things in the North, South, East and West." When someone at a rally booed Robinson, the vice president responded: "Any man who boos Jackie has no business here." The crowd applauded. Val Washington received "glowing reports" of Robinson's gatherings in Wilmington, Delaware, and Atlantic City, and he appreciated Robinson's "almost superhuman effort . . . to get votes" for the ticket. Toward the end of the month, Robinson told an Atlanta audience that "Kennedy goes the way the wind blows" and could not be trusted to take a vigorous stand on civil rights. In Dayton, Ohio, he proclaimed: "Dick Nixon has seen the light. He is a converted man. . . . He will stand his ground and give us exceptional leadership in the field of civil rights."[19]

Henry Cabot Lodge spoke on a variety of issues during the race. After the contest, he was accused of running "a leisurely campaign," but Tom Wicker, assigned to cover Lodge for his first presidential campaign as a *New York Times* reporter, offered a more nuanced assessment. Lodge's campaign looked lazy, he wrote, only in comparison to the frenzy of Nixon, Kennedy, and Johnson. In hindsight, Wicker thought Lodge looked "better and better."[20]

Nixon discovered that his running mate was a tremendous asset to the ticket. Handsome, suave, reserved, and affable, especially to women, Lodge drew enthusiastic responses everywhere. His speeches all followed the same pattern; he seldom mentioned political parties, routinely praised Nixon, and ignored Kennedy except to note his inexperience. He said little about domestic issues and instead highlighted his eight years as United States ambassador to the UN, sitting across a conference table from the Russians. The Soviets, he told his listeners, were intent on global domination, but "no one is going to take over the United States, and no one is going to take over the world."[21]

While Nixon was hospitalized in early September, Lodge telephoned him that the newspaper publisher William Randolph Hearst, Jr., had written an editorial urging the appointment of Ralph Bunche, who already held a major United Nations post, as United States ambassador to the UN in a Nixon administration. The vice president had "a very high regard for Bunche." He agreed with Lodge that he should be "high on the list . . . for the UN position" and told Herb Klein to tell Hearst that Bunche would "certainly be given very serious consideration."[22]

On the campaign trail, Lodge frequently spoke before black audiences. In Chicago on September 15, he met with the editorial boards of three African-American publishing companies. At a rally later that day, with three black leaders on the stage with him, he stressed that civil rights must be established as a priority at home and also argued its worldwide significance: four-fifths of the planet's population, he said, were people of color.[23]

The next day Lodge flew to Miami, where a segregated white audience applauded when he called civil rights "a national problem" and urged the United States to set an example for the world. In New York City in late September, he appealed to the real estate industry to make more housing available to African diplomats. In the first week of October, he applauded *Brown v. Board of Education*, saying it had added tremendously to American prestige at the UN. On October 7, he told a Seattle audience that Bunche "would make a wonderful United States Ambassador to the Soviet Union."[24]

Jet magazine printed a glowing tribute to Lodge and his ancestors, who had championed civil rights long before the issue was popular. Lodge himself had been an early advocate of eliminating poll taxes, making lynching a federal offense, and ending segregation of the armed forces. His African-American staff member Jewel Rogers traveled with the candidate throughout the campaign because, Lodge said, everyone needed "to get used to seeing Negroes." He called civil rights "our most vulnerable point—the Achilles' heel of our foreign policy"—and pledged to expand aid to Africa. He reminded audiences that the Declaration of Independence proclaimed all people were equal. Roy Wilkins, the NAACP executive director, said that Lodge was "straight" with African Americans: "We can't find anything against him."[25]

Reporters followed the candidate's lead. On October 9, during a nationally televised appearance on *Face the Nation*, Lodge was asked whether he would be in favor of the appointment of "a Negro member of the Cabinet." Lodge personally approved, but would not discuss the matter with Nixon until after the election. He did not advocate any specific candidate but then added that Bunche was "one of the three or four greatest living Americans." Two days later, when CBS anchor Walter Cronkite asked about the linkage between civil rights and foreign policy, Lodge responded that the United States urgently needed to solve the civil rights issue "so that every man is considered on his merits, without prejudice because of race, creed, or color." He added: "It's the right thing to do."[26]

At an evening rally in New York City's East Harlem on October 12, Lodge set out his most detailed civil rights proposals, going on the record favoring an African American in the president's cabinet, a pledge he made without consulting Nixon. When asked about it, the vice president replied that he would appoint the best people.[27]

The next day, Lodge backed off, telling reporters he could not "pledge anything." Putting an African American in the cabinet was his "own feeling," not a Republican commitment. Nixon summoned his running mate to Hartford, Connecticut, for an October 16 strategy session with his principal advisers. He took time from this gathering to meet alone with Lodge for a forty-five-minute private talk. When Lodge emerged, he said that the issue of civil rights had not been raised; Nixon then contradicted his running mate, telling reporters they had discussed it.[28]

For the remainder of the campaign, Lodge continued to predict that if elected, the vice president would choose an African American to serve in the cabinet. Toward the end of October, Jackie Robinson stated that a source close to Nixon had assured him that Nixon intended to do this. Three days before the balloting, before a crowd in Chapel Hill, North Carolina, Lodge proclaimed his and Nixon's determination that "no person in America is discriminated against because of race or creed or color."[29]

Nixon thought Lodge's statements damaged his campaign in the South. In his 1976 unpublished memoir, he commented that his running mate's statement in Harlem was disastrous. Lodge's apparent promise to appoint Bunche to a cabinet position, Nixon thought, made it look like he was pandering for black votes. A *Washington Post* story seemed to confirm that Lodge had hurt Nixon's drive in Dixie, and southern Republicans concurred. In Mississippi, Wirt Yerger wrote Lodge on October 12: "A negro as a member of the cabinet is absurd, and very damaging to the ticket in the South." Kent McKinley wrote Nixon two weeks later: "PLEASE no more references to a negro cabinet member." In the end, Nixon received a little more southern support than Ike had in his two campaigns.[30]

Despite the controversy over this issue, Nixon believed that the Kennedy campaign had peaked around the fourth debate and optimistically predicted himself on the path to victory. Three days before the end of October, he told reporter Earl Mazo, "Don't worry about me, I'm going to win." On the last day of the month, the vice president saw the tide turning; the election was trending his way.[31]

Dick, Pat, the campaign staff, and about one hundred newsmen spent the last week of October aboard the "Dick Nixon Victory Train," on a seventeen hundred–mile journey that left Washington's Union Station on October 23 for a whistle-stop tour of Pennsylvania, Ohio, Michigan, and Illinois—the states Nixon called "the guts states." He had used trains in earlier campaigns because they allowed him to meet voters in small towns and midsized cities. In traditional fashion, he would speak from the train's rear platform, always without notes, typically in front of large and enthusiastic crowds.[32]

Throughout the contest, Nixon praised Eisenhower's foreign policy. Kennedy, he said, had accused the United States of being "second-rate in everything," but then backed off his criticism of Ike's handling of the Paris summit in May and of the Quemoy-Matsu dispute with China. Finally, "in desperation, with no issues left, Senator Kennedy then tried to make a phony issue by claiming that I was afraid to debate him! Now that this sophomoric bluff has been called he is left without any issues at all." If Kennedy met with Khrushchev, Nixon concluded, the dictator would make "mincemeat" out of "that kind of man."[33]

Nixon repeatedly attacked Kennedy for his naïveté and inexperience. Kennedy's call during the debates to overthrow Castro was "shockingly reckless" and might lead to war with the Soviet Union. He then quoted from an earlier speech in which Kennedy praised Castro as "part of the legacy of Bolívar," the hero of the movements for South American independence.[34]

As for domestic policy, Nixon told his audiences that the senator promised a great deal, but "it isn't Jack's money—he's got a lot—it's your money that's going to buy all those promises." In addition, Kennedy would "raise your taxes, raise your prices," and damage farm income. He condemned Kennedy's constant references to that year's recession as "a despicable tactic" and "irresponsibility of the win-at-any price variety."[35]

In Michigan, Nixon faced labor hecklers. At an event in Jackson, for the first time in the campaign, three eggs were tossed at him. Speaking from the back of the train in Battle Creek, he promised that if he won, "I will not owe my election to any boss" in labor, management, or any other institution: "Whoever is President of this country has to owe his allegiance to only one boss and that's the American people." As he rode in a Grand Rapids motorcade with Congressman Gerald Ford, whom he called "a close personal friend" and the most valuable member of the House, agitators hurled tomatoes at his car without hitting it. He refused to be interrupted in Muskegon when a large number of pickets and hecklers threw eggs and tomatoes that landed on the platform, saying angrily, "All you do is show your own bad manners." He added: "I have been heckled by experts. So, don't try anything on me or we'll take care of you."[36]

On October 29, two days before Halloween, Nixon said his opponent was offering tricks, not treats. "It is a good time for America," he said, "to take a look at some of the hobgoblins Mr. Kennedy has been conjuring up." Kennedy's baleful predictions should not scare Americans; they knew better.[37]

Two incidents arose that week that the vice president had to address. The Nixon headquarters heard rumors that Democratic operatives were looking into certain business dealings of Don Nixon, the vice president's younger brother, and were expected "to publicize these transactions just before the election in some way that will reflect discredit" on the vice president. Robert Finch gave an interview to Peter Edson, the Washington columnist for Newspaper Enterprise Association, in which he offered a "full explanation" to end any rumors. Don Nixon owned a grocery store and by 1955 had expanded it into a restaurant called Nixon's Drive-In. He had then opened three other restaurants in Fullerton and Anaheim, California. Having overextended himself, in December 1956 he borrowed $205,000 from a family friend, Frank Waters, to save the businesses, but the following December he went into bankruptcy and defaulted on the loan. The vice president, Finch declared, had no interest in the loan or in any of his brother's failed business ventures.[38]

Drew Pearson had been following Don's business activities since 1952 and had learned about the loan three weeks earlier. In his "Washington Merry-Go-Round" column, the muckraker alleged that Finch had provided "a completely distorted version of the facts." The loan, Pearson charged, came from Hughes Tool Company, wholly owned by millionaire Howard Hughes, and after making the loan, Hughes had received favorable treatment from the federal government on airplane routes and government contracts. Pearson claimed that Don Nixon had received the loan "with the approval and knowledge" of his older brother and that it might be "the biggest conflict of interest revelation in the family of Richard M. Nixon."[39]

AP and UPI immediately filed their own stories, leading with Finch's denial.

Pearson's column, Finch said, contained "many false allegations" and was "an obvious political smear in the last two weeks of the campaign." Any charge that the vice president was involved in the loan was "absolute nonsense."[40]

Don Nixon released a statement on October 30, printed in the *New York Times* and other newspapers, describing how he came by the loan. His wife and Frank Waters's wife had gone to high school together, and the families had a close friendship. Waters was an attorney for Hughes, and when Don said he needed a loan, Frank acquired it from the Hughes Tool Company. Don never met Hughes. In the press release, he added: "I am deeply grieved and concerned to think that any individual would use my business misfortune to influence the outcome of the Presidential election." James Phelan, in *Scandals, Scamps, and Scoundrels*, found no linkage between the loan and any favors to Hughes: "There was no verifiable evidence that Nixon personally intervened at the request of Hughes."[41]

Yet the vice president should have anticipated that his brother's activities were a problem. He knew about his brother's financial difficulty. His former law partner Tom Bewley represented the Nixon family, including Don, and regularly wrote Dick about his brother's troubles. On October 17, 1955, Bewley reported that several reporters had insinuated that Dick must be connected to Don's restaurants, which were then in financial difficulties. Don's failed businesses, Bewley warned, were "going to be one of the smears during the next campaign." The attorney worried that Nixon's adversaries might link Don's problems to the vice president to cause embarrassment. Bewley had discussed these matters with Don and wanted to issue a public statement. Don had agreed that it was "a serious matter" because Democrats were looking for material to use against Dick.[42]

As Don's economic problems worsened in 1956, Bewley wrote the vice president on May 1 that Don had had "some knotty problems" that the attorney "felt had political implications." In the middle of November, Bewley asked Nixon whether his brother had explained "how really bad the situation" was. Nixon had no interest in Don's businesses and does not seem to have grasped the implications of his brother's troubles.[43]

Now, with Nixon again running for office, the old charges were being recycled. The campaign staff gave high priority to their counterattack, and by October 27 they believed Pearson's accusations were failing. In a press conference after the election, according to Pearson, Bobby Kennedy said that the loan story was one of the reasons his brother won the presidency.[44]

The arrest of Martin Luther King, Jr., occurred in the midst of this controversy. Fred Morrow begged Nixon's press secretary, Herb Klein, to draft a telegram to Atlanta's mayor. He even wrote it out, but Klein only put the draft in his pocket to "think about it," and nothing was done. The vice president's staff considered the telegram "bad strategy."[45]

William Safire, the future *New York Times* columnist who was then on Nixon's campaign staff, recalled that Jackie Robinson visited the vice president to plead with him to telephone the minister. Nixon refused, and Robinson left the hotel room with "tears in his eyes, shaking his head, ready to blow." Safire unsuccessfully tried to calm him down. Robinson, extremely upset, said "he would no longer support Nixon."[46]

Robinson eventually did calm down and continued to campaign for Nixon. Two days before the balloting, he spoke to African Americans in Chicago, telling them: "Kennedy sold out the Negroes by using Senator Johnson as a running mate to appease the southern racist senators." If the Democrats were elected, he said, blacks would be "in trouble." Sixteen days after the voting, Robinson had no regrets. He believed in Nixon and not Kennedy, and "if I had it to do over again, I would do exactly the same."[47]

When the nominating conventions ended, Eisenhower believed Nixon would win easily, but as the campaign unfolded, his opinion had changed. By October the president thought the outcome was in doubt.

Ike had come to loathe the Democratic ticket. His feelings erupted in a mid-October breakfast meeting with his White House science adviser, George Kistiakowsky, which turned into an angry monologue by the president "on how incompetent Kennedy is compared to Nixon, that even the more thoughtful Democrats are horrified by his selection and that Johnson is the most tricky and unreliable politician in Congress."[48]

By then Ike had already decided to get more involved in the campaign. At the beginning of the month, he felt that Republicans were gaining momentum but that the vice president needed "to be more hardhitting." On October 10 he held his first national campaign event of 1960, an appearance on NBC television. During a thirty-minute session, he answered questions from ten women who lived in ten different states. He heaped praise on the ticket—"We could not have two better men"—and admitted that he could hardly control his temper over the possibility of a Kennedy presidency, which would lead to inflation, or over the Democrats' charge that American prestige in the world had slipped.[49]

The president decided to help the Republican ticket by embarking on a sixty-five hundred–mile "nonpolitical tour" starting on Monday, October 17, and ending on the twenty-fifth. His first stop was in Detroit, where according to White House physician Howard Snyder, who routinely traveled with the president, his patient was shown the infamous "Liberty or Bigotry" pamphlet, showing a photograph of the Statue of Liberty, representing freedom of religion, along-side a photograph of a KKK figure, representing anti-Catholic prejudice. Snyder said Ike was "very upset" and used his speech to attack UAW president Walter Reuther for producing what he called "evil propaganda," "lies," and a "crooked statement." Later, when Mayor Louis Miriani gave the president the key to the city, Eisenhower, "his lips . . . so tight that he could hardly smile," took the occasion to protest against the pamphlet as a disservice to Americans. He had come to Detroit, he said, to "urge all our people to vote their own convictions, their own consciences, and not be swayed by any kind of false or extreme propaganda no matter what its source."[50]

On the second day of his allegedly nonpolitical tour, Ike flew into the Minneapolis–St. Paul International Airport, where he addressed a Republican rally of some two thousand people. He asked them to vote for "the man of our choice" without naming Nixon, and to reject "fear-mongering people who peddle gloom," without naming Kennedy.[51]

Eisenhower flew to San Francisco, where he proclaimed that those who spoke of declining American prestige were guilty of "debasement of truth." His administration, he admitted, could be better, but it was irresponsible to claim that the United States was becoming a second-class power.[52]

On Friday in San Diego, Ike met with Sigurd Larmon, who had worked for Citizens for Eisenhower in both of his elections; actor and media adviser Robert Montgomery; and W. Alton Jones, president of Cities Service Oil Company, to discuss a nationally televised program to be aired the day before election day, featuring the administration's accomplishments and the president's endorsement of the Nixon-Lodge ticket. (The program would be financed independently of the Nixon-Lodge organization.) With Jones and Larmon listening, Ike called Nixon; according to Snyder, he "spoke fairly firmly" and "agreed to do anything, everything, he can to help what is generally regarded as Dick's lost cause, but in his own way."[53]

On Monday, the last day of the tour, the president flew to Del Rio, Texas. His party drove to the International Bridge, crossed over the Rio Grande and proceeded to the tiny town of Ciudad Acuña. The president and Mexican President Adolfo López Mateos greeted each other, had lunch, and issued a communiqué on the construction of the Amistad Dam.[54]

Eisenhower flew next to Houston, where his welcoming committee included former governor Allan Shivers, the leader of Texas Democrats for Nixon-Lodge. Ike had been born in Texas and had won the state in 1952 and 1956. As his motorcade proceeded to his hotel, he received a tumultuous welcome from the 300,000 spectators lining Main Street, and that evening he spoke at Rice University Gymnasium at a special convocation of students and faculty. Declaring that he would make a nonpartisan speech, Ike said that the United States did not need "giant new arms programs" or a "massive economic shot in the arm." Texas Democrats objected to these veiled attacks on Kennedy, but Republicans were jubilant.[55]

Ike returned to the White House on the twenty-fifth and met with his friend George Allen, a Republican fundraiser. Dr. Snyder recorded in his diary that Ike "was very anxious to go on television at least twice before the election" and asked Allen to raise the money along with other Eisenhower fundraisers, that "the President is getting the gleam in his eye which, when translated into action, I am sure will be very helpful." Republicans had begun to worry that Kennedy was leading and "that they have an uphill fight." Pressure was mounting for Ike "to go campaigning to save Nixon."[56]

The president became further involved. On October 27, he went to Virginia's Shenandoah Valley, where Democratic Senator Harry Byrd welcomed him. Byrd had refused to back Adlai Stevenson and had helped Ike carry the state in 1952 and 1956. The president visited his mother's birthplace in Mount Sidney and gave a short speech at Mary Baldwin College in which he praised Byrd's service to the nation. He made no political statement; his appearance with Byrd was all that was needed.[57]

Mamie disapproved of her husband's campaigning. On October 28, Dr. Snyder wrote in his medical diary: "Mamie was plugging at me to tell the President he had to quit speaking and working for Nixon—that he might pop a cork. I have been cautioning him in this regard during the past several weeks since he became involved in a direct effort to elect Nixon."[58]

On the following day, Ike acknowledged these concerns in a letter to his friend Barry Leithead, a New York clothing manufacturer. The president had promised Nixon that he would "do everything I possibly could including the long 'nonpolitical' swing. . . . No one could put a higher estimate of the consequences of this election than I do. I have done everything I could think of and more to help out." But he had to defer to his wife's anxieties: "This would call down Mamie's wrath."[59]

Ike put any thought of his impartiality to rest at a Republican-sponsored dinner speech in Philadelphia that evening by discussing his administration's domestic achievements in personal income, increased gross national product, the interstate highway system, labor reforms, Social Security benefit increases, and civil rights. In foreign affairs, he had stopped the Korean War "always with honor." He listed the character traits a successful president would need, including ability, responsibility, and experience, and asserted that both Nixon and Lodge had those qualities. As for Kennedy, the senator's claim that the United States was "standing still," Ike said, "cruelly distorted the image of America." He ridiculed the senator's lack of experience and called his claims of American weakness irresponsible, adding that Kennedy would have "America galloping in reverse to what has been called a New Frontier." Of the two candidates, the vice president was clearly the "best qualified man to be the next President of the United States."[60]

The following Monday, Eisenhower, Nixon, Len Hall, and eight White House staffers met over lunch to discuss their strategy for the final week of the campaign. Ike later met with his speechwriters, and White House press secretary Hagerty announced that the president would expand his campaign appearances. These included a half-hour television broadcast in which he spoke of the nation's sound economy and attacked Kennedy for his vague promise to balance the budget and avoid inflation.[61]

By Wednesday morning, Ike felt fine and flew to New York to meet the Nixons, the Lodges, and the Rockefellers. At noon they rode in a motorcade through Manhattan, where a huge crowd gave them a tumultuous welcome and showered them with confetti. Special agent Clint Hill traveled with the president on this occasion and commented that Nixon "was in his glory, standing up in the back of the car, his arms outstretched to the cheering throng." Later the president met privately with Lodge and Rockefeller, then pulled Nixon aside and suggested that he go to Harlem to explain the Republican civil rights record. Nixon replied that he was "too busy" to make that stop. Ike was disappointed because he thought Nixon's appearance would increase black voting for the ticket. That evening the group went to the New York Coliseum, where the president spoke for fifteen minutes and then called Nixon to the podium to a rousing ovation.[62]

Certain that the momentum had shifted in his direction, Nixon intensified his efforts, setting off to campaign from coast to coast. He highlighted two "big" issues that were "hard hitting": Kennedy's lack of experience and the likelihood that he would bring high taxes and prices. There were two secondary points: Nixon was for the "little man . . . the labor man" and for peace through military strength. Americans, he told his audiences, had done far better under the peace and prosperity of the Eisenhower years than during the Korean War and the economic troubles of the Truman era.[63]

The president returned to the White House on November 3, while the vice president flew to Columbia, South Carolina, for an appearance with Billy Graham, whose presence alongside Nixon was tantamount to his blessing a Nixon presidency. From there the vice president traveled to Texas, where he predicted that he would win the state.[64]

That same day, John Roosevelt, the youngest of FDR's sons and the only one supporting Nixon, asked both presidential candidates to release their medical records to the public. He wanted more information on Kennedy's Addison's disease and Nixon's knee injury, and hoped that future legislation would require presidential candidates to undergo routine physical examination and publicly disclose the results. Pierre Salinger replied that Kennedy had "made public a complete medical statement" before the Democratic convention and that those traveling with the senator during the campaign had "no doubt" of his health. Nixon's press secretary, Herb Klein, said his candidate had also revealed the results of his physical before the Republican convention.[65]

After Roosevelt reported that many newspapers had asked for more recent information, Klein replied that Nixon would make a complete disclosure. White House press secretary Hagerty called Roosevelt's demand a "cheap, lousy, stinking political trick." The president added: "I am not making myself a party to any thing that has to do with the health of the candidates." Despite the president's stance, Dr. John Lungren, who was traveling with Nixon, issued a statement saying that except for being tired from campaigning, the candidate was in good health.[66]

Even though Kennedy did not respond, the president was interested enough in the circulating rumors that on the evening of October 26, he had Dr. Snyder brief him on Addison's disease. On November 5, an AP reporter contacted Dr. Arnold Hutschnecker about rumors that the vice president was seeing a New York psychiatrist, but the press did not follow up. Hutschnecker, who had treated Nixon for physical ailments during his vice presidency and moved into psychiatry, told the reporter he "detected no sign of mental illness in him."[67]

The president left for Cleveland on Friday, November 4, arriving just before noon for a motorcade and three public appearances. He flew to Pittsburgh for another motorcade, followed by a nationally televised speech that evening, and then spent Saturday at Camp David and Sunday on his Gettysburg farm.[68]

Nixon had no respite. On Friday, he spoke at Fort Worth and then flew to Casper, Wyoming, to fulfill his pledge to campaign in all fifty states. His plane landed in a snowstorm, frightening many of the reporters aboard. Sander Vanocur lost control, screaming: "The vice president's obsession is going to get us all killed!" The pilot circled the airport twice and landed on the third attempt. Press secretary Klein recalled: "We . . . skidded to a stop amid the ice on the snow-covered field." From there they went to Spokane, Washington, and then to Fresno, California. Don Hughes, the vice president's appointment secretary, remembered helping Nixon to bed. "You were actually out on your feet," Hughes told him later, "with one eye open." Nixon campaigned across his home state over the weekend. The Field Poll had 48 percent of the state's voters favoring

Kennedy, 45 percent Nixon, and 7 percent undecided. Nixon had to secure California to win the election.[69]

Throughout his run for the presidency, Nixon had never campaigned on a Sunday, but on this last weekend of the race, he did. In a nationally televised speech in Los Angeles, he promised that if elected, he would send Eisenhower and former presidents Truman and Hoover, if they wished to accompany Ike, on a mission to the Soviet satellites in Eastern Europe to invite their leaders to visit the United States. Ten days earlier, Nixon had announced that if elected, he would tour those nations himself, and in mid-October the Nixon staff had put out a rumor that the president might "serve as a roving ambassador of goodwill" after leaving the White House.[70]

Ike had not been consulted about this. A day before the vice president spoke, James Shepley, a Nixon staff member, dictated the suggestion to the president's private secretary, Ann Whitman. Ike "was astonished, did not like the idea of 'auctioning off the Presidency,'" and called the plan a "last-ditch hysterical action." Hagerty, at the president's direction, told Shepley to delete it from Nixon's speech. He agreed, but Nixon used it anyway. Ike "was so mad," Whitman wrote in her diary, that he called Nixon to demand he retract it. But on reflection, he had Jerry Persons, his chief of staff, send Nixon a congratulatory telegram: "Congratulations on a fine presentation. You are doing a great job."[71]

To complete his fifty-state pledge, the vice president flew to Alaska that evening and returned early the following morning, the last day of the race, to Madison, Wisconsin, and then Michigan. Both were battleground states. In Detroit, the vice president held a four-hour telethon on ABC that was carried by 157 stations, at a cost of $41,000 per hour. This was the first time a presidential candidate used television to answer telephone questions directly from the public. As the program proceeded, under a banner reading "Dial Dick Nixon," the candidate grew calmer and more confident. Actors Robert Young and Lloyd Nolan moderated; Lodge appeared on split screen, and Pat Nixon and her daughters came briefly on camera.[72]

The vice president's performance pleased Republicans, who over the campaign had spent twice as much on advertising as the Democrats. By the last day of the contest, Democrats had only 17.3 percent of their budget left, while the Republicans had 62.3 percent to spend. Nixon believed withholding advertising funds for the last few days of the race was essential if he was to win. Looking back on the election in 1962, Nixon believed the telethon was the most effective television program of his campaign. Richard Goodwin, who served on Kennedy's staff, agreed that Nixon was impressive. The senator had not viewed the telethon, but he was worried.[73]

The vice president made one last appearance in Chicago, urging voters to "put America first" when selecting the next president. On the eve of the balloting, he appeared on television with the president in the capital and with Lodge in Massachusetts. Ike gave his unqualified endorsement: Nixon would supply "the right kind of leadership to keep the nation dynamic, prosperous and free in the years ahead."[74]

While the vast majority of reporters favored Kennedy, Salinger estimated that 70 percent of daily newspapers endorsed Nixon. Of the nation's fifteen leading newspapers, nine endorsed Nixon, five favored Kennedy, and the *Washington Post*, as was its custom, remained neutral.[75]

Eisenhower, during his time in the Oval Office, had grown irritated over media coverage, but confined his criticism to his private correspondence. On May 6, 1960, he wrote his brother Edgar's wife, Lucy, about the deteriorating "quality of the information given to the public." Some newspapers had gone "to very great extremes" in their use of correspondents and columnists. Papers like the *Christian Science Monitor, Philadelphia Bulletin, Philadelphia Inquirer*, and *Baltimore Sun* carried "objective reporting," and he approved columnists like Arthur Krock and Roscoe Drummond. Some of the worst columnists, he said, were Drew Pearson, Doris Fleeson, Joe Alsop, James Reston, Marquis Childs, Walter Lippmann, and George Sokolsky. The president thought that "any newspaper that carries an unusual number of these signed columnists is an untrustworthy periodical."[76]

In the last week of November, Ike wrote John Whitney, publisher of the *New York Herald Tribune*, lamenting that "some newspapers have cheapened themselves too much by their indiscriminate use of columnists." Personal "opinions" were replacing news stories. Early in 1961, he wrote that Ralph McGill was once "one of the ablest and keenest newspaper men" he knew, but he was sad to see "a constant deterioration in the tone of" his writing in the *Atlanta Constitution*.[77]

The media also troubled Nixon. A month after the Republican convention, he had written about "the obvious unobjectivity and unfairness of most of the papers," particularly the *New York Times* and the *Washington Post*. They failed to contrast "Kennedy's personal attack on me in his acceptance speech with my 'high road' handling of him." The vice president expected his staff to hammer "home the line that they have already started on the low road." With the exception of "newspapers completely biased on our side," he had hardly read any columns or editorials pointing this out and wanted his campaign to mount a powerful letter-to-the-editor effort as a corrective.[78]

Henry Luce, owner of *Time, Life*, and *Fortune* magazines, endorsed Nixon. The Scripps Howard newspapers also backed the Republican ticket, as did the

Oakland Tribune, the *Los Angeles Times,* the Hearst newspapers, and many others. Nixon wrote after the election that the Hearst chain made certain "that the coverage on the front page is fair and objective. If all the editors and publishers who supported us had done as well as the Hearst papers did in this respect there is no doubt in my mind but that we would have won."[79]

Several publishers informed Nixon after the election that "there was never an unfavorable column or editorial written about Kennedy on which they did not get a strong complaint from someone high in his campaign organization." In addition, Nixon felt he could not get his "positions across to the voters in view of the attitude of some of the reporters covering the campaign."[80]

Although there was peer pressure to line up against Nixon, Earl Mazo, Ralph de Toledano, and a few other reporters wrote positive articles about the vice president. The vice president also put William White of *Harper's* magazine "high on the list among those who maintain standards of objectivity and fairness regardless of what their personal views on men or issues may be."[81]

The first female reporter for CBS television, Nancy Dickerson, started her career at the network in 1954. During the 1960 contest, she provided her impressions of the Nixons. The vice president "was uncomfortable with reporters" and at the completion of each trip, the Nixons "boarded our press plane as if they were traveling royalty on an imperial state visit."[82]

Some reporters' feelings toward Nixon can fairly be described as visceral hatred. Drew Pearson had attacked him since the Checkers speech in the 1952 presidential election and wrote derogatory stories throughout his vice presidency. Pearson published the story about the Hughes loan to Don Nixon specifically to damage Nixon's chances in the election. Jack Anderson, the muckraker's assistant, recalled that his boss was pleased that the scandal "had at least had a hand in keeping down Richard Nixon."[83]

New York Post editor James Wechsler had despised the vice president since the beginning of his congressional career. He felt Nixon had defeated Congressman Voorhis in 1946 and Congresswoman Douglas in 1950, "two of the ablest members of the liberal bloc in Congress," through "systematic misrepresentations of issues and personal slander." Wechsler also asserted that Nixon had unjustly accused Alger Hiss of being a Soviet spy and used money from his 1952 fund for personal needs. What differentiated him from others was "the utter mirthlessness, lack of self-consciousness and clear-eyed earnestness which he brings to his double role."[84]

Some of Wechsler's complaints were in the eye of the beholder, but the verifiable ones are without merit. Very few Hiss scholars now believe he was innocent. Nixon's victories over Voorhis and Douglas did not depend on misrepresentations and slander; both ran lackluster campaigns, while Nixon worked energetically and efficiently. And Nixon did not use campaign funds for his personal benefit.

Philip Potter from the *Baltimore Sun* described Nixon as "the scientific pitchman of politics, who coldly tries to figure what will sell, packages his products neatly, and then goes out to peddle them." Whenever one of Nixon's pitches succeeded, Potter considered it just luck. He became such a committed Kennedy supporter that *New York Times* reporter Russell Baker believed Kennedy and his staff had "brainwashed" him.[85]

William Costello, who attended the University of Minnesota with Potter, agreed with his classmate. Costello had been the White House correspondent for the Mutual Broadcasting System since the Roosevelt administration. In early 1960 he published a derogatory book, *The Facts about Nixon*, and the day before the voting, he said in a radio broadcast that the debates had "ruined Nixon" and his "stature has been shrinking." The vice president lacked "authentic intellectual content." Reviewing *Six Crises* two years later, Costello called Nixon "one of life's losers."[86]

Having completed his campaign on a positive note, Nixon went home to California to vote, and to wait for the people's verdict.

17

HOW THEY VOTED

As the campaign moved into the last six days, Roscoe Drummond, who was traveling with Senator Kennedy, wrote a column: "Kennedy's Windup . . . No Sign His Tide Is Receding." The Nixon team's assessment that Kennedy had peaked ten days earlier, he thought, lacked merit. The senator had overcome criticism of his youth and inexperience and had done well in the debates. He drew large crowds and inspired them to vote. Drummond reflected the mood of many reporters who believed Kennedy was heading toward a landslide. While the senator himself claimed that the race was "very close," the columnist thought President Eisenhower's all-out commitment to campaign for Nixon had unduly alarmed the Kennedy camp.[1]

Kennedy himself was deeply concerned, telling his friend Paul Fay that "Dick Nixon hit the panic button and started Ike speaking," which put the race "up for grabs." Thirty-two years later, Arthur Schlesinger confided in his journal that Kennedy had a comfortable lead at the end of October, and then voters started to change their opinion, preferring Nixon's experience. Had the campaign gone on for another week, Schlesinger concluded, the vice president "would probably have won."[2]

While Kennedy had a slight advantage in the polling at the start of the final week, on the day before the election the Gallup Poll found that the senator led the vice president 49 percent to 48, with 3 percent undecided. While *Newsweek, Time,* and *U.S. News and World Report* had Kennedy substantially ahead, The Roper Poll had Nixon leading, 49 percent to 47, with 4 percent undecided. Shortly after the election, Elmo Roper, who voted for the vice president, wrote: "Never since the start of scientific polling has so difficult, so volatile an election been encountered." Until the final weekend, "there was no way of telling which way the popular Presidential vote would go. . . . The undecided vote had the power to determine the outcome."[3]

Kennedy finished his campaign in Boston on Monday evening, November 7. Everyone who worked on the campaign was exhausted. The following morning, Jack and Jackie, whose legal residence was an apartment in the city, cast their ballots. She later told Schlesinger that she cast "only one vote—for Jack. It is a rare thing to be able to vote for one's husband for President of the United States, and I didn't want to dilute it by voting for anyone else."[4]

Then the couple traveled seventy-five miles to the Kennedy compound at Hyannis Port, where the entire clan assembled. The patriarch and his wife occupied the big house; Bobby's house had served as campaign headquarters; and Jack's house was just behind his younger brother's. Nearly three hundred newsmen, photographers, cameramen, and television and radio employees worked in a nearby facility. They and the Kennedys waited for the results.[5]

Lyndon Johnson and Lady Bird voted in his hometown of Johnson City, thirty miles west of Austin. After briefly visiting his campaign headquarters, he went to the Driscoll Hotel to monitor the incoming results in a suite with a direct line to the Kennedys at Hyannis Port.[6]

Nixon and his staff were just as tired. He had not slept for almost two days before election night and was "physically drained, emotionally drained, mentally drained. . . . You're just numb, and more numb." On Monday evening, he completed his campaign and flew to Ontario Airport in California. From there he drove to the Ambassador Hotel in Los Angeles and was able to get three hours of sleep before he and Pat voted in East Whittier.[7]

The vice president told Herb Klein, "I want to be away from everything today. Understand!" He would resurface at the hotel to follow the election results, but first, he wanted to escape from the ever-present press. Don Hughes, his appointment secretary, had never driven on Pacific Coast Highway, so he, Nixon, his Secret Service agent, Robert Sherwood, and John DiBella from the Los Angeles Police Department got in a convertible. The vice president insisted that they not discuss the election. Hughes mentioned that he had never been to Tijuana, Mexico. Since Nixon liked Mexican food, the four of them headed south for 150 miles and had enchiladas, tacos, and German beer at the Old Heidelberg restaurant in downtown Tijuana. While they were eating, Hughes called Klein and told him where the party was. On the return trip, Nixon wanted to stop at the San Juan Capistrano mission; he went into the chapel to pray. Then he returned to the hotel. He had celebrated election day eating lunch in a foreign country.[8]

Henry Cabot Lodge and his wife, Emily, cast their ballots in Beverly, Massachusetts. Afterward, he told reporters not to expect any landslide and that the current polling in favor of the Democratic ticket was a "major hallucination." After 4:00 he and his entourage flew to the capital to await the results at the Sheraton Park Hotel.[9]

President Eisenhower took a helicopter from the White House to Gettysburg, Pennsylvania, where he and Mamie voted. He then sent a telegram to Nixon, saying that he and his son John, along with their wives, cast the first four ballots for the Republican ticket. The Eisenhowers returned to the White House, and that evening they joined the Lodges at the Sheraton.[10]

The election was not just a contest between the Democrat and Republican tickets, it was also a battle over ratings. NBC used the RCA 501 computer and had its biggest news stars, Chet Huntley and David Brinkley, leading the network's coverage. CBS had the IBM 7090 with its anchor Walter Cronkite analyzing the returns. ABC employed UNIVAC, but in the early evening the network carried *Bugs Bunny* and *The Rifleman* before starting its election coverage in prime time.[11]

Just before the first polls closed in the East, the president gave supporters a brief pep talk and was pleased that the early projections from Kansas were going for the Republican ticket. From 8:00 p.m. to 9:00, results from New Hampshire started to trickle in. Dixville Notch gave Nixon all of its nine votes; seconds later, Hart's Location cast seven votes for the vice president and five for Kennedy; Waterville provided twenty votes for Nixon and two for the senator, and Millsfield gave four votes to Nixon and one to Kennedy. ABC and CBS prematurely predicted a Republican sweep.

Jack Kennedy watched the early returns with Jackie, who would deliver John Fitzgerald Kennedy, Jr., on the twenty-fifth of the month. The commentators changed their forecast when Connecticut gave Kennedy a ninety thousand–vote majority and large industrial cities like Philadelphia and Chicago began coming through with large pluralities. Ted Kennedy thought it looked "like a blowout," and so did other staff members.

Nixon appeared to be doing well in the South, with slight leads in Tennessee and Kentucky, and he hoped to win North and South Carolina. Maine, Vermont, and New Hampshire were going for Republicans, as expected. The NBC computer's first projection placed the senator's odds of victory at 25 to 1 in his favor, and the other two networks concurred that Kennedy was ahead.[12]

From 9:00 p.m. to 10:00, the three computers increased the odds of a Kennedy sweep. The vice president especially monitored the results in Pennsylvania, New York, Michigan, Ohio, Illinois, Texas, and California. He had to carry three of those states while Kennedy needed five. As anticipated, Massachusetts gave him an overwhelming majority. Ohio, New Jersey, and Michigan were not in the Democratic column.

Interviewed in Los Angeles, Len Hall pronounced: "I think we should put all of those electronic computers in the junk pile so far as election returns are concerned. This one is going down to the wire—a squeaker, a real close election." Nixon led in Tennessee, was victorious in Florida and Kentucky, and the results in Texas were inconclusive.[13]

From 10:00 p.m. to 11:00, with about one fifth of the national vote completed, Kennedy was a million votes ahead and easily defeating Nixon in electoral votes. NBC placed the odds of a Kennedy triumph at 250 to 1. New York City, Philadelphia, and Baltimore were giving Kennedy large pluralities and assuring him victory in their respective states. But just as a Democratic landslide appeared certain, Nixon won Virginia and Oklahoma and showed unexpected strength in New Jersey, Colorado, and Ohio. Kennedy had slight leads in Michigan and Wisconsin and was increasing his advantage in Texas and Illinois.[14]

From 11:00 to midnight, RNC chairman Thruston Morton said Republican chances were improving; Ohio moved into the Republican column. Democrats were still forging ahead in the big industrial states and doing well in the South. Texas had gone Democratic by approximately forty thousand votes. Michigan's labor unions appeared to be winning the state for the Democratic ticket. Kennedy's lead in the popular vote soared to almost two million. The president returned to the White House to watch the returns on television. At about midnight, Dr. Snyder recalled that Ike "took a large sleeping pill to blunt the hurt" and went to bed.[15]

Around midnight, Lodge told the dejected partisans at the hotel that the outcome looked bleak. Then returns coming in from the West gave Republicans some hope. Nixon won Washington, Oregon, Utah, Arizona, and Idaho, as well as Colorado. He also reduced Kennedy's advantage in California and was ahead in Hawaii. In the Midwest, the vice president had triumphed in Iowa, was ahead in Wisconsin, and was closing the gap in Michigan. Kennedy was leading in Minnesota and had won in Delaware, West Virginia, and Louisiana.[16]

From 1:00 a.m. to 2:00, *New York Times* reporter James Reston anticipated a Kennedy victory and wrote an article under the banner headline: KENNEDY ELECTED PRESIDENT. As the vice president began to gain, the newspaper, according to the managing editor Turner Catledge, "softened our prediction, and got some papers out." The third edition said that Kennedy had a commanding lead. The Democratic governor of Ohio, Mike DiSalle, still held out hope that his party would carry his state. Minnesota provided better news; it was going Democratic. But Nixon was cutting into Kennedy's advantage in Illinois.[17]

From 2:00 a.m. to 3:00, Nixon's chances decreased. Republican New York Senator Kenneth Keating became the first major Republican politician to wire congratulations to Kennedy. But then it looked like Keating might have been premature: the vice president put Wisconsin in his column, and Kennedy's lead in Illinois, Michigan, and Minnesota was dwindling. Small states grew in significance. The senator won in New Mexico and Nevada and was slightly ahead in Hawaii. Southern Democrats in Mississippi, Alabama, and Georgia held out hope that neither candidate would get a majority and the election would end up in the House of Representatives, where each state had one vote. Then the South could bargain for the candidate who offered them the better deal on civil rights.[18]

Shortly after midnight Pacific time, Dick and Pat came down to the ballroom at the Ambassador Hotel in Los Angeles. With his wife standing beside him, holding back tears, Nixon began his five-minute statement by thanking his supporters. He then said that if the present trends continued, Kennedy would be the next president. *Washington Post* reporter Julius Duscha watched the reaction from the thousand assembled partisans. "As women cried and as men bit their lips," Nixon hoped Americans would "unite behind our next President." The crowd opposed any concession; so had Pat. After offering his gloomy assessment, the vice president told his listeners that he had had four hours of sleep in the previous forty-eight hours and was going to bed.[19]

James Hagerty had expected Nixon to concede and prematurely sent Kennedy and Johnson congratulatory telegrams from the White House. He told Ike he had "goofed." Realizing that Nixon had not conceded, he telephoned Pierre Salinger to ask him not to release the telegrams until the appropriate moment.[20]

Kennedy watched Nixon's short speech, which came after 3 a.m. on the East Coast, and turned off the television. Those advisers still present were angry that the vice president had not conceded. Salinger recalled Kennedy's response: "If I were he, I would have done the same thing." With that, he left and went to bed.[21]

Between that moment and 6:00 a.m., Kennedy's popular margin slipped below a million for the first time. Even with that worrisome event, NBC announced early that morning that Kennedy needed just one electoral vote to win. David Brinkley recalled: "Those of us who had been on the air all night were beginning to drag." The race continued. Kennedy won Nevada and was ahead in Alaska and California. After the AP declared that the senator had won Michigan, CBS concluded that Kennedy had more than enough electoral votes for his victory.[22]

The morning's newspaper headlines across the nation declared Kennedy the winner. This was the closest presidential election since 1888, when Democrat Grover Cleveland barely defeated Republican Benjamin Harrison in the popular vote but lost in the Electoral College. With nine-tenths of the vote counted, Kennedy led Nixon by 770,000. Although the ballots in Illinois were still being counted, the senator appeared well ahead in California. The most skeptical pundits proclaimed Kennedy president-elect.[23]

Nixon rested for two hours. Awakening at 6:00 a.m., he knew that Kennedy had won. At dawn, Secret Service agents went to the Kennedy compound to guard the president-elect. Photographers took pictures of the family in front of the patriarch's fireplace. Some had "a touch football game on the lawn" with Jack joining in.[24]

At 9:45 a.m., Herb Klein read to a group of reporters the vice president's telegram congratulating Kennedy on his victory and pledging that he would "have the united support of all Americans as you lead the nation in the cause of peace and freedom during the next four years." The president-elect responded by thanking his rival, adding, "The nation can continue to count on your unswerving loyalty in whatever new effort you undertake and that you and I can maintain our long-standing cordial relations in the years ahead."[25]

When the president had gone to bed, the senator was an overwhelming favorite to win; Kennedy led by approximately two million votes, and the East had gone solidly for the Democratic ticket. Ike woke up between midnight and 2:00 a.m. and found Kennedy's advantage waning. Rising at 6:00 a.m., he "could not believe" that the senator's "margin had been greatly narrowed" and results were still being calculated. Ike went to the Oval Office at 8:03 a.m., and by the end of the hour, all hope had vanished; Kennedy was president-elect. The president sent telegrams to Kennedy and Johnson congratulating them on their win.[26]

When Eisenhower's son John walked into the Oval Office later that morning, he had rarely seen his father so depressed: "All I've been trying to do for eight years," Ike told him, "has gone down the drain." Ann Whitman, his private secretary, believed Ike saw this defeat as a "repudiation" of his two terms in office. To her, this was "nonsense." His campaign effort was "responsible for the surprisingly good showing of the Nixon-Lodge ticket."[27]

The president sent a telegram to Nixon, praising his "hard-fought courageous campaign to carry forward the principle of sound government" and adding that he cherished their friendship. At 12:25 p.m. Eastern time, the vice president called Ike from Los Angeles. According to Ike's diary, "He seemed controlled, not downcast particularly." He still believed he would win California when all the votes were tallied and might also take Illinois and Minnesota. Nixon had run "7% ahead of the Republican Party" and Kennedy "a little more behind the Democratic Party." He thanked the president for his "magnificent" campaign effort, adding that he "did a grand job." Ike urged him to concede, which he had already done. The president hoped Nixon would "take a good rest—sent his love to Pat," and said, "We can be proud of these last eight years."[28]

The president also wrote Pat and Dick a letter before leaving for Augusta, Georgia, "to get some sunshine, recreation and rest." He fervently hoped they "would not be too greatly disappointed by yesterday's election returns." Any sadness they felt should not be personal "but for our country and for the jeopardy in which our great hopes and aims for the future have been placed." Having lost the election, the couple would "have a happier life," especially more time "with your two beautiful daughters." Whatever they did in the future, they had "my best wishes." Ike added his "official confidence in you has not been shaken for a moment," and his and Mamie's "affection . . . for you will never grow less."[29]

The president congratulated Lodge for his "magnificent campaign in the finest tradition of a great American family." He thanked Lodge as well for his "effective service" during his two terms. The White House chief of staff, Jerry Persons, who worked closely with Cabot, added that his "brilliant accomplishments" at the UN "were unequalled" and the nation owed him "an immeasurable debt of gratitude." "If anyone lost at the polls Tuesday, it was the people who failed to recognize the unique leadership you offer in furthering the cause of peace and freedom throughout the free world."[30]

Lyndon Johnson watched the results from Austin, with a walkie-talkie at hand to check the voting in the Lone Star State. One LBJ supporter, state senator Dorsey Hardeman, asserted that "the national ticket owes its success to Lyndon Johnson." Others within the Democratic Party echoed that sentiment. He had carried his own state and was crucial in winning other southern states. On the afternoon of November 9, he went on television to declare victory and pledged to work closely with the president-elect.[31]

A state-by-state analysis demonstrates how complicated the voting was. Nixon easily won Maine, New Hampshire, and Vermont, for 12 electoral votes, but the rest of the region's 124 electoral votes went for Kennedy, who won his home state of Massachusetts with a half million majority. He also won in Connecticut, Rhode Island, New York, and Pennsylvania. The closest contests came in New Jersey and Delaware, where Kennedy received just over half of the ballots cast and Nixon had 49 percent.[32]

Pennsylvania had not voted for a Democratic presidential candidate since 1940. Its Democratic governor, David Lawrence, was a Kennedy ally and a Catholic. Kennedy needed a large urban turnout, and Democrats in Philadelphia and Pittsburgh came out for him, giving the ticket an insurmountable lead. Kennedy received 51.1 percent of the vote.[33]

Robert Finch, one of Nixon's campaign managers, admitted that Kennedy's victory in the Northeast was beyond Republican control: the region was becoming more urbanized and more Democratic. Finch heard "some loose talk" that the Republican ticket had lost because Rockefeller had not campaigned hard enough. The day after the election, he told the governor that "no one could have done more than you did in campaigning for Nixon and Lodge."[34]

The eleven states that made up the Old Confederacy—Alabama, Arkansas, Florida, Georgia, Louisiana, Mississippi, North and South Carolina, Tennessee, Texas, and Virginia—were usually reliably Democratic. In 1952, Eisenhower had won Florida, Tennessee, Virginia, and Texas (he was a native son), giving him 57 electoral votes. Four years later, he won those states again and added Louisiana, for a total of 67. During his first campaign, Eisenhower received 48.1 percent of the region's vote, increasing his share to 48.9 percent in 1956, while carrying the majorities in the cities in both elections. Turnout was low: about 38 percent in the first election and 39 percent four years later.[35]

To win in 1960, Kennedy adopted his own "southern strategy," hoping to bring those states back into the Democratic Party. He began that effort during his bid for the vice presidential nomination at the 1956 Democratic convention by presenting himself to southern delegates as a moderate who would not take a militant civil rights stand. Afterward, he avoided making belligerent statements against segregation and continued to court southern politicians. As historian Guy Land pointed out, Kennedy was "the last major Democratic candidate to tailor a campaign to the demands of the white Solid South." Lyndon Johnson complicated his plans by becoming a contender for the 1960 presidential nomination. Once Johnson became his running mate, the senator gave him the assignment of returning the South to the Democratic Party, and especially of winning his native state of Texas, with its crucial 24 electoral votes.[36]

Southern voter turnout increased in 1960 to slightly more than 40 percent. Kennedy's winning margin in Georgia was the highest in the South, 62.6 percent, and the second largest in the nation. That triumph was placed in doubt when a ballot initiative approved by Democratic primary voters authorized the state's twelve electors to vote as they pleased if Kennedy won. Even though the party predicted a landslide, citizens expressed their anti-Kennedy and anti–civil rights feelings. After the election, some Democrats urged these "free presidential electors" to withhold their votes for Kennedy, but Governor Ernest Vandiver and the other party leaders insisted that they cast their ballots for the senator.[37]

Kennedy easily won in Louisiana and North Carolina but squeaked by with only 51.2 percent of the vote in South Carolina, where an emerging Republican base promoted states' rights and objected to the civil rights plank of the Democratic platform. James Byrnes, who as governor had actively campaigned for

Eisenhower in 1952, campaigned for Nixon as the former governor; so did the influential Senator Strom Thurmond, who was friends with the Nixons.[38]

The most important prize in the South was Texas. Before Kennedy won the Democratic nomination, many pundits thought it might go to Johnson. Visiting Houston in late June, Nixon had called LBJ "one of the ablest political craftsmen of our times" and predicted that if he were the Democratic candidate, Republican chances of winning Texas would be remote.[39]

LBJ instead became the vice presidential nominee, and with Kennedy at the top of the ticket, Texas was in play. Republicans there were gaining strength. Allan Shivers, the conservative former governor, had come out for Eisenhower in both of his campaigns, and at the end of September he once more broke with his party and opened Democrats for Nixon-Lodge headquarters in Austin. His wife and children were Catholic; religion never played a part in his opposition to the Democratic ticket.[40]

Shivers routinely went on television and supported the vice president, both in Texas and in several other southern states. He excoriated the Democratic platform as an attempt at "socialized managed America" and attacked Kennedy on his foreign affairs positions. He also accused the senator of advocating federal control of public schools and planning to eliminate favorable tax treatment given to the oil industry.[41] The night before the balloting, Shivers blasted the Democratic ticket on statewide television. Nixon was far more qualified to govern the nation, and Shivers was "afraid for the country" if Kennedy won. He appealed to voters to vote their "own convictions."[42]

While Shivers was popular with Texas conservatives, he no longer controlled state patronage. His successor as governor, Price Daniel, had served with Johnson in the Senate and supported the Democratic ticket. The trio of Daniel, Johnson, and House Speaker Sam Rayburn ran the party in Texas, and LBJ managed the single statewide political organization.[43]

The Texas Republican Party recognized where this political advantage might lead. On November 1, in response to rumors of possible irregularities over ballots and the poll tax, state chairman Thad Hutcheson called for poll-watching teams at every precinct. Democratic statewide chairman J. Ed Connally reacted a day later, calling this move an "insult to the integrity" of the election judges. Hutcheson reminded Connally of the 1948 senatorial election, which Johnson won by eighty-seven votes, earning the nickname "Landslide Lyndon." No state law called for poll watchers; precinct judges decided whether or not to permit them. The Republican demand was ignored.[44]

From August through October, the most reliable Texas poll, the Belden Poll, showed a close race with large numbers of undecided voters. At the beginning of

September, Claude Robinson, Nixon's pollster, had his candidate ahead 52 percent to 48. Kennedy's pollster, Louis Harris, conducted three polls: the last one, from October 24 through 29, had the senator leading 48 to 42, with 10 percent undecided. Two days before the voting, the *New York Times* called Texas uncertain for either side. When the voting was completed, Kennedy-Johnson received 50.5 percent to Nixon-Lodge's 48.5 percent. The Democratic ticket defeated the Republicans by 46,233 votes and won the prize of twenty-four electoral votes.[45]

The Republican Party was steadily increasing its southern membership, and Nixon had visited every southern state. Despite his efforts, he took only three, with thirty-three electoral votes: Florida, Virginia, and Tennessee. In Virginia, Senator Harry F. Byrd, Sr., dominated state politics and worked energetically to ensure the vice president's victory.[46]

Like Eisenhower, Nixon captured the metropolitan areas in the South. He improved upon his predecessor's share of the Protestant vote and ran behind him with Catholics and African Americans. To protest the Democrats' civil rights pledge, many states' rights advocates voted Republican.[47]

Southern segregationists and states' rights advocates had tried to persuade voters to elect unpledged electors in order to force a deadlock and have the House of Representatives decide the election. Alabama, Arkansas, Georgia, and Mississippi all allowed electors to withhold or change their votes from the national party's nominee. In the 1948 presidential election, southerners ran Strom Thurmond as a "Dixiecrat" candidate against Harry Truman and Thomas Dewey in the hope of forcing the House to decide the victor. This movement surfaced again in 1960. Every major southern newspaper, with the exception of the *Atlanta Constitution*, endorsed an independent slate of electors to throw the election into the House and give the southern states the bargaining power to preserve segregation.[48]

Mississippi provided the strongest of these movements. Governor Ross Barnett used the primary to nominate two slates of electors under the Democratic label, one pledged to Kennedy and the other unpledged, as a protest vote against both parties' candidates. The unpledged delegates won a plurality of 39 percent of the vote, and in a close general election, Barnett hoped that neither national candidate would receive a majority. His eight unpledged electors, joined with other southern electors, might have enough political leverage to give the presidency to the candidate who pledged to maintain the old order on civil rights.[49]

Alabama, to avoid a disastrous split within the state Democratic Party, held no popular vote for president. Voters instead cast their ballots for eleven presidential electors: Kennedy's and Nixon's names did not appear on the ballots. Democrats won all eleven spots. Six went to unpledged states-rights electors who refused to support the national ticket. Frank Dixon, governor from 1939 to 1943 and an avowed segregationist, received the highest number of votes. Five of the winning electors were loyalists pledged to Kennedy. The wire services attributed all of Alabama's votes for Democratic electors to Kennedy, even though he did not receive a single vote.[50]

Eisenhower had won the states on the southern periphery by appealing to the urban and industrial areas that, according to political scientists Earl and Merle Black, had "large white middle classes sympathetic to the economic conservatism of the Republican party." Kennedy took Maryland, Missouri, and West Virginia, with thirty electoral votes, while Nixon managed Kentucky and Oklahoma for seventeen electoral votes.[51]

An Oklahoma elector named Henry Irwin was pledged to Nixon, but he later admitted in a CBS interview that he "could not stomach" the vice president and tried to create "a conservative coalition" that would reject both Nixon and Kennedy. Irwin sent out a telegram to the other Republican electors stating that while they could not alone deny the election to Kennedy, if "sufficient [electors among] southern Democrats" defected from the "Socialist labor nominee," the Democratic slate might be replaced by Byrd as president and Goldwater as vice president. Even though his scheme failed, he became a "faithless elector" and voted for Byrd, bringing his electoral vote total, including Mississippi's eight and six from Alabama, to fifteen.[52]

The six states in the industrial Midwest had all gone to Eisenhower in both of his campaigns. This time, Kennedy easily won Michigan with high turnout from the unions. The polls in Minnesota were much closer, even though Hubert Humphrey raised a great deal of money and worked energetically for the Kennedy-Johnson ticket. Many voters did not make their decision until very late in the race, and 51 percent of them voted a straight party line. Kennedy won by 22,000 votes. The outcome in Illinois was not decided until midnight. Ballots were usually counted first in Chicago, which was heavily Democratic, followed by the rest of the state, which was Republican. With almost 4.75 million ballots, Kennedy won by 8,858. From those three states, the Democratic ticket gained fifty-eight electoral votes.[53]

Nixon also won three industrial states: Indiana, Ohio, and Wisconsin, for fifty electoral votes. Ohio's Democratic governor, Mike DiSalle, had predicted a Kennedy landslide, but only one county voted for the senator. The governor's state tax increases and overconfidence in his party's victory had sapped enthusiasm, while Republican state chairman Ray Bliss blanketed the state with radio, television, and newspaper advertisements. In addition, the president campaigned for the ticket in the state.[54]

Democrats were hoping that the farm states would be so disenchanted with Secretary Benson that they would abandon the Republican Party. But North and South Dakota, Nebraska, Kansas, and Iowa steadfastly voted Republican, adding thirty-two electoral votes to Nixon's total. North Dakota gave the vice president his lowest majority in the region, 55.4 percent, and Nebraska the highest with 62.1 percent.[55]

As for the West, traditionally a Republican region in any race without Franklin Roosevelt, Nixon did slightly less well than Eisenhower, who had swept all thirteen states in both of his elections. Nixon won the West by a margin of ten states to three, receiving seventy-five electoral votes to Kennedy's ten. The popular vote was close: Republicans received 51.1 percent and the Democrats 48.5 percent. Seven of the thirteen states were decided by margins of less than 3 percent.[56]

The major prize was California, the second-most-populous state, with thirty-two electoral votes. Just two years earlier, in 1958, Democrats had crushed the Republican candidates, William Knowland for governor and Goodwin Knight for senator. This disaster had left the statewide Republican Party in disarray and short of money. To win his home state, Nixon needed to unite and energize California Republicans. From the start of the race until election day, he assigned Stanley McCaffrey to work with the state's Republican Party. McCaffrey organized fundraising events and solicited cooperation between the party and volunteer groups. He also mounted a massive telephone campaign aimed at persuading Republicans to vote by absentee ballot.[57]

Registered Democrats outnumbered Republicans in the state, 3.7 million to 2.6 million. Governor Pat Brown initially predicted that Kennedy would win by a million votes, but by October, seeing a very tight race, he said he would "be satisfied, if he carries it by one vote." The last statewide poll, at the end of October, had Kennedy leading Nixon 48 percent to 45 percent, with 7 percent undecided. On election night, when Kennedy jumped out to a substantial early lead, the three major television networks prematurely gave him the victory. A week later, after the 243,000 absentee ballots had been counted, the senator's lead disappeared. Nixon had won the state, 50.1 percent to 49.6. In taking the state by 35,000 votes, he had outperformed California's Republican registration by 10 percent.[58]

Harold Leventhal, the general counsel for the Kennedy campaign, wrote Bobby Kennedy on December 7, saying he doubted that any abuse had occurred. The senator's lead had vanished because of late tallies from Orange County, where the overwhelmingly Republican majority had voted five-to-two for the vice president. Leventhal also doubted there had been any "hanky-panky," and while he would "dearly love to do something in California, . . . it would be un-

Table 1. 1960 Presidential General Election Results

Candidate	Political Party	Popular Vote	Electoral Vote	EV Percentage
John Kennedy	Democratic	34,220,984	303	56.4
Richard Nixon	Republican	34,108,157	219	40.8
Unpledged Electors	Democratic	286,359	15	2.8
Others		216,983		
Total		68,832,483	537	

Source: CQ Almanac Online Election Edition.

wise to bring a court action." Instead, the campaign could ask "the Senate Committee to send out an investigator." He thought that might "put a little scare into the Nixon camp, who wouldn't know exactly what we had in mind."[59]

Kennedy won only three western states. Even though Democrats held a two-to-one registration advantage in Nevada, his margin of victory there was just 1,493 votes. His margin in New Mexico was a little better: 2,294 votes. Nixon was initially declared the winner in Hawaii by 141 votes. Democrats challenged the results in court, and Judge Ronald Jamieson ordered the first recount in the island's history. The counting continued past the December 19 deadline for the states to certify presidential electors. To resolve this dilemma, three Republican electors certified Nixon the winner, followed by three Democratic electors who chose Kennedy. On December 30, Judge Jamieson ruled that Kennedy had carried Hawaii by 115 votes. Governor William Quinn, a Republican, accepted that decision and signed a certificate in favor of Kennedy's electors on January 4, 1961—two days before Nixon was scheduled to preside over Congress as it counted the electors' votes. When Hawaii was called, its Democratic senator, Oren Long, and Democratic congressman, Daniel Inouye, were prepared to start a floor fight if the vice president rejected the Democratic electors in favor of a slate who would vote for him. He did not and gave Hawaii to Kennedy. In February 1961, Nixon wrote that he probably carried Hawaii, "but under the circumstances I did not feel it was worth while to contest the result since the national outcome would not have changed."[60]

There were approximately 109,159,000 registered voters in 1960, of whom some 68,832,000, about 63 percent, voted in the presidential election.

Kennedy's popular vote margin was slim. It is generally given as approximately 113,000 votes, a figure many have accepted without question. But there is no satisfactory way to determine the exact popular vote because Alabama did not have one. Neither Nixon nor Kennedy even received a single write-in vote. The two wire services, UPI and AP, avoided this dilemma by assigning Kennedy 324,050 votes, the highest vote given to a Democratic elector, and Nixon 237,981, the amount received by the sole Republican elector on the ballot. Authors have argued over the popular vote count that was assigned to Kennedy in Alabama and have suggested four ways to determine it: (1) keep the status quo (324,050); (2) assign Kennedy the highest number given to a Democratic loyalist (318,303); (3) give Kennedy five-elevenths of the total Democratic vote, since he won five of the eleven Democratic electors; or (4) give neither candidate any votes. If the second option were applied, Kennedy's margin of victory nationwide would decrease by 5,747 votes, but he would still barely win the popular vote. With the third option, Kennedy would receive credit for 147,300 Alabama votes and would lose the national popular vote. Under the fourth option, Kennedy would have won the popular vote by 26,758. Whichever you choose, the 1960 presidential election results were razor thin.[61]

Kennedy ran almost 8 percent behind his congressional or party ticket, and Nixon ran 5 percent to 7 percent better than his party's ticket. He ran ahead of 235 Republican House candidates in 359 districts; he outpolled all 34 Republican Senate candidates in their respective states; and of the 27 gubernatorial races that year, he outpolled the Republican candidate in 19. For the first time in the twentieth century, the presidential candidate who won the White House failed to pick up any congressional seats. Also for the first time, the candidate who won the majority of the states (twenty-six) lost. Kennedy was victorious in twenty-two states and received five of the eleven elector votes from Alabama. (One state, Mississippi, chose a slate of unpledged electors, who voted for Harry Byrd.) Republicans gained two seats in the Senate, but Democrats still had a commanding advantage, 64 to 36. In the House, Republicans had a net gain of 21 seats, but Democrats still had an overwhelming majority of 262 to 175. As for governors, the Democrats gained one, and they dominated, 34 to 16.[62]

Eisenhower had carried all eight geographical regions of the United States in 1956. Nixon carried five: East North Central, West North Central, Border, Mountain, and Pacific. He did particularly well in the farming, mountain, and Pacific states. Kennedy did exceptionally well in New England and the Middle Atlantic states, and made his poorest showing in the South in comparison with the other regions. In the border and southern states, however, the Republican share almost reached the 1952–1956 levels. Nixon outran his party in the East and the industrial Midwest. Kennedy, even with heavy losses, carried the South.[63]

Metropolitan areas were critical to the Democrats. In both of his elections,

Eisenhower had rolled up record margins in the suburbs that blunted Democratic big city turnouts. Kennedy focused more on the cities, where the Democratic political machines brought out their voters in large numbers that enabled them to counteract the Republican suburban majorities. Prophetically, Al Smith, the first Catholic Democratic presidential nominee, was also the first Democratic candidate to capture the majority in urban areas. Kennedy did especially well among young couples with children. During the campaign he went to 237 cities, while Nixon went to 168. Nixon did not win any of the nation's ten largest cities. The closest he came was Los Angeles, where he got 49.6 percent of the vote. Three examples are startling. Kennedy won Chicago by more than 475,000 votes, New York City by almost 800,000, and Philadelphia by more than 300,000. In the ten largest cities combined, Nixon received 34.6 percent of the vote.[64]

To win, Kennedy needed a large turnout of minority voters who traditionally cast their ballots for Democratic presidential nominees. The largest group were the Roman Catholics, then commonly accorded "minority" status; they made up about 85 percent of minority voters; Jews and African Americans accounted for most of the remaining 15 percent. Recognizing that many of these voters had twice cast their ballots for Eisenhower, Kennedy had to persuade them to return to the Democratic Party if he hoped to win.[65]

The issue of Kennedy's religion was critical in the election. When he attempted to win the 1956 Democratic vice presidential nomination, he listed fourteen states that were more likely to vote Democratic with a Catholic nominee. In 1960, he carried ten of these states; in 1956, Stevenson carried none; and in 1948, Truman won eight.[66]

When Eisenhower faced Stevenson in 1952, the Gallup Poll had Ike securing 44 percent of the Catholic vote; four years later the number increased to 49 percent. The poll in 1960 found a massive swing, with Republicans losing 29 percent of their Catholic voters from 1956. Sixty-two percent of Catholic Democrats who voted for Ike switched to Kennedy, who received about 78 percent of the Catholic vote.[67]

When Kennedy's numbers are compared in congressional districts with heavy concentrations of Catholic voters, he ran behind the down-ballot Democratic candidates. He ran best where the Catholic population approximated the national average of 20 percent.[68]

Of the twelve states with the largest percentages of Catholic voters, Kennedy won eight: Pennsylvania, Massachusetts, Connecticut, Rhode Island, New York, New Jersey, Louisiana, and New Mexico. Nixon carried New Hampshire, Vermont, Ohio, and Wisconsin. Of the ten states with the lowest percentages of

Catholics, Kennedy won four: North and South Carolina, Georgia, and Arkansas. He ran 21 percent behind the Democratic ticket in states where Catholics made up less than 10 percent of the population. As for the other six states with the lowest Catholic populations, Tennessee, Virginia, Utah, and Oklahoma voted for Nixon; Alabama's six electors and Mississippi's entire slate of unpledged electors cast their ballots for Byrd.[69] Kennedy did run ahead of the Democratic ticket in Washington, Delaware, and West Virginia, each with low Catholic population. Protestant voters remained constant. They cast 62 percent of their votes for Eisenhower in both 1952 and 1956, and 63 percent for Nixon in 1960.[70]

Jews voted for Kennedy more disproportionately than did Catholics. The Gallup Poll had Kennedy winning 81 percent of the Jewish vote, while the University of Michigan News Service placed the number at 88 percent. The five million or so American Jews amounted to only 3.3 percent of the U.S. population and were heavily urbanized, with three-fourths living in the Northeast and around half in greater New York City.[71]

In 1952, Jews gave Stevenson 77 percent of their vote, and in 1956, 73 percent. There were early signs of disapproval of Kennedy from Jewish groups because of Joseph Kennedy's anti-Semitism, but the patriarch remained in virtual seclusion during the campaign, and his son's disassociation from Catholic dogma eliminated this as a major issue. According to Saul Brenner, Kennedy projected an "image of a fighter against religious bigotry, of a supporter of the separation of church and state against the advocates of a religious test for presidential office, and of a liberal."[72]

The extraordinary Jewish vote for Democrats came from a belief that Republicans were anti-Semitic, a charge that included Eisenhower and Nixon. Former New Dealer Raymond Moley in a column published in September 1960, "Nixon and Anti-Semitism," undercut that claim, reporting that the Anti-Defamation League of the B'nai B'rith had absolved Nixon of charges of anti-Semitism. But Moley also refused to bring up Joseph Kennedy's history as an anti-Semite and a Hitler appeaser. Several months after the campaign, he could not understand why so many prominent Jews gave credence to the Republican Party's reputation "of being anti-Israeli—or, for that matter, pro-Arab." He thought the Eisenhower administration's Middle Eastern policies should have ended these myths.[73]

Ever since Franklin Roosevelt's landslide reelection in 1936, African Americans had typically given the Democrats two-thirds of their vote. According to the Gallup Poll, Eisenhower won 21 percent of blacks' votes in 1952, but that number jumped to 39 percent in 1956. Gallup's numbers have been challenged, however. Other pollsters reported a less dramatic swing, crediting Eisenhower with nearly 30 percent of the black vote in 1952, and 36 percent four years later. Even those numbers are misleading, because fewer black Democrats voted in 1956, and that decline accounted for part of the president's percentage increase.[74]

The Eisenhower administration had pursued a positive program on civil rights from which Nixon expected gains in African-American voting, but the black attachment to the Democratic Party was unshaken. In 1960 some ten million African Americans were eligible to vote, of whom about half were registered. Almost three-quarters lived in cities, mostly in segregated neighborhoods. Between 1950 and 1960, the twelve largest U.S. cities had lost 3.6 million white residents and added 4.5 million black residents.[75]

As the election approached, the black press began highlighting the significance of the African-American vote. Toward the end of October, the *Cleveland Call and Post* stated that five million blacks "may" vote. On November 3, the *Los Angeles Sentinel* anticipated a "Record Negro Vote." Two days later, the *Baltimore Afro-American* asked: "Has GOP Written Off the Negro Vote?"[76]

The anticipation of an enormous turnout did not take into account segregation and racism. About six million, or 60 percent, of black citizens eligible to vote were southerners, and of these, just 1,463,000 were registered. The NAACP and other civil rights groups tried to increase African-American registration, but massive resistance, including by racist organizations like the KKK, thwarted much of the effort.[77] In Mississippi, 22,000 blacks had been allowed to register—just 5.2 percent of those eligible—and Alabama had registered just 66,000, 13 percent of the eligible total. Tennessee had the highest percentage in the South of eligible black voters who were registered, 58.9 percent.

Nixon won Florida, Tennessee, and Virginia even though black voters broke two or three to one for Kennedy. In Georgia, where Kennedy got his biggest winning margin in the South, even Daddy King's promise to campaign for him in Atlanta did not work: all twelve predominantly black precincts went for Nixon. But in Arkansas, Louisiana, North and South Carolina, and Texas, blacks also voted heavily for Kennedy, helping him carry those states.[78]

Outside of the South, in cities with more than 100,0000 people, African Americans formed a significant voting bloc. The four black congressmen then in the House—William Dawson in Chicago, Adam Clayton Powell, Jr., in Harlem, Charles Diggs, Jr., in Detroit, and Robert Nix in Philadelphia—all ran powerful machines. In four predominantly black wards in Chicago, Kennedy beat Nixon by about 80,000 to 21,000. In Detroit, of the estimated 240,000 black voters, fewer than 35,000 went for Nixon. In Harlem, almost 97,000 voted for Kennedy and just 28,500 for Nixon. In Philadelphia's seventeen predominantly black wards, about 78 percent of the 170,000 voters cast their ballots for Kennedy.[79]

The assistant to the executive secretary of the NAACP, John Morsell, sent out

Table 2. Gallup Poll of the White Vote for President,
1952–1960

	1952	1956	1960
Republicans	57%	59%	51%
Democrats	43%	41%	49%

Source: Gallup, *Gallup Poll*, Vol. 3, pp. 1694–1695.
National Election Studies results were similar: 29 percent
of blacks voted for Nixon as well as 52 percent of whites;
email, Luevano to Gellman, Gellman mss.

a letter across the nation in the first week of December to at least forty prominent leaders nationwide, asking them to fill out a form describing how each black precinct or ward voted for president, Congress, and governor, as well as any African Americans elected in their areas. The results of that survey were not released. While the number of black voters in 1960 greatly exceeded the numbers in 1952 and 1956, it did not come close to the 4.5 million that was claimed.[80]

In the second week of December, the Gallup Poll provided a "post-election analysis" of African-American voting in the 1960 election. Its survey stated that 68 percent voted for Kennedy and 32 percent for Nixon.

The election was also affected by the recession that started in April 1960 and ended in February 1961. Nixon thought Kennedy had used the downturn to his advantage, and Robert Finch, one of his campaign managers, agreed: "We . . . would have won if 400,000 people had not become unemployed during the last thirty days of the campaign." Pennsylvania Senator Hugh Scott felt that if not for the minirecession in his state, Nixon would have carried it. In a meeting with his economic advisers after he entered the White House, Kennedy commented that the recession "ruined Nixon . . . in the major industrial states."[81]

Arthur Burns, the former chairman of the Council of Economic Advisers (CEA), warned the vice president in the summer that a recession was possible and that its lowest dip would come in October. To prevent any damage to his campaign, Nixon proposed that the federal government pump money into the economy, a move that Secretary of Labor James Mitchell also favored. Treasury Secretary Robert Anderson and Raymond Saulnier, chairman of the CEA, vigorously opposed the idea, and the president followed their advice. Ike also refused to propose any tax cut or any new public programs. Saulnier later admitted that although the recession was slight, it might have embarrassed the administration.[82]

On the other hand, as economist Edson Bridges stated, "The 1960–1961 downward trend in the economy proved to be the least severe recession of the last 15 years." In November 1960, the unemployment rate reached 6.1 percent, not much above the average rate of 5 percent during Eisenhower's eight years in office. Historians William McClenahan and William Becker go further, arguing that the recession was short, shallow, and not a major issue in the campaign.[83]

Unemployment, however, affected labor unions, and they worked diligently for Democrats. Walter Reuther, president of the United Automobile Workers, often spoke at Kennedy's rallies. The AFL-CIO's political organization, the Committee on Political Education, registered voters and distributed pamphlets on labor issues, scoring Kennedy as having voted "right" 91.6 percent of the time and Nixon "wrong" 76.6 percent of the time. COPE raised large sums of money for its preferred candidates and brought out the vote on election day.[84]

Gallup reported that 65 percent of the labor vote went to Kennedy and 35 percent to Nixon. Catholic union members cast more than four-fifths of their votes for Kennedy, white male union members two-thirds, and blacks 77 percent.[85]

In Gallup's breakdown by gender, men gave Kennedy a 52–48 percent advantage. Both candidates paid close attention to women because for the first time in United States history, female voters outnumbered male voters, 55 million to 52 million. Philip Potter of the *Baltimore Sun* mirrored many reporters' perceptions when he wrote that Kennedy "made feminine hearts palpitate and feminine eyes moisten." Yet in the ten presidential elections since the passage of the 19th Amendment, they had voted more Republican than men. This did not change in 1960: they went 51 percent to 49 for Nixon.[86]

Five percent of Republican voters, 84 percent of Democrats, and 43 percent of independents voted for Kennedy. Nixon captured 95 percent of Republicans, 14 percent of Democrats, and 57 percent of independents. The vice president held onto his own base, cut into the Democratic base, and won independents.[87]

Three factors in the election appear to have been decisive. First, Nixon ran ahead of his party, but not enough to overcome the party's relative weakness in registration. Moreover, much of this advantage was in the wrong places. He outperformed his fellow Republicans throughout the South, and while he might have carried some of the border states such as Tennessee, he had little chance in much of the Deep South, where voters who disapproved of Kennedy's pro–civil rights platform could choose a different Democrat, Harry Byrd, whose record on civil rights appealed to them far more than Nixon's.

Second, Kennedy received a significantly greater number of black votes, with two-thirds voting Democrat and one-third for Republicans. He won a higher number and larger percentage than Adlai Stevenson did in 1956, but the most likely explanation is that Stevenson lost in a landslide, while the race in 1960 was much closer. Kennedy did no more than restore the advantage among black voters the Democrats had enjoyed since 1936, two to one. In the South, his civil rights stance cost him more votes among white voters than it gained him among African Americans. Still, in an election where every vote was critical, the higher number of black votes helped him win.

Finally, Kennedy's Catholicism worked in his favor. The myth that he would have won by a landslide if not for the anti-Catholic vote still prevails, largely propagated by Kennedy supporters, but it is belied by the fact that it was his campaign, not Nixon's, that kept the religion issue alive. One can only assume the Kennedy side thought it worked to their advantage. The Kennedy organization sent out films of the candidate's Houston speech; Truman, Johnson, and other supporters routinely urged their listeners to vote for a Catholic to prove they were not bigots; and the most inflammatory mailing on the subject, the UAW pamphlet "Liberty or Bigotry," was a pro-Kennedy effort. The Protestants who were most likely to vote against Kennedy for religious reasons also opposed him because of his liberalism, his support of unions, and his civil rights stance. Most would never have voted for him anyway. The most dramatic shift in voting came not from Protestants—who gave Nixon the same share of their vote they had given Eisenhower in the two previous races—but from Catholics, who provided just over half of Kennedy's total vote. The RNC estimated that Kennedy received six million more Catholic votes than Stevenson did in 1956. This was the biggest demographic shift, by far, between the two elections.[88]

18

BUT DID HE WIN?

On Wednesday, November 9, before his first press conference as president-elect, Kennedy greeted *New York Times* reporter Bill Lawrence on the steps of his father's house in Hyannis Port with the words "some mandate." When the reporters were assembled, he said he thought the election would be close, but not "as close as it turned out to be." Yet even though "the margin was narrow, the responsibility is clear." When a reporter asked whether his victory was a repudiation of the current administration, he replied that it was not; "it was a victory for the Democrats." Asked about his physical condition, he claimed he was in "excellent health."[1]

He met with Clark Clifford, who had advised him during the campaign, and asked him to recommend whether J. Edgar Hoover should be reappointed as FBI director. As Clifford recalled, Joseph Kennedy admired the director, and "Hoover was the only real choice we thought we had at the time." They also decided to reappoint Allen Dulles as director of Central Intelligence. Kennedy then announced that these two men were his first selections to remain at their posts.[2]

At lunch with Kennedy on Thursday the tenth, Arthur Schlesinger said the victory margin would have been bigger if not for "the prevailing sense of prosperity and peace and . . . anti-Catholic sentiment." The same day, reporter Homer Bigart published an article in the *New York Times* stating that "some of Senator John F. Kennedy's closest associates" thought Nixon "ran one of the 'worst' Presidential campaigns in recent years." He had concentrated on the South, had given the black and Hispanic vote "by default" to the Democrats, should not have agreed to the debates, and had waited too long to bring Ike into the campaign. Despite these blunders, one of Kennedy's "chief strategists" said, it had taken a "miracle" to defeat the vice president. Heavy advertising had gained Kennedy "1 or 2 percent." The religious issue also reemerged: Protestants who might have voted for a different Democrat instead chose Nixon. Kennedy, these unnamed advisers argued, had "prevailed over the major handicaps of his religion and his youth plus the fact that he was running at a time of peace and relative prosperity." He had made some mistakes, but "he was exceedingly good at extricating himself."[3]

Like the senator, the vice president was exhausted, and the defeat depressed him. Don Hughes, his appointments secretary, believed he never thought he would lose. At breakfast that Wednesday morning in the Ambassador Hotel, Herb Klein watched his candidate "very painstakingly" explain to his daughter Julie that he had lost. After regaining their composure, Nixon and his family smiled for reporters and admirers as they left the hotel.[4]

They boarded a chartered Boeing 707 to take them back to Andrews Air Force Base, outside the capital. Although Kennedy was easily winning the electoral vote, his popular-vote lead had dropped from 800,000 to 600,000. During the flight, campaign manager Len Hall told the vice president that the Democrats had committed fraud in Illinois, Texas, Missouri, and New Mexico and argued forcefully that the vice president should contest the election.[5]

President Eisenhower had gone to bed at 10:30 on election night with the vice president behind and had awakened the next morning to learn that Kennedy had won. He told Mamie that "there was only one other occasion in his life when he felt that life was not worth living, and that was the occasion when it was determined that he could not play football any more because of his injured knee."[6]

Ike left the White House for a golfing vacation at the Augusta National Golf Club, where he stayed in a cottage built expressly for him after the 1953 Masters tournament. Nixon had never asked him how to manage his campaign even after he offered his media consultant, the movie star Robert Montgomery, as an adviser. Montgomery, said Ike, would have made sure the vice president looked better in the first debate. Lodge should not have mentioned an African American in the cabinet because it cost votes in the South. According to his personal physician, Howard Snyder, Ike rested during the flight. After arriving in Augusta, he played eighteen holes of golf, experiencing joint and muscular pain "across his shoulders and into his right elbow." Snyder believed Nixon's defeat had caused "shock to the President's emotional system."[7]

Talking with his brother Milton the following morning, Ike expressed some optimism. At first, the president, who often wrote in the third person, had "felt that his work of eight years was down the drain. But now he feels Kennedy has been talking more responsibly since the election than he did before."[8]

Eisenhower's son John welcomed the Nixons back to Washington just before midnight on November 9. On the flight, Nixon listed some reasons he had lost: urban Democratic machines; southern Democrats, especially Lyndon Johnson; Democratic governors; the Democrats' registration drive and union backing. By that time, Kennedy's lead nationwide had slipped to about 273,000 votes.[9]

RNC chairman Thruston Morton refused to concede. On November 10, he said the RNC had received messages from thousands of voters, reporting irregularities in eleven states: Delaware, Illinois, Michigan, Minnesota, Missouri, Nevada, New Mexico, New Jersey, Pennsylvania, South Carolina, and Texas. He encouraged party officials in those states to file complaints with the local United States attorney offices that could lead to statewide recounts. In a radio interview the next day, he said there were "no charges of fraud" but that he was looking closely at asking for recounts in Chicago and Texas.[10]

The Kennedy campaign chairman, Senator Henry Jackson from Washington, commented that these allegations from Republicans seemed "to be based merely on the fact that they've lost a close election." He demanded they offer concrete proof, not a "fishing expedition on a grand scale."[11]

Nixon discouraged any initiative from the RNC, telling reporters he knew nothing about any recount. On November 11, Herb Klein and Robert Finch held a press conference acknowledging "hundreds" of complaints alleging irregularities and fraud but maintained that they were "just hearsay." Finch said that Morton had not consulted Nixon, and the candidate had no role in the RNC's actions. "As far as Mr. Nixon is concerned, we are standing on the vote as it comes in. . . . There is no grand national design at all to affect the situation." Klein acknowledged a "mathematical possibility" that the vice president could win, but reiterated: "We ran a race, the votes have been cast and we accept the decision."[12]

Kennedy, meanwhile, behaved like the president-elect. At a news conference on November 11, he announced that he would appoint his White House liaison for the transition of government within twenty-four hours, but would postpone further appointments until Thanksgiving. He also would fly to his father's winter home in Palm Beach, Florida, for a "two-week working vacation." The following day, he and his family boarded the *Caroline* and took off for Washington, where Jackie and Caroline left the plane. She was expecting her second child in December and wanted to remain close to her doctor because of previous complications.[13]

Nixon had also taken a Florida vacation, arriving with his family at the Key Biscayne Hotel, about sixty miles south of Palm Beach, on the evening of November 11. He would not comment on political issues.[14]

Kennedy invited a group of reporters to his father's mansion to discuss the outcome of the election. Henry Brandon, a foreign correspondent for the *London*

Sunday Times, recalled that the senator was greatly disconcerted by his tiny margin of victory because many had predicted he would win in a landslide. Kennedy also worried that rumors of fraud in Chicago would prompt Nixon to challenge the election results. Brandon added: "Those were uncomfortable hours in the Kennedy camp."[15]

Amid this uncertainty, the president-elect decided to reach out to the vice president. Former president Herbert Hoover, eighty-six years old, had backed Nixon during the 1960 race, but as soon as the results came in he pledged to support Kennedy. On Saturday, November 12, shortly after 6:00 p.m., the president-elect tried to telephone Hoover at his apartment in the Waldorf Towers in New York City, but he was sleeping. Joseph Kennedy, a close friend of Hoover's, called at 7:00. Joe suggested that since his son and Nixon were both in Florida and not far from each other, they should meet and be photographed shaking hands. Hoover thought this was an excellent idea.[16]

At 7:45, Hoover telephoned Nixon, who was eating dinner at the Jamaica Inn in Key Biscayne with some of his staff and friends. The maître d' informed the vice president that he had an urgent telephone call. Herb Klein took it, and Hoover told him that Joe Kennedy had asked whether the vice president "would be willing to meet with the president-elect sometime soon, to discuss the fact that the country was divided." Klein handed the phone to Nixon, whose first response was "that's a cheap publicity stunt." Hoover snapped that Jack Kennedy did not need any publicity and that this was a "generous gesture on his part and you ought to meet it with equal generosity." Nixon consented.[17]

At 7:50, Hoover called Jack Kennedy. While they were talking, Nixon called the president. Ike, according to Nixon's memoirs, disliked any suggestion of a coalition government, but he approved the meeting. While Ike and Nixon were talking, the senator telephoned. Nixon offered to come to Palm Beach, but Kennedy decided to take a helicopter to Key Biscayne.[18]

The day before the meeting, Pierre Salinger announced that Kennedy had asked to meet with Nixon for "two major objectives: (1) to congratulate his opponent on the vigorous campaign that he waged, and (2) to resume their fourteen-year cordial relations." Salinger did not rule out the possibility that the president-elect might ask Nixon to accept a position in his administration.[19] Forty years later, television journalist Barbara Walters asked Nixon's appointment secretary, Don Hughes, why the meeting took place. He replied: "Kennedy wanted to be sure that perhaps that there was not going to be a, a recount. This was speculation on my part. . . . That probably was the real purpose of the meeting."[20]

On Monday afternoon, Nixon and Kennedy posed smiling for photographers and then went to a screened-in sun porch, where they had an animated

private discussion for just over an hour. Nixon remembered Kennedy's first remarks: "Well, I guess it's hard to tell who won this election." The vice president
answered: "Well, it's pretty clear that it's over now." Kennedy, Nixon recalled,
offered him a cabinet post, but he said he preferred to be "the voice of the loyal
opposition." The senator then broached the subject of bringing two Republicans, Douglas Dillon and Henry Cabot Lodge, into his government. If he did,
the vice president replied, he should use them to make policy and not just as
window dressing. (Kennedy later made Lodge the United States ambassador to
South Vietnam and Dillon the secretary of the treasury.) The two then commis-
erated about the "madness" of campaigning, the miles covered, and the number
of hands shaken.[21]

After their discussion, they held separate press conferences. Kennedy, appearing first, emphasized that his primary goal was to resume their cordial relationship. When asked whether they had talked about a post for Nixon in the new
administration, the senator refused to comment, nor would he discuss bringing
other Republicans into his government. Nixon, at his conference, said that Kennedy had been very gracious to arrange the meeting. As for the election results,
he accepted his defeat and was not asking for a recount in any state. He would
not comment on Kennedy's offering him a position and said he would lead the
opposition.[22]

Nixon was more forthcoming with Eisenhower, telling him that "the substance of his conversation with Kennedy" was the appointment of Lodge and
Dillon to diplomatic posts. He had suggested that Kennedy consult the president
on those decisions, and said Kennedy would not do anything until he and Nixon
had talked further.[23]

Pat Nixon was urging her husband to demand a recount. She thought the race
had been stolen but that little could be done about it. After smiling in public for
several weeks, she expressed her feelings in a letter to her close friend Helene
Drown: "The Florida trip was almost like a nightmare—tenseness everywhere,
office hours for Dick, the girls hearing . . . too much ugly discussion, etc. Also I
was in a state of numbness, with faith in the 'right' shaken to the point I could not
discuss the situation any more."[24]

On November 12, Lyndon Johnson announced that he expected Kennedy to
spend several days at his Texas ranch talking about domestic and international
problems. On the fifteenth, the day before Kennedy's arrival, his victory in California was overturned and the state's 32 electoral votes given to Nixon. With Kennedy's popular vote margin now below 200,000, speculation revived that the
vice president could win the contest with a recount. If Republicans could prevail
in Illinois and Texas, Nixon would triumph. At that moment, with the 3 electoral

votes from Hawaii undecided and 15 electoral votes committed to Harry Byrd, Kennedy had 300 electoral votes, far more than the 269 he needed for victory, but if he lost Illinois and Texas, he would slip to 249. Nixon had 219 electoral votes, and with Texas and Illinois added, he would reach 270 and be the winner.[25]

Johnson greeted Kennedy on November 16 outfitted in a leather jacket, "tight pants," cowboy boots, and a tan Stetson hat. The president-elect wore a gray pin-stripe suit and refused to put on "a five-gallon Stetson" for photographers. LBJ took his guest on a tour of his ranch, and the next day they talked over their plans for the new administration while hunting deer.[26]

Morton's hope of challenging the election results appeared to be fading. Re-publican politicians in Michigan, South Carolina, Illinois, New Mexico, New Jersey, Pennsylvania, and Delaware decided not to sue for a recount; Nevada and Missouri were doubtful. The RNC leaders in the capital persisted, sending repre-sentatives to eight states to argue for recounts. At the end of the month, Morton called the election a fraud and "a national disgrace," with Illinois and Texas top-ping his list. There was little chance to change the outcome, he conceded, but he had "a responsibility to expose any irregularities I can document."[27]

The president remained at Augusta National until just before Thanksgiving, when he returned to the White House. At first he accepted the outcome, writing to White House staffer Stephen Hess on November 20 that Nixon "would have made a fine President—in fact I tried to do my best to make others share this opinion. But remember that one of the great strengths of our country is that the President is chosen by the people themselves."[28]

By the end of the month, Ike too was questioning the outcome. After a meeting with Postmaster General Arthur Summerfield, who expressed outrage over the alleged fraud, Ike telephoned Attorney General Rogers that "he was very much disturbed about continuing allegations of fraud in the election. He wanted the Federal government to exercise whatever rights and responsibilities were in-herent in the situation." Even if the election was over, "we owed it to the people of the United States to assure them . . . that the Federal government did not shirk its duty." Rogers replied that the FBI was conducting an investigation, but Nixon did not appear to feel "as strongly about the matter as the President." Rogers had been a close adviser to Nixon during the campaign and had spent several days vacationing with him in Nassau just before Thanksgiving. Deputy Attorney Gen-eral William Walsh had begun legal research and wanted to investigate election violations in Illinois and Texas, but Rogers stopped him after Nixon objected.[29]

On the last day of November, the president held the first of two white-tie din-ners for administration leaders. At the end of the celebration, he offered Nixon a toast: "The Vice President will be the head of the Republican Party for the next four years, and he will have my support and the support of all those who are here tonight."[30]

Much as the Republicans tried to reconcile themselves to Nixon's defeat, the potential criminal activities in Chicago were clear, and Mayor Richard Daley had led the effort. Daley had supervised the Kennedy campaign in Illinois, and according to the political analyst Len O'Connor, ward bosses knew before the voting "that the man who failed to deliver a massive vote was going to be permanently maimed politically."[31]

Political scientist James Wilson, in his study of African-American politics in Chicago, noted that there as elsewhere, ward organizations acted as welfare services for their black constituents, providing food, money, clothing, and other necessities. On election day, precinct captains received money for expenses. "Buying votes is a relatively uncommon procedure," Wilson wrote, "but hiring workers with large families for precinct work is not." In 1960, the Daley machine continued the tradition of hiring regular precinct workers who did not buy large numbers of votes. They used other practices like ghost voters to raise their totals.[32]

The mayor's overriding obligation to the machine was to win local offices, and his highest priority that year was to defeat the incumbent Republican state's attorney, Benjamin Adamowski, who was running for reelection. He was embarrassing the mayor by prosecuting Chicago traffic court employees who were pocketing parking ticket fines instead of putting them in the city's treasury. He investigated a lieutenant in the police department who toured Europe with a head of a Chicago crime family. The biggest scandal broke in January 1960, when it emerged that some policemen in a Chicago suburb, Summerdale, were involved in a burglary ring. Adamowski's office made headlines charging the culprits, prompting Daley, who worried about local politics above all else, to put the state's attorney election at the top of his list. Defeating Adamowski was even more of a priority than winning the state for Kennedy. Adamowski lost by twenty-five thousand votes. Historian Edmund Kallina has calculated that he should have received at least 31,284 more votes than he was credited with, and that he "was cheated out of the election."[33]

Kallina also examined Nixon's defeat and concluded that there were not enough voting errors to declare him the winner in Illinois. He had lost the state by 8,858 votes. Using the results from the Chicago Board of Election Commissioners, the accounting done by Adamowski's lawyers in his litigation, and other information, Kallina calculated that Nixon should have been credited with at least 7,968 additional votes, which still left him 890 votes short. Kallina ended by suggesting "there will never be a completely satisfactory account of the election in Illinois," but "Republican charges that the election was stolen must be presently regarded as unproven." He did not, however, do a ward-by-ward analysis of the Chicago vote.[34]

Nixon and his staff, of course, followed the returns from Illinois on election night. They were pleased with the "good reports," Herb Klein remembered, until they noticed that Chicago's precincts were reporting slowly. Klein understood that Daley "was holding back voting boxes until he determined how many ballots were necessary to carry the state." Campaign manager Len Hall believed the Democrats were rigging the election. Late that evening, Kennedy was declared the winner, Klein recalled, by "a suspicious boost from Cook County. . . . Republicans began raising questions."[35]

John Bartlow Martin, who reported from Chicago during Daley's rise, wrote that "tales abounded of ballots dumped in the river, of votes cast by dead men or by voters registered from vacant lots. No doubt mostly true." A local joke had it that Robert Kennedy telephoned Daley the night before the election and asked, "How many votes do we have in Cook County?" and Daley answered, "How many do you need?"[36]

Republicans would not have found this joke funny, and they would have been even less amused had they overheard that evening's dinner conversation between Jack Kennedy and Ben Bradlee. The president-elect told him that Daley had called and told him that "with a little bit of luck and the help of a few close friends, you're going to carry Illinois." Bradlee had no doubt that Kennedy understood he had won the state by fraud.[37]

Every major biography of Daley, without exception, asserts that the mayor used fraudulent practices to secure Kennedy's victory. Mike Royko, the famous *Chicago Daily News* columnist, wrote in his memoirs: "The fraud was so obvious that Daley had to permit a special prosecutor to be appointed to investigate." The judge chosen for this task happened to be a staunch Democrat, and "most of the charges were wiped out." Historian Roger Biles underlined that for the Daley machine, vote stealing was a way of life.[38]

Donald Schilke, a Republican poll watcher on election day, recalled forty-five years later that when ballot counting started at 10:00 a.m. at City Hall, the paper ballots were put into three piles: straight Democratic and Republican, and split ballots. Some were declared spoiled, meaning they were voided. "All the spoiled ballots," Schilke reported, "were straight Republican votes—none were Democrats!"[39]

Professor Larry Sabato has said of the election fraud, "The truth is, the Republicans in downstate Illinois stole thousands of votes, too, and Nixon knew if he pursued it he'd expose his allies." An internal memorandum by Harold Leventhal, general counsel for the Kennedy campaign, on December 5, 1960, disputed that conclusion. Illinois Democratic chairman James Ronan told the Kennedy campaign committee's general counsel that Republicans did not commit any significant fraud downstate.[40]

From November 10 until the end of the month, as the national press and local Chicago papers reported on the alleged theft of the election, Daley expressed outrage that election judges in his city were accused of wrongdoing. He called for an investigation of the vote in the downstate counties, where Republicans, he alleged, had given Nixon majorities as large as those Kennedy had received in the city. Former president Truman called the Republican complaints "a lot of hooey" by "a bunch of poor losers." By the end of the month, Daley was accusing Republicans of "Hitler type" propaganda. Where, he asked, was the evidence?[41]

Republicans and others answered. Francis Connell, the Republican chairman of Cook County, declared on November 13: "There is no question that . . . [the Democrats] stole the election." State Republicans supported Daley's demand for a downstate recount, including recounts in three downstate counties that were Democratic strongholds. Five days later, Frank Durham, vice chair of the Committee on Honest Elections, a committee that monitored local elections to assure that they were honest, said that the fraud in Chicago was "the worst he has seen in more than two decades of poll watching." Meade Alcorn, the RNC's general counsel, said that with a fair count, "Illinois could wind up in the Nixon column."[42]

While fraud allegations were being flung back and forth, on November 14 State's Attorney Adamowski filed a petition with the Chicago Board of Election Commissioners for recounts of the races for president, state's attorney, and state auditor. That board, composed of four Democrats and one Republican, ordered 460 election judges to be questioned about counting errors. When they appeared on November 23, the questioning was so limited that Republicans called it a whitewash. The board then accepted the presidential vote as official, and Republicans announced that they were considering going to court.[43]

Chicago gave Kennedy 1,064,951 votes to Nixon's 608,639, a margin of 456,312. The vice president won three wards out of fifty. The turnout of registered voters was 89.3 percent, more than 25 percent above the national average. In 1956 it had been 85.5 percent, and in 1952, 87.4 percent. Even conceding that Eisenhower won both of his elections in landslides, corrupt practices in voting were the norm. Daley consolidated his control over Democratic ward bosses after his reelection in 1959, and voting fraud in the 1960 city-wide elections increased to defeat first Adamowski and second Nixon.[44]

Between 1950 and 1960, the African-American population in Chicago had almost doubled. Chicago also had the highest segregation rate of any big city, with its black population largely concentrated within five miles of downtown. In 1960, the city's 812,000 African Americans made up 23 percent of the population; 471,000 of them were eligible to vote.[45]

The city's six predominantly black wards were controlled by African-American Congressman William Dawson, who had first won his seat in 1942 and had strongly supported Daley in his first run for mayor in 1955. According to historian John Allswang, even though "Daley was provincial, insensitive, and unsympathetic to the plight of urban blacks," he still won a heavy share of their votes. Dawson, a proponent of gradualism in civil rights, avoided any discussion of race. He instead served as an effective ward boss, promising his constituents jobs in exchange for large turnout.[46]

During the 1960 presidential election, Dawson headed the DNC's minority division and cochaired Kennedy's civil rights operation along with Sargent Shriver, who rented an entire floor in Washington, D.C. Everyone had desks and phones on an open floor, but Dawson insisted on an enclosed office in the middle of the room. Dawson's biographer, Christopher Manning, writes that some of the black staffers named it Uncle Tom's Cabin. Dawson actively campaigned for Kennedy, and a week before the election, he predicted the senator would get 75 percent of the African-American vote. He delivered much more.[47]

On election day, the joint civic committee on elections to prevent corruption sent fifteen hundred poll watchers to monitor the 750 Chicago precincts and "to patrol the notorious river wards" including the six black wards controlled by Dawson. Starting at 4:00 a.m., they visited 28 precincts, not one of which had a Republican precinct captain, and found that some voters were denied the right to cast their ballots because they were Republicans.[48]

The *Chicago Tribune* reported eyewitness accounts claiming that some of the worst fraud came in these wards, including false voting lists and "ghost voters," who were registered in vacant lots or were deceased. One newspaper account reported that in ward 2, precinct 50, with twenty-two registered voters, there were seventy-four votes for Kennedy and three for Nixon. When Marie Suthers, the sole Republican commissioner on the Chicago Board of Election Commissioners, asked the other commissioners to produce the ballots in the event of a probe, the other four Democratic members denied her demand. In the meantime, the ballots had disappeared. In ward 3, according to one eyewitness, a voter left without casting his vote, so a Democratic judge voted for him.[49]

The witnesses reported other irregularities. In ward 4, precinct 4, two election judges helped Clifford Jones, who was not registered and "who appeared intoxicated and partially blind," to vote. In precinct 6, a judge demanded that a Republican voter cast his ballot for Democrats. In precinct 8, Estes Hempill voted, without being registered and with an address that could not be located. So did James and Lenna Evenes. In precinct 31, Ed Myles and his son Jimmy cast ballots, even though the father had died and the son no longer lived at the listed address. In precinct 77, the precinct captain voted twice under different names. In ward 6, precinct 28, with 42 registered voters, the voting machine counted 404 votes for Kennedy and 79 for Nixon.[50]

In 1956, the six predominantly black wards had given Stevenson a total of 113,464 votes, or 65.9 percent of the vote. Eisenhower received 59,443, or 33.6 percent, close to his national average of 36 to 39 percent of the black vote. The Democratic candidate had a plurality of 54,021. Four years later, Kennedy received 137,674 votes, 79.9 percent, to Nixon's 33,950 or 19.4 percent—far below his national average of 32 percent of the African-American vote. Kennedy's winning margin among black voters of 103,724 was the highest in the city's history. Compared with 1956, Kennedy increased the Democratic vote by 24,210 and his winning percentage by 14.0 percent. Stevenson had beaten Eisenhower in the city by 54,021, but Kennedy ran ahead of Nixon by almost twice that.[51]

A superficial argument can be made that Kennedy outperformed Stevenson because he was simply a more attractive candidate, and Nixon was far less popular than Eisenhower. But that argument ignores the fact Daley admitted to the fraud and had the means, motive, and opportunity to pull it off—and many in Chicago thought he had done it. Because any evidence has been destroyed, the charges cannot be verified.

While there is a convincing possibility of fraud in the predominantly black wards, there is far less evidence to support claims that the Mafia stole the election. Crime boss Sam Giancana and others within his family claimed in their memoirs that the mob delivered the votes to win Illinois for Kennedy. Seymour Hersh, in *The Dark Side of Camelot,* has a chapter entitled "The Stolen Election" in which he describes the mob's alleged responsibility for Kennedy's victory in Illinois and several other states. His account relies primarily on interviews and secondary sources, without any documents to prove his allegations. Hersh's main argument was that Joe Kennedy, using Frank Sinatra as a go-between, made a deal with Giancana to elect his son. If Jack won the presidency, he would repay Giancana by stopping federal investigations of organized crime.[52]

Ward 1, where the mob had the most influence, voted 70.1 percent Democratic in 1956 and gave Stevenson a plurality of 9,680 votes; four years later, those numbers increased to 79.7 percent Democratic and a 12,802-vote plurality. Hersh does not give any reason why the Daley machine would yield control to the mob. John Binder, who investigated the allegations of mob participation, dis-

Table 3. Vote Total in Predominately Black Chicago Wards in 1956 and 1960

1956	Vote for President Democrats	%	Vote for President Republicans	%	Democratic Plurality
Ward 2	18,282	67.6	8,578	31.9	9,704
Ward 3	18,700	64.9	9,950	34.5	8,750
Ward 4	20,491	62.6	12,083	36.9	8,408
Ward 6	17,398	55.9	13,572	43.6	3,826
Ward 20	17,572	60.2	11,281	38.6	6,291
Ward 24	21,021	83.9	3,979	15.9	17,042
Total	113,464		59,443		54,021
1960					
Ward 2	21,100	79.1	5,353	20.1	15,747
Ward 3	19,990	79.4	5,003	19.9	14,987
Ward 4	25,895	77.8	7,117	21.6	18,778
Ward 6	24,837	75.9	7,701	23.5	17,136
Ward 20	21,641	76.0	6,645	23.4	14,996
Ward 24	24,211	91.6	2,131	8.1	22,080
Total	137,674		33,950		103,724

Sources: Scammon, *America Votes*, pp. 393–397, and *America Votes 4*, pp. 389–393.

missed any deal between Joe Kennedy and Giancana. Alluding to the aggressive prosecution of crime figures by Bobby Kennedy's Department of Justice, Binder wrote: "John Kennedy did not double cross the Chicago Mob because they never supported him on election day." Hersh's accusations "appear to have no basis in fact."[53]

Unlike Illinois, Texas was a one-party state where Democratic control was virtually absolute. As James Anderson pointed out in *Texas Politics*, the state's politics had always "been basically an Anglo affair." But in the 1950s, Texan voters cast their presidential ballots for Eisenhower, a native son, who twice won the state with convincing majorities. In 1960, helped by conservative Democrats who disapproved of their party's civil rights platform and other liberal positions—and by voter turnout that was up by 18 percent—Nixon outpolled the president's 1956 showing by 41,080 votes. Governor Allan Shivers had backed Ike in both of his campaigns, and as former governor he energetically campaigned for Nixon. After leaving the governor's mansion, however, he had lost much of his political power, and all his patronage.[54]

Price Daniel, a conservative, segregationist Democrat who had been elected to the Senate in 1952 and had closely aligned himself with Lyndon Johnson, resigned in 1956 to run for governor. After his victory, he controlled the party machinery and patronage in the state and won reelection in 1958. In 1960 he was trying for his third term.[55]

In 1956, Eisenhower received 1,080,619 votes, or 55.3 percent, to Stevenson's 859,958 or 44.0 percent, a winning margin of 220,661. Seventy percent of the state's vote came from eleven cities and fourteen large counties, and the president won in all these areas. According to David McMillan, "Eisenhower's victory in Texas was overwhelming and decisive." Four years later, the state had a record turnout of 2,311,845. Kennedy won 1,167,932, or 50.5 percent, against Nixon's 1,121,699, or 48.5 percent. The senator won by 46,233 votes. In a state that pollsters determined on election day was too close to call, Nixon lost 6.8 points from Eisenhower's 1956 share. Of the 254 counties, 166 voted as they had in 1956. Democrats flipped 69 counties that had voted Republican in the 1956 presidential race, and Republicans flipped 19 that had voted Democratic. Kennedy won large majorities in East Texas, especially among African Americans; he won the coastal plain; and he won West Texas, where Mexican-American voters gave him 91 percent of the vote. Houston, Dallas, and Fort Worth went for Nixon, but by smaller majorities than Ike's.[56]

Ronnie Dugger, who founded the *Texas Observer* in 1954 and spent more than forty years as its editor and then publisher, covered Johnson before and during the 1960 presidential campaign. Late in his life, he told me in an interview that statewide elections in Texas rested on the premise of "competitive corruption" and that the "likelihood of significant fraud, enough to change the presidential outcome in 1960, was great." John Tower, who ran against Johnson for the Senate that year, allowed that "anyone unscrupulous enough to rig an election the first time around is more likely to rig it . . . a second time."[57]

As we have seen, in 1941, Lyndon Johnson had lost a special Senate election to former governor W. Lee O'Daniel by 1,311 votes. The result, announced after several days of late returns, led Johnson to say his opponent "out-stole him." Seven years later, he earned the nickname "Landslide Lyndon" by winning election to the Senate by 87 votes, stuffing the ballot boxes with late returns from Jim Wells County. George Parr, who ran the Democratic machine there and in Duval County, made certain Johnson out-stole his 1948 opponent, Coke Stevenson.[58]

The fourth volume of Robert Caro's LBJ biography, *The Passage of Power*, documented radical changes in various localities that demonstrated fraud.

Within limits, he wrote, a change in presidential voting patterns from 1956 to 1960 was plausible, but "the shift was outside those limits, and the majorities recorded for the Kennedy-Johnson ticket were startling in comparison with those recorded in the previous presidential election." Caro concluded that Kennedy had picked Johnson as his running mate "to take back Texas for the Democratic presidential ticket, and Johnson had done it."[59]

Forty-five years after the election, Brian Shivers recalled that his father had called Nixon "and told him that he had proof of fraud in Texas and Illinois that could turn the election in his favor." Nixon replied that he did not intend to challenge the outcome.[60]

Few questioned that fraud happened, but could the number of stolen votes have exceeded Kennedy's 46,233-vote victory margin?

Many counties had abandoned the custom of giving the Democratic Party the top line on the general election ballot, and some counties let the parties draw for position. The Texas ballot was poorly designed: rather than check the boxes beside their preferred candidates, voters had to scratch out the party columns or candidates they did not want to vote for. This change confused many voters, who failed to scratch out the Constitution and Prohibition parties. Precinct judges had the discretion to determine whether these ballots should be counted.[61]

Republicans charged that Democratic precinct judges invalidated too many votes marked for Nixon and too few marked for Kennedy. Paper ballots accounted for about 1,250,000 ballots—roughly half the total—and Republicans charged that at least 10 percent of them, or between 100,000 and 200,000, were improperly ruled invalid. In Bell County, about 5 percent of ballots were not counted; in Travis County about 6 percent; in Titus County, 10 percent; in Hunt County about 15 percent. In Starr County, heavily Democratic, only 1.5 percent were voided, but in Waller, a Republican county, 25 percent were disallowed. In Cameron, Marion, Montgomery, and Navarro counties, in addition to the issues over ballots being voided, the number of votes cast exceeded the number of registered voters.[62]

Republicans demanded a recount, while Democrats denied any wrongdoing. In Harris County, precinct judge Bill Elliott refused to admit to any mistakes and challenged Republicans to file complaints. Irregularities like those described in the *Houston Post*, which reported that witnesses saw election judges going into ballot booths with voters, were ignored. Thad Hutcheson, chairman of the Texas Republican executive committee and a Houston lawyer, wrote Nixon after the election that there "was a deep and significant irregularity in the handling of the Texas votes and we put forth every reasonable effort to contest the election here." Texas's "negative ballot" law disqualified votes if the voters did not cross out the minor parties along with the major ones. Hutcheson claimed to have evidence that precinct judges overwhelmingly accepted inadequately marked ballots for Kennedy but voided those marked for Nixon.[63]

In 1956, Eisenhower finished in a dead heat with Stevenson in the state's fifteen southern counties, losing the region by only 198 votes out of more than 120,000 cast. That winter, the FBI reported on a conversation with Truman Phelps, an attorney in Laredo, part of Webb County. Phelps told the FBI that LBJ considered "Laredo his private county" and would prevent any investigation of the voting. The agency decided against any inquiry. Four years later, Kennedy defeated Nixon by 41,164 votes; Kennedy's average vote in the fifteen counties was 63.7 percent and Nixon's was 36.1. The swing from 1956 to 1960 amounted to nearly 41,000 votes. Webb County had given 85 percent of its vote to the Democrats. Duval County, notorious for stuffing ballot boxes for LBJ in 1948, gave Kennedy 82 percent. The *Houston Chronicle* reported that Duval officials carried pistols to coerce Mexican Americans to vote Democratic. Politicians there also purchased poll tax certificates for $1.75 each in order to bribe between three hundred and three thousand voters in precincts near the Mexican border.[64]

If the suspicions over throwing out 100,000 to 200,000 ballots and widespread fraud in the southern counties were not enough reason to call the outcome into question, African-American voting provided more. Black citizens made up the large majority of registered voters, about 140,000, in the rural eastern part of the state, called the Black Belt. The percentage of black voters in this region illustrates how significant their vote was. In eighty-four counties, black voters made up more than 10 percent of the electorate; in forty-four they made up at least 40 percent, and 36 percent of black voters lived in towns with populations of more than 10,000.[65]

According to political scientist Harry Holloway, the black vote was manipulated by white politicians and filled with "chicanery and corruption." White paternalism forced blacks to "go along with the whites." Anyone over sixty years old in a town with a population under 10,000 could vote "on affidavit," meaning that he or she did not need to present identification at the polling place. Elderly voters sometimes voted twice or more, absentee ballots were often fraudulent, and vote buying was common.[66] These practices were not confined to counties with large numbers of African Americans and Mexican Americans. But the ability to manipulate their vote was widely practiced.

Democrats, faced with reports of ballot fraud in the *Houston Chronicle*, the *Texas Observer*, and other state newspapers, denied any wrongdoing. At the end of November, J. Ed Connally, the chairman of the Texas Democratic executive

Table 4. Voting for President in Southern Texas Counties for 1956 and 1960

Texas Counties (South)	Vote for Kennedy	Vote %	Vote for Nixon	Vote %	1956 Vote for Stevenson	Vote %	1956 Vote for Eisenhower	Vote %
Brooks	1,934	77	567	23	1,108	58	802	42
Cameron	12,416	55	10,190	45	8,829	42	11,952	57
Dimmit	886	58	648	42	427	37	705	62
Duval	3,803	82	809	18	3,110	68	1,459	32
Hidalgo	18,663	58	13,628	42	9,804	42	13,270	57
Jim Hogg	1,255	85	224	15	617	68	282	31
Jim Wells	5,330	66	2,773	34	2,752	45	3,348	55
Kenedy	78	51	74	49	10	7	125	93
Kleberg	3,773	64	2,092	36	2,436	53	2,121	46
La Salle	718	69	326	31	574	56	449	44
Nueces	29,361	61	18,907	39	19,912	50	19,985	50
Starr	4,051	93	280	6	2,727	83	547	17
Webb	10,059	85	1,802	15	2,744	32	5,827	68
Willacy	2,109	60	1,367	39	1,261	43	1,656	56
Zapata	675	72	260	28	886	58	637	42
Total	95,111	63.6	53,947	36.1	57,197	47.2	63,165	52.2

Sources: Scammon, *America Votes*, pp. 393–397, and *America Votes 4*, pp. 389–393.

committee, denounced "headline-hunting" Republicans and said they needed to "stop their picayunish propaganda." They were "prolonging a senseless controversy by efforts to try their case in the press with irresponsible and childish statements."[67]

The national columnists, while conceding that Kennedy's winning margin was close, avoided any mention of fraud. Walter Lippmann wrote on November 10 that "Kennedy is indisputably the President-elect" and found him clearly a better choice than Nixon. Joseph Alsop, "supremely optimistic" about the senator's triumph, said he would be "a fresh breeze" as president. Marquis Childs declared that Kennedy had a "restricted" mandate but thought the large Democratic majorities in Congress would pass much of his legislation. Childs showered praise on Lyndon Johnson for contributing to the victory by helping to win the South, and Texas in particular.[68]

Two days before the end of November, a reporter asked Kennedy about Republican demands for a recount. He approved of a recount, he said, where the votes "ought to be counted," but in this case he thought it would not change the outcome. The votes needed to be correct; but "my information is the count has been accurate."[69]

RNC chairman Morton objected. At the beginning of December, he asserted that evidence showed "shocking irregularities and fraud" in the voting. To prove his accusations, he flew to Chicago to examine the claims that Nixon had won Illinois, but after spending a few days there, he conceded that any possibility of Nixon's being declared the winner was "so remote I don't think it is in the realm of consideration." Even so, by the first week of December he was still refusing to concede the election to Kennedy. Republicans, he affirmed, would challenge the Texas and Illinois results in the courts, even though it would take several years. By then, of course, Kennedy would have already been inaugurated.[70]

New York Herald Tribune reporter Earl Mazo added to the outrage by writing four articles in early December in what originally was going to be a twelve-part series on the fraud allegations in Chicago and Texas. He had a cordial relationship with Nixon and had covered him sympathetically throughout his vice presidency. Shortly after the fourth article's publication, Nixon asked Mazo to come to his office. The vice president called the articles "interesting" but said, "No one steals the presidency of the United States." At first, Mazo said, he thought Nixon was joking, but he was earnest and asked Mazo to discontinue the series. The vice president reasoned: "The country can't afford the agony of a constitutional crisis—and I damn well will not be a party to creating one just to become President or anything else."[71]

Nixon's decision not to challenge the election results did not prevent Texas Republicans from demanding a recount, even though no statewide election there had ever been overturned. Twice after the election, Attorney General Will Wilson rejected Republican requests to impound votes. On November 25, Secretary of State Zollie Steakley certified that the Democratic ticket had won. Four days later, Republicans insisted that the State Board of Canvassers respond to a formal contest for an immediate hearing on a recount. That board was composed of Wilson, Steakley, and Governor Daniel, all Democrats who had run for reelection on the same ballot line as Kennedy and Johnson. The board delayed meeting until December 8 to give Democrats the legally permitted time to reply to the Republican charges. That day, Lyndon Johnson, acting independently, telephoned Houston lawyer Leon Jaworski. They had met several times, but Jaworski had not been active politically. After a two-hour conversation, he accepted Johnson as a client.[72]

Republicans had asked for a hearing before the canvassing board to recount paper ballots from 236 of the state's 254 counties, amounting to 1,277,184 ballots in 4,061 precincts. They claimed that between 100,000 to 200,000 votes had been improperly eliminated. Texas DNC committeeman Byron Skelton denounced the Republicans for "running down the prestige of the country with phony claims the election was stolen by the Democratic Party." Jaworski, acting as the spokesman for the legal team, called the allegations "baseless." The opposition, he said, had not presented sufficient proof to change the outcome, and their suit came too late.

Besides filing a request before the canvassing board, Republicans brought suit in the United States District Court in Houston before Judge Ben Connally. On the evening of Wednesday, December 7, he was handling a case in another jurisdiction and could not be contacted. In his place, Judge Joe Ingraham granted a temporary restraining order to prevent the canvassing board from certifying the Kennedy-Johnson victory.[73]

Jaworski had been in Austin that day, and Johnson telephoned him that evening about the restraining order. Jaworski could not believe that Ingraham, his close friend, would issue it without a hearing, but LBJ confirmed that he had. Jaworski, telephoning the judge at his home, was told that Ingraham had granted the order "to preserve the status quo." On Thursday, December 8, Republicans went to the hearing at the canvassing board. It refused to render any decision because of the restraining order, saying it would be in contempt of court if it made a ruling. The Republican lawyers argued that the board could render a decision, but it refused to budge.[74]

The next morning in the district court, Judge Connally held a three-and-a-half-hour pretrial conference. Jaworski, who had known the judge since high school, argued that he had no jurisdiction in the matter. On Monday, after another three-and-a-half-hour hearing, Judge Connally threw out the suit because there was insufficient evidence of any civil rights violations that would change the outcome. In addition, he said, he had no jurisdiction to hear the complaint. He dismissed it and dissolved the temporary restraining order. That evening, Johnson called Jaworski to praise him for winning the lawsuit. Johnson asked whether there was anything he could do for the lawyer. Jaworski jokingly answered that there was "only one thing. . . . I wish you'd run on up to Washington and get inaugurated as fast as you can . . . because I'm getting tired of handling these lawsuits for you."[75]

Almost immediately after Connally handed down his ruling in Houston, the state canvassing board convened without any Republicans present. Relying on Connally's decision, the board said it had no authority under state law to order a recount and that none of the allegations, even if true, would have changed the outcome. The board certified the victory for the Kennedy-Johnson ticket.[76]

The Republican Party announced on December 13 that it was dropping its fight for a recount and would concentrate on new legislation to prevent any recurrence. Six days later, the state's electors gathered in the Texas Senate chamber and took forty-four minutes to cast their votes for the Democratic ticket.[77]

Unlike the Texas Democrats, Daley controlled only Chicago. At the end of November, Illinois Governor William Stratton, a Republican who had run for a third term in 1960 and lost to Otto Kerner by 524,000 votes, threatened that the state's Election Board might refuse to certify Kennedy's election. The mayor recognized that Stratton could carry out his warning, because he chaired the board and controlled it, with four Republicans to one Democrat.[78]

Daley answered Stratton by accusing Republicans of a "conspiracy" to prevent Kennedy from receiving the state's twenty-seven electoral votes. The mayor added that he had not said there was no fraud, only that there was no proof. The same day he said this, however, Sidney Holzman, the Democratic chairman of Chicago's Board of Election Commissioners, acknowledged that there appeared to have been fraud. Marie Suthers, the only Republican on the board, released the results of her findings in ward 2, precinct 50: twenty-two registered voters, eighty-four votes cast, of which Kennedy received seventy-eight and Nixon four. When she asked for the ballot applications, they turned out to have disappeared from the election board vault.[79]

This embarrassment stimulated more charges from both sides. Former president Truman called the Republicans "poor losers. . . . They got beat and it hurts them." Republicans alleged that Nixon votes had been erased and replaced with Kennedy votes. They asserted without proof that more than ten thousand ballots were invalid, and demanded a recount.[80]

On December 5, Harold Leventhal, the Kennedy campaign's general counsel, wrote a four-page memo to Robert Kennedy after speaking with Illinois Democratic chairman James Ronan about the status of the recount, which had been prompted by Adamowski's formal petition (he publicly conceded it would not prevent his defeat). The Nixon recount committee, Leventhal wrote, was making "wild claims" about picking up ten votes per precinct; in fact, the recount was giving the vice president meager gains with no proof of irregularities. Democrats had requested "recounts down-state in [a] few places," including the fifteenth congressional district: "By and large there seem to be only minor discrepancies—no pattern of fraud." Leventhal concluded that if the state board refused to certify any electors from Illinois, it would reduce the necessary electoral majority from 269 to 259. He quoted the Twelfth Amendment: "The person having the greatest number of votes for President, shall be the President, if such number be a majority of the whole number of Electors appointed." Kennedy would still be elected.[81]

Over the next four days, the Chicago Board of Election Commissioners recounted the paper ballots in 863 precincts. The Republicans complained of massive irregularities while Democrats called the incidents minor discrepancies or "honest errors." On December 9, the board voted four-to-one to reject the fraud allegations.[82]

The state board met on December 14 in Springfield. Governor Stratton said it found no "showing of overwhelming fraud" in Cook County and "not sufficient evidence to change the canvass." With that statement, the board unanimously confirmed Kennedy's victory. In an interview twenty-six years later, Stratton recalled briefly delaying the certification "until Nixon asked him to validate Kennedy's victory." Five days later, the state certified its twenty-seven electors for Kennedy.[83]

The Constitution called for the electors to "meet in their respective states and vote by ballot for President and Vice President." When the fifty states' electors convened on December 19, they gave Kennedy 303 votes, Nixon 219, and Byrd 15. With the voting completed, the Constitution instructed that the "ballots [be] sealed and sent to the President of the Senate." Nixon, who held that post, counted the ballots aloud on January 6, 1961, before a joint session of Congress.[84]

Reflecting on the Chicago vote while serving as ambassador to South Vietnam, Henry Cabot Lodge admitted that he had helped rig elections in Massachusetts and that he had rigged the 1952 Republican convention to nominate Eisenhower. He thought Nixon "would have taken Chicago in 1960 if there had been an honest count." Republicans "didn't have anyone watching the polls. But I don't blame Democrats for that, I blame the Republicans."[85]

Nixon told a Chicago audience in the spring of 1961 that the Illinois returns were what swayed him to make his concession statement on election night. He decided not to contest the election, even with the fraud accusation, because a recount would have taken a year and a half: "No responsible candidate for President would thus cause administrative chaos with the inevitable world reaction." He did learn "a big lesson. . . . The time to stop stealing at the polls is before and on election day. . . . From now on, every precinct in every city must be adequately manned. Then we will do alright."[86]

Nixon understood that fraud in Texas was widespread, but he recognized that no state law allowed him to challenge the result in a presidential race. Former governor Shivers also advised him against contesting the election: "It's an old political axiom in Texas that people don't like a poor loser."[87]

Nixon agreed. Reminiscing about the election twenty-three years later, he acknowledged the massive fraud in Texas and Chicago; Eisenhower and many others had urged him to contest the election and would have supplied the money to finance a legal challenge. "My heart told me to do it," Nixon reflected. "My head said no." First, it would mean the nation would be without a president for a year while the challenges were being resolved. Second, he had visited many developing nations that were beginning on a democratic path, but where elections meant "very little." America was the great example for the merits of electoral politics. "If in the United States an election were found to be fraudulent, it would mean that every pipsqueak in every one of these countries, if he lost an election, would simply bring a fraud charge and have a coup." Considering this possibility, he decided that "the United States couldn't afford to have a vacuum in leadership for that period of time without knowing who was president, and . . . even though we were to win it, the cost in world opinion and the effect on democracy in the broadest sense would be detrimental."[88]

Rather than examine the aftermath of the election and the overwhelming evidence of fraud in Texas and Chicago, those who have written about the 1960 presidential election largely ignore this aspect of it.

Kennedy partisans asserted that Republicans never pushed for a Chicago recount because they did not want to expose their own fraud in downstate voting. Schlesinger, in his biography of Robert Kennedy, wrote that "in Illinois one party stole as many votes as the other." Sorensen maintained in his memoir that fraud downstate was "as large-scale or worse" compared with Chicago, and exposing both would not have changed the outcome. Larry O'Brien wrote in his memoirs that there had been "some vote-stealing" downstate—little if any actually occurred—and falsely claimed that reporters found no evidence that Daley stole the election. Equally far-fetched is O'Brien's insistence that "Republican pollwatchers had the Chicago polling places covered like a blanket." In fact, Democratic politicians controlled the vast majority of the voting precincts, and only a few Republican poll watchers were available across the city.[89]

The historian Gary Donaldson, in his 2007 book *The First Modern Campaign*, states without any proof that there was "strong evidence that downstate Illinois Republicans had initiated their own election fraud" on Nixon's behalf. Herbert Block agreed in two memoirs. The vice president's claim that fraud in Chicago cost him the election was a lie, he said, and Nixon was "a lying S.O.B. who has consistently robbed children's piggy banks."[90]

All these authors simply repeat rumors and Democratic charges circulated after the election. Against these and other assertions, based on no discernible evidence, we have the word of James Ronan, the Democratic state chairman in 1960, who privately informed the Kennedy campaign on December 5 that there was no evidence of fraud downstate even as he publicly mimicked Daley in claiming that Republican "errors" downstate balanced "Democratic errors" in Chicago.[91]

John Jackson and Herb Russell, two Illinois political scientists who have studied the state's elections, told me that even if you consider "downstate" to encompass every county in Illinois outside of Cook County, they could not point to any concrete evidence of Republican fraud in the 1960 election. David Kenney, who wrote a biography of Governor Stratton and lived in Springfield, Illinois, for many years, agreed.[92]

As for Texas, Sorensen offered his opinion, without any supporting evidence, that "Kennedy's margin there was too large to reverse, even had a recount been available. . . . He won it by outworking, outorganizing, outdebating, and outthinking his Republican opponent."[93]

Not only did Kennedy win the election fairly, his defenders argue, but in the aftermath of the campaign, Nixon's behavior was unacceptable. Pierre Salinger wrote in his memoirs that when he watched Nixon's press secretary read the loser's concession on television, Kennedy was "disgusted." The vice president should have read his own statement. Nixon, said JFK, "went out the way he came in — no class."[94]

Kennedy's advisers also offered recollections of the Key Biscayne meeting. Kenny O'Donnell, who accompanied Kennedy, asserted that his boss met with Nixon at Herbert Hoover's request rather than at the senator's initiative. On the helicopter ride to Key Biscayne, O'Donnell recalled, Kennedy did not know what he would say to Nixon. O'Donnell was not present when the two met, but he nonetheless reported that Nixon did most of the talking. After O'Donnell and Kennedy climbed into the helicopter to return to Palm Beach, Jack reflected: "It was just as well for all of us that . . . [Nixon] didn't quite make it." Sorensen told a similar story, saying Hoover arranged the meeting. Sorensen admitted that the meeting did help certify the election outcome and end calls for recounts, but he gives Nixon no credit for that.[95]

Historian Robert Dallek used these flawed remembrances in constructing his account in An Unfinished Life. The senator and vice president, he writes, had nothing to discuss except that they wanted to give an appearance of national unity. Nixon did most of the talking, and Kennedy thought it best for the country that the vice president lost.[96]

In his two-volume Johnson biography, Dallek does not mention any 1960 election irregularities in the text of his first volume, commenting only in the next-to-last endnote, on page 699. There he simply repeats Schlesinger's unsubstantiated opinion that both sides stole votes in Illinois and Jaworski's assertion that there was "no real proof."[97]

One of the most recent accounts comes in *The Road to Camelot,* by two former *Boston Globe* reporters, Thomas Oliphant, a Pulitzer Prize–winning journalist who campaigned for Kennedy as a teenager, and Curtis Wilkie. Their volume relied almost exclusively on collections at the Kennedy presidential library, oral histories, and interviews with his advocates. The authors did not use the vast FBI files on the Kennedy family, never set foot in the Nixon presidential library, and never made the twenty-minute drive from the JFK presidential library to the Massachusetts Historical Society, which houses the Henry Cabot Lodge, Jr., papers.[98]

Based only on accounts from the Kennedy camp, Oliphant and Wilkie assert that Nixon lied about not challenging the election. He could have told RNC Chairman Morton to stop, but "he didn't, making him tacitly complicit in what followed." The authors claim that Nixon failed to note in *Six Crises* that Eisenhower considered contesting the result immediately after the election but then changed his mind, and that Robert Finch supported a challenge.

As for fraud in the election, the authors admit that there is some anecdotal evidence in Texas but nothing more: "Not then, nor in subsequent decades, has any direct evidence of fraud surfaced that would come within a country mile of overturning the official result." In Chicago, "what evidence there is remains far from conclusive." When Nixon conceded in mid-December, he acknowledged that Kennedy had, as Oliphant and Wilkie write "just barely won the election, but he had won legitimately."[99]

This is a seriously flawed account. First, Nixon could not have prevented Morton from calling for statewide recounts, since thousands of Republican state and party officials were demanding it. Second, immediately after the election, Ike did not urge a challenge but advised Nixon to concede, which he had already done. It was only later, at the end of November, that the president considered demanding a recount. Third, Robert Finch vigorously opposed any recount effort. Fourth, Oliphant and Wilkie never mentioned that every major work on Richard Daley categorically stated that he won his state for Kennedy by fraud and Robert Caro, Ronnie Dugger, and others hold that Johnson won Texas for the ticket by fraud, nor did Oliphant and Wilkie conduct any investigation of the fraud allegations. They are correct that anecdotal evidence of fraud existed. They did not add that in sixty years since the election, no one, with the exception of Edmund Kallina, has published a detailed account of how the fraud in Chicago was committed, and there are no accounts to this day of how fraud in Texas was accomplished.

While the Kennedy apologists repeat the same accounts, a few are moving in another direction. Edward Foley, who runs the election law center at Ohio State University's Moritz College of Law and is one of America's leading experts on elections, included a section on the 1960 presidential election in his 2016 book *Ballot Battles.* He concluded that the voting in Chicago and Texas had been manipulated to give those states to Kennedy. "Given this unsettling but unavoidable possibility," he writes, "the 1960 presidential election must be viewed as a failure of American government to operate a well-functioning democracy." William Safire, who was on Nixon's staff during the campaign, reached the same conclusion more succinctly: "We wuz robbed."[100]

19

In with the New

Ike had been planning the transition for months. Budget director Maurice Stans had been the first to raise the move to a new administration during a cabinet meeting on July 1. He "hoped that assurances could be given to the American people that this Administration is acting to minimize the problems." The president needed to appoint a White House staffer to work with the federal bureaucracy and, if he wished, both major parties' candidates "on a nonpartisan basis."

Eisenhower recalled the difficulties his own transition had faced in 1952. He deeply resented Truman's personal attacks on him during the campaign, and his only meeting with the president, on November 18, had been charged with animosity. He wanted the president-elect well briefed. If Nixon won, passing the torch would be easy because he understood the nation's issues and the administration's approach to them.[1]

Five days later, at a White House press conference, Roscoe Drummond of the *New York Herald Tribune* asked Ike about the transition. He responded that if the winner wanted to consult with him, "he will certainly find me quite ready and willing." The incoming president would need to review the upcoming budget and other pressing matters. These preliminary discussions had to be more than "just talks."[2]

Ike avoided any discussion of the transition during the campaign, but five days before the voting, he told his chief of staff, Jerry Persons, to send an immediate congratulatory telegram to Kennedy if he won. Ike assumed that the victor would appoint some representative to consult with members of the executive departments to effect "an orderly transfer of responsibilities and duties." There would be no immediate transfer of power; cabinet members could advise the incoming administration.[3]

On the day after the election, the president announced that his cabinet would meet the next morning to study the transition. He entered the Oval Office at 8:03 a.m.; three and a half hours later, he convened the cabinet and then sent a telegram to the president-elect saying he would meet with him "at any mutually convenient time to consider problems of continuity of government and orderly transfer of Executive responsibility on January 20 from my Administration to yours." To assist in this transfer, Ike appointed Persons to coordinate meetings between Kennedy's representatives, the director of the budget bureau, secretary of the state, and others. Kennedy accepted Ike's invitation the following day and named Clark Clifford as his White House liaison.[4]

The president's only instruction to Persons was "that he wished to leave this place as much of a going concern as it was humanly possible to do." Persons and Clifford met on November 14, and afterward, Clifford told reporters that the conference was "most satisfactory." The two men had cordial meetings usually three times a week and spoke by phone several times a day.[5]

Meanwhile, Kennedy arranged his first meeting with the president. They had been briefly introduced at the end of World War II, but their first extended conversation happened on the morning of December 6. When the president-elect emerged from his car at the White House's north portico, the Marine Band played "The Stars and Stripes Forever." Kennedy shook the president's hand, and after posing for photographs, they went into the Oval Office and talked for almost two hours. The president-elect asked for information on the situations in Berlin, the Far East, and Cuba—then the dominant international trouble spots—and for Ike's opinion of British Prime Minister Harold Macmillan, French President Charles de Gaulle, and German Chancellor Konrad Adenauer. The president, who had known all three leaders for years, supplied some information on the global crises but told Kennedy he would have to form his own opinions of the trio. The incoming president also asked about the National Security Council; Ike explained that the weekly NSC meeting was his most important government meeting. No votes were taken, but everyone was asked to give his frank opinion.

The president talked about the United States balance-of-payments deficit and the resulting outflow of gold, which he saw as a major problem. Kennedy asked Ike whether he would serve in some appropriate manner if called upon, and the president pledged to consult in areas where he had "some experience."[6]

Afterward, they met for an hour in the Cabinet Room with Secretary of State Christian Herter, Secretary of Defense Thomas Gates, and Secretary of the Treasury Robert Anderson, along with Persons and Clifford. Ike and Kennedy issued a joint statement about their "informal personal meeting on continuing problems," especially in foreign affairs. The president would maintain absolute control of all governmental operations until the inauguration. In the interim, both men would work toward an "orderly transfer of Executive responsibility."[7]

While the president recalled the transition as smooth and without "unpleasantness," that did not translate into approval of his successor. Eisenhower deeply resented Kennedy's attacks on his administration during the campaign. Six days after the president-elect's visit, he met with Mansfield Sprague, who had completed a study of "the psychological aspects" of American foreign policy and its security implications. Ike had commissioned the report on the assumption that Nixon would succeed him. Even though Kennedy and his supporters had moderated their attacks on the administration since election day, the president "did not want to provide them with a vehicle to make unfounded charges against the present administration at a time when it would no longer have a voice."[8]

For the rest of the president's term, his successor assumed an air of victory while trying to avoid any mention of a recount. He had won the election by a tiny margin, garnering just under 50 percent of the popular vote. He was painfully aware of being a minority president.

The press did not question him about a recount. Reporters followed him wherever he went, reporting on his trips, camping out in front of his Georgetown home at 3307 N Street, following him to Georgetown University Hospital when he visited Jackie and their newborn son, and even attending John Jr.'s baptism. Kennedy focused on such continuing crises as the standoff with the People's Republic of China over Quemoy and Matsu and the Algerian revolt against the French.

He also began assembling his administration. He chose his White House staff from people he knew well and made other high-ranking political appointments on the basis of talent searches. He had task forces review various subjects he would have to address as chief executive. Most controversially, he named his brother Bobby to be his attorney general.[9]

While in Palm Beach shortly after his victory, Kennedy met with vice president–elect Johnson and Speaker Rayburn to discuss legislative proposals. The president-elect anticipated that LBJ would maintain his control over the Senate, and Rayburn pledged to help move the House in a liberal direction.[10]

Drew Pearson's column for December 7 concerned Jack Kennedy's having "spent two hours with a mysterious friend in the Waldorf Tower—probably a woman." When a correspondent asked press secretary Salinger about it, he answered: "It's purely personal." Reporters did not follow up.[11]

Until the new Senate convened in January, Johnson remained the majority leader. His chosen successor, Mike Mansfield of Montana, and the assistant majority leader and whip, Hubert Humphrey, were Johnson's close allies. Mansfield would take Johnson's seat in the front row on the aisle but allowed him to keep his palatial majority leader's office; Johnson also took over the vice president's ornate ceremonial office.[12]

As vice president, Johnson would be the Senate's presiding officer. When asked about his new job, he answered that the senators would choose their own leader (in fact Johnson had already chosen him), but he would "be very interested in the work of the Senate." Some columnists predicted that LBJ would continue to "run the Senate" even though the vice president was usually considered an outsider. When the new Congress convened in early January, the Democratic senators voted to have Johnson chair the party caucus. The vote, however, was far from unanimous. Seventeen senators opposed the decision, asserting the tradition that only senators had a voice in the chamber's business. Mansfield rejected that argument: "Lyndon will be invited to sit in on steering and policy committees and to preside over caucuses." Even with this assurance, Johnson would no longer be the master of the Senate.[13]

The president remained widely popular. A Gallup Poll in late December listed him as the "most admired man" in the world. In an earlier poll, he had received a 58 percent job approval rating, with 99 percent of Republicans, 38 percent of Democrats, and 62 percent of independents approving his performance. He continued to govern, working on the budget, the worsening balance of payments, and foreign policy issues concerning the Soviet Union, Cuba, and Laos.[14]

Eisenhower had cultivated an air of detachment from partisan politics, but behind the scenes he was heavily involved—never more so than that fall. In an hourlong strategy session on December 15, attended by Nixon, RNC Chairman Morton, and other party operatives, Ike held forth on the Republican Party's future. The two Republican minority leaders in Congress, Senator Everett Dirksen of Illinois and Congressman Charles Halleck from Indiana, were not listening to his recommendations. The party was growing divided between extreme factions: conservatives led by Goldwater and liberals led by Rockefeller. Ike was determined not to "allow the Party to lose control of the middle of the road in the American public." Those who supported a consensus "without an axe to grind don't have an adequate platform," and he would provide one. He offered to hold informal gatherings at his Gettysburg farm several times a year, attended by himself, Nixon, and other influential centrists.

Nixon believed that with Kennedy as president, the congressional leaders would be outspoken at first but would soon understand that they had a limited constituency and needed the president for his national following. Kennedy would try to seize the middle of the road, and that possibility had to be prevented. Nixon encouraged Morton to bring in fresh young Republican activists to add energy and work to enlarge the party. Morton wanted to resign as party chairman to run for reelection to the Senate in 1962, but he had not yet found a successor. He would soon appoint a new executive committee of "vigorous, forward-looking Republican leaders" to help the party prepare for the 1962 congressional races.[15]

Two days later, the president met with Republican Congressman John Byrnes from Wisconsin to discuss party unity. Nixon's defeat meant that Ike would "have to remain more active politically than he had planned." He told the congressman of his plan for periodic meetings for party leaders; Byrnes recommended that the president's weekly Republican leadership meetings be continued, with Morton as chairman.[16]

Nixon had a variety of concerns after the election. Within days after the balloting and continuing through the inauguration, he received thousands of letters expressing condolences and admiration. Republicans were already speculating that he would run for governor of California in 1962 or for the presidency in 1964. Several politicians called for him to remain active in Republican politics, fearing that without Nixon as a consensus builder, the party would be divided between conservatives and liberals. He already was emerging as de facto head of the party and leader of the opposition. By the third week of November, he was urging Democrats not to begin a spending spree and to maintain close scrutiny over the Castro regime. Rumors also circulated that he might join a prestigious California law firm.[17]

The vice president liked his assistant Charles McWhorter's suggestion that Eisenhower's final state of the union message should set the stage for Republican legislative proposals during the Kennedy administration. McWhorter hoped the message would not only review the administration's major achievements but also inspire an ongoing fight for its policies. "This would have the effect," he wrote in a memo to Nixon, "of lining the President up behind the Vice President in the future activities of the Republican Party and help to isolate the Goldwater and Rockefeller wings."[18]

Nixon took a vacation, and in the third week of December, he and Pat went to New York City to see some Broadway shows. They attended an evening performance of the musical *Fiorello!*, based on the career of longtime New York City mayor Fiorello La Guardia, and when the vice president stood up in the aisle during intermission, the audience recognized him and applause broke out throughout the theater.[19]

Henry Cabot Lodge traveled to the Virgin Islands shortly after the election. He accepted condolences about the outcome and defended himself against the charge that his suggestion of appointing a black cabinet official had cost Nixon the presidency. It did not, he insisted, lose the ticket "any votes." He also praised Rockefeller, who had "some very remarkable qualifications for high office," and congratulated Kennedy on his win. The incoming president replied that he hoped they would work "together for the best interests of the American people."[20]

Shortly after the election, rumors spread among Massachusetts Republicans that with Kennedy's resignation from the Senate, Lodge would run in 1962 to take back his old seat. He denied these rumors. He harbored no hard feelings toward Kennedy and believed Kennedy felt the same. Columnists speculated that the president-elect might offer him a diplomatic assignment. Lodge added to the gossip by congratulating Dean Rusk on his appointment as secretary of state.[21]

Lodge also maintained a cordial relationship with Nixon. They had had some disagreements during the campaign, he admitted, but there never was any personal friction. After the election, they exchanged letters expressing mutual admiration. Lodge wrote that his running mate was "a strong man" and "a generous man." He had lost "an election," but won "the battle for life." Nixon answered that Lodge had made a "tremendous contribution" to the contest, and he "was always proud to appear with my running-mate in any state in the nation." A year after the voting, Nixon wrote Lodge to say that he was "deeply grateful" for Lodge's "magnificent effort on behalf of our cause."[22]

Goldwater was looking to the future. Even before the 1960 election, he had begun building his own coalition, particularly in the South and Midwest. On October 1, he declared that in another four years, the conservative movement would "be strong enough to make our weight felt in the party." If Nixon lost, he said, he would run for the nomination the next time. He had vigorously supported Nixon during the campaign, giving 177 speeches across the nation, but he and other Republican conservatives believed the vice president had abandoned them, adopted too many Democratic positions, and become a "me-too" candidate. That belief crystallized three years later in Phyllis Schlafly's speech "How Political Conventions Are Stolen" and the best-selling book it gave rise to, *A Choice, Not an Echo*, which would help propel Goldwater to the Republican nomination in 1964.[23]

As for Nixon, the senator advised him to run for some California office to maintain his leadership in the Republican Party. Without any elected office, he warned, Nixon would lose his political base. When the new Senate convened in January 1961, Goldwater won reelection as chairman of the Republican Senate campaign committee, the Senate Republicans' chief fundraising arm.[24]

Goldwater also started to taunt Rockefeller. The senator expected "to figure in 1964 — not necessarily as the top candidate. But I don't want Rockefeller in that spot." In the first week of January, Goldwater observed that while Republicans had done well in the West, the ticket had lost decisively in New York, and that was the governor's fault. He did not stop there. Possibly referring to Rockefeller's character, he charged: "We cannot afford and we will not gloss over any attempts which ambitious men make to tear down, as an aid to their own careers," the president, vice president, or other party leaders.[25]

Rockefeller ignored Goldwater and pushed his own agenda. The day before the election, he predicted that Nixon would win New York's forty-five electoral votes. Instead, he lost by nearly 400,000 votes; four years earlier, Ike had won the state by 1.6 million. Some thought Rockefeller had not worked hard enough. Nixon rejected that assertion: "No one in the country worked harder for the Nixon-Lodge ticket than did Gov. Rockefeller."[26]

The governor called the president on November 11, asking to talk with Nixon "about his future plans." Four days later, the governor requested a conference with Ike and Nixon to "have the opportunity of talking with both of you about the future of the party and the steps that can be taken for its unity and strength."[27]

At the end of the month, Rockefeller announced his candidacy for reelection in 1962. In the meantime he would attempt to strengthen the party for 1964, with RNC chairman Morton leading the effort to take the GOP from the minority party to a majority. As for his competitors, he called Nixon a "vital" force and had no issues with Goldwater. It was all about unity.[28]

On Thursday afternoon, December 1, Rockefeller met privately with the president. That evening Ike hosted a formal White House dinner to bid farewell to those in the administration, with the vice president, the governor, and Lodge present. At the end of the evening, the president toasted Nixon as the leader of the Republican Party for the next four years. Rockefeller sat expressionless.[29]

On Friday afternoon, Ike talked to several friends, flattering himself over his toast to the vice president and rehashing Rockefeller's refusal to accept Nixon as the head of the party. "No one," Ike said, "should use the Party for personal aggrandizement. . . . The Party should seek the man for the office, not the man seek the office."[30]

Earlier that day, Rockefeller and Nixon had met for breakfast and were questioned by reporters afterward. Nixon had little comment, but the governor insisted that they would not engage in any power struggle and would enjoy the "closest cooperation."[31]

Over the same weeks, Kennedy was busy fulfilling several obligations. He flew to Boston on January 9, 1961, to attend a meeting of the Harvard Board of Overseers. Mobbed by students, he joked that he had come to review their grades with

President Nathan Pusey, and he would protect their interests. The same day, he went before the Massachusetts legislature to say goodbye to his state's senatorial duties for the presidency and promised to act with courage, integrity, and dedication as president: "These are the qualities which, with God's help, this son of Massachusetts hopes will characterize our government's conduct in the four stormy years that lie ahead."[32]

He also tried to mend fences with Protestants. Right after the election, Senator Smathers had suggested that the president-elect telephone Billy Graham to invite him to come to lunch in Palm Beach. Before agreeing, the evangelist tried to contact Nixon. When that failed, he called former South Carolina governor James Byrnes, who encouraged him to accept. Graham did, but the birth of Kennedy's son in late November postponed the meeting.[33]

Instead, they waited until January 16, 1961. After the two men talked, they held a press conference in which Graham stated that Kennedy had promoted a better understanding between Catholics and Protestants. He believed that Kennedy's triumph had reduced the possibility that religion might be an issue in future presidential elections. Kennedy, he added, "will become the most prayed-for man in the world." The meeting was widely reported; Graham assured Nixon that his "loyalty" was "undiminished."[34]

On January 3, 1961, Speaker Rayburn called the 87th Congress to order. It was his twenty-fifth term in the House and his tenth as speaker. His seventy-ninth birthday happened to be three days later. Ike wished him a happy birthday. He had been born in Rayburn's congressional district, and the two had known each other for decades. Rayburn always called him "Captain Eisenhower," and shortly before the president left office, the speaker left him a parting message: "I am glad I can at last call you 'Captain Eisenhower' again." He died of cancer the following November.[35]

On his birthday, Rayburn presided over the joint session of Congress that formally recognized Kennedy's electoral victory. Vice President Nixon was in charge of counting the votes certifying Kennedy the winner. After finishing the count, Nixon concluded: "Those who lose accept the verdict and support those who win." He offered his "heartfelt best wishes" to Kennedy and Johnson. Rayburn, who had never applauded any speech during his speakership, clapped his hands.[36]

By then, Ike was not feeling so magnanimous. He wrote his friend Robert Woodruff a "Top Secret Personal Confidential Eyes Only" letter about his "complete lack of enthusiasm for the majority of the recent appointments." The one exception was the incoming secretary of state, Dean Rusk, whom Eisenhower had worked with during World War II. Otherwise, the president-elect's state department nominations were "a menagerie . . . comprising one individual who is no less than a crackpot, another noted for his indecisiveness, and still another of demonstrated stupidity, and, finally one famous only for his ability to break the treasury of a great state." Kennedy's choice of automobile executive Robert McNamara as secretary of defense drew particular scorn. McNamara, Ike told Nixon and Morton, "took the job . . . because he knows nothing about the problems of the Defense Department." He did not confine his criticism to political appointees; he also could not understand how Kennedy "let Frank Sinatra and Sammy Davis, Jr. become so prominent in his pre-election activities."[37]

C. Douglas Dillon was undersecretary of state for economic affairs. Before joining the Eisenhower administration in 1953, he had been a New York investment banker, and while not taking an active role in the 1960 election, he had donated twelve thousand dollars to Nixon's campaign. Sargent Shriver, who was in charge of the incoming administration's "talent hunt," had recommended Dillon to Kennedy as secretary of the treasury because he was acceptable to the financial community.[38]

At first, Eisenhower approved the nomination, believing Dillon would prevent a gold drain and protect the United States currency, but then he reversed himself, feeling Kennedy would blame the Republicans if the administration mismanaged the economy. Nixon disapproved for similar reasons. Dillon recalled that the president called Kennedy "so radical and he'll ruin the country and he just wants you to save face." Nixon told Dillon that Kennedy wanted "some Republicans in some meaningless jobs."[39]

Opposition from both the outgoing and incoming administrations (many on JFK's team considered Dillon too conservative) did not dissuade Kennedy from appointing him; he accepted the post in mid-December. Since Ike disapproved, Dillon, who had intended to remain in office until the end of the president's term, offered his resignation on December 21, and on January 4, 1961, Ike accepted it. The president was disappointed but not angry. Nixon thought Dillon was unwise to take the new job, but sent him a warm letter.[40]

Eisenhower often saw Nixon in his last three weeks in office. On the day of the joint session of Congress that certified the election results, the president wrote Nixon that he was sorry he could not address him as "Mr. President." A few days later, Ike was the principal speaker at a dinner to celebrate Nixon's forty-eighth birthday. He was supposed to leave immediately after the first course, he said, but he wanted to pay "tribute to one who has served his country well, and certainly in these long 8 years has been one of the mainstays of the Republican administration and to me personally has been not only an invaluable associate in Government but a warm friend." He remained for the entire event. In the middle of the month, Nixon thanked Ike, writing, "Never in this nation's history has one man in public life owed so much to another as I owe to you."[41]

Eisenhower continued to address the future of the Republican Party. Speaking at an RNC luncheon on January 6, he noted that the party had failed to win congressional majorities from 1954 through 1960, and "no matter how hard we have worked, we can still do better." He encouraged his listeners to work hard to regain a congressional majority in 1962. He held breakfast gatherings with Republican senators and congressmen at which he emphasized that the party was "necessary" to the future of the United States and that he would "be available" for consultation.[42]

Ike had a private breakfast on January 9 with Goldwater, who chaired the Senate fundraising committee. He and Congressman William Miller of New York, who was not present, wanted the president to assist in raising money. Goldwater and Miller, both conservatives, would be running mates on the Republican ticket in 1964. They asked Ike to speak before their groups that summer, and he agreed. Goldwater, stressing the need for party unity, predicted that if Republicans did not win the 1962 congressional elections, the "presidential nomination might not mean much to anyone."[43]

Eight days later, the president met with New York Senator Jacob Javits, a leader of the party's liberal wing, who likewise urged him to remain active in Republican politics. Ike noted that Javits thought the party courted "the dangers of returning to isolationism and turning hard right in domestic political philosophy." Ike disapproved of the "liberal" and "conservative" labels, saying, "Let's be just Republicans," and he was resolved to stay active to help "save the Party from these twin threats." The Republicans, he wrote, needed to be "a balanced Party committed to balanced National programs."[44]

The president delivered a written state of the union message to Congress on January 12, highlighting a long, detailed list of accomplishments. In foreign affairs, his administration had ended the Korean War and confronted crises in Suez, Lebanon, the islands of Quemoy and Matsu, and Cuba without resorting to military intervention. The United States had adequate deterrents with missiles, aircraft, and nuclear-powered vessels. As for Kennedy's campaign accusations of a "bomber gap" and a "missile gap," they were "fiction."

His administration, he continued, had invested in the economy with the expansion of the St. Lawrence Seaway and the beginning of the interstate highway system. He had cut taxes and balanced the government's budget. Alaska and Hawaii had been admitted to the union as states. In the field of agriculture, there were improvements, but more was necessary. Education, science, and technology were advancing with the passage of the National Defense Education Act and the creation of the National Aeronautics and Space Administration. His administration had passed the Civil Rights Acts of 1957 and 1960, provided better health care for the aged and veterans, and promoted urban renewal.

He concluded that peace had been maintained through military preparedness. Despite these achievements, the communists had made advances in Laos, Cuba, and Africa. The status of Berlin remained potentially explosive. At home, the nation had to expand economic growth and create more jobs. This was more than just an enumeration of Eisenhower's record. The statement answered the Democratic charge that he had been "a do-nothing president" who would rather play golf than run the country, and it challenged the incoming government to match his successes.[45]

The next day, January 13, the president met with his cabinet for the last time to say goodbye. According to Dr. Snyder, "The President was sputtering like mad because he couldn't get away to Camp David as early as he wanted to." The reason was Mamie. Their son John, who served as a presidential aide, had "learned of the President's high blood pressure," and Mamie was demanding that the doctor take Ike's blood pressure again and call her with the result. Snyder refused.[46]

Eisenhower spent the last weekend of his presidency at Camp David, working on a speech he had been contemplating for many months. He gave his farewell address to a national radio and television audience on January 17. In it, he wished his successor "Godspeed" and urged him to govern in a cooperative, not a partisan spirit. Kennedy was about to assume leadership of the world's strongest nation, with a mission to keep the peace and fight the advance of communism.

Ike warned his countrymen about two major concerns. First, "we must guard against the acquisition of unwarranted influence . . . by the military-industrial complex." Second, "we must also be alert to the equal and opposite danger that public policy could itself become the captive of a scientific-technological elite."[47] The first warning, of course, famously introduced the phrase "military-industrial complex" and its many variations. The second is far less well remembered, but it could have served to describe the Kennedy administration's overreliance on technocratic expertise.

More than three hundred reporters attended Eisenhower's final White House press conference the next morning. May Craig of the *Portland* (Maine) *Press Herald* asked what he saw as his successes and failures. His greatest disappointment, he replied, was that no "permanent peace with justice is really in sight," and there was no "real disarmament." At the same time, he was proud that even with serious communist threats, he had avoided a war. Lillian Levy of Science Service asked about the threat of the scientific technological elite, and the president answered that a "responsible citizenship" had to guard against all abuses.[48]

William Eaton of UPI asked the president whether the time given to the transition period was sufficient. Ike argued for an amendment "to change the time of the inauguration and to give dates for election and assumption of office in such fashion that a new President ought to have at least 80 days or something of that kind before he meets his first Congress." Ray Scherer of NBC News then asked how the transition was going: it was "going splendidly" and Ike had "no complaints."[49]

On his last day as president, Ike met with Kennedy alone in the Oval Office. The president "felt very strongly about discussing . . . plans for the continuity of government in case of an emergency." That included nuclear weapons and the role of Anglo-American cooperation. After that conversation, they went to the Cabinet Room and talked with Ike's secretaries of state, defense, and the treasury, along with the president-elect's counterparts. The top priority was the Laotian crisis. Kennedy quizzed the president on how he should respond, and Ike advised that unilateral intervention should be only a last resort. But the United States could not allow another Southeast Asian nation to fall under communist domination. If Laos collapsed, he said, the rest of the region would become communist satellites. Kennedy then asked for advice on Cuba, and the president once more cautioned against unilateral action, but said the United States should openly support Castro's removal and should remain silent about the training of Cuban exiles in Guatemala.[50]

Other topics came up: the Congo, the Dominican Republic, and the country's capability to conduct a limited war. Kennedy had been well briefed on Algeria, Berlin, and nuclear test ban and disarmament talks and had no need to discuss these subjects. At the end of the meeting, Kennedy and Clifford thanked Ike and his administration "for the very fine cooperation and assistance during the transition period." The president appreciated their statements and promised to be available along with his staff if more information was needed.[51]

Snow was starting to fall as Kennedy left the White House; it fell continuously throughout the day. By evening, Dr. Snyder wrote, "the roads were so bad, traffic was at a standstill." The doctor took the snowstorm as "evidence that supernatural powers are not in sympathy with the action taken by the populace on November 8, 1960." Thousands of cars were stalled and abandoned. The Eisenhowers were confined to the mansion. The storm was so bad that many White House staff members spent the evening in the bomb shelter. No one had slept there during Eisenhower's entire presidency.[52]

On the morning of the inauguration, seven hundred plows and trucks cleared Washington's main streets of about eight inches of snow. The temperature that morning was twenty-two degrees. Ben Bradlee recalled: "The inauguration itself took place on a day so cold, no one could have survived without special pre-cautions." On Friday morning, January 20, the *Washington Post's* headline read: "Best Prepared President in History Takes Oath Today."[53]

The president telephoned Kennedy suggesting that, because of the weather, he and Jackie arrive a half-hour early. The president-elect gladly accepted. Just before noon, Ike waited in a suit as the Kennedys arrived at the White House north portico. The Nixons and Johnsons followed, joining the Eisenhowers and Kennedys for coffee. The snow had stopped falling when the outgoing and in-coming presidents were driven to Capitol Hill in a bubble-top limousine, with Johnson and Nixon in the car just behind. The four men, formally dressed in black topcoats and carrying top hats, arrived at the inaugural platform on the Capitol's east portico; the president sat next to his successor, and across the aisle the incoming vice president sat next to his predecessor.[54]

The Constitution made Kennedy president at the stroke of noon, but the cere-mony was delayed. At 12:41 p.m., Rayburn swore in Johnson as vice president, and ten minutes later, Chief Justice Earl Warren read the oath of office to Ken-nedy. In the bitter cold, the newly elected president spoke without a hat or top-coat.[55]

Sorensen had begun drafting his address in November, but it was not finished until the day before the inauguration. The new president began by saying this was not a party victory "but a celebration of freedom." The world had changed, and "the torch has been passed to a new generation of Americans." He proclaimed to the world "that we shall pay any price, bear any burden, meet any hardship, support any friend, oppose any foe to assure the survival and the success of lib-erty." He encouraged America's adversaries to cooperate with the United States to reach the goal of a peaceful world. Toward the end of the address, he appealed to the nation: "Ask not what your country can do for you: ask what you can do for your country."[56]

Recalling the address more than two decades later, Nixon thought JFK had delivered it "very, very well. It had a great impact." As for the content, he "could just hear Eisenhower's teeth . . . grating." Paraphrasing Kennedy's proclama-tion as "Let the world know that we will fight any place, any time, in defense of freedom," Nixon said he had been certain Ike was thinking of the time during the campaign when Kennedy suggested that he apologize to Khrushchev over the U-2 episode and later recommended that the president abandon Quemoy and Matsu in case of a Chinese military attack.[57]

Eisenhower had been quite open about his misgivings. Four days before the inauguration, he talked with reporters at the White House correspondents' dinner. One mentioned that he seemed to get along well with Kennedy at their

December 6 meeting, and Ike dodged: "I don't know whether you could put it that way. . . . But I could see that he was willing to learn."[58]

Six years after the election, Ike criticized the new "personality cult" that minimized the achievements of his administration. His former press secretary James Hagerty believed Ike was deeply distressed by the partisan tendency to "equate oratorical strength with editorial bombast" and "achievement with exaggerated use of the vertical pronoun."[59]

In the summer of 1967, when he sat for an oral history, Ike recalled that Kennedy ignored several problems during the transition, "but there was no unpleasantness of any kind." As for JFK's performance as president, he did not do his "job well" and never took the "job seriously." He took himself "seriously, and to hell with the job."[60]

Nixon hid his feelings about the inaugural address. With a smile on his face, he was one of the first to congratulate Kennedy and Johnson. The outgoing vice president then escorted his wife to their car, where Republican congressmen and senators cheered the couple as they left. The Nixons went to the F Street Club for a luncheon and then went home for dinner with their daughters, who wanted to talk only about election fraud.[61]

Later that evening, with snow still falling, Nixon took a last car ride around the Capitol. At midnight he would no longer have a driver. He watched women dressed in ball gowns and men in white tie and tails on their way to inaugural balls. The parties were not for him and Ike; Washington was no longer theirs. The town belonged to the Kennedys. Arriving at the Capitol, he headed upstairs and through the empty hallways to one of the building's balconies to take in his favorite view, looking west down the Mall toward the Lincoln and Washington memorials. He stood for about five minutes and left.[62]

In an interview nearly twenty-three years later, he said of those last moments standing on the balcony looking out at the capital's monuments: "Suddenly a thought just rushed into my mind—not consciously, but then it seemed almost to overwhelm me. And it was, 'I'll be back.'"[63]

Pat Nixon's thoughts centered on allowing her daughters to finish the school year in Washington while she looked for a home in some smog-free area near Los Angeles. They eventually settled in Brentwood, an upscale Los Angeles subdivision. Dick joined a prominent Los Angeles law firm to support his family and pay for his daughters' educations. His partners hoped wealthy clients would seek him out for his legal advice. They did, and that permitted Nixon the time to remain an active force in the Republican Party. His net worth when he left office was less than fifty thousand dollars; he owned no stocks or bonds and had long been giving his speaking fees to charity. Vice presidents did not receive a pension. He left Washington "a relatively poor man by most standards." He did not know his future but was satisfied with his past.[64]

Many liberals and partisans were excited that Kennedy represented a new era. They ignored the fact that the "Best Prepared President in History" was about to take charge of the most complicated bureaucracy on the planet with no executive training or experience. He had underperformed his party in the election, and the vast majority of Democrats who had served with him in Congress considered him mediocre at best. They did not owe him any political debts.

Lyndon Johnson, as a senator, had been one of the most powerful politicians in the nation. He would find that as vice president his influence was severely diluted. He was an outsider looking in on the tight Kennedy circle, and JFK did not significantly expand Johnson's authority.

Eisenhower left the presidency feeling a duty to keep his party from drifting to either the right or the left. He would remain active and try to promote a centrist consensus. But despite his overwhelming popularity with the American public, he could not thwart Goldwater or prevent his conservative insurgency. He lived long enough to see Nixon's presidential inauguration. Within a decade after his passing, the Republican Party moved farther to the right by electing Ronald Reagan president.

Nixon had lost one of the closest presidential elections in American history. At forty-eight years old, he still was young enough to stage a comeback.

20

BETWEEN MYTH AND REALITY

Speaking at a luncheon shortly after the publication of *The Making of the President* 1960, Theodore White underscored his book's overarching theme: Kennedy was the candidate who most wanted and deserved to win. JFK, he added, would "make a very great President."[1]

Kennedy's assassination less than two years later transformed him into a legendary figure. Within a month after his murder, White, prompted by Jackie Kennedy, made him almost literally mythic by writing an article that cast JFK as King Arthur in the kingdom of Camelot, an allusion to the popular musical then playing on Broadway. White knew that this idyll had "never existed" in real-life Washington and that Kennedy himself would never have approved of having his presidency compared to a fable.[2]

Fifteen years later, in his memoirs, White acknowledged his bias. Even before drafting his landmark book, he had conceived of it "as a novel." He initially liked Kennedy, a favorable impression that grew into a friendship and ultimately hero worship. On the other hand, he disliked Nixon from their first encounter but found him "essential" in the role of "the villain."[3]

Subsequent writers, largely ignoring White's admission that he fictionalized the campaign, have portrayed the 1960 presidential election as an epic struggle between good and evil. The rave reviews for White's book never ended. When the Book-of-the-Month Club released a new edition in 1988, *New York Times* columnist James Reston, one of the most influential journalists in the nation, wrote in the foreword that it was "the best account we have of the tactics and strategy, the mysteries, trickeries and accidents of American presidential elections." The book was "a model of political reporting" that captured not only the campaign but the panorama of American history. Reston, who while covering the election as a reporter had made no secret that he favored Kennedy, called White's book "the finest . . . ever written on an American presidential election."[4]

In 2009 the book was reissued, this time with a foreword by the historian Robert Dallek, who highlighted an element Reston had not: "Perhaps the book's greatest weakness is its romantic depiction of President Kennedy as a kind of knight in shining armor." Still, he added, in 1960 "the country was yearning for a sense of direction and inspired leadership," a view that excluded from "the country" the half of the electorate who were satisfied with Eisenhower's presidency and wanted his policies to continue under Nixon.[5]

Although Dallek criticized the depiction of Kennedy as a mythic character, his best-selling *An Unfinished Life: John F. Kennedy, 1917–1963* also painted its subject as charismatic and Nixon as a blunderer. The underlying theme that White laid out had not changed. Regarding the allegations of fraud, Dallek conceded that "Daley's machine probably stole Illinois from Nixon." Yet in the same paragraph, he seems to dismiss his own conclusion: "No one could demonstrate significant fraud anywhere."[6]

James MacGregor Burns released the first biography of Kennedy in 1960. Until the publication of his memoirs in 2006, he kept secret his own conflict of interest: while running for the House of Representatives in 1958, he had occasionally campaigned with Kennedy, who was seeking reelection to the Senate. After they did a joint interview at a Boston radio station, Kennedy "slipped a small wad of bills into my coat pocket as a contribution to my meager store of campaign funds."[7]

In the biography, that contribution went unmentioned. Burns informed readers that he had been given "unrestricted access to [Kennedy's] official and personal files." In his memoirs, Burns admitted that he was not permitted to see Kennedy's medical records and that he purposely did not include anything about the senator's "sexual adventurism." He also left out Kennedy's mediocre legislative record and his family's use of money to bribe officials and voters.

Clinging to his original proposition, Burns maintained that Kennedy "was of high presidential quality and promise." In his memoirs, he called Kennedy a "great man." Citing no supporting data, he asserted that anti-Catholicism had cost Kennedy millions of Democratic votes but that "Jack's youthful vigor and charisma drew a healthy celebrity vote and only just edged out Nixon's gravitas and experience."[8]

Ted Sorensen worked with Burns on his biography and pressured him to make changes regarding the Kennedy family and to reject the claims about Kennedy's having Addison's disease. Sorensen remained Kennedy's staunchest apologist throughout his life. Beginning with his hagiographic 1965 biography, he frequently spoke and published articles, opinion pieces, and books on the Kennedy presidency. In his last memoir, *Counselor*, released in 2008, he asserted without any evidence that if voters had known about Kennedy's illnesses, they still would have elected him. He maintained that Kennedy had won the 1960 election fairly while failing to mention any reasons for thinking otherwise.[9]

In 2007, reporter and television commentator Elizabeth Drew published a brief Nixon biography that embellished White's themes while highlighting her own prejudices. The vice president "envied and resented" Kennedy for his "privilege, wealth, charm, charisma, and prominent connections." His performance in the first debate reminded "people why Nixon was so widely disliked." As the campaign progressed, "Nixon became increasingly tense and wound up." He lost, Drew charged, because of these character flaws. There is no evidence that the inevitable tension of the campaign affected either his performance or his relationships. As for his being "widely disliked," Nixon's approval ratings throughout 1960 were about even with Kennedy's.[10]

A few have challenged these characterizations. Historian William Rorabaugh published *The Real Making of the President* in 2009, and in the History News Network *Newsletter* that June, he argued that the time had come to admit that White's narrative of JFK "as the virtuous white knight who defeated the dark and sinister Richard Nixon" was a naïve oversimplification. The election was much more complex. It marked a turning point in American political history in which the Kennedys took advantage of their family fortune, an excellent organization, and the new medium of television to gain the presidency. A year later, in *Nixon v. Kennedy*, Edmund Kallina independently confirmed many of Rorabaugh's findings. In a chapter titled "The Myths of 1960," he wrote: "One must abandon the eloquent hagiography of Theodore White, give more credit to Richard M. Nixon, and rediscover the realities of John F. Kennedy's close victory." The 1960 presidential election was not good versus evil. It was a battle between two ambitious, experienced politicians who desperately wanted to win the White House.[11]

These scholars' contributions fell on deaf ears. The parade of books repeating White's version of events continued.

Nixon's charges of press bias have never been taken seriously but instead have been seen as evidence of his paranoia. After the election, his press secretary, Herb Klein, said he could not attribute Nixon's loss to any one factor and certainly not to the press coverage. He described his experience with the press as "pleasant." Contrary to the gossip that was circulating, Nixon was not "hot mad" at reporters and had entertained many of them during the last month of the campaign. He did see some bias, though he could not tell how much.[12]

The *Boston Herald-Traveler*, in an editorial on November 16, 1960, disagreed.

Some reporters with "strong Democratic inclinations" had written pieces that were unfair to Nixon. During the fourth debate, some correspondents had cheered, "Give it to him, Jack." The editorial concluded that Nixon had "endured some inexcusable hostility from some of the correspondents with him."[13]

On January 1, 1961, Fletcher Knebel, the capital correspondent of the *Minneapolis Tribune*, wrote on the front page that Nixon had privately told friends he thought "a pro-Kennedy attitude by reporters covering the campaign provided Senator John Kennedy with his narrow victory margin" and that he felt resentful toward "a number of Washington correspondents." He was especially upset because he and his wife "had gone out of their way to be on friendly terms with newspapermen and TV commentators." He was shocked that the majority of those reporters who covered the campaign had favored Kennedy. The press had treated him unfairly, and on one occasion he "blew his stack with reporters" because of their "double standard." The press attacked his speeches and asked hostile questions at press conferences while treating Kennedy much more kindly. At one point, the vice president made a list of reporters' overheard remarks about the candidate and what they had written.[14]

Klein responded to the article that neither Nixon nor his staff had any "vendetta against the press," and they had not singled out biased reporting as the cause of the vice president's defeat. There was no "little list" or "black list" of reporters Nixon felt were against him. Nixon had heard a rumor that Republican congressmen were "about to launch a political attack against newsmen," but he had dismissed it.[15]

Klein waited until the summer of 1965 to express his antipathy toward White, who he said had attacked him unfairly, and the inaccuracies in his book. Later, in his memoirs, Klein wrote that Kennedy had wooed the press while Nixon had allowed "himself to be needled by reporters and lost his perspective." Klein had no doubt that press bias damaged Nixon during the race.[16]

In the first week of January 1961, Willard Edwards, the Capitol Hill correspondent for the *Chicago Tribune*, gave a talk entitled "Did Biased Reporters Cost Nixon the Election?" Edwards had covered the Nixon campaign from late July through November 8. He had listened to every speech and was present at all of Nixon's press conferences. After the campaign, he surveyed one hundred correspondents who covered the race and found that half of them favored Kennedy. "They were not only opposed to Nixon," Edwards observed; "they were outspoken in their hatred and contempt of him. . . . They regarded service with Kennedy as a lover regards a honeymoon and assignment to Nixon as a penalty—an enforced association with a discreditable character."

Edwards listed two examples. On October 26, Mario Remo, a New York department store executive who had served as finance chairman of the DNC Nationalities division, switched his support to Nixon because he feared Kennedy would quickly take the nation into a war. Len Hall, the vice president's campaign manager, brought Remo onto the campaign train for maximum press exposure. When he was introduced, one or two reporters called out "turncoat," and one New York newspaper covered his appearance with a two-paragraph piece on the bottom of page 27. Edwards's other example was an editor who sent a young reporter to cover the Nixon campaign only after assuring himself that the reporter was a Kennedy fan. Edwards thought Nixon had "a prima facie case for the charge that animosity for Nixon . . . did creep into dispatches."

After the election, Edwards said, he heard gossip that the vice president had lost because he staged "a me-too campaign" and did not attack Kennedy "hard enough." He told his audience that the vice president regularly blasted Kennedy on foreign and domestic issues, but voters did not hear this message. He noted that Pierre Salinger had appeared at a Sigma Delta Chi convention a few days after the election and said that a majority of reporters preferred his candidate. While Nixon had lost for a variety of reasons, Edwards concluded, "slanted reporting which did not fully and fairly acquaint a portion of the voting public with his words and actions during the campaign—that condition demands exposure."[17]

Paul Niven, a CBS News television commentator, wrote the vice president in the middle of January, saying that as "a reformed 'Nixon-hater'" he still differed with him "on most political issues," but he appreciated his eight years of service and would "always remember with admiration the enormous ability and dedication you brought to every aspect of your work."[18]

Six months later, Niven, who followed Nixon throughout the campaign except for three weeks he spent with Kennedy, devoted a television broadcast to arguing that Nixon and his staff never viewed the press as a "hostile conspiracy" and that not all journalists were happy to be transferred to the Democratic campaign, where they merrily sang anti-Nixon songs. Even though Niven believed that 80 percent of the Washington press corps was Democratic, many who rejoiced over Kennedy's triumph had grown to respect the vice president enormously. Only a few referred to him as "Tricky Dick." Nixon flattered reporters, just as Kennedy did, because they enjoyed it. The senior members of the vice president's staff were readily available to speak with correspondents.[19]

In 1994, Richard Bean, Klein's assistant during the campaign, offered a far different recollection. Toward the end of the contest, he recalled, after an evening rally in St. Louis, a local reporter joined the Nixon press bus. A White House correspondent took the seat beside him and began telling him what an incompetent campaigner the vice president was. Then he switched to demeaning Pat Nixon. Said Bean, "This was an out-and-out attempt to enlist the newcomer to join those who were not giving Nixon a fair shake." Some reporters did support the Nixons, "but they were sorely outnumbered."[20]

When Arthur Schlesinger's *Journals* were released in 2007, they included his account of a dinner party that Katharine Graham, heiress to the *Washington Post*, gave on the evening of October 11, 1960, for columnist Joseph Alsop's fiftieth birthday. Schlesinger described the affair as "great fun" and was "particularly" struck by "the extent to which the senior commentators—not only Joe [Alsop] but [Walter] Lippmann, [James] Reston and Phil [Graham] himself— are emotionally engaged in this campaign. They cannot stand the thought of a Nixon victory, and they have a confidence in Jack [Kennedy]." Emmet Hughes, Eisenhower's disgruntled former speechwriter, was also there "and talked quite unguardedly about his preference for Kennedy and his fears about Nixon."[21]

Jackie Kennedy sent a note to Alsop that was read at the party: "I cannot express—& become tearful when I try—in this supercharged emotional time— how we appreciate your friendship." After the balls ended on inauguration night, Jack Kennedy stopped off at Alsop's Georgetown house for champagne.[22]

In their books, however, when journalists and historians mention Nixon's resentment of press bias, they almost never acknowledge that he may have had a point. Donald Ritchie, in *The Columnist: Leaks, Lies, and Libel in Drew Pearson's Washington* (2021), reports that Pearson always distrusted Nixon and never conceded that his charges of press prejudice might have been accurate. James Reston, in his memoir published three decades after the election, admitted that he never liked Nixon, "was relieved by Kennedy's victory over Nixon and felt sure he would bring new energy and imagination to Washington."[23]

The journalist Jack Germond released a memoir in 1999 in which he declared that most of the press corps favored Kennedy in the 1960 election. Germond had written his first story on Nixon in 1954 and continued to follow him throughout his career, which "was colored by controversy over his relationship with the press." Most reporters, himself included, disliked Nixon, but during the 1968 presidential campaign, he and several colleagues "felt some collective guilt for the way Nixon had been treated by the press in 1960. . . . The first result was that we bent over backward to be 'fair.'"[24]

The media focused on Kennedy's attractive attributes and excluded his history of physical infirmities. He had been a sickly child with a host of chronic illnesses: in addition to Addison's disease, he developed back problems that required surgery and intestinal troubles that required him to eat a bland diet. He had become sexually active during his senior year in high school. Since he did not wear a condom, from 1940 on he repeatedly contracted and was treated for sexually transmitted diseases, ailments his medical record politely labeled "non specific." Dr. William Herbst, Jr., a urologist, began treating him for venereal disease in 1953 and continued until Kennedy's death.[25] The family withheld this information from the public for more than forty years afterward.

JFK also presented himself as a family man with a devoted wife, pregnant with their second child during the campaign, and a young daughter. Some knew about his many sexual liaisons outside this marriage, but the press largely ignored them. One affair surfaced when Gunilla von Post published *Love, Jack* in 1997. She was eighteen years old in 1953 when she met Jack, who was twice her age, on the French Riviera, where he told her about his impending marriage to Jackie. After von Post returned home, Jack sent letters and telegrams asking to visit her in 1954. He had to postpone that trip because of spinal surgery, but in August 1955 he traveled to Sweden, where they spent a week living together. They stayed in touch until 1956, when Jack informed Gunilla that Jackie was pregnant.[26]

On October 19, 1961, Florence Kater, whose photographic evidence of JFK leaving the apartment of his Senate receptionist, Pamela Turnure, had failed to gain media traction in 1958, wrote Attorney General Robert Kennedy about his appearance a few days earlier on the NBC television show *David Brinkley's Journal*, in which he described himself as a "moralist." During the 1960 campaign, Kater wrote, the candidate had been depicted "as a devoted husband worthy to head up the First Family of the nation." Once he was in the White House, Ms. Turnure had been appointed Jackie's press secretary, and according to Kater, the president had continued "to be the debaucher of a girl young enough to be his daughter." The press was covering this up, but Bobby knew about the affair. If he were truly a moralist, he needed to stop his brother's "present criminality in the White House for the good of the country." Not surprisingly, she never received a reply.[27]

The press and later commentators also ignored the role of money, a hallmark of Kennedy's campaign. He hired a large and excellent staff and had ample amounts of literature to distribute to voters. He was the first presidential candidate to travel the nation in his own private airplane.

Kennedy's seemingly endless supply of funds also had a sinister side. Bobby Kennedy, who managed the money, asked for and received a bribe from Disneyland's president in order to set up a Disney booth at the Democratic convention. Bobby also funneled money to local politicians to buy their allegiance. In the Wisconsin primary, for example, he employed Paul Corbin to send out anti-Catholic pamphlets falsely attributed to Senator Humphrey; in West Virginia, Corbin stood outside the polling places handing out money and whiskey to people who promised to vote for Kennedy. After those primaries, Corbin went to New York to assist in the general election. He remained a shadowy figure, and his activities were not revealed during the campaign. Evan Thomas was the first to describe Corbin's role, in his biography of Robert Kennedy. To replace Corbin, the Kennedys hired Dick Tuck, who remained a nemesis of Nixon's for the rest of Nixon's political career.[28]

Nixon did not have the funds that Kennedy had at his disposal. Unlike his opponent, he had no sexual adventures and no long-term health issues. Claude Robinson, the vice president's pollster, concluded shortly after the voting that Nixon had lost because of "partisanship and religion."[29]

The Democratic Party had an enormous advantage in voter registration, and if Kennedy could have held on to that majority, he would have won easily. But polls published after the election showed that he captured just 84 percent of Democrats, while 96 percent of Republicans voted for the vice president. The South, where Lyndon Johnson's presence on the ticket was not enough to overcome conservative Democrats' aversion to Kennedy's civil rights platform, probably accounted for much of Kennedy's underperformance.

Religion is a more complicated issue. Ike had received almost half of the Catholic vote in 1956, but four years later, 62 percent of Catholic Democrats who had voted for Eisenhower returned to their party. Religion in general did not overcome party affiliation: Catholic Democrats went 94 percent for Kennedy and Catholic Republicans just 18 percent. Independent Catholic voters broke for Kennedy, 71–29 percent. In the eight states with the highest Catholic populations, five voted Democratic and three Republican.[30] Of the nine states with the lowest Catholic populations, meanwhile, Kennedy won five, Nixon four. Factors other than religion, such as local issues like the recession, the power of labor unions, and the specific candidates, seem to be more powerful explanations for these outcomes.[31]

Since the election, several authors have offered their opinions on whether Kennedy won or lost votes due to his religion. They pretend to speak authoritatively, but none has done the rigorous research needed for definitive conclusions. Thomas Carty in *A Catholic in the White House?* provided some anecdotal evidence in several states, while Shaun Casey in *The Making of a Catholic President* presented conjecture. Both assert that Kennedy would have won by a larger margin if not for the anti-Catholic vote. Robert Dallek, in *An Unfinished Life*, makes the same claim. Like the others, he presents no supporting data but simply assumes that Kennedy's victory "marked a great leap forward in religious tolerance."[32]

Surprisingly, there is no definitive study of the role of religion in the 1960 presidential election, even though the abundance of articles and books on the influence of Catholicism in elections gives the impression that the subject has been covered. Polling results are available for the ways Catholics, Protestants, and Jews voted in the election. Only a handful of studies focus on statewide Catholic voting that year, and these show mixed results.[33]

While there are studies of the 1960 presidential election in about twenty-five states, only a few concentrate on religion. The *Western Political Quarterly* devoted its March 1961 issue to analyzing the elections in the western states. The authors who discussed religion concluded that it was not the deciding factor in any of these states. But until an analysis of all fifty states is conducted, the examination of religion's role in the election remains incomplete.[34]

The significance of the debates is another area where the consensus seems impervious to facts. Many of Nixon's advisers urged him not to debate. Kennedy would have the advantage of attacking the status quo, while Nixon would have to defend it. Given that Nixon was the better-known candidate, this effect probably worked slightly to his disadvantage. But the vice president felt he had no choice. During the campaign, reporters called the first debate even or gave a slight edge to Kennedy, and Nixon gained the advantage in the next three.[35]

The perception going into the campaign was that Nixon was a far better debater than Kennedy. Even though most reporters and commentators called the first debate a draw, Democrats saw this as a victory. Kennedy had done well enough to overcome the charges of inexperience and youth. The polls, however, did not materially change after any debate, including the first. After the election, Kennedy partisans like Schlesinger and Sorensen exaggerated the debates' significance as the turning point in the campaign. There is no convincing evidence of this.

The question of whether the election was stolen is occasionally raised, but only in order to dismiss it. Paul Rosenberg in *Salon* and Paul von Hippel in the *Washington Post*, for instance, have both criticized the allegation of fraud in the election. A frequent columnist on this theme is David Greenberg, a journalist turned academic historian, who has written several op-ed pieces with the intent of proving that Nixon lost fair and square. Relying on "long-lost newspaper articles" and acknowledging "a lack of good secondary sources," he argued in a November 2000 piece published in the *Los Angeles Times* that "there exists no conclusive evidence, or historical consensus, that the election was stolen." This is correct. The evidence had not been assembled and a consensus had not formed because no one, including Greenberg, had examined the massive archives of documents detailing how the election was conducted in key states.

Those who allege that Nixon lost the election through fraud in Chicago and

Texas, Greenberg argued, refused to acknowledge the reality of Kennedy's victory. This claim ignores the fact that major biographers of Richard Daley, such as scholars Edmund Kallina and Roger Biles, and Chicago veteran reporters Len O'Connor and Mike Royko, have stated categorically that the Daley machine committed fraud to win Illinois. As for Lyndon Johnson, his principal biographer, Robert Caro, as well as Ronnie Dugger, a journalist who followed Johnson's career for four decades, declared that LBJ won the Texas vote by fraud. Other Johnson biographers steer clear of the subject. Randall Woods, in *LBJ: Architect of American Ambition*, and Robert Dallek, in *Lone Star Rising: Lyndon Johnson and His Times*, both spend chapters on corruption in Johnson's 1941 and 1948 Senate races but not on 1960. Woods mentions the irregularities in 1960 in a single sentence, saying Republicans claimed that Texas and Illinois had been won by fraud, "but nothing came of it." Dallek does not address the charges at all in his narrative.

Besides those omissions, Greenberg made a number of other factual errors. He speculated, for example, that Nixon could have stopped RNC chairman Morton from calling for a recount. In fact, Morton was under tremendous pressure from Republicans nationwide to contest the election, and he had to respond to their outrage. Greenberg also alleged that Nixon's campaign manager, Robert Finch, vigorously advocated a recount; he did just the opposite.[36]

The picture that emerges from Greenberg's account has Nixon publicly supporting the results while privately fighting to have them overturned. This led Greenberg to a predictable conclusion: "There was nothing patriotic or honorable about Nixon's behavior in 1960. . . . His hypocrisy in feigning to take the high road while allowing his allies to do his dirty work does not deserve our admiration."[37]

Nixon could have challenged the election results, but doing so might have caused a constitutional crisis. Privately, he was convinced Kennedy had won the election through fraud, and he may well have been right. His belief that Democrats had unscrupulously robbed him of the nation's highest office would later have disastrous consequences for his career. Publicly, for now, he graciously accepted his defeat for the sake of American democracy.

Probably the most egregious misinterpretation of Kennedy's victory concerns African-American voting. The importance of African-American participation in the 1960 election has been grossly exaggerated. Far fewer than half of black registrants voted, partly because of racism and intimidation, and those who did successfully cast ballots did not behave differently from black voters since 1936.

The perception that they did otherwise perhaps begins in the black press, which greatly embellished the power of African-American voters. Approximately 10 million black citizens age twenty-one or older were eligible to vote, and about half were registered. The black press anticipated a huge turnout. After the election, the *Pittsburgh Courier* proclaimed that blacks were "the 'power balance' in the political scales" that swung the election to Kennedy. The *New York Amsterdam News* stated that blacks "helped to insure Kennedy win." The *New York Times* reinforced this message, declaring that blacks gave Kennedy "a powerful assist."[38]

In his Pulitzer Prize–winning *Parting the Waters: America in the King Years, 1954–63*, Taylor Branch claimed that there was a tsunami of black voters to Kennedy. Using poll numbers that never existed, he asserts a 30 percent increase in the Democratic share of the black vote between 1956 and 1960, from a 60–40 split for Eisenhower to a 70–30 split for Kennedy. The source he cites for this information, Gloster Current's "Why Nixon Lost the Negro Vote" in the January 1961 issue of the *Crisis*, contradicts it: "The Gallup report indicated that Senator Kennedy gained seven percentage points among Negroes in comparison with those of 1956." This is not the historic realignment both Current and Branch claim; it is regression to the mean. The 1956 election was a landslide, 1960 was very close, and the only significant changes in the voting pattern were that several million more Catholics voted for Kennedy and the Catholic percentage for him jumped by 29 percent.[39]

In *From Slavery to Freedom*, the prominent black scholar John Hope Franklin provides the standard interpretation: both political parties concentrated on African Americans because they "held the balance of power in closely contested elections." In 1960, however, according to Franklin, the Democrats did a better job courting black voters, primarily because of JFK's telephone call to Coretta King after her husband was arrested and sent to a Georgia prison. Eisenhower and Nixon failed to respond, and their silence, coupled with JFK's response, ignited the black community to vote Democratic, "assisted by the distribution in Negro churches and elsewhere of more than a million pamphlets telling of their deed." African Americans, believing that Kennedy would advance the cause of civil rights, "were responsible for the election of John F. Kennedy."[40]

Simeon Booker, chief of *Jet*'s Washington bureau, wrote shortly after the election that Eisenhower had never gotten more than 30 percent of the black vote. In fact, the Gallup organization gave Eisenhower 39 percent in 1956; other pollsters used 36 percent for the president's share.[41] (Booker seems to have started the tradition of misstating the black vote in this era. Conrad Black wrote in his 2007 book *The Invincible Quest* that African-American voting for Democrats went from 60 percent in 1956 to 80 percent in 1960.)

Booker was not a fan of either candidate at first, but he came to admire Kennedy. Shortly after the election, he admitted Kennedy's civil rights record was "spotty and not particularly impressive," but he would begin a new era in black progress. In an *Ebony* article at the start of 1961, he predicted that the Kennedy era would "become the most hopeful, the most encouraging period for racial progress in U.S. history."[42]

Booker quoted Nixon as saying he had "great respect" for King and believed that Democrats had been "unethically using the King case to woo black voters" and to paint a false picture of "my unconcern in an all-out drive in the big city Negro areas. And because we were so weak at the local level, our own eight years of racial progress was erased from the minds of many voters." In Booker's view, Nixon did not realize how effective Democrats were in promoting the King case and failed to understand that if he remained silent, "such a call could swing an election." Nixon believed "that Negroes would examine our record and not be swayed by one particular thing."[43]

The influential black columnist Carl Rowan was less kind. Before the election, he interviewed Nixon for an extended period and described him as "formal, in fact cold," and not to be trusted. On the other hand, "millions of black voters saw Kennedy as a friend." Rowan believed Kennedy would "make America's Negroes first-class citizens." He later took a job in the Kennedy administration.[44]

The *Chicago Defender* editorialized on November 19, 1960, that Kennedy was "a man with deep convictions, and who had the moral courage to stand up for what he believed to be just and proper. We predict John Kennedy will be a great President."[45]

RNC Chairman Morton lent credence to the incorrect perception of the importance of the black vote. At a press conference on the day after the election, he primarily blamed African Americans for Nixon's loss. He mistakenly said that Nixon had received just 10 to 12 percent of the black vote, compared with Eisenhower's 26 percent. When a reporter pointed out that Democrats had allocated considerably more money to black voters and begun wooing them earlier, while Republicans did not start targeting them until the middle of October, Morton agreed.[46]

Nixon and Eisenhower shared Morton's view that the black vote had swung the election. In mid-December, the three met in the Oval Office. A "sanitized" version of the meeting memorandum was released in 1984, and the entire memo was made available in 1997.[47]

The reason for the delay, clearly, was to prevent the release of the participants' remarks. Eisenhower complained that he had "made civil rights a main part our effort these past eight years but have lost Negro support, instead of increasing it." No one was "more sincere" than he was about "bettering opportunities" for black people, "but to rely entirely upon law for remedies of this problem is entirely wrong." He concluded that Nixon had lost North and South Carolina because "Negroes 'just do not give a damn.'"

Nixon commented that Lodge's promise to put an African American in the cabinet "just killed us in the south." Republicans had received "slightly more Negroes votes" in 1960 than 1952, and they helped "a little." But those voters were "a bought vote, and it isn't bought by civil rights." He probably meant that Democrats had paid African-American leaders to have their constituents vote for Kennedy. Morton agreed: "The hell with them."[48]

The president and vice president approached civil rights from different viewpoints. Eisenhower, throughout his presidency, had taken a gradualist position: all Americans were equal under the law, and civil rights was a moral issue that had to be approached with caution. Two years after leaving the White House, he told reporters that "the country's racial problems must be solved by evolutionary processes rather than by force." He said in an oral history in 1967 that "the worst enemies of the Civil Rights thing have been a great group or section of the Democratic Party, and yet most of our Negroes go and vote Democratic. It's a strange thing."[49]

Nixon had anticipated that the administration's civil rights record would bring gains in the black vote. In a memorandum written eighteen months after the election, he conceded that these efforts had not paid dividends: "Right or wrong, the image seems to persist that we are, as a Party, 'bad' for the Negro and apathetic at best in enlisting his support. This is an image we must erase — not just through words and promises but by active and creative leadership, in Congress and in various statehouses right now and eventually in the White House."[50]

Twenty-three years after the election, Nixon reminisced that black preachers had "greatly influenced" their parishioners' vote, and both parties tried to get their support. Len Hall, his campaign chairman, came from New York, had been bribing preachers for years to support his candidates, and had "a pretty good fund" to "subsidize" some of them during the campaign. But after trying in 1960, Hall said to Nixon: "My God, I've never seen anything like it." He paid them more than they had ever received, and the Kennedys came "in there and raised me every time. We didn't get one of 'em."[51]

The vice president got advice from southerners to abandon black voters as a lost constituency. As early as the summer of 1959, John Temple Graves, a syndicated columnist who was read in every southern state, wrote Nixon that rather than keep trying to capture the African-American vote, he should instead try to lure southern Democrats (meaning white Democrats) into the Republican Party. In the spring of 1960, Graves wrote Nixon again: "The South is the wave of your future since you'll never win the Negro or labor votes." Nixon thanked the columnist for his favorable columns about him.[52]

Graves was not the only one making such recommendations. W. N. Ethridge, an attorney in Oxford, Mississippi, wrote Nixon in early January 1961 to say that the recent campaign had turned Mississippi into a two-party state. Republicans had to stop "trying to reduce the Southern white man and woman to the second class citizenship the negroes admit they rate, and encourage the conservative white South to join with them in maintaining a sound economy and Nation. If the Republican Party and the Democrat Party continues to woo the negroes, jews, catholics and labor unionists and down grade the other segments of the U. S. population, it won't be long before there is a third party in the North and South."[53]

Nixon ignored this advice. But the belief that there was a massive shift of black voters to Kennedy prevailed in both parties. Many of those who later wrote on African-American participation in the election failed to recognize the obvious. In presidential elections from 1936 through 1956, blacks had voted approximately two-thirds Democratic and one-third Republican, and they did so again in 1960. The claim that Kennedy swung the election with his telephone call to Coretta King following Martin Luther King's arrest cannot be supported by a demographic analysis of the results. The overwhelming movement of black voters to the Democratic Party did not begin until 1964.

Until now, the presidential election of 1960 has been told from the winner's perspective. Kennedy was more charismatic; he outshone Nixon in the debates; he struck an important blow for religious toleration, and he made a telephone call to Coretta King that brought an outpouring of African-American votes. The weaknesses that led him to underperform relative both to his party's registration advantage and to candidates down the ballot—such as his mediocre legislative record, conflicting campaign positions, and lack of qualifications—have all been minimized. The charges of fraud are trivialized, as is the role of his father's money in getting him the presidency. Minimized as well is the fact that, with the complicity of the press, Kennedy lied about his health and his sexual escapades. Contemporary reporters and many of those who wrote about the race afterward rationalized that even with these weaknesses, Kennedy was far preferable to Nixon.

For Theodore White, Nixon made a convenient villain, and others readily embraced that proposition. But those who insist on seeing Nixon only as a dark and devious character intent on exploiting the worst impulses of the American people overlook the fact that he ran by far the more honorable, and honest, campaign.

In finishing essentially even with Kennedy in the popular vote, he overcame his party's overwhelming minority status. He refused to appeal to anti-Catholic bigotry, and even though he believed he lost through fraud, he accepted the results rather than create a constitutional crisis.

Kennedy and Nixon ran one of the closest elections in American history. While JFK had an enormous margin in Democratic registration, the vote for each was almost identical. Kennedy appeared before enthusiastic crowds, but so did Nixon. Many argued that JFK ran a masterful campaign and criticized Nixon for pledging to visit all fifty states, a pledge he fulfilled. They overlook the fact that JFK visited forty-five states. Kennedy and his partisans held that anti-Catholicism stopped him from winning by a landslide, but ignore the fact that the only significant change in the voting pattern was that Kennedy received 29 percent more Catholic votes than Eisenhower did in his 1956 landslide.

How did such a close election engender the presumption that one candidate was the hero and the other a villain?

Kennedy's assassination turned him into a martyr and for a time made any realistic assessment of his career seem uncharitable and beside the point. The only existing biography of him published before that tragic event was by the committed Democrat James MacGregor Burns, who had changed his narrative after receiving complaints from Kennedy and Sorensen. Theodore White's *The Making of the President 1960*, already hugely influential, became preserved in amber as the definitive account of the election. After the president's death, Theodore Sorensen, Kennedy's alter ego, spent the rest of his life popularizing the perception of his boss's greatness. Others in the administration, like Pierre Salinger and Arthur Schlesinger, Jr., followed a similar course. Friends like Paul Fay, Kenny O'Donnell, and David Powers wrote memoirs eulogizing the president. Ben Bradlee, Joseph Alsop, James Reston, and other reporters who had depicted Kennedy in a flattering light during his lifetime continued to do so. That is understandable. They were staying true to what they had already written. Even had they wanted to present more balanced accounts, doing so would have courted outrage from admirers of the fallen president who defined an era.

Current historians, however, have no excuse for distorting or falsifying facts, yet they continue to do so. Jeffrey Frank's *Ike and Dick*, which purports to be a "portrait of a strange political marriage" that had nothing strange about it, asserts that Eisenhower was ambivalent about whether he wanted Nixon to win the election. The president in fact desperately wanted his vice president to carry out his legacy. Robert Dallek and Randall Woods devote much attention to the corruption that occurred during Lyndon Johnson's first two senatorial races but ignore the issue in his race for the vice presidency. Thomas Carty and Shaun

Casey hold, with little support other than the opinions of partisans, that Kennedy's Catholicism cost him votes, yet both campaigns' behavior as well as a demographic analysis of the vote show that just the opposite occurred.

The few historians, like Ed Kallina and Bill Rorabaugh, who have tried to correct parts of the record have generally been ignored.

The youngest people who were eligible to vote in 1960 are now in their eighties. Nearly all of the significant players in that election — the candidates and their wives, the journalists who wrote about them, the senators, congressmen and -women, party leaders, local officials, businesspeople, union leaders, priests and pastors, activists and volunteers — have passed from the scene. The time has come to remove partisan blinders and to understand Nixon and Kennedy, two complex, driven, powerfully ambitious men, on the basis of what they actually said and did.

ABBREVIATIONS

AC	*Atlanta Constitution*
ADW	*Atlanta Daily Worker*
AS	*Austin Statesman*
B	Box
BAA	*Baltimore Afro-American*
BG	*Boston Globe*
CCP	*Cleveland Call and Post*
CD	*Chicago Defender*
CDN	*Chicago Daily News*
COHP	Columbia Oral History Project
CSF	California State College [now University] Fullerton
CST	*Chicago Sun-Times*
CT	*Chicago Tribune*
DDE	Dwight D. Eisenhower
DDEL	Dwight D. Eisenhower Presidential Library
DDEP	Dwight D. Eisenhower Papers
DMN	*Dallas Morning News*
DNC	Democratic National Committee
DTH	*Dallas Times Herald*
ER	Eleanor Roosevelt
ERP	Eleanor Roosevelt Papers
F	Folder
FBI	Federal Bureau of Investigation
FG	Frank Gannon Interviews
GOP	Grand Old Party

GPO	Government Printing Office
HC	*Houston Chronicle*
HEW	Department of Health, Education and Welfare
HL	Henry Cabot Lodge, Jr., Papers
HP	*Houston Post*
HSTL	Harry S. Truman Presidential Library
HUAC	House Committee on Un-American Activities
JFK	John F. Kennedy
JFKI	U.S. Senate, *Speeches of JFK*
JFKL	John F. Kennedy Presidential Library
JFKRN	U.S. Senate, *Joint Appearances of JFK and RN*
JG	*Journal and Guide*
LAS	*Los Angeles Sentinel*
LAT	*Los Angeles Times*
LBJL	Lyndon B. Johnson Presidential Library
NAACP	National Association for the Advancement of Colored People
NYAN	*New York Amsterdam News*
NYHT	*New York Herald Tribune*
NYP	*New York Post*
NYT	*New York Times*
OAS	Organization of American States
OH	Oral History
P	Part
PAES	Johnson, *Papers of AES*
PC	*Pittsburgh Courier*
PN	Pat Nixon
PPA	Public Papers and Addresses of Presidents: DDE
PRC	People's Republic of China
R	Reel
RN	Richard Nixon
RNI	U.S. Senate, *Speeches of RN*
RNC	Republican National Committee
RNL	Richard M. Nixon Presidential Library
SAST	*San Angelo Standard-Times*
SHO	Senate Historical Office
TO	*Texas Observer*
USNWR	*U.S. News and World Report*
WP	*Washington Post*

Notes

PREFACE

1. United States Constitution, Article 1, Section 3; calendar, Jan. 3, PPS212(1961).1, *NYT*, Jan. 3, 1961; PPS336(1961).21 and 22, *LAT*, Jan. 6, 1961; B 333, Henry, B, Series 320, *WP*, Jan. 3–4, 1961; *NYT*, Jan. 3–4, 1961.

2. Constitution, Article II, Section 1; PPS336(1961).21 and 22, 20th Amendment to the Constitution.

3. Calendar, Jan. 6, 1961, PPS212(1961).5, RNL; DDEP XXI, p. 2236; *NYT* and *WP*, Jan. 7, 1961; Peirce and Longley, *People's President*, 72–73.

4. Bryce Harlow—I—63 and —II—15, Reedy—III—57, and Clifford—I—17, LBJL OH Collection; Dulaney and Phillips, "*Speak, Mister Speaker*," 253–254, 406, 417; DDEP XXI, p. 2236; Douglas, *Court Years*, 353.

5. Davis, *Breckinridge*, 228–258; Klotter, *Breckinridges*, 118.

6. *U.S. Congressional Record*, Vol. 107, P 1, p. 291; *WP* and *NYT*, Jan. 7, 1961; Peirce and Longley, *People's President*, 72–73.

7. RN, *Six Crises*, 415.

8. RN remarks, Jan. 6, 1961, B 150, F 3, Series 207, RNL; *U.S. Congressional Record*, Vol. 107, P 1, p. 291; *NYT*, Jan. 7, 1961; *WP*, Jan. 7, 9, 1961.

9. Alger to RN, Jan. 11, 1961, B 26, Alger, B, Series 320, RNL; *U.S. Congressional Record*, Vol. 107, P 1, pp. 278–279, 284; *Time*, Jan. 13, 1961; RN, *Six Crises*, 416.

10. Miller, "Making of White's *Making*," 389–390; Brands, "Burying Theodore White," 364–367.

11. White, *In Search of History*, 209–211.

12. White Biography, White mss. (Harvard); Miller, "Making of White's *Making*," 391–392.

13. *NYT Book Review*, July 9, 1961; White, *Making of the President*, p. ix.

14. Nielsen Pubtrack, Adoption Report, July 25, 2016.

15. White, *In Search of History*, 453–454, 457–470; Thompson, *White at Large*, 20–22;

Jacqueline Kennedy worked energetically to keep her husband's positive image intact. Hogan, *Afterlife of John Fitzgerald Kennedy*, passim.

16. *NY Post*, Feb. 11, 1962; B 813, White, Te, Series 320, RNL.

17. Hoffmann, *White and Journalism as Illusion*, 107–136, 145–175.

18. White, *Making of the President*, 104.

19. Goldwater, *With No Apologies*, 105–107; see chapter 5 for the West Virginia primary.

20. White, *Making of the President*, 65, 300; White, *In Search of History*, 454.

21. White, "Gentlemen from California," 41, 47.

22. Memo to RN, undated (probably Jan. 1956), B 162, *Collier's* and Memo, Jan. 23, 1956, B 813, White, Te, Series 320, RNL.

23. White to RN, Nov. 25, 1960, B 813, White, Te, Series 320, RNL; Lungren and Lungren, *Healing Richard Nixon*, 64–65.

24. White to RN, Nov. 25, White to Klein, Nov. 25, Klein to White, Nov. 29, 1960, B 813, White, Te, Series 320, RNL.

25. Lasky to Editor, Oct. 11, 1961, B 813, White, Te, Series 320, RNL; White, *Making of the President*, 178.

26. Woods to Potter, Oct. 19, 1958, B 606, Potter, P, Series 320, RNL; White, *Making of the President*, 333–334, 338; Klein, *Making It Perfectly Clear*, 85, 86, 93, 98; Lawrence, *Six Presidents, Too Many Wars*, 239; Bradlee, *Conversations with Kennedy*, 18–20; Baker, *Good Times*, 317, 324, 325; Roberts, *First Rough Draft*, 180–181; Donaldson, *First Modern Campaign*, 141–143.

27. White, *Making of the President*, 336–337.

28. Bradlee, *Conversations with Kennedy*, 9–12, 18, 22.

29. Woods to Potter, Oct. 19, 1958, B 606, Potter, P, Series 320, RNL; Baker, *Good Times*, 324–325; RN, *Six Crises*, 396–397.

30. RN to Lasky, Aug. 24, 1961, B 440, Lasky (1 of 3), Series 320, memo by RN, Sept. 12, 1961, Wilderness Years, Series VIII, B 5, PPS257, RNL; Henggeler, *Kennedy Persuasion*, 78–79.

31. RN, *Six Crises*, 323–324, 337–342, 344–347, 351–352, 356–357, 418.

32. Ibid., 327–328, 365, 367–368, 419.

33. Ibid., 310, 362–363, 411–413.

34. Ibid., 353.

35. Ibid., 406; Bradlee, *Conversations with Kennedy*, 74; Reeves, *Question of Character*, 189–190.

36. See Stebenne, "Who Really Won the 1960 Election?"

37. Gizzi, "Historian Dallek Maligned Nixon's Campaign," 7; Dallek, *Camelot's Court*, 2.

38. Email, Martinez (Nixon Archives) to Gellman, Aug. 19, 2016, Gellman mss.

39. Rorabaugh, "Moral Character, Policy Effectiveness, and the Presidency," 448.

40. Belafonte, *My Song*, 219.

41. Kendrick and Kendrick, *Nine Days*, 209–224; Louis Martin OH, #1, #2 and #3, JFKL.

1. JACK AND DICK

1. Day 1, Tape 5, 00:38:27 [RN], FG; Warne OH, 113, HSTL; Brands, *American Dreams*, 162; Felknor, *Dirty Politics*, 77–78; Arnold, *Back when It All Began*, 1–3; Gellman, *Contender*, 25–60.

2. Hamilton, *JFK*, 674, 863.

3. O'Neill, *Rogues and Redeemers*, 128.

4. O'Brien, *John F. Kennedy*, 189–206; Nasaw, *Patriarch*, 593–604; O'Donnell and Powers, "*Johnny, We Hardly Knew Ye*," vii–ix, 43–71; Smith, *Nine of Us*, 222–223; Hamilton, *JFK*, 737–797; Lasky, *J.F.K.*, 91–98; Parmet, *Jack*, 135–164; Burns, *John Kennedy*, 57–70; Blair and Blair, *Search for JFK*, 476.

5. Sutton OH, 7, JFKL; Matthews, *Kennedy and Nixon*, 45.

6. Day 8, Tape 1, 00:29:19 [RN], FG; Gellman, *Contender*, 97.

7. RN to Jackie, Nov. 23, 1963, PPS320.106.119(2) and Graham to RN, Sept. 9, 1957, B 299, Graham (3 of 3), Series 320, RN to Parmet, Dec. 10, 1986, RNL; Day 1, Tape 5, 00:50:32 [RN], Day 8, Tape 1, 00:33:10 [RN], Day 8, Tape 1, 00:33:30 [RN], Day 8, Tape 1, 00:36:18 [RN], Day 8, Tape 1, 00:29:19 [RN], FG mss.; Smathers OH, 23, SHO; Smathers OH, Interview #6, p. 4 and Sutton OH, 4, JFKL; interview with Dorothy Donnelly, Sept. 6, 2001; JFK Foundation, *Listening In*, 38; Gellman, *Contender*, 97; Arnold, *Back when It All Began*, 6.

8. Parmet, *Jack*, 174–195; Burns, *John Kennedy*, 71–97; Lasky, *J.F.K.*, 99–128; Shaw, *JFK in the Senate*, 15–27; Nasaw, *Patriarch*, 638–655; Sorensen, "*Let the Word Go Forth*," 80, 146, 330; Reeves, *Question of Character*, 91–92.

9. Hardeman and Bacon, *Rayburn*, 434; Dulaney and Phillips, "*Speak, Mister Speaker*," 299; Hébert, *Last of the Titans*, 257; Trohan, *Political Animals*, 327; Galbraith, *Life in Our Times*, 373; Elliott and D'Orso, *Cost of Courage*, 129–130.

10. RN to Daletto, May 31, 1960, PPS320.106.53 and memoirs, March 22, 1976, RNL; Day 8, Tape 1, 00:29:19 [RN], FG; Gellman, *Contender*, 105.

11. Day 1, Tape 5, 00:51:39 [RN] and Day 8, Tape 1, 00:30:48 [RN], FG; JFK Foundation, *Listening In*, 48; Matthews, *Kennedy and Nixon*, 51–52; Gellman, *Contender*, 102–103.

12. Day 1, Tape 5, 00:51:39 [RN] and Day 8, Tape 1, 00:30:48 [RN], FG; Gellman, *Contender*, 43.

13. Woods to RN, May 3, 1960, PPS320.106.47A, RNL; Day 8, Tape 1, 00:36:34 [RN], FG; Arnold, *Back when It All Began*, 6; Matthews, *Kennedy and Nixon*, 70; Gellman, *Contender*, 306–307.

14. Gellman, *Contender*, 253–343; RN, *RN*, 71–78.

15. *NY Post*, Oct. 3, 1952, PPS6.284, RNL; Warne OH, 113, HSTL; Douglas OH, 12, 25, E. Roosevelt; Douglas OH, Tape 2, p. 7, LBJL; Arnold, *Back when It All Began*, 11; Felknor, *Dirty Politics*, 78–81; Felknor, *Political Mischief*, 130–132; Edwards, *Pulling No Punches*, 132, 150; Gellman, *President and Apprentice*, 368.

16. Logevall, *JFK*, 477; Lepore, *If Then*, 39.

17. Day 8, Tape 1, 00:37:28 [RN], FG; Mallan, "Massachusetts," 10–11; Dallek, *Unfinished Life*, 162–163; Matthews, *Kennedy and Nixon*, 74; Gellman, *Contender*, 75.

18. O'Donnell and Powers, *"Johnny, We Hardly Knew Ye,"* 77–105; O'Brien, *No Final Victories*, 5–37; O'Donnell, *Irish Brotherhood*, 57–85; Tye, *Bobby Kennedy*, 95–101.

19. Whalen, *Kennedy versus Lodge*, 34–142, 154, 163–165; O'Brien, *John F. Kennedy*, 238–259; Lasky, *J.F.K.*, 102–103; Shaw, *JFK in the Senate*, 29–46; Nasaw, *Patriarch*, 652–670; Tye, *Bobby Kennedy*, 87–91; Nelson, *John William McCormack*, 456–476, 511.

20. Haynes, Klehr, and Vassiliev, *Spies*, 1–31.

21. Gellman, *Contender*, 84, 455–456.

22. Gellman, *President and Apprentice*, 29–54.

23. JFK to RN, early Aug, PPS320.106.1 and RN to JFK, Aug. 9, 1952, PPS320.106.2, RNL; Day 8, Tape 1, 00:42:45, FG.

24. Memoir, March 22, 1976, RNL; Matthews, *Kennedy and Nixon*, 89.

25. Interview with Evarts, Sept. 6, 2001; interview with Walton, Sept. 10, 2001; interview with Hughes, July 8, 2003; Crispell, *Testing the Limits*, 226; Matthews, *Kennedy and Nixon*, 90–91; Lincoln, *My Twelve Years with John F. Kennedy*, 52, 56; Sorensen, *Counselor*, 55, 102; June 13, 1983, Part I, 00:28:20 [RN], FG.

26. Memoirs, March 22, 1976, diary, April 29, PPS212(1953).1, Beale to PN, April 30, PPS267.90, diary, May 29, PPS212(1953),1, RN to Whitaker, Dec. 31, 195, JFK to RN, Feb. 4, PPS320.106.5, calendar, July 13, 1954, RNL.

27. Memoirs, March 22, 1976, diary, April 29, PPS212(1953).1, Beale to PN, April 30, PPS267.90, diary, May 29, PPS212(1953).1, RN to Whitaker, Dec. 31, 1953, PPS267.90, diary, May 29, PPS212(1953).1, RN to Whitaker, Dec. 31, 1953, RNL. JFK to RN, Feb. 4, PPS320.106.5, calendar, July 13, 1954, RN to Jackie, Nov. 23, 1963, PPS320.106.119(2), RNL; Day 8, Tape 1, 00:33:30 [RN], FG.

28. RN to Jackie, Aug. 5, PPS320,106.15. Jackie to RN, Aug. 23, PPS320.106.1B, RN to JFK, Nov. 29, 1957, PPS320.106.20, Jackie to RN, Jan. 8, 1958, PPS320.106.24, RNL; Beschloss, *Jacqueline Kennedy: Historic Conversations*, 76; email, Scott to Gellman, Aug. 3, 2017, Gellman mss.

29. Kesaris, *Presidential Campaigns: JFK*, P II, Speeches, April 15, 24, 27, Dec. 2, 17, 1953, April 30, May 11, June 5, 1954, R 1; Nov. 17, 22, 1955, Jan. 26, Feb. 16, March 17, 1956, R 2; Sorensen, *"Let the Word Go Forth,"* 38–43, 81–83, 91–94, 370–373; JFK, *Strategy of Peace*, 87–91; Shaw, *JFK in the Senate*, 47–116.

30. *JFKI*, pp. 1001–1005; appointment calendar, June 3, 1953, PPS212(1953).2.297 and *Arizona Daily Star*, April 21, telephone logs, Aug. 18, 1954, PPS212(1954).4 (v.5), RNL; JFK Foundation, *Listening In*, 235–236; *NYT*, April 4, 11, 1954.

31. Smathers OH, 71, 80, SHO; Schmidt, *Margaret Chase Smith*, 289; Saltonstall, *Salty*, 183–185.

32. Shaw, *JFK in the Senate*, 192–193; Beschloss, *Jacqueline Kennedy: Historic Conversations*, 28–29.

33. J. Kennedy to RN, Dec. 5, 1954, PPS320.106.6, RNL; Sorensen, *Kennedy*, 55; Matthews, *Kennedy and Nixon*, 100–101.

34. RN to JFK, Feb. 5, 1955, PPS320.106.7, RNL; Goodwin, *Fitzgeralds and Kennedys*, 776; Matthews, *Kennedy and Nixon*, 101.

35. RN to JFK, Jan. 11, PPS320.106.10 and RN to Thomas, Jan. 17, 1956, PPS320.106.11,

RNyl; Parmet, *Jack*, 312–333; Matthews, *Kennedy and Nixon*, 106; Beschloss, *Jacqueline Kennedy: Historic Conversations*, 59–62.

36. Day 8, Tape 3, 00:22:53 [RN], FG.

37. Telephone logs, Feb. 24, PPS212(1954).4.68 and March 3, 1954, PPS212(1954).4.78 and diary April 20, 1955, PPS212(1955).2 and Woods to Novello, March 15, 1959, B 405, Kennedy, R, Series 320, RNL; Day 8, Tape 3, 00:17:07 [RN], FG.

38. Day 8, Tape 3, 00:17:07 [RN], FG.

39. Memoirs, March 15, 1976, RNL; Saltonstall, *Salty*, 212.

40. M. Eisenhower to Roorda, July 19, 1983, Gellman mss.; Gellman, *President and Apprentice*, 232–258.

41. Gellman, *President and Apprentice*, 240–258.

42. RN, *RN*, 163.

43. Memoirs, March 14–16, 1976, RNL; RN, *RN*, 166; Swift, *Pat and Dick*, 134–135.

44. Gellman, *President and Apprentice*, chapter 18.

45. De Toledano, *Notes from the Underground*, 216, 236, 238; Gellman, *President and Apprentice*, 285–313.

46. Memoirs, March 17, 1976, RNL; Hillings, *Irrepressible Irishman*, 71–75; Gellman, *President and Apprentice*, 314–330.

47. *JFKI*, pp. 431–432, 437–438, 450–453, 570–571.

48. *JFKI*, p. 1024; Oliphant and Wilkie, *Road to Camelot*, 35–52.

49. JFK Foundation, *Listening In*, 35; Lasky, *J.F.K.*, 587–598; O'Donnell and Powers, *"Johnny, We Hardly Knew Ye,"* 116–126; O'Brien, *John F. Kennedy*, 310–313; Nasaw, *Patriarch*, 701; Martin, *Ballots and Bandwagons*, 373–455.

50. *Face the Nation*, July 1, 1956, PPS320.106.13, RNL.

51. Smith, *Hostage to Fortune*, 673–675.

52. Ibid., 676–677; Nasaw, *Patriarch*, 701–705; Parmet, *Jack*, 334–335.

53. Parmet, *Jack*, 344–346; O'Brien, *John F. Kennedy*, 304–310; Sorensen, *Counselor*, 169–170; Nelson, *John William McCormack*, 519–522; Beschloss, *Jacqueline Kennedy: Historic Conversations*, 6–14, 30.

54. Sorensen, *"Let the Word Go Forth,"* 83–86; Parmet, *Jack*, 356–357; Sorensen, *Counselor*, 171.

55. Sorensen, *"Let the Word Go Forth,"* 87; Smathers OH, Interview #4, pp. 5–8, JFKL; Schlesinger, *Robert Kennedy and His Times*, 130–132; Sorensen, *Counselor*, 171; Nelson, *John William McCormack*, 522–527; Martin and Plaut, *Front Runner, Dark Horse*, 17–108.

56. Martin and Plaut, *Front Runner, Dark Horse*, 106.

57. JFK Foundation, *Listening In*, 34–36; Smith, *Nine of Us*, 226–227; Schlesinger, *Robert Kennedy and His Times*, 130–132; Nasaw, *Patriarch*, 706–708; O'Brien, *John F. Kennedy*, 318–319; Beschloss, *Jacqueline Kennedy: Historic Conversations*, 33–34; memoirs, March 22, 1976, RNL; Day 8, Tape 1, 00:41:03 [RN], FG.

58. Schlesinger, *Letters*, 136.

59. Smathers OH, Interview III, p. 8f and Interview #4, p. 9, JFKL; Parmet, *Jack*, 382–383; O'Brien, *John F. Kennedy*, 322–324; Reeves, *Question of Character*, 138; Lincoln, *My Twelve Years with John F. Kennedy*, 85.

60. DeLoach memo, April 19, 1960, JFK File, No. 96, Sec 1, JEH O & C, FBI; Lang to Gellman, email, Jan. 13, 2017, Gellman mss.; NYT, Nov. 6, 1959, April 5, Sept. 11, and Nov. 21, 1962, Aug. 1, 1963, July 16, 1969.

61. Kesaris, *Presidential Elections JFK*, P II, R 2, Speeches, Sept. 21, Oct. 3, 4, 15, 19, and Nov. 2, 1956; Sorensen, *Counselor*, 100, 169–179; O'Brien, *John F. Kennedy*, 324–325.

62. Interview, Dec. 7, 1966, Kennedy, R., B 1, F 37, J. B. Martin mss.; O'Donnell, *Irish Brotherhood*, 149–172; Schlesinger, *Robert Kennedy and His Times*, 133–136; Thomas, *Robert Kennedy*, 73–74; Lasky, *Robert F. Kennedy*, 96–100; Oliphant and Wilkie, *Road to Camelot*, 53–61.

63. Gellman, *President and Apprentice*, 331–359.

64. O'Donnell, *Irish Brotherhood*, 149–172; Schlesinger, *Robert Kennedy and His Times*, 132–133; Martin and Plaut, *Front Runner, Dark Horse*, 197.

2. TEAM KENNEDY

1. Smith, *Nine of Us*, 1–2 and 227; Kennedy, *True Compass*, 116; Sorensen, *Kennedy Legacy*, 45.

2. Memo by McWhorter, Jan. 20, PPS320.104.24 and Wyatt to Finch, Sept. 23, 1959, B 119, F 1, Series 207, RNL; *Newsweek*, July 27, p. 23 and Dec. 7, 1959, p. 34.

3. J. Alsop to Lawrence, Aug. 3, 1959, B 15, Aug. 1959, Alsop mss.; NYT, Oct. 24, 1957; *Newsweek*, Jan. 26, 1957, p. 26; *Time*, Nov. 9, 1959; Olson, *Stuart Symington*, 316–354; Clifford, *Counsel to the President*, 312–314; McFarland, *Cold War Strategist*, 77–96; Barrett, *CIA and Congress*, 301–313.

4. Quotations, Caro, *Path to Power*, xx, xx–xxii, 718–740; Caro, *Means of Ascent*, 303–317, 385–402; Caro, *Master of the Senate*, 115–116; Dugger, *Politician*, 233–236, 322–341; Reston, *Lone Star*, 139–155.

5. Wunderlin, *Taft*, Vol. 4, p. 490; Smathers OH, pp. 45–46, SHO; Price Daniel OH—I—LBJL; Caro, *Master of the Senate*, 485; Woods, *LBJ*, 253–265.

6. RN excerpts, June 11, 1955, B 32, F 4 [2 of 2], Series 207, RN; *PAES*, IV, p. 364; NYT, May 7, 1954; Gibbons, *U.S. Government and the Vietnam War*, 222–225; Reedy OH, 3–5, LBJL; Dallek, *Lone Star Rising*, 426–464 and 467–478; Woods, *LBJ*, 268–272; Caro, *Master of the Senate*, 557.

7. Shesol, *Mutual Contempt*, 41–60.

8. LBJ to Alsop, Aug. 27, 1956, B 13, F Aug. 1956, Alsop mss.; Reedy OH—IX—25, 37 and 40, Donnerly OH, 1–2, Knowland OH—I—28, LBJL; Unger and Unger, *LBJ*, 181–192; Woods, *LBJ*, 291–310; Dallek, *Lone Star Rising*, 467–496; Caro, *Master of the Senate*, 619–629; Baker OH, 81, SHO; Beschloss, *Reaching for Glory*, 441; Reedy, *U.S. Senate*, 28.

9. J. Alsop to LBJ, March 18 and LBJ to J. Alsop, March 21, 1958, B 14, Jan–March 1958, Alsop mss.; memo, March 26, 1958, B 364, Hutchenson, Series 320, RN; Clifford OH—Interview I—15, LBJL; Gellman, *President and Apprentice*, 379–401; Reston, *Sketches in the Sand*, 379–381.

10. J. Alsop to Rowe, Aug. 11, 1959, B 15, Aug. 1959, Alsop mss.; *Newsweek*, Sept. 28, p. 31, Dec. 14, 1959; *Time*, Nov. 16, Dec. 21, 1959.

11. *Newsweek*, Aug. 10, 31, Nov. 16, 1959; *Time*, Nov. 2, Dec. 14, 1959; *PAES*, VII, pp. 306, 318, 320, 344–345, 348–349, 369–370, 373, 380, quotation 381; Schlesinger, *Journals*, 58–59.

12. *PAES*, VII, p. 306, quotations 343, 344.

13. Ibid., VII, Nov. 5, 1958, p. 350, quotation 351.

14. Henry, *Eleanor Roosevelt and Adlai Stevenson*, 3–29, 34–179; Sorensen, *Counselor*, 168; Schlesinger, *Letters*, 156.

15. Black et al., *Eleanor Roosevelt, John Kennedy, and the Election*, excerpt, March 8, CBS, March 30, Canfield to ER and Morris enclosure, April 30, ER to Canfield, May 3, JFK to ER, May 29, 1958; Schlesinger, *Letters*, 156–157; Martin and Plaut, *Front Runner, Dark Horse*, 75.

16. Black et al., *Eleanor Roosevelt, John Kennedy, and the Election*, JFK to ER, Dec. 11, ER to JFK, Dec. 18 and JFK to ER, Dec. 29, 1958, ER to JFK, Jan. 6, JFK to ER, Jan. 10 and ER to JFK, Jan. 20, 1959; Sandler, *Letters of John F. Kennedy*, 54–63; Lash, *Eleanor*, 258, 280–282, 287.

17. Black et al, *Eleanor Roosevelt, John Kennedy, and the Election*, JFK to ER, Jan. 22, ER to JFK, Jan. 29, 1959; Sandler, *Letters of John F. Kennedy*, 63–64.

18. Photograph of JFK, Jean Kennedy, and McCarthy, summer 1947, by Mimi Blankenhorn, RNL; Smathers OH, Interview #1, p. 26, JFKL; Smathers OH, 69, SHO; Heale, *McCarthy's Americans*, 210–212; Whalen, *Kennedy versus Lodge*, 140–141; Farrell, *Tip O'Neill and the Democratic Century*, 141–143; Reeves, *Life and Times of Joe McCarthy*, 442–444, 512–513; Nasaw, *Patriarch*, 667, 672–674, 685.

19. Amory OH, 5–8, JFKL.

20. Schlesinger, *Journals*, 57–58; Crosby, *God, Church, and Flag*, 193–215; O'Brien, *John F. Kennedy*, 275–279; Sorensen, *Counselor*, 152–155; O'Donnell and Powers, *"Johnny, We Hardly Knew Ye,"* 98–99, 110–112.

21. Burke OH, 18, JFKL.

22. Nasaw, *Patriarch*, passim; Smith, *Grace and Power*, 16; Smith, *Nine of Us*, 39; *Newsweek*, June 27, 1960, pp. 41–42.

23. Nasaw, *Patriarch*, 3–104; Sheldon M. Stern, "The Still Elusive Joseph P. Kennedy," History News Network, http://historynewsnetwork.org/article/155961, June 29, 2014; O'Brien, *John F. Kennedy*, 1–48; Smith, *Nine of Us*, 18; Hannaford, *Drew Pearson Diaries*, 453.

24. Hannaford, *Drew Pearson Diaries*, 453; Miller, *Plain Speaking*, 186.

25. Sorensen, *"Let the Word Go Forth,"* 88–89; Clifford, *Counsel to the President*, 310–312.

26. Sorensen, *Kennedy*, 100; Bradlee, *Good Life*, 206; Smith, *Hostage to Fortune*, 693–694; David, *Presidential Election and Transition*, 120–121.

27. *Newsweek*, June 27, 1960, p. 41; O'Donnell, *Irish Brotherhood*, 21–36; Smith, *Nine of Us*, 29–31; Martin, *It Seems Like Only Yesterday*, 173–174; Sorensen, *Counselor*, 250–251; Farrell, *Tip O'Neill and the Democratic Century*, 177; Schlesinger, *Robert Kennedy and His Times*, 3–94, 214; Thomas, *Robert Kennedy*, 29–49, 90–92; Beschloss, *Jacqueline Kennedy: Historic Conversations*, 94–95; Galbraith, *Life in Our Times*, 495.

28. RFK bio, undated, P I, R 10, JFK pre-presidential mss.; *NYT*, Sept. 11, 1959.

29. Edward Kennedy bio, undated, P I, R 10, JFK pre-presidential mss.; Clymer, *Edward M. Kennedy*, 9–24; Kennedy, *True Compass*, 17–118.

30. Novak, *Prince of Darkness*, 72–73; Sorensen, *Counselor*, 256; Clymer, *Edward M. Kennedy*, 26–28; *Newsweek*, June 27, 1960, p. 41.

31. O'Brien, *No Final Victories*, 58–59; Bohrer, *Revolution of Robert Kennedy*, 109; Schlesinger, *Robert Kennedy and His Times*, 192; White, *Making of the President*, 51.

32. Stossel, *Sarge*, 111–143, 140, 155; Kennedy, *True Compass*, 122; Tye, *Bobby Kennedy*, 95–103; Wofford, *Of Kennedys and Kings*, 44–46; "History and Future," theMART, https//www.themart.com/about/history-and-future/.

33. Lawford OH #1, pp. 2, 3, 5, 14–16, 18, 20, JFKL; Spada, *Peter Lawford*, 132–140, 159–217, 224; Sheridan, *Sinatra and the Jack Pack*, 132–133.

34. *NYT*, July 7, 1960; Sorensen, *Counselor*, 13–115, 181, 184–185, 519; *Newsweek*, June 27, 1960, p. 42; Martin and Plaut, *Front Runner, Dark Horse*, 250–258; O'Brien, *John F. Kennedy*, 260–264; Sorensen, "Counselor," *After Words*, C-SPAN 2, Book TV, May 14, 2008.

35. *WP*, Jan. 2, 1960.

36. Memo from Goodwin, May 16, memo from Feldman, June 27, 1960, P I, R 6, JFKL; O'Brien to RFK, Nov. 13, 1959, Political Files, General Subject Files, RFK mss.; *Time*, Feb. 15, p. 60; *Newsweek*, June 27, 1960, p. 42; *Philadelphia Inquirer*, March 4, 2007; *NYT*, March 3, 2007; O'Brien, *No Final Victories*, 58–62; Goodwin, *Remembering America*, 13–65.

37. Sorensen, *Counselor*, 180; Fay, *Pleasure of His Company*, 6–7; Beschloss, *Jacqueline Kennedy: Historic Conversations*, 57–58.

38. Kaufman, *Henry M. Jackson*, 64–69, 71–93, 95–105; Ognibene, *Scoop*, 114, 120; Prochau and Larsen, *A Certain Democrat*, 124–178.

39. E. Kennedy to J. Alsop, Aug. 4, 1958, B 14, Aug.–Sept. 1958, and J. Alsop to Tyreman, Feb. 20, 1959, B 15, Feb. 1959, Alsop mss.; Merry, *Taking On the World*, 341–342; Herken, *Georgetown Set*, 246; Ferrell and Coleman, "John F. Kennedy," 43.

40. *WP*, Aug. 10, 1959, P I, R 10, JFK pre-presidential mss.

41. J. Alsop to Roger, July 23, 1959, B 15, July 1959, Alsop mss.

42. Bradlee, *Good Life*, 190, 194, 204–205, 214; Herken, *Georgetown Set*, 246.

43. Novak, *Prince of Darkness*, 53.

44. Baker, *Good Times*, 311; Shuman OH, 164, SHO.

45. Sloyan, *Politics of Deception*, 2.

46. *JFKI*, pp. 486–496; Sorensen, "*Let the Word Go Forth*," 43–49; Schlesinger, *Letters*, 137–140; Shaw, *JFK in the Senate*, 141–165.

47. *JFKI*, pp. 503–504, 535–544; Baker OH and Shuman OH, Interview #3, 161 and 163, SHO; Mitchell OH—Interview I-11, LBJL; Land, "John F. Kennedy's Southern Strategy," 53; Berg, "*Ticket to Freedom*," 194–197; Sorensen, *Counselor*, 270–271; Bryant, *Bystander*, 13–207; Mayer, *Running on Race*, 11–15; O'Brien, *John F. Kennedy*, 364–374.

48. Bryant, *Bystander*, 61–79.

49. O'Brien, *John F. Kennedy*, 351–356; Filipink, *Eisenhower and American Foreign Policy*, 19.

50. Sorensen, *"Let the Word Go Forth,"* 331–337; JFK, *Strategy of Peace*, 96–111.

51. JFK, *Strategy of Peace*, 111–112; Schlesinger, *Letters*, 145–148; Martin, *Stevenson and the World*, 415.

52. JFK, *Strategy of Peace*, 113–130; O'Brien, *John F. Kennedy*, 361–363.

53. Mieczkowski, *Eisenhower's Sputnik Moment*, 11–33, 95–111; Divine, *Sputnik Challenge*, vii–viii; Dickson, *Sputnik*, 110–122; Kolodziej, *The Uncommon Defense and Congress*, 253–254; Zaloga, *Kremlin's Nuclear Sword*, 54–57.

54. JFK remarks, Oct. 18, 1957, P 2, R 5, JFK pre-presidential mss.

55. *JFKI*, pp. 705–718; JFK, *Strategy of Peace*, 60–73; Preble, *Kennedy and the Missile Gap*, 3–18, 100, 176; Aliano, *American Defense Policy*, 230–236; Roman, *Eisenhower and the Missile Gap*, 140; Preble, *"Who Ever Believed?"* 803–808; Sorensen, *Counselor*, 188–189.

56. Quotation, Kaplan, *Wizards of Armageddon*, 248; Preble, *Kennedy and the Missile Gap*, 153–155, 164.

57. Democratic dinner, May 23 and Jefferson-Jackson, June 15, II, R 3, and also see Young Democrats, Nov. 8, 1957, II, R 4, JFK pre-presidential mss.

58. JFK, *Strategy of Peace*, 142–151, 206–212, 228–231; Woman's Club, Jan. 20, II, R 5, and Israeli Independence, May 11, 1958, II, R 5, JFK pre-presidential mss.

59. Harris survey, Oct. 1958 and JFK bio, undated, II, R 1, JFK; Celeste to Finch, Aug. 5, 1960, B 139, Celeste, Series 320, RNL; Scammon, *America Votes 3*, pp. 177, 184; O'Donnell, *Irish Brotherhood*, 213–219; Lee, *Eisenhower and Landrum-Griffin*, 94; O'Brien, *John F. Kennedy*, 386–388; Kennedy, *True Compass*, 121–126; Nelson, *John William McCormack*, 535–537; Beschloss, *Jacqueline Kennedy: Historic Conversations*, 34.

60. RFK, *Enemy Within*, 6; Hilty, *Robert Kennedy*, 90; Heyman, *RFK*, 89–93, 98–101, 134; Schlesinger, *Robert Kennedy and His Times*, 115–118.

61. Baltakis, *"Agendas of Investigation,"* 131–132, 176–178, 214–215, 335–356, 362–380, 409–413, 415–417; Lee, *Eisenhower and Landrum-Griffin*, 18–73, 97–137, 160–174; Stebenne, *Arthur J. Goldberg*, 188–197; Schlesinger, *Robert Kennedy and His Times*, 137–169, 183–184; Novak, *Prince of Darkness*, 42–43; 52–54; Hilty, *Robert Kennedy*, 100–119; Sorensen, *Kennedy*, 51.

62. Lee, *Eisenhower and Landrum-Griffin*, 169; *Newsweek*, May 4, p. 25, Sept. 7, 1959, p. 31.

63. *JFKI*, p. 872, quotation p. 874; JFK, *Strategy of Peace*, 217–220.

64. Speeches, Jan. 31, Feb. 24, March 6, 7, P II, R 5, May 22, Aug. 3, P II, R 6, July 13, P II, R 1, Nov. 19, Dec. 1, 1959, P II, R 7, JFK pre-presidential mss.; JFK, *Strategy of Peace*, 169–177, 235–241.

65. RN v. JFK, Oct. 1957, R 2, California, March, Oregon, Florida, and Maryland, Aug., Ohio, Sept., and Massachusetts, Oct. 1958, R 1, JFK pre-presidential mss.; Jacobs and Shapiro, *"Issues, Candidate Image, and Priming,"* 527–537; Sorensen, *Kennedy*, 107; JFK to Harris, Jan. 8, 1958, B?, JFKL; *Newsweek*, Aug. 31, 1959, pp. 18–19.

66. Gallup, *Gallup Poll*, 3: 1588, 1590, 1597, 1601–1602, 1607, 1613, 1617, 1622–1624, 1630, 1633–1634, 1640, 1646; *Newsweek*, Nov. 9, 1959.

67. California Poll, March 16, 1959, P I, R 10, JFK pre-presidential mss.

68. Memo to Mohr, Oct. 27, 1961; *Thunderbolt*, May 1963, File No. 3, Section 3, JEH O & C, FBI mss.; Lincoln, *My Twelve Years with John F. Kennedy*, 119–120.

69. Travell to JFK, July 21, 1959, P I, R 4, JFK pre-presidential mss.

70. Giglio, "Growing Up Kennedy," 366, 369, 371–373.

71. Ibid., 377–378; Mandel, "Endocrine and Autoimmune Aspects," 351; Blair and Blair, *Search for JFK*, 569–571.

72. Burke OH, 2, 4, 6, JFKL; O'Donnell, *Irish Brotherhood*, 48–49; Salinger, *With Kennedy*, 41.

73. Beschloss, *Jacqueline Kennedy: Historic Conversations*, 15–21, quotations 21, 90–91.

74. Mandel, "Endocrine and Autoimmune Aspects," 350–351; Giglio, "Growing Up Kennedy," 375–377; Blair and Blair, *Search for JFK*, 556–567; Lundberg, "Closing the Case in *JAMA*," 1736–1738; Roueché, *Incurable Wound*, 139–145.

75. Schlesinger, *Journals*, 58.

76. Giglio, "Growing Up Kennedy," 359–366; Giglio, "Medical Afflictions of President Kennedy," 343–346.

77. Giglio, *Presidency of John F. Kennedy*, 9; Giglio, "Medical Afflictions of President Kennedy," 345; Giglio, "Growing Up Kennedy," 379–380; O'Brien, *John F. Kennedy*, 347.

78. Mandel, "Endocrine and Autoimmune Aspects," 351; email, Mandel to Gellman, July 13, 2016, Gellman mss.

79. Sandler, *Letters of John F. Kennedy*, 68–69.

3. THE UNIFIER

1. Elections, May 1957, PPS31.B 1, RNL; Gellman, *President and Apprentice*, 346.

2. Gallup, *Gallup Poll*, 2: 1584, 3: 1647.

3. Memoirs, March 20, 1976, RNL; Gellman, *President and Apprentice*, 425–426.

4. NEA Daily News, April 15, 1958, B 236, Edson, Series 320, RNL.

5. Memo, Sept. 15, B 617, Racial 1958, memo, Sept. 22, 1958, B 694, Sidwell, Cushman to Fleetwood, Jan. 2, 1959, B 546, NAACP (3 of 5), Lyle to Gandy, Oct. 19, 1960, B 694, Sidwell, Series 320, RNL; *NYT*, Sept. 11, 1958; MacKaye and MacKaye, *Mr. Sidwell's School*, 165–173; Zug, *Long Conversation*, 191–199; Jennings, "A Long March to Equality," 15–21; Jennings, "Editor's Corner," 5.

6. Hughes OH, 62–67, U.S. Air Force; Cushman OH, 42, DDEL; NEA Daily News, April 15, 1958, B 236, Edson, Series 320, RNL; *NYT*, July 17, 1957; Holeman, "Curious Quaker," 142; Hughes interview, March 24, 2014.

7. Interviews with Marje Acker and Dorothy Cox, Sept. 29, 2001; NEA *Daily News*, April 15, 1958, B 236, Edson, Series 320, RNL; Roberts OH #266, p. 671, DDEL.

8. *Orange County Register*, Jan. 4, 2001; *NYT*, Jan. 4, 2001; Lungren and Lungren, *Healing Richard Nixon*, 47–48; Klein, *Making It Perfectly Clear*, 308; Goodpaster interview, Jan. 8, 2002.

9. Jamison to Baughman, Dec. 7, PPS325A.12, Rogers to RN, Dec. 10, 1956, Aug. 22, 1957, B 652, Rogers (4 of 4), Series 320, *Parade*, March 9, 1958, B 3, PPS272, RNL; Roberts OH, #266, p. 671, DDEL; Goodpaster interview, Jan. 8, 2002; Lungren and Lungren, *Healing Richard Nixon*, 47–48; Gellman, *Contender*, 20, 205, 266.

10. Gellman, *President and Apprentice*, 372–382, 393–401, 415–417, 421–424, 478–479.

11. Ibid., 402–407.

12. Ibid., 486–489.

13. Ibid., 364–365.

14. Memo, Feb. 29, B 213, de Toledano, Alcorn to DDE, Dec. 15, 1960, B 24, Alcorn, Series 320, RNL; Bridges, "Year End Review," 9; May, "President Eisenhower," 421–422; Morgan, *Eisenhower versus "the Spenders,"* 179–180; Sundquist, *Politics and Policy*, 20–28; Gellman, *President and Apprentice*, 450–453.

15. *NYT*, Nov. 9, 1958; Gellman, *President and Apprentice*, 438–447.

16. Memoirs, Feb. 16, 1976, RNL; Gellman, *President and Apprentice*, 445.

17. *LAT*, Nov. 2, 1958, PPS42.B 2, RNL; Gellman, *President and Apprentice*, 427, 433, 435, 438, 445.

18. *PPA* 1958, pp. 827–830, 832–833.

19. DDE to Macmillan, Nov. 11, 1958, Macmillan, R 14, OF, DDEL.

20. RN to Abele, Nov. 7, B 18, Abele, H, Moley to RN, Nov. 7, 1958, B 524, Moley—Correspondence 2 of 2, Series 320, RNL; *NYT*, Nov. 5, 1958; *CT*, Nov. 11, 1958; *Newsweek*, Nov. 17, 1958, p. 29; Scott, *Come to the Party*, 159.

21. RN to Staff, Dec. 11, 1958, B 1, London, Subject: U.S., Series 384, RNL; Mazo interview with RN, Nov. 13, 1958, Gellman mss.

22. RN to Hamilton, Nov. 20, B 315, Hamilton, R, memo, Nov. 23, B 05, McWhorter, RN to Brownson, Dec. 30, B 108, Brownson, Series 320, RN to Parker, Nov. 22, 1958, B 94, F 8, Series 207, RNL; Lavine, *Smoke-Filled Rooms*, 180–187.

23. Eisenhower, *Waging Peace*, 374.

24. Goldberg, *Barry Goldwater*, 3–99.

25. *Phoenix Gazette*, Dec. 23, 1953, PPS336(1953).195 and *Rochester Times-Union*, Jan. 10, 1956, B 44, F 18, Series 207, RNL; Goldberg, *Barry Goldwater*, 109–110.

26. Goldwater, *With No Apologies*, 11, 87; Goldberg, *Barry Goldwater*, 113–115; Edwards, *Goldwater*, 82–87.

27. Memo, March 1 and radio reports, July 2, 1956, B 293, Goldwater [2/2], Series 320, RNL.

28. RN to Goldwater, May 28, B 293, Goldwater [1/2], Goldwater to RN, Oct. 21, 1957, B 79, F 8, Series 207, RN to Goldwater, Feb. 22, 1958, B 293, Goldwater [2/2], Series 320, RNL.

29. Goldwater, *With No Apologies*, 88–93; Edwards, *Goldwater*, 49–50, 89–100; Goldberg, *Barry Goldwater*, 121–132; Pulliam, *Publisher*, 195–202.

30. Goldwater to RN, Dec. 16, 1958, B 293, Goldwater [2/2], Series 320, RNL.

31. RN to Goldwater, Dec. 30, 1958, B 293, Goldwater [2/2], Series 320, RNL.

32. Gellman, *Good Neighbor Diplomacy*, 143, 148–151, 154, 164–167, 198–201, 203–206, 209, 215–216, 218–223, 225, 228; Reich, *Life of Nelson A. Rockefeller*, 493–634; Smith, *On His Own Terms*, 7–289.

33. RN to Rockefeller, March 17, 1954, B 18, F 9, Series 207, calendar, July 8, 1953, PPS212 (1953).2.392, calendar, June 5, PPS212(1954).3.156, Mrs. Rockefeller to PN, July 13, 1954, PPS269.112, calendar, Feb. 2, PPS212(1955).1, Oct. 4 and Dec. 5, PPS212(1955).2, King to Rockefeller, May 19, Rockefeller to RN, May 2, Oct. 22, Nov. 21, and Dec. 8, 1955, B 650, Rockefeller 1955, Series 320, RNL; Reich, *Life of Nelson A. Rockefeller*, 623–633.

34. Memo, Aug. 19, Rockefeller to RN, early Sept, RN to Rockefeller, Oct. 13, 1956, B 650, Rockefeller 1955, Series 320, RNL; Reich, *Life of Nelson A. Rockefeller*, 637–649.

35. RN to Rockefeller, Jan. 15, Rockefeller to RN, April 3, RN to Rockefeller, April 29 and May 2, 1957 and Rockefeller to RN, Jan. 20, 1958, B 650, Rockefeller 1955, Series 320, RNL.

36. *NYT*, Jan. 26, 1958, B 77, F 11, Series 207, RNL; Reich, *Life of Nelson A. Rockefeller*, 671–707.

37. Press release, Aug. 27, B 650, Rockefeller 1955, Reid to RN, Aug. 27, 1958, B 625, Reid (1 of 2), Series 320, RNL; telephone call, Aug. 26, 1958, R 18, Diaries DDE; *PDDE* XIX, p. 1088; Keating OH, 30–31, COHP; Reich, *Life of Nelson A. Rockefeller*, 723–726.

38. Gerhardt to RN, Nov. 13, 1958, B 286, Gerhart, EC, Series 320, RNL; *WP*, Oct. 24, PPS42.B 1, *NY Herald Tribune*, Oct. 25, PPS42.B 4, memo, Oct. 27, 1958, B 397, Katzen (1 of 2), Series 320, RNL; "Does TV Mold Candidates' Image?" March 23, 1959, pp. 84–86; Reich, *Life of Nelson A. Rockefeller*, 727–769; Smith, *On His Own Terms*, 265–291; *NYT*, Oct. 24–25, 1958; Irwin, "Money Isn't Everything," 56–57; Klein, *Making It Perfectly Clear*, 236; Roberts, *First Rough Draft*, 272; Nissenson, *Lady Upstairs*, 186–188.

39. DDEP XIX, pp. 1240–1241; Slater, *The Ike I Knew*, 186; Eisenhower, *Waging Peace*, 590.

40. BBC television, Nov. 28, B 95, F 17, Series 207, *NY Herald Tribune*, Nov. 29, 1958, B 1, London Trip, Series 386, memo, Nov. 19, 1958, B 650, Rockefeller 1955, Series 320, RNL; *NYT*, Nov. 23, 1958; *Times* (London), Nov. 24, 1958; *Newsweek*, Dec. 1, 1958, p. 20; Eisenhower, *Waging Peace*, 244, 636.

41. DDE to RN, Dec. 18, 1958, B 96, F 6, Series 207, RNL; DDEP XXI, p. 2445; *NYT*, Jan. 23, 1959; Scott, *Come to the Party*, 160.

42. Memo, March 9, 1959, R 20, Diaries DDEL.

43. Memo, May 21, 1959, PPS324.129, RNL; notes on legislative leadership meeting, May 6, 1959, R 21, Diaries DDEL; DDEP XXI, p. 2478; Scott, *Come to the Party*, 161.

44. RN remarks, June 19, B 107, F 6, *Rocky Mountain News*, June 20, 1959, B 107, F 8, Series 207, RNL.

45. Isaacson to Goldwater, Jan. 14, B 372, Isaacson, RN to Haney, Feb. 9, *Jackson Daily News*, April 17, B 293, Goldwater [1/2], *Face the Nation*, April 19, 1959, B 293, Goldwater [2/2], Series 320, RNL.

46. Rockefeller, *Memoirs*, 190.

47. *NYT*, Jan. 18, 1959; memo, Dec. 11, B 529, Moley to Finch, Dec. 29, B 524, Moley— Correspondence (2 of 2), memo, Dec. 30, 1958, B 277, Fulton, James, Morano, UPI,

Feb. 7, B 668, Sallade, memo, March 9, B 117, Bush, D, memo, April 3, 1959, B 144, Childs, memo, Feb. 26, 1960, B 824, Wilson [2/2], Series 320, memoirs, March 31, 1976, RNL; Smith, *On His Own Terms,* 292–309.

48. Grit, Feb. 1, B 4, Penn Apr.–June, Series 303, memo, Feb. 18, B 157, Clay, L, Wilson to RN, Feb. 20, B 824, Wilson [2/2], memo, Feb. 21, B 476, Markham, Har, memo, Feb. 28, 1959, B 388, Johnston, V, Series 320, RNL; *Human Events,* Dec. 15, 1958.

49. DDEP XX, p. 1553; Slater, *The Ike I Knew,* 200; *NY Herald Tribune,* July 22, 1959.

50. *NY Herald Tribune,* Aug. 2, 3, 1959; *NYT,* Aug. 2, 3, 1959.

51. *PPA* 1959, pp. 573–580, 592–593.

52. DDE to RN, Aug. 18, 1959, R 22, Diaries DDEL.

53. Memo, April 23, B 310, Haffner, memo, May 19, B 772, Underwood [2/2], *Oakland Tribune,* Nov. 9, 1959, B 52, Arthur, C (1), Series 320, RNL; meeting, May 2, B 9, F 17, Wilson to RN, Aug. 11, 1959, B 11, F 24, Klein mss.

54. Memo, June 4, B 764, Trohan, memo, Nov. 2, 1959, B 509, Memo, F, Series 320, RNL; memo, Oct. 28, 1959, B 9, F 63, Klein mss.; *Newsweek,* Nov. 16, 1959, p. 41.

55. Memo, Oct. 27, 1959, B 104, Brock, M, Series 320, RNL; *NYT,* Nov. 12, 1959; *Newsweek,* Nov. 16, 1959, pp. 33–36; *Time,* Nov. 16, 1959.

56. *NYT,* Nov. 13, 1959; *Newsweek,* Nov. 23, 1959, pp. 32–33; *Time,* Nov. 23, 1959; Smith, *On His Own Terms,* 315.

57. Washington *Daily News* (DC), May 15, 1959, B 293, Goldwater [1/2], Series 320, RNL; *NYT,* Nov. 14, 1959; *Newsweek,* Nov. 23, 1959, p. 32; Shadegg, *What Happened to Goldwater?* 241, 245.

58. Hatfield to RN, June 16, B 325, Hatfield 2 of 2, Cross to Clayton, Aug. 25, B 193, Cross, T, Series 320, Baker to Hall, Nov. 24, B 1, Wash—1960, Martin to Hancock, Nov. 25, 1959, B 1, Cal, Jan. 1960, Series 54, RNL; *NYT,* Nov. 14, 15, 1959; *Newsweek,* Nov. 23, 1959, p. 32; *Time,* Nov. 23, 1959.

59. Viehman to Finch, Dec. 3, B 6, Minn—1960 [2], Series 52, memo, Dec. 4, B 412, King (2 of 2), Regan to RN, Dec. 15, B 624, Regan [1/3], Brown to RN, Dec. 23, B 107, Brown, TF, Rockefeller statement, Dec. 26, 1959, B 650, Rockefeller 1955, Series 320, RNL; Bean to Klein, Nov. 16, B 9, F 10, memo, Dec. 18, 1959, B 9, F 63, Klein mss.; *USNWR,* Jan. 11, 1960, pp. 38–40; Lawrence, *Six Presidents, Too Many Wars,* 231; Scott, *Come to the Party,* 161–163.

60. Memos, Sept. 1, 8, 23, 28, Texas trip, Oct. 8, 9, *Dallas Times Herald,* Oct. 9, B 118, F 4, Series 207, Carlson to Finch, Oct. 29, Carlson to RN, Oct. 21, 1959, B 134, Carlson [1/2], Series 320, RNL.

61. Rockefeller statement, Dec. 26, 1959, B 650, Rockefeller 1955, Series 320, RNL; *NYT,* Dec. 27–29, 1959; *Time,* Jan. 4, 11, 1960; *Newsweek,* Jan. 4, pp. 12–13 and Jan. 11, 1959, pp. 37–40.

62. *NYT,* Dec. 28, 1959; *PPA* 1960–61, p. 23.

63. DDE to RN, Dec. 29, 1959, PPS324.133, RNL; meeting, Nov. 27, 1959, Cabinet DDEL.

64. RN statement, Dec. 26, 1959, B 650, Rockefeller 1955, Series 320, RNL; *NYT,* Dec. 28, 1959.

65. MacKinnon to RN, Dec. 28, RN to MacKinnon, Dec. 30, B 470, MacKinnon, GE,

Series 320, RN to Alcorn, Dec. 30, B 124, F 13, Series 207, RN to Annenberg, Dec. 30, 1959, PPS238.4.1, RNL.

66. Day 9, Tape 2, 00:15:48 [RN] and 00:17:08 [RN], FG.

4. THE LEAST ATTRACTIVE CANDIDATE

1. RN appearance at Oxford, Nov. 28, 1958, B 95, F 17, Series 207, RNL.
2. Humphrey to RN, June 15, 1951, B 3, F 11 (1 of 2), Series 207, *Minneapolis Star*, Sept. 22, 1954, PPS336(1954).S378, RNL; Offner, *Hubert Humphrey*, 9–151.
3. Humphrey to RN, Aug. 2, PPS320.104.1, RN to Humphrey, Aug. 9, 1955, PPS320.104.2.1, RNL.
4. RN to Humphrey, Sept. 25, 1959, PPS320.104.29, RNL; *NYT*, Nov. 12, 20, 1959.
5. Memo, Oct. 21, 1957, B 742, Symington, S, Harkness radio, Jan. 12, B 320, Harkness, R, Series 320, *LAT*, Jan. 13, 1959, B 96, F 14, Series 207, RNL; *PPA* 1959, p. 25; Gellman, *President and Apprentice*, 248–249, 488–489; Olson, *Stuart Symington*, 348–351.
6. Reedy OH, III, p. 56 and XII—p. 31, Rowe OH, VI, p. 10, Hagerty OH, I, p. 33, Case OH, I, pp. 17–18, LBJL.
7. Johnson, *Vantage Point*, 547–548.
8. Day 8, Tape 2, 00:56:17 [RN], Day 8. Tape 3, 00:48:51 [RN] and Day 9, Tape 4, 00:57:35 [RN], FG; R. Johnson OH, 9, WC; Kuchel OH, I, pp. 3–4, LBJL.
9. Day 8, Tape 3, 00:45:37 [RN], FG.
10. Diary, July 16, 1953, E. Hughes mss.; Mazo, *Richard Nixon*, 292.
11. Memo, May 1954, B 21, F 18, Series 207, RNL; memo of telephone conversation, June 28, 1954, R 2, Dulles mss.; *NYT*, May 7, 1954; Ferrell, *Diary of James Hagerty*, 55; Gibbons, *U.S. Government and the Vietnam War*, 222–225; PAES IV, p. 364.
12. *Chicago Defender*, Aug. 17, 1957, PPS337.B 3, RNL; Gellman, *President and Apprentice*, 390–392, 395–396.
13. Memo, June 25, PPS18.2490, Woods to Dargavel, June 30, PPS18.2492, memo, Aug. 16, PPPS18.2495, RN to LBJ, Sept. 27, 1954, PPS320.105.2B, RNL.
14. LBJ to RN, Oct. 5, 1954, PPS320.105.3, RNL; Reedy OH, VII, p. 41, LBJL; Caro, *Master of the Senate*, 427; Conkin, *Big Daddy from the Pedernales*, 123–124; Dallek, *Lone Star Rising*, 463–464.
15. Reedy OH, 3–5, LBJL; White, *The Professional*, 187–188.
16. RN to LBJ, Aug. 26, B 34, F 1 [1 of 2], Series 207, LBJ to RN, Aug. 30, 1955, PPS320.105.6, RNL; *NYT*, July 31, Aug. 1, 1955; Reedy OH—VIII—p. 56, LBJL; Caro, *Master of the Senate*, 628–629; Mazo, *Richard Nixon*, 260.
17. LBJ to RN, Jan. 5, PPS320.105.10, and Jan. 9, PPS320.105.11, RN to LBJ, Jan. 12, PPS320.105.12, Jamison to Baughman, Feb. 1, 1956, PPS325A.7, RNL; Caro, *Master of the Senate*, 655; Mazo, *Richard Nixon*, 260.
18. Memo, May 9, PPS320.105.14, LBJ to RN, Aug. 4, PPS320.105.16, RN to LBJ, Aug. 9, PPS320.105.17, LBJ to RN, Sept. 14, PPS320.105.22, RN to LBJ, Dec. 15, 1956, PPS320.105.24, RNL.
19. LBJ to RN, Feb. 4, PPS320.105.26, autograph, Feb. 12, 1957, PPS320.105.27, RNL;

Roger Johnson OH, 9, WC; Day 8, Tape 3, 00:48:51 [RN], Day 9, Tape 4, 00:57:35 [RN], FG.

20. LBJ to RN, Sept. 15, 1959, PPS320.105.53, RNL; Roberts, *First Rough Draft*, 273; Mazo, *Richard Nixon*, 260.

21. Mazo, *Richard Nixon*, 49.

22. RN, *Six Crises*, 306.

23. Murphy to RN, Jan. 28, 1957, B 541, Murphy, TJ, Series 320, RNL.

24. Legislative meeting, July 2, 1957, R 2, Diaries DDEL.

25. Memo, Aug. PPS320.106.16.2a, memo, Aug. 13, Treat to McWhorter, Sept. 9, 1957, B 762, Treat, Series 320, RNL.

26. News release, April 8, 1958, PPS320.106.25, RNL.

27. Memo, April 27, 1958, PPS320.106.26, RNL.

28. Memo, Sept. 22, B 334, Herter 83, Series 320, *NYT*, Nov. 1, 1958, PPS42.B 1, RNL; RN, *Six Crises*, 307.

29. Memoirs, March 22, 1976, RNL.

30. Cronin to Editor, July 6, 1959, B 447, Letters (1959), Series 320, RNL; *NYT*, June 12, 1959.

31. *NYT*, June 20, 1959.

32. *NY World-Telegram*, Aug. 16, PPS320.106.37, RN autograph, Aug. 23, 1959, PPS320 .106.38, RNL; Lincoln, *My Twelve Years with John F. Kennedy*, 124.

33. *Newsweek*, Nov. 23, 1959, pp. 33–34; Kistiakowsky, *Scientist at the White House*, 208– 210; Van Atta, *With Honor*, 45–47.

34. Roberts, *First Rough Draft*, 276.

35. *PAES* VII, pp. 299–300; Martin, *Stevenson and the World*, 444.

36. Halsey, "Beware the Tender Trap," 7–9, and letter to editor, *New Republic*, June 16, 1958, p. 23; *PAES* VII, pp. 154, 165.

37. Memo, May 8, 1958, B 557, *New Republic* [2/2], Series 320, RNL.

38. Robinson to Frankel, March 12, 1958, B 5, F 3, Frankel mss.; Arndorfer, "Nixon Protagonistes."

39. Newt to Frankel, March 19, updated but 1958, B 5, F 3, Frankel mss.

40. Blair to Frankel, June 3, 1958, B 5, F 3, Frankel mss.; *PAES* VII, pp. 380–381; Marovitz, "Steinbeck and Stevenson," 51–62.

41. Tree to Frankel, July 15, 1958, B 5, F 3, Frankel mss.; Schlesinger, *Letters*, 158–160; Seebohm, *No Regrets*, 197–240.

42. Costello, *Facts about Nixon*, xiii; memos, Nov. 26, 1958 and Jan. 22, Costello to McWhorter, Dec. 23, 1959, B 183, Costello, Series 320, RNL; Costello OH biography, LBJL.

43. Memo, Aug. 11, Costello to Pose, Dec. 16, 1959, B 183, Costello, advertisement, Jan. 11, B 557, *New Republic*, [2/2], *NYT Book Review*, Feb. 7, 1960, B 183, Costello, Series 320, RNL; *PAES* VII, p. 385; Costello, *Facts about Nixon*, xiii.

44. Costello, *Facts about Nixon*, xiii.

45. Costello to Pose, Dec. 16, Costello to McWhorter, Dec. 23, B 183, Costello, memo, Dec. 23, 1959, B 213, de Toledano, 2/3, Series 320, news summary, July 2, 3, 4, PPS69

.104, memo, Sept. 17, 1960, B 213, de Toledano-Costello, Series 320, RNL; *PAES* VII, p. 519.

46. *Washington Daily News*, Dec. 22, 1955, PPS336(1955).618, RNL; Gallup, *Gallup Poll*, Vol. 3: 1647; Lash, *Eleanor*, 243, 261; Wallace, *Between You and Me*, 40–41; Gellman, *President and Apprentice*, 60, 243, 302–303, 334, 368.

47. *St. Louis Post Dispatch*, Oct. 4, PPS6.287 and Oct. 22, PPS6.350; *NY Herald Tribune*, Oct. 7, 1952, PPS6.300, RNL; Gellman, *Contender*, 55, 106, 184–185, 196, 239–249, 260, 264, 274, 300, 356, 371.

48. NYT, Oct. 28, PPS365, *LAT*, Nov. 27, 1955, PPS299.81S.4, *LAT*, Feb. 5, B 48, F 1, Series 207, *NY Herald Tribune*, Sept. 9, PPS299.81S.4, Hall to Truman, Sept. 17, B 764, Truman, H, Series 320, *Milwaukee Journal*, Oct. 2, 1956, PPS336os(1956), RNL; *San Antonio Express*, Oct. 28, Hechler to Boss, July 12, 1956, General Correspondence, Post-Presidential, Hechler mss.; Day 3, Tape 3, 00:07:37 [RN], Day 8, Tape 1, 00:14:31 [RN] and 00:15:51 [RN], FG; Hechler OH, 79–81 and Daniel OH, 71–76, HTL; *Newsweek*, Dec. 12, 1956, p. 96; Hechler, *Working with Truman*, 276–278; Miller, *Plain Speaking*, 178, 299; Kornitzer, *The Real Nixon*, 230–232; Gellman, *President and Apprentice*, 22, 24, 37, 61, 63, 303, 334, 431; Hechler interview, Sept. 14, 2006.

49. RN to Metzger, March 13, B 764, Truman, H, Series 320, *LAT*, Oct. 10, PPS299.81S.23, *NY Herald Tribune*, Oct. 19, PPS299.81S.24, Washington *Daily News*, Oct. 24, 1958, PPS299.81S.30, RNL; Mazo interview with Nixon, 11–12, 1958, Gellman mss.; *NYT*, June 16, Sept. 10, 1957, March 18, Oct. 1, 29, 1958.

50. Gray, *Eighteen Acres under Glass*, 284; Trohan, *Political Animals*, 369; Baker, *Good Times*, 313.

51. RN to de Toledano, Oct. 1, 1957, B 213, de Toledano, 2/3, RN to Hillings, Dec. 9, 1958, B 341, Hillings [1/2], Series 320, RNL; Gellman, *Contender*, passim; Gellman, *President and Apprentice*, 216, 366–367; Gray, *Eighteen Acres under Glass*, 284; Trohan, *Political Animals*, 369.

52. RN to Frankel, Dec. 18, 1958, B 447, Letters (1958–59), Series 320, RNL.

53. Meeting, Jan. 21, 1957, B 50, Confidential Memoranda, Record Series 26/20/12, Reston mss.; *WP*, Feb. 7, B 1, Trip, Series 357, MacKinnon to RN, Oct. 19, 1955, MacKinnon, GE, memo, Jan. 2, B 320, Harkness, R, Series 320, *NYT*, April 27, B 84, F 14, Series 207, Estabrook to Humes, Oct. 21, 1958, B 801, *WP* ad, Series 320, RNL; Rabe, "Reporter in a Troubled World," 173–194; Feldstein, "Fighting Quakers," 76–85; Stacks, *Scotty*, 295–296; Block, *Herblock Special Report*, 9–52; Block, *Herblock*, 135, 153–163, 224–225, 332–333; Roberts, *First Rough Draft*, 276; Rovere, *Final Reports*, passim; Bradlee, *Good Life*, 197–198; Anderson, *Confessions of a Muckraker*, 310; Kornitzer, *The Real Nixon*, 233; RN, *Six Crises*, 397; Gellman, *President and Apprentice*, 38–39, 124, 328.

54. Donovan to RN, Nov. 12, 197, B 221, Donovan, R, Series 320, RNL; memo, Oct. 22, 1957, B 1, B II, 308A, Krock mss.; Reston, *Deadline*, 129–131; Roberts, *First Rough Draft*, 273, quotation 174; Donovan, *Boxing the Kangaroo*, 58.

5. NOT A POLITICAL TYPE

1. Sorensen, *"Let the Word Go Forth,"* 89–90.

2. *WP*, Jan. 3, 1960.

3. *Time*, Feb. 2, 1960; *Newsweek*, Feb. 22, p. 29, June 27, 1960, p. 10.

4. JFK Foundation, *Listening In*, 27–50; Ferrell and Coleman, "John F. Kennedy," 41–44; Naftali et al., *Presidential Recordings*, Vol. 1, p. xviii.

5. California poll, March 16, 1959, P I, R 10, JFKL; Gallup, *Gallup Poll*, Vol. 3: 1663; *Newsweek*, May 16, 1960, pp. 39–40.

6. Primaries in Florida, Michigan, and Indiana, Jan. 1960, R 1, JFKL.

7. *Time*, Feb. 15, 1960; *Newsweek*, June 27, 1960, p. 10.

8. *Newsweek*, Jan. 11, p. 27, June 27, 1960, pp. 40–42; *Time*, Feb. 15, 1960; Schlesinger, *Journals*, 56–57; Goodman, *Letters to Kennedy*, 1–4, 29; Parker, *John Kenneth Galbraith*, 324, 327, 332–336; Aldous, *Schlesinger*, 204–209.

9. O'Brien, *John F. Kennedy*, 401–403; Sorensen, *Counselor*, 178–179; Sawyer to Clark, June 27, 2016, Gellman mss.

10. O'Brien, *John F. Kennedy*, 404–407.

11. Ibid., 401.

12. Ibid., 410.

13. Schaffer, *Chester Bowles*, 164–173.

14. Bowles to JFK, May 18, JFK to Bowles, June 5, P 5, JFK to Bowles, Nov. 18, 1959, Bowles to JFK, Feb. 2, 11, 1960, Series 1, B 210, Kennedy, J, Bowles to Jean, Oct. 13, 1959, Feb. 29, 1960, P 5, Series 1, B 210, Joyce, J, "Some observations," Dec. 31, 1960, P 9, Series III, B 392, F 153, Bowles mss.; Schaffer, *Chester Bowles*, 174, 179–181; *Newsweek*, March 7, p. 21, June 27, 1960, p. 42; *WP*, Feb. 24, 1960.

15. *WP*, Jan. 29, Feb. 2, 22, 1960; *Time*, Jan. 11, 1960; *USNWR*, Jan. 11, pp. 21, 36, Jan. 18, p. 73, Feb. 15, 1960, p. 56; *Newsweek*, Jan. 11, p. 20, April 18, 1960, p. 21.

16. *Time*, Jan. 25, March 21, May 2, 1960; *Newsweek*, Jan. 11, pp. 13, 20, March 14, p. 32, May 9, 1960, pp. 30–33; *USNWR*, Jan. 11, p. 36, Jan. 18, pp. 73, 75, Feb. 15, 1960, pp. 53–55; Clifford, *Counsel to the President*, 303–314; Olson, *Stuart Symington*, 348–353.

17. Dulaney and Phillips, *"Speak, Mister Speaker,"* 360, 385–386; Caro, *Master of the Senate*, 154–158.

18. McLellan and Acheson, *Among Friends*, 171.

19. *WP*, Jan. 22, 1960; *Newsweek*, May 2, 1960, pp. 34–35.

20. *Honolulu Star-Bulletin*, Jan. 31, 1960, B 327, Hayes, AJ, Series 320, RNL; *PAES VII*, pp. 384–385, 436, 449–450, 460–461, 472–473, 475–476; *WP*, Jan. 12, 1960; *Newsweek*, Jan. 11, pp. 10, 24, 27–28, Feb. 29, pp. 22–23, April 25 and 30, June 6, 1960, p. 33; *USNWR*, Jan. 11, p. 36, Jan. 18, p. 75, Feb. 15, 1960, p. 55; *Time*, Jan. 25, Feb. 8, March 28, April 25, 1960.

21. *PAES VII*, pp. 386–389; Martin, *Stevenson and the World*, 472–473.

22. "My Day," April 22, May 13, 1960, ERP; Lash, *Eleanor*, 279–280, 285–296; Galbraith, *Life in Our Times*, 375–376; Sorensen, *Counselor*, 168.

23. Miller, *Plain Speaking*, 187; Miller wrote incorrectly that Truman spoke in Richmond;

it was Charlottesville. Besides the Miller volume, Schlesinger claims Truman said this; Schlesinger, *Letters*, 194. Truman does say this on his recording; Randy Sowell, Harry Truman Presidential Library archivist, telephone call, Aug. 25, 2017.

24. *NY Post*, Dec. 30, 1959; *WP*, Jan. 7, 9, 26, 31, 1960; *NYT*, Jan. 21, 1960; *Newsweek*, March 21, 160, pp. 40, 60; *USNWR*, Feb. 29, p. 81, March 21, 1960, p. 60; *Time*, Feb. 8, March 7, 1960; Sorensen, *Kennedy*, 132–133; O'Brien, *No Final Victories*, 62–63; Smith, *Nine of Us*, 225.

25. Powell to RN, Jan. 13, memo, March 7, B 607, Powell, W, Spargo to RN, March 8, 1960, B 715, Spargo, Series 320, RNL; *WP*, March 8, 1960; Sorensen, *Kennedy*, 133; O'Brien, *No Final Victories*, 64.

26. Klein to Loeb, March 15, 1960, B 458, Loeb (1 of 2), Series 320, RNL; Fact Sheet #3, P I, R 10, JFKL; Congressional Quarterly, *Guide to U.S. Elections*, Vol. 1, p. 404; *WP*, March 7, 9, 10, 1960; *USNWR*, March 21, 1960, pp. 60, 62–63; *Newsweek*, March 7, p. 28, March 21, 1960, p. 40; *Time*, March 21, 1960.

27. *NYT*, Nov. 15, 1959; Schlesinger, *Letters*, 177–178; Proxmire OH #1, pp. 1–5, JFKL; O'Donnell, *Irish Brotherhood*, 308–309.

28. *Time*, Feb. 1, 8, 1960; Dulce and Richter, *Religion and the Presidency*, 137–139.

29. Speeches, March 9, April 1, 1960, P II, R 1, and Lucey OH, 2, 32–36, 46, 49, JFKL; JFK Foundation, *Listening In*, 33; *New Republic*, Feb. 22, 1960, p. 7; *NYT*, Jan. 31, Feb. 17, 21, 1960; *WP*, Jan. 14, 20, Feb. 26, 1960; *Time*, Feb. 1, March 28, 1960; Kennedy, *True Compass*, 139; Blake, *Liking Ike*, 180; Wofford, *Of Kennedys and Kings*, 41; Martin and Plaut, *Front Runner, Dark Horse*, 210–249; Beschloss, *Jacqueline Kennedy: Historic Conversations*, 77; Schlesinger, *Robert Kennedy and His Times*, 194–197; Silvestri, "John F. Kennedy," 12–28.

30. Lucey OH, 35–40, JFKL; Thomson to RN, March 21, 1960, B 775, Thomson, V, Series 320, RNL; Silvestri, "John F. Kennedy," 44–52; *NYT*, Feb. 17, 1960; *WP*, March 15, 1960; *Newsweek*, March 28, 1960, pp. 30–31; *USNWR*, March 14, pp. 106–108; *Time*, March 21, April 4, 1960; Kennedy, *True Compass*, 140–142; Beschloss, *Jacqueline Kennedy: Historic Conversations*, 80.

31. *WP*, Jan. 30, Feb. 2, 6–8, 22, 24, March 7, 1960; *Newsweek*, Oct. 5, 1959, p. 29; *USNWR*, March 14, 1960, p. 108; *Time*, Feb. 1, 29, March 7, 21, April 4, 1960; Silvestri, "John F. Kennedy," 52–53.

32. Day 8, Tape 2, 00:37:06 [RN], FG; *Time*, March 28, 1960; Silvestri, "John F. Kennedy," 28–29.

33. Bohrer, *Revolution of Robert Kennedy*, 30–33; Schlesinger, *Robert Kennedy and His Times*, 196; Matthews, *Bobby Kennedy*, 168; *Capital Times* (Wis.), Jan. 2, 1961, File 142964-0 FBI.

34. Congressional Quarterly, *Guide to U.S. Elections*, Vol. 1, p. 404; Fact Sheet #3, P I, R 10 and Lucey OH, 22 and 43, JFKL; Silvestri, "John F. Kennedy," 40–43; *Time*, April 18, 1960; *USNWR*, April 18, 1960, pp. 41, 44–50; Lisle, "Catholic Press and Kennedy," 32–37; David, *Presidential Election and Transition*, 6; Sorensen, *Counselor*, 60.

35. *Time*, March 28, 1960.

36. Bradlee, *Conversations with Kennedy*, 26; Bradlee, *Good Life*, 207–208.

37. *Newsweek*, May 2, 1960, pp. 22, 90–92; Schlesinger, *Letters*, 195–196; Sorensen, *Counselor*, 162–163; Silvestri, "John F. Kennedy," 55–60.

38. Congressional Quarterly, *Guide to U.S. Elections*, Vol. 1, pp. 404–405; Fact Sheet #3, P I, R 10, JFKL; *USNWR*, April 25, p. 58, May 23, 1960, p. 65; *Newsweek*, May 9, p. 25, May 16, 1960, pp. 32–33; *Time*, Feb. 15, May 9, 1960; O'Brien, *No Final Victories*, 77–78.

39. Memo by Goodwin, April 18, 1960, P I, R 4, JFKL; Fleming, *Kennedy vs. Humphrey*, 15; *Time*, March 28, 1960; Bradford, "John F. Kennedy," 161–163.

40. *Newsweek*, April 18, 1960, pp. 34–35; Lisle, "Catholic Press and Kennedy," 37–42; Bradford, "John F. Kennedy," 169; McDonough OH, 1, JFKL; Bradford, "John F. Kennedy," 165; Ernst, *Primary That Made a President*, 16–17; Loughry, *Don't Buy Another Vote*, 3–27; Fleming, *Kennedy vs. Humphrey*, 5, 13.

41. *Newsweek*, April 18, pp. 34–35, May 9, 1960; *Time*, May 9, 23, 1960; Silvestri, "John F. Kennedy," 61–64; Ernst, *Primary That Made a President*, 3, 14–15, 18–19; Fleming, *Kennedy vs. Humphrey*, 52; Offner, *Hubert Humphrey*, 234; Vander Zee OH Interview #1, pp. 31, 36, SHO.

42. O'Brien, *No Final Victories*, 2; O'Donnell, *Irish Brotherhood*, 318.

43. Speech, April 30, 1960, P II, R 1, and McDonough OH, 38–64, Haught OH, 1–12, and Peters, Jr., 1–17, JFKL; *Time*, March 28, May 9, 1960; *Newsweek*, April 18, pp. 34–35, April 25, p. 30, May 2, pp. 22–23, June 27, 1960, p. 41; *USNWR*, April 25, p. 57, May 2, 1960, p. 35; O'Donnell, *Irish Brotherhood*, 319–324; Kennedy, *True Compass*, 142–145; O'Brien, *No Final Victories*, 66–75; Sorensen, *Counselor*, 160–162; Fleming, *Kennedy vs. Humphrey*, 29–50, 158–160; Ernst, *Primary That Made a President*, 7–19; David, *Presidential Election and Transition*, 7–8.

44. WP, Feb. 9, 1960; Peters, Jr. OH, 11–13, JFKL; Beschloss, *Jacqueline Kennedy: Historic Conversations*, 80; Silvestri, "John F. Kennedy," 66–94.

45. Hannaford, *Drew Pearson Diaries* 53; Schlesinger, *Letters*, 367, 371; Day 8, Tape 2. 00: 37:06 [RN], FG; Silvestri, "John F. Kennedy," 64; Fleming, *Kennedy vs. Humphrey*, 50–52; Lasky, *Robert F. Kennedy*, 133–134; Offner, *Hubert Humphrey*, 231–233.

46. Fact Sheet #3, July 8, 1960, P I, R 10, JFKL; Congressional Quarterly, *Guide to U.S. Elections*, Vol. 1, p. 405; Ernst, *Primary That Made a President*, 32; Silvestri, "John F. Kennedy," 95–110; JFK speech, May 11, 1960, P I, R 4, JFKL; *Newsweek*, May 23, 1960, p. 56; Offner, *Hubert Humphrey*, 234; Bradlee, *Conversations with Kennedy*, 28; O'Donnell, *Irish Brotherhood*, 326–328; Fleming, *Kennedy vs. Humphrey*, 59–61.

47. Humphrey, *Education of a Public Man*, 208; Kennedy, *True Compass*, 146; Day 8, Tape 2, 00:37:06 [RN]. FG.

48. Hoblitzell to McWhorter, May 20, 1960, B 345, Hoblitzell, Series 320, RNL; Fleming, *Kennedy vs. Humphrey*, 154–156; Day 8, Tape 2, 00:37:06 [RN], FG.

49. Chafin and Sherwood, *Just Good Politics*, 115–149; Fleming, *Kennedy vs. Humphrey*, 97–106; Silvestri, "John F. Kennedy," 111–118.

50. Memo, Jan. 16, 1961, 1429664-0-File 3, FBI; *Time*, June 6, 1960; Bohrer, *Revolution of Robert Kennedy*, 34.

51. Goldwater, *With No Apologies*, 101, 105–107.

52. Memo, July 13, 1960, File No. 96, Sec 1, JEH O & C, FBI mss.; Hannaford, *Drew Pearson Diaries*, 28–29; Fleming, *Kennedy vs. Humphrey*, 109–118.

53. *Newsweek*, April 18, p. 35, April 25, 1960, p. 31; *USNWR*, May 2, p. 57, May 23, 1960, p. 65; Fleming, *Kennedy vs. Humphrey*, 64–67.

54. Fact Sheet #3, July 8, 1960, P I, R 10, JFKL; Congressional Quarterly, *Guide to U.S. Elections*, Vol. 1, p. 405; *NYT*, May 12, 18, 1960; *USNWR*, May 23, 1960, p. 65; O'Brien, *No Final Victories*, 76–77.

55. Harris survey, Jan, P I, R 2, Fact Sheet #3, July 8, 1960, P I, R 10, JFKL; *NYT*, May 22, 1960; *USNWR* April 25, 1960, p. 58; *Time*, Nov. 9, 1959, May 30, 1960; Drukman, *Wayne Morse*, 335–337; Lee, *Eisenhower and Landrum-Griffin*, 158.

56. *PAES* VII, pp. 520–521; Schlesinger, *Journals*, 66–67; O'Brien, *No Final Victories*, 79–80.

57. *PAES* VII, pp. 501–503, 505; Schlesinger, *Letters*, 200; Schlesinger, *Journals*, 67–68.

58. O'Brien, *John F. Kennedy*, 407–409.

59. JFK Foundation, *Listening In*, 39–40.

60. Memo, March 3, Los Angeles office memo, March 29, SAC to director, April 1 and DeLoach to Mohr, April 19, 1960, File No. 96, Sec 1. JEH O & C, FBI mss.; Hannaford, *Drew Pearson Diaries*, 47.

61. Memo, March 3, Los Angeles office memo, March 29, SAC to director, April 1 and DeLoach to Mohr, April 19, 1960, File No. 96, Sec 1. JEH O & C, FBI mss.; Hannaford, *Drew Pearson Diaries*, 47.

62. Exner, *My Story*, 86–149.

63. *Newsweek*, May 23, 1960, p. 56; Bradlee, *Good Life*, 208; Beschloss, *Jacqueline Kennedy: Historic Conversations*, 81.

64. *Thunderbolt*, May 1963, File No. 3, Section 3, JEH O&C, FBI mss.

65. Ibid.; Hannaford, *Drew Pearson Diaries*, 53.

66. Silvestri, "John F. Kennedy," 144–164.

6. THE WHIPPERSNAPPER AND THE RIVERBOAT GAMBLER TEAM UP

1. Harris polls, North Dakota, April, North Carolina, May, South Carolina and Iowa, June 1960, R 1, JFKL; Gallup, *Gallup Poll, Vol.* 3: 1657, 1660, 1664, 1669, 1674; *USNWR*, May 9, 1960, pp. 47–49; *Newsweek*, May 9, 1960, pp. 39–40, 42.

2. *USNWR*, April 4, 1960, pp. 86–89; *NYT*, April 19, 1960; Bryant, *Bystander*, 134.

3. Belknap, May 1960, B 39, Political File, General Subject Files, RFK mss.; Bryant, *Bystander*, 127–137.

4. *PAES* VII, pp. 511–512.

5. *Time*, May 23, 1960; *NYT*, May 27, 1960; Sarantakes, "Johnson, Foreign Policy, and the Election," 156–158.

6. *PAES* VII, pp. 510–511; *Time*, May 30, 1960; *Newsweek*, July 11, 1960, p. 38. Sarantakes, "Johnson, Foreign Policy, and the Election," 154–159.

7. Sorensen, *"Let the Word Go Forth,"* 216–220; JFK, *Strategy of Peace*, v–xv; *USNWR*, June 27, 1960, pp. 64–65.

8. Memo, April 4, 1960, B I, Book II, Krock mss.; Hagerty OH – 1–3, Harlow OH – II – 13, Halleck OH, LBJL.

9. Schlesinger, *Journals*, 68.

10. Memo by Reedy, Lyndon Johnson misc., Feb. 22, 1961, White mss. Harvard; *Time*, June 13, 1960; Smathers OH, 85, SHO; Harlow OH – 13, LBJL; memoirs, March 31, 1976, RNL; Smathers OH, Interview III, pp. 13, 11G, Interview 4, p. 12, JFKL.

11. *Time*, June 6, 13, 1960; *Newsweek*, June 20, 35, June 27, 1960, p. 35; *USNWR*, Feb. 15, pp. 26, 28, June 13, pp. 48–49, June 27, 1960, pp. 88–93.

12. *PAES* VII, pp. 499–500.

13. Ibid., 505–506, 508–510, 517; *USNWR*, June 6, 1960, pp. 46–47.

14. *NYT*, June 8, 1960; *PAES* VII, p. 512.

15. *PAES* VII, pp. 513–515, 517; "My Day," June 11, 13, July 7, 1960, ERP; *Newsweek*, June 20, 1960, p. 36.

16. *PAES* VII, pp. 507, 509, 512; Schlesinger, *Letters*, 202–203.

17. *PAES* VII, pp. 519–524.

18. Schlesinger, *Letters*, 204, 207–208; Schlesinger, *Journals*, 56–57, 63–64, 67–70; Beschloss, *Jacqueline Kennedy: Historic Conversations*, 31–32, 115–116; Attwood, *Reds and the Blacks*, 6–7.

19. Olson, *Stuart Symington*, 354–357; *USNWR*, June 13, 1960, pp. 50–51.

20. *NYT*, May 14, July 1, 4, 1960; *Time*, July 11, 1960; *Newsweek*, July 11, 1960, p. 24; Sorensen, *Counselor*, 182–183; Clifford, *Counsel to the President*, 321–322; Wofford, *Of Kennedys and Kings*, 49; Sand, *Truman in Retirement*, 73; Poen, "Truman and Kennedy," 303–305; RN to Pew, July 2, 1960, B 592, Pew, JN, Series 320, RNL.

21. *NYT*, July 5, 1960; Sorensen, *"Let the Word Go Forth,"* 91–94; Wofford, *Of Kennedys and Kings*, 49–50.

22. *NYT*, July 5, 1960; *USNWR*, July 11, 1960, pp. 45, 52; *Time*, July 18, 1960; Smathers OH, Interview #4, p. 20, JFKL; Edwards, *Pulling No Punches*, 7–230; Reston, *Lone Star*, 1–192; Bradlee, *Conversations with Kennedy*, 68–69; Bradlee, *Good Life*, 206, 209; Schlesinger, *Robert Kennedy and His Times*, 205; Dallek, *Lone Star Rising*, 572–573.

23. *NYT*, July 5, 1960.

24. Travell and Cohen to JFK, June 11, 1960, R 4, P 1, JFKL.

25. *NYT*, July 5, 1960.

26. *NYT*, July 5, 6, 1960; Edwards, *Pulling No Punches*, 227–228.

27. VP Physical Examination, April 25, 1960, RNL; *NYT*, April 26, 1960; *Time*, July 18, 1960.

28. *NYT*, July 4–6, 8, 1960; Olson, *Stuart Symington*, 356.

29. *NYT*, May 3, 1973, July 17, 18, 1999; Cohen did not talk about this burglary to close colleagues Dr. Robert Boxer, interview, June 10, 2003, and Dr. Reuben Cooper, interview, June 9, 2003.

30. Travell, *Office Hours*, passim; Travell OH, 22, JFKL.

31. Cohen to JFK, Nov. 11, 1961, Series 14.1, Medical Records, Attending Physician's Records, General, B 50, Cohen to JFK, May 9, 1962, Series 14.1, Dr. Travell/Lists and Correspondence, B 45, Cohen to Burkley (#1), Addition 2005-187, Series 14.1, Medical Records, B 50, JFK Personal Papers JFKL.

32. Dallek, *Unfinished Life*, 286; Dallek, "Medical Ordeals of JFK," 50; Hughes interview, May 19, 2011; Lungren and Lungren, *Healing Richard Nixon*, 62–64.

33. Dallek, "Medical Ordeals of JFK," 49, 61.

34. Sorensen, *Counselor*, 192–193.

35. Telephone conversations with Dr. Mandel.

36. *Chicago Daily News*, July 13, 1960, B 144, Chicago Daily, RN memoirs, March 1976, Lasky to Editor, Sept. 23, 1960, B 222, Douglas, H, Series 320, RNL; Gellman, *Contender*, 306.

37. Gellman, *Contender*, 87, 92–93, 102–106; General Belknap May, B 39, Hollywood-Rand, B 34, July 1960, Political Files, General Subject Files, Pre-Administration, RFK mss.; press conference, March 25, 1960, B 649, Robinson (1 of 2), Series 320, RNL; Long, *First Class Citizenship*, 66–72, 83–84, 92–93; Robinson, *I Never Had It Made*, 137–146; Allen, *Jackie Robinson*, 206–217.

38. NY *Post*, May 23, 1960, B 649, Robinson (1 of 2), Series 320, RNL; Long, *First Class Citizenship*, 86, 106–107; NY *Post*, March 16, 1960, *Time*, April 11, 1960, p. 93; Rampersad, *Jackie Robinson*, 232.

39. NY *Post*, June 3, 10, 15, 1960; Long, *First Class Citizenship*, 95–96.

40. RN to Jackie, June 14, B 649, Robinson (2 of 2), Series 320, RN to Robinson, June 3 (probably July 3), B 139, F 20, Series 207, RNL; Long, *First Class Citizenship*, 97–101; Falkner, *Great Time Coming*, 278–280; Rampersad, *Jackie Robinson*, 343–344.

41. JFK to Robinson, July 1, 1960, B 5, F 18, Political File: Presidential Campaigns 1960, Democratic Party, Robinson mss.; Long, *First Class Citizenship*, 107–108.

42. NY *Post*, July 6, 1960; Long, *First Class Citizenship*, 107; Robinson, *I Never Had It Made*, 149; Rampersad, *Jackie Robinson*, 345.

43. Tree to Ronnie, July 11, 1960, as quoted in Seebohm, *No Regrets*, 247.

44. *PAES VII*, pp. 506, 511; Attwood, *Reds and the Blacks*, 7–8; Wofford, *Of Kennedys and Kings*, 50; O'Brien, *No Final Victories*, 81.

45. "My Day," July 12, 1960, ERP; Lash, *Eleanor*, 292.

46. *Newsweek*, July 18, 1960, p. 11; Clifford, *Counsel to the President*, 314–316; Olson, *Stuart Symington*, 356–357.

47. *Time*, July 11, 18, 1960; *Newsweek*, July 11, pp. 22–24, July 18, 1960, pp. 18–22; *USNWR*, July 11, pp. 48–50, July 18, 1960, pp. 46–48; Lawrence, *Six Presidents, Too Many Wars*, 230, 233–234; Baker, *Good Times*, 320–321.

48. *Newsweek*, July 11, 1960, p. 15; *Time*, July 11, 1960; Salinger, *With Kennedy*, 36; O'Donnell, *Irish Brotherhood*, 345–346; Bradlee, *Good Life*, 209; Schlesinger, *Thousand Days*, 33; Beschloss, *Jacqueline Kennedy: Historic Conversations*, 83.

49. Memo to DeLoach, July 26, 1960, File No. 96, Sec 1, O & C, FBI.

50. Exner, *My Story*, 162–166.

51. *Newsweek*, July 18, 1960, p. 19; O'Brien, *No Final Victories*, 80–81; Schlesinger, *Robert Kennedy and His Times*, 193; Schlesinger, *Thousand Days*, 34–35; Tillet, *Inside Politics*, 25–39.

52. *Time*, July 11, 1960; Goodman, *Letters to Kennedy*, 134; O'Donnell, *Irish Brotherhood*, 345–346; Sorensen, *Kennedy*, 154; Schlesinger, *Thousand Days*, 33–34; Stossel, *Sarge*, 149–155; Clymer, *Edward M. Kennedy*, 27–29; Schlesinger, *Journals*, 297.

53. Kaplan, *Sinatra*, 329–331; Sheridan, *Sinatra and the Jack Pack*, 152–153; Spada, *Peter Lawford*, 228; Blake, *Liking Ike*, 184–185.

54. Lindquist, *In Service to the Mouse*, 62–67.

55. Scott to JFK, June 19 and RN to Scott, June 22, 1960, B 679, Scott (4 of 6), Series 320, RNL; Long, *First Class Citizenship*, 113.

56. NYT, July 11, 12, 1960; Weber, *Don't Call Me Boss*, 364; Lee and Buchanan, "1960 Election in California," 312–313.

57. "Some observations," Dec. 31, 1960, pp. 24–27, 29–33, Part 9, Series III, B 392, F 153, Bowles mss.; "My Day," July 14, 1960, ERP; NYT, July 13, 1960; David, *Presidential Election and Transition*, 32–36, 51–56; O'Brien, *No Final Victories*, 81; Wofford, *Of Kennedys and Kings*, 51–52; Schaffer, *Chester Bowles*, 174–176.

58. David, *Presidential Election and Transition*, 96; Schlesinger, *Thousand Days*, 38.

59. Sorensen, *Kennedy*, 158–161; O'Brien, *No Final Victories*, 82–83.

60. RN to Coleman, July 6, B 162, Coleman, S, RN to Anderson, July 12, B 40, Anderson, D, RN to Choate, July 12, B 146, Choate, J, RN to Nichols, July 13, B 560, Nichols, Lo, RN to Moley, July 13, B 524, Moley—Correspondence 2 of 2, RN to Ruark, July 13, B 661, Ruark, RN to Sokolsky, July 13, 1960, B 712, Sokolsky [1 of 3], Series 320, RNL.

61. Schlesinger, *Letters*, 205; *Time*, May 23, July 4, 1960; *Newsweek*, July 4, p. 13, July 11, pp. 32–33, July 25, 1960, p. 26; Bradlee, *Conversations with Kennedy*, 30–31; Prochnau and Larsen, *A Certain Democrat*, 194; Kaufman, *Henry M. Jackson*, 120–121; Ognibene, *Scoop*, 117.

62. NYT, July 11, 15, 1960; Newsweek, July 25, 1960, pp. 21–22; Baker OH, 26–27, SHO; Clifford, *Counsel to the President*, 316–319; Olson, *Stuart Symington*, 358–360.

63. Hannaford, *Drew Pearson Diaries*, 70; Smathers OH, Interview #4, pp. 21–22, 33–34, JFKL; O'Donnell, *Irish Brotherhood*, 360–365; O'Donnell and Powers, "*Johnny, We Hardly Knew Ye*," 205–225; Shesol, *Mutual Contempt*, 25–40; Schlesinger, *Robert Kennedy and His Times*, 206–210; Thomas, *Robert Kennedy*, 96–99; Reston, *Lone Star*, 193–196; Weeks, *Texas in the 1960 Election*, 38.

64. Beschloss, *Reaching for Glory*, 441–442; Thomas, *Front Row at the White House*, 171; Douglas, *Court Years*, 353; Morris, *Price of Fame*, 519; Reedy, *Lyndon B. Johnson*, 129.

65. "Some observations," Dec. 31, 1960, Part 9, Series III, B 392, F 153, Bowles mss.; Schlesinger, *Journals*, 75–78; Reuther, *Brothers Reuther*, 438; Lichtenstein, *Most Dangerous Man in Detroit*, 355.

66. "My Day," July 16, 1960, ERP.

67. *NY Post*, July 15, 18, 1960; NYT, July 16, 1960; Long, *First Class Citizenship*, 111; Falkner, *Great Time Coming*, 277–279; Rampersad, *Jackie Robinson*, 345.

68. McLellan and Acheson, *Among Friends*, 186.

69. "New Frontier," July 15, 1960, II, R 1, JFKL; *Newsweek*, July 11, 1960; *Time*, July 25, 1960; David, *Presidential Election and Transition*, 96; Sorensen, *Kennedy*, 166; Schlesinger, *Thousand Days*, 59–60.

70. JFK's acceptance speech, July 16, 1960; memos, July 18, July 19, 1960, Finch mss.; memo, July 22, 1960, R 11, JFD mss.

71. Goodman, *Letters to Kennedy*, 10–12; Schlesinger, *Thousand Days*, 61.

72. *Newsweek*, July 11, 1960, p. 31; Case statement, July 20, 1960, B 137, Case 1/2, Series

320, memoirs, March 31, 1976, RNL; Day 8, Tape 2, 00:21:20 [RN], FG; RN, *Six Crises*, 305.

73. RN to M. Eisenhower, July 13, 1960, B 238, Eisenhower 1/2, Series 320, RNL; Gallup, *Gallup Poll*, Vol. 3: 1676.

74. RN to Percy, April 18, B 588, Percy [2/3], RN to Campbell, June 14, B 130, Campbell 1/2, RN to Sokolsky, July 13, B 712, Sokolsky [1 of 3], Series 320, News Summary, July 15, 1960, PPS69.113, RNL; RN, *Six Crises*, 309.

75. JFK speech, June 14, PPS320.106.56, RN to Sokolsky, July 13, B 712, Sokolsky [1 of 3], RN to Robinson, July 13, 1960, B 647, Robinson (3 of 3), Series 320, RNL.

76. Memo, July 18, 22, 1960, Finch mss.

77. DDEP XX, p. 1886; memo, Jan. 13, 1960, R 29, Lodge mss.

78. Memos, April 7, B 1, Book II, July 7, 1960, B 1, Book III, Krock mss.; DDEP XXI, p. 2230.

79. Beschloss, *Jacqueline Kennedy: Historic Conversations*, 133–134; Smathers OH, interview III, July 10, 1964, JFKL.

80. Memo, July 7, 1960, B 1, Book III, Krock mss.; Telephone call, July 19, 1960, R 26, DDEL Diary; Eisenhower, *Waging Peace*, 593–594.

81. D. Eisenhower OH, 25, 28, HHPL; Hagerty OH, I, pp. 2–3, 10, 33, 52, 66, Knowland OH, I, p. 29, Saltonstall OH, 24, McCormack OH, 10, Baskin OH, I, p. 35, Brooks OH, I, pp. 10–11, Halleck OH, and Chapman OH, I, pp. 33–34, LBJL; Smathers OH, 45–46, SHO; RN OH #111, p. 19, Russell mss.; Eisenhower, *Mandate for Change*, 493; Unger and Unger, *LBJ*, 161–176; Caro, *Path to Power*, 306–334; Ewald, *Eisenhower the President*, 27–28; Kistiakowsky, *Scientist at the White House*, 402.

82. PPA 1960–61, p. 582.

7. THE WAITING GAME

1. RN to Sherrad, Nov. 2, B 1, Cal Jan. 1960, Series 54, Finch to Jossey-Bass, Dec. 7, B 259, Finch 1959 [1/2], RN to Duke, Dec. 10, 1959, B 227, Duke, J, Series 320, memo, Jan. 5, B 16, DC-Jan. 1960 [1/2], Series 54, memo, Jan. 15, B 17, DCo April 1960 [2/2], Series 54, RNL; WP, Jan. 4, 1960.

2. RN to Helene, Jan. 6, DR 201, PH to L. Annenberg, Jan. 10, B 44, Annenberg, Klein to Bond, Feb. 1, B 221, Dodd, Mead, Series 320, *Detroit News*, Feb. 15, B 126, F 1, Series 207, Kahn to Jacobs, March 15, 1960, B 757, *Time*, Series 320, RNL; *Newsweek*, Feb. 22, 1960, pp. 28–29.

3. WP, Jan. 9, 1960.

4. RN to Auchincloss, Jan. 22, B 55, Auchincloss, Series 320 and *Gainesville Daily Sun*, Jan. 17, 1960, B 123, F 1 (2 of 2), Series 207, RNL; WP, Jan. 10, 1960; USNWR, Jan. 11, pp. 42–44, Feb. 15, 1960, pp. 50–51; *Time*, Jan. 18, 1960.

5. RN to Duke, Dec. 10, 1959, B 227, Duke, J, Finch to Frayn, Feb. 10, B 258, Finch 1960 [2/2], RN to Widnall, Feb. 13, B 597, Pike (2 of 3), Klein to St. John, Feb. 16, B 360, Hughes, Em, Woods to Linville, Feb. 24, 1960, B 454, Linville, B, Series 320, RNL.

6. *Gainesville Daily Sun*, Jan. 15, 17, *Miami Herald*, Jan. 18, B 123, F 1 (2 of 2) Series 207, RNL; WP, Jan. 19, 1960; Kesaris, *Papers of the Republican Party*, excerpts, Jan. 15, 16,

1960, R 2; *Newsweek*, Jan. 11, pp. 20, 25, 30, Feb. 15, 1960, p. 25; *Time*, Jan. 25, Feb. 15, 1960.

7. *Gainesville Daily Sun*, Jan. 17, 1960, B 123, F 1 (2 of 2), RN q & a, April 11, 1960, B 131, F 16, Series 207, RNL; *Newsweek*, Jan. 25, 1960, p. 30; *Time*, Jan. 25, 1960.

8. Address, installation luncheon, Feb. 6, B 125, F 1, *LAT*, Feb. 6, 7, B 124, F 19, Series 207 and interview, Feb. 6, 1960, B 160, Coates, P, Series 320, RNL; *WP*, Feb. 7, 9, 16, 1960; *NYT*, Feb. 24, 1960.

9. News conference, Jan. 16, B 123, F 4, Installation luncheon, Feb. 6, B 125, F 1, RN transcript, Feb. 15, B 127, F 4, RN q & a, April 11, 1960, B 131, F 16, Series 207, RNL; notes, Feb. 16, 1960, R 24, DDEL Diary; *WP*, Jan. 19, 26, 1960; *USNWR*, May 30, 1960, p. 119; Gellman, *President and Apprentice*, 543–551.

10. RN q & a, April 11, 1960, B 131, F 16, Series 207, RNL; Gellman, *President and Apprentice*, 462–482; Pruden, *Conditional Partners*, 217–222.

11. RN to Manfridi, Feb. 12, B 474, Manfridi, Series 320, *Evening Star* (DC), Feb. 4, B 124, F 11, RN remarks, April 23, 1960, B 132, F 9, Series 207, RNL; *NYT*, April 24, May 15, 1960; *USNWR*, May 30, 1960, pp. 120–121.

12. McClenahan and Becker, *Eisenhower and the Cold War Economy*, 124–151; Conkin, *Revolution Down on the Farm*, 126–130.

13. Schapsmeier and Schapsmeier, "Farm Policy from FDR to Eisenhower," 367–371; Schapsmeier and Schapsmeier, "Eisenhower and Ezra Taft Benson," 369–376; Schapsmeier and Schapsmeier, "Religion and Reform," 531–534; Schapsmeier and Schapsmeier, "Eisenhower and Agricultural Reform," 147–160; Benson, *Cross Fire*, 204–207. RN to Coleman, June 7, 1954, B 161, Coleman, CC, Riley to Gainey, Sept. 3, B 279, Gainey [2/2], Case to RN, Sept. 5, 1957, B 137, Case, F, Andersen to RN, Jan. 7, B 40, Andersen, NC, RN to Emanuel, Dec. 15, 1959, B 242, Emanuel 1959–60, Series 320, Galer to RN, Jan. 18, B 3, Io [2 of 2], Series 52, memo, Feb. 26, B 40, Andersen, HC, memo, Feb. 26, 1960, B 72, Belcher, Series 320, RNL; Reedy—VI— pp. 7, 10–11, LBJL; Kistiakowsky, *Scientist at the White House*, 216–217; Gray, *Eighteen Acres under Glass*, 106–107; Heidepriem, *Fair Chance for a Free People*, 134–135; Cochrane and Ryan, *American Farm Policy*, 89–92.

14. Memo, Dec. 15, 1959, B 759, Tollefson, *Meet the Press*, Jan. 17, 1960, B 76, Benson, 1960–61, Series 320, RNL; *WP*, Dec. 31, 1959, Feb. 15, 1960; *USNWR*, May 30, 1960, p. 121; Schapsmeier and Schapsmeier, "Eisenhower and Ezra Taft Benson," 376–378; Benson, *Cross Fire*, 421–423, 456–457, 492–493, 511–513; Schapsmeier and Schapsmeier, *Ezra Taft Benson*, 242–249.

15. *Newsweek*, Jan. 18, 1960, p. 11; *PPA* 1960–61, p. 301; *NYT*, April 19, 1960.

16. RN to Harris, June 11, 1960, B 322, Harris, RJ, Series 320, RNL; Dulaney and Phillips, "*Speak, Mister Speaker*," 386, 393; Douglas, "Trends and Developments," 82–86; Nichols, *Matter of Justice*, 252–257; Thurber, *Politics of Equality*, 109; Caro, *Passage of Power*, 75–80; Laird, *Republican Papers*, 235–238; Mann, *Legacy to Power*, 201–202; Talmadge, *Talmadge*, 185–187; Gellman, *President and Apprentice*, 402–408, 418–421.

17. DDEP XX, p. 1937.

18. *USNWR*, March 7, pp. 1, 46, March 14, pp. 41–42, 44–46, April 4, p. 89, April 18, pp.

52–54, 56, May 20, 1960, p. 121; Chafe, *Civilities and Civil Rights*, 99–141; Rentschler to McWhorter, June 9, 1959, B 385, Johnson, JH, Series 320, RNL; Gellman, *President and Apprentice*, 408–410, 413–415, 419–420.

19. Memo, May 5, Hughes to Phoebus, May 21, memo, June 22, B 595, Phoebus, Series 320, *Sun* (Baltimore), June 23, 1960, B 139, F 8, Series 207, RNL.

20. RN to Robinson, Feb. 5, 1958, B 75, F 5, Series 207, *Sun* (Baltimore), April 24, 1960, PPS337.B4, RNL; Gellman, *Contender*, 434; Rampersad, *Jackie Robinson*, 261, 324.

21. *NY Post*, Dec. 30, 1959; Long, *First Class Citizenship*, 84–85.

22. *NY Post*, Jan. 20, 1960; Long, *First Class Citizenship*, 85.

23. Memo, March 30, 1960, B 649, Robinson (1 of 2), Series 320, RNL; Long, *First Class Citizenship*, 88–89.

24. Memo, April 10, RN to Robinson, April 13, Cunningham to Hughes, April 29, memo, May 10, B 649, Robinson (1 of 2), Robinson to RN, May 11, 1960, B 649, Robinson (2 of 2), Series 320, RNL; Long, *First Class Citizenship*, 89–90, 94–95, 97; Rampersad, *Jackie Robinson*, 343–345.

25. Quotations, April 26, B 428, Krock, A, Series 320, RN to Robinson, June 3, B 139, F 20, Series 207, RN to Jackie, June 14, B 649, Robinson (2 of 2), memo, June 16, B 440, Lasky (2 of 3), schedule, June 29, 1960, PPS212 (1960).344, RNL; Long, *First Class Citizenship*, 97–98, 101.

26. *Gainesville Daily Sun*, Jan. 17, B 123, F 1 (2 of 2), installation, Feb. 6, B 125, F 1, RN transcript, Feb. 15, B 127, F 4, RN q & a, April 11, B 131, F 16, Series 207, RNL; WP, Feb. 24, 1960; Lungren and Lungren, *Healing Richard Nixon*, 65–67.

27. RN speech, May 11, 1960, B 133, F 25, Series 207, RNL; conversation with RN, May 3, 1960, B 1, Krock mss.

28. RN speech, Jan. 27, 1960, B 124, F 2, Series 207, RNL; WP, Jan. 17, 28, 1960; DDEP XXI, pp. 2526–2559.

29. DDEP XX, pp. 1793–1796, 1802–1804; *PPA* 1960–61, pp. 119–121, 133.

30. *PPA* 1960–61, pp. 144, 147.

31. *Evening Star* (DC), March 15, 1960, B 263, Fleeson 1/2, Series 320, RNL; *Time*, March 28, 1960; *Newsweek*, March 28, 1960, p. 84.

32. *PPA* 1960–61, pp. 293–295; telephone calls, March 16, 21, 1960, R 25, Diary DDEL.

33. Memo, April 7, 1960, B I, Book II, Krock mss.; Roberts OH #226, p. 555, DDEL; Anderson OH #521, pp. 12–14, 25–26, DDEL; Persons OH #161, COHP; DDEP XX, pp. 1794, 1942.

34. DDEP XX, pp. 1935–1941.

35. Kraft, "IKE vs. NIXON," 83–87; *Newsweek*, Jan. 4, p. 9, Jan. 11, p. 17, April 4, 1960, p. 31; USNWR, April 4, 1960, p. 35; Gellman, *President and Apprentice*, passim.

36. Klein to Smart, March 21, Smart to Klein, March 23, Klein to Smart, March 24, Klein to Hagerty, March 28, B 700, Smart, Klein to Shein, April 19, 1960, B 426, Kraft, Jo, Series 320, RNL.

37. Telephone call, April 19, 1960, R 10, Dulles mss.; telephone call, April 21, 1960, R 25, Diary DDEL.

38. RN interview, CIA-RDP80B0167R000900010017-6, released Aug. 21, 2002, CIA mss.; Battaglio, *David Susskind*, 57.

39. RN to Robinson, May 13, B 649, Robinson, WE, Series 320, RN speech, May 17, B 134, F 9, Series 207, Celler to Rogers, May 18, B 653, Rogers 1960 (2 of 2), Series 320, *Syracuse Herald-Journal*, May 18, B 134, F 5, Series 207, memo, May 23, B 271, Foster, RN to Goodfellow, May 24, 1960, B 295, Goodfellow, Series 320, memoirs, March 23, 1976, RNL; *WP*, May 19, 1960; *Newsweek*, May 30, 1960, p. 31; Strout, *TRB*, 202.

40. Press conference, May 27, B 135, F 10, Series 207, RN to Graham, June 4, 1960, B 299, Graham {2 of 3}, Series 320, RNL; RN to Kersten, May 24, 1960, B 1, Series 9, Kersten mss.; *NYT*, May 28, 1960; *WP*, May 28, 1960; *Time*, June 13, 1960.

41. Memo, May 23, B 814, Whitman, An, RN to Cramer, June 22, B 187, Cramer, J, McGill to RN, June 16, B 498, McGill [2/3], memo, June 28, 1960, B 814, Whitman, An, Series 320, RNL; Public Opinion News Service, June 15, Woods to Whitman, June 28, 160, B 28, RN 1958 (1), Administrative Series, DDEL.

42. RN to Loeb, March 18, B 102, Bridges (2), Series 320, Daily News (DC), Jan. 9, B 122, F 21, Series 207, *Manchester Union-Leader*, March 10, B 458, Loeb (1 of 2), MacIsaac to RN, March 11, B 469, MacIsaac, D, Series 320, RNL; NY *Post*, Dec. 30, 1959; *WP*, March 9, 1960; Congressional Quarterly, *Guide to U.S. Elections*, Vol. 1, p. 404; RN, *Six Crises*, 309.

43. Memo, May 26, B 680, Scott (5 of 6), Klein to RN, June 23, 1959, B 417, Klein 1957 (1 of 2), special report, Feb, B 181, Corbett, R, memo, Feb. 25, B 679, Scott (4 of 6), RN to Hamilton, April 30, 1960, B 315, Hamilton, Wilb, Series 320, RNL; *WP*, Feb. 23, 1960; *Newsweek*, May 9, 1960, p. 28; *Time*, May 9, 1960; Congressional Quarterly, *Guide to U.S. Elections*, Vol. 1, p. 404.

44. Scranton to RN, July 11 and Dec. 7, 1959, Scranton to RN, April 29, Scranton to DDE, May 3, memo, Feb. 3, 1960, B 681, Scranton, memo, undated, B 175, Series 320, RNL; Wolf, *William Warren Scranton*, 5–58. Scranton won his race against Stanley Prokop by seventeen thousand votes.

45. Congressional Quarterly, *Guide to U.S. Elections*, Vol. 1, pp. 404–405; memo, April 22, B 603, Polls, RN to Annenberg, April 25, B 44, Annenberg, *Philadelphia Inquirer*, April 25, B 315, Hamilton, Wilb, Heffelfinger to RN and *NYT*, April 27, B 330, Heffelfinger [1/2], memo, May 23, B 725, Stassen [1/4], Hamilton to Stassen, May 26, 1960, B 315, Hamilton, Wilb, Series 320, RNL; Scott, *Come to the Party*, 163–164.

46. *Tulsa Tribune* (OK), Feb. 16, B 74, Bellmon, Woolaway to RN, June 6, 1960, B 830, Woolaway, Series 320, RNL; David, *Presidential Election and Transition*, 4.

47. Memo, June 7, RN to Pike, June 8, 1960, B 125, California primary, Series 320, RNL; *Newsweek*, June 6, 1960, p. 27.

48. Finch to Niekum, Jan. 22, B 4, California—Indefinite [3/4], Series 54, Sacramento and Fresno, Feb. 18–19, 1960, B 128, F 3, Series 207, RNL; memos, April 10, 14, 1960, Finch mss.

49. O'Brien to Woods, May 30, B 567, O'Brien, G, Ducommun to RN, June 8, B 226, Ducommun, C, Hillings to Finch, June 23, 1960, B 341, Hillings 1958, Series 320, RNL.

50. Congressional Quarterly, *Guide to U.S. Elections*, Vol. 1, p. 405; *NYT*, June 8, 1960; Hotchkis to RN, June 8, B 355, Hotchkis, Cotton to RN, June 8, B 183, Cotton, A, Brown to RN, June 10, B 107, Brown, W, Finch to Kuhrts, June 13, B 431, Kuhrts, Finch

to Planteen, June 18, B 258, Finch 1960 [1/2], Milias to Finch, June 24, 1960, B 515, Milias, Series 320, RNL; *San Diego Union*, June 9, 1960, Vol. 9, Scrapbook, R. Wilson mss.; USNWR, June 20, 1960, pp. 47–48; *Time*, June 20, 1960.

51. Congressional Quarterly, *Guide to U.S. Elections*, Vol. 1, p. 405.

52. RN to Moley, March 31, 1960, B 524, Moley—Correspondence (1 of 2), Series 320, RNL; de Toledano, *Notes from the Underground*, 325; *Time*, April 11, 1960; USNWR, April 18, pp. 41–49, April 25, 1960, pp. 80–83.

53. RN to Bricker, April 18, B 102, Bricker, J, Borgelt to RN, April 21, 1960, B 94, Borden, J, Series 320, RNL.

54. USNWR, May 9, 1960, p. 47.

55. Hesburgh to RN, March 11, 1960, B 335, Hesburgh, Series 320, RNL.

56. Memo, June 1, B 249, F Facts Con, RN to Robinson, June 15, 1960, B 647, F (3 of 3), Series 320, RNL; Gallup, *Gallup Poll*, Vol. 3: 1652, 1657, 1660, 1666, 1668, 1672–1673, 1676; WP, Feb. 6, 1960; USNWR, May 9, 1960, pp. 47–49; *Time*, June 20, 1960.

57. Memo, Sept. 5, B 93, F 1, Series 207, RN to Robinson, Sept. 15, 1958, B 1, Nov. 26 Dedication, Series 380, RNL.

58. NY *Herald Tribune*, Jan. 20, 1960, B 405, Kennedy, JP, Series 320, RNL.

59. Day 8, Tape 1, 00:34:27 [RN], FG.

60. Smith, *Hostage to Fortune*, 686, 688.

61. News conference, Jan. 16, 1960, B 123, F 4, Series 207, RNL; RN Excerpts, Jan. 16, 1960, Kesaris, *Papers of the Republican Party*, R 2; NYT, Jan. 17, 1960.

62. Thomson to RN, March 21, 1960, B 755, Thomson, V, Series 320, RNL; NYT, April 9, 1960, B 131 F 13, Series 207, RNL.

63. *Chicago American*, April 11, 1960, PPS337.B1, RNL; memo, April 18, 1960, B 9, F 62, Klein mss.; memo, April 18, 1960, Finch mss.

64. Krock to RN, May 11, 1960, B 428, Krock, A, Series 320, RNL.

8. NO CAPACITY FOR SENSIBLE ADVICE

1. Memo, Jan. 8, B 98, Bradshaw (1), Series 320 and RN remarks, Feb. 15, 1960, B 127, F 9, Series 207, RNL; NYT, Dec. 28, 1959; WP, Jan. 5, 1960; USNWR, Jan. 18, 1960, p. 4; Smith, *On His Own Terms*, 317–319; RN, *Six Crises*, 305, 309.

2. Klein to Crabtree, July 5, 1960, B 186, Crabtree, N, Series 320, RNL; *Newsweek*, Jan. 4, pp. 12–13, April 25, 1960, pp. 29–30; WP, Jan. 11, 28, Feb. 12, 1960; *Time*, Feb. 8, 1960.

3. WP, Feb. 1, 1960; Smith, *On His Own Terms*, 300.

4. Memo, Nov. 25, "The Open Mind," Dec. 6, 1959, B 360, Hughes, Em, Series 320, RNL; Smith, *On His Own Terms*, 310, 311, 317, 320–321, 338; Reich, *Life of Nelson A. Rockefeller*, 609–613.

5. Kissinger, *Nuclear Weapons and Foreign Policy*, passim; Smith, *On His Own Terms*, 254–256; Reich, *Life of Nelson A. Rockefeller*, 614, 622, 637–667.

6. DDE to Herter, Aug. 6, 1957, B 18, Herter (5), Administrative Series, DDEL; Herter to RN, Aug. 19, 1957, B 1, European Trip, Series 380, RNL; Lodge, *As It Was*, 202.

7. Ferguson, *Kissinger*, 421, 423–424, 427–428, 433, 443–446.

8. RN to Kissinger, July 7, B 414, Kissinger, HA, Series 320 and Elliott to RN, July 31,

1958, PPS325 uncatalogued, memoirs, March 22, 1976, Reid to RN, Oct. 16, 1957, B 625, Reid (1 of 2), Elliott to RN, Aug. 13, 1958, B 239, Elliott 2/2, Series 320, RNL; Kluger, *The Paper*, 467–481.

9. RN to Kissinger, July 7, 18, 1958, June 10, 1959, B 414, Kissinger, HA, Series 320, Kissinger to RN, May 29, 1959, B 1, F College Forum, Series 317, Kissinger to RN, July 1, 1959, B 414, Kissinger, HA, Series 320, Bowie to RN, Aug. 26, 1959, B 4, Series 313, RN to Kissinger, Sept. 15, 1959, B 414, Kissinger, HA, Series 320, RNL; Kissinger, "Khrushchev Visit," 5, 44–46.

10. Interview with Kissinger, Aug. 15, 1958, B 681, Scribner, F, Series 320, RNL; *Newsweek*, June 20, 1960, p. 30; Ferguson, *Kissinger*, 438–442.

11. *Tulsa Tribune* (OK), Nov. 20, 1959, B 288, Gifford, F, Series 320, *Miami News*, Nov. 20, 1959, PPS337.B4, Blaik to Gifford, Dec. 14, 1959, B 86, Blaik, Emanuel to Hughes, Dec. 16, 1959, B 263, Flanigan, P, RN to McElroy, Feb. 1, 1960, B 496, McElroy, Series 320, RNL; *NYT*, Nov. 16, 20, 1959.

12. Telephone call, March 21, 1960, R 25, Diary DDEL; *PPA* 1960–61, p. 323; memo, April 7, 1960, B I, Book II, Krock mss.

13. *Newsweek*, May 2, 1960, p. 21.

14. Memo, May 2, 1960, B 681, Scranton, Series 320, RNL.

15. DDE to Rockefeller, May 5, 1960, R 25, Diary DDEL; Eisenhower, *Waging Peace*, 592.

16. *NYT*, May 29, 1960; *Newsweek*, May 23, p. 57, June 6, 1960, pp. 33–36; *USNWR*, May 23, pp. 67–70.

17. Memo, March 22, B 97, Bradshaw, McWhorter to Cobb, May 10, 1960, B 160, Cobb, Wm, Series 320, RNL; *NYT*, May 16, 1960; *Time*, May 23, 1960.

18. Memo, May 24, 1960, B 381, Javits [2/3], Series 320, RNL; *WP*, Feb. 1, 1960; *NYT*, June 9, 1960.

19. RN to Bullitt, Dec. 16, 1959, B 62, F 1510, Bullitt mss.; Motley to Finch, Dec. 28, 1959, B 9, F 5, Klein mss.; memo, Feb. 19, 1960, B 428, Krock, A, Series 320, RNL; Gallup, *Gallup Poll*, Vol. 3: 1651, 1668; *USNWR*, Jan. 4, 1960, p. 77.

20. RN remarks, Feb. 15, 1960, B 127, F 9, Series 207, RNL.

21. Krock interview, May 3, 1960, B I, Book III, Krock mss.

22. *NYT*, May 16, 1960.

23. *NYT*, June 4, 1960; *Newsweek*, June 13, 1960, p. 31.

24. Memo, June 2, 1960, B 138, F 4, Series 207, RNL.

25. *Newsweek*, June 13, 1960, p. 32.

26. *NYT*, June 4, 1960; *Newsweek*, June 13, 1960, p. 31.

27. *NYT*, June 4, 5, 1960; *Newsweek*, June 13, 1960, p. 32.

28. *Newsweek*, June 13, 1960, pp. 31–32.

29. McLellan and Acheson, *Among Friends*, 125; Smith, *On His Own Terms*, 339; Rockefeller Brothers Fund, *Prospect for America*, passim; telephone messages, June 7, 1960, R 26, Diary DDEL; *NYT*, June 8, 1960; *Newsweek*, June 20, 1960, p. 31.

30. *Newsweek*, June 20, 1960, pp. 31–32; *USNWR*, June 20, 1960, p. 46; Eisenhower, *Waging Peace*, 592; Smith, *On His Own Terms*, 339.

31. *NYT*, June 9, 1960; Eisenhower, *Waging Peace*, 592.

32. Hannaford, *Drew Pearson Diaries*, 23; Slater, *The Ike I Knew*, 228.

33. Brown to Rockefeller, June 8, B 106, Brown, memo, June 8, B 650, Rockefeller (2 of 2), Vann to RN, June 8, B 780, Vann, Murphy to RN, June 10, B 541, Murphy, TJ, Nichols to RN, June 27, 1960, B 560, Nichols, Lo, Series 320, RNL; *Newsweek*, June 20, 1960, pp. 32–33.

34. *NYT*, June 9, 1960; *Time*, June 20, 1960; *Newsweek*, June 20, 1960, p. 30; Michener, *Report of the County Chairman*, 54–56; RN, *Six Crises*, 305.

35. NSC meeting, June 8, 1960, R 26, Diary DDEL; *Newsweek*, June 20, 1960, p. 32; Eisenhower, *Waging Peace*, 592.

36. Legislative leadership meeting, June 9, 1960, R 26, Diary DDEL; *Newsweek*, June 20, 1960, p. 32; Eisenhower, *Waging Peace*, 593.

37. *NYT*, June 10, 1960; memo, April 10, 1960, Finch mss.; schedule, June 9, 1960, PPS 212(1960).291, memoirs, March 31, 1976, RNL; legislative leadership meeting, June 9, 1960, R 26, Diary DDEL; *USNWR*, June 20, 1960, pp. 98–100; RN, *Six Crises*, 313.

38. DDE to RN, June 12, PPS324.139, RN to Hayden, June 15, B 327, Hayden, M, RN to Pinkley, June 15, 1960, B 598, Pinkley [1/2], Series 320, memoirs, March 31, 1976, RNL.

39. Memo, June 9, 1960, R 26, Diary DDEL.

40. Telephone calls and memo, June 11, 1960, R 26, Diary DDEL.

41. Ibid.

42. https://levysheetmusic.mse.jhu.edu/collection/154/003.

43. Memo, June 10, B 650, Rockefeller 1960–61, memo, June 11, 1960, B 640, Rhyne 1960, Series 320, RNL; DDEP XX, p. 1976; *Newsweek*, June 20, 1960, p. 30; *Time*, June 20, 1960.

44. RN to M. Eisenhower, June 15, B 238, Eisenhower 1/2, Series 320, RN to Masaoka, June 22, PPS320.51.176, memo, June 27, B 484, May, Ca, Series 320, RNL.

45. *USNWR*, June 27, 1960, p. 113.

46. RN to McClure, June 15, B 492, McClure, R, RN to Murphy, June 16, B 541, Murphy, TJ, RN to Miller, June 24, B 517, Miller, P (Gannett), RN to Coleman, June 27, 1960, B 162, Coleman, S, Series 320, RNL.

47. *NYT*, June 18, 1960.

48. Memo, April 26, 1960, Finch mss.; DDEP XX, p. 1975; *Newsweek*, June 13, p. 25, June 27, 1960, p. 36; *USNWR*, June 20, p. 48, July 11, 1960, p. 51.

49. Press conference and q and a, June 20, B 138, F 2 and 3, *Fargo Forum*, June 21, B 138, F 7 (1 of 2) Series 207, Klein to Jacobs, July 5, 1960, B 374, Jacobs (1 of 4), Series 320, *Fargo Forum* and *Minot Daily News*, June 21, B 138, F 7 (1 of 2), memo, June 30, B 139, F 21, Series 207, Davis to RN, June 25, 1960 B 204, Davis, J, Series 320, RNL; *NYT*, June 21, 1960.

50. Davis to RN, June 25, B 204, Davis, J, RN to Emanuel, July 11, B 241, Emanuel 1/2, Finch to Froeschek, July 13, 1960, B 276, Froeschek, RP, Series 320, RNL.

51. N.D. Election, July 5, 1960, R 26, Diary DDEL; Gainey to RN, July 6, 1960, B 279, Gainey 1960, Series 320, RNL; *NYT*, June 29, 30, July 1, 6, 1960; *USNWR*, July 11, 1960, p. 51; Congressional Quarterly, *Guide to U.S. Elections*, 79.

52. Memo, July 5, 1960, R 26, Diary DDEL.

53. Memo, June 10, B 139, F 1, "Eye on St. Louis," June 21, 1960, B 139, F 5, Series 207, RNL; *NYT*, June 22, 1960; *Newsweek*, July 4, pp. 24, 65–66, July 11, 1960, pp. 26–27; *Time*, July 4, 1960.

54. *Evening Star* (DC), June 22, 1960, PPS337.B 4, RNL; *Time*, July 4, 1960.

55. *NYT*, June 22, July 18, 1960; *Time*, June 27, 1960; *Newsweek*, June 27, 1960, p. 36.

56. Gallup, *Gallup Poll*, 3: 1674.

57. RN to Thyne, June 8, B 135, F 13, *Baltimore Sun*, June 15, 1960, B 136, F 21, Series 207, RNL.

58. RN to M. Eisenhower, June 15, M. Eisenhower to RN, June 28, 1960, B 238, Eisenhower 1/2, Series 320, RNL.

59. Press conference, June 30, 1960, B 139, F 23, Series 207, RNL; *NYT*, July 1, 1960.

60. *PPA* 1960–61, pp. 554–555, 561; memo, July 7, 1960, B 1, Book III, Krock mss.

61. Rockefeller to Silverman, Jan. 29, B 650, Rockefeller 1960–61, Series 320, *NYT*, May 5, 1960, B 133, F 18, Series 207, RNL; *USNWR*, April 25, 1960, pp. 80–83; *Newsweek*, Jan. 4, p. 11, April 18, p. 39, April 25, p. 29, May 16, 1960, p. 25; Smith, *On His Own Terms*, 318, 337.

9. "ONE OF US"

1. Skinner, Anderson, and Anderson, *Reagan*, 37, 147, 438; Gellman, *Contender*, 117.

2. RN to Reagan, June 18, 1959, B 149, Christenberry, Series 320, RNL; Morgan, *Reagan*, 59; Morris, *Dutch*, 292–293.

3. Reagan speech, June 1959, B 149, Christenberry, Series 320, RNL.

4. Reagan to RN, July 15, 1960, B 621, Reagan, R, Series 320, RNL; Skinner, Anderson, and Anderson, *Reagan*, 704–705.

5. *Prescott Evening Courier* (AZ), July 18, 1960, Vol. 90, July 11–22, 1960, Goldwater Scrapbooks, Goldwater mss.; *Newsweek*, July 11, 1960, p. 26; *Time*, July 11, 1960; Smith, *On His Own Terms*, 341–342.

6. Memo, July 8, 1960, R 26, Diary DDEL; Van Atta, *With Honor*, 47–48; Murray, *Charles Percy of Illinois*, 47–48.

7. *Time*, July 18, 1960; *Newsweek*, July 25, 1960, pp. 32–33.

8. Telephone call, July 19, 1960, R 26, Diary DDEL; Eisenhower, *Waging Peace*, 595.

9. RN to Ruark, July 13, B 661, Ruark, Series 320, memo, July 20, 1960, uncatalogued, RNL; memo, July 12, 1960, Finch mss.; Smith, *On His Own Terms*, 343; Critchlow, *Phyllis Schlafly and Grassroots Conservatism*, 113.

10. Press conference, July 23, 1960, B 140, F 6, Series 207, memoirs, March 31, 1976, RNL; memo, Dec. 17, 1960, White mss. (Harvard); *NYT*, July 24, 1960; Berle and Jacobs, *Navigating the Rapids*, 715; *Newsweek*, Aug. 1, 1960, p. 16; RN, *Six Crises*, 314–315; Smith, *On His Own Terms*, 344–346; Eisenhower, *Waging Peace*, 595; Klein, *Making It Perfectly Clear*, 99–101; Murray, *Charles Percy of Illinois*, 47–48; Van Atta, *With Honor*, 48–49; Scott, *Come to the Party*, 169–170.

11. RN press conference, July 23, 1960, B 140, F 6, Series 207, RNL; *NYT*, July 24, 1960.

12. Goldwater, *Conscience of a Conservative*, passim; *Time*, May 2, 1960; Critchlow, *Phyllis Schlafly and Grassroots Conservatism*, 111, 115–116.

13. *NYT*, June 10, 1960; *Newsweek*, April 11, p. 34, May 30, p. 50, July 4, 1960, p. 26; *USNWR*, April 25, p. 81, June 13, 1960, p. 53.

14. *NYT*, July 24, 1960; Goldwater, *Goldwater*, 119; Goldwater, *With No Apologies*, 109–112; Critchlow, *Phyllis Schlafly and Grassroots Conservatism*, 110–112.

15. *NYT*, July 24, 1960; Critchlow, *Conservative Ascendancy*, 50–52.

16. *NYT*, July 24, 1960.

17. Calendar, July 8–24, telephone calls, July 23, 1960, R 26, Diary DDEL; *NYT*, July 24, 1960; David, *Presidential Election and Transition*, 30.

18. Conversation with Percy, July 24, 1960, R 26, Diary DDEL; Eisenhower, *Waging Peace*, 596; Murray, *Charles Percy of Illinois*, 49; Van Atta, *With Honor*, 49–50; Smith, *Iron Man*, 229.

19. Conversation with RN, July 24, 1960, R 26, Diary DDEL; *PPA* 1960–61, pp. 600–602; Eisenhower, *Waging Peace*, 596.

20. Memo, July 22, 1960, B 140, F 7, Series 207, RNL; Baughman, *Secret Service Chief*, 250; Klein, *Making It Perfectly Clear*, 102.

21. *Meet the Press*, July 24, 1960, PPS501.2.32, RNL.

22. RN to Viehman, Feb. 10, B 786, Viehman, Series 320, memo, June 8, 1960, Finch mss.; DDEP XVI, pp. 1699–1700; *NYT*, June 9, 26, 1960; Best, *Herbert Hoover*, 441–443; Edwards, *Missionary for Freedom*, 247–251.

23. Memo, July 22, 1960, B 140, F 7, Series 207, RNL; DDEP *XXI*, p. 2565; memo, July 20, 1960, R 26, Diary DDEL; *PPA* 1960–61, pp. 589–601, quotation 590; *NYT*, July 26, 1960; Roberts OH #266, pp. 827–829, DDEL; David, *Presidential Election and Transition*, 96; Eisenhower, *Waging Peace*, 597.

24. *NYT*, July 27, 28, 1960; *WP*, July 6, 1965; RN, *Six Crises*, 315; Hatfield, *Against the Grain*, 122, 132–134.

25. Shorey to Curran, June 28, 1960, B 196, Curran, R, Series 320, RNL; *NYT*, July 25–28, 1960; Goldwater, *With No Apologies*, 112–117; Goldwater, *Goldwater*, 119.

26. DDEP XX, pp. 2018–2019.

27. RN to Ford, Aug. 17, 1959, B 268, Ford, GR [2/2], Series 320, RNL; *Newsweek*, June 27, 1960, p. 17; DeFrank, *Write It when I'm Gone*, 100–101, 202.

28. Ford to RN, June 24, B 33, F 3 [2 of 2], *Grand Rapids Press* (MI), Nov. 4, 1955, PPS336(1955).602, RN to Ford, Jan. 12, Ford Remarks, March 15, Ford to DDE, July 28, Ford to Martin, Aug. 7, B 268, Ford, GR [2/2], Ford to RN, Oct. 11, 1956, PPS23. Michigan, Ford to RN, June 24, 1958, memo, May 21, Ford to RN, May 27, 1959, B 1 F College Forum, Series 317, Meyer to Ford, Jan. 15, B 97, F 4, Series 207, Ford to RN, April 21, B 1, Series 303, RNL; Arnold, *Back when It All Began*, 6; DeFrank, *Write It when I'm Gone*, 100–101; Gellman, *Contender*, 268, 275.

29. Ford to RN, Nov. 12, 1958, B 268, Ford, GR [2/2], RN to Ford, May 29, B 4, Series 313, memo, June 6, B 268, Ford, GR [2/2], Ford to Editor, July 21, 1959, B 447, Letters (1959), *Baltimore Sun*, Sept. 30, *Detroit Free Press*, Dec. 5, *Detroit News*, Dec. 5, *Detroit Times*, Dec. 5, B 268, Ford, GR [2/2], RN to Moley, Dec. 30, 1959, B 524, Moley—Correspondence 1 of 2, Series 320, RNL.

30. *Daily News* (DC), June 18, *NYT* and *WP*, June 20, B 268, Ford, GR [1/2], memos, July

19, 22, 1960, B 213, de Toledano, memoirs, March 22, 31, 1976, RNL; OH Scott, 10200, B 290, p. 31, Scott mss.; *Newsweek*, July 11, 1960, pp. 31–32, 86; RN, *Richard Nixon*, 216.

31. "Political Pulse," July 23, *Globe*, July 27, 28, *Monitor*, July 29, *Globe*, July 31, 1960, R 31, Lodge mss.; Nichter, *Last Brahmin*, 7–169.

32. *BG*, June 5, Sept. 24, 28, Oct. 10, 1959, *NY Herald*, Jan. 20, *BG*, Jan. 20, 25, Feb. 2, 23, R 31, Cole to Cabot, March 15, 1960, R 3, Lodge mss., May 29, 1960, B 226, Drummond 1/2, Series 320, RNL; *NY Herald Tribune*, Jan. 12, 1960; *NYT*, Jan. 20, 1960; *Newsweek*, May 30, 1960, p. 19.

33. *BG*, June 13, 1960, R 31, Burger to Gainey, July 1, R 2, Dewey to Cabot, July 15, R 4, Howard to Cabot, July 20, R 7, *Traveler*, July 22, *BG*, July 22, 25, 26, *Christian Science Monitor*, July 25, 1960, R 31, Lodge mss.; *Life*, July 11, 1960, Vol. 49, Part I, p. 32.

34. DDE to Lodge, Dec. 30, 1957, confidential journal, Jan. 24, 1958, and memo 1959, spring 1959, DDE to Lodge, Sept. 29, 1959, R 29, Lodge mss.; Slater, *The Ike I Knew*, 186; *Newsweek*, Sept. 21, 1959, p. 35; Eisenhower, *Strictly Personal*, 254–255.

35. Telephone call, July 19, schedule, July 27, 1960, R 26, Diary DDEL; *BG*, July 25, 1960, R 31, Lodge mss.; DDEP XX, pp. 2018–2019; OH Roberts #266, pp. 829–830, DDEL.

36. Lodge to Nixon, Oct. 26, 1954, Aug. 15, 27, RN to Lodge, Sept. 11, Lodge to RN, Oct. 18, Nov. 7, 1956, R 12, Lodge mss.; Lodge to RN, Aug. 27, 1956, B 457, Lodge (2 of 2), Series 320, RNL.

37. Lodge to RN, Nov. 29, 1957, RN to Lodge, Jan. 31, Lodge to RN, May 13, Lodge to Mazo, Aug. 8, 1958, Lodge to RN, Jan. 19, Nov. 24, RN to Lodge, Dec. 15, Lodge to RN, Dec. 28, RN to Lodge, Dec. 30, 1959, R 12, Lodge mss.; Lodge to RN, Nov. 29, Dec. 16, 1957, RN to Lodge, Jan. 31, April 22, 1958, RN to Lodge, Nov. 16, Lodge to RN, Nov. 24, B 457, Lodge (2 of 2), RN to Lodge, Dec. 15, B 457, Lodge (1 of 2), Lodge to RN, Dec. 28, 1959, B 457, Lodge (2 of 2), Lodge to RN, Jan. 26, memo, Feb. 27, 1960, B 457, Lodge (2 of 2), Series 320, RNL; Lodge to RN, Jan. 15, R 12, memo, Jan. 25, Lodge to RN, Jan. 26 and 29, R 12, memo, March 9 and April 7, 1960 R 17, Lodge mss.

38. Hall to Lodge, July 9, 1960, R 6, Lodge mss.; RN to Lodge, July 9, 1960, B 457, Lodge (2 of 2), Series 320, RNL.

39. *BG*, July 27, 1960, R 31, Lodge mss.; Scott, *Come to the Party*, 173.

40. I could not find any contemporaneous notes of this meeting. "The Vice Presidential Nomination at the Republican National Convention in Chicago 1960," undated, B 47, F 47.12 (Speeches and Writings), Judd mss.

41. *NYT*, July 27, 28, 29, 1960; Lodge to Bricker, Jan. 13, 1961, R 2, *BG*, July 28, 29, 1960, R 31, Lodge mss.; *Newsweek*, Aug. 1, 1960, p. 25; memoirs, March 14, 31, 1976, RNL; OH Scott, 10200, B 290, p. 31, Scott mss.; RN, "Second Office," 89; RN, *RN*, 215–216; Eisenhower, *President Is Calling*, 369; Scott, *Come to the Party*, 172–173; Kleindienst, *Justice*, 3–4, 28–29; RN, *Six Crises*, 317–318; Lodge, *As It Was*, 211.

42. *BG*, July 28, 29, 1960, R 31, Lodge mss.; Lodge, *As It Was*, 211; RN, *Six Crises*, 318.

43. *NYT*, July 27, 28, 1960; Ford speech, July 28, 1960, B 268, Ford, GR [1/2], Series 320, RNL.

44. Nichter, *Last Brahmin*, 170–174.
45. *NYT*, July 29, 1960; RN, *Six Crises*, 318; Scott, *Come to the Party*, 173.
46. *NYT*, July 29, 1960.
47. RN to Percy, May 6, B 133, F 28, Series 207, *Washington Daily News* (DC), July 29, 1960, PPS61S.4, memoirs, March 31, 1976; memo, April 19, 1960, Finch mss.; memo, telephone call, July 22, 1960, R 11, Dulles mss.
48. RN, *Six Crises*, 319, 450–455.
49. Ibid., 455.
50. Memo, July 31, 1960, B 140, F 13, Series 207, RNL; RN, *Six Crises*, 457, 459–460.
51. DDE to RN and Lodge, July 28, B 237, Eisenhower 2/2, Cherne to RN, July 29, B 143, Cherne, Anderson to RN, July 29, B 40, Anderson, D, Burns to RN, July 29, B 115, Burns 3/3, Dart to RN, July 29, B 202, Dart 1/3, Snyder to RN, July 30, B 711, Snyder, HM, Flemming to RN, Aug. 2, B 264, Flemming 1/2, Woods to Key, Aug. 9, B 409, Key, W, Woods to Irwin, Aug. 25, B 371, Irwin (2 of 4), Series 320, Cowles to RN, Aug. 1, 1960, B 145, F 14, Series 207, memoirs, March 31, 1976, RNL.

10. MENDING FENCES

1. *JFKI*, p. 1271.
2. *JFKI*, pp. 3–4, 6–11, 64–66, 959–961, 976, 1274; *NYT*, Aug. 4, 27, 1960.
3. *NYT*, Aug. 2, 5, 1960; *JFKI*, pp. 1–3, 29–30, 33–38, 969–970.
4. *JFKI*, pp. 1272–1274.
5. Memo for the President, Aug. 3, 1960, B 13, F Dulles, Allen (1), Dulles mss.; *JFKI*, p. 60; *NYT*, July 24, 29, 1960; Dulles to Salinger, Aug. 22, CIA-RDP80B01676R00090004 0065-0, memo of phone call, Aug. 31, CIA-RDP80B0167R002600120036-4, memo for Record, Aug. 31, CIA-RDP80B01676R002600120033-7 and Executive Officer to Salinger, Sept. 2, 1960, CIA-RDP80B01676R000900040055-1, CIA mss.
6. *JFKI*, pp. 39, 50–55, 57–63, 971–973.
7. Bowles to JFK, Aug. 22, Kennedy, John, B 210, Series 1 and "Some observations," Dec. 31, 1960, B 392, F 153, Part 9, Series III, p. 46, Bowles mss.; *JFKI*, p. 963; *NYT*, Aug. 2, 1960; Lash, *Eleanor*, 299; Lawrence, *Six Presidents, Too Many Wars*, 235; Schaffer, *Chester Bowles*, 176–180.
8. Offner, *Hubert Humphrey*, 151–156.
9. Olson, *Stuart Symington*, 361–366.
10. *PAES* VII, pp. 532–541, 544–545, 562; Martin, *Stevenson and the World*, 469–519, 528–539.
11. *PAES* VII, pp. 544–549; *NYT*, Aug. 1, 1960.
12. *PAES* VII, pp. 545, 549, 551–555, 562–563, 556–557.
13. ER to Degeest, July 22, 1960, B 654, Roosevelt, E (FDR), Series 320, RNL; *ERP*, July 26, 1960.
14. ER to Lasker, Aug. 15; "My Day," Aug. 17, 1960, ERP; *JFKI*, pp. 18–21; Schlesinger, *Letters*, 212; Lash, *Eleanor*, 297–298.
15. ER to Lasker, Aug. 15; "My Day," Aug. 17, 23; ER to Lasker, Aug. 15, 1960, *ERP*.
16. "My Day," Aug. 17, 23, 1960, ERP; Schlesinger, *Letters*, 213.

17. NYT, Aug. 3, 1960; *JFKI*, pp. 25–26; *Time*, Aug. 22, 1960; Neal, *Harry and Eleanor*, 224.

18. *JFKI*, pp. 24–28. NYT, Aug. 21, Sept. 10, 1960; *Time*, Aug. 29, 1960; *Newsweek*, Aug. 29, 1960, p. 20; Poen, "Truman and Kennedy," 305–306.

19. *JFKI*, pp. 1274–1275; NYT, July 17, 21, 22, 27, 31, 1960; Bowen to Rasor, July 22, 1960, B 215, Senate Political Files and Jacobsen OH, LBJL.

20. NYT, July 25, 1960; *JFKI*, pp. 1274–1275; Beschloss, *Jacqueline Kennedy: Historic Conversations*, 84–85; Evans and Novak, *Lyndon Johnson*, 291–292.

21. Rowe to LBJ, July 25, 1960, B 262, Senate Political Files, LBJL; "Periscope," *Newsweek*, Aug. 29, 1960; Caro, *Passage of Power*, 144.

22. *JFKI*, pp. 970–971; Smathers OH, Interview #6, p. 4, March 31, 1964, and Interview II, July 10, 1964, JFKL; Crispell, *Testing the Limits*, 225–227, 243–246. The eleven states were: Florida, Georgia, Alabama, Arkansas, North Carolina, South Carolina, Virginia, Tennessee, Kentucky, Mississippi, and Louisiana; Thorburn, *Red State*, 72.

23. Memos from Rosen, Dec. 12, 13, 14, 1956, Sec 1, File No. 022, O & C, FBI mss.

24. Gamarekian OH, 30–31, JFKL; Hannaford, *Drew Pearson Diaries*, 36, 621; USNWR, Aug. 8, 1960, p. 67; *Newsweek*, Aug. 1, p. 29, Sept. 5, 1960, p. 10; Smith, *Grace and Power*, 160–166.

25. *JFKI*, p. 77; Nasaw, *Patriarch*, 740–743; *Newsweek*, Sept. 12, 1960, cover and 26–30.

26. Schlesinger, *Journals*, 80–81; Schlesinger, *Letters*, 210–211, 214–216, 220; USNWR, July 25, 1960, p. 56; Aldous, *Schlesinger*, 210–211.

27. Schlesinger, *Letters*, 214–216.

28. Ibid., 213, 228; J. Alsop to Schlesinger, Sept. 30, 1960, B 16, Sept.–Oct., 1960, Alsop mss.; Lamb interview with Schlesinger, *In Depth*, C-SPAN, Dec. 3, 2000; Schlesinger, *Thousand Days*, 64; Aldous, *Schlesinger*, 204, 213–215.

29. Galbraith to JFK, Aug. 25, 1960, R 4, P 1, JFKL; Goodman, *Letters to Kennedy*, 12; Sandler, *Letters of John F. Kennedy*, 77–79; NYT, Aug. 16, 1960; USNWR, July 25, 1960, p. 56; Galbraith, *Life in Our Times*, 152.

30. NYT, Aug. 8–9, 1960; *Newsweek*, Aug. 8, 1960, p. 15; David, *Presidential Election and Transition*, 73–74.

31. NYT, Aug. 9–11, 1960; *JFKI*, pp. 12–13, 68–69, 1273–1274.

32. *JFKI*, pp. 12–17, 21–23, 40–41. 964; *Newsweek*, Aug. 8, 1960, p. 15.

33. NYT, Aug. 17, 1960; *Time*, Sept. 5, 1960; Truman and Acheson, *Affection and Trust*, 245.

34. Truman and Acheson, *Affection and Trust*, 194; LBJ OH, June 3, 1963, p. 13, LBJL; Smathers OH, 80, SHO; Shaw, *JFK in the Senate*; "The Kennedys," Part I, Nov. 17, 2003, *American Experience*, PBS.

35. PAES VII, pp. 155–156, 345–346, 360, 368–369, 383–384, 385 (quotation), 390–392, 415, 432, 474, 509–510, 518, 530, 545; Brodie, *Richard Nixon*, 306–315.

36. Truman and Acheson, *Affection and Trust*, 242, 246.

37. Lash, *Eleanor*, 289, 299.

38. Martin, *It Seems Like Only Yesterday*, 197; Reston, *Lone Star*, 184; Dallek, "Medical Ordeals of JFK," 39; Hamilton, *JFK*, xix, xxiv, 342, 351–352, 776–779.

39. Blair and Blair, *Search for JFK*, 130–135; Hamilton, *JFK*, 419–494; Faris, *Inga*, passim;

Hannaford, *Drew Pearson Diaries*, 36, 52; von Post, *Love, Jack*, 19–142; Exner, *My Story*, 174–176, 178; Stadiem, "Behind Claude's Doors," 308, 310; for Kennedy's encounters in the White House, see Alford, *Once upon a Secret*, passim.

40. Jones to DeLoach, July 13, 1960, JEH O & C, File No. 96, Sec 1, FBI; Theoharis, *From the Secret Files*, 31–33; Gentry, *J. Edgar Hoover*, 467–471; Sullivan, *Bureau*, 48; RFK, *Enemy Within*, 177; DeLoach, *Hoover's FBI*, 37–38.

41. Jones to DeLoach, July 13, 1960, JEH O & C, File No. 96, Sec 1, FBI; Theoharis, *From the Secret Files*, 31–33; Gentry, *J. Edgar Hoover*, 467–471; Sullivan, *Bureau*, 48; RFK, *Enemy Within*, 177; DeLoach, *Hoover's FBI*, 37–38.

42. *Time*, July 25, 1960; *USNWR*, July 25, 1960, pp. 41–43, 63, 65–67.

43. Schlesinger, *Letters*, 210, 223–225.

11. UNITING REPUBLICANS

1. RN to Meeman, July 13, 1960, B 507, Meeman, Series 320, RNL; Day 9, Tape 2, 00: 11:45 [RN]. FG; *NYT*, July 29–31, 1960; *USNWR*, Aug. 8, 1960, pp. 35–37, 64, 66, 89, 91–92, 94–99; *Newsweek*, Aug. 8, 1960, pp. 16–17, 24; *Time*, Aug. 8, 1960; David, *Presidential Election and Transition*, 96–98; Gray, *Eighteen Acres under Glass*, 288.

2. *NYT*, July 30, 31, 1960; Sevareid, *This Is Eric Sevareid*, 111–113.

3. Lodge to Pinkley, May 7, 1971, R 13, Memo, 1952, p. 62, R 28 and memo, Oct. 18, 1962, R 29, Lodge mss.; *NYT*, July 30, 1960; memoirs, March 14, 31, 1976, RNL; Day 9, Tape 1, 00:03:51 [RN], FG.

4. *Christian Science Monitor*, Aug. 1, *BG*, Aug. 3, 6, *NYT*, July 30, Aug. 3, R 31 Lodge to Editor, Aug. 8, 1960, R 14, Lodge mss.; Lodge, *As It Was*, 211–212; Pruden, *Conditional Partners*, 311–314.

5. DDEP XXI, p. 2056; *NY Herald Tribune*, Aug. 19, 24, *BG*, Aug. 19, 20, R 31, *NYT*, Aug. 20, Lodge to DDE, Aug. 17 and DDE to Lodge, Aug. 19, 1960, R 29, Lodge mss.

6. Roberts OH #266, pp. 831–832, 838, DDEL.

7. DDEP XXI, pp. 2034–2035.

8. Campaign of 1956, Oct. 8, 1956, Hughes mss.; Roberts OH #226, p. 590, DDEL; memoirs, March 22, 1976, RNL.

9. Roberts OH #266, p. 857, DDEL; Eisenhower, *President Is Calling*, 368; Slater, *The Ike I Knew*, 229; Kistiakowsky, *Scientist at the White House*, 402; Filipink, *Eisenhower and American Foreign Policy*, 21–23, 63–64.

10. Kistiakowsky, *Scientist at the White House*, 402; D. Eisenhower OH, July 13, 1967, p. 28, HHPL.

11. *Newsweek*, Aug. 1, 1960, p. 19; Goldwater, *Goldwater*, 119.

12. *NYT*, Aug. 2, 3, 5, 1960; *USNWR*, Aug. 8, 1960, p. 61; memo, Aug. 25, 1960, Finch mss.

13. News release, July 28, press release, Aug. 11, and RN to Ford, Aug. 13, 1960, B 268, Ford, GR [1/2], Series 320, RNL.

14. *NYT*, July 29, Sept. 1, 1960; Benson to RN, July 29, 1960, B 76, Benson, 1960–61, Series 320, RNL; RN, *Six Crises*, 334; Schapsmeier and Schapsmeier, *Ezra Taft Benson*, 250–259.

15. *Newsweek,* June 13, 1960, p. 33; press release, Aug. 8, 1960, B 266, Folger, Series 320, RNL.

16. Golden interview, July 2 and Hughes interview, July 3, 2001, Gellman mss.; Day 3, Tape 3, 00:49:29 [RN] and Day 9, Tape 4, 00:43:35 [RN], FG.

17. *USNWR,* Aug. 8, 1960, p. 63.

18. *NY World-Telegram,* Jan. 11, 1960, B 313, Hall [1/3], Series 320, RNL; *NYT,* July 30, 1960; *Newsweek,* June 13, p. 33, July 25, p. 22, Aug. 13, 1960, p. 34; Cannon, *Politics U.S.A.,* 105–106, 113–114; Allen, *Eisenhower and the Mass Media,* 178–179; Gellman, *President and Apprentice,* 288–289, 307, 321.

19. Finch to Editor, July 6, B 258, Finch Personal, Finch to Spindell, Aug. 6, Finch 1960 [1/2], Finch to Brand, Aug. 12, 1960, B 99, Brand, G, Series 320, RNL; *USNWR,* Aug. 8, 1960, p. 62; Congressional Quarterly, *Weekly Report,* 1601; Finch OH, 10, CSF.

20. Meeting, May 2, 1959, B 9, F 17, Klein mss.; *Newsweek,* June 13, p. 34; *USNWR,* Aug. 8, 1960, p. 62; Congressional Quarterly, *Weekly Report,* 1603; Gellman, *Contender,* 139; Gellman, *President and Apprentice,* 518–519.

21. Klein to Parkinson, June 29, 1967, B 1, F 10 [3 of 3], Klein mss.; Klein, *Making It Perfectly Clear,* 12.

22. Memo, March 24, and meeting, April 1, 2, 1960, B 9, F 1, Klein mss.; Maruyama to Ehrlichman, Aug. 15, B 141, F 9, Series 207 and Hughes to Black, Dec. 12, 1960, B 86, Black, W, Series 320, RNL; Congressional Quarterly, *Weekly Report,* 1602; Klein, *Making It Perfectly Clear,* 86.

23. Memos, July 18, Aug. 1, 1960, Finch mss.

24. Memos, April 26, Aug. 1, 1960, Finch mss.

25. Memos, Aug. 1, 22, 1960, Finch mss.

26. Memo, Aug. 1, 1960, Finch mss.

27. Memos, Aug. 1, 1960, Finch mss.

28. Memo, July 14, 1960, Finch mss.

29. Memo, Aug. 27, 1960, Finch mss.

30. *RNI,* pp. 1120–1123; *NYT,* Aug. 2, 3, 1960; RN, *Six Crises,* 420; Mazo, *Richard Nixon,* 291.

31. RN speech, Aug. 2, B 141, F 7, Series 207, Bassett to Lindemer, Aug. 5, 1960, B 6, To Be—Mich, Series 52, RNL; RN, *Six Crises,* 321; *RNI,* pp. 1124–1129.

32. *RNI,* pp. 1129–1133.

33. Ibid., 1139–1143; press conference, Aug. 2, 1960, B 141, F 4, Series 207, RNL; *NYT,* Aug. 3, 1960.

34. *RNI,* pp. 1134–1139; RN speech, Aug. 2, 1960, B 141, F 6, Series 207, RNL; *NYT,* Aug. 3, 1960; *Time,* Aug. 15, 1960.

35. Press conference, Aug. 3, B 566, Nuclear I, Crossley to RN, Aug. 15, B 193, Cross, T, Blaisdell to Seaton, Aug. 19, B 86, Braisdell, N, Series 320, press conference, Aug. 3, B 141, F 12, Series 207, RN speech, Aug. 4, B 141, F 16, RN remarks, Aug. 4, B 141, F 13, RN speech, Aug. 4, B 141, F 15, RN speech, Aug. 4, 1960 B 141, F 14, Series 207, RNL; *RNI,* pp. 1143–1177; *Newsweek,* Aug. 15, p. 26, Aug. 22, 1960, p. 19; *NYT,* Aug. 4, 5, 1960.

36. McWhorter to Cohn, Aug 4, B 161, Cohen, L, RN to Harkabus, Aug. 8, 1960, B 320, Harkabus, Series 320, RNL; *RNI*, pp. 1179–1182; appointments and memo, Aug. 9, 1960, R 26, Diary DDEL; *NYT*, Aug. 2, 9, and 11, 1960; RN, *Six Crises*, 312.

37. RN to Stetler, Aug. 24, 1960, B 506, Medicare, Series 320, RNL; *RNI*, pp. 33–38, 1185, 1187–1188; DDEP XXI, 2567–2568; *NYT*, Aug. 21, 1960.

38. RN speech and press conference, Aug. 17, 1960, B 142, Series 207, RNL; Holt to Hodge, Aug. 22, 1960, B 14, political file, general subject file, RFK mss.; *RNI*, pp. 1–8, 1191–1197; *NYT*, Aug. 27, 1960; *Newsweek*, Aug. 29, 1960, p. 20; *Time*, Aug. 22, 1960; RN, *Six Crises*, 325.

39. *Gadsden Times*, Aug. 27, 1960, B 278, Gadsden, Series 320, RNL; *RNI*, pp. 39–45; *NYT*, Aug. 27, 1960.

40. RN speech, Aug. 26, B 142, F 12, Series 207, Snodgrass to RN, Aug. 29, B 711, Snodgrass, R, Series 320, *Savannah Morning News*, Aug. 29, 1960, B 6, To Be—Ga, Series 54, RNL; *RNI*, pp. 46–52; *NYT*, Aug. 27, 1960; Melton, "1960 Presidential Election in Georgia," 145–147; RN, *Six Crises*, 325.

41. *RNI*, pp. 24–32; *NYT*, Aug. 25, 1960.

42. *JFKRN*, pp. 1–11; *NYT*, Aug. 26, 1960; report and memo, Aug. 26, 1960, B 142, F 10, Series 207, RNL; Schlesinger, *Letters*, 218.

43. Press conference, Aug. 20, NB 142, F 3, Series 207, and *Pittsburgh Press*, Aug. 21, 1960, B 13, Pa—Oct.–Dec. 1960 [3/3], Series 54, RNL; *Newsweek*, Aug. 29, 1960, p. 20.

44. *NYT*, Aug. 28, 1960; Pillion to RN, Aug. 30, B 598, Pillion and Jones to RN, Aug. 31, 1960, B 389, Jones, AF, Series 320, RNL.

45. *PPA* 1960–61, pp. 620–626, 631; *Time*, Aug. 29, Sept. 12, 1960; *Newsweek*, Aug. 15, 1960, pp. 16–17.

46. Telephone call, Aug. 8, 1960, R 26, Diary DDEL.

47. *PPA* 1960–61, p. 625; *NYT*, Aug. 11, 1960.

48. DDEP XXI, pp. 2043–2044.

49. Ibid., 2034.

50. *PPA* 1960–61, pp. 621, 642; *NYT*, Aug. 20, 1960; *Newsweek*, Aug. 22, 1960, pp. 19–20; *Time*, Aug. 22, 1960.

51. DDEP XXI, pp. 2036, 2052–2053.

52. Telephone call, Aug. 19, 1960, R 26, Diary DDEL.

53. Roberts to RN, Aug. 29, 1960, B 645, Roberts, Cl, Series 320, RNL; DDEP XI, p. 2068; Roberts OH #266, pp. 639–842, DDEL; Slater, *The Ike I Knew*, 228–229; Allen, *Eisenhower and the Mass Media*, 179.

54. *PPA* 1960–61, pp. 652–658; Rives to Gellman, Feb. 4, 2016, email, Gellman mss.; Day 9, Tape 1, 00:04:55 [RN], FG; memoirs, March 22, 1976, RNL.

55. McClendon, *My Eight Presidents*, 45–46; Witcover, *Making of an Ink-Stained Wretch*, 70.

56. *RNI*, pp. 11, 33.

57. Memo, Aug. 25, 1960, Finch mss.

58. Leyerzapf to Gellman, July 14, 2008, email, Gellman mss.; Hess, *Bit Player*, 32.

59. Gale to Birkner, May 30, 2004, Gellman mss.; Allen, *Eisenhower and the Mass Media*,

181; Branyan and Larsen, *Eisenhower Administration*, Vol. 2, p. 1315; Hess, *Bit Player*, 31–32.

60. Conv. No. 541-2 (cont.), July 21, 1971, White House tapes; memoirs, March 22, 1975, RNL; Day 9, Tape 1, 00:04:55 [RN] and Day 9, Tape 2, 00:22:14 [RN], FG.

61. Knowland OH, 84–85, COHP; Day 9, Tape 1, 00:04:55 [RN], FG; Herskowitz, *Duty, Honor, Country*, 179–180.

62. Wills, *Nixon Agonistes*, 114–138; Frank, *Ike and Dick*, 205–208; Dallek, *Camelot's Court*, 26.

63. Stassen to RN, Aug. 4, 1960, B 725, Stassen [1/4], Series 320, RNL.

64. Kissel, "Presidential Campaign 1960, I," p. 9.

65. *NYT*, Aug. 7, 1960.

66. McCaffrey to Goldman, May 6, B 4, F NG, Series 54, McCaffrey to Lipscomb, May 24, B 455, Lipscomb, G, McCaffrey to Mason, May 28, B 481, Mason, T, McCaffrey to Gubser, June 3, B 307, Gubser, McCaffrey to Robinson, June 13, B 588, NY Post, McCaffrey to Davies, B 203, Davies, P, McCaffrey to Crofoot, B 190, Crofoot, memo, Aug. 13, B 488, McCaffrey [2/2], McCaffrey to Krehbiel, Aug. 30, 1960, B 427, Krehbiel, Series 320 and press release, Jan. 25, 1961, B 151, F 10, Series 207, RNL; memo, April 18, 20, 1960, Finch mss.; McCaffrey to Klein, March 8 and press release, May 13, and McCaffrey to Klein, Aug. 8, 1960, B 9, F 58, Klein mss.; *USNWR*, Aug. 8, 1960, p. 63; *LAT*, March 11, 2002.

67. Martin to McCaffrey, June 23, B 478, Martin, Jo, memo, Aug. 9, B 310, Haffner, memo, Aug. 11, B 430, Kuchel [1/2], memo, Aug. 11, B 633, Republican Groups, Finch to Preston, Aug. 16, B 610, Preston, H, Hamilton to Woods, Aug. 19, B 315, Hamilton, R, memo, Aug. 25, B 427, Krehbiel, Lipscomb to RN, Aug. 26, B 455, Lipscomb, G, Pike to Finch, Aug. 26, B 156, Clark 1 of 2, Brennan to RN, Aug. 26, 1960, B 100, Brennan (1), Series 320, RNL; Wilson to Hitt, Aug. 8, 1960, B 266, Political Affairs 18, Wilson mss.

12. STARTING THE CONTEST

1. Hoover Logs, April 19, May 11, 17, 19, 24, June 13, 23, Daily Logs, Jan. to June 30, 1960, File 66-1855-A-2860, FBI mss.; memos, May 16, 24, 1960, PPS320.103.233*C, Edgar to Dick, June 9, 1960, PPS320.103.234C.1, RNL.

2. Hoover's logs, July 2, 18, 20, 1960, daily logs, July through Dec. 1960, File 66-1855-A-2860, FBI mss.; Hoover to RN, July 7, PPS320.103.234**G.1-2, *Wall Street Journal*, July 6, Hoover to Woods, July 7, 1960, PPS320.103.234***, G, Edgar to Dick, no date, PPS320.103.332N, RNL.

3. Memo, July 21, 1960, PPS320.103.235A, RNL.

4. Greensboro appearance, Aug. 18, PPS69.139, and press release, Aug. 29, 1960, PPS421, RNL; RN, *Six Crises*, 325; Baughman, *Secret Service Chief*, 249–250; Scalettar interview, June 27, 2001, Gellman mss.

5. *NYT*, Aug. 30, 1960; memoirs, March 31, 1976, RNL; Hughes interview, July 3, 2001, Gellman mss.; RN, *Six Crises*, 326.

6. *NYT*, Aug. 30, 1960; Scalettar interview, June 27, 1960, Gellman mss.

7. Memo, Jan. 21, 1996, LBM168a, RNL; Raymond Scalettar, M.D., D.Sc., Gellman mss.; Scalettar interview, June 27, 2001, June 26, 2003, Gellman mss.

8. *NYT*, Aug. 30, 1960; RN to Graham, Sept. 8, 1960, B 299, Graham (2 of 3), Series 320, RNL and Collection 685, Series I, Notebooks 10, 14, Graham mss.; Scalettar, "Presidential Candidate Disability," 2811; Scalettar interview, June 27, 2001, Hughes interview, July 8, 2003, Gellman mss.

9. *NYT*, Aug. 30, Sept. 2, 3, 1960; Schedule, Aug. 30, 1960, PPS212(1960).422, Bowers to McGovern, Sept. 28, 1960, RNL; Scalettar, "Presidential Candidate Disability," 2811; Scalettar interview, June 27, 2001, Gellman mss.; Klein, *Making It Perfectly Clear*, 105.

10. *NYT*, Aug. 31, 1960; *Time*, Sept. 12, 1960; Scalettar interview, June 27, 2001, Gellman mss.; Donovan, *Confidential Secretary*, 258.

11. *NYT*, Sept. 2, 1960; *Newsweek*, Sept. 12, 1960, pp. 24–25.

12. RN to JFK, Aug. 31, 1960, PPS320.106.63, RNL.

13. RN to LBJ, Aug. 31, 1960, RNL; *NYT*, Sept. 3, 1960.

14. Medical bulletins, Aug. 30, 31, Sept. 1, 2, 6, 8, 1960, RNL: *NYT*, Sept. 5, 6, 1960.

15. Memos, Aug. 29, Sept. 7, 9, 1960, Finch mss.; memo, Sept. 8, 1960, B 9, F 62, Klein mss.

16. Memo, Sept. 3, 1960, Finch mss.; Klein to de Toledano, Sept. 9, 1960, B 213, de Toledano 3/3, Series 320, RNL.

17. Memos, Aug. 29, 1960, Finch mss.

18. Memo, Aug. 29, Sept. 5, 1960, Finch mss.; McCaffrey to Coolidge, Sept. 2, B 179, Coolidge, G and Hillings to McCaffrey, Sept. 8, 1960, B 341, Hillings 1958, Series 320, RNL.

19. Memo, Sept. 7, 1960, Finch mss.

20. Memos, Sept. 6, 9, 1960, Finch mss.; memo, Sept. 5, press release, Sept. 9, 1960, B 179, Cooper, John [1/2], Series 320, RNL; *RNI*, pp. 54–56.

21. Hoover to RN, Aug. 17, PPS320.103.239.1, Aug. 30, PPS320.103.240, Hoover to Woods, Sept. 3, Finch mss., Hoover to RN, Sept. 8, PPS320.103.247, Oct. 5, 1960, PPS320 .103.256, RNL; Sullivan, *Bureau*, 48–49.

22. Woods to Pinkley, Sept. 6, B 599, Pinkley 1956 (2 of 2), McCaffrey to Kolombatovich, Sept. 9, B 315, Hamilton, R, RN to Alcorn, B 25, Alcorn, RN to Kefauver, Sept. 19, B 401, Kefauver, Series 320, PN to McCrary, Sept. 10, B 10, NY—Sept.–Oct. 1960 [1/4], Series 54, memo, undated Sept. 1960, PPS421, RNL; *NYT*, Sept. 10, 1960; RN, *Six Crises*, 328.

23. *JFKI*, pp. 68–197; *LAT*, Sept. 1, 1960.

24. Gallup, *Gallup Poll*, Vol. 3: 1603, 1610, 1645, 1682, 1686, 1689; *WP*, Oct. 15, 1960.

25. *JFKI*, pp. 68–197; memo, Aug. 24, 1960, R 3, P 1, JFKL; *Time*, Aug. 22 and Sept. 5, 1960; *Newsweek*, Aug. 22, pp. 17–19, Aug. 29, pp. 18–19, Sept. 5, 1960, pp. 16–17.

26. *USNWR*, Jan. 4, p. 76, July 18, 1960, pp. 37, 43; *Time*, Aug. 8, 1960; *Newsweek*, Sept. 12, 1960, p. 26; *WP*, Sept. 4, 6, 1960.

27. Corey to Finch, Aug. 2, 1960, B 72, Opinion of Voters, Wilson mss.; Robinson to RN, Sept. 1, B 647, F (2 of 3), Series 320, Polls, Sept. 3–5, PPS69.153, and Sept. 27, 1950, PPS69.172, RN; Gallup, *Gallup Poll*, Vol. 3: 1681–1684, 1686; *USNWR*, Sept. 5, pp. 33–

36, Sept. 19, pp. 52–62, Sept. 26, 1960, pp. 50–52; *Newsweek*, Sept. 5, pp. 15–16, Sept. 26, 1960, pp. 41–45; *Time*, Sept. 5, 1960; *WP*, Sept. 2, 7, 9, 1960; RN, *Six Crises*, 320.

28. Memo, June, R 6, P I, and memo, analysis of RN, Sept. 14, 1960, R 10, P I, JFKL; *PAES* VII, p. 571; interview with Schlesinger, Dec. 3, 2000, *In Depth*, C-SPAN; Bradlee, *Conversations with Kennedy*, 32.

29. Attwood, *Reds and the Blacks*, 8–11.

30. *NYT*, Aug. 25, 1960; *JFKI*, p. 75.

31. *WP*, Sept. 9, 1960; *Time*, Sept. 12, 1960.

32. Powell, "Reactions to Kennedy's Delivery Skills," 59–68; *HP*, Sept. 10, 1960; *WP*, Sept. 11, 12, 1960; *SAST*, Sept. 11, 1960.

33. *WP*, Sept. 11, 1960.

34. *NYT*, Sept. 1, 1960; *WP*, Sept. 3, 9, 1960; *SAST*, Sept. 9, 1960; *DMN*, Sept. 9, 1960; *HP*, Sept. 10, 1960.

35. *SAST*, *DMN*, and *WP*, Sept. 9, 1960; *HP*, Sept. 12, 1960; Evans and Novak, *Lyndon Johnson*, 297.

36. Rowe to LBJ, Aug. 24, B 262, Senate Political File, Rasor to Mann, Sept. 1, B 217, Senate Political File, and Sanders OH, LBJL; *HP*, Sept. 11, 1960; *SAST*, Sept. 11, 1960; *DMN*, Sept. 11, 12, 1960.

37. Bowen to Rasor, July 22, 1960, B 215, Senate Political Files, LBJL; *USNWR*, July 11, pp. 100–101, Aug. 1, p. 33, Aug. 8, 1960, p. 40; *WP*, Sept. 8, 11, 1960.

38. *SAST*, Sept. 6, 11, 1960; *DMN*, Sept. 11, 12, 1960.

39. *SAST*, Sept. 6, 11, 1960; *DMN*, Sept. 11, 12, 1960.

40. Jacobson OH and Blundell II, OH, pp. 11, 18, LBJL; Jamieson, *Packaging the Presidency*, 155–157.

41. Robinson to RN, Sept. 1, 1960, B 647, F (2 of 3), Series 320, RNL; *NYT*, Sept. 1, 1960. *WP*, Sept. 1, 2, 3, 5, 6, 11, 1960.

42. *Newsweek*, Aug. 8, 1960, pp. 18–19; *USNWR*, p. 68; *Time*, Sept. 26, 1960.

43. RN to Lodge, Sept. 5, 1960, B 458, Lodge (1 of 2), memo, Aug. 13, B 845, Zionist, McWhorter to ?, Sept. 1960, B 457, Lodge (1 of 2), Series 320, RNL; *RNI*, pp. 52–54; memos, Aug. 1, 25, 1960, Finch mss.; *NYT*, Aug. 28, 1960 *Time*, Sept. 26, 1960; Lodge, *As It Was*, 208–210.

44. Lodge to Goldwater, Nov. 5, 1960, R 5, Lodge mss.

45. Lodge to Nelson, Nov. 5, 1958, and Lodge to Shapiro, Feb. 4, Nelson to Cabot, Feb. 17, Lodge to Nelson, Nov. 16, 1959, R 13, Lodge mss.

46. *NYT*, Aug. 27, 1960.

47. RN to Lefkowitz, Aug. 12 and Lefkowitz to RN, Aug. 18, B 445, Lefkowitz, Series 320, memo, Aug. 13, 1960, B 10, NY—Sept.–Oct. 1960 [1/4], Series 54, RNL; memos, Aug. 29, 1960, Finch mss.; *NYT*, Aug. 27, 1960.

48. Memo, Aug. 29, 1960, Finch mss.; memo, Sept. 3–5, 1960, B 10, NY—Sept.–Oct. 1960, [1/4], Series 54, RNL; *NYT*, Sept. 2–4, 1960; *BG*, Aug. 31, Sept. 4, 1960, R 31, Lodge mss.

49. Lodge to DDE, Sept. 30, 1958, R 29, and Lodge to Thompson, March 9, 1960, R 15, and *NYT*, Sept. 4. 8–10, and *BG*, Sept. 4, 8–10, 1960, R 31, Lodge mss.; cabinet meeting, Dec. 18, 1959, R 10, Cabinet DDEL; *Newsweek*, Aug. 8, 1960, p. 99.

50. Memo, Aug. 29, 1960, Finch mss.; memo, Sept. 3–5, 1960, B 10, NY—Sept.–Oct. 1960 [1/4], Series 54, RNL; *BG*, Sept. 6–8, 1960, R 31, and Rockefeller to Lodge, Oct. 5, 1960, R 13, Lodge mss.; *NYT*, Sept. 8, 1960.

51. *BG*, Sept. 7, 1960, R 31, Lodge mss.

52. Memo, Sept. 7, 1960, Finch mss.; *NYT*, Sept. 8, 1960.

53. *BG*, Sept. 8–10, 1960, R 31, Lodge mss.; *NYT*, Sept. 10, 1960.

54. *PPA* 1960–61, pp. 694–696; *WP*, Sept. 13, 1960.

55. *WP*, Sept. 13, 1960.

56. *WP*, Nov. 4, 1960.

57. Lungren and Lungren, *Healing Richard Nixon*, 61–65.

58. Scalettar, "Presidential Candidate Disability," 2811; Scalettar interview, June 27, 2001, Gellman mss.

59. Scalettar interview, June 27, 2001, June 26, 2003, Gellman mss.; Golden interview, July 2, 2001, Gellman mss.

13. THE CATHOLIC CANDIDATE

1. Lasky, *J.F.K.*, Appendix B; *USNWR*, Aug. 1, 1960, pp. 68–72; Sorensen, *Counselor*, 156–166.

2. Slayton, *Empire Statesman*, 237–263; also see Marlin, *American Catholic Voter*, 173–191; Smith, "Smith and Kennedy"; McClerren, "Southern Baptist State Newspapers."

3. Campbell et al., *American National Election Study*, 87; Fenton, *In Your Opinion*, 208–211; David, *Presidential Election and Transition*, 155–156; Kellstedt and Noll, "Religion, Voting for President, and Party Identification," 359–362.

4. Memoirs, March 15, 1976, RNL; Day 1, Tape 1, 00:44:25 [RN], FG.

5. RN speech, Feb. 1, 1953, B 9, F 2, *WP*, Oct. 25, 1955, B 40, F 4, Series 207, Miller to RN, Oct. 13, 1955, B 517, Miller, RP, Todd to RN, Feb. 8, 1957, B 757, Todd, R, Series 320, Miller to Hoover, April 20, 1957, PPS320.102.42.2, RNL; Erskine, "Dick and Pat Nixon," 33; *NYT*, June 6, 1960.

6. Cronin to Reuben, June 24, 1974, CCRO 2/25, Cronin mss.; Donovan, *Crusader in the Cold War*, 130, 147, 160–163; Gellman, *Contender*, 99–100, 233, 251; Gellman, *President and Apprentice*, 80, 269, 302, 326.

7. Spellman to RN, July 30, 1956, B 717, Spellman, RN to Cushing, July 16, B 197, Cushing, Series 320 and Cushing to Hoover, Sept. 2, 1959, PPS320.103.183, Series 320, Catholic Standard, April 30, 1954, B 21, F 2, memo, Aug. 29, B 34, F 7, RN to Pinkley, Dec. 12, 1955, B 43 F4 [2 of 2] Series 207, memoirs, April 5, 1976, RNL.

8. Gallup, *Gallup Poll*, Vol. 2: 1222, 1252–1253, 1293–1294, 1389, 1479, 1481, Vol. 3: 1649; Hudnut-Beumler, *Looking for God in the Suburbs*, 32–33; Bellah, "Civil Religion in America," 40–55.

9. Memo, Sept. 3, 1959, B 608, Prendergast, W, Series 320, RNL; *Time*, Sept. 12, 1960; Fenton, *In Your Opinion*, 195, 204; Lisle, "Canonical Impediment," 164; Herberg, *Protestant—Catholic—Jew*, 59–60, 138–139, 167–174; Wuthnow, *Restructuring of American Religion*, 72–97; Allitt, *Catholic Intellectuals and Conservative Politics*,

16–48; Ahlstrom, *Religious History of the American People,* 950–954; McGreevy, "Thinking on One's Own," 127–129.

10. Knebel, "Democratic Forecast," 13–17; U.S. Constitution, Article VI; McAndrews, "Avoidable Conflict," 283–287.

11. Lisle, "Catholic Press and Kennedy," 14–27, 85, 87–88; Wiessler, "Presidential Elections," 162–165.

12. *Newsweek,* Dec. 21, 1959, pp. 27–30.

13. *USNWR,* Jan. 25, 1960, pp. 42–44.

14. *Time,* April 18, 1960; Fenton, *In Your Opinion,* 203, 212–215; Lisle, "Canonical Impediment," 32–44; Marlin, *American Catholic Voter,* 250–251.

15. Sorensen, *"Let the Word Go Forth,"* 125–130; *Time,* May 2, 1960; Schlesinger, *Letters,* 184, 186.

16. Fleming, *Kennedy vs. Humphrey,* 67.

17. *PAES* VII, pp. 502–503; *USNWR,* July 4, 1960, pp. 48–51; Lisle, "Catholic Press and Kennedy," 42–48.

18. Sorensen, *"Let the Word Go Forth,"* 97.

19. *JFKI,* pp. 123, 137, 1285–1289; Sandler, *Letters of John F. Kennedy,* 95–96; Schlesinger, *Letters,* 184, 186; Sorensen, *"Let the Word Go Forth,"* 29; Fenton, *In Your Opinion,* 194–195.

20. RFK to Moulder, Aug. 31, 1960, Part I, R 6, JFKL; RFK to Bowles, Aug. 31, 1960, B 210, Kennedy, R, Part 5, Series 1, Bowles mss.; Maier, *Kennedys,* 340–341.

21. RFK to Moulder, Aug. 31, 1960, Part I, R 6, Sorensen to Cope, Sept. 5 and Wine to Blake, Sept. 7, 1960, R 7, P I, JFKL; *NYT,* Aug. 25 and Sept. 4, 1960; Sorensen, *Counselor,* 162.

22. Kinneally to RFK, Aug. 8, R 8, P I, Brademas to Sorensen, Aug. 11 and White to Cloud, Aug. 25, R 7, P I, Ernest to JFK, Aug. 29, R 3, P I, Lazell to Gurney, Aug. 31, R 6, P I and Lazell to Guthrie, Sept. 5, 1960, R 8, P I, JFKL; Sandler, *Letters of John F. Kennedy,* 92–95.

23. Nasaw, *Patriarch,* 709–725; Maier, *Kennedys,* 298–312.

24. Briggs, "Religious Issue," 47–48.

25. *WP,* Aug. 6, 1960; Carty, *Catholic in the White House?* 78, 86.

26. Galbraith to JFK, Aug. 25, 1960, R 4, P I, JFKL; Schlesinger, *Letters,* 226.

27. Gellman, *President and Apprentice,* 73–74.

28. *DDEP* XV, pp. 1049–1050; *WP,* Oct. 20, 1964; Sears and Osten, *Soul of an American President,* 178; Keller, "Intellectuals and Eisenhower," 281–292.

29. *PPA* 1960–61, p. 363.

30. *NYT,* Aug. 25, 1960.

31. *PPA* 1960–61, pp. 678–679.

32. *NYT,* Nov. 1, 1958.

33. RN to Davis, May 27, B 693, Polls and RN to Murphy, June 6, 1959, B 626, Religious [1/2], Series 320, RNL.

34. News conference, Feb. 15, 1960, R 2, Kesaris, *Papers of the Republican Party;* RN to Irwin, May 19, 1960, B 371, Series 320, RNL.

35. RN to M. Eisenhower, July 13, 1960, B 238, M. Eisenhower, Series 320, RNL.

36. RMW to Irwin, Aug. 25, and memo, Aug. 29, B 371, Irwin (2 of 4), Series 320, RNL; memo, Sept. 8, 1960, Finch mss.

37. *NYT*, July 31, 1960.

38. Miller, *Piety along the Potomac*, 125–131; Ahlstrom, *Religious History of the American People*, 956–958; Miller, "Popular Religion of the 1950's," 72–73.

39. Graham to DDE, Nov. 18, 1959 and May 20, Aug. 4, 1960, Notebook 2: Eisenhower, Bell to Moore, Feb. 24, 1971, Series I, Notebooks 5, 6, Collection 685, Graham mss.; Paddon, "Modern Mordecai," 70–92, 117–149; Gellman, *President and Apprentice*, 147; Graham, *Just As I Am*, 188–192, 202–203; Martin, *Prophet with Honor*, 207–208; Martin, *With God on Our Side*, 32–33; email, Rives to Gellman, Nov. 19, 2019, Gellman mss.

40. Graham to DDE, March 16, 1959, Series I, Notebook 2: Eisenhower, Collection 685, Graham mss.

41. Graham to DDE, April 12, May 20, Aug. 4, 1960, Series I, Notebook 2: Eisenhower, Collection 685, Graham mss.

42. Graham to DDE, Aug. 4, Sept. 1, 1960, Series I, Notebook 2: Eisenhower, Collection 685, Graham mss.

43. Graham to RN, Oct. 8, 1955, Series I, Notebooks 10, 14, and introduction at Pittsburgh crusade, undated, Series I, Notebook 14, Collection 685, Graham mss.; Gellman, *President and Apprentice*, 79, 148; Frady, *Billy Graham*, 269; Martin, *Prophet with Honor*, 146; Martin, *With God on Our Side*, 30–31.

44. Graham, *Just As I Am*, 319.

45. Graham to RN, Dec. 2, 1957, B 299, Graham {3 of 3}, Series 320, RNL.

46. RN to Graham, Aug. 12, PPS320.103.147, Graham to RN, Aug. 27, 1958, Nov. 17, 1959, B 299, Graham {3 of 3}, RN to Graham, March 25, B 319, Hare, R, Series 320, and Graham to RN, Dec. 29, 1959, B 1, Ill—Jan.–Mar. 1960, Series 52, RNL.

47. RN to Graham, June 4, Graham to RN, May 27, July 22, 1960, Series I, Notebooks 10, 14, Collection 685, Graham mss.

48. Graham to RN, Aug. 23, 1960, B 299, Graham {2 of 3}, Series 320, RNL and Series I, Notebooks 10, 14, Collection 685, Graham mss.

49. Graham to RN, Aug. 22, 1960, B 299, Graham {2 of 3}, Series 320, RNL and Series I, Notebooks 10, 14, Collection 685, Graham mss.

50. Graham to RN, Aug. 22, 1960, B 299, Graham {2 of 3}, Series 320, RNL and Series I, Notebook 10, 14, Collection 685, Graham mss.

51. *Time*, Aug. 29, 1960; Sandler, *Letters of John F. Kennedy*, 104–105.

52. Graham to *Time*, Aug. 28, 1960, B 229, Graham {2 of 3}, Series 320, RNL; Graham to RN, Sept. 1, and RN to Graham, Sept. 8, 1960, Series I, Notebooks 10, 14, Collection 685, Graham mss.

53. RN to Graham, Aug. 29, 1960, B 299, Graham {2 of 3}, Series 320, RNL and Series I, Notebooks 10, 14, Collection 685, Graham mss.

54. *Time*, Sept. 19, 1960; Miller, *Piety along the Potomac*, 132–143; Miller, "Popular Religion of the 1950's," 67–71; George, *God's Salesman*, 190–193.

55. Peale to RN, Feb. 20, 1956, B 583, Peale, Series 320, RNL.

56. *USNWR*, April 25, 1960, p. 56; *Newsweek*, April 25, 1960, p. 30; the incident occurred

on December 15, 1947, not 1950; see Kemper, "John F. Kennedy before the Greater Houston Ministerial Association," 98–109.

57. Peale to RN, April 5, and Peale to Dear, May 20, B 583, Peale and McElroy to Hamlin, Aug. 23, B 496, McElroy, Series 320, RNL; memo, April 19, 1960, Finch mss.

58. McCrary to Finch, May 25, B 494, McCrary [2/4] and Peale to RN. Aug. 1, 1960, B 582, Peale, Series 320, RNL.

59. Vinz, "Politics of Protestant Fundamentalism," 248, 259; Martin, *With God on Our Side*, 47–48; Marty, *Righteous*, 250–251.

60. *USNWR*, Sept. 12, 1960, p. 94.

61. *NYT*, Sept. 4, 1960; *USNWR*, Sept. 12, 1960, p. 94; *Time*, Sept. 12, 1960; Bell to JFK, Aug. 13, 1960, B 134, Byron White, DNC mss.; Kittrell to RFK, April 27, 1960, B 16, Political Files, General Subject Files, RFK mss.; Weeks, *Texas in the 1960 Election*, 58–59.

62. *USNWR*, Sept. 12, 1960, p. 94.

63. *NYT*, Sept. 8, 1960; *Time*, Sept. 19, 1960; Peale, *Tough-Minded Optimist*, 47–49; George, *God's Salesman*, 190–200; Massa, "Catholic for President," 297–317; Kemper, "John F. Kennedy before the Greater Houston Ministerial Association," 23–32; Ingle, *Nixon's First Cover-Up*, 100–105.

64. JFK to Poling, June 20, 1960, Part I, R 6, JFKL.

65. *USNWR*, Sept. 19, 1960, p. 96; *Newsweek*, Sept. 19, 1960, p. 38; *Time*, Sept. 19, 1960.

66. *USNWR*, Sept. 19, 1960, pp. 96–97; Peale, *Tough-Minded Optimist*, 50–51.

67. *Time*, Sept. 19, 1960.

68. *WP*, Sept. 16, 19, 1960; Peale, *Tough-Minded Optimist*, 51–56.

69. *USNWR*, Sept. 19, 1960, p. 97; *Newsweek*, Sept. 19, 1960, p. 38; *Time*, Sept. 19, 1960; George, *God's Salesman*, 202–205; Kemper, "John F. Kennedy before the Greater Houston Ministerial Association," 23–24; Ingle, *Nixon's First Cover-Up*, 105–107.

70. Schlesinger, *Letters*, 223; Miller, *Piety along the Potomac*, 146–157; Fox, *Reinhold Niebuhr*, 271–272; Kemper, "John F. Kennedy before the Greater Houston Ministerial Association," 24–30.

71. Smith, *Hostage to Fortune*, 692; Nasaw, *Patriarch*, 741.

72. *JFKI*, pp. 176, 183–185; *NYT*, Sept. 10, 12, 1960.

73. *HP* and *WP*, Sept. 10, 1960.

74. Memoirs, March 31, 1976, and RN to Pollock, Dec. 30, 1986, RNL; George, *God's Salesman*, 206–207; RN, *Six Crises*, 327–329.

75. Reid to RN, July 5, B 624, Reid and RN to Luce, Sept. 9, 1960, B 464, Luce [2/2], Series 320, RNL; *WP*, Sept. 5, 1960; Morris, *Price of Fame*, 515.

76. *JFKRN*, pp. 14–15.

77. *JFKI*, p. 1014; *WP*, Sept. 12, 14, 1960; Kemper, "John F. Kennedy before the Greater Houston Ministerial Association," 33–34.

78. O'Donnell, *Irish Brotherhood*, 372–375; Briggs, "Religious Issue," 56–57.

79. *JFKI*, pp. 196–206, 1014–1015; *HP* and *WP*, Sept. 12, 1960; Briggs, "Religious Issue," 58.

80. Kemper, "John F. Kennedy before the Greater Houston Ministerial Association," 12–39, 191–194; Briggs, "Religious Issue," 56–61.

81. O'Donnell, *Irish Brotherhood*, 374–375.

82. *USNWR*, Sept. 26, 1960, pp. 74–76; *JFKI*, pp. 206–210; Sorensen, *"Let the Word Go Forth,"* 130–136; Kemper, "John F. Kennedy before the Greater Houston Ministerial Association," 33, 43–142, 150–153; Briggs, "Religious Issue," 61–65, 68.

83. *Time*, Oct. 24, 1960; Briggs, "Religious Issue," 69–71, 77–81, 84–89; Dobbs, "Continuities in American Anti-Catholicism," 85–93; Hughes, "Texas Churches and Presidential Politics," 58–59, 86–128, 139–144; Viser, "John F. Kennedy and the Religious Issue," iii–iv; Weeks, *Texas in the 1960 Election*, 58–59; Dulaney and Phillips, *"Speak, Mister Speaker,"* 411; Briggs, "Religious Issue," 74–75; O'Donnell, *Irish Brotherhood*, 377.

84. *WP*, Oct. 11, 1960; *The State* (SC), Oct. 12, 1960; *Florida Times-Union*, Oct. 13, 1960; *DMN*, Oct. 14, 1960; *Time*, Oct. 24, 1960.

85. *JFKI*, p. 289; *HP*, Oct. 31, 1960.

86. *NYT*, Sept. 13, 1960; *WP*, Sept. 16, 1960; Kemper, "John F. Kennedy before the Greater Houston Ministerial Association," 184–187.

87. *WP*, Sept. 13, 1960.

88. Graham to RN, Sept. 24, 1960, Series I, Notebooks 10, 14, Collection 685, Graham mss.

89. *WP*, Sept. 16, Oct. 30, 1960.

90. *DMN*, Oct. 11, 13, 1960; *HP*, Oct. 12, 17, 1960; *SAST*, Oct. 12, 1960; *WP*, Oct. 13, 1960.

91. Memo, Oct. 18, 1960, B 2, Republican Party, 1960 Campaign, Seaton mss.; *Newsweek*, Oct. 31, 1960, p. 21; Kemper, "John F. Kennedy before the Greater Houston Ministerial Association," 187.

92. Marlin and Miner, *Sons of Saint Patrick*, 238–240.

93. Smith, *Hostage to Fortune*, 682–684, 686–687, 692, 696–697; Marlin and Miner, *Sons of Saint Patrick*, 239–240; Cooney, *American Pope*, 265–270.

94. Morris, *Price of Fame*, 515.

95. Memo, June 30, B 687, Shanley, Spellman to RN, Oct. 7, and PN to Spellman, Oct. 31, 1960, B 717, Spellman, Series 320, RNL; Sorensen, *"Let the Word Go Forth,"* 137; *NYT*, Oct. 20, 1960; *AC*, Oct. 22, 1960.

96. Sorensen, *"Let the Word Go Forth,"* 138–139.

97. *NYT* and *WP*, Oct. 20, 1960; Schlesinger, *Journals*, 90.

98. *WP*, Oct. 24, 27, 1960; *AC*, Oct. 26, 1960; *Time*, Oct. 31, 1960; *USNWR*, Nov. 7, 1960, pp. 59–61; Fischman, "Church in Politics," 832–835.

99. RN memo, Sept. 12, 1961, Wilderness Years Collection, Series VIII, Six Crises, B 5, PPS257, RNL; RN, *Six Crises*, 367–368, 421.

100. New Yorkers for Nixon, Oct. 1959, R 12, Lodge mss.; Flanigan to Dear, July 11, B 791, Volunteers and press release, Aug. 15, 1960, B 263, Flanigan, P, Series 320, RNL; Congressional Quarterly, *Weekly Report*, 1603; Flanigan interview, July 17, 2003, Gellman mss.

101. RN memo, Sept. 12, 1961, Wilderness Years Collection, Series VIII, Six Crises, B 5, PPS257, RNL.

102. Sorensen, *Kennedy*, 193–194.

103. Casey, *Making of a Catholic President,* 205, and also see 123–150, 191–194; Williams, "Richard Nixon's Religious Right," 145–146; Dallek, *Lone Star Rising,* 584–585.

14. THE GREAT DEBATES

1. White, *Making of the President,* 279–294.

2. Schlesinger, *Journals,* 151; Schlesinger, *Thousand Days,* 69–70; Sorensen, *Kennedy,* 195–204, 213; Sorensen, *Kennedy Legacy,* 59; Sorensen, "When Kennedy Met Nixon."

3. Kennedy, *True Compass,* 156–157; Clifford, *Counsel to the President,* 325–326; Salinger, *With Kennedy,* 47, 54; Goodwin, *Remembering America,* 112–116; O'Brien, *No Final Victories,* 92–93; O'Donnell and Powers, *"Johnny, We Hardly Knew Ye,"* 237–241.

4. *Indianapolis News,* June 15, 1960, PPS61S.1, RNL; Mazo et al., *Great Debates,* 3; Kennedy, *True Compass,* 154.

5. Pastore to RN, April 22, 1960, B 580, Pastore, Series 320, RNL; *PAES VII,* pp. 488–495; *NYT,* July 25, 1960; David, *Presidential Election and Transition,* 90–93; Self, "First Debate over the Debates," 61–65; Freeley, "Presidential Debates and the Speech Profession," 60–63; Lang and Lang, *Politics and Television,* 98–100; *Newsweek,* Sept. 25, 2000, p. 11.

6. RN to Pastore, May 9, B 580, Pastore, *Honolulu Star-Bulletin,* Dec. 29, 1960, B 147, Chotiner 1960, Menzies to RN, Feb. 14 and RN to Menzies, March 4, 1963, Series 320, and memoirs, March 31, 1976, RNL; *NYT,* May 17, 1960; *USNWR,* Nov. 14, 1960, p. 59. Mazo et al., *Great Debates,* 2–3.

7. Gallup, *Gallup Poll,* Vol. 3: 1684; *NYT,* Aug. 12, and *NYT Magazine,* Sept. 25, 1960, pp. 18–19; *NY Post,* Aug. 25, 1960; *WP,* Sept. 7, 21, 1960; Gilbert, *Television and Presidential Politics,* 161.

8. *NYT,* July 28 and 29, 1960; *JFKRN,* p. 617; "architect of triumph," *Broadcasting,* Nov. 14, 1960; Klein, *Making It Perfectly Clear,* 102–103.

9. Salinger to Klein, Sept. 1, PPS320.106.64 and Klein to Frandsen, Sept. 21, 1960, B 773, United Press I, Series 320, RNL; *USNWR,* Aug. 29, 1960, p. 44; *NYT,* Sept. 1, 1960; *WP,* Sept. 25, 1960.

10. *Baltimore Sun,* Sept. 1, 1960, PPS61S.9, RNL; Klein, *Making It Perfectly Clear,* 103; Wilson, *Confessions of a Kinetic Congressman,* 96–97; Sorensen, *Kennedy,* 195–196; Friel, "Influence of Television," 242.

11. Memo from Hewitt, Oct. 5, 1960, B 723, Stanton, Series 320, RNL.

12. *JFKI,* pp. 358–361, 363–366; *JFKRN,* pp. 1051–1055; *SAST,* Sept. 25, 26, 1960; *NYT,* Sept. 26, 1960; Salinger, *P.S.,* 83–84; Sorensen, *Kennedy,* 198; Goodwin, *Remembering America,* 112–114.

13. Diary, Sept. 15, 1960, B 10, 1 Sept. 1960–31 Dec. 1960, Snyder mss.; *DDEP XXI,* p. 2091–2092; *NYT,* Sept. 17, 1960; Kistiakowsky, *Scientist at the White House,* 408. *Newsweek,* Oct. 24, 1960, p. 35.

14. Schedule, Sept. 25, 1960, PPS212(1960).528, RNL; telephone calls, Sept. 25, 1960, R 27, Diary DDEL; *SAST,* Sept. 26, 1960; RN, *Six Crisis,* 333–336.

15. Javits to RN, Sept. 19, B 380, Javits (1 of 2), and Stahlman to RN, Sept. 21, 1960, B 721, Stahlman [3/4], Series 320, RNL.

16. Memo, Aug. 1, 1960, Finch mss.

17. Schedule, Sept. 26, 1960, PPS212(1960).528, RNL; *Newsweek*, Oct. 3, 1960, pp. 37–38.

18. RN to Thompson, May 39, 1958, PPS320.82.37 and memo, Sept. 21, PPS320.106.80A, Rogers to RN, Sept. 29, B 652, Rogers (1 of 4), Finch to Rogers, Oct. 7, 1959, B 258, Finch 1959 [1/2] and memo, early Sept. 1961, B 652, Rogers (2 of 4), Series 320, RNL; Gellman, *President and Apprentice*, 43, 45–46; *LAT*, March 26, 2003.

19. WP and NYT, Sept. 27, 1960; memo, Sept. 28, B 145, F 7, Series 207, and clipping, Sept. 28, 1960, PPS61S.34, RNL.

20. Stanton to RN, Oct. 6, 1960, B 773, Stanton, Series 320, RNL.

21. Memo by Hewitt, Oct. 5, 1960, B 773, Stanton, Series 320, RNL; Hewitt, *Tell Me a Story*, 67–69; Kennedy, *True Compass*, 156.

22. WP, Sept. 27, 1960; *Commercial Appeal* (TN), Sept. 27, 1960, PPS61S.65, memo, early Sept. 1961, B 652, Rogers (2 of 4), Series 320, RNL; Sorensen, *Kennedy*, 198; RN, *Six Crises*, 338 and 341; Smith, *Events Leading Up to My Death*, 263; Hewitt, *Tell Me a Story*, 67–69; O'Donnell, *Irish Brotherhood*, 388; Klein, *Making It Perfectly Clear*, 105–106.

23. First debate, Sept. 26, 1960, YouTube Video; for reactions to the first debate, see *NYT*, *WP*, and *DMN*, Sept. 27, 1960. I watched all the videos of the four debates.

24. *JFKRN*, pp. 73–75; also Sorensen, *"Let the Word Go Forth,"* 103–105; for another transcript of the debates, see Kraus, *Great Debates*, 348–368.

25. *JFKRN*, pp. 75–78; conversation with Mazo, Oct. 28, 1960, White mss.

26. *JFKRN*, p. 78.

27. Ibid., 78–81.

28. Ibid., 82–90.

29. Ibid., 81–82.

30. RN, *Six Crises*, 339; memoirs, March 20, 1976, RNL; interview with Vanocur, Oct. 19, 2005; Vanocur OH, pp. 23–24, JFKL.

31. *JFKRN*, pp. 89–92.

32. *Commercial Appeal* (TN), Sept. 27, 1960, PPS61.S.65, RNL; O'Donnell, *Irish Brotherhood*, 389.

33. NYT and LAT, Sept. 28, 1960; David, *Presidential Election and Transition*, 80; Mazo et al., *Great Debates*, 4.

34. Smith, *Events Leading Up to My Death*, 263–264.

35. *Commercial Appeal* (TN), Sept. 27, PPS61S.65, and *CST*, Sept. 27, 1960, PPS61S.40, RNL.

36. Costa to Klein, Sept. 30, 1960, B 411, King F, Series 320, RNL; RN, *Six Crises*, 340–341.

37. *BG*, Sept. 27, 1960, PPS61S.88, RNL; *Newsweek*, Sept. 25, 2000, p. 11; *DMN*, Sept. 27, 1960, and clipping, Sept. 28, 1960.

38. *Newsweek*, Sept. 25, 2000, p. 11; clipping, Sept. 28, 1960; Sorensen, *Kennedy*, 202.

39. Baker, *Good Times*, 325–326.

40. TV Debates, Sept. 28, PPS69.173, and *CST*, Sept. 29, 1960, PPS61.S, 152, RNL; *WP*, Sept. 27, 28, 1960; *NYT*, Sept. 28, 1960; Bradlee, *Good Life*, 211.

41. Polls, Sept. 30, 1960, PPS69.178, RNL; Gallup, *Gallup Poll*, Vol. 3: 1685, 1686, 1689; *WP*, Sept. 14, 25, 28, Oct. 2, 5, 16, 1960; *DMN*, Sept. 14, 21, 1960; *NYT*, Oct. 3, 1960.

42. O'Donnell, *Irish Brotherhood*, 389–390; Bradlee, *Conversations with Kennedy*, 32.

43. Sorensen, *Kennedy*, 200–202; Schlesinger, *Thousand Days*, 69; Clifford, *Counsel to the President*, 323–325; Kraus, *Great Debates*, 10–14, 18; Mazo et al., *Great Debates*, 3–4; David, *Presidential Election and Transition*, 88–89, 99–102, 106, 109–110; Michener, *Report of the County Chairman*, 124–127; Goodman, *Letters to Kennedy*, 14; Rorabaugh, *Real Making of the President*, 149–157.

44. *WP* and *NYT*, Sept. 28, 1960; *SAST*, Sept. 30, 1960; Salinger, *P.S.*, 84.

45. *NYT*, Sept. 28, 1960; *Atlanta Journal*, Sept. 27, 1960, PPS61S.33, RNL; *Springfield State Register* (IL), Sept. 28, 1960, PPS61S.132, RNL; *DMN*, Sept. 28–29, 1960; *HP*, Sept. 29, 30, 1960; *WP*, Sept. 30, Oct. 1, 1960; *NYT*, Oct. 1, 1960.

46. Swim to RN, Sept. 27, B 742, Swim, D, Series 320, *CDN*, Sept. 30, PPS61S.165, and *Philadelphia Inquirer*, Oct. 3, 1960, PPS61S.184, RNL; Strober and Strober, "*Let Us Begin Anew*," 32; Dallek, *Camelot's Court*, 20–21.

47. *Broadcasting*, Nov. 7, 1960; I have mostly depended on Bruschke, "Debunking Nixon's Radio Victory," 67–75; also see Druckman, "Power of Television Images"; Kraus, "Winners of the First 1960 Debate"; Vancil and Pendell, "Myth of Viewer-Listener Disagreement"; Self, "First Debate over the Debates."

48. Memo, Sept. 27, 1960, B 145, F 7, Series 207, and for examples see: Clarke to RN, Sept. 27, B 156, Clarke 1 of 2, Jarvis to McCaffery, Sept. 27, B 380, Jarvis, Bullis to RN, Sept. 27, B 111, Bullis, memo, Sept. 27, B 805, Weeks, O'Donnell to McWhorter, Sept. 28, B 568, O'Donnell, P, Crutcher to RN, Sept. 28, B 195, Crutcher, R, Simpson to RN, Sept. 28, B 696, Simpson, M, Longinotti to RN, Sept. 29, B 460, Longinotti, Gainey to Finch, Sept. 29, B 279, Gainey [1/2], Rhodes to Finch, Sept. 30, B 639, Rhodes, JJ, Allard to RN, Oct. 4, B 26, Allard, J, Bond to RN, Oct. 5, B 92, Bond, W, Series 320, RNL; *NYT*, Oct. 1, 1960; *Newsweek*, Oct. 10, 1960, p. 25; Klein, *Making It Perfectly Clear*, 106, 236–237; Lang and Lang, *Politics and Television*, 102–120.

49. Memo, Oct. 1, B 647, F (2 of 3), Series 320 and memo, Oct. 5, 1960, B 1, PPS61, F Opinion Research [1/2], RNL.

50. *NYT*, Sept. 26, 1960; Strober and Strober, "*Let Us Begin Anew*," 33; Fromson interview, part 3, https://interviews.televisionacademy.com/interviews/Murray-Fromson?clip=chapter3#interview-clips; Fromson interview, USC Living History Project (2015).

51. Memo, Sept. 27, 1960, B 457, Lodge (1 of 2), Series 320, RNL.

52. *Time*, Aug. 13, 1973; Ingwerson, "Where Dick Tuck Goes"; Miller, "Tricky Dick"; Felton, "Bugging of Mack the Knife," 28–31; Gershen, "Past Full of Pranks," 2; *Tucson Sentinel*, May 29, 2018; *NYT* obituary, May 29, 2018; *WP* obituary, May 30, 2018; Trout, "Political Prankster," May 30, 2018.

53. Trout, "Political Prankster"; *Time*, Aug. 13, 1973; *Tucson Sentinel*, Aug. 9, 1974.

54. Day 8, Tape 2, 00:34:15 [RN], FG; conversation no. 147-9, Oct. 7, and conversation nos. 365-7, 797-30, 797-33, Oct. 13, 1972, WH tapes; *WP*, June 17, 1997, p. A01;

Brinkley and Nichter, *Nixon Tapes*, 1973, 149, 186, 222, 257, 738; Klein, *Making It Perfectly Clear*, 139.

55. NYT and WP, Sept. 27, 28, 1960; Horne, *Macmillan*, 2: 280; Hagerty OH 91, p. 125, COHP; Roberts OH 266, pp. 842–845, DDEL.

56. Memo, Oct. 1, 1960, R 27, Diary, DDEL.

57. Hagerty OH 91, pp. 124–125, COHP; Allen, *Eisenhower and the Mass Media*, 180–181.

58. DDE to Gosden, Sept. 28, 1960, B 28, RN 1958 (1), Administrative Series, DDEL.

59. *HP*, Sept. 27; *WP*, Oct. 1, 1960.

60. *JFKI*, pp. 416–517, 1071–1087; *JFKRN*, pp. 114–145, 402, 437–438, 487–488; *WP*, Oct. 4–6, 1960; NYT, Oct. 2, 3, 1960; *HP*, Oct. 5, 6, 1960; SAST, Oct. 5, 1960; *Newsweek*, Oct. 10, 1960, pp. 26–27; *Time*, Oct. 10, 1960; *HP* and *WP*, Oct. 3, 1960; Truman and Acheson, *Affection and Trust*, 242, 246, 248–249; Poen, "Truman and Kennedy," 305–306; Sand, *Truman in Retirement*, 74–76.

61. *JFKI*, quotations on pp. 447, 427, 490, 574, 895–896, 1115, 1206, 1208; Kaplan, *Wizards of Armageddon*, 286–290; Helgerson, *Getting to Know the President*, 54–58; Preble, *Kennedy and the Missile Gap*, 108–110, 188; Taubman, *Secret Empire*, 323; Beschloss, *Crisis Years*, 25–28.

62. *DMN*, Oct. 2, 5, 7, 1960; *WP*, Oct. 2, 4, 7, 8, 1960; SAST, Oct. 2, 6, 1960; *HP*, Oct. 5, 6, 1960; *Montgomery Advertiser* and NYT, Oct. 4, 1960.

63. *RNI*, pp. 373–480, 1236–1245; NYT, Oct. 3–7, 1960; *WP*, Oct. 3, 5–7, 1960; *HP*, Oct. 2, 4, 6, 7, 1960; AC, Oct. 5, 6, 1960; SAST, Oct. 4–7, 1960; *Newsweek*, Oct. 10, 1960, p. 25 RN, *Six Crises*, 342.

64. NYT and WP, Oct. 2, 1960; *Time*, Oct. 10, 1960; USNWR, Oct. 10, 1960, p. 85.

65. Memo, Oct. 1, 1960, B 11, F Oct. 1960 (1), Diary DDEL; *WP* and *DMN*, Oct. 5, 1960; Allen, *Eisenhower and the Mass Media*, 181.

66. RN to Scott, Oct. 3, 1960, B 1, 10,200-N-P, Scott mss.; Report 1960, B 765, Truth S, Series 320, RNL; NYT, Oct. 4, 1960.

67. WP and NYT, Oct. 6–8, 1960; conversation with Mazo, Oct. 28, 1960, White mss.; Jamieson, *Packaging the Presidency*, 150–153; RN, *Six Crises*, 345.

68. Second debate, Oct. 7, 1960, YouTube Video; schedule, Oct. 6, 1960, PPS212(1960).593, RNL; NYT and WP, Oct. 7, 8, 1960; *Newsweek*, Oct. 10, 1960, p. 25.

69. Friel, "Influence of Television," 259; David, *Presidential Election and Transition*, 80, 102; Mazo, *Great Debates*, 4.

70. JFK to RN, Oct. 4, 1960, PPS320.106.83, RNL; LAT, Oct. 8, 1960, PPS61.202, RNL; WP and NYT, Oct. 8, 1960; *Time*, Oct. 17, 1960.

71. Kraus, *Great Debates*, 369–389; *JFKRN*, pp. 149–164; NYT, Oct. 8, 1960; *WP*, Oct. 8, 10, 1960; *HP*, Oct. 8, 1960; Time, Oct. 17, 1960; *National Review*, Oct. 22, 1960, p. 236; *Newsweek*, Oct. 17, 1960, pp. 108–115; Friel, "Influence of Television," 260–261; RN, *Six Crises*, 345.

72. Kraus, *Great Debates*, 386–387.

73. Michener, *Report of the County Chairman*, 164–167.

74. NYT and WP, Oct. 8, 1960; *Time*, Oct. 17, 1960.

75. *Time*, October 17, 1960; Schlesinger, *Journals*, 86–87.

76. Schlesinger, *Journals*, 86–87.
77. Sulzberger, *Last of the Giants*, 696.
78. *JFKI*, pp. 517–520; *WP* and *NYT*, Oct. 8, 9, 1960.
79. *NYT* and *WP*, Oct. 8, 9, 1960; *Time*, Oct. 17, 1060.
80. Telephone call, Oct. 7, 1960, R 27, Diary DDEL; *WP*, Oct. 8, 9, 11, 12, 1960; *NYT*, Oct. 8, 9, 1960; Beall to RN, Oct. 8, B 68, Beall, J, Moley to RN, Oct. 10, B 524, Moley—Correspondence 1 of 2, Alcorn to RN, Oct. 12, B 25, Alcorn, and Anthony to RN, Oct. 12, B 45, Anthony, E, and Simpson to RN, Oct. 19, 1960, B 696, Simpson, M, Series 320, RNL; Friel, "Influence of Television," 261.
81. Finch to Roper, Oct. 12, B 656, Roper, E, Series 320, and memo, Oct. 13, 1960, B 1, F Opinion Research, PPS61 and voting intentions, Oct. 14–15, 1960, B 2, PPS71, RNL; Gallup, *Gallup Poll*, Vol. 3: 1686–1687; *WP*, Oct. 9, 12, 1960; *DMN*, Oct. 12, 1960; *HP*, Oct. 13, 1960; *USNWR*, Oct. 10, 1960, pp. 64–68.
82. Finch to Byrnes, Oct. 10, B 119, Byrnes, Jo, and RN to Morlan, Oct. 15, 1960, B 530, Morlan, Series 320, RNL.
83. *JFKI*, pp. 521–614, 1088–1115, quotation on 1107; *JFKRN*, pp. 106–112, 521–524; Sorensen, "*Let the Word Go Forth*," 186–188; *WP*, Oct. 8–11, 13, 1960; *AC* and *HP*, Oct. 10, 11, 13, 1960; *The State* (SC), Oct. 11, 1960.
84. *RNI*, pp. 489–557; memo by Washburn, Oct. 8, 1960, PPS320.106.86, RNL; *NYT* and *WP*, Oct. 9–12, 1960; Klein, *Making It Perfectly Clear*, 94–97; Cull, *Cold War and the United States Information Agency*, 181–183.
85. *NYT*, Oct. 10, 1960; memos, Oct. 11–12, 1960, B 2, Republican Party Series, 1960 Campaign Subseries, Seaton mss.; RN speech, Oct. 13, 1960, B 147, F 16, Series 207, RNL.
86. *WP* and *NYT*, Oct. 13, 1960.
87. *WP* and *NYT*, Oct. 13, 1960.
88. *NYT*, Oct. 14, 1960; *DMN*, Oct. 13, 1960; quotation *WP*, Oct. 17, 1960; Friel, "Influence of Television," 262–263; David, *Presidential Election and Transition*, 104.
89. Kraus, *Great Debates*, 390–410; *JFKRN*, pp. 204–222; *Newsweek*, Oct. 24, 1960, pp. 39, 80–83; Friel, "Influence of Television," 263–264; RN, *Six Crises*, 346–347; memo, Sept. 12, 1961, PPS257, RNL; Lungren and Lungren, *Healing Richard Nixon*, 65–67.
90. Conversation with Mazo, Oct. 28, 1960, White mss.; DDEP XXI, pp. 2130–2131; *NYT*, Oct. 14, 1960; Friel, "Influence of Television," 263–265; Allen, *Eisenhower and the Mass Media*, 181.
91. *LAT*, *WP*, and *NYT*, Oct. 14, 15, 1960, quotation *NYT*, Oct. 14.
92. *JFKI*, pp. 505–686, 1125–1175; *JFKRN*, pp. 222–223, 240–252, 504–505; *WP*, Oct. 15 and 17–21, 1960; *NYT*, Oct. 16–21, 1960; *HP*, Oct. 13, 17, 19, 21, 1960; *AC*, Oct. 18–21, 1960; Sorensen, "*Let the Word Go Forth*," 49–54, 109–117; Goodman, *Letters to Kennedy*, 29–31; Schlesinger, *Thousand Days*, 72–73.
93. *RNI*, pp. 557–696, 1246–1252; *NYT* and *WP*, Oct. 14–21, 1960; *AC*, Oct. 14–15, 1960; RN to MacArthur, Oct. 15, B 468, MacArthur, H, RN to Bennett, Oct. 15, B 75, Bennett, W, McCaffery to Herter, Oct. 15, B 216, DiMaggio, D, and Alcorn to RN, Oct. 19, 1960, B 25, Alcorn, Series 320, RNL; Friel, "Influence of Television," 265.

94. *WP*, Oct. 16, 21, 1960; TV debate, Oct. 14, 1960, PPS69.188, Benson to DDE, Oct. 19, B 76, Benson, 1960–61, and RN to Yorty, Oct. 23, 1960, B 837, Yorty, Series 320, RNL; memo, Oct. 16, 1960, B 2, Republican Party Series, 1960 Campaign Subseries, Seaton mss.

95. O'Donnell to McWhorter, Oct. 19, B 568, O'Donnell and *CST*, Oct. 21, B 147, Chotiner (1960), Series 320 and schedule, Oct. 20, PPS212(1960).595 and Oct. 21, PPS212 (1960).595, *Cleveland Plain Dealer*, Oct. 22, PPSA61S.287, RNL; *NYT*, Oct. 21, 22, 1960.

96. Fourth debate video, Oct. 21, 1960, YouTube; Kraus, *Great Debates*, 411–430; *JFKRN*, pp. 260–278; *WP* and *NYT*, Oct. 22, 1960; Flanders to RN, Oct. 22, 1960, B 263, Flanders, Series 320, RNL; Friel, "Influence of Television," 266; RN, *Six Crises*, 351, 356.

97. Memo, Oct. 25, 1960, B 2, Republican Party Series, 1960 Campaign Subseries, Seaton mss.; *WP*, Oct. 19, 21, 1960; Thompson, *Proud Highway*, 234–235; David, *Presidential Election and Transition*, 80; Mazo et al., *Great Debates*, 4–5; Gilbert, *Television and Presidential Politics*, 116; Rider, "Charleston Study," 104–107.

98. *JFKI*, pp. 1115, 1173; *NYT*, Oct. 13, 16, 24, 25, 27, 30, 1960; *WP*, Oct. 18, 20, 23, 24, 25, 30, Nov. 1, 1960; Friel, "Influence of Television," 271.

99. In Kraus, *Great Debates*, 286–288.

100. Memo, Oct. 25, 1960, and Rogers to RN, Sept. 1, 1961, B 652, Rogers (1 of 4), and memo, early Sept. 1961, B 652, Rogers (2 of 4), Series 320, RNL.

101. RN, *Six Crises*, 339.

102. *Honolulu Star-Bulletin*, Dec. 29, 1960, B 147, Chotiner (1960), Series 320, RN to Lawson, April 17, 1961, uncatalogued, and RN to Menzies, March 4, 1963, B 510, Menzies, Series 320, RNL.

103. Schwerin Research Corporation, *Bulletin*, Jan. 1961, Vol. 9, No. 1, Gellman mss. Horace Schwerin was my father-in-law, and we often discussed the debates and their significance.

15. THE DEMOCRATS' FRANTIC FINALE

1. *JFKI*, pp. 689–759, 1173–1200; *WP*, Oct. 23–26, 1960; *NYT*, Oct. 23–26, 1960; *AC*, Oct. 26, 1960; *DMN*, Oct. 26, 1960; *Time*, Oct. 31, 1960; *Newsweek*, Oct. 31, 1960, pp. 22, 86; Mullen, "Newspaper Advertising in the Kennedy-Nixon Campaign," 3–10.

2. Martin OH, I, pp. 5–9, and Martin OH, II, pp. 9–15, 22–24, 32–33, LBJL; Bryant, *Bystander*; O'Brien, *John F. Kennedy*, 364–368; Brauer, *John F. Kennedy and the Second Reconstruction*, 11–29.

3. Belafonte, *My Song*, 213–216.

4. Wofford, *Of Kennedys and Kings*, 60; Felknor, *Dirty Politics*, 62–63; *Evening Star* (DC), July 12, 1957, PPS337.B 5, and press release, Oct. 7, 1960, B 607, Powell (1 of 2), Series 320, RNL; *Time*, March 21, 1960; *LAS*, Nov. 3, 1960; *CD*, Nov. 5 to 11, 1960; *NYT*, Nov. 5, 8, 1960; Long, *First Class Citizenship*, 102; Carty, *Catholic in the White House?* 91; Hamilton, *Adam Clayton Powell, Jr.*, 333–337; Haygood, *King of the Cats*; *Evening Star* (DC), July 12, 1957, PPS337.B 5, and press release, Oct. 7, 1960, B 607, Powell (1 of 2), Series 320, RNL; Gellman, *Contender*, 347–348.

5. Wofford OH, 81, and Shriver OH, 46, JFKL; Bowles, *Promises to Keep*, 444–446, quotation on 444; Wofford, *Of Kennedys and Kings*, 43–44.

6. Kennedy-Nixon debate, Sept. 26, 1960, video YouTube; *JFKI*, p. 432.

7. *Montgomery Advertiser* (AL), Oct. 19, 1960; Kuhn, "There's a Footnote to History!" 584–594; the best description of this episode is still Lewis, *King*, 125–130; Branch, *Parting the Waters*, 356–373; Levingston, *Kennedy and King*, 90–100; Garrow, *Bearing the Cross*, 145–149.

8. AC, Oct. 24, 26, 27, 1960; NYT, Oct. 26, 27, 1960.

9. Carson, *Papers of Martin Luther King, Jr.*, Vol. 5: 535; AC, Oct. 27, 1960; NYT, Oct. 27, 1960; *LA Sentinel*, Oct. 27, 1960; ADW, Oct. 27, 1960; *Jet*, Nov. 3, 1960, p. 5; BAA, Nov. 5, 1960; NYAN, Nov. 5, 1960; King, *My Life with Martin Luther King, Jr.*, 195; Shriver OH, 53, JFKL; Stossel, *Sarge*, 163–165; Wofford, *Of Kennedys and Kings*, 17–18; Schlesinger, *Robert Kennedy and His Times*, 215–216; Lewis and the *New York Times*, *Portrait of a Decade*, 116.

10. AC, Oct. 28, 29, 1960; NYT and DMN, Oct. 28, 1960; CCP, Oct. 29, Nov. 5, 1960; LAS, Nov. 3, 1960; NYAN, Nov. 5, 1960; CD, Nov. 5–11, 1960; *Jet*, Nov. 10, 1960, p. 4; Carson, *Papers of Martin Luther King, Jr.*, 5: 535–536, 543; Wofford, *Of Kennedys and Kings*, 20–23; Belafonte, *My Song*, 218–219; Stossel, *Sarge*, 165–166; Smith, *Events Leading Up to My Death*, 295; King, *Daddy*, 175–176; Guthman and Shulman, *Robert Kennedy in His Own Words*, 68–69; Thomas, *Robert Kennedy*, 100–103; Hilty, *Robert Kennedy*, 171–174; for an exaggerated description of RFK's role, see Tye, *Bobby Kennedy*, 123–129.

11. NY Post, Nov. 1, 1960, PPS320.107.710s, RNL; AC, Nov. 2, 7, 1960; *Montgomery Advertiser*, Nov. 2, 1960; Carson, *Papers of Martin Luther King, Jr.*, 5: 537, 544–552; Belafonte, *My Song*, 218–219.

12. Carson, *Papers of Martin Luther King, Jr.*, 5: 40, 538; PC, Nov. 19, 1960; Shriver OH, 23–25, JFKL; Wofford, *Of Kennedys and Kings*, 23–25; Stossel, *Sarge*, 167; Wolseley, *Black Press, U.S.A.*, 11; Roberts and Klibanoff, *Race Beat*, 76; I spoke with Wofford several times by telephone about reports that two million pamphlets were sent by Greyhound Bus across the United States to black churches. He could not confirm this event. I doubt that they ever happened due to time constraints and a number of other reasons. Many authors repeat this claim without any archival evidence. For Shriver OH, 24, JFKL; Wofford, *Of Kennedys and Kings*, 24; Carson, *Papers of Martin Luther King, Jr.*, 5: 40; Stossel, *Sarge*, 168–169; Branch, *Parting the Waters*, 371–373; Levingston, *Kennedy and King*, 100.

13. Interview with Wofford, Jan. 3, 2002; Wofford, *Of Kennedys and Kings*, 46–48.

14. Gellman, *President and Apprentice*, 125–156, 372–424; interview with Tyler, May 27, 2003, Gellman mss.

15. Lautier to McWhorter, Oct. 10, 1960, B 442, Lautier, Series 320, RNL.

16. AC, Oct. 27, 1960; NY Post, Nov. 1, 1960, PPS320.107.710s, RNL.

17. Silber, *With All Deliberate Speed*, 255–257; Walsh, *Gift of Insecurity*, 161–181; Walsh interview, Dec. 1, 2005, Gellman mss.; Tyler interview, May 27, 2003, Gellman mss.

18. Suggested Statement, Oct. 31, 1960 (received Jan. 9, 1960), Central Files, O.F. 142-A-4, DDEL; NYT, Dec. 14, 15, 1960; memo, Dec. 14, 1960, B 9, F 62, Klein mss.; Sil-

ber, *With All Deliberate Speed*, 270–272; Walsh, *Gift of Insecurity*, 179; Walsh interview, Dec. 1, 2005, Gellman mss.; RN, *Six Crises*, 362.

19. RN to Robinson, Nov. 4, 1960, B 649, Robinson (2 of 2), Series 320, RNL.

20. *NYT*, Dec. 14, 1960.

21. Shriver OH, 35, JFKL; Sorensen, *Counselor*, 272; *LAS*, Nov. 3, 1960; Branch, *Parting the Waters*, 374–378, quotation 378; Wilkins, *Standing Fast*, 279; Booker, *Black Man's America*, 22.

22. *ADW*, Nov. 9, 1960; *AC*, Nov. 6, 12, 1960; *PC*, Nov. 19, 1960, Martin OH, II, pp. 43–44, LBJL; Melton, "1960 Presidential Election in Georgia," 251–253.

23. *JFKRN*, pp. 165–174, 179–186; *WP* and *DMN*, Oct. 8, 10, 1960; *NYT*, Oct. 10, 1960.

24. Parker, *Capitol Hill in Black and White*, 16.

25. Hunt to Barrie, Oct. 13, 1960, B 206, Senate Political Files, LBJL; Alsop to Summers, Oct. 15, 1960, B 16, Sept.–Oct. 1960, Alsop mss.; Baker OH, 3536, SHO; *WP*, Oct. 8, 11–15, 17, Nov. 6, 1960; *The State* (SC), Oct. 11, 12, 1960; *Macon Telegraph* (GA), Oct. 15, 1960; *AC*, Oct. 12, 13, 1960; *Times-Union* (FL), Oct. 13, 1960; *Tampa Times*, Oct. 13, 1960; *Miami Herald*, Oct. 13, 1960; *Montgomery Advertiser* (AL), Oct. 10, 13, 14, 1960; *Birmingham News* (AL), Oct. 12, 13, 1960; *DMN*, Oct. 11–14, 1960; *HP*, Oct. 12–14, 1960; *NYT*, Oct. 15, 1960; *NYT Magazine*, Oct. 23, 1960, pp. 19–22; *Newsweek*, Oct. 24, 1960, p. 42; *Time*, Oct. 24, 1960; Marvin Watson OH, I, pp. 37–38, 41, LBJL; Caro, *Passage of Power*, 145–148; Baker, *Johnson Eclipse*, 80–82; Baker, *Wheeling and Dealing*, 73; Reedy, *Lyndon B. Johnson*, 130; McPherson, *Political Education*, 180–181; Trest, *Nobody but the People*, 320–324; Fite, *Richard B. Russell, Jr.*, 375–376; RN, *Six Crises*, 379.

26. Reedy, *Lyndon B. Johnson*, 130; Smathers OH, #4, pp. 23–26, JFKL.

27. *WP*, Oct. 19–22, 26–28, 1960; *SAST*, Oct. 19, 20, 1960; *HP*, Oct. 19, 21, 1960; *DMN*, Oct. 26, 28, 1960; *NYT*, Oct. 27, 1960; *Newsweek*, Oct. 24, p. 75, Oct. 31, 1960, pp. 24–25.

28. *Baltimore Sun*, Oct. 11, PPS299.81S.73, and *New Orleans Times-Picayune*, Oct. 23, 1960, PPS299.81S.84, RNL; *SAST*, Oct. 16, 1960.

29. *PAES* VII, p. 390, quotation 545.

30. *PAES* VII, pp. 572–575; *NYT*, Oct. 19, 1960; *WP*, Oct. 26, 1960; Smathers OH, Interview III, pp. 7G, 8, JFKL; Martin, *Stevenson and the World*, 539–551.

31. Emblidge, *My Day*, 289; Lash, *Eleanor*, 289, 299.

32. *DMN*, Oct. 29–31, Nov. 4, 1960; *WP*, Oct. 29, 31, Nov. 3, 1960; *SAST*, Oct. 29, 1960.

33. *WP*, Nov. 4, 1960.

34. Arbuthnot to Stover, Nov. 17, 1960, B 48, Arbuthnot and Alger to RN, Jan. 11, 1961, B 26, Alger, B, Series 320, RNL; *DTH*, Nov. 3, 1960; *DMN*, Nov. 4, 1960; Dobbs, "Dallas Republicans and the Adolphus Hotel Incident," 1, Gellman mss.; Olien, *From Token to Triumph*, 139–140; Green, "Far Right Wing in Texas Politics," 258–259.

35. *DMN*, Nov. 4, 1960; *HP*, Nov. 6, 1960; Dulaney and Phillips, "*Speak, Mister Speaker*," 420; Johnson OH (Aug 19, 1968), p. 1, LBJL; Johnson, *Vantage Point*, 5; Baker, *Johnson Eclipse*, 84–88; Caro, *Passage of Power*, 149–150; Stephenson, "Democrats of Texas and Texas Liberalism," 107–109; Dobbs, "Dallas Republicans and the Adolphus Hotel Incident," 1–2, 9, Gellman mss.

36. *DMN*, Nov. 7, 8, 1960, B 26, Alger, B, Series 320, RNL; Field Report, Nov. 10, 1960, B 215, Senate Political Field, LBJL; Dobbs, "Dallas Republicans and the Adolphus Hotel Incident," 9, Gellman mss.; Clifton Carter OH, AC 74-194, and Harold Sanders OH, AC 74-248, and Marvin Watson OH, I, p. 38, II, pp. 4–5, and Cecil Burney OH, I, pp. 42–43, and George Reedy OH, XVI, pp. 74–75, LBJL.

37. *HP*, Nov. 6–8, 1960; *DMN*, Oct. 31, Nov. 6–8, 1960; *AC*, Nov. 8, 1960; *NYT*, Nov. 1, 7, 1960; *WP*, Nov. 8, 1960; Fite, *Richard B. Russell, Jr.*, 378–379; William Jordan OH, II, p. 6, and Charles Boatner OH, III, p. 29, LBJL.

38. Belden Poll, Oct. 18, 1960, B 262, Senate Political File, LBJL; *SAST*, Oct. 19, 23, Nov. 2, 4, 1960; *DMN*, Sept. 12, Oct. 30, Nov. 7, 8, 1960; *HP*, Oct. 17, 18, Nov. 7, 8, 1960; *WP*, Sept. 14, Oct. 16, 1960.

39. *JFKI*, 760–839, 1201–1206, 1213–1221; *JFKRN*, pp. 333–342, 620–624; *SAST*, Nov. 1, 1960; *WP*, *DMN*, and *HP*, Oct. 27–31, 1960; *USNWR*, Nov. 7, 1960, pp. 41–42; *Newsweek*, Nov. 7, 1960, pp. 32–34; *Time*, Nov. 7, 1960; Sevareid, *This Is Eric Sevareid*, 113–128; Salinger, *P.S.*, 84–85; White, *In Search of History*, 473–478.

40. *JFKI*, pp. 840–958, 1227–1267; *JFKRN*, pp. 343–346, 359–362, 568–569, 578; *DMN* and *HP*, Nov. 4, 1960; *WP*, Nov. 2–8; *NYT*, Nov. 2–8, 28, 1960; *NYT Magazine*, Oct. 23, 1960, pp. 19–23, 113–115, 117–118; Sorensen, *"Let the Word Go Forth,"* 117–122.

41. *Time*, July 25, Oct. 24, 1960, Jan. 2, 13, 1961; Salinger, *With Kennedy*, 31–33, 46; Pierpont, *At the White House*, 98; Baker, *Good Times*, 259.

42. Journal, Nov. 26, 1962, R 17, Lodge mss., journal, Nov. 26, 1962, R 17 Lodge mss.; Bradlee, *Conversations with Kennedy*, 18–20, 31; J. Alsop to Gagain, July 20, 1959, B 15, July 1959, J. Alsop to Devens, June 14, J. Alsop to Mrs. RFK, Aug. 4, B 16, July–Aug. 1960, J. Alsop to Barrett, Nov. 8, and J. Alsop to RFK, Nov. 10, 1960, B 17, Nov.–Dec. 1960, Alsop mss.; *Time*, July 25, 1960; Schlesinger, *Journals*, 88.

43. Memo for RN, Sept. 7, and memo from Nixon, Nov. 28, 1960, B 9, F 62, Klein mss.; RN to Zweng, July 21, 1961, B 845, Zweng (2 of 3), Series 320, RNL; Lawrence, *Six Presidents, Too Many Wars*, 230–240, 243; Baker, *Good Times*, 317, 324; Klein, *Making It Perfectly Clear*, 98.

44. McClendon, *My Eight Presidents*, 3–23; McClendon, *Mr. President, Mr. President!* 68, 74; Sloyan, *Politics of Deception*, 4.

45. Kendrick, *Prime Time*, 447; Sevareid, *This Is Eric Sevareid*, 116–118; Pierpont, *At the White House*, 228–229; Klein, *Making It Perfectly Clear*, 223; interview with Vanocur, Jan. 6, 2003.

46. Salinger, *With Kennedy*, 46; Bradlee, *Good Life*, 212; Baker, *Good Times*, 289, 313; Roberts, *First Rough Draft*, 181; Novak, *Prince of Darkness*, 73; Germond, *Fat Man in a Middle Seat*, 93; Rovere, *Final Reports*.

47. Blair and Blair, *Search for JFK*, 587.

48. "Canons of Journalism," 305–306; Saalberg, "Canons of Journalism," 731–734; Ward, "Journalism Ethics," 298.

49. Gallup, *Gallup Poll*, Vol. 3: 1689; *SAST*, Oct. 23, Nov. 6, 8, 1960; *WP*, Nov. 4, 6, 8, 1960; *NYT*, Nov. 7, 1960; *HP*, Nov. 7, 8, 1960; *DMN*, Nov. 7, 1960.

50. Fay, *Pleasure of His Company*, 65.

51. Mullen, "Newspaper Advertising in the Kennedy-Nixon Campaign," 3–10.

52. *Thunderbolt*, May 1963, File No. 3, Section 3, JEH O & C, FBI mss.; Hannaford, *Drew Pearson Diaries*, 45.

53. Ribicoff OH—5, p. 150, COHP; *NYT*, Nov. 7, 1960; Roberts, *First Rough Draft*, 181; O'Brien, *John F. Kennedy*, 350.

54. *USNWR*, Nov. 21, 1960, p. 34.

55. Beschloss, *Reaching for Glory*, 208.

16. NIXON'S PLAN FOR WINNING

1. Graham to RN, Sept. 26, 1960, Notebooks 10, 14, Series I, Collection 685, Graham mss.; Graham to Kornitzer, Oct. 20, 1960, B 8, F 6, Kornitzer mss.; Graham, *Just As I Am*, 390–392; Frady, *Billy Graham*, 442–444; Miller, *Billy Graham and the Rise of the Republican South*, 77–81.

2. RN speech, Oct. 3, and *Life* article, Oct. 16, 1960, B 299, Graham {2 of 3}, Series 320, RNL; also draft and Jan. 15, 1961, letter in Notebooks 10, 14, Series I, Collection 685, Graham mss.

3. Graham to RN, Jan. 15, June 12, 1961, B 229, Graham {2 of 3}, Series 320, RNL and Notebooks 10, 14, Series I, Collection 685, also *Life* draft, Oct. 23, 1960, Graham mss.; Schlesinger, *Journals*, 90–91; Graham, "We Are Electing a President of the World," 109–110.

4. RN to Graham, May 31 and Graham to RN, July 17, and RN to Graham, Aug. 18, 1961, B 299, Graham {2 of 3}, Series 320, RNL and Notebooks 10, 14, Series I, Collection 685, also RN to Pollack, Dec. 30, 1986, Graham mss., uncatalogued at RNL; RN, *Six Crises*, 365.

5. Graham to RN, Oct. 17, 1960, Notebooks 10, 14, Series I, Collection 685, Graham mss.

6. Rockefeller to Republicans, Oct. 31, 1960, OF, Part I, R 25, DDEL and R 13, Lodge mss., Rockefeller to Lodge, Nov. 7, 1960; Rockefeller to Finch, Nov. 7, 1960, B 650, Rockefeller 1960–61, Series 320, RNL; *NYT*, Oct. 17, Nov. 4, 1960; *WP*, Oct. 29, 1960; Smith, *On His Own Terms*, 349; Novak, *Prince of Darkness*, 74.

7. Goldwater to RN, undated, B 293, Goldwater [3/3], Series 320, Shorey to Finch, Sept. 20, B 15, To Be—Sca, Series 54, memo, Sept. 27, 1960, B 147, F 22, Series 207, RNL; *Arizona Republican*, Oct. 6, 1960; *Tucson Citizen*, Oct. 8, 1960, V 98, Sept.–Oct. 1960, Scrapbooks, Goldwater mss.; *NYT*, Oct. 9, 12, 1960; *Time*, Oct. 17, 1960; Shadegg, *What Happened to Goldwater?* 273.

8. Reagan to RN, Sept. 7 and RN to Reagan, Sept. 23, 1959, B 621, Reagan, R, Series 320, RNL; Reagan, *American Life*, 132; Edwards, *Early Reagan*, 472; Evans, *Education of Ronald Reagan*, 83–144.

9. Memo, Sept. 2, B 122, Cagney and memo, Sept. 2, 1960, B 667, St. Johns [2/3], Series 320, RNL; Reagan, *American Life*, 133–135; Edwards, *Early Reagan*, 473–474.

10. Booker, "What 'Ike' Thinks about Negroes," 84, 86, 88, 90; Gellman, *President and Apprentice*, chaps 7, 8, 24–26.

11. Booker, "What Republicans Must Do," 48, 52, 54–55.

12. Val to Jackie, Oct. 24, 1960, B 5, F 19, Political File: Presidential Campaign 1960, Re-

publican Party, Robinson mss.; Booker, "What Republicans Must Do," 51–52; Morrow, *Black Man in the White House*, 295–296.

13. Memo, Nov. 10, 1958, Morrow to Morton, Dec. 30, 1959, B 532, Morrow, F, Series 320, RNL; Morrow, *Black Man in the White House*, 293.

14. Diary, Jan. 15, 1960, B 2, Morrow mss.; memo, Jan. 4 1960, B 532, Morrow, F, Series 320, RNL; memos, June 10, 13, 21, 1960, Finch mss.; Morrow, *Black Man in the White House*, 293–295.

15. Press release, Sept. 9, 1960, B 532, Morrow, F, Series 320, RNL; Morrow, *Black Man in the White House*, 295; interview with Flanigan, July 17, 2003.

16. *LAS*, Oct. 27, 1960; *CCP*, Nov. 5, 1960.

17. PN to Drown, June 30, 1960, DR 212, RNL; Long, *First Class Citizenship*, 91–92, 97–98, 100–101, 114.

18. *NYT*, Sept. 3, 1960; Long, *First Class Citizenship*, 114, 116–117; Rampersad, *Jackie Robinson*, 352–353.

19. RN speech, Oct. 4, B 146, F 17 and F 18, Series 207, and Klein to Kupcinet, Oct. 6, 1960, B 144, *Chicago Sun*, Series 320, RNL; *Jet*, Oct. 27, 1960, pp. 6–8; *ADW*, Nov. 1, 1960; *CCP*, Nov. 5, 1960.

20. Wicker OH—I, p. 9, LBJL; *NYT*, Oct. 23, 1960; Roberts, *First Rough Draft*, 278.

21. Memo, Oct. 9, 1960, B 457, Lodge (1 of 2), Series 320, RNL; *Boston Herald*, Sept. 29, and *BG*, Oct. 12, 1960, R 31, Lodge mss.; *JFKI*, pp. 540–541; *JFKRN*, pp. 186–201; *WP*, Oct. 1, 4, 7, 9, 11, 30, 1960; *NYT*, Oct. 1, 3, 10, 12, 23, 1960; *Time*, Sept. 19, 1960; *USNWR*, Oct. 24, 1960, pp. 78–79; *Newsweek*, Oct. 24, p. 42, Oct. 31, 1960, pp. 23–24.

22. Memo, Sept. 5, 1960, Finch mss., B 9, F 62, Klein mss.

23. *WP*, Sept. 16, 1960; Booker, "What Republicans Must Do," 52.

24. *NYT*, Sept. 17, Oct. 6–8, 1960; *WP*, Sept. 16, 29, 1960.

25. *Jet*, Oct. 6, 1960, pp. 14–17; Lodge to Bunch, June 3, 1976, R 16, Lodge mss.

26. *JFKRN*, pp. 193, 202–203; *NYT*, Oct. 9, 1960.

27. *WP* and *NYT*, Oct. 13, 1960; *Newsweek*, Oct. 24, p. 42, Oct. 31, 1960, pp. 23–24; *Time*, Oct. 24, 1960; *Jet*, Oct. 27, 1960, pp. 3–4; Lawrence, *Six Presidents, Too Many Wars*, 237–238; Booker, *Black Man's America*, 146; RN, *Six Crises*, 350.

28. *WP*, Oct. 15–17, 1960; *NYT*, Oct. 14–15, 17, 1960; *Time*, Oct. 31, 1960; Lawrence, *Six Presidents, Too Many Wars*, 237–238.

29. *WP*, Oct. 19, 28, 1960; *NYT*, Oct. 18, 1960; *BG*, Oct. 19, 1960, R 31, Lodge mss.; *DMN*, Oct. 27, 1960; *HP*, Nov. 6, 1960.

30. Trueblood to McCaffrey, Oct. 11, B 764, and Trueblood, E, Yerger to Lodge, Oct. 12, B 836, and Yerger, Burrow to McWhorter, Oct. 13, B 116, and Burrow and McKinley to RN, Oct. 26, 1960, B 502, and McKinley, K, Yerger to Kidgem Oct. 12, B 836, and Yerger and McKinley to RN, Oct. 26, 1960, B 501, and McKinley, K, Series 320 and memoirs, March 14, 1976, RNL; *WP*, Oct. 14, 1960.

31. Alcorn to RN, Oct. 25, B 25, Alcorn, Series 320, and *LAT*, Oct. 23, 1960, PPS61S.292, RNL; conversation with Mazo, Oct. 28, 1960, White mss.; *WP* and *NYT*, Oct. 31, 1960; Alsop, "Campaigning with Nixon," 32–33, 61–64; *Newsweek*, Oct. 31, 1960, pp. 19–20; *Time*, Oct. 31, 1960; RN, *Six Crises*, 359.

32. RN to Tanner, May 10, B 744, Tanner, Series 320, and memo, Nov. 4, 1960, uncatalogued, RNL; *WP*, Nov. 1, 1960; *Time*, Nov. 7, 1960; *Newsweek*, Nov. 7, 1960, p. 32; RN, *Six Crises*, 358, 360.

33. Memo, Oct. 24, 1960, B 2, Republican Party Series, 1960 Campaign Subseries, Seaton mss.; *WP*, Oct. 25, 26, 1960.

34. *WP*, Oct. 23, 1960; JFK, *Strategy of Peace*, 132.

35. *RNI*, p. 747; *WP* and *NYT*, Oct. 29, 1960.

36. Memo, Oct. 22, B 6, To Be—Mich, Series 52, and RN speech, Oct. 27, 1960, B 149, F 3, Series 207, RNL; *WP*, Oct. 28, 1960; Klein, *Making It Perfectly Clear*, 97–98.

37. *NYT* and *WP*, Oct. 30, 1960.

38. U.S. Senate, *Congressional Record*, Nov. 22, 1967, pp. 33663–33664; Phelan, "Nixon Family and the Hughes Loan," 21–22, 26; North-Broome, *Nixon-Hughes "Loan,"* 101–103; Charles Milhous OH, 8–11, CSF; Nixon and Olson, *Nixons*, 203; interview with Ed Nixon, July 25, 2009; RN, *RN*, 242; Klein, *Making It Perfectly Clear*, 63.

39. U.S. Senate, *Congressional Record*, Nov. 22, 1967, pp. 336, 364; *Whittier Star*, Oct. 19, B G281 [1 of 3], and information on Ortiz, April 2, 1955, B G281 [2 of 3], and Pearson column draft, Oct. 25, 1960, F 0111 [1 of 2], Pearson mss.; Phelan, "Nixon Family and the Hughes Loan," 26; North-Broome, *Nixon-Hughes "Loan,"* 103–107.

40. *WP*, Oct. 27, 1960.

41. *WP* and *NYT*, Oct. 31, 1960; Phelan, "Nixon Family and the Hughes Loan," 26: Kornitzer, *The Real Nixon*, 269; interview with Ed Nixon, July 25, 2009; Phelan, *Scandals, Scamps, and Scoundrels*, 92.

42. Bewley to Woods, Oct. 17, 1955, B 80, Bewley [1/2], and memo, Jan. 23, 1959, B 360, Hughes, H Series 320, RNL.

43. Bewley to Woods, May 1, B 80, Bewley [1/2], and Nov. 13, 1956, B 89, Bewley (1957–1958), Series 320, RNL; memo, April 26, 1956, B 14, April 56 Misc (1), Diary DDEL; RN, *RN*, 242.

44. Memo, Oct. 27, 1960, B 2, Republican Party Series, 1960 Campaign Subseries, Seaton mss.; Hannaford, *Drew Pearson Diaries*, 46.

45. Morrow, *Black Man in the White House*, 296; Booker, "Black Man's America," 86.

46. Safire, *Before the Fall*, 48–49; interview with Safire, Feb. 7, 2008; interview with Flanigan, July 17, 2003.

47. *CT*, Nov. 7, 1960; *LAS*, Nov. 24, 1960.

48. Kistiakowsky, *Scientist at the White House*, 402; Roberts OH, #266, p. 849, DDEL.

49. DDEP XXI, pp. 2109–2111, 2128–2129; *WP*, Oct. 1, 1960; *NYT*, Oct. 5, 1960; Roberts OH, #266, p. 848, DDEL; *WP*, Oct. 11, 1960.

50. DDEP XXI, p. 2583; medical diary, Oct. 17, 1960, B 10, Sept. 1–Dec. 31, 1960 (2), Snyder mss.; *WP*, Oct. 17, 18, 1960; *NYT*, Oct. 18, 1960.

51. DDEP XXI, pp. 778–781, 2583; medical diary, Oct. 18, 1960, B 10, Sept. 1–Dec. 31, 1960 (2), Snyder mss.; *WP*, Oct. 19, 1960.

52. DDEP XI, pp. 2583–2584; medical diary, Oct. 19–20, 1960, B 10, Sept. 1–Dec. 31, 1960 (2), Snyder mss.; *WP*, Oct. 21, 1960; *NYT*, Oct. 22, 1960.

53. DDEP XXI, pp. 2136, 2584; medical diary, Oct. 21, 1960, B 10, Sept. 1–Dec. 31, 1960 (2), Snyder mss.; telephone calls, Oct. 3, 14, 16, 19, 21, 1960, R 27, Diary DDEL.

54. DDEP XXI, p. 2584; medical diary, Oct. 24, 1960, B 10, Sept. 1–Dec. 31, 1960 (2), Snyder mss.; *NYT* and *WP*, Oct. 25, 1960; Roberts OH, #266, pp. 848–850, DDEL.

55. DDEP XXI, pp. 2584–2585; medical diary, Oct. 25, 1960, B 10, Sept. 1–Dec. 31, 1960 (3), Snyder mss.; *DMN*, Oct. 25, 26, 1960; *HP*, Oct. 24–26, 1960; *WP*, Oct. 25, 26, 1960; *Newsweek*, Oct. 31, 1960, p. 20; *Time*, Oct. 31, Nov. 7, 1960.

56. Blaik to Finch, Oct. 25, 1960, B 86, Blaik, Series 320, RNL; Kistiakowsky, *Scientist at the White House*, 408; Persons OH, #161, p. 136, COHP; Eisenhower, *President Is Calling*, 334.

57. DDEP XXI, p. 2585; medical diary, Oct. 27, 1960, B 10, Sept. 1–Dec. 31, 1960 (3), Snyder mss.; *WP*, Oct. 27, 28, 1960; *Time*, Nov. 7, 1960.

58. Medical diary, Oct. 28, 1960, B 10, Sept. 1–Dec. 31, 1960 (3), Snyder mss.; Slater, *The Ike I Knew*, 186; letter to the editor, *NYT*, June 18, 2000; Day 3, Tape 4, 00:18:52 [RN], and Day 9, Tape 1. 00:04:55 [RN], FG; Eisenhower, "What I Have Learned," 32–33; Harlow, "White House Watch," 14; Safire, *Before the Fall*, 622–623; Holt, *Mamie Doud Eisenhower*, 122–123.

59. DDEP XXI, pp. 2143–2144.

60. Ibid., 2586; schedule, Oct. 28, 1960, R 27, Diary DDEL; medical diary, Oct. 28, 1960, B 10, Sept. 1–Dec. 31, 1960 (3), Snyder mss.; *PPA* 1960–61, pp. 806–807, 815–821; Eisenhower speech, Oct. 28, 1960, EL-MP16-250, audiovisual dept, DDEL; *WP* and *NYT*, Oct. 29, 1960; *CBS Reports*, Oct. 12, 1961, B 237, Eisenhower 1/2, Series 320, and interview with Eisenhower, Oct. 27, 1965, PPS324.245A, RNL; M. Eisenhower to Roorda, July 19, 1983, Gellman mss.; Flanigan's negative opinion of Ike's staff on Nixon's campaign, interview with Flanigan, July 17, 2003.

61. DDEP XXI, pp. 822–823, 2144–2145, 2586; medical diary, Oct. 28–31, Nov. 1, 1960, B 10, Sept. 1–Dec. 31, 1960 (3), Snyder mss.; *NYT* and *WP*, Nov. 1, 2, 1960.

62. DDEP XXI, pp. 2157–2158, 2586; medical diary, Nov. 2, 1960, B 10, Sept. 1–Dec. 31, 1960 (3), Snyder mss.; *PPA* 1960–61, pp. 824–834; *RNI*, pp. 944–968; *WP* and *NYT*, Nov. 3, 1960; Rockefeller to RN, Nov. 15, 1960, B 659, Rockefeller 1960–61, Series 320, RNL; Nelson to Cabot, Nov. 4, 1960, R 13, Lodge mss.; RN, *Six Crises*, 364; Hill, *Five Presidents*, 81–83; interview with Hughes, July 3, 2001; Booker, "What 'Ike' Thinks about Negroes," 85.

63. Memo, Nov. 3, 1960, B 2, Republican Party Series, 1960 Campaign subseries, Seaton mss.; *RNI*, pp. 916–943; Daring to Rovensky, Nov. 1, 1960, Daring mss.; *WP*, Oct. 30, Nov. 2, 1960.

64. *RNI*, pp. 970–995; *WP* and *NYT*, Nov. 4, 1960; *The State* (SC), Nov. 8, 1960, B 756, Thurmond, Series 320, RNL; RN, *Six Crises*, 369.

65. *WP*, Nov. 4, 1960.

66. *NYT* and *WP*, Nov. 6, 1960; diary, Nov. 5, 1960, R 27, Diary DDEL; Lungren and Lungren, *Healing Richard Nixon*, 61; Edwards, *Missionary for Freedom*, 256–257.

67. Diary, Oct. 26, 1960, Snyder's Progress Reports, DDEL; Hutschnecker, "Mental Health of Our Leaders," 54.

68. Schedule, Nov. 4, 1960, R 28, Diary DDEL; DDEP XXI, pp. 836–851, 2587; medical diary, Nov. 3–6, 1960, B 10, Sept. 1–Dec. 31, 1960 (3), Snyder mss.; *WP* and *NYT*, Nov. 4, 5, 1960; RN, *Six Crises*, 369.

69. *RNI*, pp. 1003–1053; Hughes to RN, Oct. 7, 1962, B 360, Hughes, J, Series 320, RNL; Hughes OH, U.S. Air Force, 68; RN, *Six Crises*, 370; Lawrence, *Six Presidents, Too Many Wars*, 238: Lungren and Lungren, *Healing Richard Nixon*, 71–72; Klein, *Making It Perfectly Clear*, 98–99; interview with Vanocur, Sept. 23, 2007. *WP* and *NYT*, Nov. 5, 6, 1960.

70. *RNI*, pp. 1053–1060; *NYT* and *WP*, Oct. 14, Nov. 7, 1960.

71. DDE to RN, Nov. 6, 1960, B 237, Eisenhower 1/2, Series 320, RNL; memo, Nov. 7, R 28, and diary, Nov. 8, 1960, R 27, 1960, Diary DDEL; RN, *Six Crises*, 371.

72. *RNI*, pp. 1065–1119; *NYT* and *WP*, Nov. 8, 1960; Novak, *Prince of Darkness*, 76; RN, *Six Crises*, 371.

73. RN to Crider, Feb. 19, 1962, B 189, Crider, Series 320, RNL; Mullen, "Newspaper Advertising in the Kennedy-Nixon Campaign," 9; Klein, *Making It Perfectly Clear*, 61; Goodwin, *Remembering America*, 130.

74. Diary, Nov. 7, 1960, B 10, Sept. 1–Dec. 31, 1960 (3), Snyder mss.; *PPA 1960–61*, pp. 852–856; *NYT, WP,* and *Chicago Daily Tribune*, Nov. 8, 1960.

75. Salinger, *With Kennedy*, 56; Stempel, "Prestige Press Covers the Campaign," 158; nine for Nixon: *Baltimore Sun, CDN, CT, Christian Science Monitor, Des Moines Register, Kansas City Star, LAT, Miami Herald, Wall Street Journal*; those for Kennedy, *AC, Louisville Courier-Journal, Milwaukee Journal, NYT, St. Louis Post-Dispatch*, ibid., 158.

76. DDEP XX, pp. 1935–1938, and DDEP XXI, pp. 1042, 1046; Eisenhower OH, 30, HHPL.

77. DDEP XXI, pp. 2168–2169, 2230–2231.

78. Memo, Aug. 1, 1960, Finch mss.; memo, Nov. 29, 1960, B 509, memo, Series 320, RNL.

79. Luce to RN, Nov. 14, B 464, Luce [1/2], and Howard to RN, Dec. 23, 1960, B 357, Howard, R, RN to Berlin, Jan. 3, B 78, Berlin, Series 320, and RN to Knowland, Jan. 19, Series 311, Ca March (2), Series 311, and RN to Chandler, B 294, Good Articles, and Ferger to RN, Feb. 20, 1961, B 255, Ferger, Series 320, RNL; *NYT*, Aug. 5, 1960; Brinkley, *Publisher*, 421–425; Pulliam, *Publisher*, 220–224.

80. RN to Crabtree, Jan. 12, B 186, Crabtree, N, and RN to Haninghen, Jan. 14, B 317, Haninghen, and RN to MacArthur, Jan. 14, 1961, B 468, MacArthur, DA, Series 320, and RN to Hoover, PPS320.102.105, RNL; RN to Hoover, Jan. 14, 1961, B 9, F 62, Klein mss.

81. De Toledano to Finch, June 14, 1960, B 213, de Toledano, and RN to Walters, Jan. 11, B 144, *Chicago Daily*, and RN to Chandler, Feb. 11, B 294, Good Articles, and Ferger to RN, Feb. 20, quotation, RN to Fischer, B 814, White [1/2], Series 320, RNL; Pulliam, *Publisher*, 220–224, 290; Frost, *Hedda Hopper's Hollywood*, 214.

82. Dickerson, *Among Those Present*, 34–36, quotation 36.

83. Anderson, *Confessions of a Muckraker*, 324–333, quotation 333; Feldstein, "Fighting Quakers," 76–85.

84. Wechsler, *Reflections of an Angry Middle-Aged Editor*, 39, 194–207, quotations 195, 205; Nissenson, *Lady Upstairs*, 257.

85. Potter, "Political Pitchman," 69–101, quotation 69; Baker, *Good Times*, 324–325.

86. Costello OH, 1–4, 14–16, 18, 25–26, LBJL; Costello, "Nixon on the Eve," 17–21, quotations 17, 21; Costello, "Faceless Enemies, Waiting to Pounce" 22–23, quotation 22; *NYT*, June 21, 1969.

17. HOW THEY VOTED

1. *WP*, Nov. 2, 1960.
2. Fay, *Pleasure of His Company*, 65; Schlesinger, *Journals*, 731; O'Donnell and Powers, *"Johnny, We Hardly Knew Ye,"* 243–244.
3. Memo, Oct. 21, 1960, B 603, F Polls, Series 320, RNL; *WP*, Nov. 7, 1960; *Pittsburgh Press*, Nov. 8, 1960; *DMN*, Nov. 11, 1960; Roper, "Polling Post-Mortem," 10; Runyon et al., *Source Book of American Presidential Campaigns*, 276; Sorensen, *Kennedy*, 206–207, 209; O'Donnell, *Irish Brotherhood*, 415–416.
4. *HP* and *AC*, Nov. 9, 1960; Schlesinger, *Letters*, 232; O'Donnell, *Irish Brotherhood*, 417.
5. *HP* and *AC*, Nov. 9, 1960; O'Donnell, *Irish Brotherhood*, 418–420.
6. *WP*, Nov. 8, 9, 1960; *Time*, Nov. 16, 1960.
7. *Pittsburgh Press*, Nov. 8, 1960; *Time*, Nov. 16, 1960; Day 9, Tape 1, 00:08:37 [RN], FG; Klein, *Making It Perfectly Clear*, 51; RN, *Six Crises*, 375–377.
8. *Time*, Nov. 16, 1960; RN, *Six Crises*, 377–379; Klein, *Making It Perfectly Clear*, 51–52.
9. *WP*, Nov. 7–9, 1960; *NYT*, Nov. 8, 9, 1960; Lodge, *Storm Has Many Eyes*, 185–187.
10. DDEP XXI, pp. 2151, 2588; diary, Nov. 8, 1960, B 10, Sept. 1–Dec. 31, 1960 (3), Snyder mss.
11. YouTube, Election Night Coverage, Nov. 8, 9, 1960; *Time*, Nov. 16, 1960; Tanenhaus, "Computers and the Election," 5; Baughman, *Same Time, Same Station*, 291; for election night see Peter Carlson, "Another Race," *WP*, Nov. 17, 2000.
12. Memo, Nov. 8, 1960, B 671, Sarnoff, R, Series 320, RNL; *NYT*, Nov. 8, 1960; YouTube, Election Night Coverage, Nov. 8, 9, 1960; *Time*, Nov. 16, 1960; RN, *Six Crises*, 379–380; Kennedy, *True Compass*, 158; Clifford, *Counsel to the President*, 326; Salinger, *With Kennedy*, 47; O'Donnell, *Irish Brotherhood*, 420.
13. YouTube, Election Night Coverage, Nov. 8, 9, 1960; *Time*, Nov. 16, 1960; RN, *Six Crises*, 380, 383.
14. YouTube, Election Night Coverage, Nov. 8, 9, 1960; *Time*, Nov. 16, 1960; RN, *Six Crises*, 381.
15. YouTube, Election Night Coverage, Nov. 8, 9, 1960; *WP*, Nov. 9, 1960; *Time*, Nov. 16, 1960; diary, Nov. 8, 1960, B 10, Sept. 1–Dec. 31, 1960 (3), Snyder mss.; diary, Nov. 9, 1960, R 27, Diary DDEL; Eisenhower, *Strictly Personal*, 285; RN, *Six Crises*, 381–383; O'Donnell, *Irish Brotherhood*, 422–424.
16. YouTube, Election Night Coverage, Nov. 8, 9, 1960; *Time*, Nov. 16, 1960; RN, *Six Crises*, 383–384.
17. YouTube, Election Night Coverage, Nov. 8, 9, 1960; *Time*, Nov. 16, 1960; Catledge, *My Life and The Times*, 213.
18. YouTube, Election Night Coverage, Nov. 8. 9, 1960; *Time*, Nov. 16, 1960; O'Donnell, *Irish Brotherhood*, 428.

19. WP, Nov. 9, 13, 1960; RN, *Six Crises*, 385–390; Klein, *Making It Perfectly Clear*, 36.

20. Memo, Nov. 28, 1960, R 27, Diary DDEL; Salinger, *With Kennedy*, 47.

21. WP, Nov. 9, 1960; Salinger, *With Kennedy*, 47–48; O'Donnell and Powers, "*Johnny, We Hardly Knew Ye*," 253; Sorensen, *Kennedy*, 212; Sorensen, *Counselor*, 196; White, *Making of the President*, 25, 345.

22. YouTube, Election Night Coverage, Nov. 8, 9, 1960; *Time*, Nov. 16, 1960; Brinkley, *11 Presidents*, 137.

23. YouTube, Election Night Coverage, Nov. 8, 9, 1960; *Time*, Nov. 16, 1960.

24. Smith, *Nine of Us*, 230–231; Reston, *Deadline*, 289.

25. WP and NYT, Nov. 10, 1960; Klein, *Making It Perfectly Clear*, 55; RN, *Six Crises*, 395–396; Lincoln, *My Twelve Years with John F. Kennedy*, 192.

26. Diary, Nov. 9, 1960, B 10, Sept. 1–Dec. 31, 1960 (3), Snyder mss.; diary, Nov. 9, 1960, R 27, Diary DDEL; PPA 1960–61, p. 857; DDEP XXI, pp. 2157, 2158, 2161–2162, 2165–2166, 2588; M. Eisenhower OH, 30, and J. Eisenhower OH, 118, COHP; Eisenhower, *Strictly Personal*, 285.

27. Diary, Nov. 9, 1960, R 27, Diary DDEL; Persons OH, #161, p. 145, COHP; Eisenhower, *Strictly Personal*, 285; Slater, *The Ike I Knew*, 230.

28. PPA 1960–61, p. 857; diary, Nov. 9, 1960, B 54, F Telephone calls Nov. 1960, Diary DDEL; RN to DDE, Nov. 8, 1961, B 237, Eisenhower 1/2, Series 320, RNL; RN, *Six Crises*, 395.

29. DDEP XXI, p. 2156.

30. DDE to Lodge, Nov. 9, R 29, Lodge mss., Persons to Lodge, Nov. 10, 1960, R 13, Lodge II mss.

31. YouTube, Election Night, Nov. 8, 9, 1960; WP, SAST, HP, and DMN, Nov. 10, 1960; *Time*, Nov. 16, 1960.

32. *CQ Almanac Online Election Edition*. I have used this edition for the analysis of the states' voting. There are many others; see Guthrie, *Statistics 1960*, pp. 1–3, 6–10, 13–19, 21, 23–24, 29–30, 34–35, 37–38, 40–51.

33. Schneebeli to RN, Nov. 15, 1960, B 675, Schneebeli, and McCabe to RN, Jan. 5, B 488, McCabe, T, and RN to Martin, Jan. 11, Martin to RN, June 29, 1961, B 478, Martin, E; Zwikl, "Campaign and the Issues," 177–193; Preble, *Kennedy and the Missile Gap*, 124–127.

34. Finch to Rockefeller, Nov. 26, 1960, B 650, Rockefeller 1960–61, Series 320, RNL; Preble, *Kennedy and the Missile Gap*, 127–131.

35. Bartley and Graham, *Southern Politics and the Second Reconstruction*, 9, 86–92; Havard, *Changing Politics of the South*, 711; Seagull, *Southern Republicanism*, 33–34; Cosman, "Presidential Republicanism in the South," 303–305; Boynton, "Southern Republican Voting," 8.

36. Land, "John F. Kennedy's Southern Strategy," 41–63, quotation 63.

37. AC, Nov. 4, 5, 10, 1960; Davis, *Code of Georgia Annotated*, Book 12, pp. 68–91; *CQ Almanac Online Election Edition*; Novotny, "Kennedy and Georgia's Unpledged Electors," 380–396; Melton, "1960 Presidential Election in Georgia," 160–194, 220, 235, 258–259; Diamond, *Guide to U.S. Elections*, 296; Bartley and Graham, *Southern Politics and the Second Reconstruction*, 9; David, *Presidential Election and Transition*,

167–168; Lublin, *Republican South*, 35; Boynton, "Southern Republican Voting," 8, 197–198.

38. Thurmond to RN and PN, Jan. 27, 1960, B 756, Thurmond, Series 320, RNL; *CQ Almanac Online Election Edition*; Gifford, "'Dixie's No Longer in the Bag!'" 218–228; Sampson, "Rise of the 'New' Republican Party," 274–331; White, "Evolution of the Republican Right," 151–153; Fowler, *Presidential Voting in South Carolina*, 119, 122; Havard, *Changing Politics of the South*, 607.

39. *TO*, June 24, 1960.

40. Anderson to RN, July 29, B 40, Anderson, D and McWhorter to Wall, Sept. 28, 1960, B 794, Wall, R, Series 320, RNL; *DMN*, Sept. 17, 20, 23–25, 28, 30, Oct. 4, 1960; *SAST*, Sept. 25, Oct. 9, 1960; *HP*, Sept. 29, Oct. 9, 1960; Soukup, McCleskey, and Holloway, *Party and Factional Division*, 62–66; Green, *Establishment in Texas Politics*, 135–190.

41. *DMN*, Oct. 26, 28–30, Nov. 4, 6, 1960; *HP*, Oct. 13, 14, 19, 28, 1960; *SAST*, Oct. 14, 30, 1960; *AC*, Nov. 1, 1960.

42. *DMN*, Nov. 8, 1960.

43. *SAST*, Oct. 9, 1960; *DMN*, Nov. 4, 1960; Dulaney and Phillips, "*Speak, Mister Speaker*," 281–282; Green, *Establishment in Texas Politics*, 192.

44. *HP*, Nov. 2, 4, 7, 1960; *DMN*, Nov. 2, 3, 1960.

45. Robinson to RN, Sept. 1, 1960, B 647, Robinson (2 of 3), Series 320, RNL; Survey of Election in Tx, Nov. 3, 1960, R 2, P 1, JFKL; *TO*, Oct. 7, 1960; *SAST*, Oct. 30, 1960; *DMN*, Nov. 8, 1960; Weeks, *Texas in the 1960 Election*, 42, 51–53, 60; *CQ Almanac Online Election Edition*.

46. Memo, Sept. 7, 1960, Finch mss.; Robinson to RN, Nov. 22, 1960, B 646, Robinson, WS, Series 320, RNL; *WP*, Sept. 9, 17, 19, Oct. 3, Dec. 20, 1960; *CQ Almanac Online Election Edition*; Havard, *Changing Politics of the South*, 46–54, 82, 111, 125; Sweeney, "Whispers in the Golden Silence," 3–44; Seagull, *Southern Republicanism*, 33–34; Bartley and Graham, *Southern Politics and the Second Reconstruction*, 90, 92; Melton, "1960 Presidential Election in Georgia," 114–122.

47. Cosman, "Presidential Republicanism in the South," 303, 306–322; also see dissertations: Rudder, "Why Southerners Vote the Way They Do," and Boynton, "Southern Republican Voting."

48. Novotny, "Kennedy and Georgia's Unpledged Electors," 376–380; Wiessler, "Presidential Elections," 120–126.

49. *Delta Democrat-Times* (MS), Nov. 9, 11, 13, 18, 1960; Yerger to RN, Dec. 3, 1960, B 836, Yerger, Series 320, RNL; *CQ Almanac Online Election Edition*; Wilkins, "Development of the Mississippi Republican Party," 48–55; Kelley, "Mississippi Public Opinion," 94–182; Land, "Presidential Republicans," 105, 107–109, 115–118, 126–127, 129–130, 134–136; Land, "Mississippi Republicanism," 33–48; Havard, *Changing Politics of the South*, 699; Crespino, *In Search of Another Country*, 36.

50. Recapitulation Sheet, General Election, Nov. 8, 1960, Secretary of State, Election Files, SG 2554, Alabama Dept of Archives and History, Montgomery, AL; *AC*, Oct. 3, 1960; *Montgomery Advertiser*, Nov. 7, 9, 10, 12, 19, 28, Dec. 8, 19, 20, 30, 1960; *NYT*, Nov. 9, 1960; *CQ Almanac Online Election Edition*; Havard, *Changing Politics of the*

South, 430, 432, 437, 460; Elliott and D'Orso, *Cost of Courage*, 186–195; Hamilton, *Lister Hill*, 235–238; Thornton, *Dividing Lines*, 144, 318, 382.

51. *CQ Almanac Online Election Edition*; Albert, *Little Giant*, 236; Black and Black, *Rise of Southern Republicans*, 207, 209, 257–258; Pomper, "Future Southern Congressional Politics," 17–18.

52. *NYT, WP, LAT*, and *CT*, July 14, 1961.

53. *CQ Almanac Online Election Edition*; for Michigan, see memo from Robinson, Oct. 30, 1960, FI uncatalogued, RNL; Sigel, "Race and Religion as Factors," 436–447; Preble, *Kennedy and the Missile Gap*, 132–137; Carty, *Catholic in the White House?* 141–146; for Minnesota see, Lund to Wilson, Sept. 28, B 6, Minn—1960 (1) Series 52, *Minneapolis Tribune*, Oct. 23, B 279, Gainey 1960, Etzell to RN, Nov. 17, B 246, Etzell, survey, Dec. 1960, and Crabtree to Klein, Dec. 23, 1960, Crabtree top RN, March 3, B 186, Crabtree, N, and Mackinnon to RN, June 5, 1961, B 470, MacKinnon, GE, Series 320, RNL; Crabtree to Klein, Dec. 27, 1960, B 9, F 64, Klein mss.

54. *CQ Almanac Online Election Edition*; for Ohio see, Time, Nov. 21, 1960; Wirt, "Organization Man in Politics," 62–77.

55. *CQ Almanac Online Election Edition*; Smith to RN, Aug. 19, B 709, Smith, W, Mundt to RN, Nov. 11, B 537, Mundt [1/4], and Hickenlooper to RN, Nov. 14, 1960, B 337, Hickenlooper, Series 320, RNL. Heidepriem, *Fair Chance for a Free People*, 235–236, 238.

56. Anderson, "Political West in 1960," 287–299; Martin, "1960 Election in Colorado," 327–330; Martin, "1960 Election in Idaho," 339, 341–342; Diggs, "1960 Election in Nevada," 347–349; Swarthout, "1960 Election in Oregon," 355–360; Bone, "1960 Election in Washington," 373–375, 377–382; for election results from each state, I used *CQ Almanac Online Election Edition*. The thirteen states are Alaska, Arizona, California, Colorado, Hawaii, Idaho, Montana, Nevada, New Mexico, Oregon, Utah, Washington, and Wyoming.

57. McCaffrey to Hamilton, Sept. 3, B 776, Univ of Ca, Series 320, memo from McCaffrey, Sept. 27, B 5, F To Be, Series 54, memo from McCaffrey, Oct. 4, B 149, F 30, Series 207, and McCaffrey to Martin, Oct. 6, B 478, Martin, Jo, memo, Nov. 17, B 488, McCaffrey [2/2], and McCaffrey to Corley, Nov. 23, B 181, Corley, and McCaffrey to Weinberger, Nov. 29, B 806, Weinberger, McCaffrey to Brennan, Nov. 29, B 100, Brennan (1), and Behrens to McCaffrey, Dec. 13, 1960, B 72, Behrens, Series 320, RNL.

58. *WP*, Oct. 7, Nov. 17, 1960; Lee and Buchanan, "1960 Election in California," 309, 316–321, 325–326; California polling, Kesaris, *Papers of the Republican Party*, R 2; Wilson, *Confessions of a Kinetic Congressman*, 66; Rarick, *California Rising*, 219–224.

59. Leventhal to RFK, Dec. 7, 1960, Political Files, General Subject, 1959–1960, JFK Library.

60. Diggs, "1960 Election in Nevada," 347–349; *CQ Almanac Online Election Edition*; Smyser, "How Kennedy Won 1960 Recount," p. 5; RN to Richards, Feb. 21, 1961, B 641, Richards, M, Series 320, RNL.

61. Gaines, "Popular Myths about Popular Vote," 70–75; Peirce and Longley, *People's*

President, 65–68; Buell and Sigelman, *Attack Politics*, 20–21; Barone, *Our Country*, 719–720; Schlesinger, *Robert Kennedy and His Times*, 220; interview with Peirce, Aug. 15, 2003.

62. David, *Presidential Election and Transition*, 168–170, 172–173; Havard, *Changing Politics of the South*, 681; *Newsweek*, Nov. 14, 1960, EE4–6; *Time*, Nov. 16, 1960; Election Summary, Nov. 16, 1960, R 27, Diary DDEL; Kesaris, *Papers of the Republican Party*, 1–3, 42; Nelson, *John William McCormack*, 572–573; Witcover, *Party of the People*, 495–496.

63. An Analysis of the 1960 Election, Nov. 1960, B 17, Nov.–Dec. 1960, Alsop mss.; Kesaris, *Papers of the Republican Party*, R 2, p. 7; memo, Nov. 29, 1960, R 27, Diary DDEL.

64. *Time*, Aug. 8, 1960; *WP*, Nov. 6, 1960; An Analysis of the 1960 Election, Nov. 1960, B 17, Nov.–Dec. 1960, Alsop mss.; Kesaris, *Papers of the Republican Party*, R 2, p. 16.

65. Lipsky, "Electioneering among the Minorities," 428–429.

66. *USNWR*, Nov. 21, 1960, p. 69.

67. Gallup, *Gallup Poll*, Vol. 3: 1691–1692; Manza and Brooks, "Religious Factor in Presidential Elections," 38–74.

68. An Analysis of the 1960 Election, Nov. 1960, B 17, Nov.–Dec. 1960, Alsop mss.; Summary of 1960 Results, Kesaris, *Papers of the Republican Party*, R 2, pp. 11–12; *USNWR*, Nov. 21, 1960, p. 69.

69. An Analysis of the 1960 Election, Nov. 1960, B 17, Nov.–Dec. 1960, Alsop mss.; Summary of 1960 Results, Kesaris *Papers of the Republican Party*, R 2, pp. 11–12; *Newsweek*, Nov. 14, 1960, EE4–5.

70. Gallup, *Gallup Poll*, Vol. 3: 1693–1694; An Analysis of the 1960 Election, Nov. 1960, B 17, Nov.–Dec. 1960, Alsop mss.; Summary of 1960 Results, Kesaris, *Papers of the Republican Party*, R 2, pp. 11–12.

71. Gallup, *Gallup Poll*, Vol. 3: 1694; *NYHT*, Dec. 7, 1960; An Analysis of the 1960 Election, Nov. 1960, B 17, Nov.–Dec. 1960, Alsop mss.; Herberg, *Protestant—Catholic—Jew*, 210; Phillips, *Emerging Republican Majority*, 111, 116–117; Harris, *Is There a Republican Majority?* 160–163; Brenner, "Patterns of Jewish-Catholic Democratic Voting," 169; Manza and Brooks, "Religious Factor in Presidential Elections," 61–62.

72. Brenner, "Patterns of Jewish-Catholic Democratic Voting," 175–177, quotation 177.

73. *Newsweek*, Sept. 5, 1960, p. 76; RN to Dunner, May 15, 1961, B 230, Dunner, Series 320, RNL; interview, Day 6, Tape 3, 00:57:53, FG; Keller, "Intellectuals and Eisenhower," 268–271; Greenberg, "Shocked, Shocked"; Gellman, *Contender*, 341.

74. Gellman, *President and Apprentice*, 134–135.

75. Interview with Klein, Nov. 12, 2009; Gellman, *President and Apprentice*, 125–156, 379–424; Bryant, *Bystander*, 1–207; Crowley, *Nixon in Winter*, 142; Bracey and Meier, *Papers of the NAACP*, Fact Sheet, undated, R 3; O'Hare et al., *Blacks on the Move*, 6; Vickery, *Economics of the Negro Migration*, 13, 18, 41; Matthews and Prothro, "Political Factors and Negro Voter Registration," 355, 367; Polenberg, *One Nation Divisible*, 150–153; Taeuber, *Negro Population and Housing*, 96–107; Taeuber and Taeuber, *Negroes in Cities*, 1–8.

76. *CCP*, Oct. 29, 1960; *LAS*, Nov. 3, 1960; *BAA*, Nov. 5, 1960.

77. Report of Voter Registration, 1958–1960, Bracey and Meier, *Papers of the NAACP*,

R 4; Berg, *"Ticket to Freedom,"* 157–165, 188–189; Bartley and Graham, *Southern Politics and the Second Reconstruction*, 24–26; Lawson, *Running for Freedom*, 81; David, *Presidential Election and Transition*, 137.

78. *Commercial Appeal* (TN), Nov. 11, PPS342(1960), RNL; *JG* (Norfolk), Nov. 5–11, 1960; *PC*, Nov. 19 and 26, 1960; Bartley and Graham, *Southern Politics and the Second Reconstruction*, 3, 6, 29, 31, 59, 61, 93, 121, 141, 169, 201, 217, 219, 325, 327, 363; Moon, "How We Voted and Why?" 26; Holloway, "Negro and the Vote," 526–556; Middleton, "Civil Rights Issue and Presidential Voting," 209–215; Havard, *Changing Politics of the South*, 430, 432, 437, 442, 460; Fairclough, *Race and Democracy*, 196–233; Hamilton, *Lister Hill*, 193–194; Buni, *Negro in Virginia Politics*, 206–210; Carty, *Catholic in the White House?* 91.

79. *PC*, Nov. 19, 1960; *BAA*, Nov. 15, 19, 1960; *NYAN*, Nov. 11, 1960; McKenna, "Negro Vote in Philadelphia," 408, 411–412; Taeuber, *Negro Population and Housing*, 118, 124, 134; Dorsey, "American Negro and His Government," 474; Silberman, *City and the Negro*, 90–91; Moon, "How We Voted and Why?" 29; Wilson, *Negro Politics*, 21, 23, 25, 27–36, 40; Drake and Cayton, *Black Metropolis*, xlii, 376–377.

80. Dear to Morsell, Dec. 6, 1960, B A246, General Office File, Presidential Campaign of 1960, 1960 Sept.–Dec., Group III, NAACP mss.; Bracey and Meier, *Papers of the NAACP*, Bond to Patton, Nov. 25, 1964, R 1.

81. Clipping, Jan. 27, 1961, B 243, Emory, RNL; Mazo et al., *Great Debates*, 2; Scott OH, p. 32, B 290, 10200, Scott mss.; JFK Foundation, *Listening In*, 281.

82. Memo, July 8, 1960, B 115, Burns 2/3 and memoirs, March 22, 31, 1976, RNL; RN, *Six Crises*, 310; Saulnier, *Constructive Years*, 1–11, 116–129; Sundquist, *Politics and Policy*, 15–34, 59–83; Morgan, *Eisenhower versus "the Spenders,"* 152–181; May, "President Eisenhower," 418–427.

83. Bridges, "Year End Review," 9; Galambos, *Eisenhower*, 183–184; McClenahan and Becker, *Eisenhower and the Cold War Economy*, 103–109.

84. *USNWR*, Oct. 10, 1960, p. 115; David, *Presidential Election and Transition*, 136–138; Alexander, *Financing the 1960 Election*, 73–74; Reuther, *Brothers Reuther*, 439.

85. Gallup, *Gallup Poll*, Vol. 3: 1694.

86. *NYT*, Aug. 26, 1957; *USNWR*, Oct. 3, 1960, p. 61; Gallup, *Gallup Poll*, Vol. 3: 1695; Seltzer, *Sex as a Political Variable*, 33, 39, 65; also see Wassenberg et al., "Gender Differences in Political Conceptualization," passim.

87. Gallup, *Gallup Poll*, Vol. 3: 1695.

88. "Religion and the 1960 Election," Kesaris, *Papers of the Republican Party*, R 2.

18. but did he win?

1. *NYT*, Nov. 11, 1960; Lawrence, *Six Presidents, Too Many Wars*, 241.

2. UPI, Nov. 10, 1960; Clifford, *Counsel to the President*, 331–332.

3. Schlesinger, *Letters*, 232; *NYT*, Nov. 13, 1960.

4. "20/20: Nixon and the 1960 Election," ABCNEWS.com, Jan. 6, 2006; *WP*, Nov. 10, 13, 1960, Nov. 17, 2000.

5. Patterson to RN, Nov. 10, 1960, B 581, Patterson, JS, Series 320, RNL; *San Diego*

Union-Tribune, Nov. 10, 2000; *WP,* Nov. 17, 2000; "20/20: Nixon and the 1960 Election" (Transcript), ABCNEWS.com, Jan. 6, 2006; RN, *Six Crises,* 399, 400–401, 411.

6. Progress Reports, Nov. 12, 1960, B 10, Sept. 1–Dec. 31, 1960 (1960), Snyder mss.; *WP,* Nov. 9, 1960.

7. Slater, *The Ike I Knew,* 230; progress reports, Nov. 12, 1960, B 10, Sept. 1–Dec. 31, 1960 (1960), Snyder mss.

8. Diary, Nov. 10, R 27 and telephone calls, Nov. 10, 1960, R 28, Diary DDEL.

9. *WP* and *NYT,* Nov. 13, 1960.

10. *WP,* Nov. 11, 12, 14, 1960; UPI and AP sent out stories to many newspapers about Morton refusing to concede, for example, *SAST,* Nov. 11, and *HC,* Nov. 12, 1960.

11. *WP,* Nov. 12, 1960.

12. *NYT* and *WP,* Nov. 12, 1960; Klein notes, undated, B 129, F 18, Klein mss.; RN, *Six Crises,* 411.

13. *HP* and *DMN,* Nov. 12; *WP* and *NYT,* Nov. 13, 1960.

14. *WP,* Nov. 12, 13; *NYT,* Nov. 13, 14, 1960.

15. Brandon, *Special Relationships,* 154–155.

16. Sandler, *Letters of John F. Kennedy,* 109; appointment calendar 1960, Nov. 12, 1960, and MacNeil OH, HHPL; Best, *Herbert Hoover,* 383–384; Smith, *Uncommon Man,* 257, 271–272, 294, 30, 329, 343, 411, 425.

17. Appointment calendar 1960, Nov. 12, 1960 and MacNeil OH, HHPL; "20/20: Nixon and the 1960 Election," ABCNEWS.com, Jan. 6, 2006; RN, *Six Crises,* 403–404; Klein, *Making It Perfectly Clear,* 373; Smith, *Uncommon Man,* 423–424; Day 8, Tape 2, 00:45:57 [RN], FG.

18. Appointment calendar 1960, Nov. 12, 1960, HHPL; telephone calls, Nov. 12, 1960, Diary DDEL; DDEP XXI, p. 2589; RN, *Six Crises,* 405; Klein, *Making It Perfectly Clear,* 374; Smith, *Disarming Diplomat,* 108.

19. *NYT* and *AC,* Nov. 14, 1960.

20. "20/20: Nixon and the 1960 Election" (Transcript), ABCNEWS.com, Jan. 6, 2006.

21. *HP, HC, WP, CT,* and *DMN,* Nov. 15, 1960; *NYHT,* Jan. 5, B 216, Dillon, D, Series 320, RN remarks, Jan. 6, 1961, B 150, F 3, Series 207, and RN to Mazo, March 19, 1963, B 486, Mazo [1/4], Series 320, RNL; *Time,* Nov. 28, 1960, March 1, 1968; Klein interview, Nov. 12, 2002; Klein, *Making It Perfectly Clear,* 374–375; RN, *Six Crises,* 406–407, 409–410; Mazo, *Richard Nixon,* 250; David, *Presidential Election and Transition,* 296; Day 8, Tape 2, 00:45:01 [RN], FG.

22. *NYT,* Nov. 15, 1960; *San Diego Union-Tribune,* Nov. 10, 2000; Day 8, Tape 2, 00:47:56 [RN], FG.

23. Mr. President, Nov. 14, 1960, R 28, Diary DDEL; DDEP XXI, p. 2589.

24. Swift, *Pat and Dick,* 168; Crowley, *Nixon Off the Record,* 30; PN to Helene, Dec. 6, 1960, DR217.1, RNL.

25. *DMN,* Nov. 12; *HP,* Nov. 12, 17; *SAST,* Nov. 17; *NYT* and *WP,* Nov. 20, 1960.

26. *Time,* Nov. 28, 1960; *NYT,* Nov. 17; *AC,* Nov. 18, 1960.

27. *Time,* Nov. 28, 1960; *SAST,* Nov. 18; *DMN, DTH, WP,* and *CT,* Nov. 19; *Evening Star* (DC) and *DTH,* Dec. 1; *WP* and *DMN,* Dec. 2, 1960; Jaworski oral memoirs, Vol. 1, P 1, pp. 260–261.

28. DDE to Hess, Nov. 20, 1960, B 814, Whitman, An, Series 320, RNL; WP, Nov. 20, 1960; diary, Nov. 28, 1960, R 27, Diary DDEL.

29. Diary, Nov. 30, 1960, R 27, 1960, Diary DDEL; DDEP XXI, p. 2591; Walsh, *Gift of Insecurity*, 180; interview with Walsh, Dec. 1, 2005.

30. NYT and WP, Dec. 1, 1960; Bullis to RN, Dec. 2, 1960, B 111, Bullis, Series 320, RNL.

31. O'Connor, *Clout*, 157.

32. Wilson, *Negro Politics*, 54, 56, 58–59, 63–64.

33. Kallina, "State's Attorney and the President," 148–150, 159, 160, quotation 160; Kallina, *Courthouse over White House*, 225; Biles, *Richard J. Daley*, 71; Royko, *Boss*, 118–119; Cohen and Taylor, *American Pharaoh*, 245–249, 262; Rakove, *Don't Make No Waves*, 230.

34. Kallina, "Was Nixon Cheated in 1960?" 116–118; Kallina, "State's Attorney and the President," 157–160, quotation 160.

35. *San Diego Union-Tribune*, Nov. 10, 2000; NYT and WP, Nov. 12, 1960; Cohen and Taylor, *American Pharaoh*, 264–265; Rorabaugh, *Real Making of the President*, 188.

36. Martin, *It Seems Like Only Yesterday*, 106–107; Rakove, *Don't Make No Waves*, 159.

37. Bradlee, *Conversations with Kennedy*, 33. In his next memoir, Bradlee claimed that he did not know whether Daley meant that he committed fraud. When I asked Bradlee which version was accurate, he unhesitatingly declared the first version was true. Interview with Bradlee.

38. Royko, *Boss*, 119; Biles, *Richard J. Daley*, 71–72; Cohen and Taylor, *American Pharaoh*, 270–279; the mayor's son Bill Daley defended his father in *USA Today*, Sept. 26, 2010.

39. Memo, Feb. 26, 1995, LBM134a, RNL.

40. Garvey, "Bush Camp Looks to Nixon."

41. CT, Nov. 13, Dec. 1, 1960.

42. CT, Nov. 14, 16, 19, 22, 24, 26, 1960; Rentschler to RN, Nov. 14, B 627 Rentschler [1/3], and Brill to RN, Nov. 18, B 172, Committee on Honest Elections, and Klein to RN, Nov. 26, N 415, Klein (1 of 2), Series 320, RNL.

43. CT, Nov. 15, 22–24, 26, 1960.

44. CT, Nov. 8, 1956, Nov. 24, 1960; Everson, "Effects of Initiatives on Voter Turnout," 83; O'Connor, *Clout*, 157–158.

45. Kleppner, *Chicago Divided*, 17, 34, 67–68; Hirsch, *Making the Second Ghetto*, 17, 212–258; Grimshaw, *Bitter Fruit*, 15–16, 38, 94–95, 97, 100–101, 103; Kitagawa and Taeuber, *Local Community Fact Book*, xix, 2, 252; Colby and Green, "Consolidation of Clout," 1, 6, 33, 44, 49, 56; Taeuber and Taeuber, *Negroes in Cities*, 99; Taeuber and Taeuber, "Negro as an Immigrant Group," 374–382; Drake and Cayton, *Black Metropolis*, Vol. 1, Figures 21d, 21e; Reed, *Chicago NAACP and the Rise of Professional Leadership*, 149, 157–158, 190; Duncan and Duncan, *Negro Population of Chicago*, 25, 97, 107; Geisler, "Chicago Democratic Voting," 7, 104, 109, 165; Fremon, *Chicago Politics Ward by Ward*, 179.

46. *Jet*, July 19, 1956, pp. 12–14; Allswang, *Bosses, Machines, and Urban Voters*, 119, 136–137, 139–147, quotation 139; Kleppner, *Chicago Divided*, 30, 33, 35, 72, 265; Booker, *Black Man's America*, 96–97; Granger and Granger, *Lords of the Last Machine*, 111–

118, 120–121; Hirsch, *Making the Second Ghetto*, 129–130; Hirsch, "Cook County Democratic Machine," 75; Grimshaw, *Bitter Fruit*, 82–87, 97, 99–102, 119–120, 127–128; Wilson, *Negro Politics*, 21, 40, 51, 81; Lemann, *Promised Land*, 74–75, 91.

47. Wofford, *Of Kennedys and Kings*, 60–61. Lemann, *Promised Land*, 112–116; Manning, *William L. Dawson*, 145; *BAA*, Oct. 29, Nov. 15, 1960; Lemann, *Promised Land*, 76; Hirsch, "Cook County Democratic Machine," 76.

48. Spindell to RN, Nov. 14, 1960, B 718, Spindell 2 of 5, Series 320, RNL; *CT*, Dec. 2, 1960; Cohen and Taylor, *American Pharaoh*, 273–274.

49. *CT*, Nov. 12, 14, 16, 26, 27, 29, Dec. 2, 10, 1960; Cohen and Taylor, *American Pharaoh*, 271–276.

50. *CT*, Nov. 23, 24, 1960; *NYHT*, Dec. 6, 7, 1960. For allegations of fraud in other wards, see *CT*, Dec. 6, 9, 1960, and Mazo, *Richard Nixon*, 248.

51. Scammon, *America Votes* 3, pp. 105, 110, and *America Votes* 4, pp. 105, 110; *CD*, Nov. 10, 1960; Kallina, *Kennedy v. Nixon*, 146; Fremon, *Chicago Politics Ward by Ward*, 29–30, 34–35, 40, 52–53, 135; Biles, *Richard J. Daley*, 72; Cohen and Taylor, *American Pharaoh*, 271; Guylay to Loeb, July 13, 1960, B 7, F 50, Klein mss.; interview with Christopher Reed, a native Chicagoan and history professor at Roosevelt University, June 22, 2006.

52. Hersh, *Dark Side of Camelot*, 131–154; Giancana and Giancana, *Double Cross*, 290–291; Giancana et al., *JFK and Sam*, 83, 104; Mahoney, *Sons and Brothers*, 81.

53. Scammon, *America Votes* 3, p. 109, and *America Votes* 4, p. 109; Binder, "Organized Crime and the Election," 251–265, quotation 265.

54. Anderson, *Texas Politics*, 48; Green, *Establishment in Texas Politics*, 147–148; Weeks, *Texas in the 1960 Election*, 61–62; Havard, *Changing Politics of the South*, 213–222; Knaggs, *Two Party Texas*, 2–4; Stephenson, "Democrats of Texas and Texas Liberalism," 133–137.

55. Murph, *Texas Giant*, 118–197; Watson OH–II, p. 16, and Reedy OH–IX, p. 27, LBJL.

56. Scammon, *America Votes* 3, 397; Scammon, *America Votes* 4, p. 393; Weeks, *Texas in the 1960 Election*, 63–69; McMillan, "Texas and the Eisenhower Campaigns," 428–433; Knaggs, *Two Party Texas*, 5–6; Calvert, *History of Texas*, 403; Thorburn, *Red State*, 71–72, 75–76, 85, 89, 245; Banitch, "Ultraconservative Congressman from Dallas," 73–74; Casdorph, *History of the Republican Party in Texas*, 220–221; Olien, *From Token to Triumph*, 173; Reichley, *States in Crisis*, 121; Hogan, "Texas Presidential Election Victory," 99–107; García, *Viva Kennedy*, 105.

57. Interview with Dugger, Oct. 17, 2005; Tower, *Consequences*, 17.

58. Caro, *Means of Ascent*, 19–20, 145–412; Dallek, *Lone Star Rising*, 207–224, 295–348; Lynch, *Duke of Duval*, passim.

59. Caro, *Passage of Power*, 150–155. Allen Fisher, archivist at the Lyndon Johnson Presidential Library, did not "find evidence of published or unpublished works about LBJ's role in the 1960 election in Texas"; Fisher to Gellman, May 12, 2017, Gellman mss.

60. B. Shivers to Gellman, Sept. 25, 2005, Gellman mss.

61. Weeks, *Texas in the 1960 Election*, 61; McCleskey, *Government and Politics of Texas*, 49–50; Tower, *Consequences*, 16; Foley, *Ballot Battles*, 218–220.

62. *DMN*, Nov. 16–17, 22, 30, 1960; *HP*, Nov. 20, 22, 1960; *TO*, Nov. 25, 1960.

63. *HP*, Nov. 10, 11, 17, 22, 1960; *DMN*, Nov. 11, 12, 25, 1960; *TO*, Nov. 11, 1960; *SAST*, Nov. 11, 14, 1960; Hutcheson to RN, Dec. 16, 1960, B 364, Hutcheson, Series 320, RNL; Benton, *Texas*, 98–102.

64. Scammon, *America Votes*, pp. 393–397, and *America Votes 4*, pp. 389–393; Texas: Counties carried by Nixon and Kennedy, Kesaris, *Papers of the Republican Party*, R 4; Price to Rosen, Oct. 18, 1956, O & C File, File No. 022, Sec 01, FBI mss.; *HC*, Nov. 29, 1960; *WP*, Dec. 4, 1960; Anderson to RN, Nov. 16, 1960, B 40, Anderson, D, and Fay to RN, March 7, 1961, B 253, Fay, A, Series 320, and Fay to RN, Dec. 14, 1960, B 5, Texas—1961, Series 233, RNL; Soukup, McCleskey, and Holloway, *Party and Factional Division*, 128–130; Calvert, *History of Texas*, 403; Weeks, *Texas in the 1960 Election*, 69–70; Mazo, *Richard Nixon*, 245–246; Anderson, *Texas Politics*, 29–33.

65. Holloway, "Negro and the Vote," 543–556; Soukup, McCleskey, and Holloway, *Party and Factional Division*, 108–139. Twenty-four of the thirty-eight East Texas counties had black populations over 20 percent: in the Upper East, Anderson, Camp, Cass, Cherokee, Gregg, Harrison, Henderson, Morris, Panola, Red River, Smith, Trinity, and Upshur; in the Deep East, Houston, Jasper, Nacogdoches, Newton, Polk, Sabine, San Augustine, San Jacinto, Shelby, and Tyler; and in the South East, Jefferson. U.S. Dept of Commerce, *1960 Census by Population, Supplementary Report PC (S 1) 52, Negro Population by County, 1960 and 1950*, pp. 52–57.

66. Holloway, "Texas Negro as a Voter," 135–145.

67. *HC*, Nov. 29, 1960; press release, Nov. 30, 1960, Jaworski mss.

68. *WP*, Nov. 10, 11, 1960.

69. *WP*, Nov. 29, 1960.

70. *CT*, Dec. 3, 4, 12, 1960; *WP*, Dec. 3, 8, 9, 1960; *USNWR*, Dec. 12, 1960, pp. 58–60.

71. *NYHT*, Dec. 4–7, 1960; Mazo, *Richard Nixon*, 249; interview with Mazo, July 17, 2001; Kallina, "State's Attorney and the President," 153–154; Kallina, "Was the Presidential Election Stolen?" 114; *WP*, Nov. 17, 2000, p. A01; for the flaws in Mazo's accounts, see Kallina, "Was Nixon Cheated in 1960?" 138–140.

72. *DMN*, Nov. 22, 26, 30, Dec. 2–4, 6–7, *HP*, Nov. 21, Dec. 4, 6–7, *SAST*, Dec. 4, 6–7, *HC*, Nov. 29, Dec. 4, 7, *DTH* and *AS*, Dec. 7, 1960; Jaworski oral memoir, Vol. 1, Part I, Interview #4, pp. 255, 261, and billing sheet, Nov. 29–Dec. 12, and Winters to Jaworski, Dec. 1, draft, Dec. 3, and *McDaniel v. Daniel*, Civil Act, No. 13441, Dec. 5, 1960, Jaworski mss. Mazo has claimed that Attorney General Wilson helped to fix the election for the Democrats, and Lyndon Johnson promised that Wilson would receive the Democratic nomination for governor in 1962. Johnson reneged and supported John Connally. Interview with Mazo, July 17, 2001.

73. *DMN, AS, HP* and *SAST*, Dec. 8, 1960; Hutcheson to McWhorter, Dec. 8, 1960, B 364, Hutcheson, Series 320, RNL.

74. *TO, DTH, HC*, and *AS*, Dec. 9, 1960; *HP, HC, DMN*, Dec. 10, 1960; *SAST*, Dec. 11, 1960; Jaworski oral memoir, Vol. 1, Part I, Interview #4, pp. 256–258, Jaworski mss.

75. *SAST, DTH, HP*, and *AS*, Dec. 12, 13, 1960; *McDaniel v. Daniel*, Civil Action No. 13,441, Dec. 12, 1960, and Jaworski oral memoir, Vol. 1, Part I, Interview #4, p. 259, Jaworski mss.

76. AS, *DMN, HP*, and *HC*, Dec. 13, 1960.

77. AS and *SAST*, Dec. 14, 1960; *HP* and *DMN*, Dec. 14, 20, 1960; Hutcheson to Mc-Whorter, Dec. 13, B 364, Hutcheson, B 354, and Hutcheson and Smith to RN, Dec. 22, 1960, B 706, Smith, Series 320, RNL; Foley, *Ballot Battles*, 218–220.

78. *CT*, Dec. 1, 1960; Spindell to RN, May 9, 1961, Election, 1960, and Spindell, Jr., RNL; Kenney, *Political Passage*, 169–179.

79. *CT*, Dec. 2, 1960; Kallina, "State's Attorney and the President," 151–153.

80. *CT*, Dec. 2–5, 9, 1960.

81. Leventhal to RFK, Dec. 5, 1960, Stratton files, 1960 Campaign & Transition, General Subject, 1959–1960, RFK mss. Leventhal's count was incorrect. Subtracting Illinois's 27 electoral votes from the 1960 total would have made the electoral majority 256.

82. *CT*, Dec. 5–12, 1960; Kallina, "Was the Presidential Election Stolen?" 114.

83. *CT*, Dec. 13–15, 1960; press release, Dec. 19, 1960, B 627, Rentschler [1/3], Series 320, and Spindell, May 9, 1961, Election, 1960, and Spindell, Jr., RNL; Kenney, *Political Passage*, 179, and note 230; Cohen and Taylor, *American Pharaoh*, 270–279.

84. *NYT*, Dec. 19, 20, 1960.

85. Ellsberg, *Secrets*, 107.

86. *CT*, May 6, 1961.

87. Kinch and Long, *Allan Shivers*, 4; Rorabaugh, *Real Making of the President*, 187–188; Foley, *Ballot Battles*, 226.

88. Day 8, Tape 2, 00:41:22 [RN], FG; Crowley, *Nixon Off the Record*, 30; Kallina, "State's Attorney and the President," 154; Foley, *Ballot Battles*, 226–228.

89. Schlesinger, *Robert Kennedy and His Times*, 220; Sorensen, *Counselor*, 195; O'Brien, *No Final Victories*, 96–97.

90. Donaldson, *First Modern Campaign*, 151; Block, *Herblock*, 177; Block, *Herblock Special Report*, 59–60.

91. *CT*, Nov. 9, Dec. 15, 1960; Lawrence, *Six Presidents, Too Many Wars*, 254; Kallina, *Courthouse over White House*, note 273; Biles, *Richard J. Daley*, 74.

92. Interviews with John Jackson, Herb Russell, and David Kenney, first week of July 2008.

93. Sorensen, *Counselor*, 195.

94. Salinger, *With Kennedy*, 76; *WP*, Nov. 17, 2000; RN, *Six Crises*, 386.

95. O'Brien, *John F. Kennedy*, 499; O'Donnell and Powers, *"Johnny, We Hardly Knew Ye,"* 258; Sorensen, *Kennedy*, 231–232.

96. Dallek, *Unfinished Life*, 301; Dallek, *Camelot's Court*, 22.

97. Dallek, *Lone Star Rising*, 699.

98. Oliphant and Wilkie, *Road to Camelot*, book jacket, acknowledgments, notes, and bibliography.

99. Oliphant and Wilkie, *Road to Camelot*, 355–358.

100. Foley, *Ballot Battles*, 228; Safire, *Before the Fall*, 152.

19. IN WITH THE NEW

1. Cabinet, July 1, 1960, R 26, Diary DDEL; Benedict, "Changing the Watch in Washington," 15–29.

2. *PPA* 1960–61, p. 561; David, *Presidential Election and Transition*, 209–210.

3. Notes, Nov. 3, 1960, R 27, Diary DDEL; *Time*, Nov. 14, 1960; David, *Presidential Election and Transition*, 206–208.

4. DDEP, XXI, p. 2588; progress reports, Nov. 9, 1960, B 10, Sept. 1–Dec. 31, 1960 (1960), Snyder mss.; Benedict, "Changing the Watch in Washington," 29–33; *WP*, Nov. 11, 1960; Clifford, *Counsel to the President*, 319–320, 330, 332–334; David, *Presidential Election and Transition*, 212–213; Shaw, *Rising Star, Setting Sun*, 126–130, 168, 171–175, 179.

5. *WP*, Nov. 15, 1960; Persons OH 161, interview #4, pp. 137–138, COHP; Shaw, *Rising Star, Setting Sun*, 130–132.

6. DDEP XXI, pp. 2189–2195, 2199–2200, 2205–2206; *Time*, Dec. 19, 1960; Shaw, *Rising Star, Setting Sun*, 133–137; Baier, *Three Days in January*, prologue.

7. *PPA* 1960–61, pp. 872–873; DDEP XXI, p. 2195.

8. Memo, Dec. 16, 1960, R 28, Diary DDEL; *PPA* 1960–61, p. 1041; D. Eisenhower OH, 34, HHPL.

9. *NYT*, Nov. 10, 1960; Schlesinger, *Journals*, 91; *Time*, Dec. 12, 19, 26, 1960, Jan. 2, 13, 20, 1961; *Newsweek*, Dec. 28, 1960, p. 20, Jan. 9, pp. 20–24, Jan. 16, 1961, p. 24; *USNWR*, Nov. 21, 1960, p. 152; Shaw, *Rising Star, Setting Sun*, 184–197; Schlesinger, *Thousand Days*, 118–161; Sorensen, *Kennedy*, 227–233, 251–287.

10. *Newsweek*, Jan. 16, 1961, p. 26.

11. Hannaford, *Drew Pearson Diaries*, 51.

12. *CT*, Nov. 21, 1960; *Newsweek*, Jan. 2, 1961, p. 18; *Time*, Jan. 13, 1961.

13. *NYT*, Dec. 11, 1960; *WP*, Jan. 4, 1961; *Evening Star* (DC), Jan. 6, 1961; *Newsweek*, Jan. 2, pp. 18–20, Jan. 16, 1961, p. 26; *Time*, Jan. 13, 1961; *USNWR*, Nov. 21, 1960, p. 71.

14. Gallup, *Gallup Poll*, Vol. 3: 1696; *WP*, Nov. 16, Dec. 25, 1960; schedule, Dec. 7, 8, memo, Dec. 15, 1960, R 28, Diary DDEL; DDEP XXI, pp. 2593–2594; Shaw, *Rising Star, Setting Sun*, 139–151.

15. Appointments, Dec. 15, R 28, and diary, memo for the record, Dec. 28, 1960, B 55, staff notes, Diary DDEL; DDEP XXI, p. 2594; Morton to McWhorter, Dec. 1, B 532, Morton, T, Republican strategy, Dec. 5, B 536, Mueller, F, Series 320, memo, Dec. 9, B 149, F 48, Series 207, and schedule, Dec. 30, 1960, PPS212(1960).721, RNL; *WP*, Dec. 18, 1960.

16. Memo, Dec. 17, 1960, R 28, Diary DDEL.

17. Davies to RN, Nov. 11, 14, B 203, Davies, P, and Baker to RN, Nov. 15, B 60, Baker, L, and Adams to RN, Dec. 1, B 19, Adams, K, and Wright to RN, Dec. 2, B 832, Wright, C, and Cotton to McCaffrey, Dec. 8, B 183, Cotton, A, and RN to Abernethy, Dec. 14, B 18, Abernethy, T, and Hillings to RN, Dec. 21, B 341, Hillings 1958, Series 320, and Hoover to RN, Nov. 11, PPS320,102.103, and Helene to PN, Nov. 28, 1960, RNL; memo, Dec. 17, and mail situation, Dec. 30, 1960, Finch mss.; Kersten to RN, Nov. 21, 1960, Kersten mss.; *SAST*, Nov. 10, 13, 27, Dec. 27, 1960; *Newsweek*, Nov. 11, pp. EE-2, 9, 14, and Dec. 12, p. 27, Dec. 26, p. 21, 1960; *NYT*, Nov. 11, 24, Dec. 25, 29, 1960; *CT*, Nov. 13, 21, 25, 1960; *WP*, Nov. 11, 23, 26, 28, Dec. 2, 10, 31, 1960, Jan. 12, 1961; *Time*, Dec. 12, 1960; David, *Presidential Election and Transition*, 327–328.

18. Memo, Nov. 25, 1960, B 320, Harlow, Series 320, RNL.

19. *CT*, Jan. 6, 1961, B 149, F 47, Series 207, and schedule, Dec. 21, PPS212(1960).718, and Dec. 22, 1960, PPS212(1960).719, RNL; *NYT*, Dec. 23, 1960; RN, *Six Crises*, 414.

20. *USNWR*, Nov. 21, 1960, p. 71; JFK to Lodge, Jan. 2, 1961, R 8, Lodge II mss.

21. Lodge to Georgie, Nov. 14, R 10, Brown to Lodge, Nov. 17, and Lodge to Alexander, Nov. 30, R 2, *BG*, Dec. 2, 1960, Feb. 3, March 5, 1961, Lodge to Rusk, Dec. 12, R 14, and Lodge to Dillon, Dec. 17, 1960, R 4, Lodge II, *BG*, March 5, 1960, Lodge mss.

22. Gray to Lodge, Jan. 5, R 29, Lodge mss., RN to Lodge, Jan. 9, 16, June 19, Nov. 8, R 12, Lodge II, and *BG*, March 5, 1961, R 31, Lodge mss.; Lodge to RN, Feb. 8, Nov. 20, 1961, B 457, Lodge (1 of 2), Series 320, RNL.

23. *Evening Star* (DC), Oct. 2, PPS610s.23, and *NYT*, Oct. 9, 1960, PPS501.2,83.5, RNL; RNL; *Tucson Citizen*, Oct. 8, 1960, Vol. 98, Sept.–Oct. 1960, and *Arizona Republic*, Nov. 15, Vol. 100, Nov. 4–15, 1960, and *Arizona Daily Star*, Dec. 11, 1960, Vol. 102, Nov. 30–Dec. 13, 1960, Goldwater Scrapbooks, Goldwater mss.; *USNWR*, Nov. 21, 1960, p. 142; Goldwater, *Goldwater*, 142–147; Goldwater, *With No Apologies*, 120–126; Shadegg, *What Happened to Goldwater?* 10–11, 30, 37; Edwards, *Goldwater*, 140–143; Middendorf, *Glorious Disaster*, 5; Shadegg, *What Happened to Goldwater?* 37; Novak, *Prince of Darkness*, 74–75; Wilkins, "Development of the Mississippi Republican Party," 49–59; Melton, "1960 Presidential Election in Georgia," 168–178.

24. *NYT*, Nov. 13, 1960; *WP*, Nov. 23, Dec. 2, 1960, Jan. 6, 1961; *Time*, Nov. 21, 1960; *Newsweek*, Nov. 14, 1960, pp. EE-9, 10.

25. *WP*, Nov. 11, 1960, Jan. 7, 12, 1961; *Time*, Nov. 21, 1960.

26. *NYT*, Nov. 8, 1960; *Time*, Nov. 21, 1960; *DMN*, Nov. 28, 1960.

27. Memo, Nov. 11, R 27 and Rockefeller to DDE, Nov. 15, 1960, OF Part 1, Rockefeller 1960, R 25, Diary DDEL.

28. *WP* and *NYT*, Nov. 30, 1960.

29. DDEP XXI, p. 2591; schedule and appointments, Dec. 1, 1960, R 28, Diary DDEL; *NYT*, Dec. 2, 1960; *BG*, Nov. 30, 1960, R 31, Lodge mss.

30. Progress reports, Dec. 2, 1960, B 10, Sept. 1–Dec. 31, 1960(4), Snyder mss.

31. *NYT*, *WP*, and *CT*, Dec. 3, 1960; *Newsweek*, Dec. 5, 1960, p. 31; *Time*, Dec. 12, 1960; Rockefeller to Reece, Jan. 4, 1961, B 650, Rockefeller 1960–61, Series 320, RNL.

32. *Time*, Jan. 20, 1961; *Newsweek*, Jan. 23, 1961, p. 15; Sorensen, *Kennedy*, 233–234; Schlesinger, *Thousand Days*, 162.

33. Memo, Nov. 23, 1960, B 299, Graham {2 of 3}, Series 320, RNL; Graham to J. Graham, Nov. 22, Graham to JFK, Nov. 28, Notebook 3: Series I, Collection 685, and Graham to RN, Nov. 28, 1960, Notebooks 10, 14, Series I, Collection 685, Graham mss.

34. *NYT*, Jan. 17, 1960; Graham to RN, Nov. 9, 28, 1960, Notebooks 10, 14, Series I, Collection 685, Graham mss.; Graham to RN, Nov. 28, 1960, and RN to Graham, Jan. 15, 1961, B 299, Graham {2 of 3}, Series 320, and schedule, Dec. 18, 1960, PPS212(1960).715, RNL.

35. DDEP XXI, p. 2236; Eisenhower OH, 27–28, HHPL; Elliott and D'Orso, *Cost of Courage*, 204–205.

36. *WP*, Jan. 7, 9, 1961; *Time*, Jan. 13, 1961; MacGregor to RN, Feb. 11, 1961, B 459, MacGregor, C, Series 320, RNL; RN, *Six Crises*, 415–416.

37. DDEP XXI, pp. 2230–2232; memo, Dec. 28, 1960, B 55, staff notes, Diary DDEL;

Slater, *The Ike I Knew*, 239–240; *USNWR*, Nov. 21, 1960, p. 142; *Time*, Dec. 19, 1960; Filipink, *Eisenhower and American Foreign Policy*, 23–24; Shaw, *Rising Star, Setting Sun*, 138.

38. *Newsweek*, Jan. 30, 1961, pp. 27–29; Dillon OH, 39, 91–92, COHP; Stossel, *Sarge*, 179; Brauer, *Presidential Transitions*, 91–94.

39. Dillon OH, 43, COHP; FR, 1958–1960, Vol. 4, p. 144; telephone calls, Dec. 15, memo, Dec. 28, 1960, B 55, staff notes, 2, Diary DDEL; DDEP XXI, pp. 2202–2204; Dillon to RN, Dec. 18, 1960, RN to Dillon, Jan. 5, 1961, B 216, Dillon, D, Series 320, RNL; Schlesinger, *Journals*, 93–94; WP, Nov. 19, 21, 1960, Jan. 5, 9, 13, 1961; *SAST*, Dec. 21, 1960; Wofford, *Of Kennedys and Kings*, 76–77; Guthman and Shulman, *Robert Kennedy in His Own Words*, 40.

40. Dillon to DDE, Dec. 21, 1960, R 10, OF, DDEL; DDEP XXI, pp. 2133–2134; *WP*, Jan. 3, 1961; *Time*, Jan. 2, 1961; Slater, *The Ike I Knew*, 239.

41. DDEP XXI, p. 2600; progress reports, Jan. 9, 1961, B 10, Jan. 1, 1961–Nov. 4, 1963 (1), Snyder mss.; schedule, Jan. 9, 1961, R 28, Diary DDEL; *PPA* 1960–61, pp. 904–905; *NYT* and *WP*, Jan. 10, 1961; calendar, Jan. 9, PPS212(1961).11, and RN to DDE, Jan. 15, B 237, Eisenhower 1/2, and Nov. 8, 1961, PPS324.166(1), RNL.

42. DDEP XXI, pp. 2600–2601; *PPA* 1960–61, pp. 897, 1045, 1048; appointments, Jan. 4, 5, 11–13, 1961, R 28, and cabinet, Jan. 7, 13, 1961, R 10, Diary DDEL; *NYT*, Jan. 14, 1961.

43. DDEP XXI, pp. 2241–2242, 2600.

44. Memo, Jan. 19, 1961, R 28, Diary DDEL; DDEP XXI, p. 2602.

45. *USNWR*, Jan. 16, pp. 62, 64, Jan. 23, 1961, pp. 102–107; *Time*, Jan. 20, 1961.

46. Progress reports, Jan. 13, 1961, B 10, Jan. 1, 1961–Nov. 4, 1963 (1), Snyder mss.; DDEP XXI, p. 2601; *WP*, Jan. 15, 1961.

47. *PPA* 1960–61, pp. 1035–1040, quotations 1038, 1039; *Time*, Jan. 27, 1961; Griffin, "New Light on Eisenhower's Farewell Address," 469–477; Hartung, "Eisenhower's Warning," 39–43; Baier, *Three Days in January*, chapters 5–9.

48. Progress reports, Jan. 18, 1961, B 10, Jan. 1, 1961–Nov. 4, 1963 (1), Snyder mss.; *PPA* 1960–61, pp. 1041–1050, quotations 1043, 1044, 1045.

49. *PPA* 1960–61, pp. 1041–1043.

50. DDEP XXI, p. 2603; progress reports, Jan. 19, 1961, B 10, Jan. 1, 1961–Nov. 4, 1963 (1), Snyder mss.; memo, Jan. 19, 1961, post presidential, JFK 1960–61 (1), Augusta, Walter Reed Series, DDEL; *Newsweek*, Jan. 30, 1961, p. 22; Clifford, *Counsel to the President*, 342–345; Lemitzer—I, 13, OH, LBJL; Greenstein and Immerman, "What Did Eisenhower Tell Kennedy?" 573–585; Filipink, *Eisenhower and American Foreign Policy*, 25–29; Shaw, *Rising Star, Setting Sun*, 180–181.

51. Memo, Jan. 19, 1961, post president, JFK 1960–61 (1), Augusta, Walter Reed Series, DDEL.

52. Progress reports, Jan. 19, 1961, B 10, Jan. 1, 1961–Nov. 4, 1963 (1), Snyder mss.; WP, Jan. 20, 1961; Snyder to RN, Jan. 19, 1961, B 711, Snyder, HM, Series 320, RNL; Eisenhower, *Strictly Personal*, 287; *Time*, Jan. 27, 1961; *Newsweek*, Jan. 30, 1961, p. 22.

53. *NYT*, Jan. 21, 1961; *Time*, Jan. 27, 1961; Klein, *Making It Perfectly Clear*, 9; Gray, *Eighteen Acres under Glass*, 292; Bradlee, *Good Life*, 217.

54. Memo, Dec. 28, 1960, B 150, F 13, Series 207, RNL; *NYT*, Jan. 21, 1961; *Newsweek*, Dec. 12, 1960, p. 27, Jan. 23, 1961, pp. 18, 20; *Time*, Jan. 27, 1961; Eisenhower, *Strictly Personal*, 287.

55. Inauguration of JFK, Jan. 20, 1961, U.S. History, C-SPAN 3; *NYT*, Jan. 21, 1961; *Time*, Jan. 27, 1961; Lincoln, *My Twelve Years with John F. Kennedy*, 227; Sorensen, *Kennedy*, 244–245.

56. Sorensen, *Kennedy*, 240–248.

57. Day 9, Tape 1, 00:13: 42 [RN], FG.

58. Roberts, *First Rough Draft*, 172.

59. Allen, *Eisenhower and the Mass Media*, 198; Hagerty OH (1966), pp. 101–102; DDE to Hagerty, Nov. 1966, post presidency DDEL.

60. Eisenhower OH, 32–34, HHPL.

61. Memoirs, April 5, 1976, RNL; diary, luncheon, Jan. 20, 1961, R 28, DDEL; *WP*, Jan. 21, 1961; Day 9, Tape 1, 00:15:53 [RN], FG.

62. Day 9, Tape 1, 00:15:53 [RN] and 00:18:36 [RN], FG; memoirs, April 5, 1976, RNL; Klein, *Making It Perfectly Clear*, 372; RN, *Six Crises*, 417.

63. Day 9, Tape 1, 00:18:36 [RN], FG; also see memoirs, April 6, 1976, for a similar recollection, RNL.

64. RN to Freeman, Jan. 7, B 274, Freeman, B, Series 320, and PN to Helene, Jan. 6, 1961, DR 220, and memoirs, April 5, 1976, RNL; RN, *Six Crises*, 423, 426.

20. BETWEEN MYTH AND REALITY

1. *WP*, Feb. 15, 1962.

2. White, *In Search of History*, 518, 525.

3. Ibid., 454–455.

4. White, *Making of the President* (1988 ed.), ix–xi.

5. Ibid. (2009 ed.), xi–xiii.

6. Dallek, *Unfinished Life*, 294–296.

7. Burns, *Running Alone*, 2; Lincoln, *My Twelve Years with John F. Kennedy*, 123.

8. Burns, *John Kennedy*, v–vii; Burns, *Running Alone*, 1, 31–33, 42.

9. Sorensen, *Counselor*, 195.

10. Drew, *Richard M. Nixon*, 7.

11. Rorabaugh, "Why It's Time to Get Past White's Account"; Kallina, *Kennedy v. Nixon*, 201–214, quotation 214; also see Hoffmann, *White and Journalism as Illusion*, Brands, "Burying Theodore White," and Miller, "Making of White's *Making*."

12. Klein to Leake, Jan. 18, 1961, B 416, Klein 1960 (1 of 2), Series 320, RNL; Klein to Ladd, Aug. 16, 1965, B 1, F 9 [2 of 3], Klein mss.; Klein, *Making It Perfectly Clear*, 85–86.

13. *BH*, Nov. 16, 1960, RN to Choate, Jan. 11, and Choate to RN, Jan. 16, 1961, B 146, Choate, R, Series 320, RNL; *Time*, Aug. 8, Oct. 24, 1960.

14. Clipping, Jan. 1, B 86, Blair, W RN to Berlin, Jan. 3, 1961, B 78, Berlin, Series 320, RNL; RN to H. Hoover, Jan. 14, 1961, B 9, F 62, Klein mss. *NYT* and *WP*, Jan. 2, 1961.

15. Klein to Editor, Jan. 12, 1961, B 235, Editor & Pub, Series 320, RNL; Klein to Ladd,

Aug. 16, 1965, B 1, F 9 [2 of 3], Klein mss.; Conboy to RN, Aug. 5, 1961, B 173, Committee Appt, Series 320, RNL; Blair and Blair, *Search for JFK*, 587–588.

16. Klein to Ladd, Aug. 16, 1965, B 1, F 9 [2 of 3], Klein mss.

17. Willard Edwards, "Did Biased Reporters Cost Nixon the Election?," address to a *Human Events* Political Action Conference, Jan. 6, 1961, Edwards OH, 60–61, HSTL; RN, *Six Crises*, 396.

18. Niven to RN, Jan. 13, 1961, B 562, Niven, P, Series 320, RNL.

19. Niven broadcast, July 8, 1961, B 562, Niven, P, Series 320, RNL; Bradlee, *Good Life*, 211.

20. Bean to Naulty, June 25, 1994, LBM122, RNL.

21. Schlesinger, *Journals*, 86, quotation on 88.

22. Herken, *Georgetown Set*, 250, 257–258, 263.

23. Ritchie, *Columnist*; interview with Ritchie, July 15, 2020; Reston, *Deadline*, 407, quotation 286.

24. Germond, *Fat Man in a Middle Seat*, quotations 87, 93, and see 88.

25. Blair and Blair, *Search for JFK*, 584; Hersh, *Dark Side of Camelot*, 230–233; Giglio, "Growing Up Kennedy," 365–366, 368–369.

26. Von Post, *Love, Jack*, passim.

27. Kater to RFK, Oct. 19, 1961, JEH O & C, File no. 96, Section 1, FBI mss.

28. Thomas, *Robert Kennedy*, 94, 99, 175, 290–291, 299.

29. Memo, Nov. 11, 1960, B 647, F (1 of 3), Series 320, RNL.

30. Gallup, *Gallup Poll*, Vol. 3: 1691–1963; *Newsweek*, Nov. 14, 1960, p. EE4; *NYHT*, Dec. 6, 1960; *USNWR*, Nov. 21, 1960, p. 69; Kesaris, *Papers of the Republican Party*, Election Results, R 2; Dawidowicz and Goldstein, *Politics in a Pluralist Democracy*, 91–97. Catholic voting and percentages: for Kennedy, Rhode Island 60 percent, Connecticut 48 percent, Massachusetts 50 percent, New Jersey 35 percent, and New York 35 percent; for Nixon, New Hampshire 40 percent, Ohio 30 percent, and Wisconsin 35 percent.

31. Gallup, *Gallup Poll*, Vol. 3: 1963–1694; *NYHT*, Dec. 7, 1960; *Newsweek*, Nov. 14, 1960, p. EE-5; *USNWR*, Nov. 21, 1960, p. 26; Kellstedt et al., "Faith Transformed," 272. Protestant voting percentages for Kennedy: Arkansas 3.5 percent, Georgia 2 percent, North Carolina 1 percent, South Carolina 2.6 percent, and West Virginia 5 percent; Catholic voting percentages for Nixon: Oklahoma 5 percent, Tennessee 2 percent, Utah 4 percent, and Virginia 3.2 percent.

32. Carty, *Catholic in the White House?*; Casey, *Making of a Catholic President*; Dallek, *Unfinished Life*, 296.

33. Cosman, "Religion and Race"; Fair, "Reaction of Pennsylvania Voters"; Briggs, "Religious Issue"; Baggaley, "Religious Influence on Wisconsin."

34. See Chapter 13.

35. *Honolulu Star-Bulletin*, Dec. 29, 1960, B 147, Chotiner (1960), Series 320, and memos, Sept. 12, 19, 1961, PPS257, B 5, F Campaign and memoirs, March 23, 31, 1976, RNL; Hughes, *Ordeal of Power*, 280.

36. Greenberg, "Was Nixon Robbed?"; Greenberg, "It's a Myth"; Greenberg, "Trump's

Attitude Is Not 'Unprecedented,'"; Coker, "Dick of Honor"; Stebenne, "Who Really Won the 1960 Election?"; Maier, "Why Al Gore Is No Richard Nixon"; Rosenberg, "Debunking the Right's Enduring Myth"; von Hippel, "Here's a Voter Fraud Myth." I emailed Greenberg about some of his errors after his *LAT* op-ed appeared; he did not change any of his arguments in subsequent articles, Gellman mss. Kallina, *Courthouse over White House*; Biles, *Richard J. Daley*; O'Connor, *Clout*; Royko, *Boss*; Woods, *LBJ*, 375; Dallek, *Lone Star Rising*, 699.

37. Greenberg, "Trump's Attitude Is Not 'Unprecedented.'"
38. PC, Nov. 19, 1960; *LAS*, Nov. 3, 17, 1960; *BAA*, Oct. 29, Nov. 19, 1960; *NYT*, Nov. 11, 1960; *NYAN*, Nov. 12, 19, 1960; *CCP*, Oct. 29, Nov. 12, 1960; *JG*, Nov. 12, 19, 1960; *Ebony*, Nov. 1960, p. 40; *Newsweek*, Oct. 24, 1960, pp. 42–43; Wilkins to Lasker, Dec. 30, 1960, R 2, and Annual Report of Voter, 1961, Bond to Patton, Nov. 25, 1964, R 1, and Morsell to Anderson, Jan. 6, 1961, R 3, in Bracey and Meier, *Papers of the NAACP*; Taeuber, *Negro Population and Housing*, 115, 118–119, 124, 132; Banfield, *Big City Politics*, 293; Horton and Smith, *Statistical Record of Black America*, 479; Parsons and Clark, *Negro American*, 430, 439, 444, 759; Berg, *"Ticket to Freedom,"* 200–202.
39. Branch, *Parting the Waters*, 374.
40. Franklin and Moss, *From Slavery to Freedom*, 528–529.
41. Booker, *Black Man's America*, 22; Black, *Invincible Quest*, 414.
42. *Jet*, Nov. 17, 1960, pp. 13–14; *Ebony*, Jan. 1961, pp. 33–36, 38; Booker, "What 'Ike' Thinks about Negroes," 85; Booker, *Black Man's America*, 202–205, 207, 209–210.
43. Booker, "What Republicans Must Do," 48, 50–51.
44. *Ebony*, Nov. 1960, pp. 41–42, 44; Rowan, *Breaking Barriers*, 165–170.
45. CD, Nov. 19, 1960.
46. WP, Nov. 10, 1960; Jackson to DDE, Nov. 14, 1960, B 374, Jackson, LK, Series 320, RNL.
47. Memo, Dec. 28, 1960, diary, B 55, staff notes Dec. 1960, DDEL. Although the memo was dated Dec. 28, the meeting took place on Dec. 15; email Leyerzapf to Gellman, Oct. 31, 2005, Gellman mss.; Nichols, *Matter of Justice*, 261–263.
48. Memo, Dec. 28, 1960, diary, B 55, staff notes Dec. 1960, DDEL.
49. *SF Chronicle*, Dec. 2, 1962; Eisenhower OH, 31, HHPL; Goodpaster interview, Jan. 8, 2002.
50. RN to Gillespie, May 29, 1961, B 288, Gillespie, GK, Series 320, and memo, May 25, 1962, FE446.3, Ferman and memoirs, March 19, 1976, RNL; Klein interview, Nov. 12, 2002.
51. Day 8, Tape 2, 00:35:25 [RN], FG.
52. Graves to RN, June 17, 1959, Graves to RN, Jan. 28, Feb. 24, March 12, 29, B 301, Graves (2 of 2), Graves to RN, May 21, and RN to Graves, July 14, 1960, B 301, Graves (1 of 2), Series 320, RNL.
53. Ethridge to RN, Jan. 9, 1961, B 246, Ethridge, Series 320, RNL.

BIBLIOGRAPHY

UNITED STATES DOCUMENTS

Library of Congress, Legislative Reference Service. *John Fitzgerald Kennedy: A Compilation of Statements and Speeches Made during His Service in the United States Senate and House of Representatives.* Washington, DC: GPO, 1964.

Public Papers of the Presidents of the United States: Dwight D. Eisenhower 1960/61. Washington, DC: GPO, 1961.

U.S. Congressional Record, 1956–1961.

U.S. Department of Commerce. *Census of Population: 1960,* Vol. 1, P. 1, Table 46. Washington, DC: GPO, 1963.

———. *Census of Population: 1960,* Vol. 1, P. 1. Washington, DC: GPO, 1964.

U.S. Department of Labor. *Handbook of Labor Statistics.* Washington, DC: Bureau of Labor Statistics, 1970.

U.S. Department of State. *Foreign Relations of the United States,* 1953–1961. Washington, DC: GPO, 1991–1996.

U.S. Senate. *The Speeches, Remarks, Press Conferences, and Statements of Senator John F. Kennedy, August 1 through November 7, 1960.* Part I. Washington, DC: GPO, 1961.

———. *The Speeches, Remarks, Press Conferences, and Study Papers of Vice President Richard M. Nixon, August 1 through November 7, 1960.* Part II. Washington, DC: GPO, 1961.

———. *The Joint Appearances of Senator John F. Kennedy and Vice President Richard M. Nixon and Other 1960 Campaign Presentations.* Washington, DC: GPO, 1961.

U.S. Supreme Court, 140 SCt, 918, Peter B. CHIAFALO, Levi Jennet Guerra, and Esther Virginia John, Petitioners v. WASHINGTON, No. 19-465.

FEDERAL BUREAU OF INVESTIGATION (FBI), WASHINGTON, DC

Corbin, Paul

Cronin, John, Part 2, 95-35404

Johnson, Lyndon, File 022, Section 01

Hoover, J. Edgar, O & C, JFK, No. 96, Sec 1

Hoover, J. Edgar, O & C, RN, No. 8, Sec 1

LIBRARY OF CONGRESS, WASHINGTON, DC

Alsop, Stewart and Joseph

Martin, John Bartlow

MICROFILM MANUSCRIPTS

Bracey, John H., and August Meier, eds. *Papers of the NAACP.* Supplement to Part 4, Voting Rights, General Office Files, 1956–1965. Bethesda, MD: University Publications of America.

Eisenhower, Dwight D. *Diaries of Dwight D. Eisenhower, 1953–1961.* Ed. Robert E. Lester. Frederick, MD: University Publications of America, 1986.

Hoff-Wilson, Joan, ed. *Papers of the Nixon White House.* Frederick, MD: University Publications of America, 1987.

Kesaris, Paul, ed. *Papers of the Republican Party.* Part II, *Reports and Memoranda of the Research Division of the Headquarters of the Republican National Committee, 1938–1980.* Frederick, MD: University Publications of America, 1986.

———. *President Eisenhower's Meetings with Legislative Leaders, 1953–1961.* Frederick, MD: University Publications of America, 1986.

———. *Presidential Campaigns: The John F. Kennedy 1960 Campaign.* Part I, *Polls, Issues, and Strategy.* Frederick, MD: University Publications of America, 1986.

———. *Presidential Campaigns: The John F. Kennedy 1960 Campaign.* Part II, *Speeches, Press Conferences, and Debates.* Frederick, MD: University Publications of America, 1986.

Kesaris, Paul, and Jean Gibson, eds. *Minutes and Documents of the Cabinet Meetings of President Eisenhower, 1953–61.* Washington, DC: University Publications of America, 1980.

Lester, Robert E., ed. *Papers of John Foster Dulles and of Christian A. Herter, 1953–1961: The White House Correspondence and Memoranda Series.* Frederick, MD: University Publications of America, 1986.

———, project coordinator. *President Dwight D. Eisenhower's Office Files, 1953–1961.* Part 1, Eisenhower Administration Series. Bethesda, MD: University Publications of America, 1990.

National Association for the Advancement of Colored People. *NAACP, 1940–55: General Office File.* Bethesda, MD: University Publications of America, 1994.

———. *NAACP, Administrative File, General Office File [Richard M. Nixon], 1956–1960.* Bethesda, MD: University Publications of America, 1997.

MANUSCRIPT COLLECTIONS AND
UNPUBLISHED ORAL HISTORIES

ACADEMY OF TELEVISION ARTS AND SCIENCES, LOS ANGELES

Fromson, Murray, interview

ALABAMA

Recapitulation of the Voting of Electors in the 1960 Presidential Election.

ARIZONA STATE UNIVERSITY, TEMPE

Goldwater, Barry

BAYLOR UNIVERSITY, WACO, TX

Baylor Institute for Oral History

Jaworski, Leon, OH

Special Collections

Jaworski, Leon

CALIFORNIA STATE UNIVERSITY, FULLERTON ORAL HISTORY PROJECT

Finch, Robert
Kraushaar, I. N., #994
Milhous, Charles, #995

Milhous, William, #912
Neyer, John, #921
Yates, Harriet, #991

CALIFORNIA STATE UNIVERSITY AT SAN DIEGO

Wilson, Robert

COLUMBIA UNIVERSITY ORAL HISTORY COLLECTION,
COLUMBIA CENTER FOR ORAL HISTORY, NEW YORK

Oral History Project

Eisenhower, John
Eisenhower, Milton
Hagerty, James
Klein, Herbert

Knowland, William
Persons, Wilton, #161 and #334
Ribicoff, Abraham
Roberts, Clifford

LIBRARY ARCHIVES

DREW UNIVERSITY, MADISON, NJ

Kornitzer, Bela

DWIGHT EISENHOWER PRESIDENTIAL LIBRARY, ABILENE, KS

Audio-Visual Department

Cabinet Files
Central Files
Cushman, Robert (OH)
Dulles, Allen
Dulles, John F.
Gellman, Gloria Gae
Halleck, Charles (OH)

Official File Series
Roberts, Clifford (OH)
Seaton, Fred
Shanley, Bernard, Diaries
Snyder, Howard, Medical Diary
Whitman, Ann Series

BILLY GRAHAM CENTER ARCHIVES, WHEATON COLLEGE, WHEATON, IL

Graham, Billy

HARVARD UNIVERSITY, CAMBRIDGE, MA

White, Theodore

HERBERT HOOVER PRESIDENTIAL LIBRARY, WEST BRANCH, IA

Eisenhower, Dwight (OH)
Trohan, Walter (OH)

JOHN F. KENNEDY PRESIDENTIAL LIBRARY, COLUMBUS POINT, MA

Almond, J. Lindsay (OH)
Amory, Robert (OH)
Burke, Grace (OH)
Gamarekian, Barbara (OH)
Kennedy, John, Medical Files
Kennedy, Robert, Political Files,
    Pre-Administration
Lawford, Peter (OH)
Lucey, Patrick (OH)

Martin, Louis (OH)
Proxmire, William (OH)
Shriver, Sargent (OH)
Smathers, George (OH)
Sutton, William (OH)
Travell, Janet (OH)
Vanocur, Sandur (OH)
White, Theodore
Wofford, Harris (OH)

LYNDON B. JOHNSON PRESIDENTIAL LIBRARY, AUSTIN, TX

Oral History Collection

Boatner, Charles
Burney, Cecil
Carter, Clifton
Clifford, Clark
Daniel, Price
Donnelley, Dixon
Douglas, Helen Gahagan
Griffin, Robert
Halleck, Charles
Harlow, Bryce
Humphrey, Hubert
Johnson, Lyndon

Jordan, William
Knowland, William
Martin, Louis
McPherson, Henry
Mitchell, Clarence
Mundt, Karl
Reedy, George
Rowe, James, Jr.
Sanders, Harold
Watson, W. Martin
Wicker, Tom

Senate Political Files

WALTER BROWN MEDIA ARCHIVES AND PEABODY AWARDS
COLLECTION, UNIVERSITY OF GEORGIA, ATHENS

Gannon, Frank, Interviews
Nixon, Richard (OH)

MASSACHUSETTS HISTORICAL SOCIETY, BOSTON

Lodge, Henry Cabot, Jr.

MEMORIAL LIBRARY, SPECIAL COLLECTIONS,
MARQUETTE UNIVERSITY, MILWAUKEE

Kersten, Charles

MILLER CENTER OF PUBLIC AFFAIRS,
UNIVERSITY OF VIRGINIA, CHARLOTTESVILLE

Kennedy, Edward (OH)

MINNESOTA HISTORY SOCIETY, ST. PAUL

Judd, Walter

HENRY MUDD LIBRARY, MANUSCRIPT COLLECTION,
PRINCETON UNIVERSITY, PRINCETON, NJ

Hughes, Emmet, Diaries
Krock, Arthur
Stevenson, Adlai

NATIONAL ARCHIVES, COLLEGE PARK, MARYLAND

CREST, CIA Records Search Tool, third floor library

RICHARD NIXON PRESIDENTIAL LIBRARY AND MUSEUM, YORBA LINDA, CA

Finch, Robert
Vice presidential archives
White House Tapes

NORTHWESTERN UNIVERSITY, EVANSTON, IL

Frankel, Stanley

FRANKLIN D. ROOSEVELT PRESIDENTIAL LIBRARY, HYDE PARK, NY

Douglas, Helen Gahagan (OH), Eleanor Roosevelt Archives

SAN DIEGO STATE UNIVERSITY

Wilson, Robert

SENATE HISTORICAL OFFICE, ORAL HISTORY, WASHINGTON, DC

Baker, Robert   Smathers, George
Shuman, Howard   Vander Zee, Rein J.

STERLING MEMORIAL LIBRARY, YALE UNIVERSITY, NEW HAVEN, CT

Bowles, Chester

HARRY S. TRUMAN PRESIDENTIAL LIBRARY, INDEPENDENCE, MO

Babcock, Gaylon (OH)
Warne, William (OH)

UNITED STATES AIR FORCE

Office of Air Force History, Newburg, New York

Hughes, Donald (OH)

UNIVERSITY OF ILLINOIS, URBANA

Archives

Reston, James

UNIVERSITY OF IOWA SPECIAL COLLECTIONS, IOWA CITY

Darling, Ding

UNIVERSITY OF NOTRE DAME ARCHIVES, SOUTH BEND, IN

Cronin, John

UNIVERSITY OF SOUTHERN CALIFORNIA, LOS ANGELES

Klein, Herbert

Living History Project

Fromson, Murray, Interview

WHITTIER COLLEGE ORAL HISTORY COLLECTION, WHITTIER, CALIFORNIA

Brownfield, Lyman   Drown, Jack
Claw, Marshall   Harris, Clinton
Cloes, Elizabeth   Johnson, Geneva, #1

BOOKS, ARTICLES, FILMS, AND OTHER SOURCES

Abelson, Herbert, and Reuben Cohen. "Fragmentary Observations on a Close Election." *American Behavioral Scientist*, Vol. 4, No. 4, Dec. 1960.

Acacia, John. *Clark Clifford: The Wise Man of Washington*. Lexington: University Press of Kentucky, 2009.

Ahlstrom, Sidney. *Religious History of the American People*. New Haven: Yale University Press, 1972.

Albert, Carl. *Little Giant: The Life and Times of Speaker Carl Albert*. Norman: University of Oklahoma Press, 1990.

Aldous, Richard. *Schlesinger: The Imperial Historian*. New York: Norton, 2017.

Alexander, Herbert. *Financing the 1960 Election*. Princeton, NJ: Citizens' Research Foundation, 1962.

Alford, Mimi. *Once upon a Secret: My Affair with President John F. Kennedy and Its Aftermath.* New York: Random House, 2012.

Aliano, Richard A. *American Defense Policy from Eisenhower to Kennedy: The Politics of Changing Military Requirements, 1957–1961.* Athens: Ohio University Press, 1975.

Allen, Craig. *Eisenhower and the Mass Media: Peace, Prosperity, and Prime-Time TV.* Chapel Hill: University of North Carolina Press, 1993.

Allen, Maury. *Jackie Robinson: A Life Remembered.* New York: F. Watts, 1987.

Allitt, Patrick. *Catholic Intellectuals and Conservative Politics in America, 1958–1985.* Ithaca, NY: Cornell University Press, 1993.

Allswang, John M. *Bosses, Machines, and Urban Voters.* Baltimore: Johns Hopkins University Press, 1986.

Alsop, Joseph. *"I've Seen the Best of It": Memoirs.* New York: Norton, 1992.

Alsop, Stewart. "Campaigning with Nixon," *Saturday Evening Post,* Vol. 233, Issue 19, Nov. 5, 1960.

———. *Nixon and Rockefeller: A Double Portrait.* Garden City, NY: Doubleday, 1960.

———. *Stay of Execution: A Sort of Memoir.* Philadelphia: Lippincott, 1973.

Ambrose, Stephen. *Eisenhower,* vol. 2, *The President.* New York: Simon and Schuster, 1984.

———. *Nixon: The Education of a Politician, 1913–1962.* New York: Simon and Schuster, 1987.

Anderson, Jack. *Confessions of a Muckraker: The Inside Story of Life in Washington during the Truman, Eisenhower, Kennedy, and Johnson Years.* New York: Random House, 1979.

Anderson, James. *Texas Politics: An Introduction.* 2nd ed. New York: Harper and Row, 1975.

Anderson, Totton J. "The Architect of a Triumph on Television." *Broadcasting,* Vol. 59, No. 20, Nov. 14, 1961.

———. "The Political West in 1960," *Western Political Quarterly,* Vol. 14, No. 1, March 1961, p. 2.

Andrew, John, III. "Cracks in the Consensus: The Rockefeller Brothers Fund Special Studies Project and Eisenhower's America," *Presidential Studies Quarterly,* Vol. 28, No. 3, Summer 1998.

———. "The Struggle for the Republican Party in 1960." *Historian,* Vol. 59, Spring 1997.

Arndorfer, Jim. "Nixon Protagonistes." *NYT,* Oct. 14, 2012.

Apter, David, ed. *Ideology and Discontent.* New York: Free Press, 1964.

Arnold, William. *Back when It All Began: The Early Nixon Years.* New York: Vantage, 1975.

Ashby, LeRoy, and Rod Gramer. *Fighting the Odds: The Life of Senator Frank Church.* Seattle: University of Washington Press, 1994.

Attwood, William. *The Reds and the Blacks: A Personal Adventure.* New York: Harper and Row, 1967.

Axelrod, Robert. "Communication." *American Political Science Review,* Vol. 76, No. 2, June 1982.

———. "Where the Votes Come From: An Analysis of Electoral Coalitions, 1952–1968." *American Political Science Review,* Vol. 66, No. 1, March 1972.

Baggaley, Andrew R. "Religious Influence on Wisconsin, 1928–1960 Voting," *American Political Science Review,* Vol. 56, March 1962.

Baier, Bret, with Catherine Whitney. *Three Days in January: Dwight Eisenhower's Final Mission*. New York: Morrow, 2017.

Baker, Bobby. *Wheeling and Dealing: Confessions of a Capitol Hill Operator*. New York: Norton, 1978.

Baker, Leonard. *The Johnson Eclipse: A President's Vice Presidency*. New York: Macmillan, 1960.

Baker, Russell. *The Good Times*. New York: Morrow, 1989.

Baltakis, Anthony. "Agendas of Investigation: The McClellan Committee, 1957–1958." Ph.D. thesis, University of Akron, 1997.

Banfield, Edward C. *Big City Politics: A Comparative Guide to the Political Systems of Atlanta, Boston, Detroit, El Paso, Los Angeles, Miami, Philadelphia, St. Louis, Seattle*. New York: Random House, 1965.

Banfield, Edward C., and James Q. Wilson. *City Politics*. Cambridge: Harvard University Press and MIT Press, 1963.

Banitch, George. "The Ultraconservative Congressman from Dallas: The Rise and Fall of Bruce Alger, 1954–1964." M.A. thesis, University of Texas at Arlington, 2001.

Barone, Michael. *Our Country: The Shaping of America from Roosevelt to Reagan*. New York: Free Press, 1990.

Barrett, David M. *The CIA and Congress: The Untold Story from Truman to Kennedy*. Lawrence: University Press of Kansas, 2005.

Barrett, Patricia. "Religion and the 1960 Presidential Election." *Social Order*, Vol. 12, No. 6, June 1962.

Bartels, Larry. "Partnership and Voting Behavior, 1952–1996." *American Journal of Political Science*, Vol. 44, No. 1, Jan. 2000.

Bartley, Numan, and Hugh Graham. *Southern Politics and the Second Reconstruction*. Baltimore: Johns Hopkins University Press, 1973.

Bass, Jack, and Marilyn Thompson. *Ol' Strom: An Unauthorized Biography of Strom Thurmond*. Atlanta: Longstreet, 1998.

Battaglio, Stephen. *David Susskind: A Television Life*. New York: St. Martin's, 2010.

Baughman, James L. *Same Time, Same Station: Creating American Television, 1948–1961*. Baltimore: Johns Hopkins University Press, 2007.

Baughman, U. E., with Leonard Wallace Robinson. *Secret Service Chief*. New York: Harper and Row, 1962.

Beatty, Jack. *The Rascal King: The Life and Times of James Michael Curley, 1874–1958*. Reading, MA: Addison-Wesley, 1992.

Beck, Kent, "Necessary Lies, Hidden Truths: Cuba in the 1960 Campaign." *Diplomatic History*, Vol. 8, Winter 1984.

Behrens, Earl. "California: The New Men." In Reichley, *States in Crisis*.

Belafonte, Harry. *My Song: A Memoir*. New York: Knopf, 2011.

Bellah, Robert. "Civil Religion in America." *Daedalus*, Vol. 134, No. 4, Fall 2005.

Benedict, Stephen. "Changing the Watch in Washington," *Virginia Quarterly Review*, Vol. 37, Winter 1961.

Benson, Ezra Taft. *Cross Fire: The Eight Years with Eisenhower*. Garden City, NY, Doubleday, 1962.

Benton, Wilbourn E. *Texas: Its Government and Politics.* Englewood Cliffs, NJ: Prentice-Hall, 1961.

Berg, Manfred. *"The Ticket to Freedom": The NAACP and the Struggle for Black Political Integration.* Gainesville: University Press of Florida, 2005.

Berle, Beatrice Bishop, and Travis Beal Jacobs, eds. *Navigating the Rapids, 1918–1971: From the Papers of Adolf A. Berle.* New York: Harcourt Brace Jovanovich, 1973.

Berman, Daniel M. *A Bill Becomes a Law: The Civil Rights Act of 1960.* New York: Macmillan, 1962.

Bernard, Richard M., ed. *Snowbelt Cities: Metropolitan Politics in the Northeast and Midwest since World War II.* Bloomington: Indiana University Press, 1990.

Beschloss, Michael. *The Crisis Years: Kennedy and Khrushchev, 1960–1963.* New York: HarperCollins, 1991.

———. *Mayday: Eisenhower, Khrushchev, and the U-2 Affair.* New York: Harper and Row, 1986.

———. *Reaching for Glory: Lyndon Johnson's Secret White House Tapes, 1964–1965.* New York: Simon and Schuster. 2001.

———, ed. *Jacqueline Kennedy: Historic Conversations on Life with John F. Kennedy, Interviews with Arthur M. Schlesinger Jr., 1964.* New York: Hyperion, 2011.

Best, Gary. *Herbert Hoover: The Postpresidential Years, 1933–1964,* vol. 2, 1946–1964. Stanford: Hoover Institution Press, 1983.

Biles, Roger. *Richard J. Daley: Politics, Race, and the Governing of Chicago.* DeKalb, IL: Northern Illinois University Press, 1995.

Binder, John. "Organized Crime and the 1960 Presidential Election." *Public Choice,* Vol. 130, Nos. 3–4, March 2007.

Birdwhistell, Ira. "Southern Baptist Perceptions of and Responses to Roman Catholicism, 1917–1972." Ph.D. thesis, Southern Baptist Theological Seminary, 1975.

Black, Allida M., ed. *What I Hope to Leave Behind: The Essential Essays of Eleanor Roosevelt.* New York: Carlson, 1995.

———, et al., eds. *Eleanor Roosevelt, John Kennedy, and the Election of 1960: A Project of The Eleanor Roosevelt Papers.* Columbia, SC: Model Editions Partnership, 2003.

Black, Conrad. *The Invincible Quest: The Life of Richard Milhous Nixon.* Toronto: McClelland and Stewart, 2007.

Black, Earl, and Merle Black. *The Rise of Southern Republicans.* Cambridge: Belknap Press of Harvard University Press, 2002.

Blair, Joan, and Clay Blair, Jr. *The Search for JFK.* New York: Berkley, 1976.

Blake, David. *Liking Ike: Eisenhower, Advertising, and the Rise of Celebrity Politics.* New York: Oxford University Press, 2016.

Block, Herbert. *Herblock: A Cartoonist's Life.* New York: Macmillan, 1993.

———. *Herblock Special Report.* New York: Norton, 1976.

Boase, Paul, et al., eds. "Presidential Campaign 1960, a Symposium," Part 1, "Contest for the Nomination." *Quarterly Journal of Speech,* Vol. 46, No. 3, Oct. 1960.

Bohrer, John. *The Revolution of Robert Kennedy: From Power to Protest after JFK.* New York: Bloomsbury, 2017.

Bone, Hugh A. "The 1960 Election in Washington." *Western Political Quarterly*, Vol. 14, No. 1, March 1961.

Booker, Simeon. *Black Man's America*. Englewood Cliffs, NJ: Prentice-Hall, 1964.

———. "What 'Ike' Thinks about Negroes." *Ebony*, Vol. 18, No. 2, Dec. 1962.

———. "What Republicans Must Do to Regain Negro Votes." *Ebony*, Vol. 17, No. 6, April 1962.

Boomhower, Ray. *John Barlow Martin: A Voice for the Underdog*. Bloomington: Indiana University Press, 2015.

Bowles, Chester. *Promises to Keep: My Years in Public Life, 1941–1969*. New York: Harper Colophon, 1972.

Boynton, George, Jr. "Southern Republican Voting in the 1960 Election." Ph.D. thesis, University of North Carolina, 1963.

Bradford, Richard, "John F. Kennedy and the 1960 Presidential Primary in West Virginia." *South Atlantic Quarterly*, Vol. 75, No. 2, Spring 1976.

Bradlee, Benjamin. *Conversations with Kennedy*. New York: Norton, 1975.

———. *A Good Life: Newspapering and Other Adventures*. New York: Simon and Schuster, 1995.

Bradley, Mark Philip, and Marilyn B. Young, eds. *Making Sense of the Vietnam Wars: Local, National, and Transnational Perspectives*. New York: Oxford University Press, 2008.

Bradley, Rulon. "The Use of the Mass Media in the 1960 Election." Ph.D. thesis, University of Utah, 1962.

Brady, Steven J. *Eisenhower and Adenauer: Alliance Maintenance under Pressure, 1953–1960*. Lanham, MD: Lexington, 2010.

Branch, Taylor. *Parting the Waters: America in the King Years, 1954–63*. New York: Simon and Schuster, 1988.

Brandon, Henry. *Special Relationships: A Foreign Correspondent's Memoirs from Roosevelt to Reagan*. New York: Atheneum, 1988.

Brands, Hal. "Burying Theodore White: Recent Accounts of the 1960 Presidential Election." *Presidential Studies Quarterly*, Vol. 40, No. 2, June 2010.

Branyan, Robert L., and Lawrence H. Larsen, eds. *The Eisenhower Administration, 1953–1961: A Documentary History*, vol. 2. New York: Random House, 1971.

Brashler, William. *The Don: The Life and Death of Sam Giancana*. New York: Harper, 1977.

Brauer, Carl. *John F. Kennedy and the Second Reconstruction*. New York: Columbia University Press, 1977.

———. *Presidential Transitions: Eisenhower through Reagan*. New York: Oxford University Press, 1988.

Brenner, Saul. "Patterns of Jewish-Catholic Democratic Voting and the 1960 Presidential Vote." *Jewish Social Studies*. Vol. 26, No. 3, July 1964.

Bridges, Edson. "A Year End Review of the 1961 Economy." *Financial Analysis Journal*, Vol. 16, No. 6, Nov.–Dec. 1961.

Briggs, Linda. "The Religious Issue in the 1960 Campaign in Texas." M.A. thesis, Lamar State College of Technology, 1969.

Brinkley, Alan. *The Publisher: Henry Luce and His American Century.* New York: Knopf, 2010.

Brinkley, David. *11 Presidents, 4 Wars, 22 Political Conventions, 1 Moon Landing, 3 Assassinations, 2,000 Weeks of News and Other Stuff on Television, and 18 Years of Growing Up in North Carolina.* New York: Random House, 1995.

Brinkley, Douglas, and Luke A. Nichter, eds. *The Nixon Tapes, 1973.* Boston: Houghton Mifflin Harcourt, 2016.

Broadwater, Jeff. *Adlai Stevenson and American Politics: The Odyssey of a Cold War Liberal.* New York: Twayne, 1994.

Brodie, Fawn. *Richard Nixon: The Shaping of His Character.* New York: Norton, 1981.

Bruschke, Jon, and Laura Divine. "Debunking Nixon's Radio Victory in the 1960 Election: Re-analyzing the Historical Record and Considering Currently Unexamined Polling Data." *Social Science Journal,* Vol. 52, No. 1, 2017.

Bryant, Nick. *The Bystander: John F. Kennedy and the Struggle for Black Equality.* New York: Basic, 2006.

Buell, Emmett H., and Lee Sigelman. *Attack Politics: Negativity in Presidential Campaigns since 1960.* Lawrence: University Press of Kansas, 2008.

Bundy, McGeorge. *Danger and Survival: Choices about the Bomb in the First Fifty Years.* New York: Random House, 1988.

Buni, Andrew. *The Negro in Virginia Politics, 1902–1965.* Charlottesville: University of Virginia Press, 1967.

Burns, James MacGregor. *John Kennedy: A Political Profile.* New York: Harcourt, Brace, 1959–1960.

———. *Running Alone: Presidential Leadership from JFK to Bush II.* New York: Basic, 2006.

Calvert, Robert, et al. *The History of Texas.* 3rd ed. Wheeling, IL: Harlan Davidson, 2002.

Campbell, Angus. "Surge and Decline: A Study of Election Change." *Public Opinion Quarterly,* Vol. 24, No. 3, Autumn 1960.

———, et al. *American National Election Study.* Revised ICPR ed. Ann Arbor, MI: Inter-University Consortium for Political Research, 1970.

Campbell, Tracy. *Deliver the Vote: A History of Election Fraud, An American Political Tradition, 1742–2004.* New York: Carroll and Graf, 2005.

Cannon, James M., ed. *Politics U.S.A.: A Practical Guide to the Winning of Public Office.* Garden City, NY: Doubleday, 1960.

"Canons of Journalism: Prohibition and Its Enforcement." *Annals of the American Academy of Political and Social Science,* Vol. 109, Sept. 1923.

Caro, Robert, *The Years of Lyndon Johnson,* vol. 1, *The Path to Power.* New York: Knopf, 1982. Vol. 2, *The Means of Ascent.* New York: Knopf, 1990. Vol. 3, *Master of the Senate.* New York: Knopf, 2002. Vol. 4, *The Passage of Power.* New York: Knopf, 2012.

Caroli, Betty. *First Ladies.* New York: Oxford University Press, 1987.

Carson, Clayborne, ed. *The Papers of Martin Luther King, Jr.,* vol. 5, *Threshold of a New Decade, January 1959—December 1960.* Berkeley: University of California Press, 2005.

Carter, Richard. "Some Effects of the 'Great Debates.'" *Abstracts of Papers of the American Sociological Association,* 56th Annual Session, 1961.

Carty, Thomas. *A Catholic in the White House? Religion, Politics, and John F. Kennedy's Presidential Campaign.* New York: Palgrave, 2004.

Casdorph, Paul D. *A History of the Republican Party in Texas, 1865–1965.* Austin: Pemberton, 1965.

Casey, Shaun. *The Making of a Catholic President: Kennedy vs. Nixon, 1960.* New York: Oxford University Press, 2009.

Catledge, Turner. *My Life and The Times.* New York: Harper and Row, 1971.

Catterall, Peter, ed. *The Macmillan Diaries,* vol. 2, *Prime Minister and After, 1957–1960.* New York: Macmillan, 2009.

Chafe, William. *Civilities and Civil Rights: Greensboro, North Carolina, and the Black Struggle for Freedom.* New York: Oxford University Press, 1980.

Chafin, Raymond, and Topper Sherwood. *Just Good Politics: The Life of Raymond Chafin, Appalachian Boss.* Pittsburgh: University of Pittsburgh Press, 1994.

Childs, Marquis. *Witness to Power.* New York: McGraw-Hill, 1982.

"The Church-State Legacy of JFK." *Journal of Church and State,* Vol. 6, Winter 1964.

Clay, William. *Just Permanent Interests: Black Americans in Congress, 1870–1991.* New York: Amistad, 1992.

Cleveland, Martha. *Charles Percy: Strong New Voice from Illinois.* Jacksonville, IL: Harris-Wolfe, 1968.

Clifford, Clark. *Counsel to the President: A Memoir.* New York: Random House, 1991.

Clymer, Adam. *Edward M. Kennedy: A Biography.* New York: Morrow, 1999.

Cochrane, Willard W., and Mary E. Ryan. *American Farm Policy, 1948–1973.* Minneapolis: University of Minnesota Press, 1976.

Cohen, Adam, and Elizabeth Taylor. *American Pharaoh: Mayor Richard J. Daley, His Battle for Chicago and the Nation.* Boston: Little, Brown, 2000.

Cohodas, Nadine. *Strom Thurmond and the Politics of Southern Change.* New York: Simon and Schuster, 1993.

Coker, Matt. "Dick of Honor." *Orange County Register,* Nov. 22, 2000.

Colby, Peter, and Paul Green. "The Consolidation of Clout." In Gherardini, *Illinois Elections.*

Congressional Quarterly. *Guide to U.S. Elections.* 6th ed. Vol. 1. Washington, DC: Congressional Quarterly Press, 2010.

Conkin, Paul K. *Big Daddy from the Pedernales: Lyndon Baines Johnson.* Boston: Twayne, 1986.

———. *A Revolution Down on the Farm: The Transformation of American Agriculture since 1929.* Lexington: University Press of Kentucky, 2009.

Conley, Brian. "Party People: Bliss, Brock, and the Rise of the Modern Republican Party." Ph.D. thesis, New School, 2008.

Connally, John. *In History's Shadow: An American Odyssey.* New York: Hyperion, 1993.

Converse, Jean. *Survey Research in the United States: Roots and Emergence, 1890–1960.* Berkeley: University of California Press, 1987.

Converse, Philip. "The Nature of Belief Systems in Mass Publics." In Apter, *Ideology and Discontent.*

———, et al. "Stability and Change in 1960: A Reinstating Election." *American Political Science Review*, Vol. 55, No. 2, June 1961.

Cooney, John. *The American Pope: The Life and Times of Francis Cardinal Spellman.* New York: Dell, 1986.

Cosman, Bernard. "Presidential Republicanism in the South, 1960." *Journal of Politics*, Vol. 24, No. 2, May 1962.

———. "Religion and Race in Louisiana Presidential Politics, 1960." *Southwestern Social Science Quarterly*, Vol. 43, Dec. 1962.

Costello, William. "Faceless Enemies, Waiting to Pounce." *New Republic*, Vol. 146, No. 15, April 9, 1962.

———. *The Facts about Nixon: An Unauthorized Biography.* New York: Viking, 1960.

———. "Nixon on the Eve." *New Republic*, Vol. 143, No. 20, Nov. 7, 1960.

Cotton, Norris. *In the Senate: Amidst the Conflict and Turmoil.* New York: Dodd, Mead, 1978.

Cox, Edward. "Congressional District Party Strengths and the 1960 Election." *Journal of Politics*, Vol. 24, No. 2, May 1962.

Cox, Patrick. *Ralph W. Yarborough: The People's Senator.* Austin: University of Texas Press, 2001.

Crespino, Joseph. *In Search of Another Country: Mississippi and the Conservative Counterrevolution.* Princeton, NJ: Princeton University Press, 2009.

Crispell, Brian. *Testing the Limits: George Amistad Smathers and Cold War America.* Athens: University of Georgia Press, 1999.

Critchlow, Donald. *Conservative Ascendancy: How the GOP Right Made Political History.* Cambridge: Harvard University Press, 2007.

———. *Phyllis Schlafly and Grassroots Conservatism: A Woman's Crusade.* Princeton, NJ: Princeton University Press, 2005.

———. *Republican Character: From Nixon to Reagan.* Philadelphia: University of Pennsylvania Press, 2018.

Cronkite, Walter. *A Reporter's Life.* New York: Knopf, 1996.

Crosby, Donald. *God, Church, and Flag: Senator Joseph R. McCarthy and the Catholic Church, 1950–1957.* Chapel Hill: University of North Carolina Press, 1978.

Crowley, Monica. *Nixon in Winter.* New York: Random House, 1998.

———. *Nixon Off the Record.* New York: Random House, 1996.

Cull, Nicholas J. *The Cold War and the United States Information Agency: American Propaganda and Public Diplomacy, 1945–1989.* Cambridge: Cambridge University Press, 2008.

Cunningham, Sean. *Cowboy Conservatism: Texas and the Rise of the Modern Right.* Lexington: University Press of Kentucky, 2010.

Current, Gloster. "Why Nixon Lost the Negro Vote." *Crisis*, vol. 68, Jan. 1961.

Dallek, Robert. *Camelot's Court: Inside the Kennedy White House.* New York: HarperCollins, 2013.

———. *Lone Star Rising: Lyndon Johnson and His Times.* New York: Oxford University Press, 1991.

———. "The Medical Ordeals of JFK." *Atlantic*, Vol. 290, No. 5, Dec. 2002.

———. *An Unfinished Life: John F. Kennedy, 1917–1963.* Boston: Little, Brown, 2003.

Daniels, Maurice. *Saving the Soul of Georgia: Donald L. Hollowell and the Struggle for Civil Rights.* Athens: University of Georgia Press, 2013.

Danielson, Wayne, and John Adams. "Completeness of Press Coverage of the 1960 Presidential Campaign." *Journalism Quarterly*, Vol. 38, Autumn 1961.

David, Paul T., ed. *The Presidential Election and Transition, 1960–1961.* Washington, DC: Brookings Institution, 1961.

Davidson, Bill. "Lyndon Johnson: Can a Southerner Be Elected President?" *Look*, Vol. 23, Aug. 18, 1959.

Davis, Wiley, recompiler. *Code of Georgia Annotated.* Atlanta: Harrison, 1962.

Davis, William. *Breckinridge: Statesman, Soldier, Symbol.* Baton Rouge: Louisiana State University Press, 1974.

Dawidowicz, Lucy, and Leon J. Goldstein. *Politics in a Pluralist Democracy: Studies of Voting in the 1960 Election.* Westport, CT: Praeger, 1974.

"Debate Score: Kennedy Up, Nixon Down." *Broadcasting*, Vol. 59, No. 19, Nov. 7, 1960.

DeFrank, Thomas M. *Write It when I'm Gone: Remarkable Off-the-Record Conversations with Gerald R. Ford.* New York: Putnam, 2007.

DeLoach, Cartha. *Hoover's FBI: The Inside Story by Hoover's Trusted Lieutenant.* Washington, DC: Regnery, 1995.

Demaris, Ovid. *The Director: An Oral Biography of J. Edgar Hoover.* New York: Harper's Magazine Press, 1975.

De Roche, Andy. "Betting on the Africans: John F. Kennedy's Courting of African Nationalist Leaders." *H-Diplo Roundtable Review*, Vol. 14, No. 3, 2012.

de Toledano, Ralph. *Lament for a Generation.* New York: Farrar, Straus and Cudahy, 1960.

———. *Nixon:* New York: Holt, 1960.

———. *Notes from the Underground: The Whittaker Chambers–Ralph de Toledano Letters, 1949–1960.* Washington, DC: Regnery, 1997.

Diamond, Robert, ed. *A Guide to U.S. Elections.* Washington, DC: Congressional Quarterly Press, 1973.

Dickerson, Nancy. *Among Those Present: A Reporter's View of Twenty-five Years in Washington.* New York: Random House, 1976.

Dickson, Paul. *Sputnik: The Shock of the Century.* New York: Walker, 2001.

Divine, Robert. "Eisenhower, Dulles, and the Nuclear Test Ban Issue: Memorandum of a White House Conference, 24 March 1958." *Diplomatic History*, Vol. 2, No. 3, Summer 1978.

———. *The Sputnik Challenge.* New York: Oxford University Press, 1993.

Dobbs, Ricky. "Continuities in American Anti-Catholicism: The Texas Baptist Standard and the Coming of the 1960 Election." *Baptist History Heritage*, Vol. 42, No. 1, Winter 2007.

———. *Yellow Dogs and Republicans: Allan Shivers and Texas Two-Party Politics.* College Station: Texas A&M University Press, 2005.

"Does TV Mold Candidates' Image?" *Broadcasting*, Vol. 56, No. 12, March 23, 1959.

Donaldson, Gary. *The First Modern Campaign: Kennedy, Nixon, and the Election of 1960.* Lanham, MD: Rowman and Littlefield, 2007.

Donovan, John. *Crusader in the Cold War: A Biography of Fr. John S. Cronin, S.J., 1908–1994.* New York: Peter Lang, 2003.

Donovan, Robert. *Boxing the Kangaroo: A Reporter's Memoir.* Columbia: University of Missouri Press, 2002.

———. *Confidential Secretary: Ann Whitman's Twenty Years with Eisenhower and Rockefeller.* New York: Dutton, 1988.

Douglas, Helen. *A Full Life.* Garden City, NY: Doubleday, 1982.

Douglas, Paul. "The 1960 Voting Rights Bill: The Struggle, the Final Results, and the Reasons." *Journal of Intergroup Relations*, Vol. 1, Summer 1960.

———. "Trends and Developments: The 1960 Voting Rights Bill." *Journal of Intergroup Relations*, Vol. 1, Summer 1960.

Douglas, William. *The Court Years, 1939 to 1975.* New York: Random House, 1980.

Dorsey, Emmett. "The American Negro and His Government, 1961." *Crisis*, Oct. 1961.

Drake, St. Clair, and Horace R. Cayton. *Black Metropolis: A Study of Negro Life in a Northern City*, vol. 1. New York: Harper and Row, 1945.

Drew, Elizabeth. *Richard M. Nixon.* New York: Times Books, 2007.

Driggs, Don W. "The 1960 Election in Nevada." *Western Political Quarterly*, Part 2, Vol. 14, No. 1, March 1961.

Druckman, James. "The Power of Television Images: The First Kennedy-Nixon Debate Revisited." *Journal of Politics*, Vol. 65, No. 2, May 2003.

Drukman, Mason. *Wayne Morse: A Political Biography.* Portland: Oregon Historical Society Press, 1997.

Dudley, Robert, and Eric Shiraev. *Counting Every Vote: The Most Contentious Elections in American History.* Washington, DC: Potomac, 2008.

Dugger, Ronnie. *The Politician: The Life and Times of Lyndon Johnson—the Drive for Power, from the Frontier to Master of the Senate.* New York: Norton, 1982.

Dulaney, H. G., and Edward Hake Phillips, eds. *"Speak, Mister Speaker."* Bonham, TX: Sam Rayburn Foundation, 1978.

Dulce, Berton, and Edgar Richter. *Religion and the Presidency: A Recurring American Problem.* New York: Macmillan, 1962.

Duncan, Otis, and Beverly Duncan. *The Negro Population of Chicago: A Study of Residential Succession.* Chicago: University of Chicago Press, 1957.

Edgerton, Gary, ed. *The Columbia History of American Television.* New York: Columbia University Press, 2007.

Edwards, Anne. *Early Reagan: The Rise to Power.* New York: Morrow, 1987.

Edwards, India. *Pulling No Punches: Memoirs of a Woman in Politics.* New York: Putnam's, 1977.

Edwards, Lee. *Goldwater: The Man Who Made a Revolution.* Washington, DC: Regnery, 1995.

———. *Missionary for Freedom: The Life and Times of Walter Judd.* New York: Paragon, 1990.

Eisenhower, David, and Julie Nixon Eisenhower. *Going Home to Glory: A Memoir of Life with Dwight D. Eisenhower, 1961–1969.* New York: Simon and Schuster, 2010.

Eisenhower, Dwight, "What I Have Learned," *Saturday Review*, Vol. 49, Sept. 10, 1966.

————. *The White House Years*, vol. 1, *Mandate for Change, 1953–1956*. Garden City, NY: Doubleday, 1963. Vol. 2, *Waging Peace, 1957–1961*. Garden City, NY: Doubleday, 1965.

Eisenhower, John. *Strictly Personal*. Garden City, NY: Doubleday, 1974.

Eisenhower, Julie Nixon. *Pat Nixon: The Untold Story*. New York: Simon and Schuster, 1986.

Eisenhower, Milton. *The President Is Calling*. Garden City, NY: Doubleday, 1974.

Eisenhower, Susan. *Mrs. Ike: Memoirs and Reflections in the Life of Mamie Eisenhower*. New York: Farrar, Straus and Giroux, 1996.

Elliott, Carl, Sr., and Michael D'Orso. *The Cost of Courage: The Journey of an American Congressman*. Tuscaloosa: University of Alabama Press, 2001.

Ellsberg, Daniel. *Secrets: A Memoir of Vietnam and the Pentagon Papers*. New York: Viking, 2002.

Emblidge, David, ed. *My Day: The Best of Eleanor Roosevelt's Acclaimed Newspaper Columns, 1936–1962*. New York: Da Capo, 2001.

English, Bella, et al. *Last Lion: The Fall and Rise of Ted Kennedy*. Ed. Peter S. Canellos. New York: Simon and Schuster, 2009.

Ernst, Harry. *The Primary That Made a President: West Virginia, 1960*. New York: McGraw-Hill, 1962.

Erskine, Hazel, ed. "Revival: Reports from the Polls." *Public Opinion Quarterly*, Vol. 25, No. 1, Spring 1961.

Erskine, Helen. "Dick and Pat Nixon: The Team on Ike's Team." *Colliers*. Vol. 134, July 9, 1954.

Evans, Rowland, and Robert Novak. *Lyndon Johnson: The Exercise of Power, a Political Biography*. New York: New American Library, 1966.

Evans, Thomas. *The Education of Ronald Reagan: The General Electric Years and the Untold Story of His Conversion to Conservatism*. New York: Columbia University Press, 2006.

Everson, David H. "The Effects of Initiatives on Voter Turnout: A Comparative State Analysis." *Western Political Quarterly*, Vol. 34, No. 3, Sept. 1981.

Ewald, William Bragg, Jr. *Eisenhower the President: Crucial Days, 1951–1960*. Englewood Cliffs, NJ: Prentice-Hall, 1981.

Exner, Judith. *My Story*. New York: Grove, 1977.

Fair, Daryl. "The Reaction of Pennsylvania Voters to Catholic Candidates." *Pennsylvania History*, Vol. 32, No. 3, July 1965.

Fairclough, Adam. *Race and Democracy: The Civil Rights Struggle in Louisiana, 1915–1972*. Athens: University of Georgia Press, 1995.

Falk, Stanley. "The National Security Council under Truman, Eisenhower, and Kennedy." *Political Science Quarterly*, Vol. 79, No. 3, Sept. 1964.

Falkner, David. *Great Time Coming: The Life of Jackie Robinson from Baseball to Birmingham*. New York: Simon and Schuster, 1995.

Farrell, John. *Tip O'Neill and the Democratic Century*. Boston: Little, Brown, 2001.

Farris, Scott. *Inga: Kennedy's Great Love, Hitler's Perfect Beauty, and J. Edgar Hoover's Prime Suspect*. Guilford, CT: Lyons, 2016.

Fauntroy, Michael. *Republicans and the Black Vote*. Boulder, CO: Lynne Rienner, 2007.

Fay, Paul B., Jr. *The Pleasure of His Company*. New York: Harper and Row, 1966.

Feldman, Glen, ed. *Painting Dixie Red: When, Where, Why, and How the South Became Republican*. Gainesville: University of Florida Press, 2011.

Feldstein, Mark. "Fighting Quakers: The 1950s Battle between Richard Nixon and Columnist Drew Pearson." *Journalism History*, Vol. 30, No. 2, Summer 2004.

———. *Poisoning the Press: Richard Nixon, Jack Anderson, and the Rise of Washington's Scandal Culture*. New York: Farrar, Straus and Giroux, 2010.

Felknor, Bruce L. *Dirty Politics*. New York: Norton, 1960.

———. *Political Mischief: Smear, Sabotage, and Reform in U.S. Elections*. New York: Praeger, 1992.

Felton, David. "The Bugging of Mack the Knife." *Rolling Stone*, Issue 145, Oct. 11, 1973.

Fenton, John. *In Your Opinion . . . : The Managing Editor of the Gallup Polls Looks at Polls, Politics, and the People from 1945 to 1960*. Boston: Little, Brown, 1960.

Ferguson, Niall. *Kissinger*. New York: Penguin, 2015.

Ferman, Dave. *Journalism in Ireland: How Two Irish Newspapers Covered the 1960 Presidential Election of John F. Kennedy*. Berlin: VDM Verlag Dr. Muller, 2007.

Ferrell, Jessica, and David Coleman. "John F. Kennedy on His Entry into Politics." *Miller Center Report*, Vol. 20, No. 1, Spring–Summer 2004.

Ferrell, Robert, series ed. *The American Secretaries of State and Their Diplomacy*, vol. 18, *Christian A. Herter*, vol. ed. G. Bernard Noble. New York: Cooper Square, 1970.

———, ed. *The Diary of James Hagerty: Eisenhower in Mid-course, 1954–1955*. Bloomington: Indiana University Press, 1983.

Fischman, Jerome. "The Church in Politics: The 1960 Election in Puerto Rico." *Western Political Quarterly*, Vol. 18, No. 4, Dec. 1965.

Filipink, Richard, Jr. *Dwight Eisenhower and American Foreign Policy during the 1960s: An American Lion in Winter*. Lanham, MD: Lexington, 2015.

Fite, Gilbert. *Richard B. Russell, Jr.: Senator from Georgia*. Chapel Hill: University of North Carolina Press, 1991.

Fleming, Dan, Jr. *Kennedy vs. Humphrey, West Virginia, 1960: The Pivotal Battle for the Democratic Presidential Nomination*. Jefferson, NC: McFarland, 1992.

Foladare, Irving. "Determining of Voting Decision in the 1960 Presidential Election: Buffalo, N.Y., A Case Study." Ph.D. thesis, Columbia University, 1966.

Foley, Edward. *Ballot Battles: The History of Disputed Elections in the United States*. New York: Oxford University Press, 2016.

Fontenay, Charles. *Estes Kefauver: A Biography*. Knoxville: University of Tennessee Press, 1980.

Fowler, Donald. *Presidential Voting in South Carolina, 1948–1964*. Columbia, SC: Bureau of Governmental Research and Service Publication, 1966.

Fox, Richard. *Reinhold Niebuhr: An Intellectual Biography*. New York: Pantheon, 1985.

Frady, Marshall. *Billy Graham: A Parable of American Righteousness*. Boston: Little, Brown, 1979.

Frank, Jeffrey. *Ike and Dick: Portrait of a Strange Political Marriage*. New York: Simon and Schuster, 2013.

Frankel, Max. *The Times of My Life and My Life with The Times*. New York: Random House, 1999.

Franklin, John Hope, and Alfred A. Moss, Jr. *From Slavery to Freedom: A History of African Americans*. 8th ed. Boston: McGraw Hill, 2000.

Freeley, Austin. "The Presidential Debates and the Speech Profession." *Quarterly Journal of Speech*, Vol. 47, No. 1, Feb. 1961.

Fremon, David. *Chicago Politics Ward by Ward*. Bloomington: Indiana University Press, 1988.

Friel, Charlotte. "The Influence of Television in the Political Career of Richard M. Nixon, 1946–1962." Ph.D. thesis, New York University, 1968.

Frost, Jennifer. *Hedda Hopper's Hollywood: Celebrity Gossip and American Conservatism*. New York: New York University Press, 2011.

Gaines, Bryan. "Popular Myths about Popular Vote–Electoral College Splits." *PS: Political Science and Politics*, Vol. 34, No. 1, March 2001.

Galambos, Louis. *Eisenhower: Becoming the Leader of the Free World*. Baltimore: Johns Hopkins University Press, 2018.

Galambos, Louis, and Daun van Ee, eds. *The Papers of Dwight David Eisenhower: The Presidency, Keeping the Peace*. Vols. 15, 20, and 21. Baltimore: Johns Hopkins University Press, 2001.

Galbraith, John Kenneth. *A Life in Our Times: Memoirs*. Boston: Houghton Mifflin, 1981.

Gallup, George, ed. *The Gallup Poll: Public Opinion, 1935–1971*, vols. 1–3. New York: Random House, 1972.

Gannon, Robert. *The Cardinal Spellman Story*. Garden City, NY: Doubleday, 1962.

García, Ignacio M. *Viva Kennedy: Mexican Americans in Search of Camelot*. College Station: Texas A&M University Press, 2000.

Garment, Leonard. *Crazy Rhythm: My Journey from Brooklyn and Jazz, and Wall Street to Nixon's White House, Watergate, and Beyond*. New York: Times Books, 1997.

Garrow, David. *Bearing the Cross: Martin Luther King, Jr., and the Southern Christian Leadership Conference*. New York: Morrow, 1986.

Garvey, Megan. "Bush Camp Looks to Nixon in '60." *LAT*, Nov. 12, 2000.

Geelhoed, E. Bruce. *Diplomacy Shot Down: The U-2 Crisis and Eisenhower's Aborted Mission to Moscow, 1959–1960*. Norman: University of Oklahoma Press, 2020.

Geisler, R. Gene. "Chicago Democratic Voting, 1947–1957." Ph.D. thesis, University of Chicago, 1958.

Geisler, R. Gene, and Anthony Edmonds. *Eisenhower, Macmillan, and Allied Unity, 1957–1961*. New York: Palgrave Macmillan, 2005.

Gellman, Irwin F. *The Contender: Richard Nixon, The Congress Years, 1946–1952*. New York: Free Press, 1999.

———. *Good Neighbor Diplomacy: United States Policies in Latin America, 1933–1945*. Baltimore: Johns Hopkins University Press, 1979.

———. *The President and the Apprentice: Eisenhower and Nixon, 1952–1961*. New Haven: Yale University Press, 2015.

———. "The Richard Nixon Vice Presidency: Research without the Nixon Manuscripts." In Small, *A Companion to Richard M. Nixon*.

————. "Ruining Murray Chotiner: Chotiner, A Forgotten Chapter in the Rivalry between the Kennedys and Nixon." *Presidential Studies Quarterly*, forthcoming.

Gelman, Morris. "Television and Politics: '62." *Television*, Oct. 1962.

Gentry, Curt. *J. Edgar Hoover: The Man and the Secrets.* New York: Norton, 1991.

George, Carol. *God's Salesman: Norman Vincent Peale and the Power of Positive Thinking.* New York: Oxford University Press, 1993.

Gerard, Emmanuel, and Bruce Kuklich. *Death in the Congo: Murdering Patrice Lumumba.* Cambridge: Harvard University Press, 2015.

Germond, Jack. *Fat Man in a Middle Seat: Forty Years of Covering Politics.* New York: Random House, 1999.

Gershen, Howard. "A Past Full of Pranks." *Columbia Daily Spectator*, Vol. 105, No. 36, Oct. 30, 1980.

Gherardini, Caroline, et al. *Illinois Elections.* 2nd ed. Springfield, IL: Sangamon State University, 1982.

Giancana, Antoinette et al. *JFK and Sam: The Connection between the Giancana and Kennedy Assassinations.* Nashville, TN: Cumberland House, 2005.

Giancana, Sam, and Chuck Giancana. *Double Cross: The Explosive, Inside Story of the Mobster Who Controlled America.* New York: Warner Books, 1992.

Gibbons, William. *The U.S. Government and the Vietnam War: Executive and Legislative Roles and Relationships,* part 1, 1945–1960. Princeton, NJ: Princeton University Press, 1986.

Gibbs, Nancy, and Michael Duffy. *The Preacher and the Presidents: Billy Graham in the White House.* New York: Center Street, 2007.

Gifford, Laura Jane. *The Center Cannot Hold: The 1960 Presidential Election and the Rise of Modern Conservatism.* DeKalb: Northern Illinois University Press, 2009.

————. "'Dixie's No Longer in the Bag!' South Carolina Republicans and the Election of 1960." *Journal of Policy History*, Vol. 19, No. 2, April 2007.

Gifford, Laura Jane, and Daniel K. Williams, eds. *The Right Side of the Sixties: Reexamining Conservatism's Decade of Transformation.* New York: Palgrave Macmillan, 2012.

Giglio, James. "Growing Up Kennedy: The Role of Medical Ailments in the Life of JFK, 1920–1957." *Journal of Family History*, Vol. 31, No. 4, Oct. 2006.

————. "The Medical Afflictions of President John F. Kennedy." *White House Studies*, Vol. 6, No. 4, 2006.

————. *The Presidency of John F. Kennedy.* 2nd ed. Lawrence: University Press of Kansas, 2006.

Gilbert, Robert E. *Television and Presidential Politics.* Boston: Christopher, 1972.

Gizzi, John. "Historian Dallek Maligned Nixon's 1960 Campaign." *Human Events*, Jan. 6, 2003.

Glantz, Oscar. "The Negro Voter in Northern Industrial Cities." *Western Political Quarterly*, Vol. 13, No. 4, Dec. 1960.

Goble, Danny. *Little Giant: The Life and Times of Speaker Carl Albert.* Norman: University of Oklahoma Press, 1990.

Goldberg, Robert Alan. *Barry Goldwater.* New Haven: Yale University Press, 1995.

Goldsmith, John A. *Colleagues: Richard B. Russell and His Apprentice, Lyndon B. Johnson.* Macon, GA: Mercer University Press, 1998.

Goldwater, Barry M. *The Conscience of a Conservative.* Shepherdsville, KY: Victor, 1960.

———. *Goldwater.* Garden City, NY: Doubleday, 1988.

———. *With No Apologies: The Personal and Political Memoirs of United States Senator Barry M. Goldwater.* New York: Morrow, 1979.

Goodman, James, ed. *Letters to Kennedy: John Kenneth Galbraith.* Cambridge: Harvard University Press, 1998.

Goodwin, Doris Kearns. *The Fitzgeralds and the Kennedys: An American Saga.* New York: Simon and Schuster, 1987.

Goodwin, Richard. *Remembering America: A Voice from the Sixties.* Boston: Little, Brown, 1988.

Gormley, Ken. *Archibald Cox: Conscience of a Nation.* Reading, MA: Addison-Wesley, 1997.

Graham, Billy. *Just As I Am: The Autobiography of Billy Graham.* San Francisco: Harper-Collins, 1997.

———. "We Are Electing a President of the World." *Life,* Vol. 50, Nov. 7, 1960.

Granger, Bill, and Lori Granger. *Lords of the Last Machine: The Story of Politics in Illinois.* New York: Random House, 1987.

Gray, Charles. "Coalition, Consensus, and Conflict in the U.S. Senate, 1957–60." Ph.D. thesis, University of Colorado, 1962.

Gray, Robert Keith. *Eighteen Acres under Glass: Life in Washington as Seen by the Former Secretary of the Cabinet.* Garden City, NY: Doubleday, 1962.

Green, George N. *The Establishment in Texas Politics: The Primitive Years, 1938–1957.* Westport, CT: Greenwood, 1979.

———. "The Far Right Wing in Texas Politics, 1930's–1960's." Ph.D. thesis, Florida State University, 1966.

Green, John Clifford, ed. *Politics, Professionalism, and Power: Modern Party Organization and the Legacy of Ray C. Bliss.* Lanham, MD: University Press of America, 1994.

Greenberg, David. "It's a Myth That Nixon Acquiesced in 1960," *LAT,* Nov. 10, 2000. Opposing view, John Taylor, "Setting the Revisionist Record on 1960 Straight," *Orange County Register,* Dec. 3, 2000.

———. "Shocked, Shocked." *Forward,* Oct. 10, 2003.

———. "The Time Nixon's Cronies Tried to Overturn a Presidential Election." *Politico,* Oct. 11, 2020.

———. "Trump's Attitude Is Not 'Unprecedented,'" *WP,* Oct. 26, 2016.

———. "Was Nixon Robbed?" *Slate,* Oct. 16, 2010.

Greenstein, Fred. *The Hidden-Handed Presidency: Eisenhower as Leader.* New York: Basic, 1982.

Greenstein, Fred, and Richard Immerman. "What Did Eisenhower Tell Kennedy about Indochina? The Politics of Misperception." *Journal of American History,* Vol. 79, No. 2, Sept. 1992.

Griffin, Charles. "New Light on Eisenhower's Farewell Address." *Presidential Studies Quarterly,* Vol. 22, No. 3, Summer 1992.

Grimshaw, William. *Bitter Fruit: Black Politics and the Chicago Machine, 1931–1991.* Chicago: University of Chicago Press, 1995.

Grose, Peter. *Gentleman Spy: The Life of Allen Dulles.* Boston: Houghton Mifflin, 1994.

Gulman, Morris. "Television and Politics, '62." *Television,* Oct. 1962.

Gustafson, Melanie, Kristie Miller, and Elisabeth I. Perry, eds. *We Have Come to Stay: American Women and Political Parties, 1880–1960.* Albuquerque: University of New Mexico Press, 1999.

Guthman, Edwin O., and Jeffrey Shulman, eds. *Robert Kennedy in His Own Words: The Unpublished Recollections of the Kennedy Years.* New York: Bantam, 1988.

Guthrie, Benjamin, compiler. *Statistics of the Presidential and Congressional Election of November 8, 1960.* Washington, DC: GPO, 1961.

Halsey, Margaret. "Beware the Tender Trap." *New Republic,* Jan. 13, 1958.

Hamilton, Charles. *Adam Clayton Powell, Jr.: The Political Biography of an American Dilemma.* New York: Atheneum, 1991.

Hamilton, Nigel. *JFK: Reckless Youth.* New York: Random House, 1992.

Hamilton, Virginia. *Lister Hill: Statesman from the South.* Chapel Hill: University of North Carolina Press, 1987.

Hannaford, Peter, ed. *The Drew Pearson Diaries, 1960–1969.* Lincoln: University of Nebraska Press, 2015.

Hardeman, D. B., and Donald C. Bacon. *Rayburn: A Biography.* Austin: Texas Monthly Press, 1987.

Hardy, Henry, and Jennifer Holmes, eds. *Enlightening Letters, 1946–1960: Isaiah Berlin.* London: Chatto and Windus, 2009.

Harlow, Bryce. "White House Watch." *New Republic,* May 13, 1978.

Harper, Paul, and Joann Krieg, eds. *John F. Kennedy: The Promise Revisited.* New York: Greenwood, 1988.

Harris, Louis. *Is There a Republican Majority?* New York: Harper, 1954.

———. "Why the Odds Are Against a Governor Becoming President." *Public Opinion Quarterly,* Vol. 23, No. 3, Autumn 1959.

Hartung, William. "Eisenhower's Warning: The Military-Industrial Complex Forty Years Later." *World Policy Journal.* Vol. 18, No. 1, Spring 2001.

Harvey, Anna. *Votes without Leverage: Women in American Electoral Politics, 1920–1970.* New York: Cambridge University Press, 1998.

Hasenfus, William. "Managing Partner: Joseph W. Martin Jr., Republican Leader of the United States House of Representatives, 1939–1959." Ph.D. thesis, Boston College, 1986.

Hatfield, Mark O., with Diane N. Solomon. *Against the Grain: Reflections of a Rebel Republican.* Ashland, OR: White Cloud, 2001.

Havard, William C., ed. *The Changing Politics of the South.* Baton Rouge: Louisiana State University Press, 1972.

Havard, William C., Rudolf Heberle, and Perry Howard. *The Louisiana Election of 1960.* Baton Rouge: Louisiana State University Press, 1963.

Havard, William C., and Perry Howard. "The Louisiana Bifactional System and the Long Era: The Beginning of the End?" *Southwestern Social Science Quarterly,* Vol. 44, No. 2, Sept. 1963.

Haygood, Wil. *King of the Cats: The Life and Times of Adam Clayton Powell, Jr.* Boston: Houghton Mifflin, 1993.

Haynes, John Earl, Harvey Klehr, and Alexander Vassiliev. *Spies: The Rise and Fall of the KGB in America.* New Haven: Yale University Press, 2009.

Heale, M. J. *McCarthy's Americans: Red Scare Politics in State and Nation, 1935–1965.* New York: Palgrave, 1998.

Hébert, F. Edward. *Last of the Titans: The Life and Times of Congressman F. Edward Hébert.* Lafayette: Center for Louisiana Studies, University of Southwestern Louisiana, 1976.

Hechler, Ken. *Working with Truman: A Personal Memoir of the White House Years.* Columbia: University of Missouri Press, 1986.

Heidepriem, Scott. *A Fair Chance for a Free People: Biography of Karl E. Mundt, United States Senator.* Madison, SD: Leader, 1988.

Heinemann, Ronald. *Harry Byrd of Virginia.* Charlottesville: University of Virginia Press, 1996.

Helgerson, John. *Getting to Know the President: CIA Briefings of Presidential Candidates 1952–1992.* Washington, DC: Center for the Study of Intelligence, 1996.

Henderson, Harold. *Ernest Vandiver, Governor of Georgia.* Athens: University of Georgia Press, 2000.

Henggeler, Paul. *The Kennedy Persuasion: The Politics of Style since JFK.* Chicago: Ivan Dee, 1995.

Henry, Richard. *Eleanor Roosevelt and Adlai Stevenson.* New York: Palgrave, 2010.

Herberg, Will. *Protestant—Catholic—Jew: An Essay in American Religious Sociology.* Garden City, NY: Doubleday, 1955.

Herken, Gregg. *The Georgetown Set: Friends and Rivals in Cold War Washington.* New York: Knopf, 2014.

Hersh, Seymour. *The Dark Side of Camelot.* Boston: Little, Brown, 1997.

Herskowitz, Mickey. *Duty, Honor, Country: The Life and Legacy of Prescott Bush.* Nashville, TN: Rutledge Hill, 2003.

Herzstein, Robert. *Henry R. Luce: A Political Portrait of the Man Who Created the American Century.* New York: Scribner, 1994.

Hess, Stephen. *Bit Player: My Life with Presidents and Ideas.* Washington, DC: Brookings Institution Press, 2018.

Hewitt, Don. *Tell Me a Story: Fifty Years and 60 Minutes in Television.* New York: Public Affairs, 2001.

Heyman, C. David. *RFK: A Candid Biography of Robert F. Kennedy.* New York: Dutton, 1998.

Hill, Clint. *Five Presidents: My Extraordinary Journey with Eisenhower, Kennedy, Johnson, Nixon, and Ford.* New York: Gallery, 2016.

Hillings, Pat. *The Irrepressible Irishman: A Republican Insider, the Story of a Political Life.* N.p.: Harold D. Dean, 1993.

Hilty, James. *Robert Kennedy: Brother Protector.* Philadelphia: Temple University Press, 1997.

Hirsch, Arnold. "The Cook County Democratic Machine and the Dilemma of Race, 1931–1987." In Bernard, *Snowbelt Cities*.

———. *Making the Second Ghetto: Race and Housing in Chicago, 1940–1960*. Cambridge: Cambridge University Press, 1983.

Hoffmann, Joyce. *Theodore H. White and Journalism as Illusion*. Columbia: University of Missouri Press, 1995.

Hogan, J. Harris, III. "The 1960 Texas Presidential Election Victory of Senator John F. Kennedy." M.A. thesis, University of Massachusetts, 1963.

Hogan, Michael. *The Afterlife of John Fitzgerald Kennedy: A Biography*. New York: Cambridge University Press, 2017.

Holeman, Frank. "The Curious Quaker: Richard M. Nixon." In Sevareid, *Candidates 1960*.

Holloway, Henry. "The Negro and the Vote: The Case of Texas." *Journal of Politics*, Vol. 23, No. 3, Aug. 1961.

———. "The Texas Negro as a Voter." *Phylon*, Vol. 24, No. 2, 1963.

Holt, Marilyn. *Mamie Doud Eisenhower: The General's First Lady*. Lawrence: University Press of Kansas, 2007.

Horne, Alistair. *Harold Macmillan*, vol. 2, *1957–1986*. London: Macmillan, 1989.

———. "The Macmillan Years and Afterwards." In Louis and Bull, *"Special Relationship."*

Horton, Carrell, and Jesse Smith. *Statistical Record of Black America*. Detroit: Gale Research, 1990.

Howard, Gene. *Patterson for Alabama: The Life and Career of John Patterson*. Tuscaloosa: University of Alabama Press, 2008.

Hoyt, Edwin. *The Nixons: An American Family*. New York: Random House, 1972.

Hudnut-Beumler, James. *Looking for God in the Suburbs: The Religion of the American Dream and Its Critics, 1945–1965*. New Brunswick, NJ: Rutgers University Press, 1994.

Hughes, Emmet John. *The Ordeal of Power: A Political Memoir of the Eisenhower Years*. New York: Atheneum, 1963.

Hughes, Richard. "Texas Churches and Presidential Politics, 1928 and 1960." Ph.D. thesis, St. Louis University, 1968.

Hulsey, Byron C. *Everett Dirksen and His Presidents: How a Senate Giant Shaped American Politics*. Lawrence: University Press of Kansas, 2000.

Humphrey, Hubert H. *The Education of a Public Man: My Life and Politics*. Ed. Norman Sherman. Garden City, NY: Doubleday, 1976.

Hutschnecker, Arnold. "The Mental Health of Our Leaders." *Look*, July 15, 1969.

Ingle, H. Larry. *Nixon's First Cover-Up: The Religious Life of a Quaker President*. Columbia: University of Missouri Press, 2015.

Ingwerson, Marshall. "Where Dick Tuck Goes, Political Pranks Follow." *Christian Science Monitor*, Oct. 28, 1982.

Irwin, Don. "Money Isn't Everything—Nelson A. Rockefeller." In Sevareid, *Candidates 1960*.

"Jackie Robinson Changes Mind about Kennedys." *Jet*, Vol. 20, No. 5, May 25, 1961.

Jacobs, Lawrence R., and Robert Y. Shapiro, "Issues, Candidate Image, and Priming: The Use of Private Polls in Kennedy's 1960 Presidential Campaign." *American Political Science Review*, Vol. 88, Sept. 1994.

———. "The Rise of Presidential Polling: The Nixon White House in Historical Perspective." *Public Opinion Quarterly*, Vol. 59, 1995.

Jacobs, Seth. "No Place to Fight a War: Laos and the Evolution of U.S. Policy toward Vietnam, 1954–1963." In Bradley and Young, *Making Sense of the Vietnam Wars*.

———. *The Universe Unraveling: American Foreign Policy in Cold War Laos*. Ithaca, NY: Cornell University Press, 2012.

Jamieson, Kathleen. *Packaging the Presidency: A History and Criticism of Presidential Campaign Advertising*. 2nd ed. New York: Oxford University Press, 1992.

Javits, Jacob K. *Javits: The Autobiography of a Public Man*. Boston: Houghton Mifflin, 1981.

———. *Order of Battle: A Republican's Call to Reason*. New York: Atheneum, 1964.

Jeffries, John. "The 'Quest for National Purpose' of 1960." *American Quarterly*, Vol. 30, No. 4, Autumn 1978.

Jennings, Matt. "The Editor's Corner," *Sidwell Friends Alumni Magazine*, Summer 2001.

———. "A Long March to Equality," *Sidwell Friends Alumni Magazine*, Spring 2011.

John F. Kennedy Foundation. *Listening In: The Secret White House Recordings of John F. Kennedy*. Ed. Ted Widmer. New York: Hyperion, 2012.

Johnson, Donald Bruce, compiler. *National Party Platforms*, vol. 2, 1960–1976. Urbana: University of Illinois Press, 1978.

Johnson, Lyndon B. *The Vantage Point: Perspectives of the Presidency, 1963–1969*. New York: Holt, Rinehart and Winston, 1971.

Johnson, Walter, ed. *The Papers of Adlai E. Stevenson*, vols. 4–7. Boston: Little, Brown, 1977–1979.

Jumonville, Neil. *Henry Steele Commager: Midcentury Liberalism and the History of the Present*. Chapel Hill: University of North Carolina Press, 1999.

Kalb, Madeline. *The Congo Cables: The Cold War in Africa — From Eisenhower to Kennedy*. New York: Macmillan, 1982.

Kallina, Edmund F., Jr. *Courthouse over White House: Chicago and the Presidential Election of 1960*. Orlando: University Presses of Florida, 1988.

———. *Kennedy v. Nixon: The Presidential Election of 1960*. Gainesville: University Press of Florida, 2010.

———. "The State's Attorney and the President: The Inside Story of the 1960 Presidential Election in Illinois." *Journal of American Studies*, Vol. 12, No. 2, 1978.

———. "Was Nixon Cheated in 1960?" *Journalism Quarterly*. Vol. 62, Issue 1, March 1985.

———. "Was the Presidential Election Stolen? The Case of Illinois," *Presidential Studies Quarterly*, Vol. 15, Winter 1985.

Kaplan, Fred. *The Wizards of Armageddon*. New York: Simon and Schuster, 1983.

Kaplan, James. *Sinatra: The Chairman*. Garden City, NY: Doubleday, 2015.

Katz, Elihu, and Jacob Feldman. "The Kennedy-Nixon Debates: A Survey of Surveys." *Studies in Public Communication*, Vol. 4, Autumn 1962.

Katz, Milton. "E. Frederic Morrow and Civil Rights in the Eisenhower Administration." *Phylon*, Vol. 42, June 1981.

Kaufman, Robert. *Henry M. Jackson: A Life in Politics*. Seattle: University of Washington Press, 2000.

Kehl, James. "Presidential Sweepstakes in Review: Seen from the 1960 Starting Gate." *Pennsylvania History*, Vol. 31, No. 2, April 1964.

Keller, Craig. "The Intellectuals and Eisenhower: Civil Religion, Religious Publicity, and the Search for Moral and Religious Communities." Ph.D. thesis, George Washington University, 2002.

Kelley, Donald. "Mississippi Public Opinion in the Presidential Elections of 1928 and 1960: A Study in the Continuity of Ideas." Ph.D. thesis, Tulane University, 1965.

Kellstedt, Lyman A., et al. "Faith Transformed: Religion and American Politics from FDR to George W. Bush." In Noll and Harlow, *Religion and American Politics*.

Kellstedt, Lyman A., and Mark A. Noll, "Religion, Voting for President, and Party Identification, 1948–1984." In Noll, *Religion and American Politics*.

Kelly, Robert. *Neck and Neck to the White House: The Closest Presidential Elections, 1798–2000*. Jefferson, NC: McFarland, 2011.

Kemper, Deane. "John F. Kennedy before the Greater Houston Ministerial Association, September 12, 1960: The Religious Issue." Ph.D. thesis, Michigan State University, 1968.

Kempton, Murray. *America Comes to Middle Age: Columns, 1950–1962*. Boston: Little, Brown, 1963.

———. "The Underestimation of Dwight D. Eisenhower." *Esquire*, Vol. 68, No. 3, Sept. 1967.

Kendrick, Alexander. *Prime Time: The Life of Edward R. Murrow*. Boston: Little, Brown, 1969.

Kendrick, Paul, and Stephen Kendrick. *Nine Days: The Race to Save Martin Luther King Jr.'s Life and Win the 1960 Election*. New York: Farrar, Straus and Giroux, 2021.

Kennedy, Edward M. *True Compass: A Memoir*. New York: Twelve, 2009.

Kennedy, John F. "A Democrat Looks at Foreign Policy." *Foreign Affairs*, Vol. 36, No. 1, Oct. 1957.

———. *The Strategy of Peace*. Ed. Allan Nevins. New York: Popular Library, 1961.

Kennedy, Robert F. *The Enemy Within*. 1960; rpt. Westport, CT: Greenwood, 1982.

Kenney, David. *A Political Passage: The Career of Stratton of Illinois*. Carbondale: Southern Illinois University Press, 1990.

Keogh, James. *This Is Nixon*. New York: Putnam, 1956.

Key, V. O., Jr., with the assistance of Milton C. Cummings, Jr. *The Responsible Electorate: Rationality in Presidential Voting, 1936–1960*. Cambridge: Belknap Press of Harvard University Press, 1966.

Kiepper, James J. *Styles Bridges: Yankee Senator*. Sugar Hill, NH: Phoenix, 2001.

Kinch, Sam, and Stuart Long. *Allan Shivers: The Pied Piper of Texas Politics*. Austin: Shoal Creek, 1978.

King, Coretta Scott. *My Life with Martin Luther King, Jr.* New York: Holt, 1969.

King, Martin Luther, Sr., with Clayton Riley. *Daddy King: An Autobiography*. New York: Morrow, 1980.

Kirby, Alec. "Childe Harold's Pilgrimage: A Political Biography of Harold Stassen." Ph.D. thesis, George Washington University, 1992.

Kirby, Alec, David G. Dalin, and John F. Rothmann. *Harold E. Stassen: The Life and Perennial Candidacy of the Progressive Republican*. Jefferson, NC: McFarland, 2013.

Kissel, Paul. "Presidential Campaign 1960: A Symposium. Part I, Contest for the Nomination." *Quarterly Journal of Speech* 46, no. 3, Oct. 1960.

Kissinger, Henry A. "The Khrushchev Visit—Dangers and Hopes." *New York Times Magazine*, Sept. 6, 1959.

———. *Nuclear Weapons and Foreign Policy*. New York: Harper, for the Council on Foreign Relations, 1957.

Kistiakowsky, George B. *A Scientist at the White House: The Private Diary of President Eisenhower's Special Assistant for Science and Technology*. Cambridge: Harvard University Press, 1976.

Kitagawa, Evelyn M., and Karl E. Taeuber, eds. *Local Community Fact Book: Chicago Metropolitan Area*. Chicago: University of Chicago Press, 1960.

Klarman, Michael. *From Jim Crow to Civil Rights: The Supreme Court and the Struggle for Racial Equality*. New York: Oxford University Press, 2004.

Klein, Herbert G. *Making It Perfectly Clear: An Inside Account of Nixon's Love/Hate Relationship with the Media*. Garden City, NY: Doubleday, 1980.

Kleindienst, Richard G. *Justice: The Memoirs of Attorney General Richard Kleindienst*. Ottawa, IL: Jameson, 1985.

Kleppner, Paul. *Chicago Divided: The Making of a Black Mayor*. DeKalb: Northern Illinois University Press, 1985.

Klotter, James. *The Breckinridges of Kentucky, 1760–1981*. Lexington: University Press of Kentucky, 1986.

Kluger, Richard, with Phyllis Kluger. *The Paper: The Life and Death of the New York Herald Tribune*. New York: Knopf, 1986.

Knaggs, John. *Two-Party Texas: The John Tower Era, 1961–1984*. Austin: Eakin, 1986.

Knebel, Fletcher. "Democratic Forecast: A Catholic in 1960." *Look*, March 3, 1959.

Koeth, Stephen M. "The Strengths and Limits of American Catholic Conference: John F. Cronin, S.S., and His Political Friendship with Richard M. Nixon, 1947–1960." *Journal of Church and State*, Vol. 56, No. 4, Dec. 2014.

Kolodziej, Edward A. *The Uncommon Defense and Congress, 1945–1963*. Columbus: Ohio State University Press, 1966.

Kornitzer, Bela. *The Real Nixon: An Intimate Biography*. New York: Rand McNally, 1960.

Kraft, Joseph. "IKE vs. NIXON." *Esquire*, April 1960.

Kraus, Sidney. "Winners of the First 1960 Televised Presidential Debate between Kennedy and Nixon." *Journal of Communication*, Vol. 46, No. 4, Dec. 1996.

———, ed. *The Great Debates: Background, Perspectives, Effects*. Bloomington: Indiana University Press, 1962.

Kraus, Sidney, et al. "Political Issues and the TV Debates." *Abstracts of Papers of the American Sociological Association*. 56th Annual Session, 1961.

Krieg, Joann P., ed. *Dwight D. Eisenhower: Soldier, President, Statesman*. New York: Greenwood, 1987.

Krock, Arthur. *Memoirs: Sixty Years on the Firing Line*. New York: Funk and Wagnalls, 1968.

Kuhn, Clifford. "There's a Footnote to History! Memoir and the History of Martin Luther

King's October 1960 Arrest and Its Aftermath." *Journal of American History*, Vol. 84, No. 2, Sept. 1997.

Kurtzman, Neil. "President Kennedy and Addison's Disease." *Journal of the American Medical Association*, Vol. 201, 1967.

Lacroix, Patrick. *John F. Kennedy and the Politics of Faith*. Lawrence: University Press of Kansas, 2021.

———. "John F. Kennedy and the Politics of Faith, 1960–1963." Ph.D. thesis, University of New Hampshire, 2017.

Laird, Melvin R., ed. *Republican Papers*. New York: Praeger, 1968.

Land, Guy. "John F. Kennedy's Southern Strategy, 1956–1960." *North Carolina Historical Review*, Vol. 56, No. 1, Jan. 1979.

———. "Mississippi Republicanism and the 1960 Presidential Election." *Journal of Mississippi History*, Vol. 40, Issue 1, Feb. 1978.

———. "Presidential Republicans and the Growth of the Mississippi Republican Party, 1952–1960." M.A. thesis, University of Georgia, 1974.

Lang, Kurt, and Gladys Engel Lang. "Ordeal by Debate: Viewers Reaction." *Public Opinion Quarterly*, Vol. 25, Summer 1961.

———. *Politics and Television*. Chicago: Quadrangle, 1968.

Larres, Klaus. *Churchill's Cold War: The Politics of Personal Diplomacy*. New Haven: Yale University Press, 2002.

Lash, Joseph P. *Eleanor: The Years Alone*. New York: Norton, 1972.

Lasky, Victor. *J.F.K.: The Man and the Myth*. New York: Macmillan, 1963.

———. *Robert F. Kennedy: The Myth and the Man*. New York: Trident, 1968.

Lavine, Harold. *Smoke-Filled Rooms: The Confidential Papers of Robert Humphreys*. Englewood Cliffs, NJ: Prentice-Hall, 1970.

Lawrence, Bill. *Six Presidents, Too Many Wars*. New York: Saturday Review Press, 1972.

Lawson, Steven F. *Running for Freedom: Civil Rights and Black Politics in America since 1941*. 2nd ed. New York: McGraw-Hill, 1997.

"Leadership: An Interview with Senate Leader Lyndon Johnson." *U. S. News and World Report*, Vol. 48, June 27, 1960.

Lee, R. Alton. *Eisenhower and Landrum-Griffin: A Study in Labor-Management Relations*. Lexington: University Press of Kentucky, 1990.

Lee, Eugene C., and William Buchanan. "The 1960 Election in California." *Western Political Quarterly*, Part 2, Vol. 14, No. 1, 1961.

Lee, Eugene C., and Bruce E. Keith. *California Votes, 1960–1972*. Berkeley: Institute of Governmental Studies, University of California, 1974.

Leinster, Colin. "Nixon's Friend Bebe." *Life*, July 31, 1970.

Lemann, Nicholas. *The Promised Land: The Great Black Migration and How It Changed America*. New York: Vintage, 2011.

Lepore, Jill. "All the King's Data: Simulation, Automation, and the Election of John F. Kennedy." *New Yorker*, Aug. 3–10, 2020.

———. *If Then: How the Simulmatics Corporation Invented the Future*. New York: Liveright, 2020.

Levingston, Steven. *Kennedy and King: The President, the Pastor, and the Battle Over Civil Rights.* New York: Hachette, 2017.

Lewis, Anthony, and *The New York Times. Portrait of a Decade: The Second American Revolution.* New York: Random House, 1964.

Lewis, David Levering. *King: A Biography.* 2nd ed. Urbana: University of Illinois Press, 1978.

Lichtenstein, Nelson. *The Most Dangerous Man in Detroit: Walter Reuther and the Fate of American Labor.* New York: Basic, 1995.

Lichtman, Allan. *Prejudice and the Old Politics: The Presidential Election of 1928.* Chapel Hill: University of North Carolina Press, 1979.

Lieberman, Joseph I. *The Power Broker: A Biography of John M. Bailey, Modern Political Boss.* Boston: Houghton Mifflin, 1966.

Lincoln, Evelyn. *My Twelve Years with John F. Kennedy.* New York: McKay, 1965.

Lindquist, Jack, with Melinda J. Combs. *In Service to the Mouse: My Unexpected Journey to Becoming Disneyland's First President.* Orange, CA: Chapman University Press, 2010.

Lipsky, Roma. "Electioneering among the Minorities." *Commentary,* May 1961.

Lisle, Teddy David. "The Canonical Impediment: John F. Kennedy and the Religious Issue during the 1960 Presidential Campaign." Ph.D. thesis, University of Kentucky, 1982.

———. "The Catholic Press and the Kennedy Candidacy." M.A. thesis, University of Kentucky, 1977.

———. "Southern Baptists and the Issue of Catholic Autonomy in the 1960 Presidential Campaign." In Harper and Krieg, *John F. Kennedy.*

Lodge, Henry Cabot, Jr. *As It Was: An Inside View of Politics and Power in the Sixties.* New York: Norton, 1976.

———. *The Storm Has Many Eyes: A Personal Memoir.* New York: Norton, 1973.

Logevall, Fredrik. *JFK: Coming of Age in the American Century, 1917–1956.* New York: Random House, 2020.

Long, Michael G., ed. *First Class Citizenship: The Civil Rights Letters of Jackie Robinson.* New York: Times Books, 2007.

Longley, Kyle. *Senator Albert Gore, Sr.: Tennessee Maverick.* Baton Rouge: Louisiana State University Press, 2004.

Loughry, Allen H. *Don't Buy Another Vote, I Won't Pay for a Landslide: The Sordid and Continuing History of Political Corruption in West Virginia.* Parsons, WV: McClain, 2006.

Louis, William Roger, and Hedley Bull, eds., *The "Special Relationship": Anglo-American Relations since 1945.* Oxford: Clarendon Press, 1986.

Lubell, Samuel. *White and Black: Test of a Nation.* New York: Harper and Row, 1964.

Lublin, Robert. *The Republican South: Democratization and Partisan Change.* Princeton, NJ: Princeton University Press, 2004.

Lundberg, George. "Closing the Case in *JAMA* on the John F. Kennedy Autopsy." *Journal of the American Medical Association,* Vol. 268, No. 13, Oct. 7, 1992.

Lungren, John, and John Lungren, Jr. *Healing Richard Nixon: A Doctor's Memoir.* Lexington: University Press of Kentucky, 2003.

Lynch, Dudley. *The Duke of Duval: The Life and Times of George B. Parr.* Waco: Texian, 1976.

MacKaye, William, and Mary MacKaye. *Mr. Sidwell's School: A Centennial History, 1883–1983.* Washington, DC: Sidwell Friends School, 1983.

Macmillan, Harold. *Riding the Storm, 1956–1959.* New York: Harper Collins, 1971.

Mahoney, Richard. *JFK: Ordeal in Africa.* New York: Oxford University Press, 1983.

———. *Sons and Brothers: The Days of Jack and Bobby Kennedy.* New York: Arcade, 1999.

Maier, Thomas. *The Kennedys: America's Emerald Kings.* New York: Basic, 2003.

Maier, Timothy W. "Why Al Gore Is No Richard Nixon." *Washington Times Magazine,* Dec. 11, 2000.

Mailer, Norman. *Some Honorable Men: Political Conventions, 1960–1972.* Boston: Little, Brown, 1976.

Mallan, John. "Massachusetts: Liberal and Corrupt," *New Republic,* Vol. 127, No. 15, Oct. 13, 1952.

Mandel, Lee. "Endocrine and Autoimmune Aspects of the Health History of John F. Kennedy." *Annals of Internal Medicine,* Vol. 151, No. 5, Sept. 2009.

Mann, Robert. *Legacy to Power: Senator Russell Long of Louisiana.* New York: Paragon, 1992.

Manning, Christopher. *William L. Dawson and the Limits of Black Electoral Leadership.* DeKalb: Northern Illinois University Press, 2009.

"The Man Who Bugged Nixon." *Time,* Aug. 13, 1973.

Manza, Jeff, and Clem Brooks. "The Religious Factor in U.S. Presidential Elections, 1960–1992." *American Journal of Sociology,* Vol. 103, No. 1, July 1997.

Marlin, George J. *The American Catholic Voter: 200 Years of Political Impact.* South Bend, IN: St. Augustine's, 2004.

Marlin, George J., and Brad Miner. *The Sons of Saint Patrick: A History of the Archbishops of New York from Dagger John to Timmytown.* San Francisco: Ignatius Press, 2017.

Marling, Karal. *As Seen on TV: The Visual Culture of Everyday Life in the 1950s.* Cambridge: Harvard University Press, 1994.

Marovitz, Sanford. "John Steinbeck and Adlai Stevenson: The Shattered Image of America." *Steinbeck Quarterly,* Vol. 3, Summer 1970.

Martin, Boyd. "The 1960 Election in Idaho." *Western Political Quarterly,* Part 2, Vol. 14, No. 1, March 1961.

Martin, Curtis. "The 1960 Election in Colorado." *Western Political Quarterly,* Part 2, Vol. 14, No. 1, March 1961.

Martin, Joe. *My First Fifty Years in Politics.* New York: McGraw-Hill, 1960.

Martin, John. *Adlai Stevenson and the World: The Life of Adlai E. Stevenson.* New York: Book World Promotions, 1977.

———. *Adlai Stevenson of Illinois. The Life of Adlai E. Stevenson.* Garden City, NY: Doubleday, 1976.

———. *It Seems Like Only Yesterday: Memoirs of Writing, Presidential Politics, and Diplomatic Life.* New York: Morrow, 1986.

Martin, Ralph G. *Ballots and Bandwagons.* Chicago: Rand McNally, 1964.

Martin, Ralph G., and Ed Plaut. *Front Runner, Dark Horse*. New York: Doubleday, 1960.

Martin, William. *A Prophet with Honor: The Billy Graham Story*. New York: Morrow, 1991.

———. *With God on Our Side: The Rise of the Religious Right in America*. New York: Broadway, 1996.

Marty, Martin E. *Righteous Empire: The Protestant Experience in America*. New York: Dial, 1970.

Massa, Mark. "A Catholic for President: John F. Kennedy and the 'Secular' Theology of the Houston Speech, 1960." *Journal of Church and State*, Vol. 39, Issue 2, Spring 1997.

Matteson, Robert Eliot. *Harold Stassen: His Career, the Man, and the 1957 London Arms Control Negotiations*. Inver Grove Heights, MN: Desk Top Ink, 1991.

Matthews, Chris. *Bobby Kennedy: A Raging Spirit*. New York: Simon and Schuster, 2017.

———. *Kennedy and Nixon: The Rivalry That Shaped Postwar America*. New York: Simon and Schuster, 1996.

Matthews, Donald, and James Prothro. "Political Factors and Negro Voter Registration in the South." *American Political Science Review*, Vol. 57, No. 2, June 1963.

Matusow, Allen J. *The Unraveling of America: A History of Liberalism in the 1960s*. New York: Harper and Row, 1984.

May, Ann. "President Eisenhower, Economic Policy, and the 1960 Presidential Election." *Journal of Economic History*, Vol. 50, No. 2, June 1990.

Mayer, George. *The Republican Party, 1854–1966*. 2nd ed. New York: Oxford University Press, 1967.

Mayer, Jeremy. *Running on Race: Racial Politics in Presidential Campaigns, 1960–2000*. New York: Random House, 2002.

Mayer, Michael. *The Eisenhower Presidency and the 1950s*. Boston: Houghton Mifflin, 1998.

———, ed. *The Eisenhower Years*. New York: Facts on File, 2010.

Mazo, Earl. *Richard Nixon: A Political and Personal Portrait*. New York: Harpers, 1959.

Mazo, Earl, and the Center for the Study of Democratic Institutions. *The Great Debates: An Occasional Paper on the Role of the Political Process in the Free Society*. Santa Barbara, CA: Center for the Study of Democratic Institutions, 1962.

Mazo, Earl, and Stephen Hess. *Nixon: A Political Portrait*. New York: Harper and Row, 1968.

McAndrews, Lawrence. "The Avoidable Conflict: Kennedy, the Bishops, and Federal Aid to Education." *Catholic Historical Review*, Vol. 75, April 1990.

McClenahan, William M., Jr., and William H. Becker. *Eisenhower and the Cold War Economy*. Baltimore: Johns Hopkins University Press, 2011.

McClendon, Sarah. *My Eight Presidents*. New York: Wyden, 1978.

McClendon, Sarah, with Jules Minton. *Mr. President, Mr. President! My Fifty Years of Covering the White House*. Los Angeles: General Publishing Group, 1996.

McClerren, Beryl. "The Southern Baptist State Newspapers and the Religious Issue during the Presidential Campaigns of 1928 and 1960." Ph.D. thesis, Southern Illinois University, 1963.

McCleskey, Clifton. *The Government and Politics of Texas*. 2nd ed. Boston: Little, Brown, 1966.

McDougal, Dennis. *Privileged Son: Otis Chandler and the Rise and Fall of the L.A. Times Dynasty*. Boston: Da Capo, 2001.

McFadden, Robert. "Dick Tuck, Democrats' Political Prankster." *NYT*, May 29, 2018.

McFarland, Linda. *Cold War Strategist: Stuart Symington and the Search for National Security*. Westport, CT: Praeger, 2001.

McGrath, Joseph, and Marion McGrath. "Effects of Partisanship on Perceptions of Political Figures." *Public Opinion Quarterly*, Vol. 26, No. 2, Summer 1962.

McGreevy, John. "Thinking on One's Own: Catholicism in American Intellectual Imagination, 1928–1960." *Journal of American History*, Vol. 84, No. 1, Jan. 1997.

McGrory, Mary. "'Uneasy Politician': Adlai E. Stevenson." In Sevareid, *Candidates 1960*.

McKean, David. *Tommy the Cork: Washington's Ultimate Insider from Roosevelt to Reagan*. South Royalton, VT: Steerforth, 2004.

McKeever, Porter. *Adlai Stevenson: His Life and Legacy*. New York: Morrow, 1989.

McKenna, William. "The Influence of Religion in the Pennsylvania Elections of 1958 and 1960." *Pennsylvania History*, Vol. 29, No. 4, Oct. 1962.

———. "The Negro Vote in Philadelphia Elections." *Pennsylvania History*, Vol. 32, No. 4, Oct. 1965.

McKeough, Kevin. "Suburban Voting Behavior in the 1960 Presidential Election: The Case of Cook County, Illinois." Ph.D. thesis, University of Kansas, 1967.

McLellan, David S., and David C. Acheson, eds. *Among Friends: Personal Letters of Dean Acheson*. New York: Dodd, Mead, 1980.

McMillan, Edward. "Texas and the Eisenhower Campaigns." Ph.D. thesis, Texas Tech University, 1960.

McPherson, Harry. *A Political Education: A Washington Memoir*. Boston: Atlantic Monthly Press, 1983.

Meier, August, and Elliot Rudwick. *CORE: A Study in the Civil Rights Movement, 1942–1968*. Urbana: University of Illinois Press, 1973.

Melton, Thomas. "The 1960 Presidential Election in Georgia." Ph.D. thesis, University of Mississippi, 1985.

Menendez, Albert. *The Religious Factor in the 1960 Presidential Election: An Analysis of the Kennedy Victory over Anti-Catholic Prejudice*. Jefferson, NC: McFarland, 2011.

Meriwether, James. "'Worth a Lot of Negro Votes': Black Voters, Africa, and the 1960 Presidential Campaign." *Journal of American History*, Vol. 95, No. 3, Dec. 2008.

Merry, Robert. *Taking on the World: Joseph and Stewart Alsop — Guardians of the American Century*. New York: Viking, 1996.

Michener, James A. *Report of the County Chairman*. New York: Random House, 1961.

Middendorf, William. *A Glorious Disaster: Barry Goldwater's Presidential Campaign and the Origins of the Conservative Movement*. New York: Basic, 2006.

Middleton, Russell. "The Civil Rights Issue and Presidential Voting among Southern Negroes and Whites." *Social Forces*, Vol. 43, No. 3, March 1962.

Mieczkowski, Yanek. *Eisenhower's Sputnik Moment: The Race for Space and World Prestige*. Ithaca, NY: Cornell University Press, 2013.

Miller, Douglas. "Popular Religion of the 1950's: Norman Vincent Peale and Billy Graham." *Journal of Popular Culture*, Vol. 9, Summer 1975.

Miller, John. "The Making of Theodore H. White's *The Making of the President 1960.*" *Presidential Studies Quarterly*, Vol. 29, No. 2, June 1999.

Miller, Merle. *Plain Speaking: An Oral Biography of Harry S. Truman.* New York: Berkley, 1974.

Miller, N. Edd. "Presidential Campaign 1960: A Symposium," part 2. *Quarterly Journal of Speech*, Vol. 46, Issue 4, Dec. 1960.

Miller, Steven. *Billy Graham and the Rise of the Republican South.* Philadelphia: University of Pennsylvania Press, 2009.

———. "The Politics of Decency: Billy Graham, Evangelicalism, the End of the Solid South, 1950–1980." Ph.D. thesis, Vanderbilt University, 2005.

Miller, Tom. "Tricky Dick." *New Yorker*, Aug. 30, 2004.

Miller, Warren, et al. *American National Election Studies Data Sourcebook, 1952–1978.* Cambridge: Harvard University Press, 1980.

Miller, William Lee. "The Debating Career of Richard M. Nixon," *Reporter*, April 19, 1956.

———. *Piety along the Potomac: Notes on Politics and Morals in the Fifties.* Boston: Houghton Mifflin, 1964.

Montgomery, Gayle B., and James W. Johnson. *One Step from the White House: The Rise and Fall of Senator William F. Knowland.* Berkeley: University of California Press, 1998.

Moon, Henry Lee. "How We Voted and Why?" *Crisis*, Vol. 72, Jan. 1965.

Mooney, Booth. *The Politicians, 1945–1960.* Philadelphia: Lippincott, 1970.

Morgan, Edward. "The Missouri Compromise: Stuart Symington." In Sevareid, *Candidates 1960.*

Morgan, Iwan. *Eisenhower versus "the Spenders": The Eisenhower Administration, the Democrats, and the Budget, 1953–1960.* London: Pinter, 1990.

———. *Reagan: American Icon.* London: Tauris, 2016.

Morris, Aldon. "Black Southern Student Sit-in Movement: An Analysis of Internal Organization." *American Sociological Review*, Vol. 46, No. 6, Dec. 1981.

Morris, Edmund. *Dutch: A Memoir of Ronald Reagan.* New York: Random House, 1999.

Morris, Sylvia Jukes. *Price of Fame: The Honorable Clare Boothe Luce.* New York: Random House, 2014.

Morrow, Fred. *Black Man in the White House: A Diary of the Eisenhower Years by the Administrative Officer for Special Projects, the White House, 1955–1961.* New York: Coward-McCann, 1963.

Muehlenbeck, Philip E. *Betting on the Africans: John F. Kennedy's Courting of African Nationalist Leaders.* New York: Oxford University Press, 2012.

Mullen, James. "Newspaper Advertising in the Kennedy-Nixon Campaign." *Journalism Quarterly*, Vol. 40, Issue 1, Winter, 1963.

Murph, Dan. *Texas Giant: The Life of Price Daniel.* Austin: Eakin, 2002.

Murray, David. *Charles Percy of Illinois.* New York: Harper and Row, 1968.

Naftali, Timothy, et al., eds. *The Presidential Recordings*, vols. 1–3, *John F. Kennedy: The Great Crises.* New York: Norton, 2001.

Nasaw, David. *The Patriarch: The Remarkable Life and Turbulent Times of Joseph P. Kennedy.* New York: Penguin, 2012.

Neal, Steve, ed. *Harry and Eleanor: The Correspondence between Eleanor Roosevelt and Harry S. Truman.* New York: Citadel, 2004.

Nelson, Garrison. *John William McCormack: A Political Biography.* New York: Bloomsbury, 2017.

Neustadt, Richard. *Presidential Power and the Modern Presidents: The Political Leadership from Roosevelt to Reagan.* New York: Free Press, 1990.

Nicholas, James, et al. "Management of Adrenocortical Insufficiency during Surgery." *Archives of Surgery,* Vol. 71, No. 5, Nov. 1955.

Nichols, David A. *Ike and McCarthy: Dwight Eisenhower's Secret Campaign against Joseph McCarthy.* New York: Simon and Schuster, 2017.

———. *A Matter of Justice: Eisenhower and the Beginning of the Civil Rights Revolution.* New York: Simon and Schuster, 2007.

Nichter, Luke A. *The Last Brahmin: Henry Cabot Lodge Jr. and the Making of the Cold War.* New Haven: Yale University Press, 2020.

Nissenson, Marilyn. *The Lady Upstairs: Dorothy Schiff and the New York Post.* New York: St. Martin's, 2007.

Nixon, Edward C., and Karen L. Olson. *The Nixons: A Family Portrait.* Bothell, WA: Book Publishers Network, 2009.

Nixon, Hannah. "Nixon: A Mother's Story." *Good Housekeeping,* Vol. 150, June 1960.

Nixon, Pat. "Crisis of a Candidate's Wife." *Ladies Home Journal,* Nov. 1962.

Nixon, Richard. *Leaders: Profiles and Reminiscences of Men Who Have Shaped the Modern World.* New York: Warner, 1982.

———. "Nixon's Own Story of 7 Years in the Vice Presidency," *U.S. News and World Report,* May 16, 1960.

———. *RN: The Memoirs of Richard Nixon.* New York: Gross and Dunlap, 1978.

———. *Six Crises.* Garden City, NY: Doubleday, 1962.

Noer, Thomas. *Soapy: A Biography of G. Mennen Williams.* Ann Arbor: University of Michigan Press, 2005.

Noll, Mark A., ed. *Religion and American Politics: From the Colonial Period to the 1980s.* New York: Oxford University Press, 1990.

Noll, Mark A., and Luke E. Harlow, eds. *Religion and American Politics: From the Colonial Period to the Present.* 2nd ed. Oxford: Oxford University Press, 2007.

North-Broome, Nicholas. *The Nixon-Hughes "Loan": The Loan No One Repaid.* New York: American Public Affairs Institute, 1972.

Novak, Robert. *Prince of Darkness: 50 Years of Reporting in Washington.* New York: Crown Forum, 2007.

Novotny, Patrick. "John F. Kennedy, the 1960 Election, and Georgia's Unpledged Electors in the Electoral College." *Georgia Historical Quarterly,* Vol. 88, No. 3, Fall 2004.

O'Brien, Lawrence F. *No Final Victories: A Life in Politics—from John F. Kennedy to Watergate.* Garden City, NY: Doubleday, 1974.

O'Brien, Michael. *John F. Kennedy: A Biography.* New York: St. Martin's, 2005.

O'Connor, Len. *Clout: Mayor Daley and His City.* Chicago: Regnery, 1975.

O'Donnell, Helen, with Kenneth O'Donnell, Sr. *The Irish Brotherhood: John F. Kennedy,*

His Inner Circle, and the Improbable Rise to the Presidency. Berkeley: Counterpoint, 2015.

O'Donnell, Kenneth P., and David F. Powers, with Joe McCarthy. *"Johnny, We Hardly Knew Ye": Memories of John Fitzgerald Kennedy.* Boston: Little, Brown, 1972.

Offner, Arnold A. *Hubert Humphrey: The Conscience of the Country.* New Haven: Yale University Press, 2018.

Ognibene, Peter. *Scoop: The Life and Politics of Henry M. Jackson.* New York: Stein and Day, 1977.

O'Hare, William P., et al. *Blacks on the Move: A Decade of Demographic Change.* Washington, DC: Joint Center for Political Studies, 1982.

Olien, Roger. *From Token to Triumph: The Texas Republicans since 1920.* Dallas: Southern Methodist University Press, 1982.

Oliphant, Thomas, and Curtis Wilkie. *The Road to Camelot: Inside JFK's Five-Year Campaign.* New York: Simon and Schuster, 2017.

Olson, David, et al. *Texas Votes.* Austin: Institute of Public Affairs, 1964.

Olson, James. *Stuart Symington: A Life.* Columbia: University of Missouri Press, 2003.

O'Neill, Gerard. *Rogues and Redeemers: When Politics Was King in Irish Boston.* New York: Crown, 2012.

O'Reilly, Kenneth. *Nixon's Piano: Presidents and Racial Politics from Washington to Clinton.* New York: Free Press, 1995.

Paddon, Eric J. "Modern Mordecai: Billy Graham in the Political Arena, 1948–1980." Ph.D. thesis, Ohio University, 1999.

Parker, Richard. *John Kenneth Galbraith: His Life, His Politics, His Economics.* New York: Farrar, Straus and Giroux, 2005.

Parker, Robert, with Richard Rashke. *Capitol Hill in Black and White.* New York: Dodd, Mead, 1986.

Parmet, Herbert S. *Eisenhower and the American Crusades.* New York: Macmillan, 1972.

———. "George Aiken: A Republican Senator and His Party." In Sherman, *Political Legacy of George D. Aiken.*

———. *Jack: The Struggles of John F. Kennedy.* New York: Dial, 1980.

———. *JFK: The Presidency of John F. Kennedy.* New York: Dial, 1983.

Parry, Pam. *Eisenhower: The Public Relations President.* Lanham, MD: Lexington, 2014.

Parsons, Talcott, and Kenneth B. Clark, eds. *The Negro American.* Boston: Houghton, Mifflin, 1966.

Paterson, Thomas, et al. *American Foreign Relations,* vol. 2, *A History since 1895.* 7th ed. Belmont, CA: Wadsworth, 2010.

Patterson, James T. *Grand Expectations: The United States, 1945–1974.* New York: Oxford University Press, 1996.

Peale, Norman Vincent. *The Tough-Minded Optimist.* Englewood Cliffs, NJ: Prentice-Hall, 1961.

Peirce, Neal R., and Lawrence D. Longley. *The People's President: The Electoral College in America and the Direct Vote Alternative.* Rev. ed. New Haven: Yale University Press, 1981.

Perlstein, Rick. *Before the Storm: Barry Goldwater and the Unmaking of the American Consensus.* New York: Hill and Wang, 2001.

Phelan, James. "The Nixon Family and the Hughes Loan." *Reporter*, Vol. 27, No. 3, Aug. 16, 1962.

———. *Scandals, Scamps, and Scoundrels: The Casebook of an Investigative Reporter*. New York: Random House, 1982.

Phillips, Kevin. *The Emerging Republican Majority*. New York: Anchor, 1970.

Pierpont, Robert. *At the White House: Assignment to Six Presidents*. New York: Putnam's 1981.

Pietrusza, David. *1960: LBJ vs. JFK vs. Nixon: The Epic Campaign That Forged Three Presidencies*. New York: Union Square, 2008.

Pike, James. *A Roman Catholic in the White House*. Garden City, NY: Doubleday, 1960.

Poen, Monte. "Truman and Kennedy: The Old Guard Yields to the New." In Harper and Krieg, *John F. Kennedy*.

Poinsett, Alex. *Walking with Presidents: Louis Martin and the Rise of Black Political Power*. New York: Madison, 1997.

Polenberg, Richard. *One Nation Divisible: Class, Race, and Ethnicity in the United States since 1938*. New York: Viking, 1980.

Poling, Daniel A. *Mine Eyes Have Seen: An Autobiography*. New York: McGraw-Hill, 1959.

Polisky, Jerome. "The Kennedy-Nixon Debates: A Study in Political Persuasion." Ph.D. thesis, University of Wisconsin, 1965.

Pomper, Gerald. "Future Southern Congressional Politics." *Southwestern Social Science Quarterly*, Vol. 44, No. 1, June 1963.

Pool, Ithiel de Sola, et al. *Candidates, Issues, and Strategies: A Computer Simulation of the 1960 Presidential Election*. Cambridge: MIT Press, 1964.

Porter, Kirk, and Donald Johnson, compilers. *National Party Platforms, 1840–1968*. Urbana: University of Illinois Press, 1972.

Posner, Gerald. "Al Is Following Nixon by Contesting Vote." *Slate*, June 13, 2001.

Potter, Philip. "Political Pitchman," in Sevareid, *Candidates 1960*.

Powell, James. "Reaction to John F. Kennedy's Delivery Skills during the 1960 Campaign." *Western Speech*, Vol. 32, Issue 1, Winter 1968.

Powers, Richard Gid. *Secrecy and Power: The Life of J. Edgar Hoover*. New York: Free Press, 1987.

Preble, Christopher A. *John F. Kennedy and the Missile Gap*. De Kalb: Northern Illinois University Press, 2004.

———. "Who Ever Believed in the Missile Gap? John F. Kennedy and the Politics of National Security." *Presidential Studies Quarterly*, Vol. 33, No. 4, Dec. 2003.

Prochnau, William W., and Richard W. Larsen. *A Certain Democrat: Senator Henry M. Jackson, A Political Biography*. Englewood Cliffs, NJ: Prentice-Hall, 1972.

Pruden, Caroline. *Conditional Partners: Eisenhower, the United Nations, and the Search for a Permanent Peace*. Baton Rouge: Louisiana State University Press, 1998.

Pulliam, Russell. *Publisher: Gene Pulliam, Last of the Newspaper Titans*. Ottawa, IL: Jameson, 1984.

Rabe, Robert. "Reporter in a Troubled World: Marquis W. Childs and the Rise and Fall of Postwar Liberalism." Ph.D. thesis, University of Wisconsin–Madison, 2013.

Rakove, Milton L. *Don't Make No Waves . . . Don't Back No Losers: An Insider's Analysis of the Daley Machine.* Bloomington: Indiana University Press, 1975.

Rampersad, Arnold. *Jackie Robinson: A Biography.* New York: Knopf, 1997.

Rarick, Ethan. *California Rising: The Life and Times of Pat Brown.* Berkeley: University of California Press, 2005.

Reagan, Ronald. *An American Life.* New York: Simon and Schuster, 1990.

Reed, Christopher. *The Chicago NAACP and the Rise of Black Professional Leadership, 1910–1966.* Bloomington: Indiana University Press, 1997.

Reedy, George. *Lyndon B. Johnson: A Memoir.* New York: Andrews and McMeel, 1982.

———. *The U.S. Senate: Paralysis or a Search for Consensus?* New York: Crown, 1986.

Reeves, Richard. "JFK: Secrets and Lies." *Reader's Digest.* April 2003.

Reeves, Thomas. *The Life and Times of Joe McCarthy: A Biography.* New York: Stein and Day, 1982.

———. *A Question of Character: A Life of John F. Kennedy.* New York: Free Press, 1991.

Reich, Cary. *The Life of Nelson A. Rockefeller: Worlds to Conquer, 1908–1958.* New York: Doubleday, 1996.

Reichard, Gary. "Democrats, Civil Rights, and Electoral Strategies in the 1950s." *Congress and the Presidency,* Vol. 13, No. 1, Spring 1986.

Reichley, James, ed. *States in Crisis: Politics in Ten American States, 1950–1962.* Chapel Hill: University of North Carolina Press, 1964.

Republican Committee on Program and Progress. *Decisions for a Better America.* Garden City, NY: Doubleday, 1960.

Reston, James. *Deadline: A Memoir.* New York: Random House, 1991.

———. *Sketches in the Sand.* New York: Knopf, 1967.

Reston, James, Jr. *The Lone Star: The Life of John Connally.* New York: Harper and Row, 1989.

Reuther, Victor G. *The Brothers Reuther and the Story of the UAW: A Memoir.* Boston: Houghton Mifflin, 1976.

Rhyne, Charles S. *Working for Justice in America and Justice in the World: An Autobiography.* McLean, VA: Friends of Legal Profession Public Services, 1995.

Rider, John. "The Charleston Study: The Television Audience of the Kennedy-Nixon Debates." Ph.D. thesis, Michigan State University, 1963.

Riggs, Robert. "The South Could Rise Again: Lyndon Johnson and Others." In Sevareid, *Candidates 1960.*

Ritchie, Donald. *The Columnist: Leaks, Lies, and Libel in Drew Pearson's Washington.* New York: Oxford University Press, 2021.

———. *Reporting from Washington: A History of the Washington Press Corps.* New York: Oxford University Press, 2005.

Roberts, Chalmers M. *First Rough Draft: A Journalist's Journal of Our Times.* New York: Praeger, 1973.

Roberts, Gene, and Hank Klibanoff. *The Race Beat: The Press, the Civil Rights Struggle, and the Awakening of a Nation.* New York: Knopf, 2006.

Robertson, David. *Sly and Able: A Political Biography of James F. Byrnes.* New York: Norton, 1994.

Robinson, Jackie. "The G.O.P. for White Men Only?" *Saturday Evening Post*, Vol. 236, No. 28, Aug. 10–17, 1963.

Robinson, Jackie, with Alfred Duckett. *I Never Had It Made*. New York: Putnam, 1972.

Rockefeller, David. *Memoirs*. New York: Random House, 2002.

Rockefeller Brothers Fund. *Prospects for America: The Rockefeller Panel Reports*. Garden City, NY: Doubleday, 1961.

Rogers, Edward. "Television—Political Image Maker." *Broadcasting*, Jan. 6, 1965.

Roman, Peter J. *Eisenhower and the Missile Gap*. Ithaca, NY: Cornell University Press, 1995.

Roper, Elmo. "Polling Post-Mortem." *Saturday Review*, Vol. 43, No. 48, Nov. 26, 1960.

Rorabaugh, W. J. "The Election of 1960." In Selverstone, *A Companion to John F. Kennedy*.

———. *Kennedy and the Promise of the Sixties*. New York: Cambridge University Press, 2002.

———. "Moral Character, Policy Effectiveness, and the Presidency: The Case of JFK." *Journal of Policy History*, Vol. 10, No. 4, 1998.

———. *The Real Making of the President: Kennedy, Nixon, and the 1960 Election*. Lawrence: University Press of Kansas, 2009.

———. "Why It's Time to Get Past Teddy White's Naïve Account of the 1960 Election." *History News Network Newsletter*. June 1, 2009.

Rosen, George. "Dick and Dave's Kid Gloves as Nixon Shares Honors with Triple Spotting." *Variety*, May 18, 1960.

Rosenberg, Paul. "Debunking the Right's Enduring Myth." *Slate*, July 19, 2014.

Roueché, Berton. *The Incurable Wound: And Further Narratives of Medical Detection*. Boston: Little, Brown, 1957.

Rovere, Richard H. *Arrivals and Departures: A Journalist's Memoirs*. New York: Macmillan, 1976.

———. *Final Reports: Personal Reflections on Politics and History in Our Time*. Garden City, NY: Doubleday, 1984.

Rowan, Carl. *Breaking Barriers: A Memoir*. Boston: Little, Brown, 1980.

Royko, Mike. *Boss: Richard J. Daley of Chicago*. New York: Plume, 1988.

Rudder, Catherine. "Why Southerners Vote the Way They Do: Determinants of the Presidential Vote in the South, 1952–1968." Ph.D. thesis, Ohio State University, 1973.

Runyon, John, et al., compilers. *Source Book of American Presidential Campaigns and Election Statistics, 1948–1968*. New York: Frederick Unger, 1971.

Rust, William J. *Eisenhower and Cambodia: Diplomacy, Covert Action, and the Origins of the Second Indochina War*. Lexington: University Press of Kentucky, 2016.

———. *So Much to Lose: John F. Kennedy and American Policy in Laos*. Lexington: University Press of Kentucky, 2014.

Rymph, Catherine. *Republican Women: Feminism and Conservatism from Suffrage through the Rise of the New Right*. Chapel Hill: University of North Carolina Press, 2006.

Saalberg, Harvey. "The Canons of Journalism: A 50-Year Perspective." *Journalism Quarterly*. Vol. 50, Dec. 1973.

Safire, William. *Before the Fall: An Inside View of the Pre-Watergate White House*. Garden City, NY: Doubleday, 1975.

Salinger, Pierre. *P.S.: A Memoir*. New York: St. Martin's, 1995.

———. *With Kennedy*. Garden City, NY: Doubleday, 1966.

Saltonstall, Leverett, with Edward Weeks. *Salty: Recollections of a Yankee in Politics*. Boston: Boston Globe, 1976.

Sampson, Gregory. "The Rise of the 'New' Republican Party in South Carolina, 1948–1974: A Case Study of Political Change in a Deep South State." Ph.D. thesis, University of North Carolina, 1984.

Sand, G. W. *Truman in Retirement: A Former President Views the Nation and the World*. South Bend, IN: Justice, 1993.

Sandler, Martin, ed. *The Letters of John F. Kennedy*. New York: Bloomsbury, 2013.

Sarantakes, Nicholas Evan. *Fan in Chief: Nixon and Sports, 1969–1974*. Lawrence: University Press of Kansas, 2019.

———. "Lyndon Johnson, Foreign Policy, and the Election of 1960." *Southwestern Historical Quarterly*, Vol. 103, No. 2, Oct. 1999.

Saulnier, Raymond J. *Constructive Years: The U.S. Economy under Eisenhower*. Lanham, MD: University Press of America, 1991.

Scalettar, Raymond. "Presidential Candidate Disability." *Journal of the American Medical Association*, Vol. 251, No. 21, June 1, 1984.

Scammon, Richard M. "How the Negroes Voted." *New Republic*. Vol. 143, No. 22, Nov. 21, 1960.

———, ed. *America at the Polls: A Handbook of American Presidential Election Statistics, 1920–1964*. Pittsburgh: University of Pittsburgh Press, 1965.

———. *America Votes*. New York: Macmillan, 1958.

———. *America Votes 3: A Handbook of Contemporary American Election Statistics*. Pittsburgh: University of Pittsburgh Press, 1959.

———. *America Votes 4: A Handbook of Contemporary American Election Statistics*. Pittsburgh: University of Pittsburgh Press, 1962.

Schaffer, Howard. *Chester Bowles: New Dealer in the Cold War*. Cambridge: Harvard University Press, 1993.

Schapsmeier, Edward L., and Frederick H. Schapsmeier. *Dirksen of Illinois: Senatorial Statesman*. Urbana: University of Illinois Press, 1985.

———. "Eisenhower and Agricultural Reform: Ike's Farm Policy Legacy Appraised." *American Journal of Economics and Sociology*. Vol. 51, Issue 2, April 1992.

———. "Eisenhower and Ezra Taft Benson: Farm Policy in the 1950s." *Agricultural History*, Vol. 44, No. 4, Oct. 1970.

———. *Ezra Taft Benson and the Politics of Agriculture: The Eisenhower Years, 1953–1961*. Danville, IL: Interstate Printers, 1975.

———. "Farm Policy from FDR to Eisenhower: Southern Democrats and the Politics of Agriculture." *Agricultural History*, Vol. 53, No. 1, Jan. 1979.

———. "Religion and Reform: A Case Study of Henry A. Wallace and Ezra Taft Benson." *Journal of Church and State*, Vol. 21, Autumn 1979.

Schelle, Henry. *Charlie Halleck: A Political Biography*. New York: Exposition, 1966.

Schick, Jack. *The Berlin Crisis, 1958–1962*. Philadelphia: University of Pennsylvania Press, 1971.

Schlesinger, Arthur M., Jr. *Journals, 1952–2000*. Ed. Andrew Schlesinger and Stephen C. Schlesinger. New York: Penguin, 2007.

———. *Kennedy or Nixon: Does It Make Any Difference?* New York: Macmillan, 1960.

———. *The Letters of Arthur Schlesinger, Jr*. Ed. Andrew Schlesinger and Stephen C. Schlesinger. New York: Random House, 2013.

———. *Robert Kennedy and His Times*. Boston: Houghton Mifflin, 1978.

———. *A Thousand Days: John F. Kennedy in the White House*. Boston: Houghton Mifflin, 1965.

Schlesinger, Arthur M., Jr., and Fred L. Israel, eds. *History of American Presidential Elections*. 4 vols. New York: Chelsea House, 1971.

Schmidt, Patricia L. *Margaret Chase Smith: Beyond Convention*. Orono, ME: University of Maine Press, 1996.

Scott, Hugh. *Come to the Party*. Englewood Cliffs, NJ: Prentice-Hall, 1968.

Seagull, Louis M. *Southern Republicanism*. Cambridge, MA: Schenkman, 1972.

Sears, Alan, and Craig Osten, with Ryan Cole. *The Soul of an American President: The Untold Story of Dwight D. Eisenhower's Faith*. Grand Rapids, MI: Baker, 2019.

Seebohm, Caroline. *No Regrets: The Life of Marietta Tree*. New York: Simon and Schuster, 1997.

Self, John. "The First Debate over the Debates: How Kennedy and Nixon Negotiated the 1960 Presidential Debates." *Presidential Studies Quarterly*. Vol. 35, No. 2, June 2005.

Seltzer, Richard, et al. *Sex as a Political Variable: Women as Candidates and Voters in U.S. Elections*. Boulder, CO: Lynne Rienner, 1997.

Selverstone, Marc J., ed. *A Companion to John F. Kennedy*. Malden, MA: Wiley-Blackwell, 2014.

Sevareid, Eric, *This Is Eric Sevareid*. New York: McGraw-Hill, 1964.

———, ed. *Candidates 1960: Behind the Headlines in the Presidential Race*. New York: Basic Books, 1959.

Shadegg, Stephen C. *What Happened to Goldwater? The Inside Story of the 1964 Republican Campaign*. New York: Holt, Rinehart and Winston, 1965.

Shafer, Byron E., and Richard Johnston. *The End of Southern Exceptionalism: Class, Race, and Partisan Change in the Postwar South*. Cambridge: Harvard University Press, 2006.

Shaw, John T. *JFK in the Senate: Pathway to the Presidency*. New York: Palgrave Macmillan, 2013.

———. *Rising Star, Setting Sun: Dwight D. Eisenhower, John F. Kennedy, and the Presidential Transition That Changed America*. New York: Pegasus, 2018.

Sheridan, Michael, with David Harvey. *Sinatra and the Jack Pack: The Extraordinary Friendship between Frank Sinatra and John F. Kennedy—Why They Bonded and What Went Wrong*. New York: Skyhorse, 2016.

Sherman, Michael, ed. *The Political Legacy of George D. Aiken: Wise Old Owl of the U.S. Senate*. Montpelier: Vermont Historical Society; Woodstock, VT: Countryman, 1995.

Shermer, Elizabeth Tandy, ed. *Barry Goldwater and the Remaking of the American Political Landscape*. Tucson: University of Arizona Press, 2013.

Shesol, Jeff. *Mutual Contempt: Lyndon Johnson, Robert Kennedy, and the Feud That Defined a Decade*. New York: Norton, 1997.

Sigel, Roberta. "Race and Religion as Factors in the Kennedy Victory in Detroit, 1960." *Journal of Negro Education*, Vol. 31, No. 4, Autumn 1962.

Silber, Norman I., ed. *With All Deliberate Speed: The Life of Philip Elman, an Oral History Memoir*. Ann Arbor: University of Michigan Press, 2004.

Silberman, Charles E. *The City and the Negro*. New York: Time, 1962.

Silvestri, Vito. "John F. Kennedy: His Speaking in the Wisconsin and West Virginia Primaries 1960." Ph.D. thesis, Indiana University, 1966.

Simpson, Dick. *Rogues, Rebels, and Rubber Stamps: The Politics of the Chicago City Council from 1863 to the Present*. New York: Westview, 2018.

Sirgiovanni, George. "The 'Van Buren Jinx': Vice Presidents Need Not Beware." *Presidential Studies Quarterly*, Vol. 18, No. 1, Winter 1988.

Skinner, Kiron K., Annelise Anderson, and Martin Anderson, eds. *Reagan: A Life in Letters*. New York: Free Press, 2003.

Slater, Ellis D. *The Ike I Knew*. N.p.: Ellis Slater Trust, 1980.

Slayton, Robert A. *Empire Statesman: The Rise and Redemption of Al Smith*. New York: Free Press, 2001.

Sloan, John. "The Management and Decision Making Style of President Eisenhower." *Presidential Studies Quarterly*, Vol. 20, No. 2, Spring 1990.

Sloyan, Patrick J. *The Politics of Deception: JFK's Secret Decisions on Vietnam, Civil Rights, and Cuba*. New York: St. Martin's, 2015.

Small, Melvin, ed. *A Companion to Richard M. Nixon*. Malden, MA: Wiley Blackwell, 2011.

Smiley, Sara. "Political Career of Thruston B. Morton: The Senate Years, 1956–1968." Ph.D. thesis, University of Kentucky, 1975.

Smith, Amanda, ed. *Hostage to Fortune: The Letters of Joseph P. Kennedy*. New York: Viking, 2001.

Smith, Gerald C. *Disarming Diplomat: The Memoirs of Ambassador Gerald C. Smith, Arms Control Negotiator*. Lanham, MD: Madison, 1996.

Smith, Howard K. *Events Leading Up to My Death: The Life of a Twentieth-Century Reporter*. New York: St. Martin's, 1996.

Smith, James G. "Presidential Elections and Racial Discrimination: Campaign Promises, Presidential Performance, and Democratic Accountability, 1960–1980." Ph.D. thesis, Indiana University, 1981.

Smith, Jean Kennedy. *The Nine of Us: Growing Up Kennedy*. New York: Harper, 2016.

Smith, Kevin. *The Iron Man: The Life and Times of Congressman Glenn R. Davis*. Lanham, MD: University Press of America, 1994.

Smith, Richard Norton. *On His Own Terms: A Life of Nelson Rockefeller*. New York: Random House, 2014.

———. *An Uncommon Man: The Triumph of Herbert Hoover*. New York: Simon and Schuster, 1984.

Smith, Sally Bedell. *Grace and Power: The Private World of the Kennedy White House*. New York: Random House, 2004.

Smith, T. Lynn. "The Redistribution of the Negro Population of the United States, 1910–1960." *Journal of Negro History*, Vol. 51, No. 3, July 1966.

Smith, William David. "Alfred E. Smith and John F. Kennedy: The Religious Issue during the Presidential Campaigns of 1928 and 1960." Ph.D. thesis, University of Southern Illinois, 1964.

Smyser, A. A. "How Kennedy Won 1960 Recount in Hawaii." *Honolulu Star-Bulletin*, June 8, 1963.

Sorensen, Theodore C. *Counselor: A Life at the Edge of History*. New York: Harper, 2008.

———. "Election of 1960." In Schlesinger and Israel, *History of American Presidential Elections*, vol. 4.

———. *Kennedy*. New York, Harper and Row, 1965.

———. *The Kennedy Legacy*. New York: Macmillan, 1969.

———. "When Kennedy Met Nixon," *NYT*, Sept. 26, 2010.

———, ed. *"Let the Word Go Forth": The Speeches, Statements, and Writings of John F. Kennedy*. New York: Delacorte, 1988.

Soukup, James R., Clifton McCleskey, and Harry Holloway. *Party and Factional Division in Texas*. Austin: University of Texas Press, 1964.

Spada, James. *Peter Lawford: The Man Who Kept the Secrets*. New York: Bantam, 1991.

Stacks, John F. *Scotty: James B. Reston and the Rise and Fall of American Journalism*. Boston: Little, Brown, 2003.

Stadiem, William. "Behind Claude's Doors," *Vanity Fair*, Sept. 2014.

Stanton, Frank. "An Appeal to the American People." *TV Guide*, Jan. 14–20, 1961.

———. "The First Debate over Presidential Debates." *Newsweek*. Vol. 136, Issue 13, Sept. 25, 2000.

"State Power to Bind Presidential Electors," *Columbia Law Review*, Vol. 65, No. 4, April 1965.

St. Clair, Drake, and Horace R. Cayton. *Black Metropolis: A Study of Negro Life in a Northern City*. Rev. ed., 2 vols. New York: Harper and Row, 1962.

Stebenne, David L. *Arthur J. Goldberg: New Deal Liberal*. New York: Oxford University Press, 1996.

———. "Who Really Won the 1960 Election?" Nov. 14, 2010, historynewsnetwork.org /article/133484.

Stedman, Murray S., Jr. *Religion and Politics in America*. New York: Harcourt, Brace and World, 1964.

Steel, Ronald. *Walter Lippmann and the American Century*. Boston: Atlantic Monthly Press, 1980.

Steinberg, Alfred. *Sam Rayburn: A Biography*. New York: Hawthorn, 1975.

Stempel, Guido, III. "The Prestige Press Covers the 1960 Presidential Campaign." *Journalism Quarterly*: Vol. 38, Issue 2, Spring 1961.

Stephenson, Charles. "The Democrats of Texas and Texas Liberalism, 1944–1960: A Study in Political Frustration." M.A. thesis, Southwest Texas State College, 1967.

Stossel, Scott. *Sarge: The Life and Times of Sargent Shriver*. Washington, DC: Smithsonian Books, 2004.

Strober, Gerald S., and Deborah H. Strober, eds. *"Let Us Begin Anew": An Oral History of the Kennedy Presidency*. New York: HarperCollins, 1993.

Strout, Richard L. *TRB: Views and Perspectives on the Presidency*. New York: Macmillan, 1979.

Stumme, John. "Lutherans on Religion and the 1960 Presidential Election." *Journal of Lutheran Ethics*. Vol. 7, Issue 2, Nov. 2007.

Sullivan, William C., with Bill Brown. *The Bureau: My Thirty Years in Hoover's FBI*. New York: Norton, 1979.

Sulzberger, C. L. *The Last of the Giants*. New York: Macmillan, 1970.

———. *The World and Richard Nixon*. Englewood Cliffs, NJ: Prentice Hall, 1987.

Sundquist, James L. *Politics and Policy: The Eisenhower, Kennedy, and Johnson Years*. Washington, DC: Brookings Institution, 1968.

Swarthout, John. "The 1960 Election in Oregon." *Western Political Quarterly*, Part 2, Vol. 14, No. 1, March 1961.

Sweeney, James. "Whispers in the Golden Silence: Harry F. Byrd, Sr., John F. Kennedy, and Virginia Democrats in the 1960 Presidential Election." *Virginia Magazine of History and Biography*, Vol. 99, No. 1, Jan. 1991.

Swift, Will. *Pat and Dick: The Nixons, an Intimate Portrait of a Marriage*. New York: Threshold, 2014.

Taeuber, Karl E. *Negro Population and Housing: Demographic Aspects of a Social Accounting Scheme*. Madison, WI: Institute for Research on Poverty, 1967.

Taeuber, Karl E., and Alma F. Taeuber. "The Negro as an Immigrant Group: Recent Trends in Racial and Ethnic Segregation in Chicago." *American Journal of Sociology*. Vol. 69, No. 4, Jan. 1964.

———. *Negroes in Cities: Residential Segregation and Neighborhood Change*. Chicago: Aldine, 1965.

Talmadge, Herman E., with Mark Royden Winchell. *Talmadge: A Political Legacy, a Politician's Life: A Memoir*. Atlanta: Peachtree, 1987.

Tanenhaus, Joseph. "The Computers and the Election." *American Behavioral Scientist*, Vol. 4, No. 4, Dec. 1960.

Tanzer, Lester. *The Kennedy Circle*. Washington, DC: Luce, 1961.

Taubman, Philip. *Secret Empire: Eisenhower, the CIA, and the Hidden Story of America's Space Espionage*. New York: Simon and Schuster, 2004.

Taubman, William. *Khrushchev: The Man and His Era*. New York: Norton, 2003.

Teel, Leonard Ray. *Ralph Emerson McGill: Voice of the Southern Conscience*. Knoxville: University of Tennessee Press, 2001.

Theodoulou, Stella Z., and Nancy V. Baker. *The Louisiana Republican Party, 1948–1984: Building of a State Political Party*. Tulane Studies in Political Science. New Orleans: Tulane University, 1986.

Theoharis, Athan G. *Spying on Americans: Political Surveillance from Hoover to the Huston Plan*. Philadelphia: Temple University Press, 1978.

———, ed. *From the Secret Files of J. Edgar Hoover*. Chicago: Ivan R. Dee, 1991.

Theoharis, Athan G., and John Stuart Cox. *The Boss: J. Edgar Hoover and the Great American Inquisition*. Philadelphia: Temple University Press, 1988.

Thomas, Evan. *Being Nixon: A Man Divided*. New York: Random House, 2015.

———. *Robert Kennedy: His Life*. New York: Simon and Schuster, 2000.

Thomas, G. Scott. *A New World to Be Won: John Kennedy, Richard Nixon, and the Tumultuous Year of 1960*. Santa Barbara, CA: Praeger, 2011.

Thomas, Helen. *Dateline: White House*. New York: Macmillan, 1975.

———. *Front Row at the White House: My Life and Times*. New York: Scribner, 1999.

———. *Thanks for the Memories, Mr. President: Wit and Wisdom from the Front Row at the White House*. New York: Scribner, 2002.

Thompson, Edward T., ed. *Theodore H. White at Large: The Best of His Magazine Writing, 1939–1986*. New York: Pantheon, 1992.

Thompson, Hunter S. *The Proud Highway: Saga of a Desperate Southern Gentleman, 1955–1967*. Ed. Douglas Brinkley. New York: Villard, 1997.

Thorburn, Wayne. *Red State: An Insider's Story of How the GOP Came to Dominate Texas Politics*. Austin: University of Texas Press, 2014.

Thornton, J. Mills, III. *Dividing Lines: Municipal Politics and the Struggle for Civil Rights in Montgomery, Birmingham, and Selma*. Tuscaloosa: University of Alabama Press, 2006.

Thurber, Timothy N. *The Politics of Equality: Hubert H. Humphrey and the African American Freedom Struggle*. New York: Columbia University Press, 1999.

———. *Republicans and Race: The GOP's Frayed Relationship with African Americans, 1945–1974*. Lawrence: University Press of Kansas, 2013.

Tillet, Paul, ed. *Inside Politics: The National Conventions, 1960*. Dobbs Ferry, NY: Oceana, 1962.

Tilly, Louise A., and Patricia Gurin, eds. *Women, Politics, and Change*. New York: Sage, 1990.

Todd, John, and Kay Ellis. "Analyzing Factional Patterns in State Politics: Texas, 1944–1972." *Social Science Quarterly*, Vol. 55, No. 3, Dec. 1974.

Tomlin, Homer Ross. *Homer Thornberry: Congressman, Judge, and Advocate for Equal Rights*. Fort Worth, TX: Texas Christian University Press, 2016.

Tower, John. *Consequences: A Personal and Political Memoir*. Boston: Little, Brown, 1991.

Travell, Janet G. *Office Hours: Day and Night, the Autobiography of Janet Travell, M.D.* New York: World, 1968.

Trest, Warren. *Nobody but the People: The Life and Times of Alabama's Youngest Governor*. Montgomery, AL: NewSouth, 2008.

Trohan, Walter. *Political Animals: Memoirs of a Sentimental Cynic*. Garden City, NY: Doubleday, 1975.

Trout, Bill. "Political Prankster." Reuters, May 30, 2018.

Truman, Harry, and Dean Acheson. *Affection and Trust: The Personal Correspondence of Harry S. Truman and Dean Acheson, 1953–1971*. New York: Knopf, 2010.

Tye, Larry. *Bobby Kennedy: The Making of a Liberal Lion*. New York: Random House, 2016.

Unger, Irwin, and Debi Unger. *LBJ: A Life*. New York: Wiley, 1999.

Unruh, Gail. "Eternal Liberal: Wayne L. Morse and the Politics of Liberalism." Ph.D. thesis, University of Oregon, 1987.

Urquhart, Brian. *Ralph Bunche: An American Life*. New York: Norton, 1993.

Van Atta, Dale. *With Honor: Melvin Laird in War, Peace, and Politics.* Madison: University of Wisconsin Press, 2008.

Vancil, David L., and Sue D. Pendell. "The Myth of Viewer-Listener Disagreement in the First Kennedy-Nixon Debate." *Central States Speech Journal*, Vol. 38, No. 1, Spring 1987.

Vickery, William. *The Economics of the Negro Migration, 1900–1960.* New York: Arno, 1977.

Vinz, Warren. "The Politics of Protestant Fundamentalism in the 1950s and 1960s." *Journal of Church and State*, Vol. 14, No. 2, Spring 1972.

Viser, Edward. "John F. Kennedy and the Religious Issue in Texas." M.A. thesis, East Texas State University, 1970.

von Hippel, Paul. "Here's a Voter Fraud Myth." *WP*, Aug. 8, 2017.

von Post, Gunilla, with Carl Johnes. *Love, Jack.* New York: Crown, 1997.

Wahl-Jorgensen, Karin, and Thomas Hanitzsch. *The Handbook of Journalism Studies.* New York: Routledge, 2009.

Wallace, Mike, with Gary Paul Gates. *Between You and Me: A Memoir.* New York: Hyperion, 2003.

Walsh, Lawrence E. *The Gift of Insecurity: A Lawyer's Life.* Chicago: American Bar Association, 2003.

Ward, Stephen J. A. "Journalism Ethics." https://www.supportuw.org/wp-content/uploads/wwa_2010_ward_journalism.pdf.

Ware, Susan. "American Women in the 1950s." In Tilly and Gurin, *Women, Politics, and Change.*

Wassenberg, Pinky S., et al. "Gender Differences in Political Conceptualization, 1956–1980." *American Politics Quarterly*, Vol. 11, No. 2, April 1983.

Watson, Mary. "Television and the Presidency: Eisenhower and Kennedy." In Edgerton, *Columbia History of American Television.*

Watson, Richard. "Religion and Politics in Mid-America: Presidential Voting in Missouri in 1928 and 1960." *Midcontinent American Studies*, Vol. 5, No. 1, Spring 1964.

Wattenberg, Martin P. *The Decline of American Political Parties, 1952–1996.* 6th ed. Cambridge: Harvard University Press, 1998.

Weber, Michael P. *Don't Call Me Boss: David L. Lawrence, Pittsburgh's Renaissance Mayor.* Pittsburgh: University of Pittsburgh Press, 1988.

Wechsler, James A. *Reflections of an Angry Middle-Aged Editor.* New York: Random House, 1960.

Weeks, O. Douglas. *Texas in the 1960 Presidential Election.* Austin: Institute of Public Affairs, 1961.

Weinberger, Casper W., with Gretchen Roberts. *In the Arena: A Memoir of the 20th Century.* Washington, DC: Regnery, 2001.

Whalen, Thomas J. *Kennedy versus Lodge: The 1952 Massachusetts Senate Race.* Boston: Northeastern University Press, 2000.

White, F. Clifton, with Jerome Tuccille. *Politics as a Noble Calling: The Memoirs of F. Clifton White.* Ottawa, IL: Jameson, 1994.

White, Irving. "Research Report on Kennedy-Nixon Debates." *Abstracts of Papers of the American Sociological Association.* 56th Annual Session, 1961.

White, John. "The Evolution of the Republican Right in South Carolina, 1952–1974." In Feldman, *Painting Dixie Red.*

White, Theodore H. "The Gentlemen from California." *Collier's*, Feb. 3, 1956.

———. *In Search of History: A Personal Adventure*, New York: Harper and Row, 1978.

———. *The Making of the President 1960.* New York: Atheneum, 1961.

———. *The Making of the President 1960.* New York: Book-of-the-Month Club, 1988.

———. *The Making of the President 1960.* New York: Harper, 2009.

White, William S. *The Professional: Lyndon B. Johnson.* Boston: Houghton Mifflin, 1964.

Whitfield, Stephen. "How the Fifties Became the Sixties." *Historically Speaking*, Jan.–Feb. 2008.

Wicker, Tom, et al. "TV in the Political Campaign." *Television Quarterly*, Winter 1966.

Wiessler, David. "The Presidential Elections of 1952, 1956, and 1960 as Recorded in Selected Newspapers in Deep South Cities." M.A. thesis, University of Texas, 1970.

Wilkins, Martha Huddleston. "The Development of the Mississippi Republican Party." M.A. thesis, Mississippi College, 1965.

Wilkins, Roy, with Tom Mathews. *Standing Fast: The Autobiography of Roy Wilkins.* New York: Viking, 1982.

Williams, Daniel. "Richard Nixon's Religious Right." In Gifford and Williams, *Right Side of the Sixties.*

Williamson, David. *Separate Agenda: Churchill, Eisenhower, and Anglo-American Relations, 1953–1955.* Lanham, MD: Lexington, 2006.

Wills, Garry. *Nixon Agonistes: The Crisis of the Self-Made Man.* Boston: Houghton Mifflin, 1970.

Wilson, Bob, with Larry Bischof and William Brian Lowry. *Confessions of a Kinetic Congressman.* San Diego: San Diego State University Foundation, 1996.

Wilson, James Q. *Negro Politics: The Search for Leadership.* New York: Free Press, 1960.

———. "Two Negro Politicians: An Interpretation." *Midwest Journal of Political Science*, Vol. 4, No. 4, 1960.

Wirt, F. M. "The Organization Man in Politics: Ray Bliss and the 1960 Election." In Green, *Politics, Professionalism, and Power.*

Witcover, Jules. *The Making of an Ink-Stained Wretch: Half a Century Pounding the Political Beat.* Baltimore: Johns Hopkins University Press, 2005.

———. *Party of the People: A History of the Democrats.* New York: Random House, 2003.

Wlezien, Christopher, and Robert S. Erikson. "The Timeline of Presidential Election Campaigns." *Journal of Politics*, Vol. 64, No. 4, Nov. 2002.

Wofford, Harris, Jr. *Of Kennedy and Kings: Making Sense of the Sixties.* New York: Farrar, Straus, Giroux, 1980.

Wolf, George D. *William Warren Scranton: Pennsylvania Statesman.* University Park: Penn State University Press, 1981.

Wolfe, James. "The Religion of and about John F. Kennedy." In Harper and Krieg, *John F. Kennedy.*

———. "The Religious Issue Revisited: Presbyterian Responses to Kennedy's Presidential Campaign." *Journal of Presbyterian History*, Vol. 51, No. 1, Spring 1979.

Wolseley, Roland E. *The Black Press, U.S.A.* Ames: Iowa State University Press, 1971.

Woods, Randall B. *LBJ: Architect of American Ambition.* New York: Free Press, 2006.

Woodward, Kenneth L. *Getting Religion: Faith, Culture, and Politics from the Age of Eisenhower to the Era of Obama.* New York: Convergent, 2016.

Wuthnow, Robert. *The Restructuring of American Religion: Society and Faith Since World War II.* Princeton, NJ: Princeton University Press, 1988.

Yoder, Edwin M., Jr. *Joe Alsop's Cold War: A Study of Journalistic Influence and Intrigue.* Chapel Hill: University of North Carolina Press, 1995.

Zaloga, Steven J. *The Kremlin's Nuclear Sword: The Rise and Fall of Russia's Strategic Nuclear Forces, 1945–2000.* Washington, DC: Smithsonian Institution Press, 2002.

Zelizer, Julian. "Rethinking the History of American Conservatism." *Reviews in American History*, Vol. 38, No. 2, June 2010.

Zug, James. *The Long Conversation: 125 Years of Sidwell Friends School, 1883–2008.* Privately published, 2008.

Zwikl, Kurt. "The Campaign and the Issues: An Examination of the 1960 Presidential Election in Lehigh County, Pennsylvania." M.A. thesis, Lehigh University, 1982.

NEWSPAPERS AND MAGAZINES

Human Events

London Times

New York Post

New York Times

Newsweek

Time

U.S. News and World Report

Washington Post

BROADCAST MATERIALS

Ralph de Toledano interview, Dec. 25, 1997, C-SPAN.

The Kennedy-Nixon Debates, 1 through 4, video, YouTube.

"The Kennedys," Part 1, *American Experience*, Nov. 17, 2003, PBS.

Arthur Schlesinger, Jr., interview with Brian Lamb, *In Depth*, Dec. 3, 2000, C-SPAN.

Theodore C. Sorensen, *Counselor*, Book TV, May 14, 2008, C-SPAN 2.

UNPUBLISHED MATERIAL

Dobbs, Ricky. "Dallas Republicans and the Adolphus Hotel Incident of 1960." Paper presented Urban Houston Association, Houston, Nov. 11, 2008.

Eisenhower, Milton, to Eric Roorda, letter, July 14, 1983.

Hughes, Don, lecture, Jan. 10, 2001, RNL.

INTERVIEWS BY AUTHOR

Acker, Marje

Boxer, M.D.

Bradlee, Ben

Cooper, M.D.

Donnelly, Dorothy
Dugger, Ronnie
Flanigan, Peter
Golden, Jack
Goodpaster, Andrew
Heckler, Ken
Hughes, Don
Jackson, John
Kenney, David
Klein, Herbert
Mazo, Earl
Nixon, Edward

Peirce, Neal
Rabb, Maxwell
Reed, Christopher
Ritchie, Donald
Rogers, Edward "Ted"
Russell, Herb
Safire, William
Scalettar, Raymond
Tyler, Harold
Vanocur, Sandur
Walsh, Lawrence
Wofford, Harris, Jr.

ACKNOWLEDGMENTS

This is the third volume in my series on Richard Nixon's life and times. No one contributed more than my wife Gloria Gae, who first tricked me into going to Nixon's presidential library in Yorba Linda, California. At one point while working on this manuscript, I asked her if I could dedicate it to her parents. She was touched and immediately agreed. As I was finishing the first draft, my wife died suddenly. I do not think that she would object to my including her in the dedication. Without any question, she deserves the recognition.

Besides Gloria, several colleagues who helped with my work have also passed away. I went to graduate school with Bill Brinker and Garry Clifford. Over many decades, they encouraged me to write the best history that I could and ignore those who attacked me, not on the facts, but on political beliefs. Herb Parmet, Paul Glad, Kevin Starr, and Robert Ferrell, all distinguished historians, were always supportive. When I talked to Arthur Schlesinger, Jr., about the election and presented a different viewpoint, he laughed and admitted that he might have exaggerated his case. Horace Schwerin, a leading marketing expert and pollster, talked to me on many occasions about his analysis of the Great Debates.

Many scholars read the entire manuscript and offered constructive comments. Allen Matusow and Timothy Thurber were my referees for the press and provided cogent suggestions. Louise Stevenson, Ed Kallina, Evan Thomas, Dave Nichols, Will Swift, and Mel Small read early drafts and offered valuable insights.

I asked many scholars who were specialists on various topics to read sections of the manuscript. Luke Nichter looked at the sections on Henry Cabot Lodge, Jr.; Richard Norton Smith on Nelson Rockefeller; Arnie Offner on Hubert Humphrey; Donald Ritchie on the press; Jon Bruschke on the Great Debates;

John Shaw on John Kennedy's senatorial career and the transition from the election to the inauguration. I am not an expert on Catholicism and depended on three scholars to review my chapter: George Marlin, Vincent Cannato, and Stephen Koeth, C.S.C. Dr. Lee Mandel reviewed the material on Kennedy's health and also discussed it with James Giglio. Bill Rorabaugh shared his knowledge concerning fraud in the Texas election, and Ed Kallina did the same for corruption in Chicago. Garrison Nelson helped me to understand Massachusetts politics during Kennedy's rise. I asked Daun van Ee countless questions on Dwight Eisenhower and the election. Athan Theoharis provided information on J. Edgar Hoover and how the F.B.I. functioned. Donald Critchlow and I discussed Republican politics during this period. David Levering Lewis went over my sections on Martin Luther King, Jr., and African-American politics.

Ricky Dobbs shared his notes from the Johnson and Kennedy presidential libraries with me and sent me a paper he presented on the closing days of the campaign in Texas. John Farrell provided documents from the Theodore White manuscripts at Harvard University. John Fox, FBI historian, forwarded Hoover's files on his activities during the election and the files on Lyndon Johnson and on Joe, John, and Robert Kennedy. Robert Hartley, CIA librarian, forwarded me documents on that agency's role in the election. Joe Dmohowski emailed me the entire Whittier College oral history collection. Jonathan Movroydis at the Richard Nixon Foundation was extremely helpful in finding documents.

Librarians and archivists were essential to my research. Susan Naulty and Beverly Lindy in Yorba Linda as well as Paul Wormser and Diane Nixon in Laguna Nigel supplied me with documents from Nixon's archives. Archivists James Leyerzapf and Tim Rives efficiently responded to inquiries regarding Eisenhower's manuscripts. Archivists Sam Rushay and Randy Sowell at the Harry S Truman library found documents for me on the president's activities during the election. At the Lyndon B. Johnson presidential library, Claudia Anderson and Allen Fisher could not have been more helpful. Benna Vaughan at Baylor University assisted me with the Leon Jaworski manuscripts and oral history. Susan Luftschein and Claude Zachary at the University of Southern California assisted me in examining the Herbert Klein collection. I also thank Ryan Pettigrew at the Nixon presidential library, Michele Beckerman at the Rockefeller archives, Laurie Austin at the Truman presidential library, Maryrose Grossman at the Kennedy presidential library, Mary Burtzloff at the Eisenhower presidential library, and Chris Banks at the Johnson presidential library.

Some individuals whom I interviewed went above and beyond what I asked. Ed Nixon answered numerous inquiries about his family and his brother Dick. Herbert Klein, who acted as the vice president's press secretary, replied to many requests for additional information. Don Hughes, Nixon's appointment secretary, provided detailed accounts of the campaign. Ben Bradlee clearly recalled his conversation with the president-elect concerning the fraud in Chicago. Harris Wofford conceded that the significance of the "blue bomb" had been exaggerated. Raymond Scalettar, M.D., explained his role in treating Nixon at Walter Reed Hospital.

The librarians and staff at the Shadek-Fackenthal Library cheerfully assisted me during the research for this book. Jennifer Buch, Tom Karel, and Scott Vine found obscure material; Nicole Rearich, Denise Chmielewski, Carol Kornhauser, and Sue Wood expedited my requests for books and other material. Jill Borin, head of archives and distinctive collections at Widener University, searched out articles from journals and uncovered information that was difficult to find.

Yale University Press has done everything it could during this pandemic to turn this manuscript into the best product possible. Margaret Otzel supervised the production, and Erica Hanson fact-checked. I have worked with copy editors for a half century; I had never experienced anyone quite as good as Dan Heaton. Karen Olson applied her skills as an author and an editor. While I appreciate their kindnesses and professionalism, my editor Bill Frucht is special. He not only believed in the manuscript, he also spent an inordinate amount of time reviewing each page for grammar and content. As a result of Yale's demand for excellence, these individuals and the entire YUP team have made my work better.

Alexander Hoyt is an exceptional agent. He believed in my concept, read the entire manuscript, and offered cogent comments. Finally, my wife Joanne, who is eternally ebullient, puts up with my mess and me.

Those whom I have mentioned tried to help improve my work, and they deserve thanks. I alone am responsible for any and all errors of fact and interpretation.

Index

Numbers in square brackets refer to the (unpaged) illustrations following page 170.

Date Due
